17

1.49

CONCISE DICTIONARY OF HISTORY

CONCISE DICTIONARY OF HISTORY

EDITOR: CALLUM BRINES

TIGER BOOKS INTERNATIONAL
LONDON

This edition published in 1993 by
Tiger Books International PLC, London.

ISBN 1-85501-368-1

Printed and bound in Slovenia.

A

A1, first British car registration, issued to the 2nd Earl Russell 1903.
Aachen (Aix-la-Chapelle), founded 125; Charlemagne's capital, free city of the Holy Roman *Empire*, burnt 1656; captured by American troops 1944.
Aalto, Hugo Alvar, Finnish architect, b.1898, d.1976.
Abbado, Claudio, Italian conductor, b.1933.
Abbas I, Egyptian pasha, b.1813, assassinated 1854.
Abbas, Ferhat, Algerian nationalist leader, b.1899, d.1985.
Abbas the Great, shah of Persia, b.c.1557, d.1628.
Abbasid Dynasty, founded by Abdul Abbas 750, ended 1258.
Abbeville, Treaty of (Treaty of Paris), relinquishing English claims to several French territories, signed 20 May 1259.
Abbey, Edwin Austin, American-born painter, b.1852, d.1911.
Abbey Theatre, Dublin, founded 1904, burned down 1952, rebuilt 1966.
Abbot, Bud, American film comedian, b.1895, d.1974.
Abbot, George, archbishop of Canterbury 1611–33, b.1562, d.1633.
ABC (American Broadcasting Company), formed 1943.
Abd-el-Kader, Algerian revolutionary leader, b.1808, d.1883.
Abd-el-Krim, Rif revolutionary leader, b.1882, d.1963.
Abdication of King Edward VIII, 10 Dec. 1936.
Abdominal operation, first successfully performed by the American surgeon Ephraim McDowell, b.1771, d.1830.
Abdul Latif, Arabian writer, b.1162, d.1231.
Abdur Rahman Khan, emir of Afghanistan, b.c.1844, d.1901.
Abe, Kobo, Japanese writer, b.1924.
à Becket, Thomas, archbishop of Canterbury, b.1118, assassinated 1170.
à Beckett, Gilbert, English humorous writer, b.1811, d.1856.
Abel, Sir Frederick Augustus, scientist, inventor (1879) of apparatus for determining flashpoint of petroleum, b.1827, d.1902.
Abelard, Peter, French philosopher, lover of Héloïse, b.1079, d.1142.
Abercrombie, Lascelles, English poet, b.1881, d.1938.
Abercromby, Sir Robert, commander of the Indian forces, b.1740, d.1827.

Aberdeen, incorporated by David I, granted charter by William the Lion 1179, burnt by Edward III 1336.

Aberdeen, George Gordon, Earl of, British statesman (prime minister 1852–55), b.1784, d.1860.

Aberfan disaster, 2 million tons of coal waste slid onto a Welsh village, killing 192 people including 113 children, 21 Oct. 1966.

Aberration of light, discovered 1729 by the English astronomer James Bradley, b.1693, d.1762.

Abershaw, Jerry, English highwayman, b.*c.*1773, hanged 1795.

Aberystwyth, founded 1109, granted first charter 1277, College erected there 1872.

Abhorrers, political group (connected with Tories), first came into prominence 1680.

Abington, Mrs Frances, English actress, b.1737, d.1815.

Abjuration oath, rejecting the Stewarts, first required 1701.

ABM (Anti-Ballistic Missile) Treaty, between the USA and USSR signed 26 May 1972.

Abolition of slavery, in British possessions 1834; in French possessions 1848; throughout USA 1862.

Aboukir Bay, Battle of (the Battle of the Nile), fought by Lord Nelson 1 Aug. 1798.

About, Edmond, French writer (*Le roi des montagnes,* 1856), b.1828, d.1885.

Abraham (Abram), Hebrew patriarch, travelled from Ur to Palestine *c.*2000, d.1500 BC.

Abraham, Battle of the Heights of, fought near Quebec between British and French 13 Sept. 1759.

Abraham, Robert, English architect, b.1773, d.1850.

Abruzzi earthquake, Italy, destroying 15,000, 3 Nov. 1706.

Absolute zero (–273° C; –459° F), idea introduced by Lord Kelvin, b.1824, d.1907.

Abu Nidal, Palestinian terrorist, b. 1937.

Abu Nuwas, Arabian poet, b.*c.*756, d.810.

Abyssinia, *see* Ethiopia.

Abyssinian Expedition, carried out by British troops from India 1867–68.

Abzug, Bella, American political activist, b.1920.

Académie des Jeux Floreux, Paris, constituted an academy by Louis XIV 1694.

Académie Française, Paris, founded 10 Feb. 1635.

Academy Awards, given annually since 1927 to films, actors and technicians by the American Academy of Motion Picture Arts and Sciences for merit in the form of statuettes called Oscars.

Accademia della Crusca, Italy, leading Italian academy, founded 1582.

Accoramboni, Vittoria (Webster's 'White Devil'), b.1557, assassinated 1585.

Accordion, invented by the German Friedrich Buschmann 1822.

Accountants, Institute of Chartered, in England and Wales, founded (as the Institute of Accountants) 1870; chartered 1880.

Accountants of Scotland, The Institute of Chartered, chartered 1854.

Acetylene, discovered 1836 by the British scientist Edmund Davy, b.1785, d.1857.

Achaean League, Greece, formed *c.*280, dissolved 146 BC.

Achaemenid Dynasty, ruled Persia from *c.*550 to 300 BC.

Acheson, Dean Gooderham, US statesman, b.1893, d.1971.

Achille Lauro, Italian cruise liner hijacked by Palestinian terrorists, 7–9 Oct. 1985.

Achromatic telescope, invented *c.*1757 by the English optician John Dollond, b.1706, d.1761; and, independently, in 1733 by the English amateur Chester Moor Hall, b.1703, d.1771.

Ackermann, Rudolph, German-born publisher of illustrated books, b.1764, d.1834.

Aconcagua, highest mountain in the Andes, first climbed by the Fitzgerald Expedition 1897.

Acre, N. Israel, taken by the Crusaders 1110, captured by Saladin 1187, recaptured by Richard Coeur de Lion 1191, finally lost to Christendom 1291. Battle of Acre 1189.

Acridine, chemical compound, isolated by the German scientists Carl Graebe and H. Caro 1890.

Actinium, radioactive element, discovered 1900 by the French scientist André Debierne, b.1874.

Actinometer, invented 1825 by Sir John Herschel, b.1792, d.1871.

Actium, Battle of, between Octavian and Mark Antony, 2 Sept. 31 BC.

Act of Settlement, securing Hanoverian succession to the English throne, passed 1701.

Acton, John Dalberg, Lord, English historian, b.1834, d.1902.

Adalbert, St, b.*c.*957, martyred 997.

Adalbert, German archbishop, b.*c.*1000, d.1072.

Adam, James, Scottish architect, b.1730, d.1794.
Adam, Robert, Scottish architect and brother of James, b.1728, d.1792.
Adams, Ansell Easton, American photographer, b.1902, d.1984.
Adams, Francis William Lauderdale, Australian writer, b.1862, committed suicide 1893.
Adams, Henry, American historian, b.1838, d.1918.
Adams, John, 2nd US president (1797–1801), b.1735, d.1826.
Adams, John Bertram, English nuclear physicist, founder member of CERN, b.1920, d.1984.
Adams, John Couch, English astronomer (predicted position of the planet Neptune 1845), b.1819, d.1892.
Adams, John Quincy, 6th US president (1825–29), b.1767, d.1848.
Adams, Samuel, American statesman, b.1722, d.1803.
Adams, Sarah Flower, English hymnwriter (*Nearer to Thee*), b.1805, d.1848.
Adams, William Bridges, English inventor, b.1797, d.1872.
Addams, Charles, American cartoonist, inspired 'The Addams Family' TV series, b.1912, d.1988.
Addams, Jane, American social reformer, Nobel peace prize 1931, b.1860, d.1935.
Adding machine, first model built 1642 by the French scientist Blaise Pascal, b.1623, d.1662.
Addington, Henry, 1st Viscount Sidmouth, English statesman, Tory prime minister (1801–04), b.1757, d.1844.
Addinsell, Richard, English composer of incidental music (*Warsaw Concerto*), b.1904, d.1977.
Addis Ababa, capital of Ethiopia, founded by Menelek II 1892.
Addison, Joseph, English author – with Steele – of *The Spectator*, b.1672, d.1719.
Addison, Thomas, English discoverer 1855 of Addison's disease, b.1793, d.1860.
Addled Parliament, of James I's reign, Sat 5 April to 7 June 1614.
Adelaide, queen, wife of William IV, b.1792, d.1849.
Adelaide, South Australia, founded 1836 and named after Queen Adelaide.
Aden, annexed to British India, 16 Jan. 1839; Crown Colony 1 April 1937; became part of People's Republic of Southern Yemen 1967.

Adenauer, Konrad, German chancellor (1949–63), b.1876, d.1967.

Adler, Alfred, Austrian psychologist, b.1870, d.1937.

Adler, Larry, American harmonica player, b.1914.

Adler, Nathan Marcus, Chief Rabbi and founder 1855 of Jews' College, London, b.1803, d.1890.

Admiralty, London, founded 1512.

Admiralty Islands, part of Papua New Guinea in the Bismarck Archipelago, first colonized by the Dutch 1616.

Adoption, in England and Wales governed by the Adoption Act 1976, as amended by the Children Act 1978.

Adrenaline, a hormone, isolated 1901 by the Japanese scientist Jokichi Takamine, b.1854, d.1922.

Adrian, St, martyred 4 March 303.

Adrian, Edgar Douglas, Baron, English physiologist, b.1889, d.1977.

Adrian I, pope 772–795.

Adrian II, pope 867–872.

Adrian III, St, pope 884–885.

Adrian IV (Nicolas Breakspear), pope, first and only English Pope, 1154–59.

Adrian V, pope 1276.

Adrian VI (Adrian Florensz), pope 1522–23, b.1459, d.1523.

Adrianople, Battle of, 378; taken by the Ottomans 1360, and their capital 1366–1453.

Advent, Christian festival comprising the period encompassed by the four Sundays before Christmas.

Advertisement Duty, Newspaper, introduced in England under Cromwell, abolished 1853.

Ady, Endre, Hungarian poet, b.1877, d.1919.

'AE' (George William Russell), Irish poet, b.1867, d.1935.

Aelfric, scholar and writer, b.*c.*955, d.*c.*1020.

Aemilian Way, Roman road, constructed 187 BC.

Aerodynamics, study founded by Sir George Cayley 1809.

Aeroplane, steam model patented 1842 by W. S. Henson; successful model flown 1903 by Wright brothers; flights of Blériot, Brabazon and Cody 1909.

Aeschines, Greek orator, b.389, d.314 BC.

Aeschylus, Greek dramatist (*Seven against Thebes,* 467 BC), b.525, d.456 BC.

Aesop, Greek writer of fables, b.*c.*620, d.*c.*560 BC.

Aetius, Flavius, Roman leader (defeated Attila 451), b.c.390, murdered 454.
Afghanistan, independent republic since 1919; invaded by Soviet troops 1979, withdrawn 1988–89.
Afghan Wars, between British and Afghans 1839–42, 1879–80, 1919.
African National Congress (ANC), African nationalist movement opposed to apartheid in South Africa; founded 1912, banned 1960, leader Nelson Mandela imprisoned 1962, released 1989; negotiated new constitution with President de Klerk 1990–93.
Agadir, incident of, 1911; earthquake, 1960.
Aga Khan, heriditary title of the spiritual leader of the Ismaili sect of Islam.
Aga Khan IV, spiritual leader of the Ismaili sect of Islam, b.1936.
Agapemonites, religious sect founded 1846 by the Rev. Henry James Prince, b.1811, d.1899.
Agapitus, St, pope 535–536.
Agapitus II, pope 946–955.
Agassiz, Jean Louis Rodolphe, Swiss naturalist, b.1807, d.1873.
Agatha, St, martyred 5 Feb. 251.
Agatho, St, pope 678–681.
Agee, James, American author (*Let Us Now Praise Famous Men*, 1941), b.1909, d.1955.
Agent Orange, chemical defoliant used by US Air Force in Vietnam 1962–70.
Aghrim, Battle of, fought in Ireland against James II 12 July 1691.
Agincourt, Battle of, fought between Henry V and the French 25 Oct. 1415.
Agnes' Eve, St, 20–21 Jan.
Agnostic, term first introduced 1869 by the English scientist Thomas Henry Huxley, b.1825, d.1895.
Agricola (Georg Bauer), German 'father of mineralogy', b.1490, d.1555.
Agricola, Gnaeus Julius, Roman general, b.37, d.93.
Agriculture, administered by Ministry of Agriculture, Fisheries and Food (formerly Board of Agriculture), formed 1889.
Agriculture, Department of, USA, created 15 May 1862.
Agrigentum, Sicily, founded c.582 BC.
Agrippa, Marcus Vipsanius, Roman general, b.63, d.12 BC.

Aguilar, Grace, English writer (*The Vale of Cedars,* 1850), b.1816, d.1847.

Ahmed I, Turkish sultan (from 1603), b.1589, d.1617.

Ahmed II, Turkish sultan (from 1691), b.1643, d.1695.

Ahmed III, Turkish sultan (1703–30), b.1637, d.1736.

Ahmedabad, Indian city, founded by Ahmed Shah 1411.

Ahmediya Movement, Muslim sect founded 1889 by Mirza Ghulam Ahmed, b.1839, d.1908.

Ahmednagar, Indian city, founded by Ahmed Nizam Shah 1494.

Aidan, St, first bishop of Lindisfarne, d. 31 Aug. 651.

Aids (acquired immune deficiency syndrome), first recognized in USA 1981; retrovirus first isolated in France 1983.

Ainsworth, William Harrison, English historical novelist (*The Tower of London,* 1840), b.1805, d.1882.

Air, composition first analysed 1771 by the French chemist Antoine Laurent Lavoisier, b.1743, d.1794.

Air conditioning, first primitive system designed by Stuart W. Cramer 1906; first associated with Legionnaire's Disease 1970s.

Airdrie, Lanarkshire, founded 1695.

Air gun, invented 1656 by Guter of Nuremberg.

Airmail post, first organized in Britain by the *Empire Illustrated* 10 Aug. 1910.

Airmail Service, first regular, inaugurated by the US Government 1918.

Air pump, invented by the German scientist Otto von Guericke, b.1602, d.1686.

Airship, models constructed by Giffard in 1852 and by Renard and Krebos in 1884; rigid model constructed by Zeppelin in 1900.

Airy, Sir George Biddell, Astronomer Royal (1835–81), b.1801, d.1892.

Aisne, Battle of the, World War I, 13–28 Sept. 1914.

Aix-la-Chapelle (Aachen), founded 125. Congresses 1668, 1748 and 30 Sept.–21 Nov. 1818.

Ajaccio, Corsica, founded 1492 by Genoese.

Ajanta Cave Paintings, India, dated approximately 600.

Akbar, Jalaluddin Mohammed, Mogul emperor of India (1556–1605), b.1542, d.1605.

Akerman, John Yonge, English founder of the *Numismatic Journal,* b.1806, d.1873.

Akhnaton, heretic pharaoh of Egypt (Amenhotep IV), *fl.* 14th century BC.

Akihito, emperor of Japan (since 1989), b. 1933.

Akron, Ohio, founded 1825, chartered 1865.
Aksakov, Sergei Timofeievich, Russian writer (*Family Chronicle*, 1846–56), b.1791, d.1859.
Alabama, USA, created Territory 1817, admitted as State to the Union 1819.
Alabama, The, Confederate warship, built at Birkenhead 1862, attacked US shipping 1862–64, sunk by *Kearsage* 1864.
Alamein, Battle of, World War II, 23 Oct.–4 Nov. 1942.
Alanbrooke, Alan Brooke, Viscount, British soldier, b.1887, d.1963.
Alaric, Visigoth king, d.410.
Alaska, discovered by Vitus Bering 1741; purchased from the Russians by USA 1867; incorporated as Territory 1912; became 49th State 1959.
Alaska Highway, runs 1,523 miles (2,400 km) from Rawson Creek, British Columbia to Fairbanks, Alaska, built 1942.
Alba, Ferdinand Alvarez de Toledo, Duke of, Spanish soldier, b.1507, d.1582.
Albania, under Turkish rule 1467–1912; principality 1912–24; republic 1925–28; monarchy 1928–46; republic from 1946.
Albany, Louisa, Countess of, wife of Prince Charles Edward, b.1753, d.1824.
Albee, Edward, American playwright (*Who's Afraid of Virginia Woolf?* 1962), b.1928.
Albeniz, Isaac, Spanish composer (*Iberia*, 1906), b.1860, d.1909.
Albert, anti-pope, 1102.
Albert, prince, consort of Queen Victoria (from 1840), b.1819, d.1861.
Albert I, king of the Belgians (from 1909), b.1875, d.1934.
Alberta, Canada, organized as District 1875; created Province 1905.
Albert Hall, Kensington, built in memory of Prince Albert 1867–71.
Alberti, Domenico, Italian composer (*Endimione*), b.*c.*1710, d.1740.
Albertini, Leone Battista, Italian painter and sculptor, b.1404, d.1472.
Albert Memorial, Hyde Park, begun 1864, completed 1876.
Albert Nyanza, lake, discovered 1864 by Sir Samuel White Baker, b.1821, d.1893.
Albertus, Magnus, German philosopher, b.*c.*1200, d.1280.
Albigenses, French heretics, active *c.*1200, destroyed 1209–1229.

Albuera, Battle of, Peninsular War, fought between British and French 16 May 1811.

Albuquerque, New Mexico, founded 1706.

Alcibiades, Greek general, b.*c.*451, d.404 BC.

Alcock, Sir John William, pioneer aviator, b.1892, d.1919.

Alcoholics Anonymous (AA), self-help group founded 1935.

Alcott, Louisa May, American writer (*Little Women*, 1868–69), b.1832, d.1888.

Alcuin, English scholar, b.*c.*735, d.804.

Aldhelm, bishop of Sherborne, b.*c.*640, d.709.

Aldington, Richard, English writer (*Death of a Hero*, 1929), b.1892, d.1962.

Aldol, chemical compound discovered by the French chemist Charles Adolphe Wurtz, b.1817, d.1884.

Aldrich, Robert, American film director (*Whatever Happened to Baby Jane?* 1962), b.1918, d.1983.

Aldwych, London theatre, opened 18 Oct. 1905.

Aleichem, Sholem (Shalom Rabinovich), Yiddish writer, b.1859, d.1916.

Aleman, Mateo, Spanish writer (*Guzmán de Alfarache,* 1599–1604), b.1547, d.*c.*1616.

Alembert, Jean le Rond d', French scientist and philosopher, b.1717, d.1783.

Aleutian Islands, discovered by Vitus Bering 1725; bought from Russia by USA 1867.

Alexander, St, Pope 105–119.

Alexander, king of Yugoslavia (from 1921), b.1888, assassinated at Marseilles 9 Oct. 1934.

Alexander, Mrs Cecil Frances, hymnwriter ('There is a green hill far away'), b.1818, d.1895.

Alexander, Sir George, English actor-manager, b.1858, d.1918.

Alexander, Harold, Viscount, British soldier, b.1891, d.1969.

Alexander II (Anselmo Baggio), pope 1061–73.

Alexander III (Rolando Bandinelli), pope 1159–81.

Alexander IV (Rinaldo di Segni), pope 1254–61.

Alexander V (Peter Philargès), anti-pope 1409–10.

Alexander VI (Rodrigo Borgia), pope 1492–1503, b.1431, d.1503.

Alexander VII (Fabio Chigi), pope 1655–67, b.1599, d.1667.

Alexander VIII (Pietro Ottoboni), pope 1689–91, b.1610, d.1691.

Alexander the Great, of Macedon, ruler of Greece, (336–323 BC) and conqueror of Persia (334–330 BC), b.356, d.323 BC.

Alexander I, Russian emperor (from 1801), b.1777, d.1825.

Alexander II, Russian emperor (from 1855), b.1818, assassinated 1881.
Alexander III, Russian emperor (from 1881), b.1845, d.1894.
Alexander I, king of Scotland (from 1107), b.*c.*1078, d.1124.
Alexander II, king of Scotland (from 1214), b.1198, d.1249.
Alexander III, king of Scotland (from 1249), b.1241, d.1285.
Alexandra, queen, wife of Edward VII, b.1844, d.1925.
Alexandria, founded 331 BC; library founded during 3rd century BC, damaged 47 BC, destroyed AD 272.
Alexandria, Battle of, fought between British and French 21 March 1801.
Alexandrian Era, began 5503 BC.
Alexios Comnenos, Byzantine emperor (1081–1118), b.1048, d.1118.
Alfarabi, Arabian musician, b.*c.*900, d.950.
Alfieri, Vittorio, Italian poet (*Saul*, 1782), b.1749, d.1803.
Alfonso, *see* **Alphonso.**
'Alfred Jewel, The', Ashmolean Museum, Oxford, found at Athelney 1693.
Alfred the Great, king of England (from 871), b.849, d.899.
Algeciras, Conference of, concerning Morocco, held 1906.
Algeria, annexed to France 1842; conquered by Allies from Axis 1942; nationalist revolt began 1954; achieved independence 1962.
Algren, Nelson, American novelist (*The Man with the Golden Arm*, 1949), b.1909, d.1981.
Alhambra, The, Moorish palace near Granada, built between 1248 and 1354.
Ali, Muslim leader, b.*c.*600, killed 660.
Ali, Muhammed (Cassius Clay), American boxer, three-times world heavyweight champion (1964, 1974, 1978), b.1942.
Aliwal, Battle of, first Sikh War, fought between the British and the Sikhs 28 Jan. 1846.
Alizarin, red dye, synthetized 1868 by the German scientist Karl Liebermann, b.1842, d.1914.
Alken, Henry, English etcher, d.1831.
Allan, David, Scottish painter, b.1744, d.1796.
Allen, Grant, Canadian-born writer (*The Woman Who Did*, 1895), b.1848, d.1899.
Allen, Woody (Allen Stewart Konigsberg), American film actor, director, screenwriter, comedian (*Manhattan*, 1979), b.1935.
Allenby, Edmund, Viscount, British soldier, b.1861, d.1936.

Allende, Isabel, Chilean-born novelist (*The House of the Spirits,* 1985), b.1942.
Allende (Gossens), Salvador, Chilean politician, president 1970–73, b.1908, killed 1973.
Alleyn, Edward, English actor-manager, founder of Dulwich College 1619, b.1566, d.1626.
All Hallows' Eve, 31 Oct.
All Saints, festival, instituted 625; celebrated at Rome 13 May.
All Saints' Day, celebrated 1 Nov.
All Souls' College, Oxford University, founded 1437 by Henry Chichele, b.1362, d.1443.
All Souls' Day, celebrated 2 Nov. (except when Sunday of festival is of the first class when it is celebrated 3 Nov.).
'All the Talents', Administration of, cabinet formed under Grenville 1806, resigned 1807.
Alma, Battle of the, Crimean War, in which the Allies fought the Russians, 20 Sept. 1854.
Almack's, London club founded 1763 by William Almack, d.1781; established as Brooks's 1778.
Almanza, Battle of, War of the Spanish Succession, French fought British and Portuguese, 25 April 1707.
Alma-Tadema, Sir Lawrence, Dutch-born painter, b.1836, d.1912.
Almeida, Portugal, captured by the Spaniards 25 Aug. 1762; by the French 1810; and recaptured by the Allies under Wellington 1811.
Almond, Dr Hely Hutchinson, Scottish educational reformer, b.1832, d.1903.
Almoravides (*Murabitim*), Berber Muslim sect, ruled N. Africa and Spain during 11th and 12th centuries.
Almqvist, Karl, Swedish writer, b.1793, d.1866.
Alpaca fabrics, first manufactured (1852) in England by Sir Titus Salt, b.1803, d.1876.
Alphage, St, archbishop of Canterbury, b.954, d.1012.
Alpha rays, discovered 1896 by Lord Rutherford, b.1871, d.1937.
Alphonso I, king of Portugal (from 1112), b.1094, d.1185.
Alphonso the Fat, king of Portugal (from 1211), b.1185, d.1223.
Alphonso III, king of Portugal (from 1248), b.1210, d.1279.
Alphonso IV, king of Portugal (from 1325), b.1290, d.1357.
Alphonso Africano, king of Portugal (from 1438), b.1432, d.1481.
Alphonso VI, king of Portugal (1656–1668), b.1643, d.1675.
Alphonso I, king of Spain, 739–757.

Alphonso the Chaste, king of Spain, 789–842.
Alphonso the Great, king of Spain, 866–914.
Alphonso IV, king of Spain, 924–931.
Alphonso V, king of Spain, 999–1028.
Alphonso VI, king of Spain, 1065–1109.
Alphonso the Emperor, king of Spain, 1126–57.
Alphonso the Noble, king of Castile, 1158–1214.
Alphonso IX, king of Leon, 1188–1230.
Alphonso the Wise, king of Spain, 1252–84.
Alphonso XI, king of Spain, 1312–50.
Alphonso XII, king of Spain (from 1870), b.1857, d.1885.
Alphonso XIII, king of Spain (from 1902 – abdicated 14 April 1931), b.1886, d.1941.
Alsace-Lorraine, ruled by Germany 1871–1918, by France 1918–40, by Germany 1940–44, by France since 1944.
Altamira cave paintings, Santander, Spain, discovered by the daughter of Marcelino de Sautuola 1879.
Altdorfer, Albrecht, German artist, b.*c.*1480, d.1538.
Altman, Robert, American film director (*M.A.S.H.*, 1970), b.1922.
Altmark, Battle of the, 16 Feb. 1940.
Aluminium, isolated 1854 by the French scientist Henri Ste.-Claire Deville, b.1818, d.1881.
Amado, Jorge, Brazilian novelist (*Gabriella, Clove and Cinnamon,* 1958), b.1912.
Amateur Athletic Association, United Kingdom, founded 1880.
Amati, Niccolo, Italian violin-maker, b.1596, d.1684.
Amazon River, discovered 1500 by the Spanish navigator Vicente Yañez Pinzón, b.*c.*1460, d.*c.*1524.
Ambassadors, first legally protected in England 1708.
Amboyna, Molucca island and town, discovered by the Portuguese 1511; seized by the Dutch 1605; Massacre of, 1623.
Ambrose, St, bishop of Milan, b.*c.*340, d.397.
Ambulances, introduced 1792 by Baron Dominique Jean Larrey, b.1766, d.1842.
Amelia, princess, daughter of George III, b.1783, d.1810.
America, discovered by Christopher Columbus 1492. Vikings believed to have reached America *c.*1000.
American Academy, in Rome, founded 1905.
American Academy of Arts and Sciences, chartered at Boston 1780.
American Antiquarian Society, founded 1812.
American Bar Association, organized 1878.

American Bible Society, founded 1816.
American Civil Liberties Union, founded 1920.
American Civil War, fought 1861 to 1865.
American Civil War Veteran, last surviving, Walter Williams, b.1843, d.1959.
American Constitution, came into force 21 June 1788.
American Declaration of Independence, made 4 July 1776.
American Dialect, of English, first mentioned 1740.
American Duties Act, passed 1764; on tea 1767.
American Ephemerus and Nautical Almanac, founded 1849 by Charles Henry Davis, b.1807, d.1877.
American Federation of Labor, founded 1886.
American Football, adopted present form 1880.
American Legion, founded 1919.
American Philosophical Society, founded by Benjamin Franklin at Philadelphia 1734.
American Society for the Prevention of Cruelty to Animals, founded 1866.
American States, Organization of, formed 1948.
American War of Independence, fought 1775 to 1783.
Ames, Joseph, English bibliographer (*Typographical Antiquities*, 1749), b.1689, d.1759.
Amherst College, Hampshire Co., Mass., USA, opened 1821, chartered 1825.
Amiel, Henri Frédéric, Swiss philosopher, b.1821, d.1881.
Amiens, Treaty of, between Great Britain, France, Spain and the Netherlands, signed 25 March 1802.
Amiens Cathedral, constructed 1220–88.
Amin, Idi, Ugandan soldier and politician, military dictator (1971–79), b.c.1925.
Amines, derivatives of ammonia, discovered 1849 by the French chemist Charles Adolphe Wurtz, b.1817, d.1843.
Amis, Kingsley, British writer (*Lucky Jim*, 1954), b.1922.
Amis, Martin, British writer (*Money*, 1984), b.1949.
Amman, Jost, Swiss artist, b.1539, d.1591.
Ammonia, gas, discovered 1774 by Joseph Priestley, b.1733, d.1804.
Amnesty International, founded 1961; Nobel peace prize 1972.
Amoy, in S.E. China, one of the first treaty-ports opened to European trade (1842).
Ampère, André Marie, French physicist, b.1775, d.1836.

Amritsar, Indian city, founded 1577 by Ram Das as the holy city of the Sikhs. Riots, 10 to 15 April 1919; Golden Temple attacked by Indian troops 1981.

Amundsen, Roald, Norwegian explorer (reached South Pole 14 Dec. 1911), b.1872, d.1928.

Amyot, Jacques, French translator of Plutarch, b.1513, d.1593.

Anabaptists, religious movement, began in Münster, Germany, 1521; first reached England 1549.

Anacletus (Anencletus), **St**, pope 76–78.

Anacletus II, anti-pope 1130–38.

Anacreon, Greek poet, b.*c.*550, d.*c.*465 BC.

Anaesthesia, General, nitrous oxide used 1799 by Humphry Davy, 1844 by Horace Wells (USA); ethyl chloride used 1848 by Heyfelder; ether used 1846 by William Morton (USA); chloroform demonstrated 1847 by Robert Simpson, administered to Queen Victoria 1853 by John Snow. Local freezing used 1812 by Baron Larrey (in Napoleon's army); cocaine used 1884 by Carl Koller; procaine used 1905 by Einhorn.

Anastasia, Grand Duchess of Russia, b.1901, d.1918?

Anastasius I, St, pope 399–401.

Anastasius II, St, pope 496–498.

Anastasius, anti-pope 855–858.

Anastasius III, pope 911–913.

Anastasius IV, pope 1153–54.

Anastasius I, Roman emperor (from 491), b.*c.*430, d.518.

Anastasius II, Roman emperor (from 713), executed 721.

Anaxagoras, Greek philosopher, b.*c.*500, d.*c.*428 BC.

Anaximander, first world map designer, b.611, d.546 BC.

Anaximenes, Greek philosopher, lived during 6th century BC.

ANC, *see* **African National Congress.**

Anchor Escapement, clock-making, invented by the English clockmaker Robert Hooke, b.1635, d.1703.

Ancon, Treaty of, almost ending the War of the Pacific (1879–84), signed 20 Oct. 1883.

Andaman Islands, used as penal settlement at intervals from 1858–1942; occupied by Japanese 1942–45; administered, together with the Nicobar Islands by the Government of India.

Andersen, Hans Christian, Danish writer of fairy stories, b.1805, d.1875.

Anderson, Elizabeth Garrett, first British woman doctor, qualified 1856, b.1836, d.1917.

Anderson, Lindsay, British film director and critic (*This Sporting Life*, 1963), b.1923.

Andhra Pradesh, India, constituted separate State 1953; on enlarging boundaries assumed present name 1956.

Andorra, traditionally granted independence by Charlemagne *c.*778; created a coprincipality 1278.

Andrássy, Julius, Count, Hungarian statesman, b.1823, d.1890.

André, Major John, British spy in America, b.1751, hanged 1780.

Andrea del Sarto, Italian painter, b.1487, d.1531.

Andrée, Salomon August, Swedish polar explorer, b.1854, d.1897.

Andrew, St, martyred 30 Nov. 69.

Andrew I, king of Hungary 1047–61.

Andrew II, king of Hungary (from 1205), b.1175, d.1235.

Andrew III, king of Hungary 1290–1301.

Andrewes, Lancelot, bishop of Winchester, b.1555, d.1626.

Andrews, Julie, British film star (*The Sound of Music*, 1965), b.1934.

Andreyev, Leonid Nikolaievich, Russian playwright (*He Who Gets Slapped*, 1916), b.1871, d.1919.

Andronicus I, Comnenus, Byzantine emperor (from 1183), murdered 1185.

Andronicus II, Palaeologus, Byzantine emperor (1282–1328), b.1260, d.1332.

Andronicus III, Palaeologus, Byzantine emperor (from 1325), b.*c.*1296, d.1341.

Andronicus IV, Palaeologus, Byzantine emperor (1376–79), d.1385.

Angas, George Fife, South Australian pioneer, b.1789, d.1879.

Angel, gold coin first used in France 1340; in England 1465.

Angelico, Fra (Guido di Pietri), Italian painter, b.1387, d.1455.

Angell, Sir Norman, (Ralph Norman Angell Lane) British economist (*The Great Illusion*, 1910), b.1874, d.1967.

Angelo, Domenico, fencing-master (*L'Ecole d'armes*, 1763), b.1716, d.1802.

Angelo, Henry, fencing-master (son of Domenico), b.1760, d.*c.*1839.

Angelou, Maya (Marguerite Ann Johnson), American author, poet, singer (*I Know Why the Caged Bird Sings*, 1970), b.1928.

Angerstein, John Julius, important figure in the development of Lloyds, b.1735, d.1823.

Angiosperms, plants whose seeds ripen in a container, first defined by Paul Hermann 1690.

Angkor Vat, Kampuchea, constructed *c.*1112–52.

Anglesey, conquered by the Romans 61; by the English 1295.

Anglican Church (Church of England), established by Augustine 597, separated from Catholic Church 1534.

Anglo-Afghan Treaty, concluded by the Dobbs Mission in Kabul, 22 Nov. 1921.

Anglo-Irish Treaty, setting up the Irish Free State, signed 6 Dec. 1921.

Anglo-Persian Oil Company, now British Petroleum Company, formed April 1909.

Anglo-Saxons, first landed in Britain *c.*449.

Angola (formerly Portuguese West Africa), discovered by the Portuguese navigator Diogo Cão 1482–85; Portuguese possession from 1575 until independence in 1975.

Angstrom unit (one millionth of 1 mm), named after the Swedish physicist Anders Jöns Angström, b.1814, d.1874.

Anhydrite, discovered 1794; named 1804 by Abraham Gottleb Werner, b.1750, d.1817.

Anicetus, St, pope 155–166.

Aniline, discovered by O. Unverdorben 1826, present name given by C. J. Fritzsche 1841.

Aniline Dyes, discovered 1856 by Sir William Henry Perkin, b.1838, d.1907.

Animism, philosophical doctrine propounded in the 18th century by Georg Ernst Stahl, b.1660, d.1734.

Ankara, capital of Turkey since 1920.

Anna Comnena, Byzantine princess, b.1083, d.1148.

Annam, former kingdom (3rd cent.–1428), empire (1428–1884) and French protectorate (1884–1945) in E. Indochina, now in Vietnam.

Annapolis, Maryland, first settled (under the name Providence) 1649; assumed present name 1694; incorporated 1708.

Ann Arbor, Michigan, first settled 1824; incorporated 1851.

Anne, queen of England (from 1702), b.1665, d.1714.

Anne, Russian empress (from 1730), b.1693, d.1740.

Anne, queen of Richard III, b.1456, d.1485.

Anne Boleyn, 2nd wife of Henry VIII, b.*c.*1507, beheaded 1536.

Anne of Austria, queen of France, b.1601, d.1666.

Anne of Bohemia, first queen of Richard II, b.1366, d.1394.

Anne of Brittany, wife successively of Maximilian of Austria and of Louis XII, b.1477, d.1514.
Anne of Cleves, 4th wife of Henry VIII. b.1515, m.1540, divorced 1540, d.1557.
Anne of Denmark, queen of James I, b.1574, d.1619.
Anning, Mary, English discoverer 1811 onwards of saurian remains, b.1799, d.1847.
Annual Register, first issued 1759.
Annunciation, Feast of the, celebrated in the Christian Church 25 March each year.
Annunzio, Gabriele d', Italian writer (*Francesca da Rimini*, 1901), b.1863, d.1938.
Anselm, St, archbishop of Canterbury, b.*c.*1033, d.1109.
Anson, George, Baron Anson, explorer, sailed round the world 1740–44, b.1697, d.1762.
Ansermet, Ernest, Swiss conductor, b.1883, d.1969.
Anstey, Christopher, English writer (*The New Bath Guide*, 1766), b.1724, d.1806.
'Anstey, F.' (Thomas Anstey Guthrie), writer (*Vice-versa*, 1882), b.1856, d.1934.
Anterus, St, pope 235–236.
Antheil, George, American composer, b.1900, d.1959.
Anthesteria, Athenian festival in honour of Dionysus, 11–13 month of Anthesterion (Feb.-March).
Anthony, St, the Great, first Christian monk, b.*c.*250, d.356.
Anthony of Padua, St, b.1197, d.1231.
Anthrax bacteria, first discovered independently by Pollender and Brauell, 1849
Anthropometry, first so named 1872 by Cesare Lombroso, b.1836, d.1909.
Anthroposophy, form of theosophy founded by Rudolf Steiner, b.1861, d.1925.
Anti-aircraft Defence, first used in siege of Paris 1870.
Antibiotics, first, penicillin, discovered by Sir Alexander Fleming b.1881, d.1955.
Anti-Corn-Law League, founded 1838 by Richard Cobden, b.1804, d.1865.
Anticosti, Canadian island, first sighted 1534 by the French explorer Jacques Cartier, b.1491, d.1557.
Antietam, Battle of, American Civil War, fought 16–17 Sept. 1862.

Antigua, discovered by Christopher Columbus 1493; British colony until 1967; became independent as part of the state of Antigua and Barbuda in 1981.

Antimony, discovered (according to tradition) by 'Basilius Valentinus' (possibly a 16th-century monk).

Antinomian Controversy, between Agricola and the Lutherans, 1527–40.

Antioch, founded by Seleucus 300 BC.

Antislavery Society, USA, founded *c.*1833 by William Lloyd Garrison, b.1805, d.1879.

Antisthenes, Greek philosopher, b.*c.*444, d.*c.*365 BC.

Antitoxins, study initiated by the French scientist Pierre Paul Emile Roux, b.1853, d.1933.

Antofagasta, Chile, founded 1870.

Antonello da Messina, Italian painter, b.*c.*1430, d.1479.

Antoninus, St, b.1389, d.1459.

Antonioni, Michelangelo, Italian film director (*The Passenger*, 1974), b.1912.

Antonius, Marcus (Mark Antony), b.*c.*83, committed suicide 30 BC.

Antoninus Pius, Roman emperor (from 138), b.86, d.161.

Antraigues, Comte Emanuel d', French diplomat, b.1755, murdered 1812.

Anzac Day, first celebrated in London 25 April 1916.

Anzio Landings, World War II, 22–25 Jan. 1944.

Apartheid, South African policy of separate political and cultural development for white and black races, first so named by the Rev. J. C. du Plessis at Kroonstad 1929; official policy of the government of South Africa 1948–90.

Apollinaire, Guillaume (Wilhelm Appolinaris Kostrowicki), French poet, b.1880, d.1918.

Apollinaris, the Younger, bishop of Laodicea, d.*c.*390.

Apothecaries Company, London, incorporated 1606 and 1617.

Apperley, Charles James, 'Nimrod', the sporting writer, b.1779, d.1843.

Appian Way, Roman road, constructed 312–308 BC.

'Appleseed, Johnny' (John Chapman), American pioneer, b.*c.*1775, d.1847.

Apollo project, American space programme initiated 1962 by President J. F. Kennedy; first lunar landing Apollo 10, 24 July 1969; discontinued 1975.

Apponyi, Albert, Count, Hungarian statesman, b.1846, d.1933.

Apraksin, Feodor Matveievich, founder of the Russian Navy, b.1671, d.1728.

Apricots, first planted in England *c.*1540.

April-Fools' Day (All Fools' Day), 1 April; similar Indian custom, The Feast of Huli, 31 March.

Apsley, Sir Allen, royalist leader, b.1616, d.1683.

Apuleius, Lucius, writer of *The Golden Ass, b.c.*125.

Aquatint, invented in France 1768.

Aquinas, Thomas, Italian theologian and philosopher, b.*c.*1227, d.1274

Aquino, (Maria) Corazon, Filipino politician, president (since 1986), b.1933.

Arabella Stewart, heir to English throne, b.1575, d. in prison 1615.

Arab-Israeli Wars: Six Day War 5 –10 June 1967; Yom Kippur War 6 –24 Oct. 1973.

Arab League, founded at Cairo 1945.

Arachnidae, family to which spiders belong, first distinguished 1815 by the French naturalist Jean Lamarck, b.1744, d.1829.

Arafat, Yasser, Palestinian resistance leader, b.1929.

Arago, Dominique François Jean, French scientist, b.1786, d.1853.

Aragon, Louis, French writer, b.1897, d.1982.

Aram, Eugene, murderer, b.1704, hanged 1759.

Ararat, Mt., reputed resting-place of Noah's Ark, first climbed 1829 by the German Dr Johann Jacob Parrot, b.1792, d.1840.

Arber, Edward, English bibliographer and scholar, b.1836, d.1912.

Arber Werner, Swiss microbilogist, shared Nobel prize 1978 for work on DNA and monoclonal antibodies, b.1929.

Arblay, Madame d' (Frances Burney), English novelist (*Evelina*, 1778), b.1752, d.1840.

Arbuckle (Roscoe), 'Fatty', American comedy actor, b.1887, d.1933.

Arbuthnot, Alexander, printer of the first Bible issued 1575 in Scotland, d.1585.

Arbuthnot, John, Scottish writer (*Martin Scriblerus*), b.1667, d.1735.

Arcadius, Roman emperor (from 395), b.378, d.408.

Arc de Triomphe, Paris, constructed in honour of the Grande Armée 1806–36.

Arcesilaus, Greek philosopher, b.*c.*316, d.*c.*241 BC.

Archangel, Russia, founded 1584.
Archangel Passage, discovered 1553 by the English navigator Richard Chancellor, d.1556.
Archer, Frederick, outstanding English jockey, b.1857, committed suicide 1886.
Archer, William, drama critic, b.1856, d.1924.
Archibald, Sir Adams George, Canadian statesman, b.1814, d.1892.
Archimedes, Greek mathematician, b.*c.*287, killed 212 BC.
Archipenko, Aleksandr, Russian-born sculptor, b.1887, d.1964.
Arden, Edward, English High Sheriff, b.*c.*1542, hanged 1583.
Arderne, John, English pioneer surgeon, lived in the 14th century.
Arditi, Luigi, Italian composer, (*Il Bacio*), b.1822, d.1903.
Arensky, Anton Stepanovich, Russian composer (*Raphael*, 1894), b.1861, d.1906.
Areopagus, Greek tribunal, founded *c.*1507 BC.
Arequipa, Peru, founded 1539 by the Spanish conquistador Francisco Pizarro, b.1478, murdered 1541.
Aretino, Pietro, Italian poet and playwright, b.1492, d.1556.
Argenson, Marc, Comte d', French army reformer, b.1696, d.1764.
Argentina, discovered by the Spanish explorer Don Juan Diaz de Solis 1516; ruled by Spain until 1816; independent series of governments from 1816; constitutional republic since 1852.
Argon, inert gas, discovered 1894 by the British scientists Lord Lister, b.1827, d.1912, and Sir William Ramsay, b.1852, d.1916.
Arian movement, heretical Christian movement, founded *c.*314 by the Libyan theologian Arius, d.336.
Ariosto, Lodovico, Italian poet (*Orlando furioso*, 1516), b.1474, d.1533.
Ariovistus, German chieftain, lived in the 1st century BC.
Aristarchus of Samos, Greek astronomer at Alexandria, b.*c.*310, d.*c.*250 BC.
Aristarchus of Samothrace, Greek writer, b.*c.*214, d.143 BC.
Aristides, Athenian general, d.*c.*468 BC.
Aristippus, Greek philosopher of the 5th and 4th centuries BC.
Aristophanes, Greek playwright (*The Wasps*), b.*c.*450, d.*c.*380 BC.
Aristotle, Greek philosopher, b.384, d.322 BC.
Arithmetic of Cardinal Numbers, axiomatized by the Italian mathematician Giuseppe Peano 1899.

Arius, Libyan theologian and leader of the Arian Movement, d.336.

Arizona, USA, settled 1732; created a Territory 1863; admitted to the Union 1912.

Arkansas, USA, settled 1686; created a Territory 1819; admitted to the Union 1836.

Arkhangelsky, Aleksandr, Russian composer (*Mass for the Dead*), b.1846, d.1924.

Arkwright, Sir Richard, English inventor 1768 of the spinning frame, b.1732, d.1792.

'Arlen, Michael' (Dikran Kouyoumdjian), Armenian-born novelist (*The Green Hat*, 1924), b.1895, d.1956.

Arles, Synod of, convened by the Emperor Constantine 314.

Arletty (Leonie Bathiat), French stage and screen actress (*Les Enfants du Paradis*, 1944), b.1898, d.1992.

Armada, Spanish, assembled 1587; defeated by the English 1588.

Armaments, Limitation of, Conference held Washington DC, 1921–22.

Armani, Giorgio, Italian fashion designer, founded own label 1975, b.1935.

Armenia, former kingdom created a Soviet Socialist Republic 1920; proclaimed a constituent Republic of the USSR 1936; became independent state on dissolution of USSR 1991.

Armenian Church, separate since 451.

Arminianism, religious movement, founded by the Dutch theologian Jacobus Arminius (Hermandzoon), b.1560, d.1609.

Arminius, German leader (17 BC–AD 21), routed Roman army under Varus AD 9.

Armistice Day (Day of Remembrance), World War I, 11 Nov. 1918.

Armour Plate, first proposed for ships of war 1805 by the English scientist and politician Sir William Congreve, b.1772, d.1828.

Armstrong, (Daniel) Louis, ('Satchmo' – satchel mouth), American jazz trumpeter, b.1900, d.1971.

Armstrong, Henry Edward, English chemist and educationist, b.1848, d.1937.

Armstrong, Neil, American astronaut, first man on the moon 20 July 1969, b.1930.

Armstrong, William George, Baron, English engineer and inventor, b.1810, d.1900.

Arne, Thomas Augustine, English composer (*Rule, Britannia,* 1740), b.1710, d.1778.

Arnhem, Battle of, World War II, 19–28 Sept. 1944.

Arnold, Benedict, American soldier, b.1741, d.1801.

Arnold, Bion Joseph, American electrical engineer and inventor 1900 of the magnetic clutch, b.1861, d.1942.

Arnold, Sir Edwin, English writer (*The Light of Asia,* 1879), b.1832, d.1904.

Arnold, Matthew, English educationist and poet (*Sohrab and Rustum,* 1853) b.1822, d.1888.

Arnold, Thomas, Headmaster of Rugby (1828–42), b.1795, d.1842.

Arnolfo di Cambio, Italian architect, b.c.1232, d.c.1310.

Arnulf, bishop of Rochester, b.1040, d.1124.

Aroostook 'War', American boundary dispute between Maine and New Brunswick, 1839.

Arp, Hans, French artist, b.1888, d.1966.

Arpád, Magyar leader, d.907; dynasty ruled Hungary until 1301.

Arras, Treaty of, between Charles VII and Philip the Good, signed 1435.

Arrau, Claudio, Chilean pianist, b.1903.

Arrhenius, Svante August, Swedish chemist, b.1859, d.1927.

Arrowsmith, Aaron, English geographer and map-publisher, b.1750, d.1823.

Arsacid dynasty, ruled Persia 227 BC to AD 224.

Artagnan, Charles de Baatz d', French captain of the Musketeers, b.1611, d.1673.

Artaud, Antonin, French playwright, poet, actor and theorist (*The Theatre and it's Double,* 1938), b.1896, d.1948.

Artaxerxes I, Persian king, reigned 465–425 BC.

Artaxerxes II, Persian king, reigned 404–358 BC.

Artaxerxes III, Persian king, reigned 358–338 BC.

Artevelde, Jacob van, governor of Flanders, killed 1345.

Arthur, king, possibly real 5th- or 6th-century British chieftain.

Arthur, duke of Brittany, b.1187, murdered 1203.

Arthur, Chester Alan, 21st US president (1881–85), b.1830, d.1886.

Arthur, Sir George, governor of Bombay (1842–46), b.1784, d.1854.

Artichokes, first grown in England in the 16th century.

Articles of Religion, 6 published by King Henry VIII 1536; 42 published without Parliamentary consent 1552; reduced to 39 1563, and received Parliamentary authority 1571.

Artificial radioactivity, discovered 1934 by the French physicist Jean Frédéric Joliot-Curie b.1900, d.1958.

Artificial silk, made 1883 by the English electro-chemist Sir Joseph Wilson Swan, b.1828, d.1914. Industry founded *c.*1885 by the French scientist Hilaire, Comte de Chardonnet, b.1839, d.1924.

Artigas, José Gervasio, Uruguayan revolutionary leader, b.1774, d.1850.

Arts Council of Great Britain, London, founded as the Council for the Encouragement of Music and the Arts (C.E.M.A.) 1940; incorporated under present name 1946.

Artsybashev, Mikhail Petrovich, Russian-born writer (*Sanine,* 1907), b.1878, d.1927.

Arundel, Thomas, archbishop of Canterbury (1396–1414), b.1353, d.1414.

Asaph, St, d.*c.*596.

Asbury, Francis, English-born Methodist leader in America, b.1745, d.1816.

Ascalon, Battle of, fought between the Crusaders and the Moslems, 15 Aug. 1099.

Ascension Day, celebrated on a Thursday each year 40 days after Easter Sunday.

Ascension Island, discovered by the Portuguese navigator João da Nova on Ascension Day 1501.

Asch, Sholem, Yiddish writer (*Dos Shtelt,* 1904), b.1880, d.1957.

Ascham, Roger, English writer (*The Schoolmaster,* 1570), b.*c.*1515, d.1568.

Asclepiades, Greek physician, *fl.* 2nd century BC.

Ascot Gold Cup, instituted 1807.

Ascot Race Meeting, first held 11 Aug. 1711.

Asen dynasty, ruled Bulgaria, 1185–1258.

Ashanti, former West African kingdom, formally annexed by Britain 1901 and incorporated within the colony of the Gold Coast (now Ghana).

Ashanti Wars, 1863–64,1873–74 and 1895–1900.

Ashcroft, Dame Peggy (Edith Margaret Emily), British actress, b.1907, d.1991.

Ashdown, Battle of, between the Saxons and the Danes, 6 Jan. 871.

Ashendene Press, private press, founded and operated by C. H. St John Hornby, b.1895, d.1923.

'Ashes, The', instituted 1882.

Ashford, Daisy, English writer (*The Young Visiters,* 1919), b.1881, d.1972.

Ashkenazy, Vladimir, Russian pianist and conductor, b.1937.

Ashley, Laura, Welsh-born designer and retailer of clothes and furnishings, b.1926, d.1985.

Ashmolean Museum, Oxford, founded *c.*1677 by the English antiquary Elias Ashmole, b.1617, d.1692; opened 1682.

Ashmun, Jehudi, American reformer in Liberia, b.1794, d.1828.

Ashton, Sir Frederick, English dancer and choreographer, director of Royal Ballet (1963–70), b.1906, d.1988.

Ash Wednesday, the first day of Lent.

Aske, Robert, English leader 1536 of the Pilgrimage of Grace, executed 1537.

Aslib, London, founded as the Association of Special Libraries and Information Bureaux 1924.

Asoka, Indian emperor, b.273, d.232 BC.

Aspdin, Joseph, English stonemason and inventor (1824) of Portland cement, b.1779, d.1855.

Aspirin, developed 1899 by German physician Felix Hoffman.

Asquith, Herbert Henry, Earl of Oxford and Asquith, British statesman (prime minister 1908–16), b.1852, d.1928.

Assam, state of N.E. India, conquered by the British 1842, incorporated into Bengal by 1914, became separate province 1924.

Asser, English historian and Bishop of Sherborne, d.*c.*909.

Assignats, French Revolutionary paper money used 1789–97.

Assumption of the Blessed Virgin Mary, Feast of the, celebrated each year 15 Aug.; Catholic dogma defined 195.

Assur-Bani-Pal, Assyrian King (about 669–626 BC), d.626 BC.

Astaire, Fred (Frederick Austerlitz), American dancing film-star (*Top Hat,* 1935), b.1899, d.1987.

Asteroid, first (Ceres) discovered 1801 by the Italian astronomer Giuseppe Piazzi, b.1746, d.1826.

Astley's Circus, founded 1770 by the English equestrian Philip Astley, b.1742, d.1814.

Aston, Francis William, English inventor of the mass spectograph, b.1877, d.1945.

Astor, John Jacob, American millionaire, b.1763, d.1848.

Astor, Nancy Witcher Langhorne, Viscountess, American-born, first woman to sit (1919) in the House of Commons, b.1879, d.1964.

Astrolabe, Mariner's, adapted from the astronomer's astrolabe *c.*1480 by the German Martin Behaim, b.*c.*1459, d.1507.

Astrophysics, study founded 1855 by the English scientist Sir William Huggins, b.1824, d.1910.

Aswan Dam, Upper Egypt, completed 1902.

Atahualpa, last Inca of Peru (1532–33), executed 1533.

Atatürk, Kemal, Turkish soldier and statesman (prime minister 1923–38), b.1880, d.1938.

Athanasius, St, patriarch of Alexandria, b.*c.*298, d.373.

Athelstan, king (924) of Wessex and Mercia, b.*c.*895, d.939.

Athenaeum, British periodical, began publication 1828; absorbed into *The Nation* 1921.

Athenaeum Club, London, founded 1824.

Athens, schools closed 529; ruled by Turks 1456–1832.

Atkinson, Sir Harry, New Zealand prime minister (1876–77, 1883–84, 1887–91), b.1831, d.1892.

Atlantic Charter, signed 1941.

Atlantic Flight, First solo Trans-, New York to Paris, made 1927 by the American aviator Charles Augustus Lindbergh, b.1902, d.1974.

Atlantic Telephone Cable, first opened for traffic 1956.

Atlantic Telegraph Cable, first successfully laid by the S.S. *Great Eastern* 1866.

Atlantic Treaty, North, signed in Washington DC, 1949.

Atmosphere, composition determined by the British scientist Henry Cavendish, b.1731, d.1810.

Atom, split 1919 by the New Zealand-born scientist Lord Rutherford, b.1871, d.1937.

Atom bomb, first used in warfare on Hiroshima and Nagasaki August 1945.

Atomic bomb explosion, first carried out by the USA in New Mexico 1945.

Atomic Energy Agency, United Nations agency based in Vienna, established 1957.

Atomic nucleus, first split (and the atom's energy released) by Sir John Cockcroft and Dr Walton 1932.

Atomic numbers, of elements, determined by the British scientist Henry Gwyn Jeffreys Moseley, b.1887, killed in battle 1915.

Atomic pile, first started operating in Chicago 2 Dec. 1942.

Atomic-powered ship, world's first, the Russian ice-breaker *Lenin*, launched 1957, put to sea 1958.
Atomic shell, first fired in Nevada, USA, 1953.
Atomic theory, classical version postulated by Leucippus of Miletus *c.*475 BC; modern version developed by the English chemist John Dalton, b.1766, d.1844.
Atomic weights, pioneer work done by the Swedish chemist Baron Berzelius, b.1779, d.1848.
Atropine, drug extracted from belladonna, discovered by the German scientist Philipp Lorenz Geiger 1833.
Attenborough, Sir David, English naturalist and broadcaster, b.1926.
Attenborough, Sir Richard, British actor and film director (*Brighton Rock,* 1947), b.1923.
Atticus, Titus Pomponius, Roman scholar, b.109, d.32 BC.
Attila, 'Scourge of God', king of the Huns, b.*c.*406, d.453.
Attlee, Clement Richard, 1st Earl, British statesman (prime minister 1945–51), b.1883, d.1967.
Attorney-General, first English, William Bonneville 1277.
Atwood, Margaret, Canadian novelist and poet (*The Handmaid's Tale,* 1986), b.1939.
Auber, Daniel François Esprit, French composer (*Fra Diavolo,* 1830), b.1782, d.1871.
Aubrey, John, English antiquary and writer (*Minutes for Lives*), b.1626, d.1697.
Auchinleck, Sir Claude, British soldier, b.1884, d.1981.
Auden, Wystan Hugh, English-born poet (*The Orators,* 1932), b.1907, d.1973.
Audenarde (Oudenarde), Battle of, fought between the English and the French 30 June–11 July 1708.
Audubon, John James, American naturalist, b.1785, d.1851.
Auer von Welsbach, Karl, inventor 1885 of gas mantle, b.1858, d.1929.
Augsburg, The Confession of, Lutheran creed, prepared 1530.
Augustine, St, bishop of Hippo, N. African philosopher and theologian (*De Civitate Dei*), b.354, d.430.
Augustine, St, first archbishop of Canterbury, d.*c.*604.
Augustus, first Roman emperor (27 BC–AD 14), b.63 BC, d. AD 14.
Augustus II, king of Poland (1697–1733), b.1670, d.1733.
Augustus III, king of Poland (1736–63), b.1696, d.1763.
Aulus Vitellius, Roman emperor (69), b.15, murdered 69.
Aurangzeb, Mogul emperor of India (1659–1707), b.1618, d.1707.

Aurelian, Roman emperor (270–275), b.*c.*212, assassinated 275.
Aurelius, Marcus, Roman emperor (161–180), and author of *The Meditations*, b.121, d.180.
Auric, Georges, French composer (*Les Matelots,* 1925), b.1899, d.1983.
Auscultation by stethoscope, medical examination, introduced by the French physician René Théophile Hyacinthe Laënnec, b.1781, d.1826.
Austen, Jane, English novelist (*Pride and Prejudice,* 1813), b.1775, d.1817.
Austerlitz, Battle of, between the French, and the Austrians and Russians, 2 Dec. 1805.
Australia, circumnavigated 1642–43 by the Dutch navigator Abel Janszoon Tasman (*c.*1603–59). Reached by air from England by Ross and Keith Smith 1919.
Australia, The Commonwealth of, created 1 Jan. 1901.
Austria, ruled by Hapsburgs 1278–1918; republic 1918–38; annexed by Germany 1938; occupied 1943–55; regained independence 1955.
Austrian Succession, War of the, 1740–48.
Authorized Version of the Bible, made at order of James I, first published 1611.
Autogyro, invented by La Cierra 1920.
Avars, entered Europe *c.*555; defeated by Franks in 8th and 9th centuries.
Averroës (Ibn Rushd), Arabian philosopher, b.1126, d.1198.
Avery, 'Tex' (Frederick Bean), American animator, created Daffy Duck, Bugs Bunny, b.1907, d.1980.
Avicenna (Ibn Sina), Persian philosopher, b.*c.*980, d.1037.
Avignon, ceded to the Papacy 1274; seat of Papacy 1309–1418; annexed to France 1791.
Avoirdupois, generally superseded the merchants' pound in England 1303.
Axminster carpet, introduced into Britain from the USA *c.*1878.
Ayckbourn, Alan, British playwright and theatre director (*The Norman Conquests,* 1974), b.1939.
Ayer, Sir Alfred Jules (Freddie), English philosopher (*Language, Truth and Logic,* 1936), b.1910, d.1989.
Azañay Diaz, Manuel de, Spanish statesman (last republican president), b.1880, d.1940.
Aztec Empire, Mexico, established in the 14th century, destroyed by Spaniards in early 16th century.

B

Baader, Franz Xaver von, German theologian, b.1765, d.1841.
Baader-Meinhof Group (Red Army Faction), West German urban guerrilla group (1968–72) led by Andreas Baader, b.1943, d.1977, and Ulrike Meinhof, b.1934, d.1976; both committed suicide in prison.
Baalbek, Syrian city, destroyed by earthquake 1759.
Baal-Shem-Tov (Israel ben Eliezer), Russian founder of the modern Hasidim (Jewish sect), b.1700, d.1760.
Babar, *see* **Baber.**
Babbage, Charles, English mathematician and founder of the Royal Astronomical Society, b.1792, d.1871. Designed an 'analytical engine' (1827–47), the prototype for modern computers.
Babbitt Metal, anti-friction alloy, invented 1839 by the American Isaac Babbitt, b.1799, d.1861.
Babel, Isaac Emmanuilovich, Russian writer (*Red Cavalry*, 1926), b.1894, d.1941.
Baber, founder of the Mogul dynasty and conqueror of North India (ruled 1526–30), b.*c.*1483, d.1530.
Babeuf, François Noël, French revolutionary leader, b.1760, prepared Babouvist conspiracy 1796, guillotined 1797.
Babi, Persian religious sect, founded 1844 by Mirza Ali Mohammed, b.1821, killed 1850.
Babington Plot, to murder Queen Elizabeth I in 1585, devised by Anthony Babington, b.1561, executed 1586.
Babur, *see* **Baber.**
Babylon, Babylonian capital, chosen as capital *c.*2100 BC, declined in importance after 538 BC.
Babylonian Captivity, of the Jews, 586–516 BC.
'Babylonish Captivity', of the popes, 1309–77.
Bacall, Lauren (Betty Joan Perske), American film and stage actress (*The Big Sleep,* 1946), m. Humphrey Bogart 1944, b.1924.
Baccarat Case, in which future Edward VII gave evidence concerning gambling at Tranby Croft, tried June 1891.
Bacchelli, Riccardo, Italian novelist (*Il Diavolo al Pontelungo,* 1927), b.1891, d.1985.
Bach, Carl Philipp Emmanuel, German composer, b.1714, d.1788.
Bach, Johann Christian, German composer, b.1725, d.1782.
Bach, Johann Sebastian, German composer, b.1685, d.1750.

Bache, Alexander Dallas, American founder 1863 of the National Academy of Sciences, b.1806, d.1867.

Bacon, Francis, Baron Verulam, English statesman and writer, b.1561, d.1626.

Bacon, Francis, British artist (*Three Studies for a Crucifixion*, 1962), b.1909, d.1992.

Bacon, Roger, English philosopher, b.*c.*1214, d.*c.*1294.

Bacon's Rebellion, American revolt 1676 in Virginia, led by Nathaniel Bacon, b.1647, d.1676.

Bacteria, discovered 1680 by the Dutch scientist A. van Leeuwenhoek, b.1632, d.1723; classified by F. J. Cohn 1872.

Badajoz, Battle of, Peninsular War, between Wellington and the French, 1812.

Baden-Powell, Robert, Lord, founder 1908 of the Boy Scouts, b.1857, d.1941.

Badminton, game played with shuttlecock, first played in England *c.*1873.

Badoglio, Pietro, Italian field marshal, b.1871, d.1956.

Badon, Mount, legendary battle between British and Saxons, *c.*500.

Baedeker, Karl, German guide book compiler and publisher, b.1801, d.1859.

Baer, Karl Ernst von, Estonian scientist and discoverer 1827 of the mammalian ovum, b.1792, d.1876.

Baer, Max, world heavy-weight boxing champion 1934, b.1910, d.1959.

Baeyer, Johann Friedrich Wilhelm Adolf von, German scientist and Nobel Prize winner 1905, b.1835, d.1917.

Baez, Joan, American folk singer, b.1941.

Baffin Bay, discovered 1616 by William Baffin, b.*c.*1584, d.1622.

Bagehot, Walter, English sociologist and editor of the *Economist*, *b.*1826, d.1877.

Baghdad Railway, started 1888, completed 1940.

Bagration, Piotr Ivanovich, Russian general who fought (1812) Napoleon at Borodino, b.1765, d.1812.

Baha'i, religious sect developed from Babi by Mirza Hozain Ali, b.1817, d.1892, and his son Abbas Effendi, b.1844, d.1921.

Bahamas, West Indian islands, discovered 1492 by Christopher Columbus; British colony 1783–1964; independent within the Commonwealth since 1973.

Bahrain, Persian Gulf, British Protectorate from 1861 to independence in 1971.

Baïf, Jean Antoine de, French poet, b.1532, d.1589.
Baikie, William Balfour, Scottish explorer of West Africa, b.1825, d.1864.
Bailey bridge, invented 1941 by Sir Donald Bailey, b.1901, d.1985.
Baillie, Joanna, Scottish dramatist and poet, b.1762, d.1851.
Bain, Alexander, Scottish philosopher, b.1818, d.1903.
Baird, John Logie, Scottish inventor (1926) of television, b.1888, d.1946.
Bairnsfather, Bruce, English cartoonist and creator of the character 'Old Bill', b.1888, d.1959.
Bajazet I, Turkish sultan, b.1347, d.1403.
Bajazet II, Turkish sultan, b.1446, d.1513.
Bakelite, invented 1907 by the American Leo Hendrik Baekeland, b.1863, d.1944.
Baker, Sir Benjamin, English designer of the Forth Rail Bridge, b.1840, d.1907.
Baker, Chet (Chesney), American jazz trumpeter and vocalist, b.1929, d.1988.
Baker, Dame Janet, English mezzo-soprano, b.1933.
Baker, Josephine, American dancer, singer and civil rights activist, b.1906, d.1975.
Baker, Sir Samuel White, English explorer of Africa, discoverer (1864) of Albert Nyanza, b.1821, d.1893.
Bakerloo Line, London Underground, opened 1906.
Bakewell, Robert, English agricultural pioneer, b.1725, d.1795.
Bakst, Leon, Russian-born stage designer, b.1866, d.1924.
Bakunin, Mikhail, Russian anarchist leader, b.1814, d.1876.
Balakirev, Mili Alexeivich, Russian composer, b.1836, d.1910.
Balaklava, Battle of, scene of the Charge of the Light Brigade, fought 25 Oct. 1854.
Balanchine, George, Russian-born ballet dancer, b.1904, d.1983.
Balboa, Vasco Núñez de, Spanish discoverer (1513) of the Pacific Ocean b.1475, beheaded 1517.
Balbus, Lucius Cornelius, Roman consul defended by Cicero, *fl.* 56–40 BC.
Balchin, Nigel, English writer (*The Small Back Room*, 1943) b.1908.
Baldovinetti, Alessio, Italian painter, b.c.1425, d.1499.
Baldwin, James, American author (*Go Tell It On A Mountain*, 1953), b.1924, d.1989.
Baldwin, Robert, Canadian statesman, b.1804, d.1858.

Baldwin, Stanley, British statesman (prime minister 1923, 1924, 1924–29, 1935–37), b.1867, d.1947.

Baldwin I, emperor at Constantinople, b.1171, killed 1205.

Baldwin II, emperor at Constantinople, b.1217, d.1273.

Baldwin I, first king of Jerusalem, b.1058, d.1118.

Baldwin II, king of Jerusalem, succeeded to the throne 1118, d.1131.

Baldwin III, king of Jerusalem, b.1130, d.1162.

Baldwin IV, king of Jerusalem, b.c.1161, d.1185.

Baldwin V, king of Jerusalem, b.1178, d.1186.

Bale, John, English dramatist, b.1495, d.1563.

Balearic Islands, finally ceded to Spain by the British 1803.

Balfe, Michael William, British composer (*The Bohemian Girl*), b.1808, d.1870.

Balfour, Arthur James, **Earl Balfour**, British statesman (prime minister 1902–05), b.1848, d.1930.

Balfour Declaration, favouring the creation of a Jewish national home in Palestine, made by the British Government 2 Nov. 1917.

Bali, Indonesian island, first reached by the Dutch 1597.

Balliol, John de, king of Scots (1295–96), b.1249, d.1313.

Balliol College, Oxford University, founded *c.*1263 by John de Baliol, d.1269.

Balkan Wars, fought by the Balkan powers over the division of the Turkish empire in Europe 1912–13.

Ball, John, English priest and peasants' leader, executed 1381.

Ball, Lucy (Lucille Desirée), American comedy actress, star of TV series 'I Love Lucy' (1951–55), b.1911, d.1989.

Ballantyne, Robert Michael, Scottish writer of boys' stories, b.1825, d.1894.

Ballard, James Graham, English novelist (*Empire of the Sun,* 1984), b.1930.

Ballistite, smokeless powder, invented 1888 by the Swedish chemist Alfred Nobel, b.1833, d.1896.

Ballot, voting by, made compulsory in Britain 1872.

Balloons, invented by the brothers Joseph and Etienne Montgolfier 1783, first ascent by Montgolfier and Pilâtre de Roziers 21 Nov. 1783; first ascent in hydrogen balloon made by the physicist J. A. C. Charles 1 Dec. 1783; first ascents in Britain made 1784.

Balmoral Castle, Aberdeenshire, British royal residence, completed 1855.

Balsamo, Giuseppe, 'Count Alessandro di Cagliostro', Italian charlatan and alchemist, b.1743, d.1795.

Baltic Exchange (The Baltic Mercantile and Shipping Exchange), London, developed from informal 17th-century coffee-house transactions to the formal establishment of the Baltic Club 1823.

Baltimore, Maryland, formally founded 1729; settled about fifty years earlier.

Baluchistan, merged in West Pakistan 14 Oct. 1955.

Balzac, Honoré de, French novelist (*La Comédie Humaine,* 1829–50), b.1799, d.1850.

Bampton Lectures, delivered annually at Oxford University since 1780, founded by John Bampton, b.c.1690, d.1751.

Bancroft, George, American historian, b.1800, d.1891.

Bancroft, Sir Squire, English actor-manager, b.1841, d.1926.

Banda, Hastings Kamuzu, president of Malawi since 1966, b.1905.

Bandung Conference, of Asian-African countries, held 18–27 April 1955.

Bangalore, Mysore capital, founded 1537.

Bangkok, made capital of Thailand by Paya Tak 1782.

Bangladesh, formerly East Pakistan; became independent republic after civil war 1971.

Bank for International Settlements, founded 13 Nov. 1929.

Bank for Reconstruction and Development, International, proposed at Bretton Woods Conference 1944, constituted Dec. 1945, started operations 27 June 1946.

Bankhead, Tallulah, American stage and film actress (*Lifeboat* 1944), b.1903, d.1968.

Bank of England, founded 1694 by William Paterson, b.1658, d.1719; nationalized 1946.

Bank of France, founded by Napoleon I, 1800.

Bank of Scotland, founded by the Scottish Parliament 1695.

Bank of the United States: 1st, founded by the Federalists 1791, ended 1811; 2nd, founded 1816, ended 1836.

Bankruptcy Act, abolished imprisonment for debt 1870.

Banks, Sir Joseph, English naturalist, founder of the African Association, b.1744, d.1820.

Bannister, Sir Roger (Gilbert), English runner, physician and amateur athelete; first to run the four-minute mile 6 May 1954, b.1929.

Bannockburn, Battle of, fought between Scots and English, 24 June 1314.

Banting, Sir Frederick Grant, Canadian scientist, b.1891, killed in an air crash 1941

Banting, William, English undertaker and pioneer in slimming by diet, b.1797, d.1878.

Bantock, Sir Granville, English composer (*The Great God Pan*, 1903), b.1868, d.1946.

Bantry Bay, Battle of, when French attempted the invasion of Ireland 1689; and again in 1796.

Baptist Church, first English, formed 1609 at Amsterdam, and 1611 in London. The Baptist Union of Great Britain and Ireland formed 1891. In USA, first Baptist Church formed at the Providence settlement of Narragansett Bay 1639.

Barbados, visited by the English 1605; formally occupied by the English 1625; became part of the British Caribbean Federation 1956.

Barbarossa (Frederick I), Holy Roman emperor, b.c.1123, d.1190.

Barbarossa Brothers, Turkish pirates who terrorized Christian shipping in the Mediterranean in early 16th century.

Barbed Wire, invented 1873 by the American Joseph Farwell Glidden, b.1813, d.1906.

'Barbellion, W. N. P.' (Bruce Frederick Cummings), English writer (*The Journal of a Disappointed Man*, 1919), b.1889, d.1919.

Barber, Samuel, American composer (*Essay for Orchestra*, 1938), b.1910, d.1981.

Barbey d'Aurevilly, Jules, French writer, b.1808, d.1889.

Barbirolli, Sir John, conductor of the Hallé Orchestra from 1943, b.1899, d.1970.

Barbizon School, French art movement 1830–70.

Barbon, Nicolas (son of Praise-God Barebone), English pioneer of fire insurance, b.1640, d.1698.

Barbusse, Henri, French writer (*Le Feu*, 1916), b.1873, d.1935.

Barcelona Cathedral, erected 1298–1448.

Barcelona University, founded 1430.

Bard College, Annandale-on-Hudson, N.Y., founded 1860, chartered in its present form and name 1935.

Bardot, Brigitte, French film actress and sex symbol (*And God Created Woman*, 1956), b.1934.

Barebone's Parliament, called by Cromwell during the Commonwealth, sat 4 July to 12 Dec. 1653. Named after one of its members, Praise-God Barebone, b.*c.*1596, d.1679.

Barents Sea, named after William Barents, d.1597, Dutch explorer.

Barham, Richard Harris, English writer (*The Ingoldsby Legends,* 1837–40), b.1788, d.1845.

Barhebraeus (Abulfaraj), Armenian writer and bishop of Aleppo, b.1226, d.1286.

Baring, Maurice, English writer (*In My End is My Beginning,* 1931), b.1874, d.1945.

Baring Brothers, English merchant bankers, founded by John Baring, b.1730, d.1816, and Francis Baring, b.1740, d.1810.

Baring-Gould, Sabine, English writer and hymn-writer ('Onward, Christian soldiers', 1865), b.1834, d.1924.

Barium, first investigated by V. Casciorolus of Bologna 1602, discovered 1808 by Sir Humphry Davy, b.1778, d.1829.

Barker, Granville, English poet and novelist (*Alanna Autumnal,* 1933), b.1913.

Bar-Kochba, Simon, Jewish leader in revolt against Romans (131–135), killed fighting 135.

Barlach, Ernst, German artist, b.1870, d.1937.

Barnabites, Catholic religious order, founded 1537 by St Antony Mary Zaccaria, d.1539.

Barnard, Christian, South African surgeon, performed first heart transplant 2 Dec. 1967, b.1923.

Barnardo's Homes, Dr, founded 1867 by Dr Thomas Barnardo, b.1845, d.1905.

Barnato, Barnett, English-born South African financier, b.1852, committed suicide 1897.

Barnes, Barnabe, English poet, b.*c.*1569, d.1609.

Barnes, Thomas, English journalist (edited *The Times,* 1817–41), b.1785, d.1841.

Barnes, William, English dialect poet, b.1800, d.1886.

Barnet, Battle of, Wars of the Roses, 14 April 1471.

Barnet Fair, Hertfordshire, held during first week in Sept.

Barnfield, Richard, English pastoral poet, b.1574, d.1627.

Barnum's Show, founded 1871 by the American Phineas Taylor Barnum, b.1810, d.1891.

Baroja, Pio, Spanish novelist, b.1872, d.1956.

Barometers, invented 1644 by Evangelista Torricelli, b.1608, d.1647.

Baronet, title created by King James I of England 1611.
Barr, Robert, Scottish writer (*In the Midst of Alarms*, 1894), b.1850, d.1912.
Barren Grounds, Canada, first crossed 1770–72 by the English explorer Samuel Hearne, b.1745, d.1792.
Barrès, Maurice, French politician and writer (*Le jardin de Bérénice*, 1891), b.1862, d.1923.
Barrie, Sir James Matthew, Scottish writer (*Peter Pan*, 1904), b.1860, d.1937.
Barrington, George, Irish pickpocket who became an Australian chief constable, b.1755, d.1804.
Barrister, first English woman, qualified 25 May 1921.
Barrow, Sir John, English explorer and founder (1830) of the Royal Geographical Society, b.1764, d.1848.
Barry, Sir Charles, English architect of the House of Commons, b.1795, d.1860.
Barrymore, family of American stage and film performers: Lionel, b.1878, d.1954; Ethel, b.1879, d.1959; John, b.1882, d.1942; they appeared together only once in *Rasputin and the Empress*, 1932.
Bart, Jean, French admiral, b.1650, d.1702.
Barth, Hans, German composer, b.1897, d.1956.
Barth, Heinrich, German traveller and scientist, b.1821, d.1865.
Barth, Karl, German pianist, b.1847, d.1922.
Barth, Karl, Swiss theologian, b.1886, d.1968.
Barthes, Roland, French literary critic and philosopher (*Mythologies*, 1957), b.1915, d.1980.
Bartholdi, Frédéric Auguste, French sculptor (*Statue of Liberty*), b.1834, d.1904.
Bartholomew, John George, Scottish cartographer, b.1860, d.1920.
Bartholomew, Massacre of St, of Protestants by Catholics in Paris, 24 Aug. 1572.
Bartholomew Fair, held at West Smithfield, London, on St Bartholomew's Day (24 Aug. OS) from 1133–1855.
Barthou, Jean, French statesman b.1862, assassinated 1934.
Bartlett, John, compiler of standard collection of *Familiar Quotations* (1855), b.1820, d.1905.
Bartók, Bela, Hungarian composer (*The Castle of Duke Bluebeard*, 1918), b.1881, d.1945.
Bartolommeo, Fra, Italian painter (*The Marriage of St Catherine*), b.c.1470, d.1517.

Bartolozzi, Francesco, Italian engraver, b.1727, d.1815.
Bartram, John, first American botanist, b.1739, d.1823.
Baruch, Bernard Mannes, American financier, b.1870, d.1965.
Barye, Antoine Louis, French sculptor, b.1795, d.1875.
Baseball, invention attributed to Abner Doubleday, b.1819, d.1883, of Cooperstown, New York.
Basevi, George, English architect of the Fitzwilliam Museum, Cambridge (1837), b.1794, d.1845.
Bashkirtsev, Marie, Russian painter and writer (*Journal*, 1887), b.1860, d.1884.
Basic English, produced 1930 by C. K. Ogden.
Basie, William, 'Count', American jazz pianist and band leader, b.1904, d.1984.
Basil, St, known as Basil the Great, b.*c.*330, d.379.
Basil I, Byzantine emperor (867–886), b.*c.*813, d.886.
Basil II, Byzantine emperor (963–1025), b.*c.*958, d.1025.
Baskerville, John, British printer and type-founder, b.1706, d.1775.
Basketball, invented by James Naismith at Springfield, Mass., 1891.
Basle University, founded by Pope Pius II 1460.
Bass & Co., British brewers, founded 1777 by William Bass b.1720.
Bassano, Jacopo, Italian painter, b.1510, d.1592.
Bassompierre, François de, French field marshal at the siege of La Rochelle (1628–29), b.1579, d.1646.
Bass Strait, between Australia and Tasmania, discovered 1798 by George Bass, English naval surgeon, d.1812.
Bastien-Lepage, Jules, French painter, b.1848, d.1884.
Bastille, The, Paris, built by Hugues Aubriot 1369, d.1383; destroyed 14 July 1789.
Bataille, Henri, French writer, b.1872, d.1922.
Batavia, Java, founded by the Dutch governor-general Pieter Roth 1619.
Bates, Herbert Ernest, English writer (*My Uncle Silas*, 1939), b.1905, d.1974.
Bath, Order of the (custom in existence by 1127), founded by George I in 1725.
Batoni, Pompeo Girolamo, Italian painter, b.1708, d.1787.
Battaan, World War II, occupied 14 April 1945 by the Allies.

Battenberg, title conferred on Julia von Hanke in 1851 on the occasion of her morganatic marriage with Prince Alexander of Hesse; son Louis changed the name to Mountbatten in 1917.

Battle, Ordeal by, valid in English law until 1818.

'Battle Hymn of the Republic, The', written 1862 by the American poet Mrs Julia Ward Howe, b.1819, d.1910.

Battle of Britain, fought 8 Aug. to 5 Oct. 1940.

Battle of the Bulge, World War II, fought in France Dec. 1944 to Jan. 1945.

Battle of the Spurs, fought between Henry VIII and the French 16 Aug. 1513.

Baudelaire, Charles, French poet (*Les Fleurs du Mal*, 1857), b.1821, d.1867.

Bauhaus, architectural and design movement founded 1919 by Walter Gropius, b.1883, d.1969.

Bauxite, discovered by the Belgian P. Berthier 1821.

Bavaria, ruled by Wittelsbachs 1180–1918.

Bavarian Succession, War of the, fought 1778–79.

Bax, Sir Arnold, composer (*The Poisoned Fountain*, 1920), b.1883, d.1953.

Baxter, George, English engraver and colour printer, b.1804, d.1867.

Baxter, Richard, English nonconformist writer (*The Saints' Everlasting Rest*, 1650), b.1615, d.1691.

Bayard, Chevalier de, French general b.c.1474, killed 1524.

Bay Bridge, San Francisco, built 1936.

Bayeux Tapestry, probably embroidered in the 12th century; first recorded mention 1476.

Bayle, Pierre, French dictionary compiler, b.1647, d.1707.

Baylis, Lilian, British theatre manager, b.1874, d.1937.

Bay of Pigs, Invasion of the, abortive attempt to invade Cuba by anti-Castro exiles funded and equipped by the US government, April 1961.

Bay Psalm Book, earliest American printed book, published at Cambridge, Mass., 1640.

Bayreuth, Bavaria, founded 1194.

Bayreuth Theatre, Germany, home of Wagnerian opera, built 1872, opened 1876.

Bazin, René, French writer (*Les Oberté*, 1901), b.1853, d.1932.

Beale, Dorothea, principal of Cheltenham Ladies' College, b.1831, d.1906.

Bear-baiting, prohibited in Britain by Act of Parliament 1835

Beardsley, Aubrey, English artist (illustrated *The Yellow Book,* 1894–95), b.1872, d.1898.

Beatles, The ('Fab Four'), English pop group founded 1963, disbanded 1970: John Lennon, b.1940, d.1980, Paul McCartney, b.1942, George Harrison, b.1943, Ringo Starr, b.1940.

Beattie, James, Scottish poet (*The Minstrel,* 1771–74), b.1735, d.1803.

Beatty, David, 1st Earl Beatty, British First Sea Lord, b.1871, d.1936.

Beaufort, Margaret, Countess of Richmond and Derby, philanthropist, b.1443, d.1509.

Beauharnais, Eugène de, Prince of Venice, b.1781, d.1824.

Beaumarchais, Pierre Augustine Caron de, French playwright (*The Barber of Seville,* 1775), b.1732, d.1799.

Beaumont, Sir Francis, English dramatist (with John Fletcher, b.1579, d.1625, *The Knight of the Burning Pestle*), b.1584, d.1616.

Beaverbrook, William Maxwell Aitken, 1st Baron, Canadian-born newspaper publisher, b.1879, d.1964.

Bebop, dance movement and jazz style dating from about 1941.

Bechuanaland, *see* **Botswana.**

Becker, Boris, German tennis player, youngest competitor to win Wimbledon men's singles title 1985, b.1967.

Becket, Thomas à, archbishop of Canterbury b.*c.*1118, murdered 1170.

Beckett, Gilbert Abbott à, English humorous writer and contributor to *Punch,* b.1811, d.1856.

Beckett, Samuel, Irish-born playwright (*Waiting for Godot,* 1952), b.1906, d.1989.

Beckford, William, English writer (*Vathek,* 1787), b.1760, d.1844.

Becquer, Gustavo Adolfo, Spanish writer, b.1836, d.1870.

Becquerel, Antoine Henri, French scientist and discoverer (1896) of radioactivity in uranium, b.1852, d.1908.

Beddoes, Thomas Lovell, English writer (*The Bride's Tragedy,* 1822), b.1803, committed suicide 1849.

Bede, The Venerable, English writer and historian, b.*c.*672, d.735.

Bedlam (Bethlehem Hospital), London, founded by Simon Fitzmary 1247.

Beecham, Sir Thomas, English conductor and composer, b.1879, d.1961.

Beecher, Henry Ward, American writer, preacher and social reformer, b.1813, d.1887.

Beerbohm, Sir Max, English writer (*Zuleika Dobson,* 1911), b.1872, d.1956.

Beethoven, Ludwig van, German composer, b.1770, d.1827.

Beeton, Mrs (Isabella Mary Beeton), pioneer arbitor of British housekeeping, b.1836, d.1865.

Beet sugar, discovered 1747 by the German chemist Andreas Sigismund Maggraf, b.1709, d.1782.

Begin, Menachem, Israeli statesman, prime minister 1977–83, b.1913.

Beguines, lay sisterhoods founded *c.*1180 at Liège by Lambert le Bègue, b.*c.*1187.

Behan, Brendan, Irish playwright (*The Hostage,* 1950), b.1923, d.1964.

Behn, Mrs Aphra, English writer (*Oronooko,* 1688), b.1640, d.1689.

Behring Strait, discovered 1725 by Vitus Bering, b.1681, d.1741.

Beiderbecke, (Leon) Bix, American jazz cornetist, pianist and composer, b.1903, d.1931.

Beit, Alfred, German-born British South African financier and philanthropist, b.1853, d.1906.

Belasco, David, American actor-manager, b.1853, d.1931.

Belgian Congo, *see* **Zaire.**

Belgium, part of Burgundian and Spanish Netherlands until 1572; Spanish rule until 1700; Austrian rule 1713–94; part of Netherlands 1815–30; became independent kingdom 1830.

Belisarius, Byzantine general and defeater of Persians, Vandals and Ostrogoths, b.505, d.565.

Belize, formerly British Honduras, first settled by the English 1638; declared a British colony 1862; renamed Belize 1973; became independent 21 Sept. 1981.

Bell, Alexander Graham, Scottish-born inventor (1876) of the telephone, b.1847, d.1922.

Bell, Gertrude, English explorer in Arabia, b.1868, d.1926.

Bell, John, English bookseller and introducer *c.*1788 of 'modern face' type, b.1745, d.1831.

Bellarmine, Robert, Italian Jesuit writer (*Disputations,* 1581), b.1542, d.1621.

Belleau Wood, Battle of, World War I, fought between US Marines and Germans 6–10 June 1918.

Belle Sauvage, London, one of England's oldest coaching inns, first mentioned 1453.

Bellini, Giovanni, Italian painter (*Agony in the Garden*), b.c 1426, d.1516.
Belloc, Hilaire, Anglo-French writer (*The Path to Rome*, 1902), b.1870, d.1953.
Bell Rock Lighthouse, North Sea, completed 1812.
Bellow, Saul, American novelist (*Herzog*, 1964), b.1915.
Belmondo, Jean-Paul, French film actor (*A Bout de Souffle*, 1960), b.1933.
Belo Horizonte, capital of Minas Gerais, Brazil, founded 1895.
Belvoir Hunt, Leicestershire and Lincolnshire, dates from 1750; became a fox pack 1762.
Belzoni, Giovanni Battista, Italian archaeologist in Middle East, b.1778, d.1823.
Bembo, Cardinal Pietro, Italian poet, b.1470, d.1547.
Benavente, Jacinto, Spanish playwright, b.1866, d.1954.
Benbow, John, English admiral, b.1653, d.1702.
Benchley, Robert, American humorous writer, b.1889, d.1945.
Benedict of Nursia, St, b.*c.*480, d.*c.*544.
Benedict I, pope 575–579.
Benedict II, pope 684–685.
Benedict III, pope 855–858.
Benedict IV, pope 900–903.
Benedict V, pope 964–965.
Benedict VI, pope 973–974 (murdered).
Benedict VII, pope 974–983.
Benedict VIII (Theophylactus), pope 1012–24.
Benedict IX (Theophylactus), pope 1032–48, b.*c.*1021, d.1056.
Benedict X (Johannes Mincius), anti-pope 1058, d.1059.
Benedict XI (Niccolo Boccasini), pope 1303–04, b.1240, d.1304.
Benedict XII (Jacques Fournier), pope 1334, d.1342.
Benedict XIII (Pedro de Luna), anti-pope 1394–1417, b.*c.*1328, d.*c.*1423.
Benedict XIII (Piero Francesco Orsini) pope 1724–30, b.1649, d.1730.
Benedict XIV (Prospero Lorenzo Lambertini) pope 1740–58, b.1675, d.1758.
Benedict XV (Giacomo della Chiesa), pope 1914–22, b.1854, d.1922.
Benedict Biscop, English churchman and founder of monastery at Wearmouth, b.*c.*628, d.690.
Benedictine Order, founded 529 by St Benedict of Nursia, b.*c.*480, d.*c.*544.

Benes, Eduard, Czech statesman, b.1884, d.1948.

Benét, Stephen Vincent, American writer (*John Brown's Body,* 1928), b.1898, d.1943.

Bengal, became English settlement *c.*1652; made Chief Presidency 1773; divided between India and Pakistan 1947; East Bengal fought war of independence and became Bangladesh in 1971.

Benghazi, World War II, captured by British 7 Feb. 1941; by Rommel 3 April 1941; recaptured by British 24 Dec. 1941, and again 20 Nov. 1942.

Ben-Gurion, David (David Green), Israeli statesman, 'Father of Israel', first prime minister 1948–53, also 1955–63, b.1886, d.1973.

Benin, West Africa, incorporated into French West Africa by 1904; independent as Dahomey 1960; named changed to Benin in 1975; held first free presidential elections in 30 years in 1991.

Benn, Tony (Anthony Wedgewood), British Labour politician, b.1925.

Bennet, Alan, English actor and playwright (*Kafka's Dick,* 1986), b.1934.

Bennett, Arnold, English novelist (*The Old Wives' Tale,* 1908), b.1867, d.1931.

Benno, St, bishop of Meissen, b.1010, d.1106. Canonized 1523.

Bentham, Jeremy, English philosopher and social reformer, b.1748, d.1832.

Bentley, Richard, English literary critic (*Dissertation on the Epistles of Phalaris,* 1699), b.1662, d.1742.

'Beowulf', Anglo-Saxon epic poem written *c.*1000.

Béranger, Pierre Jean de, French songwriter (*Chansons Nouvelles,* 1830), b.1780, d.1857.

Bérard, Christian, French painter (*Seated Acrobat*), b.1902, d.1949.

Berchtold's Day, Swiss annual festival held 2 Jan.

Berdyaev, Nicholas, Russian-born philosopher, b.1874, d.1948.

Berenson, Bernhard, Lithuanian-born American art critic, b.1865, d.1959.

Berg, Alban, Austrian composer (*Wozzeck,* 1922), b.1885, d.1935.

Bergerac, Cyrano de, French writer and soldier, b.1619, d.1655.

Bergh, Henry, founder (1866) of the American Society for the Prevention of Cruelty to Animals, b.1811, d.1888.

Bergman, Ingmar, Swedish stage and film director (*The Seventh Seal,* 1957), b.1918.

Bergman, Ingrid, Swedish-born film actress (*Casablanca,* 1943), b.1915, d.1982.

Bergson, Henri, French philosopher, b.1859, d.1942.

Bering, Vitus, Danish-born Russian explorer, b.1681, d.1741.

Berkeley, George, Irish philosopher, b.1685, d.1753.

Berlin, captured by the French 1806. Decree of Berlin, 21 Nov. 1806. Congress of Berlin 1878; Treaty of Berlin signed 13 July 1878. Berlin Blockade began 28 June 1948; lifted 12 May 1949; Berlin Wall built to prevent exodus of East German citizens, Aug. 1961; Wall begins to be dismantled Nov. 1989 as democracy sweeps Eastern Europe following the collapse of the USSR.

Berlin, Irving (Israel Baline), American composer (*Alexander's Ragtime Band,* 1911), b.1888, d.1989.

Berlioz, Hector, French composer (*The Damnation of Faust*), b.1803, d.1869.

Bermuda, discovered by the Spaniard Juan Bermúdez 1503; settled by the English 1609, and formally taken over 1684.

Bernadette (Soubirous), St, of Lourdes (visions 1858), b.1844, d.1879.

Bernadotte, Count Folke, Swedish humanitarian, b.1895, assassinated 1948.

Bernadotte, Jean Baptiste, French general and Swedish king from 1818, b.1763, d.1844.

Bernanos, Georges, French writer (*Diary of a Country Parson,* 1936), b.1888, d.1948.

Bernard, St, abbot of Clairvaux, b.1091, d.1153.

Bernardin de St Pierre, Jacques-Henri, French writer (*Paul et Virginie,* 1787), b.1737, d.1814.

Bernhardt, Sarah, French actress, b.1844, d.1923.

Bernini, Giovanni Lorenzo, Italian sculptor and architect, b.1598, d.1680.

Bernoulli's Numbers, mathematics, discovered by Jacques Bernoulli, b.1654, d.1705.

Bernoulli's Principle, of the flow of liquids, formulated by Daniel Bernoulli, b.1700, d.1782.

Bernstein, Leonard, American conductor, pianist and composer (*West Side Story,* 1958), b.1918, d.1990.

Berruguete, Alonso, Spanish artist, b.c.1480, d.1561.

Berry, Chuck (Charles Edward), American rock and roll singer-songwriter ('Johnny B Goode', 1958), b.1926. **Berthelot, Marcelin**, French organic chemist, b.1827, d.1907.

Bertillon System, criminal investigation by anthropometry, devised 1880 by the Frenchman Alphonse Bertillon, b.1853, d.1914.

Bertolucci, Bernardo, Italian-born film director (*Last Tango in Paris*, 1972), b.1940.

Berwick, Peace of, signed (between England and Scotland) 1639.

Beryllium, isolated 1828 by the German scientist Friedrich Wöhler, b.1800, d.1982.

Berzelius, Baron Jöns Jakob, Swedish chemist, b.1779, d.1848.

Besant, Mrs Annie, British theosophist and reformer, b.1847, d.1933.

Bessel Functions, invented 1817, fully developed 1824, by the German astronomer Wilhelm Bessel, b.1784, d.1846.

Bessemer Converter, invented 1856 by the English engineer Sir Henry Bessemer, b.1813, d.1898.

Bessemer Steel Process, first used in USA at Phillipsburg 1856.

Beta Rays, discovered 1896 by Lord Rutherford, b.1871, d.1937.

Bethlen, Gábor, Hungarian leader, b.1580, d.1629.

Bethmann-Hollweg, Theobald von, German chancellor, b.1856, d.1921.

Betjeman, Sir John, English poet and broadcaster (*New Bats in Old Belfries*, 1945), Poet Laureate 1972, b.1906, d.1984.

Betterton, Thomas, English actor-manager, b.1635, d.1710.

Bevan, Aneurin, British statesman, b.1897, d.1960.

Beveridge Plan, national insurance scheme for Britain conceived by Lord Beveridge; published 20 Nov. 1942.

Beveridge, William Henry, 1st Baron Beveridge, British economist and author of the Beveridge Plan, b.1879, d.1963.

Bevin, Ernest, British trade-union leader and Labour statesman, b.1881, d.1951.

Bewick, Thomas, English wood engraver, b.1753, d.1828.

Béza, Theodore, French religious reformer, b.1519, d.1605.

Bhave, Vinobha, Indian social reformer and spiritual leader, b.1895, d.1982.

Bhopal, India, founded 1728; capital city of the State of Madhya Pradesh 1956; scene of worst industrial (chemical) accident in history 1984: 2,000 killed and 50,000 injured by toxic gas leak.

Bhutan, Himalayan State, concluded treaty with East India Company 1774; subsidized by British from 1865, by Indian government from 1942; new treaty with government of India, 1949;

restoration of National Assembly 1953; became democratic monarchy 1969.

Bhutto, Benazir, Pakistani politician, daughter of the former prime minister; prime minister 1980–90, b.1953.

Bhutto, Zulfikar Ali, Pakistani politician; president 1971–73, prime minister 1973–77, b.1928, executed 1979.

Bibliographical Society, London, founded 1892.

Bibliothèque Nationale, Paris, founded 1721.

Bicycles: pedal-operated model invented by the British inventor Kirkpatrick Macmillan 1838; 'penny-farthings' popular 1870s; Rover 'safety' bicycle 1885; inflated tyres invented 1888.

Bifocal Lens, invented 1780 by Benjamin Franklin, b.1706, d.1790.

Big Ben, London, hour bell cast 10 April 1858. Clock went into service 31 May 1859. Chimes first broadcast 31 Dec. 1923.

Big Bertha, German long-range gun that shelled Paris March 1918.

Big Brother Movement, scheme for emigration of boys from Britain to Australia founded by New Zealand-born Sir Richard Linton, b.1879, d.1959.

Bihar, Indian State, treaty made with East India Company 1765; separated from Bengal Province 1912 and united with Orissa. Made separate province 1936.

Bikaner, capital of Bikaner State, India, founded 1488.

Bikini Atoll, Marshall Islands, scene of atom-bomb tests started by US Navy 1946.

Bill of Rights, English, based on Declaration of Rights (Feb.) and passed by Parliament Oct. 1689.

Billiards, believed to have been invented by Henrique Devigne, French artist, *c.*1571.

Bimetallism, use of gold and silver for currency, first so termed 1869 by Henri Cernuschi, Italian economist, b.1821, d.1896.

Binomial Theorem, invented before 1676 by Sir Isaac Newton, b.1642, d.1727.

Binyon, Laurence, English poet (*For the Fallen*), b.1869, d.1943.

Bioko, island off West Africa, discovered by the Portuguese navigator Fernão de Po *c.*1470.

Birkbeck College, London University, founded (as the London Mechanics' Institution) 1823 by Dr George Birkbeck, b.1776, d.1841.

Birkenhead, Frederick Edwin Smith, 1st Earl of, British statesman, b.1872, d.1930.

Birmingham University, founded 1875 as Mason College by Sir Josiah Mason, b.1795, d.1881. Charter granted 1900.

Birrell, Augustine, English writer and statesman, b.1850, d.1933.

Birth Control Clinics, world's first, at Amsterdam 1881; first English, London 1921; first American, New York 1923 (previously opened 1916 and closed by police).

Bischof, Werner, Swiss photographer, b.1916, killed in car accident 1954.

Bisley, National Rifle Association first met at Bisley 1890. First woman (Miss M. E. Foster) to win King's Prize 19 July 1930.

Bismarck, Otto Eduard Leopold, Prinz von, German chancellor (1861–90), b.1815, d.1898.

Bismarck, World War II naval battle, 24–27 March 1941.

Bismarck Sea, Battle of the World War II, 2–4 March 1943.

Bismuth, chemical element, identified 1530 by the German scientist Georg Agricola, b.1490, d.1555.

Bizet, Georges, French composer (*Carmen*, 1875), b.1838, d.1875.

Björnson, Björnstjerne, Norwegian writer (*Synnöve Solbakken*, 1857), b.1832, d.1910.

Black, Joseph, British scientist who developed (about 1765) the theory of latent heat, b.1728, d.1799.

'Black and Tans', auxiliary police used against Irish republicans 1920–21.

Black Death, The, plague pandemic affecting Asia and N. Africa, Italy 1340, England 1348–49.

Blackfriars, Dominican convent, established in London 1276.

Blackfriars Bridge, London, erected 1865–69.

Black Friday, American financial disaster, 24 Sept. 1869.

Black Hawk, North American Indian chief, b.1767, d.1838.

Black Hole of Calcutta, scene of imprisonment of English by rebels 20–21 June 1756.

Black Letter, for English newspaper titles, first used 1679.

Blackmore, Richard Doddridge, English novelist (*Lorna Doone*, 1869), b.1825, d.1900.

Black phosphorus, first prepared by the American physicist Percy Williams Bridgman, b.1882, d.1961.

Black Prince, The, Edward, son of Edward III, b.1330, d.1376.

Black Rod, House of Lords, first appointed 1350.

Blackstone's Commentaries, (1765–69), legal guide, written by Sir William Blackstone, English jurist, b.1723, d.1780.

Black Watch, Highland regiment, formed 1725, became Royal Highland Black Watch 1739.

Blackwell, Dr Elizabeth, first (1859) British registered woman doctor, b.1821, d.1910.

Blackwood's Magazine, founded 1817 by William Blackwood, b.1776, d.1834, of Edinburgh.

Blades, William, London printer, b.1824, d.1890.

Blaeu, Willem Janszoon, founder of Dutch firm of map-makers, b.1571, d.1638.

Blair, Robert, Scottish poet (*The Grave*, 1743), b.1699, d.1746.

Blake, Robert, English admiral, b.1599, d.1657.

Blake, William, English painter and poet (*The Marriage of Heaven and Hell*, 1790), b.1757, d.1827.

Blanc, Mont, (15,782 ft.) first climbed by Jacques Balmat and Michel Paccard 1786.

Blanche of Castile, wife of Louis VIII, b.1188, d.1252.

Blanqui, Louis, French revolutionary leader, b.1805, d.1881.

Blatchford, Robert, British socialist writer, b.1851, d.1943.

Blavatsky, Madame Helena, Russian-born founder of the Theosophical Society, b.1831, d.1891.

Bleaching Powder, discovered 1798 by the English scientist Smithson Tennant, b.1761, d.1815.

Blenheim, Battle of, between the English and the French, 13 Aug. 1704.

Blenheim Palace, Oxfordshire, built 1705–22.

Blériot, Louis, French aviator, inventor of monoplane which he flew across the English Channel 27 July 1909, b.1872, d.1936.

Blessed Virgin Mary, The Assumption of The, celebrated 15 Aug.

Bligh, Admiral William, of *The Bounty*, b.1754, d.1817. Mutiny of the Bounty 28 April 1789.

Blind books, letters first printed in relief 1771 by the French philanthropist Valentin Haüy.

Bliss, Sir Arthur, Master of the Queen's Musick (1953–75), b.1891, d.1975.

Blitz (from German *Blitzkrieg*, 'lightning war'), military technique of surprise attack, 1939–41; applied in England to heavy bombing 1940–41

Bloch, Ernst, Swiss-born composer (*America*, 1926), b.1880, d.1959.

Bloch, Jean Richard, French novelist (*Et Compagnie*, 1918), b.1884, d.1947.

Blok, Alexander Alexandrovich, Russian poet, b.1880, d.1921.
Blom, Eric, English music critic and historian, b.1888, d.1959.
Blomfield, Sir Arthur William, English architect of the London Law Courts in Fleet Street, b.1829, d.1899.
Blondin, Charles, French acrobat, b.1824, d.1897. Crossed Niagara Falls on a tightrope 1859.
Blood, Colonel Thomas, Irish malcontent, attempted to steal the Crown Jewels 9 May 1671, b.*c.*1618, d.1680.
Blood circulation discovered 1615 by William Harvey, b.1578, d.1657.
Blood groups, defined 1901 by Karl Landsteiner, b.1868, d.1943.
Bloody Assizes, held 1685 by Judge Jeffreys, b.*c.*1644, d.1689.
Bloody Sunday, massacre of St Petersburg workers 22 Jan. 1905; also killing of 13 Roman Catholic protesters by British troops in Londonderry, Northern Ireland, 30 Jan. 1972.
Bloomer, Amelia Jenks, American women's rights campaigner and dress reformer, b.1818, d.1894.
Bloomfield, Robert, English poet (*The Farmer's Boy,* 1800), b.1766, d.1823.
Blow, John, English composer, b.*c.*1648, d.1708.
Blücher, Gebhard Leberecht von, German field marshal, b.1742, d.1819.
Blueprint process, for copying plans, etc, first used 1842 by the English astronomer Sir John Herschel, b.1792, d.1871.
Blum, Léon, French statesman (premier 1936, 1938, 1946), b.1872, d.1950.
Blunden, Edmund (Charles), English poet and writer (*Undertones of War*, 1928), b.1896, d.1974.
Blunt, Anthony Frederick, English Soviet spy and keeper of the Queen's pictures, b.1907, d.1983.
Blunt, Wilfrid Scawen, English writer, b.1840, d.1922.
Boadicea, British queen of the Iceni, committed suicide 62.
Board of Trade, London, founded 1661; now Department of Trade and Industry, and incorporating (since 1992) the Department of Energy.
Boccaccio, Giovanni, Italian writer (*The Decameron,* 1348–53), b.1313, d.1375.
Boccherini, Luigi, Italian composer, b.1743, d.1805.
Bodichon, Barbara, English founder 1869 of Girton College, Cambridge University, b.1827, d.1890.
Bodin, Jean, French political thinker (*Six Livres de la République,* 1576), b.*c.*1530, d.1596.

Bodleian Library, Oxford, founded 1598, opened 1602, by Sir Thomas Bodley, b.1545, d.1613; new library opened 1946.

Bodoni, Giambattista, Italian printer and typographer, b.1740, d.1813.

Boece, Hector, Scottish historian, b.*c.*1465, d.1536.

Boecklin, Arnold, Swiss painter, b.1827, d.1901.

Boer War, South Africa, began 11 Oct. 1899, ended 31 May 1902.

Boethius, Roman statesman and philosopher (*De Consolatione Philosophiae*) b.*c.*473, executed 525.

Bogarde, Dirk, English actor and author, b.1921.

Bogart, Humphrey (De Forest), American film actor (*The Maltese Falcon,* 1941), b.1899, d.1957.

Bogotá, Colombian capital, founded by Gonzalo Jiménez de Quesada 1538.

Bohemia, ruled by Hapsburgs 1526–1918; part of Czechoslovakia 1918–93.

Bohemian Brethren, Christian sect, founded among followers of Hus by Peter Chelcicky in early 15th century.

Bohr, Aage Niels, Danish nuclear physicist b.1922.

Bohr, Niels (Henrik David), Danish atomic scientist, b.1885, d.1962.

Boileau, Nicolas, French writer and critic, b.1636, d.1711.

Boito, Arrigo, Italian composer (*Mefistofele,* 1868), b. 1842, d.1918.

Bojer, Johan, Norwegian novelist (*Troens Magt,* 1903), b.1872, d.1959.

'Boldrewood, Rolf' (Thomas Alexander Browne), English-born Australian writer (*Robbery under Arms,* 1888), b.1826, d.1915.

Boleslaus I, Polish king (992–1025), d.1025.

Boleslaus II, Polish king (1058–79), b.1039, d.*c.*1081.

Boleslaus III, Polish king (1102–39), b.1086, d.1139.

Boleyn, Anne, English queen b.*c.*1507, m. Henry VIII 1533, beheaded 1536

Bolingbroke, Henry St John, Viscount Bolingbroke, English statesman and writer (*The Idea of a Patriot King*), b.1678, d.1751.

Bolívar, Simón, liberator of South America (1810–24), b.1783, d.1830.

Bolivia, proclaimed a republic 1825; boundary with Chile fixed after war 1879–82; with Paraguay after war 1932–35; with Peru after war 1935–38.

Bologna, Giovanni da, Flemish sculptor, b.1524, d.1608.

Bolsheviks, majority faction of Russian Social Democrat Party at Congress in Brussels and London, 1903; became Communist Party 1918.

Boltzmann, Ludwig, Austrian physicist b.1844, committed suicide 1906.

Bombay University, founded 1857.

Bonaparte (Buonaparte until 1796), Napoleon, emperor of France (1804–13), b.1769, d.1821; Jerome, king of Westphalia (1807–13), b.1784, d.1860; Joseph, king of Naples (1806–07) and Spain (1808–13), b.1768, d.1844; Louis, king of Holland (1806–10), b.1778, d.1846; Louis Napoleon, emperor of France (1851–70), b.1808, d.1873.

Bonar Law, Andrew, British statesman (prime minister 1922–23), b.1858, d.1923.

Bonaventura, St, b.1221, d.1274.

Bond, Edward, English playwright (*The Pope's Wedding*, 1962), b.1934.

Bondfield, Margaret, first (1929) woman privy councillor, b.1873, d.1953.

Bone, Henry, English enamel-painter, b.1755, d.1834.

Bone, Muirhead, Scottish artist, b.1876, d.1953.

Bonesetting (osteopathy), practice founded 1874 by the American surgeon Andrew Taylor Still, b.1828, d.1917.

Bonheur, Rosa, French painter, b.1822, d.1899.

Boniface, St, b.c.680, murdered 754.

Boniface I, St, pope 418–22.

Boniface II, pope 530–32.

Boniface III, pope 607.

Boniface IV, pope 608–15.

Boniface V, pope 619–25.

Boniface VI, pope 896.

Boniface VII, anti-pope 974.

Boniface VIII (Benedetto Gaetano), pope 1294–1303, b.1235, d.1303.

Boniface IX (Piero Tomacelli), pope 1389–1404, b.c.1345, d.1404.

Bonington, Chris (Christian John Storey), English mountaineer, reached summit of Everest 1985, b.1934.

Bonington, Richard Parkes, English painter (*Grand Canal, Venice*), b.1802, d.1828.

Bonn, capital of German Federal Republic 1949–90.

Book auction, first, the sale of George Dousa's library, held in Leyden 1604.

Book jackets *or* **dust-wrappers**, first used in England 1832; came into general use *c.*1890.

Book of Common Prayer, Church of England, *First* published 1549, *Second* 1552, *Elizabethan* 1559, *revised* 1662, controversial *modernized* 1980.

Bookplates, to mark ownership, first introduced in Germany *c.*1450.

Booksellers Association, of Great Britain and Ireland, founded as the Associated Booksellers 1895; assumed present name 1948.

Boole, George, English mathematician and originator of Boolean algebra, b.1815–1864.

Boone, Daniel, American explorer, b.1734, d.1820.

Booth, Edwin Thomas, American actor, b.1833, d.1893.

Booth, John Wilkes, murderer (1865) of Abraham Lincoln b.1838, shot 1865.

Booth, William, English founder (1865) of the Salvation Army, b.1829, d.1912.

Booth, William Bramwell, who succeeded (1912) his father William Booth as General of the Salvation Army, b.1856, d.1929.

Bordeaux, Henri, French novelist (*Le Feu*), b.1870, d.1963.

Borgia, Cesare, Italian statesman and general, b.1476, killed in battle 1507.

Borgia, Lucrezia, Duchess of Ferrara, b.1479, d.1519.

Borgia, Rodrigo, elected Pope Alexander VI, 1492, b.1431, poisoned 1503.

Boric acid, first prepared 1702 by the Dutch chemist Willem Homberg, b.1652, d.1715.

Boring machine, first practical invented 1769 by the English engineer John Smeaton, b.1724, d.1792.

Boris II, Bulgarian Tsar, b.1894, d.1943.

Boris Godunov, Russian Tsar, b.*c.*1551, d.1605.

Borneo, discovered by the Portuguese 1521. North Borneo made British Protectorate 1881.

Borodin, Alexander, Russian composer (*Prince Igor,* 1869–91), b.1833, d.1887.

Borodino, Battle of, fought between Napoleon and the Russians 7 Sept. 1812.

Boron, chemical element isolated 1808 by Sir Humphry Davy, b.1778, d.1829.

Borromeo, St Charles, b.1538, d.1584.

Borromini, Francesco, Italian architect, b.1599, d.1667.

Borrow, George Henry, English writer (*Lavengro*, 1851), b.1803, d.1881.

Bosanquet, Bernard, English philosopher, b.1848, d.1923.

Bosch, Hieronymus, Flemish painter (*The Temptation of St Anthony*), b.c.1462, d.1516.

Boscobel, Shropshire, scene of the hiding-place (in an oak) of Charles II in 1651.

Bose, Sir Jagadis Chandra, Indian plant expert, b.1858, d.1937.

Bosnia-Hercegovina, ruled by Austria 1878–1918; part of Yugoslavia since 1918.

Bossuet, Jacques Bénigne, French theologian, b.1627, d.1704.

Boston, Massachusetts, settled by John Winthrop 1630.

Boston Massacre, occurred 1770.

Boston Symphony Orchestra, founded 1881 by the American philanthropist Henry Lee Higginson, b.1834, d.1919.

Boston Tea Party, American revolutionary incident, 16 Dec. 1773.

Boswell, James, Scottish biographer of Dr Samuel Johnson, b.1740, d.1795.

Bosworth Field, Battle of, fought between Henry VII and Richard III, 22 Aug. 1485.

Botany Bay, New South Wales, discovered 28 April 1770 by Captain James Cook, b.1728, d.1779; became British penal settlement 1786; transportation ceased 1840.

Botha, General Louis, Boer leader (prime minister of South Africa, 1910–19), b.1862, d.1919.

Bothwell, James Hepburn, Earl of, husband of Mary, Queen of Scots, b.c.1537, d.1578.

Bothwell Bridge, Battle of, fought between the English and the Scottish Covenanters 1679.

Botswana, former British protectorate of Bechuanaland from 1885; became independent state within the Commonwealth 1981.

Botticelli, Sandro, Italian painter (*The Birth of Venus*), b.1444, d.1510.

Bottomley, Horatio, English politician, financier and founder (1906) of *John Bull*; in prison for fraud 1920–27, b.1860, d.1933.

Boucher, François, French painter (*The Toilet of Venus*), b.1703, d.1770.

Boucicault, Dion, Irish-born playwright (*The Colleen Bawn*, 1860), b.1822, d.1890.

Bougainville, Louis Antoine de, French explorer, b.1729, d.1811.

Boughton, Rutland, English composer (*The Immortal Hour*, 1913), b.1878, d.1960.

Boulanger, George Ernest Jean Marie, French general and politician b.1837, committed suicide 1891.

Boulder Dam, harnessing the Colorado River, began 1928.

Boulez, Pierre, French composer and conductor (*Memoriales*, 1975), b.1925.

Boulsover, Thomas, English inventor (1743) of Sheffield plate.

Boulton, Matthew, English engineer and inventor, b.1728, d.1809.

Bounty, Mutiny of the, 28 April 1789.

Bourbon Dynasty, ruled France 1589–1792, 1814–48; Spain 1700–1808, 1814–68, 1874–1930; Naples 1759–99, 1799–1806, 1815–60; Parma 1748–1815, 1847–60.

Bourges Cathedral, constructed between 1220 and 1260.

Bourne, Francis, English cardinal, b.1861, d.1935.

Bourse, The Paris, French Stock Exchange, founded 1724.

Bouts, Dirk, Dutch painter, b.*c.*1410, d.1475.

Bouvet Island, South Atlantic, discovered 1739 by the French navigator Jean Baptiste Lozier Bouvet; annexed by Norway 1927–30.

Bowdler, Thomas, English self-appointed censor of the classics, b.1754, d.1825.

Bowdoin College, Maine, founded 1794.

Bowen, Elizabeth, Anglo-Irish writer (*The Death of the Heart*, 1938), b.1889, d.1973.

Bowen, York (Edwin), English composer (*The Lament of Tasso*, 1903), b.1884, d.1961.

Bowles, Jane, American writer (*Plain Pleasures*, 1966), b.1917, d.1973.

Bowles, Paul, American novelist and composer (*The Sheltering Sky*, 1949), b.1910.

Bow porcelain, manufactured 1745–76.

Bow Street Runners, London, superseded by the Police 1829.

Boxer Rising, Peking, in which the Chinese rose against foreigners in China, June and July 1900.

Boxing, legalized in England 1901.

Boy Scout Movement, began with camp for 20 boys in 1907 held by Lord Baden-Powell, b.1857, d.1941. First Rally and

Conference, Crystal Palace, London, 4 Sept. 1909. Incorporated in USA 1910.

Boyce, William, English organist and composer, b.1710, d.1779.

Boycott, Captain Charles Cunningham, Lord Erne's English land agent in Co. Mayo, who was 'boycotted' from 24 Sept. 1880, b.1832, d.1897.

Boyd-Orr, John, Baron, Scottish nutritionist, b.1880, d.1971.

Boyle, Richard, Earl of Cork, British Lord High Treasurer, b.1566, d.1643.

Boyle, Robert, Irish-born scientist and discoverer (1667) of Boyle's Law, b.1627, d.1691.

Boyne, Battle of the, fought between William III and James II, 1 July 1690.

Boys' Brigade, The, founded 1883 by Sir William Alexander Smith, b.1854, d.1914.

Brabançonne, La, Belgian national anthem, composed by François van Campenhout, b.1779, d.1849.

Bracegirdle, Anne, English actress, b.c.1664, d.1748.

Bradlaugh, Charles, English politician and social reformer, b.1833, d.1891.

Bradley, Andrew Cecil, English critic, b.1851, d.1935.

Bradley, Francis Herbert, English philosopher, b.1846, d.1924.

Bradley, Henry, one of the editors of the *New (Oxford) English Dictionary*, b.1845, d.1923.

Bradshaw, John, English regicide, president of court that condemned Charles I (1649), b.1602, d.1659.

Bradshaw's Railway Guide, Great Britain, first published 1839 by George Bradshaw, b.1801, d.1853; discontinued 1961. Continental Bradshaw established 1848.

Brady, Matthew B., 'Lincoln's cameraman', American pioneer photographer, b.c.1823, d.1896.

Bragg, Sir William Henry, English scientist, b.1862, d.1942.

Brahe, Tycho, Danish astronomer, b.1546, d.1601.

Brahms, Johannes, German composer (*Hungarian Dances*, 1852–69), b.1833, d.1897.

Braid, James, Scottish pioneer in study of hypnotism, b.c.1796, d.1860.

Braille Alphabet for the Blind, invented 1834 by the blind Frenchman Louis Braille, b.1809, d.1852.

Braine, John, English novelist (*Room at the Top*, 1957), b.1922, d.1986.

Bramalea, near Toronto, Canada's first satellite city, founded 1959.

Bramante, Donato, Italian architect, b.1444, d.1514.

Brancusi, Constantin, Romanian-born sculptor, b.1876, d.1957.

Brandeis, Louis Dembitz, American chief justice, b.1856, d.1941.

Brando, Marlon, American film and stage actor (*A Streetcar Named Desire*, 1947), b.1924.

Brandt, Willy (Karl Herbert Frahm), West German statesman; chancellor 1969–74; Nobel peace prize 1971; produced Brandt Report (1980) urging increased economic aid for the Third World, b.1913, d.1993.

Brandywine, Battle of, Delaware, fought between the British and the Americans 11 Sept. 1777.

Brangwyn, Frank, British artist, b.1867, d.1935.

Brant, Sebastian, German writer (*Das Narrenschiff*, 1494), b.1457, d.1521.

Braque, Georges, French painter, b.1882, d.1963.

Brassey's Naval Annual, founded 1886 by Lord Brassey, b.1836, d.1918.

Bratby, John, English painter, b.1928.

Braun, Wernher von, German-born scientist and developer of ballistic missiles and satellites, b.1912, d.1977.

Bray, The Rev. Thomas, English pioneer in the provision of libraries, b.1656, d.1730.

Brazil, discovered 500 by Vicente Yáñez Pinzón, b.*c*.1460, d.*c*.1524; independent empire 1822–89, republic since 1889.

Breakspear, Nicolas (Adrian IV), only English Pope, b.1154, d.1159.

Breasted, James Henry, American Egyptologist, b.1865, d.1935.

Brecht, Bertolt, German dramatist (*Dreigroschenoper*, 1928), b.1898, d.1956.

Breda, Peace of, between England and the United Netherlands 1667.

Breechloading cartridge case, first adopted in principle by the Prussians *c*.1841.

'Breeches' Bible, published by the Calvinists at Geneva 1558.

Bremen, belonged to Hanseatic League 1260–85, 1358–1422, 1433–1646; became free city 1648; became German 1867.

Brendan, St, b.484, d.577.

Brenner Pass, Swiss Alps; road built 1772, railway 1864–67.

Breslau, capital of Silesia, founded *c.*1000; since 1945 included in Poland and called Wroclaw

Brest-Litovsk, Treaty of, World War I, confirming Russian Armistice with the Central Powers, signed 3 March 1918.

Breton, Nicholas, English writer, b.*c.*1545, d.*c.*1626.

Bretton Woods Conference, on international monetary policy, held July 1944.

Breughel, Pieter, the Elder, Dutch painter (*The Harvesters*), b.*c.*1525, d.1569.

Breuil, Henri, French priest and archaeologist and expert in cave paintings, b.1877, d.1961.

Brian Boru, Irish king, b.926, killed 1014.

Briand, Aristide, French statesman, b.1862, d.1932.

Bricks, size standardized in England *c.*1625, taxed in England 1784 to 1850.

Bride, St, b.453, d.523.

Bridge, first iron, built 1779 by Wilkinson and Darby at Ironbridge, Shropshire.

Bridge, card game, first recorded mention in England 1886.

Bridge of Sighs, Venice, built 1597.

Bridges, Robert, English poet (*The Testament of Beauty,* 1929), b.1844, d.1930.

Bridget, St, Swedish visionary, b.*c.*1303, d.1373.

Bridgewater Canal, Worsley to Manchester, constructed 1756–61 by the Duke of Bridgewater, b.1736, d.1806; engineer James Brindley, b.1716, d.1772.

Bridie, James (Osborne Henry Mavor), Scottish playwright, b.1888, d.1951.

Brieux, Eugène, French playwright (*Les Avariés*, 1901), b.1858, d.1932.

Briggs, Henry, English mathematician and pioneer in the study of logarithms, b.1561, d.1631.

Bright, John, English statesman, b.1811, d.1889.

Brighton bombing, IRA attack on a Brighton hotel used by Conservative politicians (including prime minister Margaret Thatcher) during the Party Conference 12 Oct. 1984.

Bright's Disease, identified 1827 by Dr Richard Bright, b.1789, d.1858.

Brillat-Savarin, Anthelme, French gastronome, b.1755, d.1826.

Brindley, James, English engineer, b.1716, d.1772.

Brisbane, Queensland capital, founded by the English explorer John Oxley 1824; named after General Sir Thomas Brisbane, b.1773, d.1860, governor of New South Wales (1821–25).
Bristol porcelain, manufactured 1750–80.
Bristol University, England, founded as University College 1876; granted Royal Charter 24 May 1909.
Britannia Royal Naval College, Dartmouth, founded 1857 at Portland; transferred to Dartmouth 1863.
British Academy, London, granted charter 8 Aug. 1902.
British Association for the Advancement of Science, founded 1831.
British Broadcasting Corporation (preceded by British Broadcasting Company, formed 1922), constituted under Royal Charter 1 Jan. 1927.
British Cameroons, *see* **Cameroon**.
British Columbia, Canada, constituted British Crown Colony 2 Aug. 1858. Became a Province of the Dominion of Canada 1871.
British Council, London, established 1935; chartered 1940.
British Empire, Order of, founded by George V in 1917.
British Empire Exhibition, Wembley, London, opened 23 April, closed 1 Nov. 1924.
British Film Institute, London, founded 1933.
British Guiana, *see* **Guyana.**
British Guiana issued the most valuable postage stamp (only one copy known) Feb. 1856.
British Honduras, *see* **Belize.**
British Interplanetary Society, founded at Liverpool 1933.
British Legion, founded in London by Earl Haig 24 May 1921; became Royal British Legion in 1971.
British Museum, London, founded 1753; opened 16 Jan. 1759.
British North American Act, by which the Dominion of Canada was created, proclaimed 1 July 1867.
British Pharmacopoeia, first published 1864.
British Railways, amalgamating existing regional railway companies under national ownership, inaugurated 1 Jan. 1948.
British Red Cross Society, founded 1905; received Royal Charter 1908.
British Somaliland, former British protectorate (1884–1960), together with Italian Somaliland became the Somali Republic in 1960.

British Standards Institution, founded 1901 as the Engineering Standards Committee; incorporated by Royal Charter 1929.

British Telecom (BT), created 1980 when the telephone service split from the Post Office; BT privatized as a public limited company 1984.

Britten, (Edward) Benjamin, Baron, English composer (*Billy Budd,* 1951), b.1913, d.1976.

Britton, John, English topographical writer (*The Beauties of England and Wales,* 1803–14), b.1771, d.1857.

Broadcasting, American daily, began from KDKA 2 November 1920, British daily, began from 2LO 14 Nov. 1922.

Broadmoor, England, criminal lunatic asylum, opened 1863.

Brod, Max, Czech writer (*Tycho Brahe,* 1914) and literary executor of Kafka, b.1884, d.1968.

Brockhaus Conversations-Lexikon, German national encyclopedia, first published 1810–11 by Friedrich Arnold Brockhaus, b.1772, d.1823.

Broglie, Prince Louis Victor de, French physicist, b.1892, d.1987.

Broken Hill, New South Wales, silver lode discovered 1883.

Bromine, discovered 1826 by Antoine Jérôme Balard, b.1802, d.1876.

Brontë sisters, English novelists: Anne (*Agnes Grey,* 1850), b.1820, d.1849; Charlotte (*Jane Eyre,* 1847), b.1816, d.1855; Emily (*Wuthering Heights,* 1847), b.1818, d.1848.

Brooke, Henry, Irish writer (*The Fool of Quality,* 1766), b.1708, d.1783.

Brooke, Sir James, Indian-born rajah of Sarawak, b.1803, d.1868.

Brooke, Rupert, English poet, b.1887, d.1915.

Brookings Institution, Washington, founded 1922 for research in administration and economics by Robert Somers Brookings, American philanthropist, b.1850, d.1932.

Brooklands motor racecourse, opened 6 July 1907.

Brooklyn Bridge, New York, built 1870–83 by the German-born engineer John Augustus Roebling, b.1806, d.1869.

Brooks's Club, London, established 1778. Formerly known as Almack's, founded 1763.

Brougham, Henry, Lord Brougham and Vaux, British statesman, b.1778, d.1868.

Brouwer, Adriaen, Dutch painter, b.c.1605, d.1638.

Brown Christy, disabled Irish writer and painter (*My Left Foot*, 1954), b.1932, d.1981.
Brown, Ford Maddox, French-born painter (*Romeo and Juliet*), b.1821, d.1893.
Brown, George Douglas ('George Douglas'), Scottish writer (*The House with the Green Shutters*, 1901), b.1869, d.1902.
Brown, John, Scottish medical pioneer, b.1736, d.1788.
Brown, John, American abolitionist, b.1800, hanged 1859.
Brown, Louise, first 'test-tube' baby, b.1978.
Browne, Hablot Knight ('Phiz'), English artist and illustrator, b.1815, d.1882.
Browne, Robert, English religious leader (founded Brownist sect – later Congregationalists – 1582), b.c.1550, d.1633.
Browne, Sir Thomas, English writer (*Hydriotaphia*, 1658), b.1605, d.1682.
Brownian Motion, physics, discovered 1828 by the Scottish botanist Robert Brown, b.1773, d.1858.
Browning, Elizabeth Barrett, English poet and wife of Robert Browning (*Aurora Leigh*, 1856), b.1806, d.1861.
Browning, Robert, English poet (*Andrea del Sarto*, 1855), b.1812, d.1889.
Browning machine gun, invented by the American John Moses Browning, b.1855, d.1926.
Brown University, Providence, Rhode Island, founded 1764 as Rhode Island College.
Bruce, Sir David, British pioneer in tropical medicine, b.1855, d.1932.
Bruce, James, Scottish explorer of Abyssinia, b.1730, d.1794.
Bruce, Lenny (Leonard Alfred Schneider), American stand-up comic, frequently prosecuted for obscenity, b.1925, d.1966.
Bruce, Robert, Scottish king, b.1274, d.1329.
Bruce, William Speirs, Scottish polar explorer, b.1867, d.1921.
Bruch, Max, German composer (*Violin concerto*, 1865–67), b.1838, d.1920.
Bruckner, Anton, Austrian composer (*Missa Solemnis*, 1854), b.1824, d.1896.
Brulé, Etienne, French explorer of North America b.c.1592, murdered 1632.
Brumaire, 2nd month (mid-Oct. to mid-Nov.) in the French Revolutionary calendar established 1793.
Brummell, 'Beau' (George Bryan Brummell), English dandy, b.1778, d.1840.

Brunei, N.W. Borneo state, sultanate placed under British protection 1888; achieved independence in 1983.

Brunel, Isambard Kingdom, English civil engineer, b.1806, d.1859.

Brunel, Sir Marc Isambard, French-born engineer, b.1769, d.1849.

Brunelleschi, Filippo, Italian architect, b.1377, d.1446.

Brunet, Jacques Charles, French bibliographer (*Manuel du libraire*, 1810), b.1780, d.1867.

Brüning, Heinrich, German statesman (chancellor 1930–32), b.1885, d.1970.

Brunner, Heinrich, German historian, b.1840, d.1915.

Brunner, Thomas, English explorer in New Zealand, b.1821, d.1874.

Bruno, St, German-born founder (1084) of the Carthusian Order, b.*c.*1030, d.1101.

Bruno, Giordano, Italian philosopher b.1548, burnt at the stake 1600.

Brussels, Belgian capital, founded by St Gery of Cambrai in the 7th century.

Brussels Treaty, concerning Western Union, signed 17 March 1948; came into force 25 July 1948.

Brutus, Marcus Junius, Roman patriot b.85, committed suicide 42 BC.

Bryan, William Jennings, American statesman, b.1860, d.1925.

Bryce, James, Viscount Bryce, British statesman, b.1838, d.1922.

Bryn Mawr College, Philadelphia, American women's college, founded 1880.

Brynner, Yul, American film actor of Swiss-Mongolian descent (*The King and I*, 1956), b.1915, d.1985.

Bubonic plague, bacillus discovered 1894 by the French scientist Alexandre Emile John Yersin, b.1863, d.1943.

Buccaneers, French and English pirates active in Caribbean between 1625 and 1700.

Bucer, Martin, German religious reformer, b.1491, d.1551.

Buchan, John, 1st Baron Tweedsmuir, Scottish statesman and writer (*Greenmantle*, 1916), b.1875, d.1940.

Buchanan, George, Scottish scholar, b.1506, d.1582.

Buchanan, James, 15th US president (1857–61), b.1791, d.1868.

Buchanites, Scottish religious sect, founded by Elspeth Buchan, b.1738, d.1791.

Buchan's days, weather predictions defined 1869 by Alexander Buchan, b.1829, d.1907.

Buchman, Frank, American evangelist and founder (1921) of Moral Rearmament, b.1878, d.1961.

Büchner, Georg, German playwright (*Dantons Tod,* 1835), b.1813, d.1837.

Buckingham, George Villiers, Duke of, favourite of James I b.1592, assassinated 1628.

Buckingham, George Villiers, 2nd Duke of, favourite of Charles II, b.1627, d.1687.

Buckingham Palace, built by the Duke of Buckingham 1703; rebuilt 1825–37.

Buckle, Henry Thomas, English historian, b.1821, d.1862.

Buddha, Gautama Siddharta, the Indian founder of Buddhism, b.*c.*568, d.*c.*488 BC.

Budé, Guillaume, French classicist, b.1467, d.1540.

Budge, Sir Ernest Alfred Wallis, English Egyptologist, b.1857, d.1934.

Buell, Abel, American map engraver, silversmith and inventor, b.1742, d.1822.

Buenos Aires, founded 1536 by Don Pedro de Mendoza, b.c.1487, d.1537.

Buenos Aires Standard, first English-language South American daily newspaper, founded 1861 by the Irish-born economist Michael George Mulhall, b.1836, d.1900.

'Buffalo Bill' (William Frederick Cody), American frontiersman and showman, b.1846, d.1917.

Buffon, Georges Louis Leclere, Comte de, French naturalist, b.1707, d.1788.

Buhl Cabinets, style introduced by the French furniture maker André Charles Boulle, b.1642, d.1732.

Bukharin, Nikolai Ivanovich, Russian Communist leader, b.1888, tried and shot 1938.

Bulawayo, mining city in Zimbabwe, founded 1893.

Bulganin, Nikolai Aleksandrovich, Soviet leader, b.1895, d.1975.

Bulgaria, established in 7th century, conquered by Byzantines in 10th century, revived in 12th century, conquered by Turks in 14th century; Principality under Turkish suzerainty 1878; independent kingdom 1908; Communist republic 1946; democratic constitution adopted 1991.

Bull-baiting, prohibited in England by Act of Parliament 1835.

Bull Run, Battles of, American Civil War, 1st, 21 July 1861; 2nd, 30 Aug. 1862.

Buller, Sir Redvers Henry, British soldier, b.1839, d.1908.

Bullinger, Heinrich, Swiss Reformation leader, b.1504, d.1575.

Bülow, Prince Bernhard von, German chancellor (1900–09), b.1849, d.1929.

Bunin, Ivan Alexeyevich, Russian writer in exile, b.1870, d.1954.

Bunker Hill, Battle of, American Revolution, fought between Americans and English 17 June 1775.

Bunsen, Christian Karl Josias, Baron, German diplomat, b.1791, d.1860.

Bunsen burner, invented for use in laboratories by the German scientist Robert Wilhelm Bunsen, b.1811, d.1899.

Bunyan, John, English religious leader and writer (*Pilgrim's Progress*, 1684), b.1628, d.1688.

Buonarroti, Philippe, French revolutionary leader, b.1761, d.1837.

Buononcini, Giovanni Battista, Italian composer (*Muzio Scevola,* 1710), b.1672, d.c.1750.

Burbage, Richard, English actor, b.c.1567, d.1619.

Burbank, Luther, American horticulturalist, b.1849, d.1926.

Burchell, William John, English explorer, b.c.1782, d.1863.

Burckhardt, Jacob, Swiss historian, b.1818, d.1897.

Burdett, Francis, English politician, b.1770, d.1844.

Burgess, Anthony (John Anthony Burgess Wilson), English novelist, critic and composer (*A Clockwork Orange,* 1962), b.1917.

Burgess, Guy Francis de Moncy, English spy, defected to the Soviet Union 26 May 1951, b.1910, d.1963.

Burghley, William Cecil, Lord, English statesman, b.1520, d.1598.

Burgkmair, Hans, German artist, b.1473, d.1531.

Burgoyne, John, English general in American Revolution, b.1723, d.1792.

Burke, Edmund, Irish-born statesman and writer, b.1729, d.1797.

Burke, Robert O'Hara, Australian pioneer, b.1820, d.1861.

Burke, William, Irish criminal (with William Hare), b.1792, hanged 1829.

Burke's Peerage, founded 1826 by Sir John Bernard Burke, b.1814, d.1892.

Burlington Arcade, Piccadilly, London, opened 20 March 1819.

Burlington House, Piccadilly, London, built *c.*1664 by Sir John Denham, b.1615, d.1669; rebuilt 1731.

Burma, gained independence as a republic 4 Jan. 1948.

Burne-Jones, Sir Edward, English painter (*Cophetua and the Beggarmaid*), b.1833, d.1898.

Burnet, Gilbert, British writer and divine, b.1643, d.1715.

Burnett, Mrs Frances Hodgson, English-born writer (*Little Lord Fauntleroy,* 1886), b.1849, d.1924.

Burney, Charles, English musicologist, b.1726, d.1814.

Burney, Fanny (Madame d'Arblay), English writer (*Evelina*, 1778), b.1752, d.1840.

Burning to death, British punishment for women, last inflicted 1729; legally abolished 1790.

Burns, John, British socialist leader, b.1858, d.1943.

Burns, Robert, Scottish poet, b.1759, d.1796.

Burr, Aaron, American statesman, b.1756, d.1836.

Burton, Decimus, English architect, b.1800, d.1881.

Burton, Richard, Welsh-born film actor (*The Spy Who Came in from the Cold,* 1965), b.1925, d.1984.

Burton, Sir Richard Francis, English explorer and translator of *The Arabian Nights*, b.1821, d.1890.

Burton, Robert, English writer (*The Anatomy of Melancholy,* 1621), b.1577, d.1640.

Bus, first in London ran from Marylebone Road to the Bank 4 July 1829.

Busch, Wilhelm, German humorous artist, b.1832, d.1908.

Bush, George Herbert Walker, 41st US president (1989–93), b.1924.

Bushell, Edward, English champion of juries, *fl.* 1670–71.

Busoni, Ferruccio, Italian composer (*Die Brautwahl,* 1912), b.1866, d.1924.

Buss, Frances Mary, English pioneer of high schools for girls, b.1827, d.1894.

Butcher, Samuel Henry, Irish classicist, b.1850, d.1910.

Bute, John Stuart, Earl of, British statesman, b.1713, d.1792.

Butler, Joseph, bishop of Durham, b.1692, d.1752.

Butler, Josephine, social reformer, b.1828, d.1906.

Butler, Samuel, English poet (*Hudibras,* 1663–78), b.1612, d.1680.

Butler, Samuel, English writer (*Erewhon,* 1872), b.1835, d.1902.

Butlin, William Edmund ('Billy'), South African-born pioneer of holiday camps, b.1900, d.1980.

Butt, Dame Clara, English contralto, b.1873, d.1936.
Butt, Isaac, Irish nationalist politician, b.1813, d.1879.
Buxtehude, Dietrich, Danish-born organist and composer, b.1637, d.1707.
Byng, George, **Viscount Torrington**, English admiral, b.1663, d.1733.
Byng, John, English admiral, b.1704, shot 1757.
Byrd, Richard Evelyn, American polar aviator, b.1888, d.1957.
Byrd, William, English composer, b.*c.*1542, d.1623.
Byrom, John, English shorthand pioneer, b.1692, d.1763.
Byron, George Gordon, Lord, English poet (*Don Juan*), b.1788, d.1824.
Byzantine empire, existed 330–1453.
Byzantium, founded 658 BC; rebuilt as Constantinople AD 330; conquered by the Turks 1453 and renamed Istanbul.

C

Cabal ministry, formed 1668 by King Charles II of England; ended 1673 (from names of members: Clifford Ashley, Buckingham, Arlington, Lauderdale).

Cabell, James Branch, American novelist (*Jurgen*, 1919), b.1879, d.1958.

Cabinet, form of British government, introduced by Charles II, formally instituted by William III, 1693, principles developed by Sir Robert Walpole, b.1676, d.1745.

Cabinet Noir, French postal censorship, instituted in reign of Louis XI, formally constituted in reign of Louis XV, abolished 1868.

Cable, first Atlantic, completed 5 Aug. 1858 by Sir Charles Tilston Bright, b.1832, d.1888; first successful cable laid completed 7 Sept. 1866.

Cabochiens, Parisian rioters led by Simon 'Caboche' (real name Lecoustellier) active 1413–14.

Cabot, John, Italian-born explorer (discovered Newfoundland 1497), b.1451, d.1498.

Cabral, Pedro, Portuguese explorer, b.*c.*1467, d.*c.*1520.

Cabrillo, Juan Rodriguez, Spanish explorer, d.1543.

Cadbury, George, English cocoa manufacturer and newspaper owner, b.1839, d.1922.

Cade, Jack, English revolutionary leader, killed 1450.

Cadets, Russian political party, formed 1905 by Paul Milyukov.

Cadillac, Antoine de la Mothe, Sieur, governor of Louisiana (1713–16), b.*c.*1656, d.1730.

Cadiz, Naval Battle of, fought between Sir Francis Drake and the Spaniards 1587.

Cadmium, chemical element, first isolated by the German scientist F. Stromeyer 1817.

Cadogan, William, 1st Earl Cadogan, Irish general, b.1675, d.1726.

Cadwalladr, Welsh prince, d.1172.

Caedmon, English poet, d.*c.*680.

Caesar, Caius Julius, Roman dictator, b.100 BC, assassinated 44 BC.

Caesarian Section, performed on living woman as early as 1500.

Caesium, chemical element first isolated 1860 by the German scientist Robert Wilhelm Bunsen, b.1811, d.1899.

Cafe Royal, London, founded 1864, bombed 1940.
'Cagliostro, Alessandro' (Giuseppe Balsamo), Italian alchemist, b.1743, d.1795.
Cagney, James, American film actor of Irish descent (*Yankee Doodle Dandy,* 1942), b.1899, d.1986.
Cahiers, statements of local grievances submitted to the French States-General 1789.
Caicos Islands, West Indies, part of British colony of Turks and Caicos Islancds, discovered *c.*1512.
Caine, Sir Hall, British novelist (*The Deemster*, 1887), b.1853, d.1931.
Caine, Michael (Maurice Joseph Micklewhite), British film actor (*Alfie,* 1966), b.1933.
Ça Ira, French revolutionary song written by Ladré 1789.
Caius, St, pope 283–296.
Caius, John, English physician to the Royal family, b.1510, d.1593.
Caius College, Gonville and, Cambridge University, founded as Gonville Hall by Edmund Gonville (d.1351) in 1348; assumed present name under Royal Charter 1557.
Cajetan, Cardinal Thomas, Italian theologian, b.1469, d.1534.
'Calamity Jane' (Martha Jane Burke), American pioneer, b.*c.*1852, d.1903.
Calamy, Edmund, English historian of nonconformity (*Account of the Ejected Ministers*, 1702), b.1671, d.1732.
Calas, Jean, French Calvinist, b.1698, tortured to death 1752.
Calcium, discovered 1808 by Sir Humphry Davy, b.1778, d.1829.
Calculating machine, first model built 1694 by the German scientist Gottfried Wilhelm Leibniz, b.1646, d.1716.
Calculus, *Infinitesimal*, invented 1675 by the German scientist Gottfried Wilhelm Leibniz, b.1646, d.1716; *Integral and Differential*, invented independently by Leibniz and Isaac Newton , b.1642, d.1727.
Calcutta, founded 1686–90 by the English official Job Charnock, d.1693; Black Hole of, episode occurred 20 June 1756.
Calderón de la Barca, Pedro, Spanish playwright (*La Vida es Sueño*), b.1600, d.1681.
Caledonian Canal, Scotland, constructed 1804–22 by the Scottish engineer Thomas Telford, b.1757, d.1834.
Calendar, French Revolutionary, instituted 1793, abolished 1806.
Calendar, Gregorian, reformed version of Julian Calendar, introduced by Pope Gregory XIII, 1582; adopted in Britain Sept. 1752.

Calendar, Hebrew, calculated from 3761 BC; system adopted AD 358.
Calendar, Julian, reformed version of Roman Calendar, introduced by Julius Caesar 46 BC.
Calendar, Mohammedan, calculated from the Hegira 622.
Calendar, Roman, calculated from the supposed date of the foundation of Rome 754 BC.
Calhoun, John Caldwell, American statesman, b.1782, d.1850.
California, first settled 1769; ceded by Mexico to the USA 1848; admitted to the Union 1850.
California, University of, founded at Berkeley 1868.
Californian gold fields, discovered Dec. 1847.
Caligula, Roman emperor (37–41), b.12, assassinated 41.
Caliphate, Egyptian, extinguished by Ottoman conquest 1517.
Caliphate of the Islamic Empire, Umayyad, 661–750; Abbasid, established 750, extinguished by the Mongols 1258.
Caliphate, Ottoman, extinguished by the Kemalist Revolution 1923.
Callaghan, James, Baron, British statesman (prime minister 1976–79), b.1912.
Callas, Maria, American opera singer, b.1924, d.1977.
Callimachus, Greek poet who lived in the 3rd century BC.
Callisthenes, Greek historian, b.*c*.360, executed 328 BC.
Callistus I, St, pope 217–222.
Callistus II (Guido), pope 1119–24.
Callistus III (Alfonso de Borja), pope 1455–58.
Callistus III, anti-pope 1168–79.
Callot, Jacques, French engraver, b.1592, d.1635.
Calloway, Cab(ell), American band leader, singer and composer, b.1907.
Calorimeters, invented 1865 by the French scientist Pierre Eugène Marcelin Berthelot, b.1827, d.1907.
Calpurnia, wife of Julius Caesar, *fl.* 50–40 BC.
Calvin, John (Jean Cauvin), French theologian (*Institutes*, 1535), and leader of the Reformation at Geneva, b.1509, d.1564.
Calvino, Italo, Italian author (*Invisible Cities,* 1972), b.1923, d.1985.
Camargo, Marie Anne, French dancer, b.1710, d.1770.
Cambodia, IndoChina, made French Protectorate 1863; granted independence 1955; 1970 Prince Norodom Sihanouk overthrown by Lon Nol and monarchy abolished; Khmer Rouge captured

Phonm Penh 1975, renamed Kampuchea; murderous regime of Pol Pot 1975–79; invasion by Vietnam 1979–89.

Cambrai, Treaty of (The Ladies' Peace), renewing Treaty of Madrid, signed 1529.

Cambrian Period, Earth history, 520 million years ago.

Cambridge University, founded in 13th century, granted Royal Charter 1231.

Cambridge University Observatory, opened 1820.

Cambridge University Press, founded 1583 by Thomas Thomas, b.1553, d.1588.

Cambyses, king of the Medes and Persians (529–522 BC), committed suicide c.522.

Camden, Battle of, American War of Independence, fought between the British and the Americans 16 Aug. 1780.

Camden, Charles Pratt, Earl, English reforming judge, b.1713, d.1794.

Camden, William, English antiquary (*Britannia*, 1586), b.1551, d.1623.

Camera, first roll-film, marketed 1888 by the American inventor George Eastman, b.1854, d.1932.

Camera lucida, invented by English scientist William Hyde Wollaston, b.1766, d.1828.

Camera obscura, described 1569.

Cameron, Sir David Young, Scottish artist, b.1865, d.1945.

Cameron, James, Scottish newspaper and TV journalist, b.1911, d.1985.

Cameroon, West Africa, German colony 1884–1916; divided 1919 into British Cameroons and French Cameroun; S. Cameroons and Cameroun united as a republic in 1961.

Camisards, French Protestant rebels in the Cevennes active from 1685 to 1705.

Camões, Luis de, Portuguese poet (*Os Lusiadas*, 1572), b.c.1524, d.1579.

Camorra, The, Neapolitan secret society, formed in the 16th century, suppressed in the late 19th century.

Camouflage, Thayer's Law of, defined 1910 by the American painter Abbott Henderson Thayer, b.1849, d.1921.

Campagnola, Domenico, Italian painter (*The Holy Family*), b.c.1490, d.c.1565.

Campaign for Nuclear Disarmament (CND), founded in Britain 1958 by Bertrand Russell and Canon John L. Collins.

Campanella, Tommaso, Italian philosopher (*Città del Sole*), b.1568, d.1639.
Campbell, Sir Colin, British field marshal, b.1792, d.1863.
Campbell, Donald Malcolm, English car and speedboat racer, set world speed records 1964 on water (276.3 mph) and land (403.1 mph), b.1921, killed in *Bluebird* crash on Lake Coniston 1967.
Campbell, Kim (Avril), first woman prime minister of Canada (since 1993), b.1947.
Campbell, Sir Malcolm, English sportsman and racer, holder of world speed records on land and water from 1927, b.1885, d.1949.
Campbell, Mrs Patrick, English actress, b.1865, d.1940.
Campbell, Thomas, Scottish poet (*Ye Mariners of England*), *b*.1777, d.1844.
Campbell-Bannerman, Sir Henry, British statesman (prime minister 1905–08), b.1836, d.1908.
Camp David, official US presidential retreat near Washington DC, named by President Eisenhower after his grandson 1953.
Campeggio, Cardinal Lorenzo, Italian divine, b.1472, d.1539.
Camperdown, Battle of, naval engagement fought between the British and the Dutch fleets 11 Oct. 1797.
Campion, Edmund, Jesuit missionary to England, b.1540, hanged 1581, beatified 1886.
Campo Formio, Treaty of, between Napoleon I and Austria, signed 1797.
Camus, Albert, French novelist (*La Peste*, 1947), b.1913, killed in car accident 1960.
Canada, granted constitution as a Dominion 1867; associated as a member of the British Commonwealth of Nations 1926.
Canadian-Pacific Railway, completed 1886.
Canadian-USA frontiers, defined 9 Aug. 1842.
Canal, chief period of construction in England, 1755–1827.
Canaletto, Antonio, Italian painter (*S. Maria della Salute*), b.1697, d.1768.
Canary Islands, Spanish territory in the Atlantic, occupation completed by Spain 1496.
Canberra, Australian federal capital, founded 1923.
Cancer Research Institute, London, founded 1902.
Candlemas, Festival of the Purification of the Virgin, 2 Feb.
Cannae, Italy, battle between Romans and Carthaginians 216 BC.
Cannes Film Festival, first held 1946.

Canning, George, British statesman (prime minister 1827), b.1770, d.1827.

Canning, to preserve food, pioneered by François Appert 1809; patented in England by Durand 1810.

Canon law, study developed by the 12th-century Italian monk Gratian, in his *Decretum* published c.1140.

Canossa, Italy, scene of penance of the emperor Henry IV 1077.

Canova, Antonio, Italian sculptor (*Perseus*), b.1757, d.1822.

Canterbury, ecclesiastical centre of England since 597.

Canterbury Cathedral, England, built 1070–1495.

Cantor, Georg, German mathematician, b.1845, d.1918.

Canute, Danish king of England (1016–35), b.c.994, d.1035.

Capa, Robert, American photographer, co-founder of Magnum Agency 1946, b.1913, killed in Indochina 1954.

Capablanca, José Raúl, Cuban chess player, world champion (1921–27), b.1888, d.1942.

Cape of Good Hope, South Africa, first doubled 1488 by the Portuguese navigator Bartolomeu Diaz, d.1500.

Cape of Good Hope Triangular Postage Stamps, first issued 1 Sept. 1853,

Cape Horn, South America, discovered by the Dutch navigator Willem Cornelis Schouten 1616.

Cape Province, settled by Dutch 1652, bought by Britain 1814.

Capek, Karel, Czech writer (*R.U.R.*, 1920), b.1890, d.1938.

Cape St Vincent, Naval Battle of, fought between British and Spanish fleets 14 Feb. 1797.

Capet Dynasty, ruled France 987–1328, Naples 1265–1435, Hungary 1308–82.

Cape Verde Islands, independent republic in the Atlantic, Portuguese overseas province until 1975, discovered by the Portuguese navigator Diogo Gomes 1460.

Capgrave, John, English theologian, b.1393, d.1464.

Capone, Al(phonso), Italian-born gangster, b.1895, d.1947.

Caporetto, Battle of, World War I, fought between Austrians and Italians 24 Oct. 1917.

Capote, Truman, American author (*In Cold Blood*, 1966), b.1924, d.1984.

Capra, Frank, American film director (*Mr Smith Goes to Washington*, 1939), b.1897, d.1991.

Capuchin Order, founded 1528 by Matteo di Bassi.

Caracalla, Roman emperor (211–217), b.188, assassinated 217.

Caractacus, English king, died in captivity in Rome c.54.

Caramanlis, Constantine, Greek statesman (premier 1955–63, 1974–80; president 1980–85), b. 1907.

'Caran d'Ache' (Emmanuel Poiré), Russian-born humorous artist, b.1858, d.1909.

Carausius, Marcus Aurelius Mausaeus, British leader in 3rd century.

Caravaggio, Michelangelo Amerighi, Italian painter (*The Supper at Emmaus*), b.1569, d.1609.

Carbolic, first used 1863 as a disinfectant by Lord Lister, b.1827, d.1912.

Carbonari, Italian secret revolutionary society, formed *c.*1810.

Carboniferous Period, Earth history, 275 million years ago.

Cardin, Pierre, French fashion designer, b.1922.

Carducci, Giosuè, Italian poet, b.1835, d.1907.

Carew, Thomas, English poet, b.*c.*1598, d.1639.

Care, George Leonard, archbishop of Canterbury since 1990, b.1935.

Carey, Henry, English poet (*Sally in our alley*), b.*c.*1690, d.1743.

Carleton, William, Irish writer (*Traits and Stories of the Irish Peasantry*, 1830), b.1794, d.1869.

Carlile, Richard, English radical, b.1799, d.1843.

Carlile, The Rev. Wilson, English founder of the Church Army (1882), b.1847, d.1942.

Carlisle, Cumbria, English city, granted charter 1158 by King Henry II.

Carlists, supporters of the claims of Don Carlos, b.1788, d.1855, and his heirs to the Spanish throne; formed early in 19th century, suppressed 1878.

Carlos, Don, heir of Philip II of Spain, b.1545, d.1568.

Carlotta, empress of Mexico (1863–67), b.1840, d.1927.

Carlowitz, Treaty of, between the Turks and the Allies, signed 1699.

Carl Rosa Opera Company, founded by Carl Rosa, b.1843, d.1889.

Carlsbad Decrees, repressing growth of German democratic movements, signed by the German states 1819.

Carlyle, Jane Welsh, wife of Thomas Carlyle, b.1801, d.1866.

Carlyle, Thomas, Scottish writer (*The French Revolution*, 1837), b.1795, d.1881.

Carmelite Order, founded *c.*1150 by the Crusader Berthold; monastic order recognized 1224.

'Carmagnole, La', French revolutionary song (possibly of Italian origin), composed 1792, suppressed 1799.

'Carmen Sylva', Elizabeth, queen of Romania, b.1843, d.1916.

Carmichael, Hoagy (Hoagland), American jazz composer and actor, b.1899, d.1981.

Carnarvon, Henry Howard Molyneux Herbert, Earl of, British statesman, b.1831, d.1890.

Carnegie, Andrew, Scottish-born philanthropist, b.1835, d.1919.

Carnegie, Dale, American salesman, lecturer and author (*How to Win Friends and Influence People*, 1936), b.1888, d.1955.

Carnegie Endowment for International Peace, Washington, founded 1910.

Carnot, Lazare Nicolas Marguerite, French revolutionary leader, b.1753, d.1823.

Carol I, Romanian king (1866–1914), b.1839, d.1914.

Carol II, Romanian king (1930–40), b.1893, d.1953.

Caroline of Anspach, queen of England, wife of George II, b.1683, d.1737.

Caroline, Queen, wife of George IV, b.1768, d.1821.

Carolingian Dynasty, ruled the Franks 751–887.

Carpaccio, Vittore, Italian painter (*The Presentation in the Temple*), b.c.1455, d.1522.

Carpenter, Edward, English writer and social reformer (*Towards Democracy*, 1905), b.1844, d.1929.

Carpetbaggers, Northern businessmen who 'invaded' the Southern States of the USA after the American Civil War 1865.

Carpet-sweeper, invented 1876 by the American businessman Melville R. Bissell.

Carracci, Ludovico, Italian painter (*Transfiguration*), b.1555, d.1619.

Carroll, Lewis (Charles Lutwidge Dodgson), English mathematician and writer (*Alice's Adventures in Wonderland*, 1865), b.1832, d.1898.

Carson, Edward, Baron, British politician, b.1854, d.1935.

Carson, Kit, American pioneer, b.1809, d.1878.

Cartagena, Colombia, founded 1533 by Pedro de Heredia; captured by Sir Francis Drake 1585.

Carter, James Earl ('Jimmy'), 39th US president (1977–81), b.1924.

Carteret, Sir George, Jersey-born English administrator, b.c.1610, d.1680.

Carteret, John, Baron, British politician, b.1690, d.1763.

Cartesian coordinates, theory first propounded 1637 by the French philosopher René Descartes, b.1596, d.1650.
Carthage, Phoenician city on north African coast, traditionally founded 814–813 BC, finally destroyed by the Arabs AD 648.
Carthusian Order, founded 1084 by St Bruno, b.*c.*1030, d.1101.
Cartier, Jacques, French discoverer 1534 of the St Lawrence River, b.1491, d.1557.
Cartier-Bresson, Henri, French photo-journalist, b.1908.
Cartland, Barbara Hamilton, English romantic novelist, the world's best-selling author, b.1901.
Cartwright, Edmund, English inventor 1785 of the power loom, b.1743, d.1823.
Cartwright, Thomas, English religious leader, b.1535, d.1600.
Caruso, Enrico, Italian opera singer, b.1873, d.1921.
Carver, John, English leader of the Pilgrim Fathers, b.*c.*1576, d.1621.
Carver, Raymond, American short-story writer (*What We Talk About When We Talk About Love,* 1981), b.1938, d.1988.
Cary, Joyce, Anglo-Irish writer (*The Horse's Mouth*, 1945), b.1888, d.1957.
Casablanca, Moroccan port, founded 1468.
Casablanca Conference, World War II, meeting between Franklin D. Roosevelt and Winston Churchill at which 'unconditional surrender' formula was agreed, held 14–20 Jan. 1943
Casals, Pablo, Catalan cellist, b.1876, d.1973.
Casanova, Giovanni Giacomo, Italian adventurer and writer (*Memoirs*), b.1725, d.1798.
Casaubon, Isaac, Swiss-born classical scholar, b.1559, d.1614.
Casca, Publius Servilius, Roman conspirator and assassin of Julius Caesar, d.*c.*42 BC.
Casement, Sir Roger, Irish leader, b.1864, hanged 1916.
Cash register, invented by the American John Ritty of Ohio 1879.
Casimir I, Polish king (1040–58), b.1015, d.1058.
Casimir II, Polish king (1177–94).
Casimir III, Polish king (1333–70), b.1310, d.1370.
Casimir IV, Polish king (1447–92), b.1427, d.1492.
Casimir V (John II Casimir), Polish king (1648–68), b.1609, d.1672.
Caslon, William, English typefounder, b.1692, d.1766.
Cassatt, Mary, American painter, b.*c.*1845, d.1926.
Cassel, Gustav, Swedish economist, b.1866, d.1945.

Cassell, John, English publisher, b.1817, d.1865.
Cassianus, Joannes, French-born pioneer founder of monasteries, b.365, d.435.
Cassini, Giovanni Domenico, Italian astronomer, b.1625, d.1712.
Cassino, Monte, monastery founded by St Benedict 529, destroyed by Allies May 1944.
Cassiodorus, Roman statesman and scholar, b.*c*.478, d.570.
Cassius, Roman conspirator against Julius Caesar, committed suicide 42 BC.
Castagno, Andrea del, Italian painter, b.1390, d.1457.
Castelnau, Michel de, French soldier and ambassador to English court, b.*c*.1520, d.1592.
Castillon, Battle of, fought between French and English, and ending the Hundred Years' War, 17 July 1453.
Castle, Barbara Anne, British Labour politician, Member of European Parliament since 1979, b.1911.
Castlereagh, Robert Stewart, Viscount, Ulster-born statesman, b.1769, committed suicide 1822.
Castro Ruz, Fidel, president of Cuba since 1959, b.1927.
Catalysis, chemical action, discovered 1836 by the Swedish scientist Baron Berzelius, b.1779, d.1848.
Catesby, Robert, English conspirator, b.1573, killed 1605.
Catherine I, Russian empress (1725–27), b.1684, d.1727.
Catherine II, 'The Great', Russian empress (1762–96), b.1729, d.1796.
Catherine Howard, 5th wife of Henry VIII, beheaded 1542.
Catherine of Aragon, 1st wife of Henry VIII, b.1485, d.1536.
Catherine of Siena, St, b.1347, d.1380. Feast: 30 April.
Catherine Parr, 6th wife of Henry VIII, b.1512, d.1548.
Cathode rays, discovered by the English scientist Sir William Crookes, b.1832, d.1919.
Catholic emancipation in Britain, April 1829.
Catholic reform, commenced *c*.1522, completed 1590.
Catilina, Lucius Sergius, Roman conspirator, b.*c*.108, killed in battle 62 BC.
Catlin, George, American artist famous for his depiction of North American Indians and their life, b.1796, d.1872.
Cato the Elder (Marcus Portius Cato), Roman statesman, b.234, d.149 BC.
Cato the Younger (Marcus Portius Uticensis), Roman statesman, b.95, committed suicide 46 BC.

Cato Street Conspiracy, unsuccessful plot to assassinate members of the British Cabinet 1820, planned by Arthur Thistlewood, b.1770, executed 1820.

Catt, Carrie Chapman, American suffragette and peace campaigner, b.1859, d.1947.

Cattermole, George, English painter, b.1800, d.1868.

Catullus, Valerius, Roman poet, b.*c.*84, d.*c.*54 BC.

Caudine Forks, Battle of the, fought between the Samnites and the Romans, 321 BC.

Caughley porcelain, manufactured 1772–99.

Caulaincourt, Armand, Marquis de, French statesman, b.1772, d.1827.

Cavalcanti, Guido, Italian poet, b.*c.*1230, d.1300.

Cavell, Edith, English nurse and patriot, b.1866, executed by the Germans 12 Oct. 1915.

Cavendish, Henry, English scientist and eccentric, b.1731, d.1810.

Cavour, Count Camillo, Italian statesman, b.1810, d.1861.

Cawnpore (Kanpur), **Mutiny of**, in which rioters murdered the English garrison and their families, 6 June 1857.

Caxton, William, first English printer, b.*c.*1422, d.*c.*1491.

Cayenne, capital of French Guiana, founded 1664.

CBS (Columbia Broadcasting System), major American TV network founded 1927.

Cecil, Robert, **1st Earl of Salisbury**, statesman, b.*c.*1563, d.1612.

Cecil, William, **Baron Burghley**, English Elizabethan statesman, b.1520, d.1598.

Cecilia, St, martyred 230. Feast: 22 Nov.

Cedar Creek, Battle of, American Civil War, 17 Oct. 1864.

Celebes, *see* **Sulawesi.**

Celestine I, St, pope 422–432.

Celestine II, anti-pope 1124–30.

Celestine II, pope 1143–44.

Celestine III (Giacinto Bobo), pope 1191–98.

Celestine IV (Godfrey Castiglione), pope 1241–43.

Celestine V (St Peter Celestine), pope 1294, b.1215, d.1296.

Cellini, Benvenuto, Italian artist and writer (*Autobiography*), b.1500, d.1571.

Cellophane, invented *c.*1900 by the Swiss scientist J. E. Brandenberger.

Cell theory, botany, developed *c.*1850 by the German botanist Hugo von Mohl, b.1805, d.1872.
Cellular composition of plant tissue, proved 1838 by the German botanist Matthias Jakob.
Celluloid, patented 1855 by the English chemist Alexander Parkes; successfully invented 1870 by the American chemist John Wesley Hyatt, b.1837, d.1920.
Cellulose nitrate, first synthetic plastic material, invented 1855 by the British chemist Alexander Parkes, b.1813, d.1890.
Celsius, Anders, Swedish astronomer and inventor (1742) of the centigrade thermometer, b.1701, d.1744.
Celsus, Aulus Cornelius, Roman medical writer (*De Medecina*) in 1st century.
Cenci, Beatrice, Italian heroine and possibly murderess, b.1577, executed 1599.
Cenozoic Era, Earth history, between 1 and 70 million years ago.
Centigrade thermometer, invented 1742 by the Swedish scientist Anders Celsius, b.1701, d.1744.
Cenotaph, Whitehall, London, memorial to the dead of both World Wars, unveiled 11 Nov 1920.
Censorship, of printed books, begun in Mainz in 1486.
Census, first in Britain made 1801.
Centlivre, Susannah, English dramatist and actress, b.c.1667, d.1723.
Central African Republic, former French colony of Ubanghi Shari took name, elected to stay in French Community 1958; became independent in 1960; parliamentary monarchy 1976; republic 1979.
Central Intelligence Agency (CIA), US organization to coordinate and analyze foreign intelligence, founded 1947.
Central London electric railway, opened 27 June 1900.
Central Treaty Organization (CENTO), set up as the Baghdad Pact Organization 1956 (Treaty signed 1955). Adopted present title 1958.
Ceres, first planetoid sighted, discovered 1801 by the Italian astronomer Giuseppe Piazzi, b.1746, d.1826.
Cerium, chemical element, isolated 1803 by the Swedish chemist Baron Berzelius, b.1779, d.1848.
CERN, Centre Européen pour la Recherche Nucléare, European research facility for particle physics, established 1954.
Cervantes, Miguel de, Spanish writer (*Don Quixote*, 1605–15), b.1547, d.1616.

Cesarewitch Stakes, Newmarket, first run in 1839.
Cetewayo, Zulu king, b.*c.*1836, d.1884.
Ceylon, *see* **Sri Lanka**.
Cézanne, Paul, French painter, b.1839, d.1906.
Chabrier, Emmanuel, French composer (*España*), b.1841, d.1894.
Chad, Equatorial Africa, became autonomous republic within the French Community 1958; became indepedent 1960.
Chadwick, Sir Edwin, English pioneer in public health, b.1800, d.1890.
Chaeronea, Battle of, fought between the Roman general Sulla and Mithridates' army 86 BC.
Chagall, Marc, Russian-born painter, b.1889, d.1985.
Chalcedon, Council of, Fourth Ecumenical Council, held 451.
Chalgrove Field, Battle of, (Oxfordshire), fought between the Royalists and the Parliamentarians 1643.
Chaliapin, Fyodor Ivanovich, Russian operatic singer, b.1873, d.1938.
Challenger disaster, explosion of US space shuttle on lift-off killing all seven astronauts on board, 28 Jan. 1986.
Châlons, Battle of, fought between the Romans and the Goths and Huns 451.
Chamber of Commerce, first in Britain, founded Glasgow 1783.
Chamberlain, Austen, British statesman, b.1863, d.1937.
Chamberlain, Houston Stewart, English-born racialist, b.1855, d.1926.
Chamberlain, Joseph, British statesman, b.1836, d.1914.
Chamberlain, Neville, British statesman (prime minister 1937–40), b.1869, d.1940.
Chamberlain porcelain, manufactured 1786–1840.
Chambers's Encyclopaedia, founded 1859–68 by the Scottish publisher William Chambers, b.1800, d.1883.
Chambre Ardente, French special court for trial of heretics, etc, instituted 1535, abolished 1682.
Chamisso, Adalbert von, German poet, b.1781, d.1838.
Champaigne, Philippe de, Flemish painter, b.1602, d.1674.
Champion Hurdle, Cheltenham, first run 1927.
Champlain, Samuel de, Lieutenant of Canada (1612–29), b.1567, d.1635.
Champlain, Battle of, fought between the Americans and the British 1814.

Champollion, Jean François, French Egyptologist and decipherer of the Rosetta Stone, b.1790, d.1832.

Chancellor, Richard, English navigator and instigator of the Muscovy Company, died in shipwreck 1556.

Chandernagor, port in S.W. Bengal, former French settlement 1686–1950.

Chandler, Raymond, American writer of detective stories and screenplays (*The Big Sleep,* 1939), b.1888, d.1959.

Chanel, Gabrielle ('Coco'), French fashion designer, b.1883, d.1971.

Channel, English: submarine cable first laid 1850; first crossed by balloon 1785 by Blanchard and Jeffries; first swum 1875 by Matthew Webb; first flown by aeroplane 1909 by Louis Blériot; first woman flier Harriet Quimby 1912; tunnel scheme abandoned by British government 1924, revived as private venture 1980s, opened 1994.

Channel Islands, under German occupation June 1940–May 1945.

Channing, William Ellery, American Unitarian leader, b.1780, d.1842.

Chantrey Bequest, to Royal Academy (and now at Tate Gallery, London), made by Sir Francis Legatt Chantrey, b.1781, d.1841.

Chaplin, Sir Charles Spencer, English-born film actor, b.1889, d.1977.

Chapman, George, English poet and dramatist (*Bussy d'Ambois*, 1607), b.*c.*1559, d.1634.

Chappaquiddick Incident, death of Senator Edward Kennedy's secretary in a car crash after leaving a party, 18 July 1969; Kennedy was driving and left the scene before help arrived.

Chapter of Mitton, battle fought between Scots and English 1319.

Chardin, Jean Baptiste Siméon, French painter (*La Bénédicité*), b.1699, d.1779.

Charge of the Light Brigade, Balaklava, Crimean War, 25 Oct. 1854.

Charlemagne, king of Franks (768–814), king of Lombards (774–814), Holy Roman emperor (800–814), b.742, d.814.

Charles II, the Bald, French king, Holy Roman emperor (875–881), b.823, d.881.

Charles III, the Fat, Holy Roman emperor (881–891), b.839, d.891.

Charles IV, Holy Roman emperor (1347–78), b.1316, d.1378.

Charles V, king of Spain, Holy Roman emperor (1519–55), b.1500, d.1558.
Charles VI, Holy Roman emperor (1711–42), b.1697, d.1745.
Charles VII, Holy Roman emperor (1742–45), b.1697, d.1745.
Charles I, Austrian emperor (1916–18), b.1887, d.1922.
Charles I, English king (1625–49), b.1600, beheaded 1649.
Charles II, English king (1660–85), b.1630, crowned at Scone 1651, d.1685.
Charles Edward, the Young Pretender to the English throne, b.1720, d.1788.
Charles, Prince of Wales, b. 14 Nov. 1948.
Charles III, the Simple, French king, b.879, d.929.
Charles IV, the Fair, French king (1322–28), b.1294, d.1328.
Charles V, the Wise, French king (1364–80), b.1337, d.1380.
Charles VI, the Foolish, French king (1380–1422), b.1368, d.1422.
Charles VII, French king (1422–61), b.1403, d.1461.
Charles VIII, French king (1483–98), b.1470, d.1498.
Charles IX, French king (1560–74), b.1550, d.1574.
Charles X, French king (1822–30), b.1757, d.1836.
Charles II, Spanish king (1665–1700), b.1661, d.1700.
Charles III, Spanish king (1759–88), b.1716, d.1788.
Charles IV, Spanish king (1788–1808), b.1748, d.1819.
Charles I to **Charles VI**, legendary Swedish kings.
Charles VII, Swedish king (1160–67), d.1167.
Charles VIII, Swedish king (1436–41, 1448–70), d.1470.
Charles IX, Swedish king (1600–11), b.1550, d.1611.
Charles X, Swedish king (1654–60), b.1622, d.1660.
Charles XI, Swedish king (1660–97), b.1655, d.1697.
Charles XII, Swedish king (1697–1718), b.1682, killed 1718.
Charles XIII, Swedish king (1809–18), b.1748, d.1818.
Charles XIV, Swedish king (1818–44), b.1763, d.1844.
Charles XV, Swedish king (1859–72), b.1826, d.1872.
Charles the Bold, Duke of Burgundy, b.1433, killed 1477.
Charles Borromeo, St, b.1538, d.1584.
Charles Martel, ruler of the Franks, b.*c.*689, d.741.
Charleston, South Carolina, founded 1670, by the Englishman William Sayle, d.1671.
Charlotte Sophia, wife of George III, b.1744, d.1818.
Charter, Great (Magna Carta) 1215; People's (Chartist) 1836.
Chartist Movement, English social reform, begun 1836, ended *c.*1858; petitions rejected by Parliament 1839, 1842 and 1848.

Chartres Cathedral, constructed 1194 to 1260.

Chartreuse liqueur, manufactured at La Grande Chartreuse Monastery near Grenoble 1607–1901, when the monks left France for Tarragona in Spain.

Chastelard, Pierre de, French poet, b.1540, hanged 1564.

Chateaubriand, François René, Vicomte de, French statesman, b.1768, d.1848.

Chatham, William Pitt, Earl of, British statesman (prime minister 1766–67), b.1708, d.1778.

Chattanooga, Battle of, American Civil War, 23 to 25 Nov. 1863.

Chatterton, Thomas, English forger and poet (*The Rowley Poems*), b.1752, committed suicide 1770.

Chaucer, Geoffrey, English poet (*The Canterbury Tales*, 1387–1400), b.c.1340, d.1400.

Chausson, Ernest, French composer, b.1855, d.1899.

Cheka, Soviet secret police, established 1917, became GPU in 1922, later OGPU which was superseded by NKVD in 1934.

Chekhov, Anton, Russian writer (*The Cherry Orchard*, 1903), b.1860, d.1904.

Chelcicky, Petz, Bohemian religious leader in 15th century.

Chelsea-Derby porcelain, manufactured 1770–84.

Cheltenham Gold Cup, first run 1924.

Chemical wood pulp, for paper manufacture, invented 1857.

Cheng-hua period, China, 1465–87.

Cheng-têh period, China, 1506–21.

Chénier, André, French poet, b.1762, guillotined 1794.

Cheops, Egyptian king, *fl. c.*2900 BC.

Cheques, first printed by the English banker Lawrence Childs *c.*1762.

Chernobyl disaster, explosion and fire at a Soviet light-water nuclear reactor in the Ukraine April 1986.

Cherokee, North American Indian people, disbanded 1906.

Cherubini, Luigi, Italian composer, b.1760, d.1842.

Cherypnin, Nikolai, Russian-born composer (*Le Pavillon d'Armide*, 1903), b.1873, d.1945.

Chesapeake Bay, battle between French and British fleets, 5 Sept. 1781.

Chess, played in India by 7th century AD, brought to Spain between 8th and 10th centuries, to England in late 13th century.

Chester Cathedral, England, founded 1093; created cathedral by Henry VIII, 1541.

Chesterfield, Philip Dormer Stanhope, Earl of, British statesman and writer of the *Letters*, b.1694, d.1773.

Chesterton, Gilbert Keith, English writer (of the Father Brown stories), b.1874, d.1936.

'Chevalier sans peur et sans reproche' (Pierre du Terrail, Chevalier de Bayard), French soldier, b.1474, died in battle 1524.

Chetham's Library, Manchester, founded 1653 by the English manufacturer Humfrey Chetham, b.1580, d.1653.

Chevalier, Albert, English music-hall artist, b.1861, d.1923.

Chevalier, Maurice, French actor, b.1888, d.1972.

Chevy Chase, Battle of, fought between Scots and English 1388.

Chia Ching period, China, 1522–66.

Chiang Kai-shek, president of China 1928–31, 1943–49; and of Republic of China 1950–75, b.1887, d.1975.

Chicago, Illinois, settled at the beginning of the 19th century; partly destroyed by fire 1871.

Chicago University, founded 1890.

Chichester, Sir Francis, English sailor and adventurer, made the first non-stop solo voyage around the world 1966, b.1901, d.1972.

Chickamauga, Battle of, American Civil War, fought 19–20 Sept. 1863.

Childermas, Holy Innocents' Day, 28 Dec.

Childers, Erskine, Irish Republican and writer (*The Riddle of the Sands*, 1903), executed 1922.

Children's Crusade, set out from France and Germany to the Holy Land 1212.

Chile, South America, settled by the Spaniards 1540-1565; national government set up 1810; independence from Spain achieved 1818; military junta seized power from Salvador Allende Sept. 1972; General Pinochet ousted by democratic elections Dec. 1989.

Chiltern Hundreds, first granted to an MP as grounds for resignation, 1750.

Chimborazo, volcanic mountain in Ecuador, first climbed 1880 by English mountaineer Edward Whymper, b.1840, d.1911.

China, empire from at least the 23rd century BC until 1912; republic since 1912; the Communist People's Republic of China, governing the whole of China except Taiwan, proclaimed 1 Oct. 1949.

Chinese Law, first codified *c.*950 BC.

Ch'ing dynasty, China, 1644–1912.

Chippendale, Thomas, English furniture maker, b.1718, d.1779.

Chirac, Jacques, French politician (prime minister 1974–76, 1986–88), b.1932.
Chirico, Giorgio de, Italian painter, b.1888, d.1978.
Chiswick Press, London, founded 1810 by the English printer Charles Whittingham, b.1767, d.1840.
Chladni figures, acoustic phenomenon discovered 1787 by the German physicist Ernst Chladni, b.1756, d.1827.
Chlorine, first isolated 1774 by the Swedish chemist Karl Wilhelm Scheele, b.1742, d.1786.
Chloroform, discovered 1831 by the German scientist Justus Liebig, b.1803, d.1873. First used as an anaesthetic 1847.
Chocolate (Cocoa), brought to Europe during 16th century.
Choiseul, Etienne François, Duc de, French statesman, b.1719, d.1785.
Cholera, bacillus, discovered 1883 by the German scientist Robert Koch, b.1843, d.1910; last major epidemic in England 1866.
Chomsky, Noam, American linguistics theorist and political activist (*American power and the New Madarins*, 1969), b.1928.
Chopin, Frédéric, Polish-born composer, b.1810, d.1849.
Chosroes I, Persian ruler (from 531), d.579.
Chosroes II, Persian ruler (from 591), murdered 628.
Chou dynasty, China, 1122 to 255 BC.
Chouans, Breton royalists, formed 1792, suppressed 1800.
Chrétien de Troyes, French poet (*Conte del Graal*), lived in the 12th century.
Christ, title of Jesus of Nazareth, founder of Christianity, born between 5 BC and AD 2, crucified between 30 and 33.
Christ Church, Oxford University, founded 1525.
Christadelphians, religious movement founded by John Thomas, b.1805, d.1871.
Christian, Fletcher, leader of the 1789 mutiny on the *Bounty*; may have lived until after 1810.
Christian I, Danish king (1448–81), b.1426, d.1481.
Christian II, Danish king (1513–23), b.1481, died in prison 1559.
Christian III, Danish king (1535–59), b.1503, d.1559.
Christian IV, Danish king (1588–1648), b.1577, d.1648.
Christian V, Danish king (1670–99), b.1646, d.1699.
Christian VI, Danish king (1730–46), d.1746.
Christian VII, Danish king (1766–1808), b.1749, d.1808.
Christian VIII, Danish king (1839–48), b.1786, d.1848.
Christian IX, Danish king (1863–1906), b.1818, d.1906.
Christian X, Danish king (1912–47), b.1870, d.1947.

Christian Era, calculated from ostensible date of Incarnation, adopted in Italy in 6th century.

Christian Science, religious movement, founded 1879 by the American Mrs Mary Baker Eddy, b.1821, d.1910.

Christian Socialism, founded 1850 by John Ludlau, b.1821, d.1911.

Christian Tract Society, London, founded 1809 by the Unitarian minister Robert Aspland, b.1782, d.1845.

Christianity, religious movement founded by Jesus of Nazareth in 1st century.

Christie, Dame Agatha, English detective-story writer and playwright, b.1891, d.1976.

Christie, John Reginald Halliday, English murderer, b.1898, hanged 1953.

Christie's, London auctioneers, founded 1766 by James Christie, b.1730, d.1803.

Christina, Swedish queen (1632–54), b.1626, d.1689.

Christmas cards, first examples designed in Britain 1843.

Christmas Day, 25 Dec. (Spain: 6 Jan.; Russia and Greece: 7 Jan.).

Christmas Island, Western Pacific, discovered 1777 by Captain James Cook; annexed 1888 by Britain; administered by Singapore 1900–58, and now by Australia; called Kiritimati from 1981.

Christophe, Henry, king of Haiti, b.1767, committed suicide 1820.

Christ's College, Cambridge University, founded as God's-House 1448 by King Henry VI; refounded and enlarged by the Lady Margaret Beaufort, Countess of Richmond and Derby, 1505.

Chromium, first isolated 1797 by the French chemist Louis Nicolas Vauquelin, b.1763, d.1829.

Chromosphere, layer of the Sun's atmosphere, so named by the English astronomer Sir Joseph Norman Lockyer, b.1836, d.1920.

Chronometers, invented 1726 by the English inventor John Harrison, b.1693, d.1776.

Church Army, founded in London 1882 by the English Rev. Wilson Carlile, b.1847, d.1942.

Churchill, Charles, English satirical writer (*The Rosciad*, 1761), b.1731, d.1764.

Churchill, Lord Randolph, British statesman, b.1849, d.1894.

Churchill, Sarah, Duchess of Marlborough, b.1660, d.1744.

Churchill, Sir Winston, British statesman (prime minister 1940–45, 1951–55), b.1874, d.1965.
Churchill College, Cambridge University, opened 1960.
Church of England, established by St Augustine 597, separated from the Catholic Church by the Act of Supremacy 1534.
Church of Ireland (Anglican), disestablished 1869.
Church of Scotland, The Reformed, established 1560.
Church of Wales (Anglican), disestablished 1919.
Churriguera, José de, Spanish architect, b.*c*.1650, d.1725.
CIA, *see* **Central Intelligence Agency.**
Ciano, Galeazzo, Italian politician, b.1903, shot 1944.
Cibber, Colley, English poet laureate (appointed 1730), b.1671, d.1757.
Cicero, Marcus Tullius, Roman statesman and writer, b.106, d.43 BC.
Cid, El (Rodrigo Diaz), Spanish hero, b.*c*.1026, d.1099.
Cigarettes, introduced into Britain 1854; link with lung cancer established 1950.
Cigars, introduced into Britain from Cuba 1762.
Cimabué, Giovanni (Cenni di Pepi), Italian painter (*St Francis*), b.*c*.1240, d.1302.
Cimarosa, Domenico, Italian composer (*Il Matrimonio Segreto*, 1792), b.1749, d.1801.
Cinchona, introduced 1860 to India from South America by the explorer Sir Clements Robert Markham, b.1830, d.1916.
Cinchonine, an alkaloid, discovered by the French scientist Pierre Joseph Pelletier, b.1788, d.1842.
Cincinnatus, Lucius Quinctius, Roman patriot, b.519, d.438 BC.
Cinema projector, first model constructed by the French inventor Etienne J. Marey 1893.
Cinematograph, first model constructed by the French brothers Auguste and Louis Lumière 1895.
Cinna, Roman consul, murdered 84 BC.
Cintra, Treaty of, concerning the French evacuation of Portugal, signed Aug. 1808.
Circumcision, Christian Feast of the, celebrated 1 Jan.
Circulation of the blood, discovered 1615 by the English physician William Harvey, b.1578, d.1657.
Cisalpine Republic, existed in N. Italy 1797–1802.
Cistercian Order, founded 1098 by St Stephen Harding, d.1134.
Cîteaux, French monastery, founded by St Robert of Molesme 1098.

City and South London Railway, first electric underground line, opened 18 Dec. 1890 between King William St. and Stockwell.
Civil Engineers, Institution of, London, founded 1818; granted Royal Charter 1828.
Civil War, American, 1861–65.
Civil War, English; first, 1642–46; second, 1648.
Civil War, Spanish, 1936–39.
Clair, René, French film producer, b.1898, d.1981.
Clairvaux, French abbey, founded 1115 by St Bernard, b.1091, d.1153.
Clapton, Eric, English rock guitarist and vocalist, b.1945.
Claque, existed in the Théâtre Français until 1878.
Clare, John, English poet (*Shepherd 's Calendar*, 1827), b.1793, d.1864.
Clare College, Cambridge University, founded 1326 as Union Hall by Richard Badew, Chancellor of Cambridge; refounded 1336 by Lady Elizabeth de Clare, b.*c.*1291, d.1360.
Clarendon, Edward Hyde, Earl of, British statesman (chief minister 1660–67), b.1608, d.1674.
Clarendon, Constitutions of, royal proclamation, issued 1164.
Clark, William George, Shakespearean editor, b.1821, d.1878.
Clarke, Arthur C(harles), British sci-fi author (*2001, A Space Odyssey,* 1968), b.1917, d.
Clarke, John, pioneer settler 1638 in Rhode Island, b.1609, d.1676.
Clarkson, Thomas, English opponent of slavery, b.1760, d.1846.
Claudel, Paul, French writer and diplomat, b.1868, d.1955.
Claudius I, Roman emperor (41–54), b.10 BC, poisoned AD 54.
Claudius II, Roman emperor (268–270), d.270.
Clausewitz, Karl von, Prussian strategist (*On War*), b.1780, d.1831.
Claverhouse, John Graham of, Scottish soldier, b.*c.*1649, died in battle 1689.
Clay, Henry, American statesman, b.1777, d.1852.
Clemenceau, Georges, French statesman (premier 1906–09, 1917–20), b.1841, d.1929.
Clement I, St, pope 88–97.
Clement II (Suidger), pope 1046–47.
Clement III (Paolo Scolari), pope 1187–91.
Clement IV (Gui Foulques), pope 1268–71.
Clement V (Bertrand de Gouth), pope 1305–14, b.*c.*1264, d.1314.

Clement VI (Pierre Roger), pope 1342–52, b.1291, d.1352.
Clement VII (Robert of Geneva), anti-pope 1378–94, d.1394.
Clement VII (Giulio dei Medici), pope 1523–34, d.1534.
Clement VIII (Aegidius Muñoz), anti-pope 1425–29, d.1446.
Clement VIII (Ippolito Aldobrandini), pope 1592–1605, b.1535, d.1605.
Clement IX (Giulio Respigliosi), pope 1667–69, b.1600, d.1669.
Clement X (Emilio Altieri), pope 1670–76, b.1590, d.1676.
Clement XI (Gian Francesco Albani), pope 1700–21, b.1649, d.1721.
Clement XII (Lorenzo Corsini), pope 1730–40, b.*c.*1652, d.1740
Clement XIII (Carlo della Torre Rezzonico), pope 1758–69, b.1693 d.1769.
Clement XIV (Lorenzo Ganganelli), pope 1769–74, b.1705, d.1774.
Clementi, Muzio, Italian composer (*Gradus ad Parnassum*, 1817), b.1752, d.1832.
Clement of Alexandria, Greek theologian in 2nd century.
Cleopatra, Egyptian queen, b.69, committed suicide 30 BC.
Cleopatra's Needle, transferred from Egypt to London 1877 by the English surgeon Sir Erasmus Wilson, b.1809, d.1884.
Clerk-Maxwell, James, Scottish physicist, b.1831, d.1879.
Clermont, the first steamship, built 1807 by the American engineer Robert Fulton, b.1765, d.1815.
Cleve, Joos van, Flemish artist, b.*c.*1518, d.1556.
Cleveland, Stephen Grover, 22nd and 24th US president (1885–89, 1893–97), b.1837, d.1908.
Clift, Montgomery, American screen and stage star (*From Here to Eternity*, 1953), b.1920, d.1966.
Clifton Suspension Bridge, opened 1864.
Clinton, William Jefferson Davis, 42nd US president (since 1993), b.1946.
Clive, Robert, Baron Clive, Indian Empire pioneer, b.1725, committed suicide 1774.
Clontarf, Battle of, between the Irish and the Danes 1014.
Clotaire I, king of the Franks 558–561.
Clotaire II, king of the Franks 584–628.
Cloth of Gold, Field of the, near Calais, conference between Henry VIII and Francis I, 6 June 1520.
Clothworkers, Livery Company, London, founded before 1480; incorporated 1523.
Cloud, St, b.*c.*520, d.560.

Cloud chamber, expansion chamber, invented by the Scottish scientist Charles Thomson Rees Wilson, b.1869, d.1959.

Clouet, Jean, French miniaturist, b.c.1485, d.c.1541.

Clovis, first Merovingian king of the Franks, b.465, d.511.

Cluny Abbey, founded 910.

Clynes, Joseph Robert, British politician, b.1869, d.1949.

Coal gas, invented 1792–96 by the Scottish engineer William Murdock, b.1754, d.1839. First used for lighting in Soho 1803.

Coal industry, in Britain, taken over by State 1938, nationalized 1947.

Coalitions, in Britain, 1757, 1782, 1852, 1915, 1931, 1940.

Coalport porcelain, manufactured from 1790.

Cobalt, first isolated by the German scientist Georg Brandt 1735.

Cobbett, William, English politician, writer (*Rural Rides*, 1830), b.1763, d.1935.

Cobden, Richard, English political reformer, b.1804, d.1865.

Cockfighting, made illegal in England 1849.

Coco-Cola®, American soft drink, the most widely consumed beverage in the world, invented 1866.

Cocos Islands, Indian Ocean, discovered by Captain William Keeling of the East India Company 1609; settled 1826; annexed by Britain 1857; a Territory of Australia since 1955.

Cocteau, Jean, French writer, b.1889, d.1963.

Code Napoléon, promulgated as the French civil law code 1804; assumed its present name 1807.

Codex Sinaiticus, purchased from the Soviet Government by Britain 1933.

Cody, Colonel Samuel Franklin, American aviation pioneer, b.1862, killed in flying accident 1913.

Cody, William Frederick ('Buffalo Bill'), American frontiersman and showman, b.1846, d.1917.

Coello, Alonzo Sánchez, Spanish painter, b.1515, d.1590.

Coello, Claudio, Spanish painter, b.c.1621, d.1693.

Coffee, brought to England *c.*1650.

Coimbra, University of, founded 1288 in Lisbon and transferred to Coimbra 1537.

Coke, Sir Edward, English statesman and jurist, b.1552, d.1634.

Coke, manufacture of, patented 1621 by Dud Dudley, the ironmaster, b.1599, d.1684.

Coke Ovens, invented by Friedrich Hoffmann 1893.

Colbert, Jean Baptiste, French statesman, b.1619, d.1683.

Colburn, Zerah, American calculating prodigy, b.1804, d.1840.

Coldstream Guards, raised 1659.

Cole, Douglas, English political writer, b.1889, d.1959.

Cole, Nat 'King' (Nathaniel Adams Coles), American jazz and popular music vocalist and pianist, b.1919, d.1965.

Colenso, William, English missionary and explorer in New Zealand, b.1811, d.1899.

Coleridge, Samuel Taylor, English poet (*The Ancient Mariner*, 1798), b.1772, d.1834.

Coleridge-Taylor, Samuel, English composer (*The Song of Hiawatha*, 1898–1900), b.1875, d.1912.

Colet, John, English divine and scholar, b.*c*.1467, d.1519.

'Colette' (Sidonie Gabrielle Colette), French novelist, b.1873, d.1954.

Coligny, Gaspard de, French statesman, b.1519, murdered 1572.

College postal stamps, first used by Keble College, Oxford University, 1871; suppressed by the Postmaster-General Dec. 1885.

Collingwood, Cuthbert Lord, English admiral, b.1750, d.1810.

Collingwood, Robin George, English historian and philosopher, b.1889, d.1943.

Collins, Michael, Irish leader, b.1890, killed 1922.

Collins, Wilkie, English novelist (*The Moonstone*, 1868), b.1824, d.1889.

Collins, William, English poet (*How Sleep the Brave*, 1746), b.1721, d.1759.

Collodion process; invented 1850 by the English photographer Frederick Scott Archer, b.1813, d.1857.

Colloidal chemistry, study initiated 1861 by the Scottish chemist Thomas Graham, b.1805, d.1869.

Collotype, illustrations printing process, invented by the French inventors Tessie du Motay and C. R. Maréchal 1865.

Colman, George, the elder, English dramatist (*The Jealous Wife*, 1761), b.1732, d.1794.

Colman, George, the younger, English dramatist (*The Heir at Law*, 1797), b.1762, d.1836.

Cologne University, founded 1388.

Colombia, achieved freedom from Spanish rule 1819; formed part of the State of Greater Colombia 1819–30; became the Republic of New Granada 1830; transformed into the Confederación Granadina 1858; adopted the name of the United States of Colombia 1863; became the Republic of Colombia 1886.

Colon, Cristobal, *see* **Columbus, Christopher**

Colorado, USA, first settled 1858; made a Territory 1861; admitted to the Union 1876.

Colorado beetle, reached Europe 1922.

Colosseum, Roman amphitheatre, built 75–80.

Colossus of Rhodes, statue built *c.*285 BC; destroyed by an earthquake 224 BC.

Colour photography, invented 1907 by the French pioneer in cinematography Auguste Lumière, b.1862, d.1954.

Colour television, first experimental transmission to include 'live' pictures made from Alexandra Palace, London, 1956.

Colt revolver, invented 1835 by the American manufacturer Samuel Colt, b.1814, d.1862.

Colum, Pádraic, Irish poet, b.1881, d.1972.

Columba, St, b.521, d.597.

Columban, St, b.*c.*540, d.615.

Columbia Broadcasting System, *see* **CBS.**

Columbia River, discovered 1792 by the American explorer Robert Gray, b.1755, d.1806.

Columbia University, New York, founded 1754 as King's College; reopened with present name 1784.

Columbium (niobium), isolated 1801 by the English chemist Charles Hatchett, b.*c.*1765, d.1847.

Columbus, Christopher, Italian-born explorer, b.1451, d.1506.

Columbus Day, commemorating the discovery of America: 12 Oct.

Combe, William, English writer (*Dr Syntax*, 1812–21), b.1741, d.1823.

Combine harvester-thresher, invented in California 1875.

Comédie-Française, Paris, instituted 1658; assumed present name 1680.

Comenius (John Amos Komensky), Moravian scholar, b.1592, d.1671.

Comets, studied 1698–1705 by Edmund Halley, b.1656, d.1742.

Comic strips, originated by the German artist Wilhelm Busch, b.1832, d.1908.

Cominform, international Communist body, founded 1947, abolished 1956.

Comintern, international Communist body, founded 1919, dissolved 1943.

Commedia dell'Arte, came into being in Italy 1567.

Commodus, Roman emperor (180–192), b.161, murdered 192.

Commonwealth, republican regime in England, 1649–53.

Commonwealth Day, British, founded as Empire Day, 24 May 1902.

Commonwealth of Nations, British, title first used during First World War 1914–18.

Commonwealth Relations Office, founded 1925 as the Dominions Office; assumed present name 1947.

Commune of Paris, revolutionary regime March–May 1871.

Communism, origins in the Parisian secret societies of the 1830s. Karl Marx's *Communist Manifesto* issued by Communist League 1848.

Commynes, Philippe de, French historian, b.1445, d.1509.

Comoro, a Protectorate of France until 1912; proclaimed a French colony 1912; attached to the Government-General of Madagascar 1914; a French Territory from 1947; became independent (except Mayotte) 1976.

Compass, magnetic, described 1269 by Peter Peregrinus of Picardy.

Compensated pendulum, invented 1722 by the English mechanician George Graham, b.1675, d.1751.

Complutensian Bible, first polyglot Bible, prepared 1514–22.

Compressibility of water, first demonstrated 1762 by the English scientist John Canton, b.1718, d.1772.

Comptometer, invented 1884 by the American inventor Dorr Eugene Felt, b.1862, d.1930.

Computer, first mechanical model discussed in Italy 1840–41 by the British mathematician Dr Charles Babbage, b.1792, d.1871; first complete (the Harvard Mark I), built by the American Howard Aiken and IBM 1939–44; first digital (ENIAC) developed 1946; first transisterized developed by IBM 1959; first personal computer Apple II, 1977.

Comstock, Anthony, American pioneer in censorship, b.1844, d.1915.

Comstock silver lode, Nevada, discovered *c.*1856 by the American trapper Henry Tompkins Paige Comstock, b.1820, d.1870.

Comte, Auguste (Isidore Xavier), French positivist philosopher, b.1798, d.1857.

Concentration camps, first used as prison camps for Afrikaner women and children by the British during the Boer War 1899–1901; used in Nazi Germany (1933–45) as part of the 'Final Solution' to exterminate Jews, Gypsies, homosexuals and other political opponents. First: Dachau 1933; most notorious:

Auschwitz, opened 1941; first to be liberated (by Red Army): Maidenek July 1944.

Concepción, Chilean city, founded 1541 by the Spanish conquistador Pedro de Valdivia, b.*c.*1510, d.1554.

Concert hall, London's first public, Hickford's Room, The Haymarket, opened 1697.

Concertina, invented 1829 by Charles Wheatstone.

Conclave of cardinals, to elect a pope (Gregory X), first held at Viterbo 1268–71.

Condé, Louis II de Bourbon, Prince de, French general, b.1621, d.1686.

Condell, Henry, first Shakespearean editor, d.1627.

Condensed milk, process invented 18S6 by the American inventor Gail Borden, b.1801, d.1874.

Conder, Charles, English painter, b.1868, d.1909.

Condillac, Etienne Bonnot de, French philosopher, b.1715, d.1780.

Condorcet, Marie Jean Antoine Nicolas Caritat, Marquis de, French philosopher, b.1743, committed suicide 1794.

Confederate States of America, formed 4 Feb. 1861; defeated by Union 1865.

Confederation of British Industries, founded 1965.

Confederation of the Rhine, Napoleonic organization of German states, formed 1806; ended 1813.

Confession of Augsburg, Lutheran creed, prepared 1530.

Confucianism, religious movement, founded *c.*531 BC by the Chinese sage Confucius, b.551, d.478 BC.

Congo River, discovered by the Portuguese navigator Diogo Cão 1482.

Congregational Movement, founded *c.*1580 by the English leader Robert Browne, b.*c.*1550, d.*c.*1633.

Congress of Industrial Organizations, USA, founded 1936.

Congress of the United States of America, instituted 1787.

Congreve, William, English playwright (*The Way of the World*, 1700), b.1670, d.1729.

Connecticut, USA, first settled 1635; organized commonwealth since 1637; one of the original states of the Union.

Connelly, Marc, American playwright (*Green Pastures*, 1930), b.1890, d.1980.

Conrad, Joseph (Teodor Josef Konrad Korzeniowski), Polish-born writer (*Lord Jim*, 1900), b.1857, d.1924.

Conrad I, German king (911–918), d.918.

Conrad II, German king (1024–39), b.*c.*990, d.1039.
Conrad III, German king (1138–52), b.*c.*1093, d.1152.
Conrad IV, German king (1250–54), b.1228, d.1254.
Conscription, in England 1916–18, 1939–60; (women) 1941–47.
Conservation of energy, principles defined 1847 by the German physicist Hermann von Helmholtz, b.1821, d.1894.
Conservation of matter, principle defined 1789 by Lavoisier.
Conservative Party, British, origins *c.*1680 in the Tories; present name began to be adopted 1824–32.
Consols, British consolidated annuitites, first consolidated between 1750 and 1757.
Constable, John, English painter (*The Hay Wain*), b.1776, d.1837.
Constans I, Roman emperor (337–350), b.*c.*320, assassinated 350
Constans II, Byzantine emperor (641–668), b.630, murdered 668.
Constant, Benjamin, French painter (*Samson et Dalilah*), b.1845, d.1902.
Constantine, pope 708–715.
Constantine, anti-pope 767.
Constantine I, Byzantine emperor (309–337), b.*c.*288, d.337.
Constantine II, Byzantine emperor (337–340), b.316, killed in battle 340.
Constantine III, Byzantine emperor (641), d.641.
Constantine IV, Byzantine emperor (668–685), d.685.
Constantine V, Byzantine emperor (740–775), b.718, d.775.
Constantine VI, Byzantine emperor (780–797), b.*c.*770.
Constantine VII, Byzantine emperor (913–919, 944–959), b.905, d.959.
Constantine VIII, Byzantine emperor (1025–28).
Constantine IX, Byzantine emperor (1042–55).
Constantine X, Byzantine emperor (1059–67), d.1067.
Constantine XI, last Byzantine emperor (1448–53), killed 1453.
Constantine I, king of the Hellenes (1913–17, 1920–22), b.1868, d.1923.
Constantinople, founded as Byzantium 658 BC; rebuilt as Constantinople AD 330; captured by the Turks 1453 and renamed Istanbul.
Constantius I, Roman emperor (305–306), b.*c.*250, d.306.
Constantius II, Roman emperor (337–361), b.317, d.361.
Constantius III, Roman emperor (421), d.421.
Consulate, The, French Napoleonic government, established 1799, abolished 1804.

Contact lenses, first suggested 1827 by the English astronomer Sir John Herschel, b.1792, d.1871; first made by the German lens maker F. E. Müller 1887.

Continental Congress, American Federal legislative body, established 1774, ended 1789.

Continental Drift, theory developed 1910 by the German geologist Alfred Wegener, b.1880, d.1930.

Continental System, blockade carried out by Napoleon 1804–12.

Conventicle Acts to suppress nonconformist worship in Britain, enacted 1593 and 1664; repealed 1689.

Convulsionaries, Jansenist group in Paris who venerated François de Paris, d.1727.

Cook, James, English explorer and mariner, b.1728, murdered 1779. First voyage 1768–71; second 1772–75; third 1776–79.

Cook, Thomas, English pioneer travel agent, b.1808, d.1892.

Cook Strait, New Zealand, discovered by Captain James Cook 1770.

Cooke, Alistair, Anglo-American journalist, author and broadcaster ('Letters from America'), b.1908.

Cooke, Jay, American financier, b.1821, d.1905.

Coolidge, Susan, American writer (*What Katy Did*), b.1845, d.1905.

Coolidge, Calvin, 30th US president (1923–29), b.1872, d.1933.

Cooper, Gary (Frank J.), American film star (*High Noon*, 1952), b.1901, d.1961.

Cooper, James Fenimore, American writer (*The Last of the Mohicans*, 1826), b.1789, d.1851.

Cooper, Samuel, English miniaturist, b.1609, d.1672.

Co-operative Congress, first, held London 1869.

Co-operative Party, Great Britain, formed 1917; first MP elected 1919.

Co-operative Societies, origins in England in the Rochdale Society, founded 1844.

Copeland, William Taylor, English potter, b.1797, d.1868.

Copenhagen, Battle of, between the British and Danish fleets, 2 April 1801.

Copenhagen University, founded 1479.

Copernicus, Nicolas (Mikdaj Kopernik), Polish astronomer, b.1473, d.1543.

Copland, Aaron, American composer (*Billy the Kid*, 1938), b.1900, d.1990.

Copley, John Singleton, American painter (*The Death of Chatham*), b.1737, d.1815.

Coppard, Alfred Edgar, English writer (*Adam and Eve and Pinch Me*, 1921), b.1878, d.1957.

Coppée, François, French writer (*Le Réliquaire*, 1866), b.1842, d.1908.

Coppola, Francis Ford, American film director (*Apocalypse Now*, 1979), b.1939.

Coptic Church, separated from Orthodox Church 451.

Coptic Era, began 29 Aug. 284.

Copyright, first Act passed in England 1709; law consolidated by Act of 1911.

Coquelin, Benoît Constant, French actor, b.1841, d.1909.

Coral Sea, Battle of the, World War II, 7–9 May 1942.

Coram, Thomas, English philanthropist, b.1668, d.1751.

Corday, Charlotte, French murderer of Marat, b.1768, guillotined 1793.

Cordite, invented by Sir Frank Augustus Abel, b.1827, d.1902, and Sir James Dewar, b.1842, d.1923, and adopted by the British Government 1891.

Corelli, Arcangelo, Italian composer (*La Follia*), b.1653, d.1713.

Corelli, Marie, English popular novelist (*Sorrows of Satan*, 1895), b.1854, d.1924.

Corinth, Lovis, German painter, b.1858, d.1925.

Corman, Roger, 'B' movie producer and director (*Little Shop of Horrors*, 1960), b.1926.

'Corn Law Rhymer, The' (Ebenezer Elliott), English poet (*Battle Song*), b.1781, d.1849.

Corn Laws, enacted in Britain 1815, 1828, 1842; repealed 1844, 1869.

Corneille, Pierre, French playwright (*Le Cid*, 1636), b.1606, d.1684.

Cornelius, St, pope 251–253.

Cornell University, Ithaca, N.Y., founded 1865 by the American financier Ezra Cornell, b.1807, d.1874.

Cornet, cavalry rank, abolished 1871.

Cornish languages, spoken until 18th century.

Cornwallis, Charles, Marquis, governor-general of India, b.1738, d.1805.

Coronado, Francisco Vásquez de, Spanish explorer of S.W. USA, b.c.1510, d.1554.

Coronation Cup, Epsom, first run 1902.

Coronation Stone (Stone of Scone), placed in Westminster Abbey 1296 by King Edward I. Stolen by the Scottish Nationalists 1950; returned to Westminster 1952.

Corot, Jean Baptiste Camille, French painter, b.1796, d.1875.

Corps of Commissionaires, founded 1859 by the English soldier Sir Edward Walter, b.1823, d.1904.

Corpus Christi, feast day, founded 1264 by Pope Urban IV, celebrated on the Thursday after Trinity Sunday.

Corpus Christi College, Cambridge University, founded by the united Guilds of Corpus Christi and of the Blessed Virgin Mary 1352.

Corpus Christi College, Oxford University, founded 1516 by the statesman Richard Foxe, b.1448, d.1528.

Corpus Juris Civilis, Roman legal code, compiled at the Emperor Justinian I's orders 528–533.

Corpuscles, Red, first discovered by the Dutch naturalist Jan Swammerdam, b.1637, d.1680.

Correggio, Antonio Allegri da, Italian painter (*The Assumption of the Virgin*), b.1494, d.1534.

Corsica, settled by the Greeks *c.* 560 BC; sold by Genoa to France 1768.

Cortés, Hernando, Spanish *conquistador* of Mexico (1519–21), b.1485, d.1547.

Cortisone, discovered 1936 by the American biochemist Edward Calvin Kendall, b.1886, d.1972.

Cortona, Pietro da, Italian artist, b.1596, d.1669.

Cortot, Alfred, Swiss pianist, b.1877, d.1962.

'Corvo, Baron' (Frederick Rolfe), English novelist (*Hadrian the Seventh*, 1904), b.1860, d.1913.

Coryate, Thomas, English traveller and writer (*Crudities*, 1611), b.*c.*1577, d.1617.

Cosgrave, Liam, Irish politician (prime minister 1973–77), b.1920.

Cosgrave, William Thomas, Irish politician (president 1922–32), b.1880, d.1965.

Cosmic rays, discovered 1925 by the American scientist Robert Andrews Millikan, b.1868, d.1953.

Costa, Lorenzo, Italian painter (*Madonna and Child Enthroned*), b.1460, d.1535.

Costa Rica, Central America, discovered 1502 by Christopher Columbus; achieved independence from Spanish rule 1821.

Costello, Lou (Louis Cristillo), American comedian, partner of Bud Abbot, b.1906, d.1959.

Cosway, Richard, English miniaturist, b.*c.*1742, d.1821.

Côte d'Ivoire, West Africa, autonomous republic within the French Community since 1960.

Cotman, John Sell, English painter, b.1782, d.1842.

Cotton, Charles, English poet (*New Year Poem*), b.1630, d.1687.

Cotton, Sir Robert Bruce, English collector of the Cottonian Collection (now in the British Museum), b.1571, d.1631.

Coué, Emile, French founder of auto-suggestion, b.1857, d.1926.

Coulomb, Charles Augustin de, French physicist, b.1736, d.1806.

Council of Chalcedon, 4th Ecumenical Council, 451.

Council of Constance, Catholic general council, 1414–18.

Councils of Constantinople, 2nd Ecumenical Council, 381; 5th Ecumenical Council, 553, 6th Ecumenical Council, 680.

Council of Elders, French revolutionary government, 1795–99.

Council of Ephesus, 3rd Ecumenical Council, convened 431.

Council of Europe, statute signed at 10-power London conference, came into effect 1949.

Council of Five Hundred, French Revolutionary government, 1795–99.

Council of Nicaea, 1st Ecumenical Council, 325; 7th Ecumenical Council, 787.

Council of Ten, Venetian cabal, set up 1310; abolished *c.*1797.

Council of Trent, Catholic General Council, began 1545; ended 1563.

Council, Vatican, Catholic General Council 1869–70.

Counter-Reformation, within the Catholic Church, began 1513; completed 1563.

Countess of Huntingdon's Connection, Calvinist Methodist sect, founded in the 1740s.

Couperin, François, French composer (*Les Nations*, 1726), b.1668, d.1733.

Couperus, Louis, Dutch writer, b.1863, d.1923.

Coupon election, held 1918.

Courbet, Gustave, French painter, b.1819, d.1877.

Courtauld, Samuel, British silk manufacturer, b.1793, d.1881.

Courtauld Institute of Art, London, established 1930, relocated to Somerset House 1990.

Courtrai, Battle of (The Battle of the Golden Spurs), between the Flemish and the French, 1302.

Cousin, Jean, French painter (*The Last Judgment*), b.*c.*1500, d.*c.*1590.

Cousins, Samuel, English engraver, b.1801, d.1887.

Cousteau, Jacques Yves, French oceanographer and underwater filmmaker, b.1910, d.

Coutts & Co., British bankers, founded by the Scottish banker Thomas Coutts, b.1735, d.1822.

Covent Garden Theatre, London, opera house built 1858.

Coventry Cathedral, built in the 15th century; destroyed in World War II 1940; rebuilt 1954–62.

Coverdale's Bible, translated into English by the English divine Miles Coverdale (1488–1568); published 1535.

Coward, Sir Noël (Pierce), English playwright (*Bitter Sweet*, 1929), b.1899, d.1973.

Cowley, Abraham, English writer (*The Mistress*, 1647), b.1618, d.1667.

Cowper, William, English poet (*The Task*, 1785), b.1731, d.1800.

Cox, David, English painter, b.1783 d.1859.

Coxwell, Henry Tracey, English balloonist, b.1819, d.1900.

Cozens, John Robert, English watercolour artist, b.1752, d.1799.

Crabbe, George, English poet (*The Borough*, 1810), b.1754, d.1832.

Craig, Edward Gordon, English theatre director and designer, b.1872, d.1966.

Craigavon, James Craig, Viscount, first prime minister of Northern Ireland, b.1871, d.1940.

Craik, Mrs (Dinah Maria Mulock), English writer (*John Halifax, Gentleman*, 1857) b.1826, d.1887.

Cramer, Johann Baptist, German-born pianist and music teacher, b.1771, d.1858.

Cranach, Lucas, German painter (*The Judgment of Paris*), b.1472, d.1553.

Crane, hydraulic, invented *c.*1845 by William George Armstrong (later Baron Armstrong), b.1810, d.1900.

Crane, Hart, American poet, b.1899, d.1932.

Crane, Stephen, American writer (*The Red Badge of Courage*, 1896), b.1871, d.1900.

Crane, Walter, English artist, b.1845, d.1915.

Cranmer, **Thomas**, archbishop of Canterbury, b.1489, burnt at the stake 1556.

Crashaw, **Richard**, English poet (*Steps to the Temple*, 1646), b.*c.*1613, d.1649.

Crassus, Marcus Licinius, Roman triumvir, b.*c.*114, murdered 53 BC.

Cream separator, first centrifugal model invented 1877 by the Swedish engineer Carl Gustaf de Laval, b.1845, d.1913.

Crébillon, Claude Prosper Jolyot de, French writer (*Le Sofa*, 1742), b.1707, d.1777.

Crébillon, Prosper Jolyot de, French playwright (*Catilina*, 1748), b.1674, d.1762.

Crécy, Battle of, between the English and the French, 26 Aug. 1346.

Creevey, Thomas, English diarist, b.1768, d.1838.

Cremona Cathedral, Italy, built 1107–1606.

Creosote, discovered 1833 by the German manufacturer Baron von Reichenbach, b.1788, d.1869.

Crespi, Giuseppe Maria ('Lo Spagnuolo'), Italian painter, b.1665, d.1747.

Crete, ruled by Venetians 1204–1645, by Turks 1645–1898; part of Greece since 1913.

Crewe, Robert Offley Ashburton Crewe Milnes, Marquess of, British statesman, b.1858, d.1945.

'Crichton, The Admirable' (James Crichton), Scottish scholar, b.1560, killed 1582.

Crick, Francis Harry Compton, British molecular biologist, b.1916, developed the double helix model of the structure of DNA with James D. Watson, b.1928; both received the Nobel prize for medicine and physiology 1962.

Cricket, played in England since 13th century; M.C.C. founded 1787.

Crimean War, between the Allies (Britain, Turkey, France) and Russia, 1854–56.

Criminology, study founded by the Italian Cesare Lombroso, b.1836, d.1909.

Crippen, Dr Hawley Harvey, American murderer in England, b.1861, hanged 1910.

Cripps, Richard Stafford, British statesman, b.1889, d.1952.

Crivelli, Carlo, Italian painter, b.*c.*1434, d.1493.

Croatia, independent 925–1102; part of Hungary 1102–1918, of Yugoslavia 1918–91; became independent from the former Yugoslavia 1991.

Croce, Benedetto, Italian philosopher, b.1866, d.1952.

Crockett, David, American pioneer, b.1786, killed in battle 1836.

Crockett, Samuel Rutherford, Scottish novelist (*The Stickit Minister*, 1893), b.1860, d.1914.

Croesus, king of Lydia (560–546 BC).

Croker, John Wilson, Irish politician, b.1780, d.1857.

Crome, John, English painter, b.1768, d.1821.

Cromer, Evelyn Baring, Earl of, British agent and Consul-General in Egypt (1883–1907), b.1841, d.1917.

Crompton, Richmal (Richmal Crompton Lamburn), English writer (*Just William*, 1922), b.1890, d.1969.

Crompton's mule, spinning machine, invented 1779 by the English weaver Samuel Crompton, b.1753, d.1827.

Cromwell, Oliver, Puritan general, Lord Protector (1653–58), b.1599, d.1658.

Cromwell, Richard, Lord Protector (1658–59), b.1626, d.1712.

Cromwell, Thomas, Earl of Essex, English statesman (chief minister 1533–40), b.*c.*1485, beheaded 1540.

Cronin, Archibald Joseph, Scottish novelist (*Hatter's Castle*, 1931), b.1896, d.1981.

Cronkite, Walter, American radio and TV broadcaster, b.1916.

Crookes tube, high vacuum tube, invented by the English scientist Sir William Crookes, b.1832, d.1919.

Crossbow, first used in Europe *c.*1090.

Crossword puzzles, first introduced in England at the beginning of 19th century.

Cruden's Concordance, published 1737, compiled by Alexander Cruden, b.1701, d.1770.

Cruikshank, George, English artist, b.1792, d.1878.

Crusades, in Eastern Mediterranean, 1095–1291.

Crusoe, Robinson, story founded on the experiences of Scottish sailor Alexander Selkirk, b.1676, d.1721.

Crystal Palace, designed by Sir Joseph Paxton, b.1801, d.1865; erected in Hyde Park 1851, moved to Penge 1854, destroyed by fire 1936.

Cuba, discovered 1492 by Christopher Columbus; achieved independence from Spanish rule 1898; declared a People's Republic under Castro in 1960.

Cube sugar, manufacturing process invented by Sir Henry Tate, b.1819, d.1899.

Cubism, art movement, founded in France *c.*1909.

Cui, César, Russian-born composer (*The Saracen*, 1899), b.1835, d.1918.

Cullen, Countée, black American poet, b.1903, d.1946.

Cullinan diamond, found at Pretoria 1905, presented to Edward VII on behalf of the people of Transvaal 9 Nov. 1907.

Culloden, Battle of, fought between the Duke of Cumberland and the Young Pretender 16 April 1746 (last battle fought in Britain).

Culpeper's Herbal, published 1653, compiled by Nicholas Culpeper, b.1616, d.1654.

Cumberland, William Augustus, Duke of, British military commander, b.1721, d.1765.

Cumberland, Richard, bishop of Peterborough and philanthropist, b.1631, d.1718.

Cummings, E(dward) E(stlin), American writer (*The Enormous Room*, 1922), b.1894, d.1962.

Cunard, Sir Samuel, Nova Scotia manufacturer, founder of the first regular Atlantic steamship service, b.1787, d.1865.

Cunard Company, founded by Samuel Cunard, George Burns and David MacIver 4 May 1839; merger of Cunard and White Star Lines 1934.

Cuneiform, writing first deciphered 1835 by Sir Henry Rawlinson.

Cunninghame Graham, Robert Bontine, Scottish writer, b.1852, d.1936.

Curaçao, island in Netherlands Antilles, discovered, became Dutch colony 1634.

Curare, discovered c.1740 by the Frenchman Charles Marie de Lacondamine, b.1701, d.1774.

'Curé d'Ars', The (Jean-Marie Vianney), patron saint of parish priests, b.1787, d.1859.

Curfew, introduced at Oxford by King Alfred to reduce fire risks 872.

Curie, Professor Frédéric Joliot-, French physicist, b.1900, d.1958.

Curie, Marie (Marie Sklodowska), wife of Pierre Curie, Polish scientist and discoverer of radium, b.1867, d.1934.

Curie, Pierre, French scientist and discoverer of radium, b.1859, d.1906.

Curll, Edmund, English bookseller, b.1675, d.1747.

Curragh, Meeting of the, Ireland, March 1914.

Curran, John Philpot, Irish judge and patriot, b.1750, d.1817.

Curtiss, Glenn Hammond, American aviation pioneer, b.1878, d.1930.

Curzon, George Nathaniel, Marquess, British statesman and Viceroy of India (1899–1905), b.1859, d.1925.
Curzon Line, dividing Poland on linguistic lines, 1919.
Cust, Sir Lionel Henry, English art historian and critic, b.1859, d.1929.
'Custer's Last Stand', made 25 June 1876 at Little Big Horn, Montana, by George Armstrong Custer, b.1839, d.1876.
Cuthbert, St, b.*c*.635, d.687.
Cuyp, Albert, Dutch painter (*Piper with Cows*), b.1620, d.1691.
Cyanide, invented 1905 by the German chemist Heinrich Caro, b.1834, d.1910.
Cyanogen, first isolated 1815 by the French scientist Joseph Louis Gay-Lussac, b.1778, d.1850.
Cyclotron, invented 1929 by the American physicist Ernest Lawrence, b.1901, d.1958.
Cymbeline (Cunobelinus), British king, d.*c*.43.
Cynewulf, Anglo-Saxon poet (*The Dream of the Cross*), lived in the 8th century
Cyprian, St, b.*c*.200, martyred 14 Sept. 258.
Cyprus, taken from the Venetians by the Turks 1571; ceded to Britain 1878; made British Crown Colony 1925; became republic 1960; partitioned in 1974 after Greek military coup and invasion by Turkey.
Cyrano de Bergerac, Savinien, French writer and duellist, b.1619, d.1655.
Cyril, St, of Alexandria, d.444.
Cyril, St, of Jerusalem, b.*c*.315, d.386.
Cyrillic alphabet, invention attributed to Saint Cyril, b.827, d.869.
Cyrus the Great, Persian emperor (563–529 BC), d.529 BC.
Cyrus the Younger, Persian satrap, b.424, killed in battle 401 BC.
Cyzicus, Naval Battle of, between Alcibiades and the Lacedaemonians 410 BC.
Czechoslovakia, Republic founded 28 Oct. 1918; annexed by Germany 1939; liberated 1944–45; Communist regime 1948–89; free elections held 1990; split into two separate states, Czech Republic and Slovak Republic 1994.
Czerny, Karl, Austrian pianist and composer (*Daily Studies*), b.1791, d.1857.

D

Dabrowski, Jan Henryk, Polish military leader and national hero, b.1755, d.1818.

Dadaism, art movement founded *c.*1915 in Zurich; ended *c.*1922.

Dagobert I, king of the Franks (629–639), d.639.

Daguerrotype process, invented between 1826 and 1839 by the French artist Louis Jacques Mandé Daguerre, b.1789, d.1851.

Dahl, Michael, Swedish painter (*Queen Christina*), b.1656, d.1743.

Dahlgren, John Adolf, American ordnance specialist and inventor, b.1809, d.1870.

Dahomey, *see* **Benin.**

Dail Eireann, Irish Free State Chamber of Deputies, formed in Dublin Jan. 1919.

Daily Courant, The, first English daily newspaper, founded 1702, ran until 1735.

Daily Express, The, British newspaper, founded 1900 by C. Arthur Pearson.

Daily Graphic, The, British newspaper, founded 1890 by W. L. Thomas; absorbed by *Daily Sketch* 1925.

Daily Herald, The, British newspaper, began publication 16 April 1912; placed under joint control of Odhams and the TUC in 1929.

Daily Mail, The, British newspaper, founded 1896 by Lord Northcliffe, b.1865, d.1922.

Daily Mirror, The, British newspaper, founded 1903 by Lord Northcliffe, b.1865, d.1922.

Daily News, The, British newspaper, founded 1846, merged in *News Chronicle* 1930.

Daily Sketch, The, British newspaper, founded 1909 by Edward Hulton.

Daily Telegraph, The, British newspaper, re-founded 1855 by Joseph Moses Levy, d.1888.

Daimler, Gottlieb, German automobile manufacturer, b.1834, d.1900.

Daladier, Edouard, French statesman (premier 1933, 1934, 1938–40), b.1884, d.1970.

Dalai Lama, highest ecclesiastical and secular official of Tibet since 15th century; present incumbent b.1935, installed 1940, assumed full power 1950, escaped to India 1959; Nobel peace prize 1989.

Dalcroze eurhythmics, music educational system, invented by the Swiss composer Emile Jaques-Dalcroze, b.1865, d.1950.

Dale, David, Scottish industrialist and philanthropist, b.1739, d.1806.

Dalhousie, James Andrew Brown Ramsay, Marquis of, governor-general of India (1848–56), b.1812, d.1860.

Dali, Salvador, Spanish-born Surrealist artist (*The Persistence of Memory,* 1931), b.1904, d.1989.

Dallas, Texas, first settled 1841, assumed present name 1845, in honour of the American statesman George Mifflin Dallas, b.1792, d.1864.

Dalmatia, ruled by Venice 1718–97, by Austria 1797–1918; part of Croatia in the former Yugoslavia 1918–91.

Dalton Plan, educational system, introduced at Dalton, Mass., by Helen Parkhurst *c.*1920.

Dalton's Law, defined 1803 by the English scientist John Dalton, b.1766, d.1844.

Daman and Diu, discovered by Vasco de Gama 1498; district of Portuguese India 1559–1961; part of Union Territory of Goa, Daman and Diu 1961–87.

Damasus I, St, pope 366–384.

Damasus II, pope July-Aug. 1048.

Damão, *see* **Daman and Diu.**

Damian, St, martyred 303.

Damiani, Pietro, Italian papal legate and reformer, b.*c.*1007, d.1072.

Damien, Father Joseph (Joseph de Veuster), French leper missionary in Hawaii, b.1840, d.1889.

Dampier, William, English navigator, b.1652, d.1715.

Damrosch, Leopold, German composer and conductor, b.1832, d.1885.

Dana, Charles Anderson, American writer and editor, b.1819, d.1897.

Dana, Richard Henry, American writer (*Two Years Before the Mast,* 1840), b.1815, d.1882.

Dance, George, English architect (Mansion House, London), b.1700, d.1768.

Dance, George, son of George Dance (*above*), English architect (College of Surgeons), b.1741, d.1825.

Danegeld, tax first levied in England 991; finally abolished 1163.

Danelaw, name applied in 11th century to area of eastern England settled by Danes in 9th and 10th centuries.

Daniel, Samuel, English writer *(Defence of Rhyme,* 1602), b.1562, d.1619.

Daniell cell, invented by the English scientist John Frederick Daniell, b.1790, d.1845.

Danish invasion of England, began *c.*835.

Dante Alighieri, Italian poet (*The Divine Comedy*), b.1265, d.1321.

Danton, Georges Jacques, French revolutionary leader, b.1759, guillotined 1794.

Danube Navigation, European Commission appointed under the Treaty of Paris 1856; Statute 2 Dec. 1861; International Commission appointed 1904.

Danzig (Gdansk), Poland, made capital of the Dukes of Pomerania 1230; Free City 1466–1793, 1807–14, 1919–39; annexed by Germany 1939; returned to Poland 1945.

Dardanelles Expedition, World War I, Feb.–March 1915.

Darien, Central America, discovered 1501 by the Spanish explorer Rodrigo de Bastidas.

Darien Scheme, Scottish overseas trading venture, conceived 1684 by the Scottish merchant William Paterson, b.1658, d.1719. Darien expedition set out for Panama 1698.

Darius I, Persian king (521–486 BC), b.548, d.486 BC.

Darius II, Persian king (423–404 BC), d.404 BC.

Darius III, Persian king (336–330 BC), assassinated 330 BC.

Darling, Grace, English heroine of the rescue of the *Forfarshire*'s survivors on 7 Sept. 1838, b.1815, d.1842.

Darling River, Australia, discovered 1828 by the English explorer Charles Sturt, b.1795, d.1869.

Darnley, Henry, husband of Mary Queen of Scots, b.1545, murdered 1567.

Dartmouth College, New Hampshire, founded 1769.

Dartmouth College (Britannia Royal Naval College), opened 1905.

Darwin, Charles, English biologist (*The Origin of Species*, 1859), b.1809, d.1882.

Darwin, Erasmus, English physician and writer (*The Botanic Garden*, 1789–92), b.1731, d.1802.

Dasent, Sir George Webbe, British Nordic scholar (*Burnt Njal*, 1861), b.1817, d.1896.

Daubigné, Théodore Agrippa, French historian, b.1552, d.1630.

Daudet, Alphonse, French writer (*Tartarin de Tarascon*, 1872), b.1840, d.1897.

Daughters of the American Revolution, Washington, DC, founded as a national society 1890.

Daumier, Honoré, French painter (*The Good Samaritan*), b.1808, d.1879.

D'Avenant, Sir William, English writer (*The Wits*, 1633), b.1606, d.1668.

Davenant porcelain, manufactured 1793–1882.

David, St (Dewi), lived in Wales in 6th century.

David, Gerhard, Flemish painter (*Pieta*), b.*c*.1450, d.1523.

David, Jacques Louis, French painter (*Madame Recamier*), b.1748, d.1825.

'David, Pierre' (David d'Angers), French sculptor (*Lafayette*), b.1789, d.1856.

David I, Scottish king (1124–53), b.*c*.1080, d.1153.

David II, Scottish king (1329–71), b.1324, d.1371.

Davidson, Randall, archbishop of Canterbury (1903–28), b.1848, d.1930.

Davies, Emily, English founder 1866–69 of Girton College, Cambridge, b.1830, d.1921.

Davies, Sir John, English poet (*Nosce teipsum,* 1599), b.1569, d.1626.

Davies, Sir Peter Maxwell, British composer and conductor, b.1934.

Davies, Sir Walford, English composer (*Everyman,* 1904), b.1869, d.1941.

Davies, William Henry, English poet (*The Autobiography of a Super Tramp,* 1906), b.1871, d.1940.

Davis, Bette (Ruth Elizabeth), American fim actress (*Dark Victory,* 1941), b.1908, d.1989.

Davis, Jefferson, president (1861–65) of the Southern Confederacy, b.1808, d.1889.

Davis, John, English explorer and discoverer (1587) of Davis Strait, b.*c*.1550, killed 1605.

Davis, Miles, American jazz trumpeter and composer, b.1926, d.1991.

Davis, Richard Harding, American writer (*Soldiers of Fortune,* 1897), b.1864, d.1916.

Davis, Sammy, Jnr, American singer, actor and dancer, b.1925, d.1990.

Davis Strait, Greenland, discovered 1587 by the English navigator John Davis.

Davitt, Michael, Irish patriot, b.1846, d.1906.

Davy, Sir Humphry, English chemist, b.1778, d.1829.

Dawes Plan, concerning reparations for World War I, devised by the American statesman Charles Gates Dawes, b.1865, d.1951.

Dawkins, Richard, British ethologist (*The Selfish Gene,* 1976), b.1941.

Dawson, Henry, English painter (*The Wooden Walls of Old England*), b.1811, d.1878.

Day, mean terrestrial, 23 hr, 56 min, 4.1 sec; mean solar, 24 hr, 3 min, 56.6 sec; mean sidereal, 23 hr, 56 min, 4.091 sec.

Day, John, English printer, b.1522, d.1584.

Day, Thomas, English writer (*Sandford and Merton,* 1783–89), b.1748, d.1789.

Daye, Stephen, English-born first New England printer, b.c.1600, d.1668.

Daylight saving, pioneered in Britain by William Willett, b.1856, d.1915. Officially adopted 1916.

Day of Atonement (*Yom Kippur*), Jewish holy day, falls during last fortnight of Sept. and first fortnight of Oct. (10th day of Tishri).

D-Day, World War II, Allies landed in Normandy, 6 June 1944.

DDT (dichloro-diphenyl-trichloroethane), insecticide, invented by the German scientist Zeidler 1874. First used as insecticide 1939.

'Deadwood Dick' (Richard W. Clarke), American pioneer, b.1845, d.1930.

Deaf and dumb school, first British, set up 1760 at Edinburgh by the Scottish teacher Thomas Braidwood, b.1715, d.1798.

Dean, James, American film actor (*Rebel Without a Cause,* 1955), b.1931, killed in a car crash 1955.

Death penalty, for murder, abolished 1965.

de Beauvoir, Simone French philosopher, novelist and essayist (*The Second Sex,* 1953), b.1908, d.1986.

Debrett's Peerage, first published 1802 by the English publisher John Debrett, d.1822.

Debs, Eugene, American socialist leader, b.1855, d.1926.

Debussy, Claude, French composer (*L'Après-midi d'un Faune*, 1892–94), b.1862, d.1918.

December Rising, Russian revolt concerning the succession of Tsar Nicolas I, 1825.

Decimal classification, for books, invented 1876 by the American Melvil Dewey, b.1851, d.1931.

Decimal curency, introduced in Britain 15 Feb. 1971.

Decimal numbers, first used extensively by Simon Stevin, b.1548, d.1620.

Decius, Roman emperor (249–251), b.201, killed in battle 251.

Decker, Sir Matthew, Dutch-born economist, b.1679, d.1749.

Declaration of Independence, American Revolution, adopted 4 July 1776.

Declaration of Right, England, Feb. 1689.

Decree of Union (Laetentur caeli), uniting the Latin and Greek Churches, issued 6 July 1439.

Dee, John, English alchemist, b.1527, d.1608.

Defender of the Faith, English royal title first bestowed by Pope Leo X on Henry VIII in 1521; continued by Parliament 1544.

Defoe, Daniel, English writer (*Robinson Crusoe,* 1719), b.c.1661, d.1731.

Degas, Edgar Hilaire Germain, French painter (*The Rehearsal*), b.1834, d.1917.

de Gaulle, Charles de, French general and statesman (president 1958–69), b.1890, d.1970.

De Grey, Walter, archbishop of York (1215–55) and chancellor of England (1205–14), d.1255.

Dehydration, of food, first extensively employed during the American Civil War, 1861–65.

Dekker, Thomas, English playwright (*The Shoemaker's Holiday,* 1599), b.*c.*1570, d.*c.*1640.

De Klerk, Frederick Willem, South African politician (president since 1989), b.1936.

de Kooning, Willem, Dutch-born American painter, b.1904, d.1988.

Delacroix, Eugène, French painter (*The Triumph of Apollo*), b.1798, d.1863.

De La Mare, Walter, English poet (*Peacock Pie,* 1913), b.1873, d.1958.

Delaroche, 'Paul' (Hippolyte Delaroche), French painter (*The Finding of Moses*), b.1797, d.1856.

De La Rue, Thomas, British printer and founder of the playing-card publishing firm, b.1793, d.1866.

Delaware, USA, first settled 1638; entered the Union 1787.

Deledda, Grazia, Italian novelist (*Cenere*), b.1875, d.1936.

Delibes, Léo, French composer (*Lakmé*, 1883), b.1836, d.1891.

Delius, Frederick, English composer (*Brigg Fair*, 1907), b.1862, d.1934.

Della Robbia, Luca, Italian sculptor, b.*c.*1400, d.1482.

Delorme, Philibert, French architect, b.*c.*1512, d.1570.

Delphin classics, published by the French printer François Ambroise Didot, b.1730, d.1804.

Demarcation, Bull of, of Pope Alexander VI, dividing discoveries in the known world between Spain and Portugal, issued 1493.

Demetrius I, king of Macedon, b.337, d.283 BC.

Demetrius II, king of Macedon, d.229 BC.

Demetrius I, Syrian king, b.*c.*187, d.150 BC.

Demetrius II, Syrian king, killed in battle 125 BC.

Demetrius III, Syrian king, d.88 BC.

De Mille, Cecil B., American film director and producer (*The Greatest Show on Earth*, 1952), b.1881, d.1959.

Democritus, Greek philosopher, d.370 BC.

De Morgan, Augustus, English logician (*Budget of Paradoxes*, 1872), b.1806, d.1871.

De Morgan, William Frend, English writer (*Joseph Vance*, 1906), b.1839, d.1917.

Demosthenes, Greek orator, b.*c.*384, committed suicide 322 BC.

Dempsey, Jack (William Harrison), American world heavyweight boxing champion 1919–26, b.1919, d.1984.

Deneuve, Catherine (Catherine Dorleac), French film actress (*Belle de Jour*, 1967), b.1943.

Dengue, disease first described 1780 by the American physician Benjamin Rush, b.1745, d.1813.

De Niro, Robert, American film and theatre actor (*Raging Bull*, 1979), b.1943.

Denmark, kingdom since the 10th century; new constitution granted 1953.

Dennis, John, English playwright (*Appius and Virginia*, 1709), b.1657, d.1734.

Denny, Sir Archibald, Scottish shipbuilder, b.1860, d.1936.

Dental forceps, invented by the English dental surgeon Sir John Tomes, b.1815, d.1895.

Depardieu, Gerard, French film actor (*Jean de Florette*, 1985), b.1948.

De Paul University, Chicago, founded 1898.

De Pauw University, Indiana, founded 1837 as the Indiana Asbury College; assumed present name 1884.

Deposition, Bull of, first issued by Pope Paul III excommunicating King Henry VIII, 1535; second issued by Pope Pius V excommunicating Queen Elizabeth I, 1570.

Depression, The, began in USA in Oct. 1929.

De Quincey, Thomas, English writer (*Confessions of an English Opium Eater*, 1821), b.1785, d.1859.

Derain, André, French painter, b.1880, d.1954.

'Derby, The', Epsom Downs, first run 4 May 1780.

Derby porcelain, manufactured 1750 to present day.

Derby-Chelsea Porcelain, manufactured 1770–84.

Derrida, Jacques, French deconstructionist literary critic and philosopher, b.1930.

Desai, Anita, Indian novelist (*Fire on the Mountain,* 1977), b.1937.

Descartes, René, French philosopher, b.1596, d.1650.

Desmoulins, Camille, French Revolutionary leader, b.1760, guillotined 1794.

De Soto, Hernando, Spanish explorer of North America, b.*c.*1498, d.1542.

Despard's Plot, against the British Government, devised by the English officer Edward Marcus Despard, b.1751, executed 1803.

Determinants, mathematical theory developed 1851 by the English scientist William Spottiswoode, b.1825, d.1883.

Detroit University, Michigan, founded 1877.

Deusdedit I, St, pope 615–619.

Deusdedit II, pope 672–676.

De Valera, Eamon, Irish statesman (prime minister 1927–48, 1951–54, 1957–59; president 1959–73), b.1882, d.1975.

De Vere, Aubrey, British poet, b.1814, d.1902.

Devil's Island (Cayenne), French Guiana, used as a penal settlement 1854–1938.

Devolution, War of, enforcing the Queen of France's claim to parts of the Spanish Netherlands, 1667–68.

Dew, nature discovered by the American-born physician William Charles Wells, b.1757, d.1817.

De Wet, Christian Rudolf, Boer patriot, b.1854, d.1922.

Dewey, John, American philosopher, b.1859, d.1952.

Dewey, Melvil, American inventor (1876) of the Decimal Classification for printed material, b.1851, d.1931.

De Wint, Peter, English painter (*A Cornfield),* b.1784, d.1849.

De Witt, Johan, Dutch statesman, b.1625, lynched 1672.

Diagnosis, medical, established as an exact science by the English physician Thomas Sydenham, b.1624, d.1689.

Diabelli, Anton, Austrian music publisher and composer, b.1781, d.1858.

Diaghilev, Sergei, Russian impresario and ballet master, b.1872, d.1929.

Diamond necklace affair, involving Queen Marie Antoinette, took place 1784–85; tried 1786.

Diamonds, first discovered in South Africa 1867.

Diamonds, carbon composition demonstrated 1796 by the English scientist Smithson Tennant, b.1761, d.1815.

Diaz, Bartolomeu, Portuguese explorer, d.1500.

Dickens, Charles, English novelist (*Pickwick Papers*, 1836–38), b.1812, d.1870.

Dickinson, Emily, American poet, b.1830, d.1886.

Dick Tracy, world's most popular comic strip, first syndicated 12 Oct. 1931.

Dictaphone, invented by the American electrician Charles Sumner Tainter, b.1854, d.1940.

Dictionary of American Biography, first published 1872; compiled by Francis Samuel Drake, b.1828, d.1885.

Dictionary of National Biography, British, founded 1882 by George Smith, b.1824, d.1901; first published 1885–1901; supplemented each decade to the present day.

Diderot, Denis, French encyclopedist, writer and philosopher, b.1713, d.1784.

Didius Julianus, Roman emperor (193), murdered 193.

Diemen, Antony van, governor-general of Batavia, b.1593, d.1645.

Diesel engine, invented 1893 by the German engineer Rudolf Diesel, b.1858, d.1913.

Diet of Worms, concerning Martin Luther's actions and writings, held 1521.

Dietrich, Marlene (Maria Magdalena von Losch), German-born film actress (*The Blue Angel*, 1930), b.1901, d.1992.

Differential motor gear, invented 1885 by the German engineer Karl Benz, b.1844, d.1929.

Digby, Sir Kenelm, English writer (*Private Memoirs*), b.1603, d.1665.

Diggers, group of English communists led by Gerrard Winstanley, active 1648–52.

Dilke, Sir Charles, British statesman, b.1843, b.1911.
Dimitrov, Georgi, Bulgarian communist leader (prime minister 1945–49), b.1882, d.1949.
Dingaan's Day, South African anniversary commemorating the rout of the Zulu chief Dingaan 16 Dec. 1838.
Diocletian, Roman emperor (284–305), b.245, d.313.
Diode valve, invented 1904 by the English electrical engineer Sir John Ambrose Fleming, b.1849, d.1945.
Diodorus Siculus, Greek historian, *fl.* 1st century BC.
Diogenes, Greek cynic philosopher, b.c.412, d.323 BC.
Dionysius, St, pope 259–269.
Diophantine equations, invented by the Greek mathematician Diophantus of Alexandria, *fl.* 3rd century.
Dior, Christian, French fashion designer, b.1905, d.1957.
Dioscorus, anti-pope 530.
Discontent, Winter of, 1978-79, time of pay freezes and strikes under the Labour government of James Callaghan, led to Labour losing the 1979 general election.
Disney, Walt (Walter Elias), American film maker and theme park entrepreneur (*Fantasia,* 1941), b.1901, d.1966.
Disneyland, Anaheim, California, the first of the Disney amusement parks, opened 1955.
Dispensing, in the USA, first dispensary opened 1785 in Philadelphia by the American physician Benjamin Rush, b.1745, d.1813.
Disraeli, Benjamin, Earl of Beaconsfield, British writer (*Coningsby,* 1844) and statesman (prime minister 1868, 1874–80), b.1804, d.1881.
d'Israeli, Isaac, English writer (*Curiosities of Literature,* 1791–93, 1823), b.1766, d.1848.
Dissolution of the monasteries, England, 1536–40.
District nursing movement introduced in Britain 1859 by the English philanthropist William Rathbone, b.1819, d.1902.
Dittersdorf, Karl Ditters von, Austrian violinist and composer, b.1739, d.1799.
Divorce, for grounds other than adultery, made legal in England 1937.
Djibouti, northeast coast of Africa, former overseas territory of the French Republic (called French Somaliland then Territory of the Afars and Issas) acquired between 1856 and 1883; became independent 27 June 1977.

DNA (deoxyribonucleic acid), complex molecule that constitutes genetic material of living organisms, its double helix structure was first identified by James Watson, b.1928, and Francis Crick, b.1916, in 1953.

Dobson, Austin, English poet (*At the Sign of the Lyre*, 1885), b.1840, d.1921.

Docking of horses' tails, prohibited by law in Britain since 1950.

Doctor Wall (Worcester) porcelain, manufactured 1751–83.

Doctor Who, British children's BBC TV series, began 1963.

Documentary film, term dates from1929; first significant example was Nanook of the North (1920) by Robert Flaherty, b.1884, d.1951.

Dodo, became extinct c.1680.

Dodsley, Robert, English publisher, b.1703, d.1764.

Dod's Parliamentary Companion, founded 1832 by the English journalist Charles Roger Phipps Dod, b.1793, d.1855.

Dog licence, required in Britain by Act of Parliament 1878.

Doggett's Coat and Badge Prize, Thames rowing competition, founded 1715 by the English actor Thomas Doggett, d.1721.

Dohnanyi, Ernst von, Hungarian composer (*Ruralia Hungarica*, 1924), b.1877, d.1960.

Dolabella, Roman general, b.c.70, d.43 BC.

Dole, British unemployment payments, first so named by the *Daily Mail* 1919.

Dollar, first issued in USA 1794, in England 1804.

Dollfuss, Engelbert, Austrian chancellor (1932–34), b.1892, assassinated 1934.

Döllinger, Johann, German theologian, b.1799, d.1890.

Dolomite rock, nature first studied 1791 by the French geologist Déodat de Gratet de Dolomieu, b.1750, d.1801.

Domagk, Gerhard, German pathologist, b.1895, d.1964, awarded Nobel prize 1938.

Domesday Book, William the Conqueror's survey of England, prepared 1085–86.

Dominic, St, b.c.1170, d.1221.

Dominican Order, founded by St Dominic 1216.

Dominican Republic, discovered 1492 by Christopher Columbus; achieved independence from Spanish rule 1821; the Republic founded 1844; new constitution granted 1924.

Dominion Day, Canada, celebrated 1 July.

Domitian, Roman emperor (81–96), b.51, assassinated 96.

Donatello (Donato di Niccolò), Italian sculptor (*St George*), b.*c.*1386, d.1466.
Dongan, Thomas, Earl of Limerick, Irish-born governor (1682–88) of New York, b.1634, d.1715.
Dönitz, Karl, German admiral (Reichsführer in May 1945), b.1891, d.1980.
Donizetti, Gaetano, Italian composer (*Lucia di Lammermoor*, 1835), b.1797, d.1848.
Donne, John, English poet and divine, b.1573, d.1631.
Donnybrook Fair, Ireland, licensed by King John 1204; suppressed 1855.
Donus, pope 676–678.
Doolittle, Hilda ('H.D.'), American poet (*Hymen*, 1921), b.1886, d.1961.
Doppler effect, physics, predicted 1842 by the Austrian scientist Christian Doppler, b.1803, d.1853.
Doré, Gustave, French artist and illustrator (Dante's *Inferno*), b.1833, d.1883.
Dorr's Rebellion, to extend the suffrage to Rhode Island, led (1841) by the American politician Thomas Wilson Dorr, b.1805, d.1854.
Dort, Synod of, held to discuss the Arminian heresy, 1618–19.
Dortmund-Ems Canal, Germany, constructed 1892–99.
Dos Passos, John, American novelist (*U.S.A.*), b.1896, d.1970.
Dostoyevsky, Fyodor Mikhailovich, Russian novelist (*The Brothers Karamazov*, 1880), b.1821, d.1881.
Douai Bible, first English Catholic translation, published 1609–10.
Double Eagle II, flight of the, the first transatlantic crossing by balloon (Maine to France, 137 hrs 18 min.) 17 Aug. 1978.
Double refraction, theory developed by the French physicist Etienne Louis Malus, b.1775, d.1812.
Double valency, study (contributing to the study of Isomerism) developed 1893 by the Swiss chemist Alfred Werner, b.1866, d.1919.
Doughty, Charles Montagu, English explorer and writer (*Arabia Deserta*, 1888), b.1843, d.1926.
Douglas, Sir James, of Douglas, Scottish patriot, b.*c.*1286, killed in battle 1330.
Douglas, Norman, Scottish writer (*South Wind*, 1917), b.1868, d.1952.

Douglas-Home, Sir Alec (Lord Home of the Hirsel), British statesman (prime minister 1963–64), b.1903.

Dover, Treaty of, to re-establish Catholicism in England, signed between Charles II and Louis XIV, 1670.

Dounreay, site in Caithness of Britain's first fast-breeder reactor; first experimental started 1955; first large-scale prototype1974.

Downing College, Cambridge University, founded by Sir George Downing, b.1684, d.1749; built 1807.

Dowland, John, English poet and composer, b.1563, d.1626.

Doyle, Sir Arthur Conan, Scottish writer of the Sherlock Holmes stories, b.1859, d.1930.

Doyle, Richard, English caricaturist, b.1824, d.1883.

D'Oyly Carte, Richard, English impresario (the Gilbert and Sullivan operas), b.1844, d.1901.

Dragonnades, expeditions by French soldiers to persecute the Huguenots in the provinces, 1685.

Drake, Sir Francis, English sailor (circumnavigated the world 1577–80), b.*c.*1540, d.1596.

Draper, Ruth, American actress and diseuse, b.1889, d.1959.

Drayton, Michael, English poet, b.1563, d.1631.

Dreadnoughts, heavily armed warships, introduced in Britain by Lord Fisher 1905.

Dresden china, originated by the German Johann Friedrich Böttger, b.1628, d.1719.

Dreyfus, Alfred, French artillery officer, b.1859; first trial for treason 1894; rehabilitated 1906; d.1935.

Drinkwater, John, English writer *(Abraham Lincoln,* 1918), b.1882, d.1937.

Drive-in bank, first British (Westminster), opened at Liverpool Jan. 1959.

Drogheda, Ireland, sacked by Cromwell 10 Sept. 1649.

Drummond, Thomas, Scottish engineer and inventor, b.1797, d.1840.

Drummond, William, of Hawthornden, Scottish writer (*The Cypresse Grove,* 1623), b.1585, d.1649.

Drury Lane, theatres in London, opened 1663, 1674, 1794, 1812.

Druses, heretical Muslim sect, followers of Egyptian Caliph al Hakim (996–1020).

Dryden, John, English poet and playwright *(All for Love,* 1678), b.1631, d.1700.

Du Barry, Madame, mistress of King Louis XV of France, b.1741, guillotined 1793.

Du Bartas, Guillaume de Sallust, Huguenot poet, b.1544, d.1590.

Du Bellay, Joachim, French poet, b.1522, d.1560.

Duchamp, Marcel, French painter and art theorist (*Nude Descending a Staircase,* 1912), b.1887, d.1968.

Duel, last fought in England at Priest Hill, Egham, Surrey, 1852.

Dufy, Raoul, French painter, b.1877, d.1953.

Dugdale, Sir William, English antiquarian writer (*Monasticon Anglicanum*, 1655–73), b.1605, d.1686.

Duhamel, Georges, French writer (*Civilization),* b.1884, d.1966.

Dukas, Paul, French composer (*L'Apprenti-Sorcier*, 1897), b.1865, d.1935.

Duke University, North Carolina, founded 1838; assumed present name 1930.

Dulles, John Foster, American statesman, b.1888, d.1959.

Dumas, Alexandre, *père*, French writer (*Les Trois Mousquetaires,* 1844), b.1802, d.1870.

Dumas, Alexandre, *fils*, French writer (*La Dame aux Camélias*, 1848), b.1824, d.1895.

Du Maurier, George, French-born novelist (*Trilby*, 1894), b.1834, d.1896.

Dumbarton Oaks Conference, at which the foundations of the United Nations were laid, held Washington, DC, 1944.

Dumdum bullets, use banned by the Hague Conference 1907.

Dunant, Henri, Swiss founder (1864) of the International Red Cross, b.1828, d.1910.

Dunbar, William, Scottish poet (*Lament for the Makaris*), b.*c.*1460, d.*c.*1522.

Dunbar, Battle of, between the English and the Scots, 3 Sept. 1650.

Duncan, Isadora, American dancer, b.1878, d.1927.

Dunes, Battle of, Dunkirk, between French and Spanish, 4 June 1658.

Dunkirk, sold to France by King Charles II 1662; Battle of, World War II, 22 May to 4 June 1940.

Duns Scotus, Scottish philosopher, b.*c.*1266, d.1308.

Dunstan, St, archbishop of Canterbury (961–988), b.*c.*910, d.988.

Dupes, Day of, dissembling the triumph of the Spanish policy in France, 12 Nov. 1630.

Dupleix, Joseph, governor-general of India under the French, b.1697, d.1763.

Durand Line, defining the frontier between India and Afghanistan, determined 1893.

Dürer, Albrecht, German artist (*St Jerome*), b.1471, d.1528.

Durham, John, Earl of, British statesman, b.1792, d.1840.

Durham University, founded by William Van Mildert, bishop of Durham, and the dean and Chapter of Durham 1832.

Durkheim, Emile, French sociologist, b.1858, d.1917.

Durrell, Lawrence, Anglo-Irish writer (*Bitter Lemons*, 1957), b.1912, d.1990.

Duse, Eleanora, Italian actress, b.1859, d.1924.

Dussek, Johann Ladislaus (Jan Ladislav Dusek), Bohemian composer (*Elégie Harmonique*), b.1760, d.1812.

Dust wrappers, for books, first used in Britain 1832; came into general use c.1890.

Duveen, Sir Joseph Joel, Dutch-born art dealer, b.1843, d.1908.

Dvorak, Antonin, Czech composer (*From the New World*, 1893), b.1841, d.1904.

Dylan, Bob (Robert Zimmerman), American folk singer and composer ('Blowin' in the Wind', 1962), b.1941.

Dynamite, discovered 1867 by the Swedish manufacturer Alfred Nobel, b.1833, d.1896.

Dynamo, invented 1823 by the English electrician William Sturgeon, b.1783, d.1850.

Dynamometer, electrical, invented 1840 by the German physicist Wilhelm Eduard Weber, b.1804, d.1891.

Dysentery, bacillus first isolated by the Danish scientist C. Sonne 1915.

E

Ealing Studios, established 1929 as Associated Talking Pictures, peaked 1946–58 with 'Ealing Comedies', dissolved late 1950s.
Earhart, Amelia, American aviator, b.1898, d.1937.
Earle, John, English divine and writer (*Microcosmographie*, 1628), b.*c.*1601, d.1665.
Earth, circumference of the, first calculated by Eratosthenes *c.*230 BC.
Earth, circumnavigation of the, by Magellan's sailors Sept. 1519–Sept. 1522.
Earth, density of the, calculated by the English mathematician Charles Hutton, b.1737, d.1823. Sir George Airy, b.1801, d.1892, Astronomer-Royal, calculated the mean density of the earth to be 6.566 in 1954.
Earth, magnetism of the, described 1600 by William Gilbert.
Earth, mass of the, first calculated 1797 by Henry Cavendish.
Earth current, discovered 1862 by the Scottish-born astronomer Johann von Lamont, b.1805, d.1879.
East, Sir Alfred, English painter, b.1849, d.1913.
East India Company, first chartered 1600, dissolved 1858.
East London, South African port, founded 1848.
East Prussia, German *land*, absorbed into Russia and Poland in 1945.
Easter, Christian Feast of the Resurrection, celebrated on the first Sunday after the first full moon after the Vernal Equinox.
Easter Island, Pacific, discovered by the Dutch navigator Jakob Roggeveen 1722.
Eastlake, Sir Charles Lock, English painter and president of the Royal Academy (1850–65), b.1793, d.1865.
Eastman, George, American pioneer developer of photographic equipment, b.1854, d.1932.
Eastwood, Clint, American screen actor and director (*The Unforgiven*, 1992), b.1930.
Eau de Cologne, traditionally invented by the Italian Johann Maria Farina, b.1685, d.1766.
Eberlein, Gustav, German sculptor (*Boy Extracting a Thorn*), b.1847, d.1926.
Ebers, Georg, German novelist (*Kleopatra*, 1894), b.1837, d.1898.
Ebert, Friedrich, German statesman (president 1919–25), b.1871, d.1925.

Ebonite (vulcanized rubber), invented 1849 by the American inventor Charles Goodyear, b.1800, d.1860.

Echegaray, José, Spanish playwright (Nobel prize 1904), b.1833, d.1916.

Echo, The, British newspaper founded 1876 by John Passmore Edwards, b.1823, d.1911.

Eckermann, Johann Peter, German friend of Goethe, b.1792, d.1854.

Eckhardt, Meister Jean, German theologian and mystic, b.*c.*1260, d.1327.

Eclipse Stakes, Sandown Park, first run 1883.

Eco, Umberto, Italian author and philosopher (*The Name of the Rose*, 1984), b.1932.

Ecole des Beaux Arts, Paris, founded 1648; adopted present name 1793.

Economist, The, British periodical founded 1843 by the Scottish economist James Wilson, b.1805, d.1860.

Ecu, international currency unit, adopted by the EC 1978.

Ecuador, achieved independence by secession from Republic of Colombia 1830; granted new constitution 1945.

Eddington, Sir Arthur Stanley, British astronomer and writer (*The Expanding Universe*, 1933), b.1882, d.1944.

Eddy, Mrs Mary Baker, American founder of Christian Science, b.1821, d.1910.

Eddystone Lighthouse, first structure erected by Henry Winstanley 1696–1700 and swept away 1703; second, by John Rudyerd, completed 1709 and burnt Dec. 1755; third, by John Smeaton, completed 1759; fourth, by J. N. Douglass, completed 1882.

Edelinck, Gérard, French engraver, b.1640, d.1707.

Eden, Sir Anthony, Earl of Avon, British statesman (prime minister 1955–57), b.1897, d.1977.

Edgar, king of the English (959–975), b.944, d.975.

Edgar Atheling, English prince, b.*c.*1050, d.*c.*1125.

Edgehill, Battle of, between King Charles I and the Parliamentary forces 23 Oct. 1642.

Edgeworth, Maria, Irish novelist (*Castle Rackrent*, 1800), b.1767, d.1849.

Edict of Diocletian, Roman measure to check speculation, issued 301.

Edict of Nantes, granting religious freedom to the Huguenots, signed by Henri IV, 1598; revoked by Louis XIV, 1685.

Edinburgh, founded *c.*617 by Edwin, king of Northumbria.
Edinburgh, Treaty of, enacting peace between England and Scotland, signed 1560.
Edinburgh Festival, founded 1947.
Edinburgh Review, British periodical, began publication Oct. 1802.
Edinburgh University, founded 1583.
Edison, Thomas Alva, American inventor, b.1847, d.1931.
Edmund, St (Edmund Rich), d.1240.
Edmund, St, king of East Anglia (855–870), b.841, killed 870.
Edmund, king of the English (940–946), b.*c.*922, d.946.
Edmund Crouchback, Earl of Lancaster, b.1245, d.1296.
Edmund Ironside, king of the English (1016), b.*c.*981, d.1016.
Edred, king of the English (946–955), d.955.
Education Acts, 1870, 1944, 1992.
Edward, the Black Prince, b.1330, d.1376.
Edward I, king of England (1272–1307), b.1239, d.1307.
Edward II, king of England (1307–27), b.1284, murdered 1327.
Edward III, king of England (1327–77), b.1312, d.1377.
Edward IV, king of England (1461–83), b.1442, d.1483.
Edward V, king of England (1483), b.1470, murdered 1483.
Edward VI, king of England (1547–53), b.1537, d.1553.
Edward VII, king of England (1901–10), b.1841, d.1910.
Edward VIII, king of England (Jan. 1936 – abdicated 10 Dec. 1936), b.1894, d.1972.
Edward, Lake, Uganda, discovered 1889 by Sir Henry Morton Stanley, b.1841, d.1904.
Edwards, Jonathan, American theologian (*Freedom of Will*, 1754), b.1703, d.1758.
Edward the Confessor, king of the English (1043–66), d.1066.
Edward the Elder, king of the Angles and Saxons (901–924), d.924.
Edwin, king of Northumbria (617–633), b.*c.*585, killed 633.
Egan, Pierce, English writer (*Life in London*, 1821), b.1772, d.1849.
Egbert, king of the West Saxons (802–839), d.839.
Egerton, Francis, Earl of Ellesmere, statesman and poet, b.1800, d.1857.
Egerton, Francis, Duke of Bridgewater, pioneer canal builder, b.1736, d.1803.
Egmont, Lamoral, Count of, Flemish statesman, b.1522, executed 1568.

Egypt, approximate extent of ancient history (1st to 31st dynasties), 3188–332 BC; Arab conquest AD 640; Turkish conquest 1517; proclaimed an independent kingdom 1922, an independent republic 1953.

Egyptian Era (Cycle of Sothis), began 19 July 4241 BC.

Ehrenburg, Ilya Grigoryevich, Russian writer (*Julio Jurenito*), b.1891, d.1967.

Ehrlich, Paul, German bacteriologist, b.1854, d.1915.

Eiffel Tower, opened 1889, built by the French engineer Gustave Eiffel, b.1832, d.1923.

Einstein, Albert, German-born physicist, b.1879, d.1955.

Eire, established as Irish Free State 1921; renamed 'Eire' 1937; became Irish Republic (*Poblacht na h'Eireann*) and left British Commonwealth 1949.

Eisenhower, Dwight David, US general and 34th president (1953–61), b.1890, d.1969.

Eisenstaedt, Alfred, American photographer and pioneer photojournalist, b.1898.

Eisenstein, Sergei, Russian film director (*The Battleship Potemkin*, 1925), b.1898, d.1948.

Eisner, Kurt, German statesman, b.1867, assassinated 1919.

Eisteddfod, Welsh national festival with a history of at least fourteen centuries, first so named in the twelfth century.

El Alamein, World War II, 8th Army offensive begun 23 Oct. 1942; victorious 4 Nov. 1942.

Elastic, first British patent issued 1832 to J. V. Desgrand.

Eldon, John Scott, Lord, English jurist, b.1751, d.1838.

Eleanor of Aquitaine, wife of Henry II of England, b.1122, d.1204.

Eleanor of Castile, wife of Edward I of England, d.1290.

Eleanor of Provence, wife of Henry III of England, d.1291.

Electors (*Kurfürsten*), of Holy Roman Empire, system established in 13th century, revised 1356; ended with Empire 1806.

Electric batteries, invented 1800 by Italian scientist Alessandro Volta, b.1745, d.1827.

Electric lamps, first publicly demonstrated by Sir Joseph Swan, b.1828, d.1914; invented simultaneously by Thomas Edison, b.1847, d.1931.

Electric light, first produced 1800 by Sir Humphry Davy, b.1778, d.1829. First used domestically in Britain 1881.

Electric locomotives, invented 1851 by American inventor Alfred Vail, b.1807, d.1859.

Electric power station, first English, opened at Godalming, Surrey, 1881.

Electrical Engineers, Institution of, founded as The Society of Telegraph Engineers 1871.

Electrified railway, first commercial line (City & South London Railway) opened 1890.

Electrocardiography, study of heart action, first developed by the Dutch physiologist Willem Einthoven, b.1860, d.1927.

Electrodynamics, theory developed 1822 by French scientist André Marie Ampere, b.1775, d.1836.

Electroencephalography, pioneered 1929.

Electrolysis, investigated 1833 by Michael Faraday, b.1791, d.1867.

Electromagnet, invented 1825 by the English electrician William Sturgeon, b.1783, d.1850.

Electromagnetic induction, laws defined 1831 by the English chemist Michael Faraday, b.1791, d.1867.

Electromagnetic waves, existence established 1864 by the Scottish physicist James Clerk Maxwell, b.1831, d.1879.

Electromagnetism, discovered 1819 by the Danish physicist Hans Christian Oersted, b.1777, d.1851.

Electron, discovered 1897 by Sir Joseph John Thomson, b.1856, d.1940; first isolated *c.*1920 by the American physicist Robert Andrews Millikan, b.1868, d.1953.

Electron microscope, constituted 1932 by Knoll and Ruska.

Electroplating, invented 1832 by the English manufacturer George Richards Elkington, b.1801, d.1865.

Eleutherius, St, pope 175–189.

Elevated railway, world's first, opened at Liverpool 1893.

Elgar, Sir Edward, English composer *(The Dream of Gerontius,* 1900), b.1857, d.1934.

Elgin Marbles, brought from the Parthenon to London 1801–03 by Lord Elgin, b.1766, d.1841.

'Eliot, George' (Mary Ann Evans), English novelist (*The Mill on the Floss*, 1860), b.1819, d.1880.

Eliot, Sir John, English Parliamentarian, b.1592, died in prison 1632.

Eliot, John, English missionary to the North American Indians, b.1604, d.1690.

Eliot, Thomas Stearns, American-born critic and poet (*The Waste Land*, 1922), b.1888, d.1965.

Elizabeth, St, b.1207, d.1231.

Elizabeth I, queen of England, b.1533, succeeded Mary 1558, d.1603.
Elizabeth II, queen of Great Britain, b. 21 April 1926, m. 20 Nov. 1947, succeeded her father King George VI, 6 Feb. 1952.
Elizabeth, Queen, the Queen Mother, b.1900.
Elizabeth, empress of Austria, b.1837, d.1898.
Elizabeth, empress of Russia, b.1709, d.1761.
Elizabeth, English queen of Bohemia, b.1596, d.1662.
Elizabethville, Zaire, founded 1910.
Ellington, Duke (Edward Kennedy), American jazz pianist, composer and bandleader, b.1899, d.1974.
Elliptical functions, discovered 1829 by Karl Gustav Jakob Jacobi, b.1804, d.1851.
Ellis, Havelock, English physician (*The Psychology of Sex*, 1901–10), b.1859, d.1939.
Ellis Island, the principal immigration port for the US 1892–1943; restored and opened as Immigration Museum 1990.
Ellison, Ralph, American writer (*Invisible Man*, 1952), b.1914.
El Paso, Texas, first settled 1659.
Elphinstone, William, Scottish bishop, b.1431, d.1514.
El Salvador, colonized by the Spanish from 1524; declared independence 1821; became a republic 1856; Civil War 1979–92.
Elssler, Fanny, Austrian dancer, b.1810, d.1884.
Elssler, Thérèse, Austrian dancer (and sister of Fanny), b.1808, d.1878.
Ely Cathedral, built 11th to 14th centuries.
Elyot, Sir Thomas, diplomatist and writer, b.c.1490, d.1546.
Elzevir, Louis, Dutch publisher of the classics, b.1540, d.1617.
Emancipation of Catholics, in Britain, enacted 1829.
Emancipation of slaves, in the USA, proclaimed 1863.
Ember Days (in W. Christendom), fasts on Wednesday, Friday and Saturday after first Sunday in Lent, after Pentecost, after 14 Sept. and after 13 Dec.
Emerson, Ralph Waldo, American writer (*Essays*, 1841–44), b.1803, d.1882.
Emin Pasha (Eduard Schnitzer), German explorer, b.1840, d.1892.
Emmet, Robert, Irish leader, b.1778, hanged 1803.
Emmett, Daniel Decatur, American composer (*Dixie,* 1859), b.1815, d.1904.
Empedocles, Greek philosopher, b.c.494, d.c.434 BC.
Empire, French, first: 1804–14, second: 1852–1870.

Empire, German, first: 962–1806, second: 1871–1918, third: 1933–45.

Empire State Building, New York, built 1930–31.

Encyclopaedia Americana, first published 1829–33.

Encyclopaedia Britannica, first produced and published by Andrew Bell, Colin Macfarquhar and William Smellie 1768–71.

Enderby Land, Antarctic, discovered 1831 by the British navigator John Biscoe, d.1848.

Enesco, Georges, Rumanian violinist, b.1881, d.1955.

Engels, Friedrich, German Marxist, b.1820, d.1895.

Enghien, Louis, Duc d', French Royalist, b.1772, shot 1804.

English Folk Dance Society, founded 1911 by Cecil Sharp, b.1859, d.1924; succeeded by English Folk Dance and Song Society 1932.

ENIAC (Electronic Numerical Integrator and Calculator), first electronic computer, first publicly demonstrated in Feb. 1946.

Eniwetok Atoll, Marshall Islands, scene of atom bomb tests started by the US Navy 1946.

Ennius, Quintus, Latin poet, b.239, d.170 BC.

Enosis, movement for the union of Cyprus with Greece, had its origins in the Greek government's demand of 1912.

Ensign, infantry rank, abolished 1871.

Entebbe raid, freeing by Israeli commandos of Jewish passengers hijacked at Entebbe airport in Uganda by members of the Popular Front for the Liberation of Palestine, 3 July 1976.

Entente, Triple, between England, France and Russia, 1904–17; **Little,** between Czechoslovakia, Yugoslavia and Romania, 1920–38.

Entropy, the relation between the total amount of heat and temperature, discovered by the German physicist Rudolf Clausius, b.1822, d.1888.

Envelope-making machine, first, invented 1851 by the British scientist Warren de la Rue, b.1815, d.1889.

Enver Pasha, Turkish leader, b.1881, killed in action 1922.

Eocene Epoch, Earth history, 60 million years ago.

EOKA (National Organization of Cypriot Combatants), guerrilla and terrorist group organized in Cyprus 1954.

Epaminondas, Greek general, b.c.418, d.326 BC.

Epée, Charles Michel, Abbé de l', French priest and benefactor of the deaf and mute, b.1712, d.1789.

Epictetus, Greek philosopher, b.c.55, d.c.120.

Epicurus, Greek philosopher, b.341, d.270 BC.

Epinay, Louise, Marquise d', French writer, b.1726, d.1783.
Epiphany, Christian Feast of the Manifestation of Christ to the Gentiles (connected with both the Nativity and the Baptism), celebrated 6 Jan.
Epsom, races first run *c*.1620.
Epsom Salts, discovered 1618.
Epstein, Sir Jacob, American-born sculptor (*Rima*, 1925), b.1880, d.1959.
Equinox, time at which day and night are of equal length; Vernal Equinox 21–22 March; Autumnal Equinox 21–22 Sept.
Erasmus, Desiderius, Dutch religious reformer and theologian, b.1467, d.1536.
Erastus, Thomas (Thomas Lüber), German-Swiss theologian, b.1524, d.1583.
Eratosthenes, Alexandrian philosopher, b.*c*.276, d.*c*.194 BC.
Erbium, chemical element, first isolated 1843 by the Swedish chemist Karl Gustav Mosander, b.1797, d.1858.
Erckmann-Chatrian, pen-name of the French writers, Emile Erckmann, b.1822, d.1899, and Alexandre Chatrian, b.1826, d.1890, who worked in collaboration between 1847 and 1889.
Erebus, Mt., volcanic mountain in the Antarctic, discovered 1841 by Sir James Ross, b.1800, d.1862.
Eric, king of Denmark, reigned 814 to 854.
Eric Eiggod, king of Denmark (1095–1101), b.*c*.1056, d.1101.
Eric Emune, king of Denmark (1131–37), assassinated 1137.
Eric Lam, king of Denmark (1137–46), d.1146.
Eric Plogpenning, king of Denmark (1241–50), b.1216, beheaded 1250.
Eric Klipping, king of Denmark (1259–86), b.*c*.1249, assassinated 1286.
Eric Menved, king of Denmark (1286–1319). b.1274, d.1319.
Eric VII, king of Denmark (1396–1438), and **XIII**, king of Sweden, b.1382, d.1459.
Eric I to V, legendary kings of Sweden.
Eric VI, king of Sweden, reigned from *c*.850 till his death *c*.880.
Eric VII, king of Sweden, d.*c*.994.
Eric VIII, king of Sweden, reigned towards the end of the 11th century.
Eric IX, St, king of Sweden and Denmark, beheaded 1160.
Eric X, king of Sweden (1210–16), d.1216.
Eric XI, king of Sweden (1222–52), b.1216, d.1252.
Eric XII, king of Sweden, b.1339, d.1359.

Eric XIII, king of Sweden (1396–1438), b.1382, d.1459, and **VII** king of Denmark (1396–1438).

Eric XIV, king of Sweden (1560–77), b.1533, d.1577.

Eric the Red, Norwegian discoverer (about 981) of Greenland, b.*c*.949.

Ericsson, John, Swedish-born inventor, b.1803, d.1889.

Ericsson, Leif, Scandinavian discoverer (about 1000) of North America, b.*c*.971.

Erie Canal, New York State, begun 1817, completed 1825.

Erie, Battle of Lake, between Americans and British, Sept. 1813.

Erigena, Johannes Scotus, Irish philosopher and theologian in 9th century.

Eritrea, conquered by Italy 1885–89; invaded by British forces 1941; sovereignty handed over by the British to Ethiopia 1952; Eritrean independence movement has fought against the government since 1961.

Erivan, Ivan Fyodorovich Paskevich, Count of, Russian field-marshal, b.1782, d.1856.

Erkel, Franz, Hungarian composer (*Bánk Bán*, 1861), b.1810, d.1893.

ERNIE (Electronic Random Number Indicating Equipment), used to select winning numbers in premium bonds, first issued by the Dept. of National Savings 1956.

Ernle, Rowland Edmund Prothero, Baron, English agricultural historian, b.1851, d.1937.

Ernst, Max, German painter, b.1891, d.1976.

Erskine, Ebenezer, Scottish church reformer, b.1680, d.1754.

Erskine, John, Scottish reformer, b.1509, d.1591.

Erskine, John, Earl of Mar, Jacobite supporter, b.1675, d.1732.

Erskine, Thomas, Baron Erskine, Scottish lawyer, b.1750, d.1823.

Ervine, St John, Ulster-born playwright (*Jane Clegg*, 1911), b.1883, d.1971.

Escalator, first in England installed at Earls Court Station, London, in 1911.

Escorial, The, Spain, palace built by King Philip II, 1563–84.

Esparto grass, first used for the manufacture of paper *c*.1855.

Esperanto, universal language, produced 1887 by the Polish scholar Lazarus Ludovic Zamenhof, b.1859, d.1917.

Essex, Robert Devereux, 2nd Earl of, English statesman and rebel, b.1566, executed 1601.

Essex, Robert Devereux, 3rd Earl of, English statesman and general, b.1591, d.1646.

Este, Beatrice d', Italian diplomat and patron of the arts, b.1475, d.1497.

Esterházy, Prince Pál Antal, Austro-Hungarian diplomat, b.1786, d.1866.

Estienne, Henri, French printer and publisher, b.*c.*1531, d.1598.

Estienne, Robert, French printer and publisher, b.1503, d.1559.

Estonia, proclaimed an independent Republic 1918; incorporated in the Soviet Union 1940; independent since the dissolution of the Soviet Union Aug. 1991.

Estrées, Gabrielle d', mistress of King Henri IV of France, b.1573, d.1599.

ETA (Euzkadi Ta Askatasuna, 'Basque Homeland of Liberty'), radical terrorist group seeking Basque independence from Spain, split from the Basque Nationalist Party 1959.

Ethelred the Unready, king of England (from 978), b.*c.*968, d.1016.

Ethelreda, St, b.630, d.679.

Ether, soporific qualities discovered 1818 by the English chemist Michael Faraday, b.1791, d.1867; first used as an anaesthetic 1846 by the American physician Crawford Williamson Long, b.1815, d.1878.

Etherege, Sir George, English playwright (*She Would If She Could*, 1667), b.*c.*1635, d.1692.

Ethiopia, independence established 1906; conquered by Italy 1935–37; independence regained 1941; monarchy abolished 1975.

Etna (Mongibello), Sicilian volcano: main eruptions 125, 121 and 43 BC; AD 1169, 1669 and 1992.

'Ettrick Shepherd', The (James Hogg), Scottish poet, b.1770, d.1835.

Etty, William, English painter (*Youth at the Prow and Pleasure at the Helm*), b.1787, d.1849.

Euclid, Greek mathematician, fl. 300 BC.

Eudocia, Byzantine empress, b.*c.*400, d.*c.*459.

Eudoxia, Byzantine empress, d.404.

Eugéne I, St, pope 654–657.

Eugene II, pope 824–827.

Eugene III (Bernardo Paganelli), pope 1145–53.

Eugene IV (Gabriel Condulmieri), pope 1431–47.

Eugene of Savoy, Prince, b.1663, d.1736.

Eugénie, wife of the Emperor Napoleon III, b.1826, d.1920.
Eulalius, anti-pope 418.
Euler, Leonhard, Swiss mathematician, b.1707, d.1783.
Eumenes, Greek general, b.*c.*360, killed 316 BC.
Euratom (European Atomic Energy Authority), established by Treaty of Rome 25 March 1957.
Eurhythmics, Dalcroze, music educational system, invented by the Swiss composer Emile Jaques-Dalcroze, b.1865, d.1950.
Euripides, Greek dramatist *(The Trojan Women,* 413 BC), b.*c.*480, d.*c.*406 BC.
European Coal and Steel Community, established by the Treaty of Paris 1951.
European Defence Community, set up 27 May 1952.
European Economic Community, established by Treaty of Rome 25 March 1957.
European Nuclear Energy Agency, founded within OEEC 1 Feb. 1958.
European Union, established by Treaty Feb. 1984; Single European Act signed Feb. 1986.
Eurovision, television link-up between European countries, first carried out on a large scale by the BBC 1954.
Eusebius, St, pope 309–311.
Eusebius of Caesarea, theologian, b.*c.*264, d.340.
Eustachian tube, anatomy, first described by the Italian anatomist Bartolommeo Eustachio, d.1574.
Eustathius, Greek literary critic, d.*c.*1196.
Euston Station, London, opened 1838.
Eutychian, St, pope 275–283.
Evans, Sir Arthur John, English archaeologist, b.1851, d.1941.
Evans, Sir John, English archaeologist, b.1823, d.1908.
Evans, Oliver, American inventor of mining machinery, b.1755, d.1819.
Evaporated milk, invented 1856 by the American surveyor Gail Borden, b.1801, d.1874.
Evaristus, St, pope 97–105.
Evelyn, John, English diarist, b.1620, d.1706.
Evening News, The, British newspaper founded 1881; absorbed the *Star* 1960.
Evening Standard, The, British newspaper, founded 1827; absorbed the *St James's Gazette* 1905.
Everest, Mt, summit reached 29 May 1953 by the New Zealander Sir Edmund Hillary, b.1919, d.1993 and the Sherpa Tensing.

Everlasting League, The, Swiss patriotic pact made 1291 between Schwyz, Uri and Unterwalden.

Evolution, by natural selection, Darwinian theory first communicated to the Linnean Society of London 1 July 1858; Charles Darwin's *Origin of the Species* first published 1859.

Ewart, William, English library pioneer, b.1798, d.1869.

Ewing, Sir James Alfred, Scottish scientist, b.1855, d.1935.

Ewing, Mrs Juliana Horatia, English writer (*Jackanapes*, 1884), b.1841, d.1885.

Exchange Rate Mechanism (ERM), stabilizing of currency (each valued in Ecus) in European Monetary System, Britain joined Oct. 1990.

Exclusion Struggle, against the succession of James, Duke of York (later James II), 1678–81.

Excursion train, world's first (Leicester-Loughborough return), organized by the English pioneer travel agent Thomas Cook, b.1808, d.1892.

Exeter Cathedral, constructed 1285–1367.

Exeter College, Oxford University, founded 1314 by Walter de Stapeldon, Bishop of Exeter, b.1261, d.1326.

Exmouth, Edward Pellew, Viscount, English admiral, b.1757, d.1833.

Expanding universe, theory developed by the Dutch scientist William de Sitter, b.1872, d.1934.

Explorer I, first American satellite, launched 31 Jan. 1958.

Exxon Valdez, oil tanker which ran aground leaking 11 million gallons of crude oil into Prince William Sound, Alaska, 24 March 1989.

Eyck, Hubert van, Flemish painter, b.*c.*1370, d.1426.

Eyck, Jan van, Flemish painter, b.*c.*1389, d.1440.

Eyre, Edward John, English explorer and statesman, b.1815, d.1901.

Eyre, Lake, South Australia, discovered 1840 by the English explorer Edward John Eyre, b.1815, d.1901.

F

Faber, Frederick William, English theologian and poet, b.1814, d.1863.
Fabian, St, pope 236–250.
Fabian Society, London, founded 1883 by the English writers Edward R. Pease and Frank Podmore, b.1855, d.1910.
Fabius Maximus, Quintus, Roman statesman, d.203 BC.
Fabre, Jean Henri, French entomologist (*Souvenirs Entomologiques*, 1879–1907), b.1823, d.1915.
Fabriano, Gentile da, Italian painter, b.*c.*1370, d.1427.
Fabricius, Hieronymus, Italian anatomist, b.1533, d.1619.
Fabricius, Johann Christian, Danish entomologist, b.1745, d.1808.
Fabritius, Carel, Dutch painter, b.1622, d.1654.
Fabyan, Robert, English historian, d.1513.
Factory Act, first in England passed 1802.
Fahd, king and prime minister of Saudi Arabia (since 1982), b.1933.
Fahrenheit scale, temperature, invented *c.*1714 by the German physicist Gabriel Daniel Fahrenheit, b.1686, d.1736.
Fairbairn, Sir William, Scottish engineer and inventor, b.1789, d.1874.
Fairbanks, Douglas, Junior American film actor (*The Prisoner of Zenda*, 1937), b.1909.
Fairbanks, Douglas, Senior American film actor (*The Thief of Baghdad*, 1924), b.1883, d.1939.
Fairbanks, Thaddeus, American inventor, b.1796, d.1886.
Fairey, Sir Charles Richard, British aviation pioneer, b.1887, d.1956.
Fairfax, Thomas, English puritan general, b.1612, d.1671.
Faisal, king of Saudi Arabia (1964–75), prime minister (1953–64), b.1906, d.1975.
Faithfull, Emily, English champion of rights for women, b.1835, d.1895.
Falange, Spanish Fascist Party, founded 1933 by José Antonio Primo de Rivera; completed control of Spain in 1939; abolished 1977.
Faliero, Marino, doge of Venice (1354–55), b.1274, executed 1355.
Falkirk, Battle of, 22 July 1298, between the English and the Scots.

Falkirk, Battle of, 17 Jan. 1746, between the Young Pretender and General Hawley.

Falkland Islands, Naval Battle of the, between the British and German fleets 8 Dec. 1914.

Falklands War, between Britain and Argentina over rival claims to sovereignty over the Falkland Islands (claimed by Britain as a Crown Colony since 1833): invaded by the Argentines April 1982, recaptured by British May–June 1982.

Falla, Manuel de, Spanish composer (*The Three-cornered Hat*, 1919), b.1876, d.1946.

Fallopian tubes, physiological function first described by the Italian anatomist Gabriello Fallopio, b.c.1523, d.1562.

Family Allowances, former name for Child Benefit, introduced into Britain 1945; general in France by 1932.

Fanshawe, Sir Richard, English diplomat and translator, b.1608, d.1666.

Fantin-Latour, Ignace Henri Jean Théodore, French painter (*Homage à Delacroix*), b.1836, d.1904.

FAO, *see* **Food and Agricultural Organization.**

Faraday, Michael, English physicist, b.1791, d.1867.

Farel, Guillaume, Swiss religious reformer, b.1489, d.1565.

Fargo, William George, American partner in the Wells Fargo express company, b.1818, d.1881.

Farinelli (Carlo Broschi), Italian *castrato* singer, b.1705, d.1782.

Farnese, Alessandro, Italian cardinal, b.1520, d.1589.

Farnese, Alessandro, Italian diplomat and soldier, b.1545, d.1592.

Farnese Palace, Rome, built c.1513–15.

Faroe Islands, Atlantic, came under Danish rule 1380; granted separate legislature and executive 1948.

Farouk, last king of Egypt (1936–52), b.1920, d.1965.

Farquhar, George, Irish-born dramatist (*The Beaux' Stratagem*, 1707), b.1678, d.1707.

Farr, William, English pioneer in the study of vital statistics, b.1807, d.1883.

Farragut, David Glasgow, American admiral, b.1801, d.1870.

Fascist Party, Italian, founded March 1919 by Mussolini; seized power 20 Oct. 1922; dissolved 28 July 1943. Spanish (Falange), founded 1933; gained control of Spain 1936–39. English (British Union of Fascists), founded 1932 by Sir Oswald Mosley; revived (British Union Movement) in 1948.

Fashoda Incident, Egypt, between British and French 1898.

Fassbinder, Rainer Werner, German film director and actor (*Lola,* 1981), b.1946, d.1982.
Fast breeder reactor, first experimental, set up by the United Kingdom Atomic Energy Authority at Dounreay, Scotland, 1957.
Fast of Ab, Jewish fast, Ab 9th.
Fastolf, Sir John, English soldier, b.*c.*1378, d.1459.
Father's Day, 3rd Sun. in June.
Fatima, daughter of Mahomet, b.*c.*605, d.632.
Fatima, Miracle of (Portugal), occurred 13 Oct. 1917.
Fatimids, caliphs in North Africa 909–1171.
Faulkner, William, American novelist (*Sanctuary*, 1931), b.1897, d.1962.
Fauré, Gabriel, French composer (*Messe basse*, 1907), b.1845, d.1924.
Faust, Johann *or* **Georg**, German magician, b.*c.*1480, d.*c.*1540.
Fauvist movement, French art group, first recognized 1905; disintegrated 1908.
Fawcett, Henry, English economist, b.1833, d.1884.
Fawcett, Millicent Garrett, English champion of women's rights, b.1847, d.1929.
Fawkes, Guy, English conspirator, b.1570, hanged 1606.
Feast of Tabernacles (*Sukkoth*), Jewish festival, 15th to 22nd Tishri inclusive.
Feast of Weeks (*Sharuoth*), Jewish festival, Sivan 6th.
Federal Reserve Bank, Washington, DC, founded 23 Dec. 1913.
Feisal I, first king of Iraq (1921-1933), b.1883, d.1933.
Feisal II, third and last king (from 1939) of Iraq, b.1935, assassinated 1958.
Felix I, St, pope 269–275.
Felix II, anti-pope 355–357, d.365.
Felix III, pope 483–492.
Felix IV, pope 526–530.
Felix V (Amadeus), anti-pope 1440–49, b.1383, d.1451.
Fell, Dr John, bishop of Oxford (from 1675), b.1625, d.1686.
Fellini, Frederico, Italian film director (*La Dolce Vita,* 1959), b.1920.
Fellowes, Edmund, English musicologist, b.1870, d.1951.
Felton, John, English assassin of the Duke of Buckingham, b.*c.*1595, hanged 1628.
Fénelon, François de Salignac de la Mothe, French theologian (*Télémaque*, 1699), b.1651, d.1715.

Fenians (Irish Republican Brotherhood), Irish-American revolutionary movement founded 1858 in the USA by John O'Mahony, b.1816, d.1877.

Feodor I, tsar of Russia (1584–98), b.1557, d.1598.

Feodor II, tsar of Russia (1605), b.1589, assassinated 1605.

Feodor III, tsar of Russia (1676–82) b.1656, d.1682.

Ferber, Edna, American writer (*Cimarron*, 1929), b.1887, d.1968.

Ferdinand I, Holy Roman emperor (1558–64), b.1503, d.1564.

Ferdinand II, Holy Roman emperor (1619–37), b.1578, d.1637.

Ferdinand III, Holy Roman emperor (1637–58), b.1608, d.1658.

Ferdinand I, king of Portugal (1367–83), b.1345, d.1383.

Ferdinand II, consort (1826–53) of Maria II of Portugal, b.1816, d.1885.

Ferdinand I, king of Castile and Leon, d.1065

Ferdinand II, king of Leon (1157–88).

Ferdinand III, king of Castile and Leon, b.1199, d.1212.

Ferdinand IV, king of Castile and Leon (1296–1312), d.1312.

Ferdinand V, king of Castile and Leon (1474–1516), b.1452, d.1516.

Ferdinand VI, king of Spain (1746–59), b.1713, d.1759.

Ferdinand VII, king of Spain (1813–33), b.1784, d.1833.

Ferdinand I, king of Naples (1458–94), b.1423, d.1494.

Ferdinand II, king of Naples (1495–96), b.1469, d.1496.

Ferguson, James, Scottish astronomer, b.1710, d.1776.

Ferguson, Patrick, Scottish inventor, b.1744, killed in action 1780.

Fermat, Pierre de, French mathematician, b.1601, d.1665.

Fermi, Enrico, Italian-born atomic physicist, b.1901, d.1954.

Fernandel (Fernand Contandin), French comedian, b.1903, d.1971.

Fernandez, Juan, Spanish explorer, b.*c*.1537, d.*c*.1603.

Fernando Po, *see* **Bioko.**

Fernel, Jean François, French scientist, b.1497, d.1558.

Ferrar, Nicholas, English religious leader, b.1592, d.1637.

Ferrara, Andrea, Italian sword-maker, active in the second half of the 16th century.

Ferrers, Laurence, Earl, last nobleman who was executed in Britain, b.1720, hanged 1760.

Ferrier, Kathleen, English singer, b.1912, d.1953.

Ferrier, Susan, Scottish novelist (*Marriage*, 1818), b.1782, d.1854.

Ferris wheel, invented for the World's Columbian Exposition 1892 by the American engineer George Washington Gale Ferris, b.1859, d.1896.

Ferro, Canary Isles, prime meridian adopted by French in 17th century (after Arab usage); superseded by Paris and in 1911 by Greenwich.

Fersen, Hans Axel, Count, Swedish diplomat, b.1755, murdered 1810.

Fervidor, French Revolutionary Calendar month, 19 July to 17 Aug.

Festival of Britain, 3 May–30 Sept. 1951.

Festival of Lights (Chanucah), Jewish festival, Kislev 25th.

Festival of the Purification of the Virgin (Candlemas), 2 Feb.

Feuchtwanger, Lion, German novelist (*Jud Süss*, 1924), b.1884, d.1958.

Feuerbach, Ludwig Andreas, German philosopher, b.1804, d.1872.

Feuillet, Octave, French novelist (*Sibylle*, 1862), b.1821, d.1890.

Féval, Paul, French novelist (*Les Mystères de Londres*, 1844), b.1817, d.1887.

Feydeau, Georges, French playwright, b.1862, d.1921.

Feynman, Richard Phillips, American physicist, shared Nobel prize 1965, b.1918, d.1988.

Fez, Treaty of, concerning the establishment of a French protectorate (1912–56) in Morocco, concluded 30 March 1912; terminated 2 March 1956.

Fianna Fail ('Soldiers of destiny'), Irish political party founded 1927 by statesman Eamon de Valera, b.1882, d.1975.

Fibreoptics, first suggested as a telecommunications medium by Charles Kao in 1966.

Fichte, Johann Gottlieb, German philosopher, b.1762, d.1814.

Fido, airfield clearance method, developed 1942 by the British engineer Arthur Clifford Hartley, b.1889, d.1960.

Field, John, Irish-born composer of nocturnes, b.1782, d.1837.

Field, Marshall, American department store pioneer, b.1834, d.1906.

Field marshal, military rank, introduced into Britain in 1736.

Field of the Cloth of Gold *see* **Cloth of Gold.**

Fielding, Henry, English novelist (*Tom Jones*, 1748), b.1707, d.1754.

Fields, Dame Gracie, British singer, b.1898, d.1979.

Fields, W. C. (William Claude Dukenfield), American comic stage and film actor (*You Can't Cheat an Honest Man,* 1939), b.1879, d.1946.

Fifth dimension, existence affirmed 1929 by Sir Owen Williams Richardson, b.1879, d.1959.

Fifth Monarchy Men, English religious movement, active 1642 to 1661.

Fifth Republic, France, constitution came into force 5 Oct. 1958.

Fiji, Polynesia, discovered 1643 by Abel Janszoon Tasman, b.*c.*1603, d.1659; British colony 1874–1970; now an independent republic.

Fillmore, Millard, 13th US president (1850–53), b.1800, d.1874.

Film, first flexible transparent, suitable for motion pictures, invented 1889 by the American inventor George Eastman, b.1854, d.1932.

Filmer, Sir Robert, English political writer (*Patriarcha,* 1680), d.1653.

Films in colour (Kinemacolour), first shown 1906.

Finland, ruled by Sweden until 1808, by Russia 1808–1918; independent republic since 1918.

Finney, Albert, British stage and film actor (*Under the Volcano,* 1984), b.1936.

Firdausi, Persian poet, b.*c.*940, d.1020.

Firearms, used in Europe in late 14th century; wheellock introduced in early 16th century; flintlock in late 16th century; percussion detonator invented 1805 by the Scottish minister Alexander Forsyth, b.1768, d.1843.

Fire engines, first acquired by London insurance company 1722.

Fire extinguisher, first portable, invented 1816 by the English barrack-master, George William Manby, b.1765, d.1854.

Fire insurance, pioneered by Nicholas Barbon 1666.

Fireplaces, in Britain, removed from the centre of the hall to the side wall in the 14th century.

Fire plugs, put into water mains in Britain 1667.

Fire rules, drawn up by the City of London 1189.

First of June, sea battle between French and British, 1794.

First Republic, France, proclaimed 22 Sept. 1792, ended 1804.

Fischer, Robert James (Bobby), American chess player, b.1943.

Fischer-Dieskau, Dietrich, German baritone, b.1925.

Fisher, John, Admiral Lord, British sailor, b.1841, d.1920.

Fishmongers Company, London, origins uncertain, first extant charter granted by King Edward III 1364.

Fiske, John, American philosopher, b.1842, d.1901.
Fisk University, Nashville, Tennessee, American negro university founded 1866.
Fitzgerald, Edward, English poet (*The Rubaiyat of Omar Khayyam*, 1859), b.1809, d.1883.
Fitzgerald, Ella, American jazz singer, b.1918.
Fitzgerald, F(rancis) S(cott), American writer (*The Great Gatsby,* 1925), b.1896, d.1940.
Fitzgerald, Lord Edward, Irish patriot, b.1763, d.1798.
Fitzherbert, Mrs Maria, wife of King George IV, b.1756, m.1785, d.1837.
Fitzwilliam Collection, bequeathed to the University of Cambridge by Viscount Richard Fitzwilliam, b.1745, d.1816.
Fiume, *see* **Rijeka-Susak.**
Flag Day, USA, celebrated 14 June.
Flagstad, Kirsten, Norwegian operatic singer, b.1895, d.1962.
Flambard, Ranulf, English statesman, d.1128.
Flaminian Way, from north of Rome to Ariminum on Adriatic coast, built 220 BC by the tribune Flaminius Gaius.
Flaminius, Gaius, Roman democratic leader, killed 217 BC.
Flammarion, Camille, French astronomer, b.1842, d.1925.
Flamsteed, John, first English Astronomer Royal, b.1646, d.1719.
Flatman, Thomas, English artist and poet, b.1637, d.1688.
Flaubert, Gustave, French novelist (*Madame Bovary*, 1857), b.1821, d.1880.
Flaxman, John, English sculptor (*St Michael*), b.1755, d.1826.
Flecker, James Elroy, English poet (*Hassan*, 1922), b.1884, d.1915.
Fleet Prison, London, founded in Norman times; burnt down 1666; rebuilt, but again destroyed 1780; rebuilt 1782; pulled down 1844.
Fleming, Sir Alexander, British biologist (discovered penicillin 1928), b.1881, d.1955.
Fleming, Ian (Lancaster), English novelist and journalist, creator of James Bond, b.1908, d.1964.
Fleming, Sir John Ambrose, English electrical engineer, b.1849, d.1945.
Fleming, Margaret, Scottish child prodigy, b.1803, d.1811.
Fleming, Sir Sandford, Scottish-born Canadian engineer, b.1827, d.1915.

Fletcher, John, English dramatist (with Francis Beaumont, *The Knight of the Burning Pestle*, 1607), b.1579, d.1625.

Fleury, André Hercule, Cardinal, French statesman, b.1653, d.1743.

Flintlocks, invented *c.*1635.

Flodden, Battle of, between English and Scots, 9 Sept. 1513.

Flogging in the British Navy, abolished through the efforts of the Irish politician John Gordon Swift Macneill, b.1849, d.1926.

Floral Games, first held at Toulouse May 1324.

Floréal, French Revolutionary calendar month, 20 April–19 May.

Florence of Worcester, English historian (*Chronicon*), d.1118.

Florida, discovered March 1512 by Juan Ponce de Leon, b.1460, d.1521. Ceded by Spain to USA 1819; granted statehood 1845.

Florio, John, English translator (Montaigne's *Essays*, 1603), b.*c.*1553, d.1625.

Flotow, Friedrich, Freiherr von, German composer (*Martha*, 1847), b.1812, d.1883.

Flour mill, first steam, erected by the Scottish engineer John Rennie at Blackfriars, London, 1784–88; burnt down 1791.

Fluorescence, nature discovered by the Irish-born scientist Sir George Gabriel Stokes, b.1819, d.1903.

Fluorescent lighting, low voltage, first marketed 1938.

Fluorine in drinking water, beneficial effects in preventing tooth decay first demonstrated by the American doctor Frederick S. McKay, b.1874, d.1959.

Fluorine, first isolated 1886 by the French chemist Henri Moissan, b.1852, d.1907.

Flying boat, invented 1912 by the American aviator Glenn Hammond Curtiss, b.1878, d.1930.

Flying bomb, first used by the Germans against the Allies 12 June 1944.

Flying Doctor Service, Australia, founded by the Australian Inland Mission of the Presbyterian Church of Australia 1928.

'Flying Saucers', first so named by the American Kenneth Arnold, June 1947.

Flynn, Errol, Australian-born Hollywood film actor (*Captain Blood*, 1935), b.1909, d.1959.

Foch, Ferdinand, French Commander-in-Chief Allied Forces during World War I, b.1851, d.1929.

Fokine, Michael, Russian ballet dancer, b.1880, d.1942.

Fokker, Anton Hermann Gerard, Dutch aviation pioneer, b.1890, d.1939.

Folger Shakespeare Memorial Library, Washington, DC, opened 1932.

Fonda, Henry, American stage and film actor (*Twelve Angry Men,* 1957), b.1905, d.1982.

Fonda, Jane, American film actress (*Klute,* 1971), b.1937.

Fontainebleau, Palace of, France, origins unknown, oldest building erected in 12th century, additions being made up to 19th century.

Fontana, Domenico, Italian architect, b.1543, d.1607.

Fontane, Theodor, German wrlter (*Stine*, 1890), b.1819, d.1898.

Fontenelle, Bernard le Bouvier de, French writer (*La Pluralité des mondes*, 1686), b.1657, d.1757.

Fontenoy, Battle of, between French and English, 11 May 1745.

Fonteyn, Dame Margot (Margaret Hookham), English ballerina, b.1919, d.1991.

Food and Agricultural Organization (FAO), UN agency established in Rome 16 Oct. 1945.

Football Association, formed 1863.

Foot, Michael, British Labour politician and journalist, b.1913.

Foote, Samuel, English playwright (*The Nabob*, 1772), b.1720, d.1777.

Footlights, in British theatres, first used 1672.

Foppa, Vincenzo, Italian painter, b.*c.*1429, d.*c.*1516.

Forbes-Robertson, Sir Johnston, English actor, b.1853, d.1937.

Ford, Gerald Rudolph, 38th US president (1974–77), b.1913.

Ford, Ford Madox, English novelist (*No More Parades*, 1925), b.1873, d.1939.

Ford, John, English dramatist (*'Tis Pity She's a Whore*, 1633), b.1586, d.*c.*1639.

Ford, John (Sean Aloysius O'Feeney), American film director (*The Searchers*, 1956), b.1895, d.1973.

Ford Motor Works, USA, founded 1903 by Henry Ford, b.1863, d.1947.

Forefathers' Day, USA, celebrating the landing (1620) of the Pilgrim Fathers at Plymouth Rock. Celebrated 21 Dec.

Formosa, *see* **Taiwan.**

Forester, C(ecil) S(cott), British writer , creator of the Hornblower series (*Ship of the Line,* 1938), b.1899, d.1966.

Forster, Edward Morgan, English writer (*A Passage to India*, 1924), b.1879, d.1970.

Forsyth, Rev. Alexander John, British inventor 1805 of the percussion lock, b.1768, d.1843.

Fort Duquesne, Pennsylvania, built 1754, burnt 1758.
Fortescue, Sir John, Lord Chief Justice, b.*c.*1394, d.*c.*1476.
Forth and Clyde Canal, begun 1768 by John Smeaton, b.1724, d.1792; completed 1790.
Forth Rail Bridge, Scotland, designed by Sir John Fowler, b.1817, d.1898, and Sir Benjamin Baker, b.1840, d.1907; constructed 1883–90 by Sir William Arrol, b.1839, d.1913.
Forth Road Bridge, construction begun 21 Nov. 1958, completed 1964.
Fort Sumter, Battle of, American Civil War, fought 12 to 14 April 1861.
Foscolo, Ugo, Italian writer (*Sepolcri*, 1807), b.1778, d.1827.
Fosse, Robert Louis (Bob), American dancer, director and choreographer (*Cabaret*, 1973), b.1927, d.1987.
Fosse Way, Lincoln to Exeter, Roman road begun as frontier line against raiding forces by Publius Ostorius Scapula AD 47.
Foster, Birket, English artist, b.1825, d.1899.
Foster, Stephen Collins, American song-writer (*Old Folks at Home*), b.1826, d.1864.
Foucault, Michel, French philosopher, psychologist and social critic (*Madness and Civilization*, 1961), b.1926, d.1984.
Foucault pendulum, to measure rotation of the Earth, constructed 1851 by the French scientist, Jean Foucault, b.1819, d.1868.
Foulis, Robert, Scottish bookseller and printer, b.1707, d.1776.
Fountains Abbey, Cistercian house in Yorkshire, founded 1132; building completed 1526.
Fouquet, Jean, French painter (miniatures in *Book of Hours*), b.*c.*1415, d.*c.*1481.
Fouquier-Tinville, Antoine Quentin, French revolutionary leader, b.1747, guillotined 1795.
Fourier, François Marie Charles, French socialist, b.1772, d.1837.
Fourier, Jean Baptiste Joseph, Baron, French mathematician, b.1768, d.1830.
'Fournier, Alain' (Henri Fournier), French writer (*Le Grand Meaulnes*, 1913), b.1886, killed in action 1914.
Fourth Republic, France, constitution came into force 1946; collapsed 1958.
Fowler, Henry Watson, expert on English usage, b.1858, d.1933.
Fowler, Sir John, English engineer, b.1817, d.1898.
Fowler, John, English engineer and inventor, b.1826, d.1864.
Fox, Charles James, British statesman, b.1749, d.1806.

Fox, George, English founder (1647) of the Society of Friends (Quakers), b.1624, d.1690.

Foxe's *Book of Martyrs* (1554–59), written by the English historian John Foxe, b.1516, d.1587.

Fra Angelico (Fra Giovanni da Fiesole), Italian painter, b.c.1387, d.1455.

Fracastoro, Girolamo, Italian physician, b.1483, d.1553.

Fragonard, Jean Honoré, French painter (*The Swing*), b.1732, d.1806.

Frame, Janet (Janet Paterson Frame Cluthal), New Zealand novelist and poet (*An Angel at my Table*, 1984), b.1924.

Frampton, Sir George, English sculptor (*Peter Pan*), b.1860, d.1928.

'France, Anatole' (Jacques Anatole Thibault), French novelist (*Penguin Island*, 1908), b.1844, d.1924.

France: monarchy, Merovingian (481–751), Carolingian (751–987), Capetian (987–1328), Valois (1328–1589), (Bourbon (1589–1792); 1st republic 1793–1804; 1st empire 1804–14; restored monarchy 1814–48; 2nd republic 1848–52; 2nd empire 1852–70; 3rd republic 1871–1940; German occupation and Vichy regime 1940–44; 4th republic 1946–58; 5th republic since 1958.

Francesca, Piero della, Italian painter (*Battista Sforza*), b.c.1415, d.1492.

Francesca da Rimini, Italian heroine, wife of Giovanni Malatesta, murdered c.1285.

Francis I, Holy Roman emperor (1745–65), b.1708, d.1765.

Francis II, Holy Roman emperor (1792–1806), b.1768, d.1835.

Francis I, king of France (1515–47), b.1494, d.1547.

Francis II, king of France (1559–60), b.1544, d.1560.

Francis Borgia, St, general of the Society of Jesus, b.1510, d.1572.

Francis de Sales, St, b.1567, d.1622.

Franciscan Order, founded 1208 by St Francis of Assisi; constitution established 1209.

Francis of Assisi, St, b.c.1182, d.1226.

Francis Xavier, St, b.1506, d.1552.

Franck, César, Belgian-born composer (*Le Chasseur Maudit*, 1882), b.1822, d.1890.

Franco (Francisco Franco Bahamonde), dictator of Spain 1939–75, b.1892, d.1975.

Franco-Prussian War, began July 1870, ended Feb. 1871.

Frank, Anna, Jewish diarist (*Diary* published 1947), b.1929, d. in Belsen 1945.

Frank, Bruno, German novelist (*Trenck*, 1926), b.1887, d.1945.

Frank, Leonhard, German novelist (*Karl und Anna*, 1928), b.1882, d.1961.

Frankenstein, monster from the novel by Mary Shelley, written 1816–18; filmed in numerous versions since 1908, most memorably in the version by Hollywood director James Whale 1931.

Frankfurter, Felix, American Supreme Court judge, b.1882, d.1965.

Franklin, Benjamin, American statesman, b.1706, d.1790.

Franklin, Sir John, Arctic explorer, b.1786, d.1847.

Franz, Robert, German composer, b.1815, d.1892.

Franz Ferdinand, Austrian archduke, b.1863, assassinated 1914.

Franz Joseph, Austrian emperor (1848–1916), b.1830, d.1916.

Franz Joseph Land, Arctic archipelago, discovered 1873 by the German explorer Karl Weyprecht, b.1838, d.1881.

Fraser, John Malcolm, Australian statesman (prime minister 1975–83), b.1930.

Fraser, Simon, American-born explorer of Canada, b.*c.*1776, d.1862.

Fraser River, British Columbia, discovered 1793 by the explorer Sir Alexander Mackenzie.

Fraunhofer lines, in solar spectrum, discovered by the English scientist William Wollaston, b.1766, d.1828, studied by German physicist Joseph von Fraunhofer, b.1787, d.1826.

Frazer, Sir James George, Scottish writer (*The Golden Bough*, 1890), b.1854, d.1941.

Fréchette, Louis Honoré, French Canadian writer, b.1839, d.1908.

Fredegunde, Frankish queen, b.*c.*546, d.*c.*598.

Frederick I (Barbarossa), Holy Roman emperor, b.*c.*1123, d.1190.

Frederick II, Holy Roman emperor (1212–50), b.1194, d.1250.

Frederick III, Holy Roman emperor (1440–93), b.1415, d.1493.

Frederick I, king of Denmark (1523–33), d.1533.

Frederick II, king of Denmark (1559–88), b.1534, d.1588.

Frederick III, king of Denmark (1648–70), b.1609, d.1670.

Frederick IV, king of Denmark (1699–1730), b.1671, d.1730.

Frederick V, king of Denmark (1746–66), b.1723, d.1766.

Frederick VI, king of Denmark (1808–39), b.1768, d.1839.

Frederick VII, king of Denmark (1848–63), b.1808, d.1863.
Frederick VIII, king of Denmark (1906–12), b.1843, d.1912.
Frederick IX, king of Denmark (1947–72), b.1899, d.1972.
Frederick I, king of Prussia (1701–13), b.1657, d.1713.
Frederick II, the Great, king of Prussia (1740–86), b.1712, d.1786.
Frederick III, emperor of Germany, b.1831, d.1888.
Fredericksburg, Battle of, American Civil War, 13 Dec. 1862.
Frederick William I, king of Prussia (1713–40), b.1688, d.1740.
Frederick William II, king of Prussia (1786–97), b.1744, d.1797.
Frederick William III, king of Prussia (1797–1840), b.1770, d.1840.
Frederick William IV, king of Prussia (1840–61), b.1795, d.1861.
Frederick William the Great, Elector of Brandenburg, b.1620, d.1688.
Free Church of Scotland, formed 1843.
Freedom, British periodical, began publication 1886.
Freeman, Edward Augustus, English historian, b.1823, d.1892.
Freemasonry, derived from Lodges of English and Scottish masons in the 17th century; Mother Grand Lodge inaugurated in London 1717.
Freetown, Sierra Leone capital, first settled 1787.
Freiligrath, Ferdinand, German poet, b.1810, d.1876.
Fremont, John Charles, American explorer, b.1813, d.1890.
French, John, Earl of Ypres, English field-marshal, b.1852, d.1925.
French Equatorial Africa, former French Overseas Territories of Chad, Gabon, Middle Congo, and Ubangi-Shari (1910–58); first settled 1839; assumed present name 1910.
French Foreign Legion, first formed 1831.
French Guiana, South America, first settled 1604; became Department of France 1947.
French language, earliest known document, the 'Strasbourg Oaths', dated 842.
French Revolution, began June 1789; Consulate established Nov. 1799.
French Revolutionary Calendar, began 21–22 Sept. 1792, ended 31 Dec. 1805.
French Revolutionary Era, First, 1792–1804.
French Revolutionary Wars, 1792–1802.
French Somaliland, *see* **Djibouti.**

French West Africa, former group of French Overseas Territories (1895–1958) comprising Senegal, Mauritania, French Sudan, Burkina-Faso, Niger, French Guinea, Ivory Coast, Dahomey.

Freneau, Philip, American poet, b.1752, d.1832.

Frenssen, Gustav, German novelist (*Jorn Uhl*, 1901), b.1863, d.1945.

Frere, Sir Bartle, Scottish-born statesman, b.1815, d.1884.

Frescobaldi, Girolamo, Italian organist and composer, b.1583, d.1643.

Freud, Anna, Austrian psychologist, daughter of Sigmund, b.1895, d.1982.

Freud, Sigmund, Austrian pioneer psychoanalyst (*The Interpretation of Dreams*, 1900), b.1856, d.1939.

Freytag, Gustav, German writer (*Soll und Haben*, 1855), b.1816, d.1895.

Frick, Henry Clay, American industrialist, b.1849, d.1919.

Fricker, Racine, English composer (*Rapsodia concertante*, 1954), b.1920, d.1990.

Friends, Society of (Quakers), founded 1647 by the Englishman George Fox, b.1624, d.1690.

Frimaire, French revolutionary calendar month, 21 Nov. to 20 Dec.

Friml, Rudolf, Czech composer (*Katinka*, 1915), b.1879, d.1972.

Frith, William, English painter (*Derby Day*), b.1819, d.1909.

Frobisher, Sir Martin, English navigator, b.*c.*1535, d.1594.

Froebel System, of kindergarten education, founded 1816 by the German educationalist Friedrich Wilhelm August Froebel, b.1782, d.1852.

Froissart, Jean, French historian (*Chroniques*), b.*c.*1337, d.1410.

Fromentin, Eugène, French artist and writer, b.1820, d.1876.

Fronde, The, French civil war, begun 1648, ended 1653.

Frontenac, Louis de Buade, Comte de, French statesman, b.1620, d.1698.

Fronto, Marcus Cornelius, Roman orator, b.*c.*100, d.*c.*166.

Frost, Robert, American poet, b.1874, d.1963.

Froude, James Anthony, English historian (*History of England*, 1856–70), b.1818, d.1894.

Fructidor, French revolutionary calendar month, 18 Aug. to 16 Sept.

Frumentius, St, apostle of Ethiopia in 4th century; feast celebrated 27 Oct.

Fry, Christopher, English playwright (*The Lady's not for Burning*, 1948), b.1907.
Fry, Elizabeth, English Quaker social reformer, b.1780, d.1845.
Fry, Joseph, English Quaker businessman, b.1728, d.1787.
Fry, Roger, English painter and art critic, b.1866, d.1934.
Fuad I, king of Egypt (1922–36), b.1868, d.1936.
Fuad II, Ahmed, king of Egypt (1952–54), b.1950.
Fuentes, Carlos, Mexican writer and diplomat (*The Old Gringo*, 1985), b.1928.
Fulk, count of Anjou and king of Jerusalem, b.1092, d.1143.
Fuller, Thomas, English religious historian, b.1608, d.1661.
Fulton, Robert, American inventor of the steamship, b.1765, d.1815.
Fulvia, wife of Marc Antony, d.40 BC.
Furfural, solvent, discovered by the German scientist Johann Wolfgang Döbereiner, b.1780, d.1849.
Furness, Christopher, Baron Furness, British shipowner, b.1852, d.1912.
Furniss, Harry, Irish-born humorous artist, b.1854, d.1925.
Furtwängler, Wilhelm, German conductor, b.1886, d.1954.
Fuseli, Henry, Swiss-born painter and illustrator, b.1741, d.1825.
Fustel de Coulanges, Numa Denis, French historian, b.1830, d.1889.
Futurism, art movement, identified 1909 by the Italian poet Filippo Tommaso Marinetti, b.1878; movement disintegrated *c.*1915.

G

Gabin, Jean (Jean Alexis Montgorgé), French actor (*Pépé le Moko,* 1937), b.1904, d.1976.

Gable, Clark (William Gable), American film actor (*Gone with the Wind,* 1939), b.1901, d.1960.

Gabon, W. central Africa; first settled by the French 1839; made part of the French Congo 1888; became independent 1960.

Gaboriau, Emile, French novelist (*Monsieur Lecoq*, 1869), b.1835, d.1873.

Gabriel, Jacques Ange, French architect b.c.1698, d.1782.

Gaddi, Taddeo, Italian painter (*Life of the Virgin*), d.1366.

Gadolinium, chemical element, first isolated 1880 by the Swiss chemist Jean Charles Galissard de Marignac, b.1817, d.1894.

Gaelic League, founded in Dublin 1893.

Gagarin, Yuri, Soviet cosmonaut, first person in space, 12 April 1961, b.1934, d.1968.

Gage, Thomas, English general, b.1721, d.1787.

Gainsborough, Thomas, English painter (*Mrs Siddons*), b.1727, d.1788.

Gaitskell, Hugh, British statesman, b.1906, d.1963.

Galápagos Islands, archipelago in the Pacific, discovered by the Spanish 1535; annexed by Ecuador 1832.

Galba, Roman emperor (68–69), b.3 BC, assassinated AD 69.

Galbraith, John Kenneth, American economist and author (*The Affluent Society,* 1958), b.1908.

Galen, Claudius, Greek physician, b.c.130, d.c.201.

Galerius, Roman emperor (305–311), d.311.

Galiani, Ferdinando, Italian economist, b.1728, d.1787.

Galicia, ruled by Poland 1372–1772, by Austria 1772–1919, by Poland 1919–39, by Soviet Union 1945–91; now part of independent republic of Ukraine.

Galileo Galilei, Italian astronomer, b.1564, d.1642.

Galle, Johann, German astronomer (observed the planet Neptune, 23 Sept. 1846), b.1812, d.1910.

Gallegos, Rómulo, Venezuelan writer (*Dona Barbara*, 1929), b.1884, d.1969.

Galli-Curci, Amelita, Italian operatic singer, b.1882, d.1963.

Galliéni, Joseph Simon, French statesman, b.1849, d.1916.

Gallienus, Roman emperor (253–268), assassinated 268.

Gallipoli, Turkey, World War I, first Allied landings 25 April 1915; withdrawal 8 Jan. 1916.

Gallitzin, Dmitri Augustin, Russian-born missionary in America, b.1770, d.1840.

Gallium, chemical element, first isolated 1875, by the French scientist Paul Emile Lecoq de Boisbaudran, b.1838, d.1912.

Gallon, Imperial standard, measure legalized in Britain 1824.

Gallus, Roman emperor (251–253), murdered 253.

Galsworthy, John, English novelist (*The Forsyte Saga*, 1906–22), b.1867, d.1933.

Galt, Sir Alexander Tilloch, British-born statesman in Canada, b.1817, d.1893.

Galt, John, Scottish novelist (*Annals of the Parish*, 1821), b.1779, d.1839.

Galton, Sir Francis, English scientist, b.1822, d.1911.

Galvani, Luigi, Italian scientist, b.1737, d.1798.

Galvanometer, mirror, invented by Lord Kelvin, b.1824, d.1907.

Gama, Vasco da, Portuguese explorer and navigator, reached Calicut (India) 23 May 1498, b.*c.*1460, d.1525.

Gambetta, Léon, French statesman, b.1838, d.1882.

Gambia, The, sold to English merchants by the Portuguese 1588; made an independent British Crown Colony 1843; incorporated in the West African settlements 1866; again made separate Crown Colony 1888; gained independence within the Commonwealth 1965; formed the Confederation of Senegambia with Senegal 1982.

Gamma rays, discovered 1900 by Paul Villard.

Gandhi, Indira, Indian politician (prime minister 1966–77, 1980–84), b.1917, assassinated 1984.

Gandhi, Mohandas Karamchand, Indian leader, b.1869, started civil disobedience campaign in India 1 Aug. 1920, and was assassinated after Independence 30 Jan. 1948.

Gandhi, Rajiv, Indian politician (prime minister 1984–90), b.1945, assassinated 1991.

Gantt Chart, industrial management, devised by the American engineer Henry Lawrence Gantt, b.1861, d.1919.

Gapon, Georgy Apollonovich, Russian priest and politician, b.1870, murdered 1906.

Garamond, Claude, French type designer, d.1561.

Garbo, Greta (Greta Lovisa Gustafsson), Swedish-born American film actress (*Mata Hari*, 1931), b.1905, d.1990.

García Lorca, *see* **Lorca.**

Garden cities, idea introduced into England (1898) by Sir Ebenezer Howard, b.1850, d.1928; Letchworth begun 1903.

Gardiner, Samuel Rawson, English historian, b.1829, d.1902.

Gardiner, Stephen, bishop of Winchester, b.*c.*1483, d.1555.

Gardner, Ava (Lavinia), American film actress (*The Night of the Iguana*, 1964), b.1922, d.1990.

Gardner, Erle Stanley, American detective-story writer (the Perry Mason series), b.1889, d.1970.

Garfield, James Abram, 20th US president (1881), b.1831, murdered 1881.

Garibaldi, Giuseppe, Italian leader, b.1807, march to Rome 1862, d.1882.

Garland, Judy (Frances Gumm), American actress and singer (*The Wizard of Oz*, 1939), b.1922, d.1969.

Garnett, David, English novelist (*Lady into Fox*, 1922), b.1892, d.1981.

Garnett, Edward, English man of letters, b.1868, d.1937.

Garnier, Francis, French explorer, b.1839, killed 1873.

'Garofalo, Il', Italian painter, b.1481, d.1559.

Garrick, David, English actor, b.1717, d.1779.

Garrison, William Lloyd, American abolitionist, b.1805, d.1879.

Garter, Order of the, founded by Edward III *c.*1348.

Garth, Sir Samuel, English poet (*The Dispensary*, 1699), b.1661, d.1719.

Garvin, James Louis, Irish-born journalist (edited *The Observer* 1908–42), b.1868, d.1947.

Gary, Indiana, founded 1905 by the US Steel Corporation, and named after Elbert Henry Gary, b.1846, d.1927.

Gas, coal, first produced in quantity by the Scottish inventor William Murdock, b.1754, d.1839.

Gas Light and Coke Company, first gas company, granted charter 1812.

Gas masks, issued to civilians in Britain 1939.

Gas, poison, first used in World War I by Germans 22 April 1915; first used by British 25 Sept. 1915.

Gas-turbined powered car, first, built by the British Rover Company 1950.

Gascoigne, George, English poet (*Jocasta*, 1575), b.*c.*1525, d.1577.

Gaskell, Mrs Elizabeth, English novelist (*Cranford*, 1853), b.1810, d.1865.

Gassendi, Pierre, French scientist, b.1592, d.1655.

Gatling gun, invented 1861–62 by the American engineer Richard Jordan Gatling, b.1818, d.1903.
GATT (General Agreement on Tariffs and Trade), signed 1947 by 23 nations; 96 nation members by 1990.
Gatty, Harold Charles, Australian-born pioneer aviator, b.1903, d.1957.
Gauden, John, bishop of Worcester, theologian and probable author of *Eikon Basilike* (1649), b.1605, d.1662.
Gaudi, Antoni, Catalan architect, b.1852, d.1926.
Gaudier-Brzeska, Henri, French sculptor, b.1891, killed in action 1915.
Gauguin, Paul, French painter, b.1848, d.1903.
Gaul (Ancient France), Roman conquest completed 51 BC.
Gaunt, John of, Duke of Lancaster, b.1340, d.1399.
Gauss, Karl Friedrich, German mathematician, b.1777, d.1855.
Gautier, Théophile, French writer (*Mlle de Maupin*, 1835), b.1811, d.1872.
'Gavarni, Paul' (Hippolyte Chevalier), French humorous artist, b.1804, d.1866.
Gaveston, Piers, Earl of Cornwall, favourite of Edward II, executed 1312.
Gay, John, English writer (*The Beggar's Opera*, 1728), b.1685, d.1732.
Gay-Lussac, Joseph Louis, French scientist, b.1778, d.1850.
Gdansk *see* **Danzig.**
Ged, William, Scottish inventor 1725 of stereotyping, b.1690, d.1749.
Geddes, Andrew, Scottish painter, b.1783, d.1839.
Geddes, Sir Eric, British statesman, b.1875, d.1937.
Geertgen Van Haarlem (Geertgen tot Sint Jans), Dutch painter (*The Bones of St John the Baptist*), b.c.1462, d.c.1490.
Geiger counter, invented 1908 by the scientists Hans Geiger, b.1882, d.1945, and Lord Rutherford, b.1871, d.1937.
Geikie, Sir Archibald, Scottish geologist, b.1835, d.1924.
Geissler's tube, invented by the German scientist Heinrich Geissler, b.1814, d.1879.
Gelasius, St, pope 492–496, d.496.
Gelasius II (John of Gaeta), pope 1118–19, d.1119.
General Agreement on Tariffs and Trade, *see* **GATT.**
General Medical Council, London, held first meeting 23 Nov. 1858.
General Strike, United Kingdom, 3–13 May 1926.

Genet, Jean, French writer (*Les Bonnes*), b.1910, d.1986.
Geneva Convention, establishing the International Red Cross, held 1864.
Geneviève, St, patron saint of Paris, d.512.
Genghis Khan (Temujin), Mongol ruler, b.1162, d.1227.
Genlis, Stéphanie Félicité Ducrest de St Aubin, Comtesse de, French writer (*Mémoires*, 1825), b.1746, d.1830.
Genovesi, Antonio, Italian philosopher, b.1712, d.1769.
Gentile da Fabriano, Italian painter, b.*c.* 1370, d.1427.
Gentleman's Magazine, The, founded 1731 by 'Sylvanus Urban' (Edward Cave), b.1691, d.1754.
Gentlemen-at-Arms, the sovereign's personal bodyguard, established by King Henry VIII, 1509.
Geoffrey of Monmouth, British divine and historian, b.*c.* 1100, d.1154.
Geographical Society, Royal, London, founded 1830 by Sir John Barrow, b.1764, d.1848.
Geologists' Association, London, founded 17 Dec. 1858.
Geometry, descriptive, study founded 1771 by the French mathematician Gaspard Monge, b.1746, d.1818.
George, Henry, American propounder of the 'single-tax' system (*Progress and Poverty*, 1879), b.1839, d.1897.
George, Stefan, German poet, b.1868, d.1933.
George I, elector of Hanover (1698–1727) and king of Great Britain (1714–27), b.1660, d.1727.
George II, elector of Hanover and king of Great Britain (1727–1760), b.1683, d.1760.
George III, elector of Hanover (1760–1815), king of Hanover (1815–20) and king of Great Britain (1760–1820), b.1738, d.1820.
George IV, Prince Regent (1812–20), king of Hanover and king of Great Britain (1820–30), b.1762, d.1830.
George V, king of Great Britain (1910–36), b.1865, d.1936.
George VI, king of Great Britain (1936–52), b.1895, d.1952.
George I, king of Greece (1863–1913), b.1845, assassinated 1913.
George II, king of Greece (1922–23), b.1890, d.1947.
George Cross and George Medal, British order instituted 23 Sept. 1940.
George Washington Bridge, New York to New Jersey, constructed 1927–31.
Georgia, USA, founded as a colony 1733; entered Union 1788.
Georgia (Gruzia, in Caucasus), acknowledged Russian suzerainty 1783; Soviet Socialist Republic, USSR, declared independent

1918; became a constituent republic of the USSR 1936; became independent republic on dissolution of the USSR April 1991.

Gerard, archbishop of York (1100–08), d.1108.

Gerard, John, English herbalist, b.1545, d.1612.

Gerard, John, English Jesuit, b.1564, d.1637.

Gerhardie, William, English writer (*The Polyglots*, 1925), b.1895, d.1977.

Géricault, Théodore, French artist, b.1791, d.1824.

German, Sir Edward, English composer (*Merrie England*, 1902), b.1862, d.1936.

German silver, alloy, discovered by the German scientist Ernst Augustus Geitner, b.1783, d.1852.

Germanicus, Roman soldier, b.15 BC, d. AD 19.

Germanium, chemical element, first isolated 1886 by the German chemist Clemens Alexander Winkler, b.1838, d.1904.

Germany, separated from France by Treaty of Verdun (843); ruled by emperors, Saxon (919–1024), Salian (1024–1125), Welf and Hohenstaufen (1125–1254), Hapsburg and Luxemburg (1273–1457), Hapsburg (1457–1806); Confederation of Rhine (1806–12); German Confederation (1812–66); North German Confederation (1867–71); German Empire (Hohenzollern) (1871–1918); Weimar Republic (1919–33); 'Third Empire' (Nazi Regime) (1933–45); Allied Occupation after 1945; Bizonia 1946 and Trizonia 1947 became German Federal Republic 1949; Russian Zone became German Democratic Republic 1949; end of the Cold War and opening of the Berlin Wall 1989 led to German reunification 1 July 1990.

Gerry, Elbridge Thomas, American founder 1874 of the American Society for the Prevention of Cruelty to Children, b.1837, d.1927.

Gershwin, George, American composer (*Rhapsody in Blue*, 1924), b.1898, d.1937.

Gerson, Jean Charlier de, French theologian, b.1363, d.1429.

Gerstäcker, Friedrich, German travel writer, b.1816, d.1872.

Gertrude, St, b.1256, d.c.1301.

Gervase of Canterbury, English historian, lived in the second half of the 12th century.

Gesenius, Heinrich Friedrich Wilhelm, Hebrew lexicographer, b.1786, d.1842.

Gesner, Konrad von, Swiss bibliographer and naturalist, b.1516, d.1565.

Gettysburg, Battle of, American Civil War, 1 to 3 July 1863; **Address of**, delivered by Abraham Lincoln 19 Nov. 1863.
Ghana (formerly Gold Coast), West Africa, settled by the Portuguese 1482; British colony established 1874; united with British Togoland 1957 and became republic within the Commonwealth 1960.
Ghazali, Abu Hamid Mohammed al (Algazel), Muslim theologian, b.1058, d.1111.
Ghent, Treaty of, between the USA and Great Britain (ending the War of 1812), signed 24 Dec. 1814.
Ghent, University of, founded by King William of Württemberg 1816.
Ghent Cathedral, built 1274–1554 (crypt 941).
Ghiberti, Lorenzo, Italian sculptor, b.c.1378, d.1455.
Ghirlandaio (Domenico Curradi), Italian painter (*Adoration of the Shepherds*), b.1449, d.1494.
Gibbon, Edward, English historian (*The Decline and Fall of the Roman Empire*, 1766–88), b.1737, d.1794.
Gibbons, Grinling, Dutch-born sculptor, b.1648, d.1720.
Gibbons, Orlando, English composer (*Fantasies*, 1610), b.1583, d.1625.
Gibbs, James, Scottish architect, b.1682, d.1754.
Gibbs, Sir Vicary, English judge, b.1751, d.1820.
Gibraltar, settled 711; conquered by Spain 1462; captured by British 1704 and ceded by Spain to Britain 1713.
Gibson, John, Welsh sculptor, b.1790, d.1866.
Gide, André, French writer (*Les Faux-Monnayeurs*, 1926), b.1869, d.1951.
Gielgud, Sir John, English actor, b.1904.
Gierke, Otto von, German legal and political thinker, b.1841, d.1921.
Gieseking, Walter, French pianist, b.1895, d.1956.
Gifford, William, English writer and editor, b.1756, d.1826.
Gigli, Beniamino, Italian operatic singer, b.1890, d.1957.
Gilbert, Sir Alfred, English sculptor (*Eros*, in Piccadilly Circus), b.1854, d.1934.
Gilbert, Sir Humphrey, English explorer, b.c.1539, drowned at sea 1583.
Gilbert, William, English pioneer in magnetism (*De Magnete*, 1600), b.c.1540, d.1603.
Gilbert, Sir William Schwenk, English playwright (*Trial by Jury*, 1875), b.1836, d.1911.

Gilbert and Ellice Islands, Western Pacific, proclaimed a British protectorate 1892; annexed by Britain 1915 and remained a British colony until 1975; achieved full independence 1979.
Gilbertines, English religious order, founded at Sempringham (Lincs.) 1135 by St Gilbert, b.1083, d.1139.
Gildas, St, British historian, b.*c.*500, d.570.
Gill, Eric, English artist, b.1882, d.1940.
Gillespie, Dizzy (John Birks), American jazz trumpeter, band-leader and composer, b.1917, d.1992.
Gillray, James, English political caricaturist, b.1757, d.1815.
Gilmore, Patrick Sarsfield, Irish-born bandmaster and composer (*When Johnny Comes Marching Home*, 1863), b.1829, d.1892.
Ginkgo tree, found in Japan (1690) by Kaempfer, introduced into Europe 1730.
Giordano, Luca, Italian painter, b.1632, d.1705.
Giordano, Umberto, Italian composer (*Andrea Chénier*, 1896), b.1867, d.1948.
Giorgione, Italian painter, b.*c.*1478, d.1511.
Giotto di Bondone, Italian painter, b.*c.*1267, d.1337.
Giraldus Cambrensis, Welsh historian, b.*c.*1146, d.*c.*1220.
Giraudoux, Jean, French writer (*Amphitryon 38*, 1929), b.1882, d.1944.
Girl Guides and Girl Scouts, World Association of, formed in London 1928.
Girl Guides Association, movement formed in Britain 1910.
Girl Scouts, USA, founded 1912 by Mrs Juliette Gordon Low, b.1860, d.1927.
Girondins, group in French Revolution 1791–94.
Girtin, Thomas, English artist (*Bolton Bridge,* 1801), b.1775, d.1802.
Girton College, Cambridge University, founded by Miss Emily Davies and others 1866; College opened 16 Oct. 1869, as the College for Women. Acquired present name and site 1872.
Giscard d'Estaing, Valery, French politician (president of France 1974–81), b.1926.
Gish, Lillian, American film and stage actress (*Broken Blossoms,* 1919), b.1896, d.1992.
Gissing, George, English novelist (*The Private Papers of Henry Ryecroft*, 1903), b.1857, d.1903.
Giulio Romano, Italian artist, b.*c.*1496, d.1546.
Gjellerup, Karl Adolf, Danish writer (*Romulus*, 1884), b.1857, d.1919.

Gladstone, Herbert John, Viscount, British statesman, b.1854, d.1930.

Gladstone, William Ewart, British statesman (prime minister 1868–74, 1880–85, 1886, 1892–94), b.1809, d.1898.

Gland secretion, discovered 1889 by Mauritius-born Charles Edouard Brown-Séquard, b.1817, d.1894.

Glanvill, Joseph, English theologian (*The Vanity of Dogmatising*, 1661), b.1636, d.1680.

Glanvill, Ranulf, English statesman, d.1190.

Glasgow Chamber of Commerce, oldest British chamber of commerce, founded 1783.

Glasgow University, founded 1450.

Glass, blown glass discovered *c.*30 BC; English glass industry established *c.*1226; plate-glass first made commercially in France.

Glass, Philip, American composer (*Einstein on the Beach*, 1976), b.1937.

Glauber's salts, discovered by the German scientist Johann Rudolf Glauber, b.1604, d.1668.

Glazunov, Aleksandr Konstantinovich, Russian composer (*Raymonda*, 1898), b.1865, d.1936.

Glencoe, Massacre of, Scotland, 13 Feb. 1692.

Glidden, Joseph Farwell, American inventor 1873 of barbed wire, b.1813, d.1906.

Glinka, Mikhail Ivanovich, Russian composer (*A Life for the Tsar*, 1836), b.1804, d.1857.

'Glorious First of June', naval battle between English and French fought off Ushant 1794.

Gloucester, Humphrey, Duke of, statesman and soldier, b.1391, d.1447.

Gloucester, Statute of, decreeing necessity of trial before the granting of the Royal pardon, 1278.

Gloucester Cathedral, built 1072–1104.

Glover, Sarah Ann, English inventor *c.*1845 of the tonic sol-fa system, b.1785, d.1867.

Glucinum, chemical element, first isolated 1828 by the German scientist Friedrich Wöhler, b.1800, d.1882.

Gluck, Christoph Willibald, German composer (*Alceste*, 1767), b.1714, d.1787.

Glycerine, discovered by the French chemist Charles Adolphe Wurtz, b.1817, d.1884.

Glycogen, discovered by Claude Bernard in 1857.

Glyndebourne Festival Opera, founded 1934 by John Christie, b.1882, d.1962.

Glyndwr, Owain (Owen Glendower), Welsh rebel leader, b.*c.*1350, d.*c.*1416.

Gmelin, Leopold, German scientist, b.1788, d.1853.

Gneisenau, August Wilhelm Anton, Graf Neithardt von, Prussian military commander, b.1760, d.1831.

Gnosticism, philosophy founded by the philosopher Valentinus, d.*c.*160.

Goa, S.W. coast of India, discovered by Vasco da Gama 1498; Portuguese overseas territory from 1510; annexed by India 1961.

Gobelins, The, tapestry works near Paris, founded 1601. First director (1662), Charles Le Brun, the painter, b.1619, d.1690.

Gobineau, Joseph Arthur, Comte de, French diplomat and writer, b.1816, d.1862.

Goddard, Jean-Luc, French film director and critic (*A Bout de Souffle,* 1959), b.1930.

Gödel's theory, mathematical philosophy, propounded 1931 by the Austrian-born US mathematician Kurt Gödel, b.1906, d.1978.

Godfrey of Bouillon, crusader and conqueror of Jerusalem, b.*c.*1060, d.1100.

Godfrey, Sir Edmund Berry, English justice of the peace, b.1621, murdered 1678.

Godfrey, Thomas, America's first playwright (*The Prince of Parthia*, 1765), b.1736, d.1763.

Godiva, Lady, wife of Leofric, Earl of Mercia, traditionally rode naked through the streets of Coventry 1040, *fl.* 1040–85.

Godolphin, Sidney, **Earl of Godolphin**, British statesman, b.1645, d.1712.

Godunov, Boris, tsar of Russia (1598–1605), b.1552, d.1605.

Godwin, earl of the West Saxons, d.1053.

Godwin, William, English writer and reformer (*Political Justice*, 1793), b.1756, d.1836.

Godwin-Austen, Robert Alfred Cloyne, English geologist, b.1808, d.1884.

Godwin-Austen, Mt (K2), Himalayas, climbed by an Italian expedition 31 July 1954.

Goebbels, Paul Joseph, German Nazi leader, b.1897, committed suicide 1945.

Goering, Hermann Wilhelm, German Nazi leader, b.1893, committed suicide 1946.

Goes, Hugo van der, Flemish painter (*The Portinari Altarpiece*), d.1482.

Goethals, George Washington, American builder (1907–14) of the Panama Canal and first governor (1914–17) of the Canal Zone, b.1858, d.1928.

Goethe, Johann Wolfgang von, German scientist and writer (*Werther*, 1774), b.1749, d.1832.

Gogh, Vincent van, Dutch painter (*Sunflowers*), b.1853, committed suicide 1890.

Gogol, Nikolai, Russian writer (*Dead Souls*, 1837), b.1809, d.1852.

Gold, found in New Granada (S. America) 1537; near Sacramento (California) 1847; on the Bluc Hills (New South Wales) 12 Feb. 1851, by Edmund Hammond Hargraves, b.1815, d.1891; in Otago (New Zealand) June 1861; at Barberton (S. Africa) 1882 and Witwatersrand (S. Africa) 1884; in Rabbit Creek (Klondike) 16 Aug. 1896 by George Washington Carmack.

Gold Coast, *see* **Ghana**.

Gold rush, California 1848; Australia 1851; South Africa 1886; Klondike 1897.

Gold standard, abandoned by Great Britain 21 Sept. 1931.

Golden Bull, on German government, promulgated by the Emperor Charles IV, 1356.

Golden Gate Bridge, San Francisco, opcned 1937.

Golden Spurs, Battle of the (Battle of Courtrai), between Flemish and French 1302.

Golding, Louis, English writer (*Magnolia Street*), b.1895, d.1958.

Golding, Sir William (Gerald) (*Lord of the Flies* 1954), b.1911, d.1993.

Goldman, Emma, Russian-born anarchist, b.1869, d.1940.

Goldoni, Carlo, Italian dramatist (*The Mistress of the Inn*, 1753), b.1707, d.1793.

Goldsmith, Oliver, Irish-born writer (*The Vicar of Wakefield*, 1766), b.1728, d.1774.

Goldwyn, Samuel (Samuel Goldfish), American film producer and Hollywood mogul, b.1882, d.1974.

Golf, origins uncertain, earliest recorded allusion Scotland 1457. Introduced in the USA 1779.

Golf Club, earliest, the Honourable Company of Edinburgh Golfers, founded 1784.

Gollancz, Victor, English publisher and writer (*My Dear Timothy*), b.1893, d.1967.

Gompers, Samuel, English-born American labour leader, b.1850, d.1924.

Gomulka, Wladyslaw, Communist leader of Poland 1956–71, b.1905, d.1982.

Goncharov, Ivan, Russian novelist (*Oblomov*, 1857), b.1812, d.1891.

Goncourt, Edmond de, French writer (*La Fille Elisa*, 1878), b.1822, d.1896.

Goncourt, Jules de, French writer (with Edmond, *Germinie Lacerteux*, 1865), b.1830, d.1870.

Gondomar, Diego Sarmiento de Acuña, Count of, Spanish diplomat (English ambassador 1613–22), b.1567, d.1626.

Gongora (Luis de Gongora y Argote), Spanish poet, b.1561, d.1627.

Gonville and Caius College, Cambridge University, founded as Gonville Hall 1348 by Edmund Gonville. Assumed present name by Royal Charter 1557.

Gonzaga, Federigo, Duke of Mantua (1530–40), b.1500, d.1540.

Gooch, Sir Daniel, English railway pioneer, b.1816, d.1889.

Good Friday, Christian commemoration of the Crucifixion, the Friday before Easter.

Goodman, Benny, American jazz clarinettist and bandleader, b.1909, d.1986.

Goodwin Sands, off S.E. coast of England, first mapped by the Dutch cartographer Lucas Janszon Waghenaer 1585.

Goodwood Cup, Goodwood, first run 1812.

Googe, Barnabe, English poet, b.1540, d.1594.

'Goon Show, The', BBC radio comedy series 1949–1960.

Goossens, Léon, English oboe player, b.1896, d.1988.

Gorbachev, Mikhail Sergeevich, Soviet political leader (president 1985–91), b.1931.

Gorchakov, Prince Aleksandr Mikhailovich, Russian statesman, b.1798, d.1883.

Gordian I, Roman emperor (238), b.*c.*158, committed suicide 238.

Gordian II, Roman emperor (238), b.192, killed 238.

Gordian III, Roman emperor (238–244), b.*c.*224, murdered 244.

Gordon, Adam Lindsay, British poet, b.1833, committed suicide 1870.

Gordon, General Charles George, governor of the Sudan (1877–80), b.1833, killed 1885.

Gordon, Lord George, leader of the Gordon Riots (1770), b.1751, d.1793.

Gordon Highlanders, raised by the Marquis of Huntly (later Duke of Gordon) 1794.

Gorges, Sir Ferdinando, pioneer in North America, b.*c.*1566, d.1647.

Gorgias, Greek philosopher, b.*c.*485 d.380 BC.

Gorki, Maxim (Alexei Maximovich Peshkov), Russian novelist (*My Universities*, 1923), b.1868, d.1936.

Gort, John, Viscount, British soldier and administrator, b.1886, d.1946.

Gorton, John Grey, Australian statesman (prime minister 1968–71), b.1911.

Goschen, George Joachim, Viscount Goschen, British statesman, b.1831, d.1907.

Gosse, Sir Edmund, English writer (*Father and Son*, 1907), b.1845, d.1928.

Gothic language, first written by Bishop Wulfila (311–383); spoken in Crimea up to 1560.

Goths, first attacked Romans 214, defeated Decius 251, became Christian *c.*340, attacked by Huns 363; **Visigoths,** crossed Danube 376, defeated Valens 378, became *foederati* 382, attacked Greece 396, invaded Italy 401, sacked Rome 410, invaded Gaul 412–470, defeated by Arabs 711; **Ostrogoths,** crossed Danube and became *foederati* 380, attacked Italy 405, occupied Italy 489–493, defeated by Byzantines 536–562.

Gottfried von Strassburg, German poet (*Tristan und Isolde*), lived in the late 12th and early 13th centuries.

Gottschalk, German theologian, b.*c.*804, d.868.

Gottsched, Johann Christoph, German critic and writer, b.1700, d.1766.

Götz von Berlichingen, German leader, b.1480, d.1562.

Goucher College, Baltimore, American women's college, founded 1885; assumed present name 1910.

Goudy, Frederick William, American type designer, b.1865, d.1947.

Gough Island, probably discovered by the Portuguese navigator Pero d'Anhaya 1505.

Goujon, Jean, French sculptor, flourished during the middle of 16th century.

Gould, Sir Francis Carruthers, humorous artist, b.1844, d.1925.

Gould, Jay, American financier, b.1836, d.1892.

Gounod, Charles, French composer (*Faust*, 1859), b.1818, d.1893.

Gourmont, Remy de, French writer (*Sixtine*, 1890), b.1858, d.1915.

Gower, John, English poet (*Speculum Meditantis*), b.c.1325, d.1408.

Goya y Lucientes, Francisco de, Spanish painter (*Charles IV*), b.1746, d.1828.

Gozzi, Count Carlo, Italian playwright (*Love for Three Oranges*, 1761), b.1720, d.1806.

Gozzoli, Benozzo, Italian painter (*The Medici Family as the Magi*), b.c.1421, d.1497.

Gracchus, Tiberius Sempronius, Roman reformer, b.c.169, murdered 133 BC.

Gracchus, Caius Sempronius, b.c.160, killed 121 BC.

Grace, Princess (Grace Kelly), American film and stage actress (*Rear Window,* 1954), b.1929, m. Prince Rainier of Monaco 19 April 1956, killed in car crash 1982.

Grace, Dr William Gilbert, English cricketer, b.1848, d.1915.

Graetz, Heinrich, German historian (*History of the Jews*, 1853–76), b.1817, d.1891.

Graf, Urs, Swiss artist, b.c.1485, d.1528.

Graf Spee, German warship, trapped by the British in a naval action 13–17 Dec. 1939; scuttled 17 Dec.

Grafton, Augustus, Duke of, English statesman, b.1735, d.1811.

Graf Zeppelin, German airship, completed first transatlantic flight 15 Oct. 1928. Circumnavigated the world 15–29 Aug. 1929.

Graham, William Franklin (Billy), American evangelist, b.1918.

Graham, John, of Claverhouse, Viscount Dundee, soldier, b.c.1649, killed in battle 1689.

Graham, Martha, American dancer, choreographer and teacher, b.1894, d.1991.

Graham, Thomas, Baron Lynedoch, Scottish soldier, b.1748, d.1843.

Graham's Law, concerning the diffusion of gas, formulated by the Scottish chemist Thomas Graham, b.1805, d.1869.

Grahame, Kenneth, Scottish writer (*The Wind in the Willows*, 1908), b.1859, d.1931.

Grahame-White, Claude, pioneer British aviator, b.1879, d.1959.

Grainger, Percy Aldridge, Australian composer (*Spoon River*, 1930), b.1882, d.1961.

Gramont, Philibert, Comte de, French courtier, b.1621, d.1707.

Gramophone (phonograph), invented 1876 by the American Thomas Alva Edison, b.1847, d.1931.

Gramsci, Antonio, Italian Marxist political theorist, b.1891, d.1937.

Granados, Enrique, Spanish composer (*Goyescas*, 1916), b.1867, d.1916.

Grand Alliance, war of, between France and the Allies, 1688–97.

Grand Canyon National Park, Arizona, established 1919.

Grand Central Station, New York, opened 1913.

Grand Junction Canal, England, built 1793–1805.

Grand National, Liverpool, first run 1837.

Grand Prix, motor race, first held at Le Mans 1906 (and won by M. Szisz in a Renault). First held in Britain at Brooklands Aug. 1926.

Grand Trunk Canal, England, built 1766 onwards by the English engineer James Brindley, b.1716, d.1772.

Granjon, Robert, French type designer, *fl.* mid–16th century.

Grant, Cary (Archibald Leach), English-born Hollywood film actor (*Bringing Up Baby,* 1938), b.1904, d.1986.

Grant, Duncan, Scottish painter, b.1885, d.1978.

Grant, Ulysses Simpson, 18th US president (1869–77), b.1822, d.1885.

Granville, George, Earl, English statesman, b.1815, d.1891.

Granville-Barker, Harley, English playwright and critic (*Waste,* 1907), b.1877, d.1946.

Grape sugar, discovered 1799 by the French scientist Joseph Louis Proust, b.1754, d.1826.

Grass, Gunter, German writer (*The Tin Drum,* 1959), b.1927.

Grasse, François Joseph Paul, Comte de, French admiral in the West Indies, b.1722, d.1788.

Gratian, Roman emperor (375–383), b.359, assassinated 383.

Grattan, Henry, Irish reformer, b.1746, d.1820.

Graves, Robert, English writer (*I, Claudius*, 1934), b.1895, d.1985.

Gravity, Law of, established 1684 by Sir Isaac Newton, b.1642, d.1727.

Gray, Elisha, American inventor, b.1835, d.1901.

'Gray, Maxwell' (Mary Glied Tuttiet), English writer (*The Silence of Dean Maitland*, 1886), b.1847, d.1923.

Gray, Thomas, English poet (*Elegy*, 1750), b.1716, d.1771.

Great Australian Basin, largest artesian basin in the world, resources discovered in northwestern New South Wales 1878.

Great Exhibition, Crystal Palace, London, 1 May–15 Oct. 1851.
Great Fire of London, 2–6 Sept. 1666.
Great Schism, between Catholic and Orthodox churches 1054–1439 and since 1472.
Great Schism, within Catholic Church, 1378–1417.
Great Train Robbery, of Glasgow to London mail train 8 Aug. 1963 (£2.5 million); 12 of the gang were tried and convicted 1964 .
Great Trek, of Boers from Cape Colony to the Orange Free State area 1836.
Great Yarmouth, granted charter by King John 18 March 1208.
Greco, El (Domenico Theotocopuli), Cretan-born painter (*El Espolio*), b.1541, d.1614.
Greece, Ancient, Greek-speaking peoples entered Greece *c.*2000 BC; Persians crossed Bosphorus 512; campaign of Xerxes 480; Confederacy of Delos 477; Peloponnesian wars 431–404; Macedonian conquest completed 338; Roman conquest completed 133; Constantinople founded AD 330.
Greece, Modern, Turkish conquest completed 1466; achieved independence from Turkey 1821–27; monarchy 1833–1922; republic 1922–35; monarchy 1935–73; German occupation 1941–44.
Greek Orthodox Era, began 5509 BC.
Greeley, Horace, American editor and politician, b.1811, d.1872.
Green, Charles, English balloonist, b.1785, d.1870.
Green, John Richard, English historian, b.1837, d.1883.
Green, Thomas Hill, English philosopher, b.1836, d.1882.
Greenaway, Kate, English illustrator of children's books (*Mother Goose*), b.1846, d.1901.
'Greenbacks', American legal tender notes, first issued by Abraham Lincoln 5 Feb. 1862.
Green Belt Scheme, approved by the London County Council 29 Jan. 1935; came into operation 1 April 1935.
Greene, Graham, English writer (*Brighton Rock*, 1938), b.1904, d.1991.
Greene, Hugh Carleton, director-general of the BBC (1959–69), b.1910, d.1987.
Greene, Maurice, English organist and composer (*Jephthah*, 1737), b.*c.*1695, d.1755.
Greene, Robert, English writer (*Friar Bacon and Friar Bungay*, 1594), b.*c.*1560, d.1592.
Greenland, discovered *c.*982 by the Norwegian explorer Eric the Red (b.*c.*949); resettled 1721; first crossed 1888 by the Norwegian

explorer Fridtjof Nansen, b.1861, d.1930; declared a dependency of Denmark 1953; granted internal autonomy 1979.

Greenpeace, international environment protection organization founded in Canada 1969.

Greenwich Mean Time, made legal time for Great Britain 1880; made prime meridian of world 1884.

Greenwich Observatory, established by Charles II, 1675; moved to Herstmonceaux during 1950s.

Greer, Germaine, Australian author and feminist (*The Female Eunuch*, 1971), b.1939.

Greg, Sir Walter Wilson, English bibliographer, b.1875, d.1959.

Gregg, Sir Cornelius, introducer (1944) of PAYE. in Britain, b.1888, d.1959.

Gregg, John Robert, Irish-born inventor 1888 of Gregg's shorthand, b.1867, d.1948.

Gregorovius, Ferdinand, German historian, b.1821, d.1891.

Gregory, Lady Augusta, Irish patroness and playwright (*Hyacinthe Halevy*, 1909), b.1852, d.1932.

Gregory, Sir Augustus Charles, English explorer of Australia, b.1819, d.1905.

Gregory I, St, pope 590–604, b.c.540, d.604.

Gregory II, St, pope 715–731, d.731.

Gregory III, St, pope 731–741, d.741.

Gregory IV, pope 827–844, d.844.

Gregory V (Bruno), pope 996–999, b.c.971, d.999.

Gregory VI (Johannes Gratianus), pope 1045–46, d.1047.

Gregory VII, St (Hildebrand), pope 1073–85, b.c.1035, d.1085.

Gregory VIII (Mauritius Burdinus), anti-pope 1118–21.

Gregory VIII (Alberto de Mora), pope 1187, d.1187.

Gregory IX (Ugolino Conti de Segno), pope 1227–41, d.1241.

Gregory X (Tebaldo Visconti), pope 1271–76, b.1208, d.1276.

Gregory XI (Pierre Roger de Beaufort), pope 1371–18, b.1330, d.1378.

Gregory XII (Angelo Coriaro), pope 1406–15, b.c.1326, d.1417.

Gregory XIII (Ugo Buoncompagno), pope 1572–85, b.1502, d.1585.

Gregory XIV (Nicolo Sfondrato), pope 1590–91, b.1535, d.1591.

Gregory XV (Alessandro Ludovisi), pope 1621–23, b.1554, d.1623.

Gregory XII (Bartolommeo Alberto Cappellari), pope 1831–46, b.1765, d.1846.

Gregory Nazianzen, St, b.c.330, d.c.390.

Gregory of Tours, St, historian, b.c.540, d.594.

Grenadier Guards, organized on a permanent basis 1740.
Grenfell, Joyce, English actress and entertainer, b.1910, d.1979.
Grenfell, Sir Wilfred, English medical missionary, b.1865, d.1940.
Grenville, George, English statesman, b.1712, d.1770.
Grenville, Sir Richard, Captain of *The Revenge*, b.*c.*1541, d. of wounds 1591.
Gresham's Law, on the question of coinage, propounded by Sir Thomas Gresham, b.*c.*1519, d.1579.
Gretchaninov, Aleksandr, Russian-born composer (*Missa festiva*, 1939), b.1864, d.1956.
Gretna Green, Scotland, scene of runaway marriages, particularly 1754 to 1856.
Grétry, André Ernest Modeste, Belgian composer (*Andromaque*, 1780), b.1741, d.1813.
Greuze, Jean Baptiste, French painter (*The Broken Pitcher*), b.1725, d.1805.
Greville, Sir Fulke, English poet, b.1554, murdered 1628.
Greville, Charles Cavendish Fulke, English political diarist (*Memoirs*, 1875–87), b.1794, d.1865.
Grey, Charles, Earl, British statesman (prime minister 1831–34), b.1764, d.1845.
Grey, Edward, Viscount Grey of Fallodon, British statesman, b.1862, d.1933.
Grey, Lady Jane, claimant to the English throne, b.*c.*1537, proclaimed queen July 1553, beheaded 1554.
Grey, Zane, American writer (*The Last of the Plainsmen*, 1908), b.1875, d.1939.
Greyhound racing, in Britain, began at White City 20 June 1927.
Grieg, Edvard, Norwegian composer (*Peer Gynt*, 1874), b.1843, d.1907.
Grierson, Sir Robert (prototype of Scott's Sir Robert Redgauntlet), b.*c.*1655, d.1733.
Griffith, Arthur, Irish patriot, b.1872, d.1922.
Griffith, David Wark, American film producer (*The Birth of a Nation*, 1915), b.1875, d.1948.
Grillparzer, Frans, Austrian poet (*Sappho*, 1819), b.1791, d.1872.
Grimald, Nicholas, English writer (*Christus Redivivus*, 1543), b.1519, d.1562.
Grimaldi, Joseph, English clown, b.1779, d.1837.
Grimbald, St, Flemish-born abbot at Winchester, b.*c.*820, d.903.

Grimm, Jakob, German writer (*Fairy Tales*), b.1785, d.1863.
Grimm, Wilhelm Karl, German writer, b.1786, d.1859.
Grimmelshausen, Hans Jacob Christoph von, German writer (*Simplicissimus*, 1669), b.c.1625, d.1676.
Grimond, Joseph, British statesman, b.1913.
Grimthorpe, Edmund Beckett, Baron, inventor and lawyer, b.1816, d.1905.
Grindal, Edmund, English divine, b.1519, d.1583.
Gringoire, Pierre, French poet, b.*c.*1475, d.1538.
Gris, Juan, Spanish-born painter, b.1887, d.1927.
Grisi, Giulia, Italian operatic singer, b.1811, d.1869.
Grocers Company, London, origins uncertain but at least as early as 1231; Hall built 1427; first charter granted by King Edward III, 1345.
'Grock' (Adrien Wettach), Swiss clown, b.1880, d.1959.
Grocyn, William, English scholar, b.c.1446, d.1519.
Grolier, Jean, French diplomat and book collector, b.1479, d.1565.
Gropius, Walter, German-born architect, b.1883, d.1969.
Gros, Baron Antoine Jean, French painter (particularly of Napoleon), b.1771, committed suicide 1835.
Grosseteste, Robert, English theologian, b.*c.*1175, d.1253.
Grossmith, George, English actor and writer (*Diary of a Nobody*, 1892), b.1847, d.1912.
Grosz, Georg, German-born painter, b.1893, d.1959.
Grote, George, English historian, b.1794, d.1871.
Grotius, Hugo, Dutch jurist (*De jure belli et pacis*, 1625), b.1583, d.1645.
Grouchy, Emmanuel, Marquis de, French general, b.1766, d.1847.
Groundnut scheme, in Tanganyika, begun 1947.
Grove, Sir George, English compiler of the *Dictionary of Music and Musicians* (first published 1879–89), b.1820, d.1900.
Grove cell, electric battery, invented 1839 by Sir William Robert Grove, b.1811, d.1896.
Gruber, Franz Xaver, Austrian composer (*Silent Night*, 1818), b.1787, d.1863.
Grünewald, Matthias (Mathis Nithart), German painter (the Isenheim altarpiece), b.*c.*1480, d.1528.
Guadalcanal Islands, World War II, evacuated by the Japanese 9 Feb. 1943.
Guam, World War II, occupied by the Americans 21 July 1944
Guardi, Francesco, Italian painter, b.1712, d.1793.

Guarneri, Giuseppe Antonio, Italian violin-maker, b.1687, d.*c.*1745.

Guatemala, Central American republic, conquered by the Spanish 1523; gained independence and annexed to Mexico 1821; became independent republic 1839.

Gucci, Guccio, Italian leatherworker and designer, b.1881, d.1953.

Guelphs, German family founded by Welf, d.*c.*825.

Guericke, Otto, German scientist, b.1602, d.1686.

Guérin, Maurice de, French poet (*Le Centaurel*, *c.*1835), b.1810, d.1839.

Guernica, Basque capital in N.W. Spain, savagely bombed during the Spanish Civil War, 26 April 1937.

Guernsey, Channel Islands, acquired 933 by William, Duke of Normandy, d.943, and attached to England since 1066.

Guesclin, Bertrand du, French leader, b.*c.*1320, d.1380.

Guest, Lady Charlotte (later Lady Charlotte Schreiber), translator of the *Mabinogion*, b.1812, d.1895.

Guevara, Ernesto Che, Argentinian revolutionary communist leader, b.1928, shot 1967.

Guggenheim, Meyer, American financier, b.1828, d.1905.

Guiana, British, *see* **Guyana.**

Guiana, French, *see* **French Guiana.**

Guicciardini, Francesco, Italian diplomat and historian, b.1483, d.1540.

Guido d'Avezzo, pioneer in musical instruction and notation, b.*c.*995, d.1050.

Guido Reni, Italian painter (*Deeds of Hercules*), b.1575, d.1642.

Guilbert, Yvette, French actress, b.1869, d.1944.

Guild Socialism, in Britain, National Guilds League formed 1915; movement collapsed by 1924.

Guillotine, introduced 1792 by the French doctor Joseph Guillotin, b.1738, d.1814.

Guinea, colony of French Guinea from 1890; became independent republic 1958.

Guinea-Bissau, formerly Portuguese Guinea, discovered 1446 by Nuno Tristão; made a separate colony of Portugal 1879; became an independent republic in 1974.

Guinness, Sir Alec, English actor, b.1914.

Guinness, Sir Benjamin Lee, Irish brewer, b.1798, d.1868.

Guise, François de Lorraine, Duc de, French soldier and politician, b.1519, assassinated 1563.

Guise, Henri de Lorraine, Duc de, French soldier, b.1550, assassinated 1588.

Guitry, Sacha, French actor and playwright (*Le Veilleur de nuit*, 1911), b.1885, d.1957.

Guizot, François Pierre Guillaume, French statesman and historian, b.1787, d.1874.

Gun, traditionally invented 1313 by Berthold Schwartz.

Gunpowder, introduced into Europe by 1300.

Gunpowder Plot, against the Houses of Parliament 5 Nov. 1605.

Gunter, Edmund, English mathematician, b.1581, d.1626.

Gurney, Sir Goldsworthy, English inventor, b.1793, d.1875.

Gustavus I, king of Sweden (1523–60), b.1496, d.1560.

Gustavus II, king of Sweden (1611–32), b.1594, killed in battle 1632.

Gustavus III, king of Sweden (1771–92), b.1746, assassinated 1792.

Gustavus IV, king of Sweden (1792–1809), b.1778, d.1837.

Gustavus V, king of Sweden (1907–50), b.1858, d.1950.

Gustavus VI, king of Sweden (1950–73), b.1882, d.1973.

Gutenberg, Johannes, German founder *c.*1440 of Western printing, b.*c.*1397, d.1468.

Guthrie, Thomas, Scottish reformer, b.1803, d.1873.

Guthrie, Woody, American folk singer and political activist, b.1912, d.1967.

Guyana (formerly British Guiana), N.E. South America, became a British colony 1831, and an independent republic within the Commonwealth 1966.

Guy de Lusignan, king of Jerusalem (1186–92), d.1194.

Guy Fawkes Day, 5 Nov., commemorating the attempt on the Houses of Parliament by the English conspirator Guy Fawkes, b.1570, executed 1606.

Guyon, Jeanne, French mystic, b.1648, d.1717.

Guyot, Arnold, Swiss geographer, b.1807, d.1884.

Guys, Constantin, French artist, b.1802, d.1892.

Guy's Hospital, London, founded 1722 by the English Thomas Guy, b.*c.*1644, d.1724.

Gwyn, Nell, mistress of King Charles II, b.1650, d.1687.

Gyrocompass, invented 1915 by the American inventor Elmer Ambrose Sperry, b.1860, d.1930.

Gyroscope, invented 1852 by the French scientist Jean Bernard Leon Foucault, b.1819, d.1868.

H

Haakon I, the Good, king of Norway (935–961), killed in battle 961.

Haakon II, the Broadshouldered, king of Norway (1161–62), b.1047, d.1162.

Haakon III, king of Norway (1202–04).

Haakon IV, the Old, king of Norway (1217–63), b.1204, d.1263.

Haakon V, king of Norway (1299–1319).

Haakon VI, king of Norway (1343–80), b.1340, d.1386.

Haakon VII, king of Norway (1905–57), b.1872, d.1957.

Habberton, John, American writer (*Helen's Babies,* 1876), b.1842, d.1921.

Habeas Corpus Act, principle stated in Magna Carta 1215, confirmed by Petition of Right 1627; became law in England 27 May 1679.

Haberdashers' Company, London, origins uncertain; bye-laws drawn up 1371; granted first charter by Henry VI 1448.

Hackney carriages, used at least as early as 1636 in London; regularized by the Carriage Act 1831.

Haden, Sir Francis Seymour, English surgeon and etcher, b.1818, d.1910.

Hadow, Sir William Henry, English musicologist (*William Byrd*, 1923), b.1859, d.1937.

Hadrian, Roman emperor (117–138), b.76, d.138.

Hadrian's Wall, Roman wall across northern England, built under the governorship of Aulus Platorius Nepos, 122–126.

Haeckel, Ernst Heinrich, German naturalist, b.1834, d.1919.

Hafiz (Shams ad-Din Mohammed), Persian poet, b.*c.*1320, d.*c.*1389.

Hafnium, a metal, first isolated by the Norwegian scientist Dirk Coster and the Hungarian scientist Georg von Hevesy 1922.

Hagedorn, Friedrich von, German poet, b.1708, d.1754.

Haggard, Sir Rider, English novelist (*King Solomon's Mines,* 1885), b.1856, d.1925.

Hahn, Otto, German nuclear physicist, b.1879, d.1968.

Hahn, Reynaldo, Venezuelan composer (*Concerto provençal,* 1930), b 1875, d.1947.

Haidar Ali, Indian leader, b.*c.*1728, d.1782.

Haig, Douglas, Earl Haig, field marshal, b.1861, d.1928.

Haile Selassie (Ras Tafari), emperor of Ethiopia 1930–36, 1941–74; king 1928–30; in exile 1936–41, b.1891, d.1975.

Haiti, discovered by Christopher Columbus 6 Dec. 1492; ruled by French 1697–1792; independence proclaimed 1803; ruled by USA 1915–41; under dictatorships of Francois Duvalier ('Papa Doc') 1957–71 and Jean-Claude Duvalier 1971–86.

Hakluyt, Richard, English historian (*Voyages*, 1598–1600), b.*c.*1552, d.1616.

Haldane, John Burdon Sanderson, British scientist, b.1892, d.1964.

Haldane, John Scott, Scottish physiologist, b.1860, d.1936.

Haldane, Richard Burdon, Viscount Haldane of Cloan, British statesman and reformer, b.1856, d.1928.

Hale, Edward Everett, American storyteller (*The Man Without a Country*, 1863), poet and Unitarian minister, b.1822, d.1909.

Hale, Sir Matthew, English jurist and writer, b.1609, d.1676.

Hale, Nathan, American patriot, b.1755, hanged 1776.

Halévy, Jacques François Fromental Elie, French composer (*La Juive*, 1835), b.1799, d.1862.

Haley, Bill, American guitarist, singer and pioneer of rock 'n' roll ('Rock around the Clock', 1955), b.1927, d.1981.

Halfpenny postage, introduced in Britain 1 Oct. 1870.

Halftone engraving, first practical process invented 1878 by the American pioneer in photography Frederick Eugene Ives, b.1856, d.1937.

Halifax, Earl of, viceroy and governor-general of India (1926–31), b.1881, d.1959.

Halifax, Charles Montagu, Earl of, British statesman and writer, b.1661, d.1715.

Halifax, Nova Scotia, founded 1749.

Hall, Sir Edward Marshall, English lawyer, b.1858, d.1929.

Hall, Joseph, English theologian and writer, b.1574, d.1656.

Hall, Marshall, English physiologist, b.1790, d.1857.

Hall, Peter, British theatre director, b.1930.

Hallam, Henry, English historian, b.1777, d.1859.

Halle, Adam de la, French troubadour, b.*c.*1240, d.1287.

Hallé Orchestra, Manchester, established 1857 by Sir Charles Hallé, b.1819, d.1895. First regular public concert 30 Jan. 1858.

Halley, Edmund, English astronomer, b.1656, d.1742.

Halley's Comet, named after Edmund Halley; appeared 1456, 1531, 1607, 1682, 1758, 1835, 1910, 1986. First photographed by astronomers 1910.

Hall of Fame, New York, US national shrine, established 1900.
Hallowe'en (All-Hallows Eve), celebrated 31 Oct.
Hall's effect, electromagnetism, discovered 1879 by the American scientist Edwin Herbert Hall, b.1853, d.1921.
Hals, Frans, Dutch painter (*Laughing Cavalier*, 1624), b.c.1580, d.1666.
Hamburg-Amerika Line, founded 1847.
Hamilcar Barca, Carthaginian general, d.228 BC.
Hamilton, Alexander, American statesman, b.1757, killed in a duel 1804.
Hamilton, Emma, Lady, mistress of Lord Nelson, b.*c.*1765, d.1815.
Hamilton, Patrick, Scottish martyr, b.*c.*1504, burnt at the stake 1528.
Hamilton, Sir Robert, governor of Tasmania (1886–93), b.1836, d.1895.
Hamilton, Sir William, diplomat, archeologist (purchaser of the Portland Vase), b.1730, d.1803.
Hamlet, story of, in existence in 12th century.
Hammarskjöld, Dag, Swedish-born secretary-general of the United Nations (1953–61), b.1905, killed in air crash 1961.
Hammer action, in modern pianos, invented *c.*1710 by the Italian harpsichord-maker Bartolommeo Cristofori, b.1655, d.173.
Hammerstein, Oscar, American impresario, b.1848, d.1919.
Hammett, Dashiell, American crime-story writer (*Red Harvest*, 1929), b.1894, d.1961.
Hammond, Joan, Australian operatic singer, b.1912.
Hammond, John, English social historian, b.1872, d.1949.
Hammurabi, king of Babylonia, reigned in the 21st century BC.
Hampden, John, English parliamentarian, refused 1636–37 to pay ship-money; b.*c.*1594, killed in battle 1643.
Hampton Court, Treaty of, alliance between Queen Elizabeth I and the Prince de Condé, signed 21 Sept. 1562.
Hampton Court Conference, of English clergy, held 1604.
Hamsun, Knut, Norwegian writer (*Hunger,* 1888), b.1859, d.1952.
Han dynasty, China, 206 BC to 220 AD.
Hancock, Tony, English comedian, b.1924, committed suicide 1968.
Handel, George Frideric, German-born composer (*The Messiah*, 1742), b.1685, d.1759.

Hannibal, Carthaginian general, b.247, invaded Italy 218–203, committed suicide *c.*182 BC.
Hannington, James, first bishop of Eastern Equatorial Africa, b.1847, murdered 1885.
Hanno, Carthaginian navigator, explored W. African coast *c.*450 BC.
Hansard, record of parliamentary debates, begun 1774 by Luke Hansard, b.1752, d.1828; present series founded 1803 by William Cobbett, b.1763, d.1835.
Hanseatic League, N. German and Baltic commercial alliance, origins *c.*1140; formal alliance 1241; last meeting 1669.
Hansen, Gerhard, Norwegian scientist, b.1841, d.1912.
Hansom cab, idea patented 1834 by the English architect Joseph Aloysius Hansom, b.1803, d.1882.
Hapsburg dynasty, ruled Austria 1278–1918, Netherlands 1482–1700 (and Belgium 1713–94), Spain 1516–1700, Bohemia 1526–1918.
Hara-kiri, Japanese obligatory suicide, abolished officially 1868.
Harald I, Haarfager, king of Norway (860–933), b.850, d.933.
Harald II, Graafeld, king of Norway (961–969), murdered 969.
Harald III, Haardraade, king of Norway (1048–66), killed in battle 1066.
Harald IV, Gylle, king of Norway (1134–36), murdered 1136.
Harcourt, Sir William, British statesman, b.1827, d.1904.
Hardaknut Knutsson, king of England (1040–42), b.*c.*1019, d.1042.
Hardie, James Keir, Scottish socialist leader, b.1856, d.1915.
Harding, Warren Gamaliel, 29th US president (1921–23), b.1865, d.1923.
Harding, Stephen, St, d.1134.
Hardinge, Henry, **Viscount Hardinge**, statesman and soldier, b.1785, d.1856.
Hardwicke, Sir Cedric, English actor, b.1893, d.1964.
Hardwicke, Philip Yorke, Earl of, Lord Chancellor, b.1690, d.1764.
Hardy, Thomas, English writer (*Tess of the D'Urbevilles,* 1891), b.1840, d.1928.
Hare, Augustus, English writer (*The Story of My Life,* 1896–1900), b.1834, d.1903.
Hare, William, Irish murderer in the Burke and Hare case, d.*c.*1865.

Hargreaves' Spinning Jenny, invented *c.*1764 by the English weaver James Hargreaves, d.1778.

Harington, Sir John, English writer (*Metamorphosis of Ajax*, 1596), b.1561, d.1612.

Harleian Library, British Museum, formed by Robert Harley, Earl of Oxford, b.1661, d.1724.

Harley, Robert, Earl of Oxford, English statesman and book collector, b.1661, d.1724.

Harlow, Jean (Harlean Carpenter), film actress, Hollywood's 'blonde bombshell' (*Red Dust*, 1932), b.1911, d.1937.

Harmonium, invented 1840 by the French organ manufacturer Alexandre François Debain, b.1809, d.1877.

Harold, king of the English (1066), b.*c.*1022, killed in battle 1066.

Harold Harefoot, king of the English (1037–40), d.1040.

Harper's Ferry, Virginia, captured by John Brown, 16 Oct. 1859.

Harpignies, Henri, French painter (*View of Capri*), b.1819, d.1916.

Harris, Frank, Irish-born writer (*My Life and Loves*, 1923–27), b.1856, d.1931.

Harris, Joel Chandler, American writer (*Uncle Remus,* 1880), b.1848, d.1908.

Harris, Thomas Lake, British-born founder of the Brotherhood of the New Life, b.1823, d.1906.

Harrison, Benjamin, 23rd US president (1889–93), b.1833, d.1901.

Harrison, Sir Rex (Reginald Carey Harrison), English stage and film actor (*My Fair Lady*, 1964), b.1908, d.1990.

Harrison, William Henry, 9th US president (1841), b.1773, d.1841.

Harrison, William, English topographer (*Description of England*, 1577), b.1534, d.1593.

Hart, Lorenz, American song-writer (*With a Song in My Heart*), b.1895, d.1943.

Harte, Bret, American writer (*The Luck of Roaring Camp,* 1870), b.1839, d.1902.

Hartley, Arthur Clifford, British inventor of 'Pluto' and 'Fido', b.1889, d.1960.

Hartley, Leslie Poles, English writer (*The Shrimp and the Anemone*), b.1895, d.1972.

Hartmann von Aue, German minnesinger, b.*c.*1168, d.*c.*1217.

Harty, Sir Hamilton, English conductor, b.1879, d.1941.

Harun-al-Rashid, caliph, b.*c.*763, d.809.

Harunobu, Suzuki, Japanese artist (*The Broken Shoestring*), b.*c.*1720, d.*c.*1770.

Harvard University, founded 1636; named after the Puritan minister John Harvard, b.1607, d.1638.

Harvard University Observatory, built 1843–47.

Harvest moon, the full moon within a fortnight of 22 or 23 Sept.

Harvester, mechanical, invented 1831 by the American manufacturer Cyrus Hall McCormick, b.1809, d.1884.

Harvey, Gabriel, English poet, b.*c.*1545, d.1630.

Harvey, Thomas, Quaker relief worker and theologian, b.1812, d.1884.

Harvey, William, English discoverer of the circulation of the blood (*De Motu Cordis,* 1628), b.1578, d.1657.

Hasdrubal, Carthaginian general (brother of Hannibal), killed in battle 207 BC.

Hasek, Jaroslav, Czechslovakian writer (*The Good Soldier Schweik,* 1920–23), b.1883, d.1923.

Hastings, Warren, first English governor-general of Bengal (1774–85); tried 1788–94, b.1732, d.1818.

Hastings, Battle of, fought at Battle between the Normans and the English 14 Oct. 1066.

Hathaway, Anne, wife of William Shakespeare, b.*c.*1556, d.1623.

Hatton, Sir Christopher, lord chancellor, b.1540, d.1591.

Hauptmann, Gerhart, German playwright (*Rose Bernd*, 1903), b.1862, d.1946.

Haussmann, Georges Eugène, Baron, French town planner, b.1809, d.1891.

Havas Agency, French press agency founded 1835 by the Frenchman Charles Havas, d.1850.

Havel, Vaclav, Czech writer, also president of Czechoslovakia (1989–92), b.1936.

Havelock the Dane, early 14th-century Anglo-Danish epic.

Havelock, Sir Henry, general in India, b.1795, d.1857.

Hawaii (formerly Sandwich Islands), Pacific, discovered 1778 by Captain James Cook; formally annexed by the USA 1898; admitted to the Union 1959.

Hawes, Stephen, English poet (*Passetyme of Pleasure,* 1509), d.*c.*1523.

Hawke, Robert James Lee, Australian statesman (prime minister 1983–91), b.1929.

Hawker, Robert Stephen, English poet ('And shall Trelawny die ?'), b.1803, d.1875.

Hawking, Stephen William, British astrophysicist and author (*A Brief History of Time,* 1988), b.1942.

Hawkins, Sir John, English naval reformer and slave-trader, b.1532, d.1595.

Hawkins, Sir Richard, English admiral, b.*c.*1562, d.1622.

Hawksmoor, Nicholas, English architect, b.1661, d.1736.

Hawthorne, Nathaniel, American writer (*The Scarlet Letter,* 1850), b.1804, d.1864.

Haydn, Franz Josef, Austrian composer (*The Creation,* 1798), b.1732, d.1809.

Haydn, Joseph, English compiler of the *Dictionary of Dates* (1841), d.1856.

Haydon, Benjamin Robert, English painter (*Lazarus*), b.1786, committed suicide 1846.

Hayes, Rutherford Birchard, 19th US president (1877–81), b.1822, d.1893.

Hays, William Harrison, American film administrator, b.1879, d.1954.

Hayworth, Rita (Margarita Carmen Cansino), Hollywood film actress (*Gilda,* 1946), b.1918, d.1987.

Hazlitt, William, English essayist (*Table Talk,* 1821), b.1778, d.1830.

H-bomb, first exploded by the Americans in the Pacific 21 Nov. 1952; first Russian explosion (USSR) 12 Aug. 1953.

Healy, Timothy Michael, Irish Free State governor-general (1922–28), b.1855, d.1931.

Heaney, Seamus, Irish poet, critic and teacher, b.1939.

Heaphy, Charles, explorer in New Zealand, awarded New Zealand's first (1867) Victoria Cross, b.1820, d.1881.

Hearn, Lafcadio, naturalized Japanese writer (*Japan,* 1904), b.1850, d.1904.

Hearst, William Randolph, American newspaper publisher, b.1863, d.1951.

Heart, surgery of, pioneered by Rehn of Frankfurt in 1896.

Heart, transplant, first performed by Christiaan Barnard 1957.

Heat, latent, existence established *c.*1765 by the British scientist Joseph Black, b.1728, d.1799; dynamical theory of, suggested by experiments of Count Rumford at Munich in 1798, and postulated 1841 by James Joule, b.1818, d.1889.

Heath, Sir Edward, British statesman (prime minister 1970–74), b.1916.

Heath, Neville, English murderer, b.1917, hanged 1946.

Heavier-than-air machine, first flight made by the American brothers Orville and Wilbur Wright 17 Dec. 1903.

Heaviside, Oliver, English scientist, b.1850, d.1925.

Heavy hydrogen (Deuterium), discovered 1931 by the American chemist Harold Clayton Urey, b.1893, d.1981.

Heavy-oil engine, first used in Britain, invented by William Priestman 1885.

Heavy water, discovered 1931 by the American chemist Harold Clayton Urey, b.1893, d.1981.

Hebbel, Friedrich, German writer (*Agnes Bernauer,* 1852), b.1813, d.1863.

Heber, Reginald, English hymn-writer ('From Greenland's icy mountains'), b.1783, d.1826.

Hébert, Jacques René, French revolutionary leader, b.1757, guillotined 1794.

Hectograph, duplicating process, invented 1780 by the Scottish engineer James Watt, b.1736, d.1819.

Hedin, Sven, Swedish explorer, b.1865, d.1952.

Hegel, Georg Wilhelm Friedrich, German philosopher, b.1770, d.1831.

Hegira, Mahommed's flight from Mecca to Medina, 13 Sept. 622.

Heidegger, Martin, German philosopher, b.1889, d.1976.

Heidelberg Catechism, instigated by the Elector Frederick III; published 19 Jan. 1563 by Zacharias Ursinus, b.1536, d.1583, and Caspar Olevianus, b.1536, d.1587.

Heidelberg University, Germany, founded 1385.

Heifetz, Jascha, Russian-born violinist, b.1901, d.1987

Heine, Heinrich, German poet (*Atta Troll,* 1843), b.1797, d.1856.

Heinsius, Daniel, Dutch classical scholar, b.1580, d.1655.

Heisenberg, Werner Karl, German physicist, Nobel prize 1932, b.1901, d.1976.

Hejaz, proclaimed independent kingdom 1916; conquered by and annexed to the kingdom of Saudi Arabia 1925–26.

Helena, St, b.*c.*248, d.*c.*328.

Helena, St, South Atlantic, discovered by the Portuguese navigator João de Nova 1502; appropriated by the British East India Company 1661; vested in the Crown 1833.

Helicopter, first successful model built 1918 by the Americans Peter Cooper Hewitt, b.1861, d.1921, and F. B. Crocker.

Heliogabalus (Elagabalus), Roman emperor (218–222), b.*c.*204, assassinated 222.

Heliograph, invented by the German mathematician and astronomer Johann Karl Friedrich Gauss, b.1777, d.1855.
Heliometer, modern form invented 1754 by the English optician John Dollond, b.1706, d.1761.
Helioscope, instrument for observing the sun, invented by the American engineer Herschel Clifford Parker, b.1867.
Heliport, Britain's first, opened in London 23 April 1959.
Helium, discovered spectroscopically in sun 1868 by Sir Joseph Norman Lockyer, b.1836, d.1920; obtained 1895 by Sir William Ramsay, b.1852, d.1916.
Helium, liquid, obtained 1913 by the Dutch scientist Heike Kamerlingh Onnes, b.1853, d.1926.
Heller, Joseph, American author (*Catch 22,* 1961), b.1923.
Hellgate Bridge, New York, built 1902–03 by Austrian-born engineer Gustav Lindenthal, b.1850, d.1935.
Hellman, Lillian Florence, American playwright (*The Little Foxes,* 1939), b.1905, d.1984.
Helmholtz, Hermann von, German scientist, b.1821, d.1894.
Helsinki, capital of Finland since 1812.
Helvétius, Claude Adrien, French writer (*De l'Esprit,* 1758), b.1715, d.1771.
Hemans, Mrs Felicia Dorothea, English hymn-writer and poet (*Casabianca,* 1829), b.1793, d.1835.
Hematin, artificial blood pigment, discovered 1928 by the German scientist Hans Fischer, b.1881, d.1945.
Heming, John, English actor-manager, d.1630.
Hemingway, Ernest, American writer (*A Farewell to Arms*, 1929), b.1898, d.1961.
Hémon, Louis, French-Canadian novelist (*Marie Chapdelaine,* 1913), b.1880, d.1913.
Henderson, Alexander, Scottish religious leader, b.*c.*1583, d.1646.
Henderson, Arthur, British statesman, b.1863, d.1935.
Hendrix, Jimi (James Marshall), American rock guitarist, b.1942, d.1970.
Henley, William Ernest, English poet (*For England's Sake*, 1900), b.1849, d.1903.
Henley regatta, Henley-on-Thames, founded 1839.
Henri I, king of France (1031–60), b.*c.*1008, d.1060.
Henri II, king of France (1547–59), b.1519, d.1559.
Henri III, king of France (1574–89), b.1551, assassinated 1589.
Henri IV, king of France (1589–1610), b.1553, assassinated 1610.

'Henri V' (Henri, Comte de Chambord), claimant to the French throne, b.1820, d.1883.
Henrietta, daughter of King Charles I and Duchess of Orleans, b.1644, d.1670.
Henrietta Maria, wife of King Charles I, b.1609, d.1669.
Henry I, king of England (1100–35), b.1068, d.1135.
Henry II, king of England (1154–89), b.1133, d.1189.
Henry III, king of England (1216–72), b.1207, d.1272.
Henry IV, king of England (1399–1413), b.1367, d.1413.
Henry V, king of England (1413–22), b.1387, d.1422.
Henry VI, king of England (1422–61, 1470–71), b.1421, murdered 1471.
Henry VII, king of England (1485–1509), b.1457, d.1509.
Henry VIII, king of England (1509–47), b.1491, d.1547.
Henry II, Holy Roman emperor (1002–24), b.973, d.1024.
Henry III, Holy Roman emperor (1039–56), b.1017, d.1056.
Henry IV, Holy Roman emperor (1056–1106), b.1050, d.1106.
Henry V, Holy Roman emperor (1106–25), b.1081, d.1125.
Henry VI, Holy Roman emperor (1190–97), b.1165, d.1197.
Henry VII, Holy Roman emperor (1308–13), b.1269, d.1313.
Henry the Fowler, German king (919–936), b.*c.*875, d.936.
Henry the Navigator, Portuguese prince, b.1394, d.1460.
Henry Christophe, king of Haiti, b.1767, committed suicide 1820.
'Henry, O' (William Sydney Porter), American writer (*Cabbages and Kings*, 1904), b.1862, d.1910.
Henry, Patrick, governor of Virginia, b.1736, d.1799.
Henry, William, English chemist, b.1774, d.1836.
Henryson, Robert, Scottish poet (*Testament of Cresseid*), b.*c.*1430, d.*c.*1506.
Henschel, Sir George, German-born composer and conductor, b.1850, d.1934.
Henslowe, Philip, English theatre manager, d.1616.
Henty, George Alfred English writer for boys, b.1832, d.1902.
Hepburn, Katherine, American stage and film actress (*Guess Who's Coming to Dinner,* 1967), b.1907.
Hepplewhite, George, English cabinet-maker, d.1786.
Hepworth, Barbara, English sculptor, b.1903, d.1975.
Heraclitus, Greek philosopher, b.*c.*540, d.475 BC.
Heraclius, Byzantine emperor (610–641), b.*c.*575, d.641.
Heralds College, London, founded 1461 by King Edward IV. Chartered 1483.

Herbart, Johann Friedrich, German philosopher, b.1776, d.1841.

Herbert, George, Welsh-born poet (*The Temple,* 1633), b.1593, d.1633.

Herbert of Cherbury, Edward Herbert, Baron, English philosopher and historian, b.1583, d.1648.

Herder, Johann Gottfried, German writer (*Der Cid*, 1805), b.1744, d.1803.

Heredia, José Maria de, Cuba-born poet (*Les Trophées,* 1893), b.1842, d.1905.

Heredity, principles of, postulated 1865 by the Austrian biologist and monk Gregor Johann Mendel, b.1822, d.1884.

Hereford Cathedral, England, constructed 1079–1148 (crypt Anglo-Saxon).

Hereward the Wake, English outlaw, lived in second half of 11th century.

Hergesheimer, Joseph, American novelist (*Java Head,* 1919), b.1880, d.1954.

Heriot, George, Scottish goldsmith and royal banker, b.1563, d.1624.

Herkomer, Sir Hubert von, German-born painter, b.1849, d.1914.

Herod Agrippa, tetrarch of Galilee and Peraea, later of Judea and Samaria, b.10 BC, d. AD 44.

Herod Antipas, tetrarch of Galilee and Peraea, d.*c.*39.

Herod the Great, king of Judea, b.*c.*68, d.4 BC.

Herodotus, Greek historian, b.*c.*485, d.*c.*425 BC.

Hero of Alexandria, Greek mathematician in 1st century.

Hérold, Louis Joseph Ferdinand, French composer (*Zampa,* 1831), b.1791, d.1833.

Herrera, Ferdinando, Spanish poet, b.*c.*1534, d.1597.

Herrick, Robert, English poet (*Hesperides*, 1648), b.1591, d.1674.

Herrings, Battle of the (Battle of Rouvray), between the English and the French, 1429.

Herriot, Édouard, French statesman, b.1872, d.1957.

Herschel, Sir John Frederick William, English astronomer, b.1792, d.1871.

Herschel, Sir William, German-born astronomer, b.1738, d.1822.

Hertford College, Oxford University, founded as Hertford Hall 1282 by Elias de Hertford; incorporated as Hertford College 1740; reincorporated 1874.

Hertzog, James Barry Munnik, South African statesman (prime minister 1924–39), b.1866, d.1942.

Herzen, Aleksandr, Russian revolutionary leader, b.1812, d.1870.

Herzl, Theodor, Hungarian-born founder of Zionism (*Der Judenstaat,* 1896), b.1860, d.1904.

Herzog, Werner, German film director (*Fitzcarraldo,* 1982), b.1942.

Heseltine, Philip ('Peter Warlock'), English composer (*Capriol Suite,* 1926), b.1894, committed suicide 1930.

Hesiod, Greek poet of the 8th century BC.

Hesperia, an asteroid, discovered 1861 by the Italian astronomer Giovanni Virginio Schiaparelli, b.1835, d.1910.

Hess, Dame Myra, English pianist, b.1890, d.1965.

Hess, Rudolf, German Nazi leader, flew to Britain 1941, b.1894, committed suicide in prison 1987.

Hesse, Hermann, German writer (*Peter Camenzind,* 1904), b.1877, d.1962.

Heston, Charlton, American fim actor (*Ben Hur,* 1959), b.1923.

Hesychasts, Greek mystic movement in 14th century.

Hetton line, Co. Durham, oldest mineral railway in Britain and first real railway on a prepared surface, built 1819–22 by George Stephenson, b.1781, d.1848; opened 1822; closed 1959.

Heuristic method, of education, suggested 1884 by Professor Meiklejohn.

Heuss, Dr Theodor, president of West Germany (1949–59), b.1884, d.1963.

Hevelius, Johannes, Polish astronomer, b.1611, d.1687.

Hewlett, Maurice, English writer (*The Forest Lovers,* 1897), b.1861, d.1923.

Heyward, DuBose, American writer (*Porgy,* 1925), b.1885, d.1940.

Heywood, John, English writer (*The Four P's,* 1569), b.*c.*1497, d.*c.*1580.

Heywood, Thomas, English writer (*A Woman Killed with Kindness*), b.*c.* 1574, d.1641.

Hibbert Trust, originally for the elevation of the Unitarian ministry, founded 1847 by the British merchant Robert Hibbert, b.1770, d.1849.

'Hickock, Wild Bill' (James Butler Hickock), American pioneer, b.1837, murdered 1876.

Hiero I, king of Syracuse (478–467 BC), d.467 BC.

Hiero II, king of Syracuse (270–215 BC), d.215 BC.
Higden, Ranulf, English historian (*Polychronicon*), d.1364.
High-pressure steam, pioneered 1800 by the English engineer Richard Trevithick, b.1771, d.1833.
Highsmith, Patricia, American thriller writer (*Strangers on a Train,* 1950), b.1921.
Hilarius, St, b.*c.*300, d.367.
Hilary, St, pope, 461–467, d.467.
Hilary Term, legal term beginning 11 Jan., ending Wed. before Easter.
Hilda, St, b.614, d.680.
Hildebert, French ecclesiastic and writer, b.*c.*1055, d.1133.
Hildebrand, Adolf von, German sculptor, b.1847, d.1921.
Hildegard, St, b.1098, d.1179.
Hill, Octavia, English social reformer, b.1838, d.1912.
Hill, Sir Rowland, English pioneer in postal services, b.1795, d.1879.
Hilliard, Nicholas, English painter (particularly of miniatures), b.*c.*1547, d.1619.
Hillsborough stadium disaster, 95 football fans crushed to death at Liverpool vs Nottingham Forest match, Sheffield, 15 Apr. 1989.
Himmler, Heinrich, German Nazi leader, b.1900, committed suicide 1945.
Hindemith, Paul, German composer (*Mathis der Maler,* 1938), b.1895, d.1963.
Hindenburg, Paul von, German general and president (1925–34), b.1847, d.1934.
Hinton, Dr William Augustus, first black American to hold a professorship, Harvard University, b.1884, d.1959.
Hipparchus, Greek astronomer, b.*c.*160, d.*c.*125 BC.
Hippocrates, Greek physician, b.*c.*460, d.*c.*370 BC.
Hippolytus, Roman heretical leader in 3rd century.
Hirohito, emperor of Japan from 1926, b.1901, d.1989.
Hiroshige, Ando, Japanese artist, b.1797, d.1858.
Hiroshima, Japanese city, destroyed by an atom bomb 6 Aug. 1945.
Hirsch, Samson Raphael, German Jewish scholar, b.1808, d.1888.
Hirsch Music Library, British Museum, founded by Paul Adolf Hirsch, b.1881, d.1951.

Hispanic and Luso-Brazilian Councils, London, incorporated 1943.

Hispanic Society of America, New York, founded 1904.

Hitchcock, Sir Alfred, English-born film director, b.1899, d.1980.

Hitler, Adolf, German Nazi leader, b.1889; German chancellor 1933, Reichsführer 1934; attempted assassination 1944; committed suicide 1945.

HIV (human immuno-deficiency virus), discovered as cause of AIDS 1984.

Hoadly, Benjamin, English theologian, b.1676, d.1761.

Hoban, James, Irish-born architect (the White House, Washington, DC), b.c.1762, d.1831.

Hobart, capital of Tasmania, founded 1804.

Hobbema, Meindert, Dutch painter (*The Water Mill*), b.1638, d.1709.

Hobbes, Thomas, English philosopher and historian (*The Leviathan*, 1651), b.1588, d.1679.

Hobhouse, Leonard Trelawney, English sociologist, b.1864, d.1929.

Ho Chi Minh (Nguyen That Thanh), North Vietnamese communist leader (president 1954–69), b.1890, d.1969.

Hoccleve, Thomas, English poet (*De Regimine Principum*, 1411–12), b.c.1369, d.c.1450.

Hoche, Lazare, French revolutionary general, b.1768, d.1797.

Hockey Association, present body formed 1886.

Hockney, David, English painter, b.1937.

Hodgson, Ralph, English poet (*The Last Blackbird*, 1907), b.1871, d.1962.

Hodler, Ferdinand, Swiss artist, b.1853, d.1918.

Hoe, horse-drawn, invented 1731 by the English farmer Jethro Tull, b.1674, d.1714.

Hoe, Richard Marsh, American inventor (1846) of the rotary printing press, b.1812, d.1886.

Hofer, Andreas, Tyrolese patriot, b.1767, executed 1810.

Hoffman, Dustin, American stage and film actor (*The Graduate*, 1967), b.1937.

Hoffmann, Ernst Theodor Amadeus, German poet, b.1776, d.1822.

Hoffmann, Heinrich, German humorous writer (*Struwwelpeter*, 1847), b.1809, d.1894.

Hoffnung, Gerard, English caricaturist, musician and social reformer, b.1925, d.1959.

Hofmannsthal, Hugo von, Austrian poet (*Ariadne auf Naxos,* 1912), b.1874, d.1929.

Hofmeyr, Jan Hendrik, South African statesman, b.1845, d.1909.

Hogarth, David George, English archaeologist, b.1862, d.1929.

Hogarth, William, English painter (*Rake's Progress*, 1735), b.1697, d.1764.

Hogg, James ('Ettrick Shepherd'), Scottish poet, b.1770, d.1835.

Hogg, Quintin, English founder (1882) of The (London) Polytechnic, b.1845, d.1903.

Hohenlinden, Battle of, Wars of the French Revolution, between the French and the Austrians 3 Dec. 1800.

Hohenstaufen dynasty, emperors of Germany 1138–1254.

Hohenzollern dynasty, ruled Brandenburg 1411–1701, Prussia 1701–1871, Germany 1871–1918.

Hokusai, Japanese painter, b.1760, d.1849.

Holbach, Paul Heinrich Dietrich, Baron d', French philosopher (*Système de la Nature,* 1770), b.1723, d.1789.

Holbein, Hans, the elder, German painter, b.*c.*1465, d.1524.

Holbein, Hans, the younger, German painter (*The Ambassadors,* 1533), b.1497, d.1543.

Holbrooke, Josef, English composer (*Queen Mab,* 1904), b.1878, d.1958.

Holcombe, Henry, English composer, b.*c.*1690, d.*c.*1750.

Holcroft, Thomas, English playwright (*The Road to Ruin,* 1792), b.1745, d.1809.

Hölderlin, Johann Christian Friedrich, German poet, b.1770, d.1843.

Holgate, Robert, archbishop of York (1545–54), b.*c.*1481, d.1555.

Holiday, Billie, American jazz and blues singer, b.1915, d.1959.

Holidays with pay, enforced by law in Britain since 1938.

Holinshed, Raphael, English historian (*Chronicles,* 1578), d.*c.*1580.

Holland, Henry, English architect (Battersea Bridge, 1771–72), b.*c.*1746, d.1806.

Holland, Henry Richard Vassal Fox, Baron, British statesman, b.1773, d.1840.

Holland, John, founder and first governor (1695) of the Bank of Scotland, d.1722.

Hollar, Wenceslaus, Bohemian artist, b.1607, d.1677.

Holles, Denzil, Baron, Puritan leader, b.1599, d.1680.

Hollywood, California, founded 1887; incorporated 1903.

Holmes, Oliver Wendell, American writer (*The Autocrat of the Breakfast Table*, 1831–58), b.1809, d.1894.

Holmes, Oliver Wendell, US Supreme Court judge, b.1841, d.1935.

Holmium, chemical element, discovered 1879 by Per Teodor Cleve.

Holocene Epoch, the time from c.8000 BC to the present day.

Holst, Gustav, English composer (*The Perfect Fool*, 1923), b.1874, d.1934.

Holstein, Friedrich von, German statesman, b.1837, d.1909.

Holy Alliance, made between the emperors of Russia and Austria and the king of Prussia, 26 Sept. 1815.

Holy Island (Lindisfarne), England, chosen for the site of his church and monastery by St Aidan 635.

Holyoake, George Jacob, English pioneer in co-operation, b.1817, d.1906.

Holyoke, Samuel, American hymn-writer (*Arnheim*, 1778), b.1762, d.1820.

Holy Roman Empire, crown first held 800 by Charlemagne; renounced by Francis II, 1806.

Holyrood Abbey, Scotland, founded by King David I, 1128; Palace begun 1498.

Holy Spirit, dogma of procession from the Father and the Son ('Filioque'), added to Catholic doctrine 589.

Holy Thursday (Ascension Day), 40th day after Easter Sunday.

Holy Week, the week from Palm Sunday to Easter Saturday.

Home, John, Scottish playwright (*Douglas*, 1756), b.1722, d.1808.

Home Guard, founded May 1940 as LDV, adopted new name July 1940, disbanded Dec. 1945.

Home Office, Great Britain, founded by 1785.

Home Rule for Ireland League founded 1870 by Isaac Butt; first Bill 1886, second Bill 1893, third Bill 1912–14; Government of Ireland Bill 1919–20.

Homer, Greek poet (*The Iliad* and *The Odyssey*), probably lived in the 10th century BC.

Homer, Winslow, American painter, b.1836, d.1910.

Homoeopathic physician, first to practice in England, Dr Frederic Hervey Foster Quin, b.1799, d.1878.

Homoeopathy, principles first enunciated 1796 by the German physician Samuel Hahnemann, b.1755, d.1843.

Homology, principle declared 1818 by the French naturalist Etienne St Hilaire.

Honduras, Central American republic, discovered by Christopher Columbus 1502; colonized by Spanish from 1524; gained independence 1821.

Honduras, British, *see* **Belize.**

Honegger, Arthur, Swiss composer (*King David*, 1921), b.1892, d.1955.

Hong Kong, leased to Britain by China 1842 (New Territories, Kowloon and Stonecutters Island, 1898); occupied by the Japanese 1941–45; to be returned to Chinese control 1997.

Honorius I, pope 625–638.

Honorius II (Pietro Cadalo), anti-pope 1061–64, d.1072.

Honorius II (Lamberto Scannabecchi), pope 1124–30, d.1130.

Honorius III (Cencio Savelli), pope 1216–27, d.1227.

Honorius IV (Giacomo Savelli), pope 1285–87, d.1287.

Honourable Corps of Gentlemen at Arms, the Queen's personal bodyguard, founded 1559.

Honthorst, Gerard van, Dutch painter (*Christ before Pilate*), b.1590, d.1656.

Hooch, Pieter de, Dutch painter (*Scene in a Courtyard*), b.1629, d.*c.*1685.

Hood, Samuel, Viscount Hood, admiral, b.1724, d.1816.

Hood, Thomas, English poet (*Eugene Aram's Dream*, 1829), b.1799, d.1845.

Hook, Theodore, English writer (*Maxwell*, 1830), b.1788, d.1841.

Hooke, Robert, English clockmaker and inventor of the anchor escapement, b.1635, d.1703.

Hooker, Richard, English theologian (*Ecclesiasticall Politie*, 1594–1648), b.*c.*1554, d.1600.

Hooker, Sir William Jackson, English botanist, b.1785, d.1865.

Hooper, John, English religious reformer, burnt at the stake 1555.

Hoover, Herbert Clark, 31st US president (1929–33), b.1874, d.1964.

Hoover, John Edgar, American civil servant (director of the FBI 1924–72), b.1895, d.1972.

Hope, Bob, American comedian, star of the 'Road' films with Bing Crosby, b.1903.

'Hope, Anthony' (Sir Anthony Hope Hawkins), English novelist (*The Prisoner of Zenda*, 1894), b.1863, d.1933.

Hope, Thomas, English designer (*Household Furniture*, 1807), b.1709, d.1831.

Hopkins, Gerard Manley, English poet (*Poems*, 1918), b.1844, d.1889.

Hopkins, Johns, American merchant and philanthropist, b.1795, d.1873.

Hopkins, Stephen, governor of Rhode Island, b.1707, d.1785.

Hopkinson, Joseph, American lawyer and writer of 'Hail, Columbia' (1798), b.1770, d.1842.

Hoppner, John, English painter (*The Countess of Oxford*), b.1758, d.1810.

Horace, Latin poet (*Odes*, *c*.24 BC), b.65, d.8 BC.

Hormisdas, St, pope 514–523.

Hormones, internal secretions, discovered 1902–03 by the English physiologists Sir William Bayliss, b.1866, d.1924, and Ernest Henry Starling, b.1866, d.1927.

Hornung, Ernest William, English author of the 'Raffles' stories, b.1866, d.1921.

Horowitz, Vladimir, Russian-born pianist, b.1904, d.1989.

Horrocks, Jeremiah, English astronomer, b.*c*.1617, d.1641.

Horsley, Samuel, English theologian, b.1733, d.1806.

Hortensius, Quintus, Roman orator, b.114, d.50 BC.

Horthy of Nagybanya, Admiral Miklos, regent of Hungary (1920–44), b.1868, d.1957.

Hot blast, in smelting process, invented 1825–28 by the Scottish engineer James Beaumont Neilson, b.1792, d.1865.

Hot Springs Conference, World War II, held 18 May–I June 1943.

Hotchkiss machine gun, invented 1872 by the American Benjamin Berkeley Hotchkiss, b.1826, d.1885.

'Hotspur' (Sir Henry Percy), b.1364, killed in battle 1403.

'Houdini, Harry' (Erich Weiss), Hungarian-born magician and conjurer, b.1874, d.1926.

Houdon, Jean Antoine, French sculptor (*Morpheus*, 1777), b.1741, d.1828.

House, Colonel Edward Mandell, American statesman, b.1858, d.1938.

House of Commons, Great Britain, origins in 13th century.

House of Lords, Great Britain, origins in 13th century.

House of Representatives, US Congress, instituted 1787.

Housman, Alfred Edward, English poet (*A Shropshire Lad*, 1896), b.1859, d.1936.

Housman, Laurence, English writer (*Palace Plays*, 1930), b.1865, d.1959.

Houston, Samuel, first Texas president (1836–44), b.1793, d.1863.

Hovercraft, started as a private venture 1953 by its English inventor Christopher S. Cockerell, b.1910; development and manufacture undertaken 1958; first Dover-Calais crossing 1959.

Howard, Catherine, fifth wife of Henry VIII, b.1521, m. 1540, beheaded 1542.

Howard, Henry, **Earl of Surrey**, English politician and poet, b.1517, beheaded 1547.

Howard, John, English prison reformer, b.1726, d.1790.

Howard, Trevor, British film and stage actor (*Brief Encounter*, 1946), b.1916, d.1988

Howard, Sidney, American playwright (*Alien Corn,* 1933), b.1891, d.1939.

Howard League for Penal Reform, founded 1866.

Howe, Elias, American inventor of the sewing-machine (1846), b.1819, d.1867.

Howe, Admiral Richard, of 'The Glorious First of June' 1794, b.1726, d.1799.

Howell, James, Welsh writer (*Epistolae Ho-Elianae*, 1655), b.*c.*1594.

Howells, Herbert, English composer, b.1892, d.1983.

Howells, William Dean, American writer and editor, b.1837, d.1920.

Howrah Bridge, Calcutta, opened 1943.

Hoyle, Edmond, English whist expert, b.1672, d.1769.

Hsüan Tê Period, China, 1426–35.

Hubbard, L. Ron, American writer and founder of Scientology, b.1911, d.1986.

Hubble, Edwin Powell, American astronomer and cosmologist, b.1889, d.1953.

Hubert, St, b.*c.*656, d.*c.*727.

Hubert de Burgh, Chief Justiciar of England, d.1243.

Huc, Evariste Régis, French missionary to Tibet, b.1813, d.1860.

Huch, Ricarda, German writer (*Ludolf Urslev,* 1883), b.1864, d.1947.

Hudson, Henry, English navigator, d.*c.*1611.

Hudson, Rock, American film and TV actor (*Giant,* 1956), b.1925, d.1985.

Hudson, William Henry, Argentine-born naturalist (*Green Mansions,* 1904), b.1841, d.1922.

Hudson's Bay, discovered 1610 by the English navigator Henry Hudson, d.1611.

Hudson's Bay Company, formed by Prince Rupert, chartered by King Charles II, 1670.

Hughes, Howard Robard, American industrialist, aviator and film producer, b.1905, d.1976.

Hughes, Thomas, English writer (*Tom Brown's Schooldays,* 1856), b.1822, d.1896.

Hugos, Victor, French writer (*Les Misérables,* 1862), b.1802, d.1885.

Huguenots, French Protestants, so called from the middle of 16th century.

Hugues Capet, king of France (987–996), b.*c.*938, d.996.

Huli, Feast of, Indian custom similar to April Fools' Day, celebrated 31 March.

Hull, Cordell, American statesman, b.1871, d.1955.

Hulme, Thomas Ernest, English writer (*Speculations,* 1924), b.1883, d.1917.

Human experiment, first planned, to test an hypothesis based on observation, undertaken 1798 by the English physician Edward Jenner, b.1749, d.1823.

Human Rights, Declaration of, adopted by the United Nations General Assembly 10 Dec. 1948.

Humboldt, Alexander von, German naturalist and explorer, b.1769, d.1859.

Hume, David, Scottish philosopher (*Political Discourses,* 1752), b.1711, d.1776.

Humperdinck, Engelbert, German composer (*Hansel and Gretel,* 1893), b.1854, d.1921.

Hundred Days, The, Napoleon's return from Elba, 20 March 1815 to 28 June 1815.

Hundred Years' War, The, between England and France, 1337–1453.

Hung Chih Period, China, 1488–1505.

Hung Wu Period, China, 1368–98.

Hungary, traditionally conquered by Magyars 896; independent kingdom from 1001; Hapsburg rule 1526–1918; republic and communist regime 1918–19; Horthy's dictatorship 1920–44; republic proclaimed 1946; Communist regime began 1949; popular revolt crushed by Soviet forces Oct.–Nov. 1956; democracy established 1989.

Huns, invaded Europe 363; defeated 454.

Hunt, Leigh, English essayist (*Imagination and Fancy,* 1844), b.1784, d.1859.

Hunt, William Holman, English painter (*The Light of the World,* 1854), b.1827, *d.*1910.

Hunt, Wilson Price, American explorer, b.*c.*1782, d.1842.

Hunter, John, Scottish surgeon, b.1728, d.1793.

Hunter, William, Scottish anatomist, b.1718, d.1783.

Hunter, Sir William Wilson, Scottish administrator in India, b.1840, d.1900.

Hunters' moon, the first full moon after the Harvest Moon.

Huntingdon, Selina Hastings, Countess of, founder of the Calvinist-Methodist 'Countess of Huntingdon's Connexion', b.1707, d.1791.

Huntington, Henry Edwards, American railway promoter, b.1850, d.1927.

Hunyadi, János, Hungarian patriot, b.*c.*1387, d.1456.

Hurricane, aeroplane, last fly-past over London commemorating the Battle of Britain, Sunday, 20 Sept. 1959.

Hurst, Fannie, American novelist (*Back Street,* 1931), b.1889, d.1968.

Hus, Jan, Bohemian religious reformer, b.*c.*1369, burnt at the stake 1415.

Huskisson, William, British statesman, b.1770, d.1830.

Hussein, king of Jordan (since 1952), b.1935.

Hussein ibn Ali, king of the Hejaz (1916–24), b.1856, d.1931.

Hussein, Saddam, president of Iraq (since 1979), b.1937.

Husserl, Edmund, Austrian philosopher, b.1859, d.1938.

Huston, John, American film director and actor (*The Maltese Falcon,* 1941), b.1906, d.1987.

Hutcheson, Francis, Irish philosopher (*System of Moral Philosophy,* 1755), b.1694, d.1746.

Hutchinson, Anne, English-born religious leader, b.1590, killed 1643.

Hutchinson, Thomas, governor of Massachusetts Bay, b.1711, d.1780.

Hutton, James, Scottish pioneer in the study of geology, b.1726, d.1797.

Huxley, Aldous, English writer (*Point Counter Point,* 1928), b.1894, d.1963.

Huxley, Sir Julian, English biologist, b.1887, d.1975.

Huxley, Thomas Henry, English scientist and educationist (*Lay Sermons,* 1870), b.1825, d.1895.

Huygens, Christiaan, Dutch scientist, b.1629, d.1695.

Huysmans, Cornelis, Flemish painter, b.1648, d.1727.

Huysmans, Joris Karl, French novelist (*A Rebours,* 1884), b.1848, d.1907.

Huysum, Jan van, Dutch painter (particularly of flower-pieces), b.1682, d.1749.

Hyder Ali, Indian leader, b.*c.*1728, d.1782.

Hyderabad, India, founded 1589; absorbed into India 1948.

Hydraulic crane, invented *c.*1845 by William George Armstrong (later Baron Armstrong), b.1810, d.1900.

Hydraulic press, invented 1796 by the English inventor Joseph Bramah, b.1748, d.1814.

Hydraulic pressure accumulator, invented 1850 by William George Armstrong (later Baron Armstrong), b.1810, d.1900.

Hydroelectric station, first example begun in Northern Ireland 1883.

Hydroelectricity, discovered 1843 by the English scientist Michael Faraday, b.1791, d.1867.

Hydrogen, properties discovered 1776 by the British scientist Henry Cavendish, b.1731, d.1810.

Hydrogen bomb, first American, exploded over Bikini Atoll 1 March 1954.

Hydrogen bomb, first Russian, exploded in the Pacific 12 Aug. 1953.

Hydrogen peroxide, obtained 1810 by the French chemist Louis Jacques Thénard, b.1777, d.1857.

Hydrophobia, effective vaccine treatment developed 1885 by the French scientist Louis Pasteur, b.1822, d.1895.

Hygiene, modern practice developed by the English physician Edmund Alexander Parkes, b.1819, d.1876.

Hyginus, St, pope 136–140.

Hygrometer, invented 1783 by the Swiss scientist Horace Benédict de Saussure, b.1740, d.1799.

Hyndman, Henry Mayers, English socialist leader, b.1842, d.1921.

Hypatia, Alexandrian scholar, murdered 415.

Hypnotism, term first introduced 1841, by the Scottish scholar James Braid, b.1796, d.1860.

Hyppolytus, St, anti-pope 217.

Hysterisis, Law of, discovered by the German-born engineer Charles Proteus Steinmetz, b.1865, d.1923.

I

Ibáñez, Vicente Blasco, Spanish novelist (*The Four Horsemen of the Apocalypse*), b.1867, d.1928.
IBM (International Business Machines), the world's largest computer manufacturer, founded 1914.
Ibn Battutah, Arab traveller, b.1304, d.1368.
Ibn Khaldun, Arab historian (*Kitab al Tbar*), b.1332, d.1406.
Ibn Saud, king of Saudi Arabia, b.*c.*1880, d.1953.
Ibrahim Pasha, viceroy of Egypt (1844), b.1789, d.1848.
Ibsen, Henrik, Norwegian dramatist (*Peer Gynt*, 1867), b.1828, d.1906.
ICAO (International Civil Aviation Organization), Montreal, proposed at an international conference at Chicago 1944; came into being 1947; 168 members in 1992.
Iceland, first settled 874; independent republic 930–1262; ruled by Denmark 1381–1918; sovereign state 1918–44; independent republic since 1944.
Ichthyosaurus, first brought to scientific notice 1811 by the English fossil collector Mary Anning, b.1799, d.1847.
Icknield Way, from Berkshire Down to the Fens, England, natural road of Celtic origin, first recorded mention 45.
Iconoclast Controversy, in Byzantine Empire, 726–843.
Idaho, USA, first permanently settled 1860; organized as a Territory 1863; admitted to the Union 1890.
Identity cards, introduced in Britain 1939; abolished 21 Feb. 1952.
Ido, revision of Esperanto, produced 1907 by Marquis de Beaufront.
Idrisi, Arab geographer, b.*c.*1099, d.*c.*1155.
Ifni, former Spanish province administered from Madrid ceded by Morocco to Spain 1860; returned to Morocco 1969.
Ignatius Loyola, St, founder 1534 of the Society of Jesus, b.1491, d.1556.
Ignatius of Antioch, St, lived in the 1st century.
Ignatius of Constantinople, St, b.*c.*800, d.*c.*878.
Ikhnaton, pharaoh of Egypt, d.*c.*1357 BC.
Illinium, chemical element, discovered 1926 by the American scientist B. Smith Hopkins, b.1873, d.1952.

Illinois, USA, discovered by the French 1673; settled 1720; ceded by France to Britain 1763; organized as a Territory 1809; admitted to the Union 1818.

Illinois University, Urbana, founded 1867.

Illium, alloy, discovered by the American chemist Samuel Wilson Parr, b.1857, d.1931.

Illuminati, German rationalist society founded 1776 by the German philosopher Adam Weishaupt, b.1748, d.1830; officially proscribed and dissolved 1785.

Illustrated London News, British periodical, began publication 1842.

Immaculate Conception, of the Virgin Mary, Catholic dogma defined 1854.

Imperial Defence College, London, for senior army, navy and air force officers, founded 1926.

Inauguration Day, USA, 20 Jan., on which American presidents take the oath of office every four years.

Incandescent electric lamp, invented 1878 by Thomas Alva Edison, b.1847, d.1931, and Sir Joseph Wilson Swan b.1828, d.1914.

Incandescent gas mantles, invented 1886 by the Austrian chemist Baron Auer von Welsbach, b.1858, d.1929.

Inchbald, Mrs Elizabeth, English actress and novelist, b.1753, d.1821.

Income tax, introduced in Britain 1799.

Incunabula, books printed in Europe before the year 1500.

Independence Day, commemorating the Declaration of Independence, 4 July 1776; celebrated in the USA 4 July each year.

Independent Labour Party, founded 1893 by the Scottish socialist James Keir Hardie, b.1856, d.1915; seceded from Labour Party 1932 under James Maxton, b.1885, d.1946; ceased to have parliamentary representation 1948.

Index Vaticanus (*Index librorum prohibitorum*), the list of books condemned by the Catholic Church, first issued 1559.

India, government of India transferred from East India Company to British Crown 1858; Indian Empire proclaimed 1877; gained independence within the Commonwealth and divided into separate dominions of Pakistan (Muslim) and India (Hindu); India became a republic 1950.

India Office Library, London, founded by the East India Company 1801.

India rubber, discovered *c.*1740 by the French traveller Charles Marie de la Condamine, b.1701, d.1774.

Indian Mutiny, against the British, 1857–58.

Indian National Congress, founded 1885 by Wedderburn and Hume.

Indian Post Office, established 24 July 1837.

Indiana, USA, first settled 1732; organized as a Territory 1800; admitted to the Union 1816.

Indianapolis, Indiana, state capital, first settled 1819.

Indium, metallic element, discovered by the German scientists F. Reich and T. Richter 1863.

IndoChina, former collective name for Cambodia, Laos and Vietnam, occupied by French 1859–85; French protectorates until Japanese occupation 1940–45; Laos and Cambodia achieved independence after World War II; French re-established colonial rule in Vietnam which led to the war against the French 1946–54; Vietnam partitioned between North and South 1954; American supported the South 1965–73 in the Vietnam War, with North Vietnam gaining control over the whole country 1975.

Indo-European Language, existence postulated 1786 by Sir William Jones.

Indonesia, settled by the Portuguese *c.*1545; ruled by the Netherlands East India Company from 1602; became Dutch East Indies 1798; declared independence 1945; became a republic 1950.

Induction, principles discovered 1830 by the English scientist Michael Faraday, b.1791, d.1867.

Industrial Revolution, in Britain, occurred roughly 1760–1840; name first applied 1884 by Arnold Toynbee.

Industrial Workers of the World, labour organization, founded in USA in 1905.

Indy, Vincent d', French composer (*Istar,* 1896), b.1851, d.1931.

Infallibility, Papal, Catholic dogma defined 1870.

Influenza, pandemics 1889–90, 1918–19.

Information, Ministry of, existed in Britain 1939–46.

Inge, Dean Ralph, English writer and divine, b.1880, d.1945.

Inglis, James, abbot of Culross, murdered 1531.

Ingoldsby, Thomas (Richard Harris Barham), English writer, b.1788, d.1845.

Ingres, Jean Auguste Dominique, French painter (*Apotheosis of Homer*), b.1780, d.1867.

Inkatha, Zulu nationalist movement in South Africa led by Chief Mangosuthu Buthelezi since 1975.

Inkerman, Battle of, between the Russians and British in the Crimean War, 5 Nov. 1854.

Inman, Henry, American painter (*William Penn*), b.1801, d.1846.

Inness, George, American painter (*Georgia Pines*), b.1825, d.1894.

Innocent I, St, pope 401–417, d.417.

Innocent II (Gregorio Papareschi dei Guideni), pope 1130–43, d.1143.

Innocent III (Lando da Sezza), anti-pope 1179–80.

Innocent III (Lotario de' Conti di Segni), pope 1198–1216, b.*c.*1160, d.1216.

Innocent IV (Sinibaldo Fiesco), pope 1243–54, d.1254.

Innocent V (Pierre de Champagni), pope 1276, b.*c.*1225, d.1276.

Innocent VI (Etienne Aubert), pope 1352–62, d.1362.

Innocent VII (Cosimo dei Migliorati), pope 1404–06, b.1339, d.1406.

Innocent VIII (Giovanni Battista Cibo), pope 1484–92, b.1432, d.1492.

Innocent IX (Giovanni Antonio Fachinetti), pope 1591, b.*1519,* d.1591.

Innocent X (Giovanni Battista Pamfili), pope 1644–55, b.1574, d.1655.

Innocent XI (Benedetto Odescalchi), pope 1676–89, b.1611, d.1689.

Innocent XII (Antonio Pignatelli), pope 1691–1700, b.1615, d.1700.

Innocent XIII (Michele Angelo Conti), pope 1721–24, b.1655, d.1724.

Inoculation, for smallpox, introduced *c.*1718 into England from Constantinople by Lady Mary Wortley Montagu, b.1689, d.1762.

Inquisition, Holy office of the, founded 1231; Spanish Inquisition reorganized 1478, abolished 1820.

Institute of Contemporary Arts, London, founded 1948.

Institute of International Law, Ghent, founded 1873 by the Swiss jurist Johann Kaspar Bluntschli, b.1808, d.1881.

Insulin, isolated 1921 by the Canadian scientists Sir Frederick Grant Banting, b.1891, d.1941, and Charles Herbert Best, b.1899, d.1978.

Insurance, earliest recorded policy 1523; fire insurance pioneered 1666 by Nicolas Barbon; earliest recorded life assurance bond 1228.

Intelligence test, IQ scale devised by Binet and Simon in 1905; Stanford-Binet scale introduced 1916.

Interdict, Papal, on England 1208–13.

Interferometry, study pioneered 1861 by the French physicist Armand Fizeau, b.1819, d.1896.

Internal combustion engine, first constructed 1860 by Lenoir.

International: *First* ('International Working Men's Association', Marxist and Anarchist), 1864–76; *Second* (Socialist), 1889–1914, revived 1918–46 (as so-called '2½th International') and again in 1948 (as 'Comisco'); *Third* ('Comintern', Communist), 1919–43, revived in 1947 (as 'Cominform'); *Fourth* (Trotskyist), formed in 1928.

International Atomic Energy Agency (IAEA), Vienna, established 1956.

International Bank for Reconstruction and Development (IBRD), *see* **World Bank.**

International Civil Aviation Organization (ICAO), Montreal, proposed at an international conference at Chicago 1944; came into being 1947.

International Code of Signals, devised by the British Government 1857; amended 1901.

International Criminal Police Commission (Interpol), formed in Vienna 1923.

International Date Line, in Pacific Ocean, represented by the meridian of 180°, for the convenience of adjusting the loss or gain of one day; established 1883.

International Labour Organization, Geneva, set up 1919.

International Monetary Fund, established 27 Dec. 1945.

International Postal Union, founded at Berne 9 Oct. 1875.

International Red Cross, founded at Geneva 22 Aug. 1864.

International Statistical Congress, first convened 1853 at Brussels by the Belgian scientist Lambert Adolphe Jacques Quetelet, b.1796, d.1874.

International Telecommunication Union, founded 1865, reorganized 1947.

Intifada, Palestinian popular uprising against Israeli authority in the West Bank, began 9 Dec. 1987.

Invar, alloy discovered 1920 by the Swiss scientist Charles Edouard Guillaume, b.1861, d.1938.

In vitro fertilization, technique to treat infertility first used successfully 1978.

Iodine, discovered 1811 in the ashes of seaweed by the French chemist Bernard Courtois, b.1777, d.1838.

Iona, home of St Columba from 563 AD.

Iona Community, founded 1938 by the Rev. George Macleod, b.1895, d.1991.

Ionization, theory developed 1887 by Swedish chemist Svante August Arrhenius, b.1859, d.1927.

Ionium, discovered 1907 by the American chemist Bertram Borden Boltwood, b.1870, d.1927.

Iowa, USA, first settled 1788; organized as a Territory 1838; admitted to the Union 1846.

IRA, *see* **Irish Republican Army.**

Iran, ruled by Achaemenids (c.550–330 BC), Arsacids (227 BC–AD 224), Sassanids (226–651), Muslims (651–1231), Mongols and Turks (1231–1502), Safavids (1502–1722), Turks (1722–79), Kajars (1779–1925); by Pahlavis 1925–79; Ayatollah Khomeini returned from exile to head new Islamic republic 1979.

Iran-Iraq War, 21–22 Sept. 1980–Aug. 1988.

Iraq, conquered by British from Turkey 1914–18; British mandate 1919–1921; Hashemite kingdom 1921–58; military republic since 1958.

Iraq-Mediterranean oil pipeline, Kirkuk to Haifa, inaugurated 14 Jan. 1935.

Ireland, first invaded by Norsemen 795, by English 1167; Act of Union 1800; Easter Rising 1916; Irish Free State recognized 1921 (*see* **Eire**).

Ireland, John, English composer (*The Forgotten Rite,* 1915), b.1879, d.1962.

Ireland, William Henry, English literary forger, b.1777, d.1835.

Irenaeus, St, bishop of Lyons, lived in the 2nd century.

Irene, Byzantine empress (797–802), b.752, d.803.

Ireton, Henry, English Puritan leader, b.1611, d.1651.

Iriarte, Ignacio, Spanish painter, b.1620, d.1685.

Iridium, discovered 1804 by the English chemist Smithson Tennant, b.1761, d.1815.

Irish Free State, title of Southern Ireland 1922–37.

Irish Land League, founded 1879 by Michael Davitt, b.1846, d.1906.

Irish Republican Army (IRA), formed 1919.

Irish Volunteers, first formed 1779; second formed 1913, and merged with IRA in 1919.

Iron bridge, first example constructed at Coalbrookdale 1773–79.

'Iron Curtain', term describing former barrier between the USSR and Western Europe, first popularized by Sir Winston Churchill 5 March 1946; had been used earlier in the sense of protection by *Pravda* 11 Oct. 1939.

Ironclad ships, first battle of, took place in the American Civil War between *Monitor* and *Merrimac* 9 March 1862.

Ironmongers Company, London origins uncertain; first recorded mention 1300; grant of arms 1455; Royal Charter 1463.

Irving, Sir Henry (John Henry Brodribb), English actor, b.1838, d.1905.

Irving, Washington, American writer (*Rip Van Winkle*, 1819), b.1783, d.1859.

Irvingites, Catholic Apostolic Church, founded 1829, by the Scottish preacher Edward Irving, b.1792, d.1834.

Isaac I, Byzantine emperor (1057–59), d.1061.

Isaac II, Byzantine emperor (1185–95, 1203–04), executed 1204.

Isabella, wife of the Emperor Frederick II, b.1214, d.1241.

Isabella I, queen of Castile and Leon, b.1451, d.1504.

Isabella II, queen of Spain, b.1830, d.I904.

Isabella of Angoulême, queen of England, d.1246.

Isabella of France, queen of England, b.1292, d.1358.

Isabey, Jean Baptiste, French painter (*The Empress Josephine*), b.1767, d.1855.

Isherwood, Christopher William Bradshaw, English-born American author (*Goodbye to Berlin,* 1939), b.1904, d.1986.

Isidore, St, bishop of Seville (*Etymologies*), b.*c.*560, d.636.

Islam, religious movement, founded *c.*610 by Mahommed, b.*c.*570, d.632.

Ismailis, Muslim sect, formed in 8th century.

Ismail Pasha, khedive of Egypt, b.1830, d.1895.

Isocrates, Greek orator, b.436, d.338 BC.

Isomorphism, chemical relationship, principle defined 1820 by the German scientist Eilhard Mitscherlich, b.1794, d.1863.

Isotopes, theory developed 1912 by the English scientist Frederick Soddy, b.1877; first identified 1910 by Sir Joseph John Thomson, b.1856, d.1940.

Israel, State of, proclaimed 14 May 1948.

Isräels, Jozef, Dutch painter (*Toilers of the Sea*), b.1824, d.1911.

Istanbul, founded (as Byzantium) 658 BC; capital of Byzantine Empire (as Constantinople) 330–1453; of Ottoman Empire (as Istanbul) 1453–1923.

Isthmian games, held in Ancient Greece, began 581 BC.

Italian language, earliest known document, the *Placito Capuano*, dated March 960.

Italian Parliament, opened 18 Feb. 1861.

Italian Somaliland, *see* **Somalia.**

Italy, kingdom 1861–1946; Fascist regime 1922–43; democratic republic since 1946.

Ito, Prince Hirobumi, Japanese statesman and reformer, b.1841, assassinated 1909.

Iturbide, Agustin de, emperor of Mexico (1822–23), b.1783, shot 1824.

Ivan I, grand duke of Vladimir, d.1341.

Ivan II, grand duke of Vladimir (1353–59), b.1326, d.1359.

Ivan III, the Great, grand duke of Muscovy (1462–1505), b.1440, d.1505.

Ivan IV, the Terrible, tsar of Muscovy (1547–84), b.1530, d.1584.

Ivan V, tsar of Russia (1682–96), b.1666, d.1696.

Ivan VI, emperor of Russia (1740–41), b.1740, murdered 1764.

Ives, St, b.1253, d.1303.

Ivo, St, bishop of Chartres, b.*c.*1040, d.1116.

Ivory Coast, *see* **Côte d'Ivoire.**

J

'Jack of Tilbury' (Sir John Arundell), b.1495, d.1561.
Jackson, Andrew, 7th US president (1829–37), b.1767, d.1845.
Jackson, Sir Barry, English theatre manager and director, b.1879, d.1961.
Jackson, Frederick George, British Arctic explorer, b.1860, d.1938.
Jackson, Glenda, British actress (*Women in Love,* 1969) and Labour MP, b.1936.
Jackson, Jesse Louis, American civil rights leader and politician, b.1941.
Jackson, Michael, American pop singer ('Thriller', 1982), b.1958.
Jackson, 'Stonewall' (Thomas Jonathan Jackson), American Confederate general, b.1824, killed 1863.
'Jack the Ripper', perpetrator of series of unsolved murders of women in London 1888.
Jacobin Club, founded in France 1789. Movement ended 1794, but was revived during the 1848 Revolution.
Jacobite glass, manufactured mainly 1745–65.
Jacobites, supporters of James II and his descendants 1688–1760.
Jacobs, William Wymark, English writer (*The Skipper's Wooing*, 1897), b.1863, d.1943.
Jacobus de Voragine, Italian writer (*The Golden Legend*), *fl.* 13th century.
Jacopone da Todi, Italian poet (*Stabat Mater*), b.*c.*1240, d.1306.
Jacquard loom, first to weave patterns, invented 1801 by the French inventor Joseph Marie Jacquard, b.1752, d.1834.
Jacquerie, The, insurrection of French peasants, May 1358.
Jadassohn, Solomon, German composer, b.1831, d.1902.
Jadwiga, Polish queen, b.*c.*1372, d.1399.
Jaggard, William, English publisher of Shakespeare, b.*c.*1568, d.1623.
Jagger, Mick, British rock singer and songwriter, leader of the Rolling Stones, b.1943.
Jagiellon dynasty, Lithuanian dynasty ruled Poland 1386–1572.
Jahangir, Mogul emperor of India (1605–27), b.1569, d.1627.
Jainism, Indian religious movement, had its beginnings in the 6th century BC.

Jalal Ad-din Rumi, Mohammed, Persian mystical poet, b.1207, d.1273.

Jalalian *or* **Seljuk Era**, began 15 March 1079.

Jamaica, discovered by Christopher Columbus 1494; under Spanish rule until 1655; captured by the British 1655, and established as a colony 1866; included in the British Caribbean Federation 1956; gained independence 1962.

Jamboree, World, of Boy Scouts, first held London 1920.

James, Henry, American theologian, b.1811, d.1882.

James, Henry, American-born novelist (*The Ambassadors*, 1903), b.1843, d.1916.

James, Jesse, American outlaw, b.1847, killed 1882.

James, William, American philosopher and psychologist, b.1842, d.1910.

James I, king of Great Britain (1603–25), b.1566, d.1625. Proclaimed king of Scotland 1567.

James II, king of Great Britain (1685–88), b.1633, d.1701.

James, the Old Pretender (James Francis Edward Stewart), b.1688, d.1766.

James I, king of Scotland (1406–37), b.1394, assassinated 1437.

James II, king of Scotland (1437–60), b.1430, killed 1460.

James III, king of Scotland (1460–88), b.1451, assassinated 1488.

James IV, king of Scotland (1488–1513), b.1473, killed in battle 1513.

James V, king of Scotland (1513–42), b.1512, d.1542.

James VI, king of Scotland (1567–1603), *see* **James I**.

Jameson, Mrs Anna, Irish-born popular writer (*Legend of the Madonna*, 1852), b.1794, d.1860.

Jameson Raid, Transvaal, led 29 Dec. 1895 to 2 Jan. 1896 by the Scottish pioneer in South Africa, Sir Leander Starr Jameson, b.1853, d.1917.

Jammes, Francis, French writer (*Le Roman du lièvre*, 1903), b.1868, d.1938.

Janacek, Leos, Czech composer (*Jenufa*, 1902), b.1854, d.1928.

Jane, Queen (Lady Jane Grey), b.*c.*1537, proclaimed queen 1553, beheaded 1554.

Janin, Jules Gabriel, French writer (*L'Ane mort et la femme guillotiné*, 1829), b.1804, d.1874.

Janissaries, Turkish troops, first levied 1330, abolished 1826.

Jan Mayen Island, Arctic, discovered 1607 by the English explorer Henry Hudson (d.*c.*1611); annexed by Norway 1929.

Jansenism, religious movement deriving from the posthumous publication of *Augustinus* (1640) by the Dutch theologian Cornelis Jansen, b.1585, d.1638.

Janssens Van Nuyssen, Abraham, Flemish painter (*Ecce Homo!*), b.c.1575, d.1632.

Japan, empire for at least 2000 years; Togukawa Shogunate 1600–1867; feudal system abolished 1871; American occupation 1945–52; new constitution granted 1947.

Jaques-Dalcroze, Émile, Swiss composer, b.1865, d.1950.

Jarry, Alfred, French writer (*Ubu Roi*, 1896), b.1873, d.1907.

Jarvis, John Wesley, English-born painter (*Alexander Anderson*), b.c.1781, d.1839.

Jasper National Park, Canada, established 1907.

Jaurès, Jean Léon, French socialist leader, b.1859, assassinated 1914.

Jay, John, American statesman, b.1745, d.1829.

Jazz, began to develop in New Orleans *c.*1893–95; first so named 1910.

Jean de Meung, French writer (second part of the *Roman de la rose*), d.c.1305.

Jeanne d'Albret, queen of Navarre, b.1528, d.1572.

Jeanne d'Arc, Ste, b.c.1412, burnt at the stake 1431.

Jeans, Sir James, English scientist (*The Stars in Their Courses*, 1931), b.1877, d.1946.

Jefferies, Richard, English writer (*The Story of My Heart*, 1883), b.1848, d.1887.

Jeffers, Robinson, American poet (*Flagons and Apples*, 1912), b.1887, d.1962.

Jefferson, Thomas, 3rd US president (1801–09), b.1743, d.1826.

Jeffreys, George, Baron, judge of the 'Bloody Assizes', b.1648, d.1689.

Jehovah's Witnesses, founded 1872 in Pennsylvania by Charles Taze Russell, b.1852, d.1916.

Jellicoe, Admiral John, Earl Jellicoe, governor-general of New Zealand (1920–24), b.1859, d.1935.

Jemison, Mrs Mary ('The White Woman of the Genesee'), b.1743, d.1833.

Jena, Battle of, between Napoleon and the Prussians, 14 Oct. 1806.

Jena University, Germany, founded 1558.

Jenghiz Khan (Temujin), Mongol ruler, b.1162, d.1227.

Jenkin's Ear, War of, between Britain and Spain, 1739–41.

Jenner, Edward, English physician and discoverer 1796 of vaccination, b.1749, d.1823.

Jenson, Nicolas, French pioneer printer in Italy, d.c.1480.

Jenyns, Soame, English writer (*Free Enquiry into the Nature and Origin of Evil*, 1756), b.1704, d.1787.

Jerome, St, (produced *Vulgate*, 382–405), b.c.340, d.420.

Jerome, Jerome Klapka, English humorous writer (*Three Men in a Boat*, 1889), b.1859, d.1927.

Jerome of Prague, Czech religious reformer, b.c.1365, d.1416.

Jerrold, Douglas, English writer (*Mrs Caudle's Curtain Lectures*, 1846), b.1803, d.1857.

Jerusalem, destroyed by Nebuchadnezzar 587–586 BC; rebuilt 536–516 BC; razed 168 BC by Antiochus Epiphanes; destroyed AD 70 by Titus; sacked by the Persians 615; captured by the Crusaders 1099; recovered by Saladin 1187; taken by the British 1917; divided between Jordan and Israel 1949; unified after the Six Day War (1967) under the Israelis.

Jervis, John, Earl of St Vincent, Admiral of the Fleet, b.1735, d.1823.

Jesus, Society of, founded 1534 by St Ignatius Loyola, b.1491, d.1556; dissolved 1773 by Pope Clement XIV; re-established by Pope Pius VII, 1814.

Jesus College, Cambridge University, founded 1496 by John Alcock, bishop of Ely, b.1430, d.1500.

Jesus College, Oxford University, founded by Queen Elizabeth I, 1571.

Jesus of Nazareth, founder of Christianity, born between 5 BC and AD 2, crucified between 30 and 33.

Jet aircraft engine, developed by Sir Frank Whittle, b.1907, d.1991, first ran on test-bed 1937.

Jewel, John, English divine and writer (*Apologia Ecclesiae Anglicanae*, 1562), b.1522, d.1571.

Jewett, Sarah Orne, American writer (*The Country of the Painted Firs*, 1896), b.1849, d.1909.

Jewish calendar, calculated from 3761 BC; fixed AD 358.

Jewish Diaspora, dispersal of the Jews, began with deportations by Assyrians 721 BC.

Jewish Disabilities Removal Act, Great Britain, passed 1858.

Jewish Era, began 7 Oct. 3761 BC.

Jex-Blake, Sophia Louisa, English physician, mathematician and champion of women's right, b.1840, d.1912.

Jhabvala, Ruth Prawer, British novelist and screenwriter (*Heat and Dust,* 1975), b.1927.
Jiménez de Cisneros, Francisco, Spanish divine and statesman, b.1436, d.1517.
Jinnah, Mohammed Ali, Indian Muslim leader and founder of Pakistan, b.1876, d.1948.
Joachim, Joseph, Bohemian violinist, b.1831, d.1907.
Joan (Fair Maid of Kent), wife of the Black Prince, b.1328, d.1385.
Joan, Pope, mythical female pope, *c.*855–858.
Joanna I, queen of Naples (1343–82), b.*c.*1327, executed 1382.
Joanna II, queen of Naples (1414–35), b.1371, d.1435.
Joan of Arc, St, born *c.*1412, burnt at the stake 30 May 1431; canonized 1920.
Jocelin de Brakelond, English historian, lived at the end of the 12th and the beginning of the 13th centuries.
Jodelle, Étienne, French playwright (*Cléopatre captive*, 1552), b.1532, d.1573.
Joffre, Joseph Jacques Césaire, French soldier, b.1852, d.1931.
Johannesburg, South Africa, founded 1886.
John, Augustus, Welsh painter (*Bella*), b.1878, d.1961.
John I, St, pope 523–526, d. in prison 526.
John II, pope 533–535.
John III, pope 561–574.
John IV, pope 640–642.
John V, pope 685–686.
John VI, pope 701–705.
John VII, pope 705–707.
John VIII, pope 872–882, murdered 882.
John IX, pope 898–900.
John X, pope 914–928.
John XI, pope 931–935.
John XII (Octavian), pope 955–963, b.*c.*938, d.963.
John XIII, pope 965–972.
John XIV, pope 983–984, died in prison 984.
John XV, pope 985–996.
John XVI (Philagathus), anti-pope 997–998.
John XVII (Sicco), pope 1003.
John XVIII, pope 1004–09.
John XIX, pope 1024–32.
John XX (non-existent: a fault in numbering).
John XXI (Pedro Giuliamo Rebulo), pope 1276–77.
John XXII (Jacques Duèse), pope 1316–34, b.1249, d.1334.

John XXIII (Baldassare Cossa), anti-pope 1410–15, d.1419.
John XXIII (Angelo Roncalli), pope 1958–63, b.1881, d.1963.
John I (Tzimisces), Byzantine emperor (969–976), b.925, d.976.
John II (Comnenus), Byzantine emperor (1118–43), b.1088, d.1143.
John III (Vatatzes), Byzantine emperor (1222–54), b.1193, d.1254.
John IV (Lascaris), Byzantine emperor (1258–61), b.*c.*1250, d.*c.*1300.
John V (Palaeologus), Byzantine emperor (1341–47), b.1332, d.1391.
John VI (Cantacuzene), Byzantine emperor (1347–55), b.*c.*1292, d.1383.
John VII, Byzantine emperor 1390.
John VIII, Byzantine emperor (1425–48), b.1390, d.1448.
John, king of England (1199-1216), b.1167, d.1216.
John I, king of Poland, 1492–1501.
John II (Casimir), king of Poland (1648–68), b.1609, d.1672.
John III (Sobieski), king of Poland (1674–96), b.1624, d.1696.
John I, king of Portugal (1385–1433), b.1357, d.1433.
John II, king of Portugal (1481–95), b.1455, d.1495.
John III, king of Portugal (1521–57), b.1502, d.1557.
John IV, king of Portugal (1640–56), b.1603, d.1656.
John V, king of Portugal (1706–50), b.1689, d.1750.
John VI, king of Portugal, b.1769, d.1826.
John Chrysostom, St, b.*c.*357, d.407.
John of Austria, Don, Austrian soldier and administrator, b.1545, d.1578.
John of Beverley, St, b.687, d.721.
John of Damascus, St, theologian, *fl.* late 7th and first half of 8th centuries.
John of Fornsete, English monk and reputed composer of *Sumer is icumen in*, d.1239.
John of Gaunt, Duke of Lancaster, b.1340, d.1399.
John of Lancaster, Duke of Bedford, b.1389, d.1435.
John of Leyden (John Beuckelszoon), Dutch anabaptist, b.1509, killed 1536.
John of Nepomuk, St, national saint of Bohemia, killed 1393.
John of Salisbury, English scholar and divine, b.*c.*1115, d.1180.
John of the Cross, St, b.1542, d.1591.
John of Trevisa, English translator (of Higden's *Polychronicon*, 1387), b.1326, d.1412.

John O'London's Weekly, British periodical, published 1919–54, revived 1959.

John Paul I, pope 1978, b.1912, d.1978.

John Paul II (Karl Jozef Wojtyla), pope since 1978, b.1920.

John Rylands Library, Manchester, founded 1899 by his widow in memory of John Rylands, b.1801, d.1888.

Johns Hopkins University, Baltimore, founded 1867 by bequest of the American philanthropist Johns Hopkins, b.1795, d.1873. Opened 1876.

Johns, Jasper, American artist (*Target with Four Faces,* 1955), b.1930.

Johnson, Amy, English aviator, b.1903, d.1941.

Johnson, Andrew, 17th US president (1865–69), b.1808, d.1875.

Johnson, Dame Celia, British stage and screen actress (*Brief Encounter,* 1945), b.1908, d.1982.

Johnson, Dr John, first colonial-surgeon in New Zealand, b.1794, d.1848.

Johnson, Lyndon Baines, 36th US president (1963–69), b.1908, d.1973.

Johnson, Dr Samuel, English writer (*Dictionary*, 1755), b.1709, d.1784.

Johnston, Joseph, American soldier, b.1807, d.1891.

Joinville, Jean, Sire de, crusader and historian, b.c.1224, d.1319.

Joliot-Curie, Professor Frédéric, French physicist, b.1900, d.1958.

Jolliet, Louis, French explorer, b.1645, d.1700.

Jolson, Al (Asa Yoelson), American stage and screen actor and singer (*The Jazz Singer,* 1927), b.1886, d.1950.

Jones, Ernest, first British psychoanalyst, b.1879, d.1958.

Jones, Henry Arthur, English playwright (*Judah*, 1890), b.1851, d.1929.

Jones, Inigo, English architect, b.1573, d.1652.

Jones, John Luther ('Casey'), American railway hero, b.1864, killed 1900.

Jones, John Paul, Scottish-born American naval adventurer, b.1747, d.1792.

Jones, Owen, British architect (*Grammar of Ornament*, 1856), b.1809, d.1874.

Jonestown Massacre, mass suicide by members of Jim Jones's People's Temple religious cult, 18 Nov. 1978.

Jonson, Ben, English dramatist (*The Alchemist*, 1610), b.c.1573, d.1637

Jonson, Cornelis, English painter (*Charles I*), b.1593, d.1661.
Jooss, Kurt, German-born choreographer, b.1901, d.1979.
Joplin, Janis, American rock singer, b.1945, d.1970.
Joplin, Scott, American pianist-composer, one of the originators of 'Ragtime', b.1868, d.1917.
Jordaens, Jacob, Flemish painter (*Triumph of Bacchus*), b.1593, d.1678.
Jordan, Hashemite Kingdom of, came under British control 1922; became independent kingdom 1946; former name Trans-Jordan 1922–49.
Jordan, Mrs Dorothy, Irish actress and mistress of William IV, b.1762, d.1816.
Joseph, Chief, American Indian leader, d.1904.
Joseph I, Holy Roman emperor (1705–11), b.1678, d.1711.
Joseph II, Holy Roman emperor (1765–90), b.1741, d.1790.
Josephine, empress of the French, wife of Napoleon I, b.1763, d.1814.
Josephus, Flavius, Jewish historian, b.*c*.37, d.*c*.95.
Joubert, Joseph, French writer, b.1754, d.1824.
Joule's Law, of electrical energy, pronounced 1841 by the English scientist James Prescott Joule, b.1818, d.1889.
Jouvenet, Jean, French painter, b.1647, d.1717.
Jovian, Roman emperor (363–364), b.*c*.331, d.364.
Jowett, Benjamin, English scholar and educationist, b.1817, d.1893.
Joyce, James, Irish-born writer (*Ulysses*, 1922), b.1882, d.1941.
Joyce, William ('Lord Haw-Haw'), British traitor, b.1906, hanged 1946.
Juan Carlos I, king of Spain since 1975, b.1938.
Juan Fernández Islands, discovered *c*.1564 by the navigator Juan Fernández, d.*c*.1603.
Juárez, Benito, Mexican president (1861–62, 1867–72), b.1806, d.1872.
Jugurtha, king of Numidia (113–106), died in prison 104 BC.
Julian calendar, introduced in Rome by Julius Caesar 46 BC.
Juliana, queen of the Netherlands, b.1909, m. 1937, succeeded to the throne 1948.
Juliana of Norwich, English mystic, b.1343, d.1443.
Julian the Apostate, Roman emperor (361–363), b.*c*.331, d.363.
Jülich-Cleves, dispute over succession 1609–14.
Julius I, St, pope 337–352.
Julius II (Giuliano della Rovere), pope 1503–13, b.1443, d.1513.

Julius III (Giovanni Maria del Monte), pope 1550–55, b.1487, d.1555.
Julius Caesar, Caius, Roman dictator, b.100, assassinated 44 BC.
July Revolution, provoked by the reactionary measures of Charles X of France, 27 July to Aug. 1830.
Juneau, Solomon Laurent, French-American founder 1846 of Milwaukee, b.1793, d.1856.
Jung, Carl Gustav, Swiss psychoanalyst, b.1875, d.1961.
Jungfrau, Swiss mountain (13,699 ft.), first climbed 1811 on the east side by the Swiss brothers Meyer of Aaravi, first climbed on the west side by Sir George Young and the Rev. H. B. George 1865.
Jungfrau railway, highest in Europe, constructed 1896–1912.
'Junius', writer of political letters published 1769–72. Pseudonym believed to conceal the authorship of Sir Philip Francis, b.1740, d.1818.
Jupiter, satellites first discovered 1610 by Galileo; Red Spot first observed 1831
Jurassic Period, 170 million years ago.
Jusserand, Jean Antoine Jules, French diplomat and historian, b.1855, d.1932.
Justice of the peace, English judicial and administrative post, first recorded reference 1264.
Justiciar, official of Anglo-Norman kings until 1234.
Justin, St, b.*c.*100, martyred *c.*165
Justin I, Byzantine emperor (518–527), b.450, d.527.
Justin II, Byzantine emperor (565–578), d.578.
Justinian I, Byzantine emperor (527–565), b.483, d.565.
Justinian II, Byzantine emperor (685–695, 704–711), b.669, assassinated 711.
Jutland, Naval Battle of, between the British and German fleets, 31 May 1916.
Juvenal, Roman satirical poet, b.*c.*55, d.*c.*140.
Juxon, William, English divine, b.1582, d.1663.

K

K2 (Mt Godwin-Austen), Himalayas, climbed by an Italian expedition 31 July 1954.

Kabalevsky, Dimitri, Russian composer (*Master of Clamecy*, 1937), b.1904, d.1987.

Kabul, capital of Afghanistan since 1774.

Kafka, Franz, Austrian novelist (*Der Process*), b.1883, d.1924.

Kagawa, Toyohiko, Japanese writer (*The Psychology of the Poor*, 1915), b.1888, d.1960.

Kaiser, Georg, German dramatist (*Die Bürger von Calais*, 1913), b.1878, d.1945.

Kaiser Wilhelm II Land, Antarctica, discovered 1903 by the German explorer Erich von Drygalski, b.1865, d.1949.

KAL 007, Korean Airlines Boeing 707 passenger jet shot down by Soviet fighters for straying from flight path, 1 Sept. 1983.

Kaleidoscope, invented 1816 by Sir David Brewster, b.1781, d.1868.

Kalevala, Finnish folk epic, first published 1822 onwards.

Kalidása, Indian writer (*The Sakuntala*), probably lived in the 4th century.

Kalinin, Mikhail Ivanovich, Russian Bolshevik leader, b.1875, d.1946.

Kalium (potassium), discovered 1817 by the English chemist Sir Humphrey Davy, b.1778, d.1829.

Kamenev, Lev Borisovich (Rosenfeld), Russian Bolshevik leader, b.1883, executed 1936.

Kamerlingh Onnes, Heike, Dutch scientist, b.1853, d.1926.

Kanchenjunga, Himalayas, climbed by a British expedition 25 May 1955.

Kandinsky, Wassily, Russian-born painter, b.1866, d.1944.

K'ang Hsi Period, China, 1662–1722.

Kansas, USA, formed into a Territory 1854; admitted to the Union 1861.

Kansas University, Lawrence, Kansas, founded 1864.

Kant, Immanuel, German philosopher (*Critique of Pure Reason*, 1781), b.1724, d.1804.

Kapitza, Pyotr Leonidovich, Russian physicist, b.1894, d.1984.

Karajan, Herbert von, Austrian-born conductor, b.1908, d.1989.

Karg-Elert, Siegfried, German composer, b.1877, d.1933.

Kariba Hydro-Electric Project High Dam, Zambezi River, construction began 6 Nov. 1956, opened 18 May 1960.

Karloff, Boris (William Pratt), British-born (horror) film and stage actor (*Frankenstein*, 1931), b.1887, d.1969.

Karlsefni, Thorfinn, Icelandic navigator, *fl.* late 10th and first half of the 11th centuries.

Karsavina, Tamara, Russian-born ballet dancer, b.1885, d.1978.

Karsh, Yousuf, Armenian-born photographer (*Sir Winston Churchill*), b.1908.

Kashmir, Jammu and, became part of the Mogul Empire 1586; British supremacy recognized 1846; the Maharajah acceded to the dominion of India 1947; disputed between India, Pakistan and China since 1947; Indian-held territory became a state 1956.

Kasparov, Gary (Garik Weinstein), Russian chess master, b.1963.

Kassem, Abdul Karim, ruler of Iraq (1958–63), b.1914, killed in a coup 1963.

Kate Greenaway Medal, British award for the most distinguished work in the illustration of children's books, awarded annually by the British Library Association since 1956.

Katherine of Aragon, queen of England, b.1485, m. Prince Arthur, m. Henry VIII, d.1536.

Kauffmann, Angelica, Swiss-born painter, b.1741, d.1807.

Kaufman, George Simon, American writer (*Of Thee I Sing*, 1931), b.1889, d.1961.

Kaulbach, Wilhelm von, German painter (*Narrenhaus*), b.1805, d.1874.

Kaunda, Kenneth, African statesman (president of Zambia 1964–91), b.1924.

Kautsky, Karl, German socialist, b.1854, d.1938.

Kaye, Danny (Daniel Kominski), American comic actor and entertainer (*The Secret Life of Walter Mitty*, 1947), b.1913, d.1987.

Kay's flying shuttle, invented 1733 by the English clockmaker John Kay, b.1704, d.1764.

Kazan, Elia, American stage and film director (*A Streetcar Named Desire*, 1951), b.1909.

Kazantzakis, Nikos, Greek author (*Zorba the Greek*, 1946), b.1883, d.1957.

Kean, Charles John, English actor, b.*c.*1811, d.1868.

Kean, Edmund, English actor, b.1787, d.1833.

Keating, Paul, Australian statesman (prime minister since 1991), b.1945.

Keaton, Buster, American silent comedy actor and producer, b.1895, d.1966.

Keats, John, English poet (*Endymion*, 1818), b.1795, d.1821.

Keble, John, English divine (*Christian Year*, 1827), b.1792, d.1866.

Keble College, Oxford University, erected 1870 as a memorial to the English divine John Keble, b.1792, d.1866.

Keene, Charles, English artist and illustrator, b.1823, d.1891.

Keir Hardie, James, Scottish socialist leader, b.1856, d.1915.

Keller, Gottfried, Swiss novelist (*Der grüne Heinrich*, 1851–53), b.1819, d.1890.

Keller, Helen, American deaf-mute and blind writer (*The Story of My Life*, 1903), b.1880, d.1968.

Kellogg-Briand Pact (The Pact of Paris), renouncing war, signed 27 Aug. 1928.

Kelly, Gene, American dancer, choreographer, actor and film director (*Singin' in the Rain,* 1952), b.1912.

Kelly, Grace, *see* **Grace, Princess.**

Kelmscott Press, private press, founded and operated (1891–98) by William Morris, b.1834, d.1896.

Kelvin, William Thomson, Baron, British physicist, b.1824, d.1907.

Kemal Atatürk (Mustafa Kemal), Turkish soldier and statesman (president 1923–38), b.*c.*1880, d.1938.

Kemble, Fanny, English actress, b.1809, d.1893.

Kemény, Zsigmond, Baron, Hungarian politician and writer, b.1814, d.1875.

Ken, Thomas, bishop of Bath and Wells and hymn-writer ('Praise God from Whom All Blessings Flow'), b.1637, d.1711.

Kennedy, John Fitzgerald, 35th US president (1961–63), b.1917, assassinated 22 Nov. 1963.

Kennedy, Robert Francis (Bobby), American politician, brother of J. F. Kennedy, b.1925, assassinated 5 June 1968.

Kenneth I, first king of Scotland, d.*c.*860.

Kenneth II, king of Scotland (971–995), assassinated 995.

Kensington Gardens, London, became generally accessible to the public at the beginning of the 19th century.

Kensington Palace, London, acquired 1661 by the Earl of Nottingham, b.1621, d.1682, purchased by King William III, 1689.

Kent, Rockwell, American artist writer (*Salamina*, 1935), b.1882, d.1971.

Kent, William, English architect, b.1684, d.1748.

Kentucky, USA, first settled 1765; admitted to the Union 1792.

Kentucky Derby, USA, first run 17 May 1875.

Kenya, annexed to the British Crown as a colony 1920; gained independence 1963; member of the Commonwealth.

Kenyatta, Jomo, Kenyan nationalist politician (first president of Kenya 1964–78), b.*c.*1895, d.1978.

Keokuk, American Indian chief, b.*c.*1780, d.1848.

Kepler, Johannes, German mathematician and astronomer, b.1571, d.1630.

Ker, William Paton, Scottish literary critic (*Epic and Romance*, 1897), b.1855, d.1923.

Kerensky, Aleksandr, Russian socialist (head of government July-Nov. 1917), b.1881, d.1970.

Kerguélen Archipelago, Southern Indian Ocean, discovered 1772 by the French explorer Yves Kerguélen Trémarec, b.1745, d.1797.

Kern, Jerome, American composer (*Sally*, 1920), b.1885, d.1945.

Kerosene oil, discovered 1852 by the Canadian geologist Abraham Gesner, b.1797, d.1864.

Kerouac, Jack, American novelist, member of the Beat generation of poets and writers in 1950s (*On the Road*, 1957), b.1922, d.1969.

Kerschensteiner, Georg, German educationist, b.1854, d.1932.

Kesey, Ken, American writer (*One Flew Over the Cuckoo's Nest*, 1962), b.1935.

Ketch, Jack, official executioner (1663–86), d.1686.

Ketelby, Albert William, English composer (*In a Monastery Garden*, 1912), b.1880, d.1959.

Kett's Rebellion, 1549, led by the English landowner Robert Kett, hanged 1549.

Kew Gardens, established by Princess Augusta, Dowager Princess of Wales, 1759.

Kew Palace, the Dutch House, purchased King George III, 1781.

Key, Francis Scott, American lawyer and poet (*The Star-spangled Banner*, 1814), b.1779, d.1843.

Keyes, Roger, **Baron of Zeebrugge**, sailor and politician, b.1872, d.1945.

Keynes, John Maynard, English economist (*General Theory of Employment, Interest and Money*, 1936), b.1883, d.1946.

KGB (Komitet Gosudarstvennoye Bezhopaznosti), Soviet Committee for State Security, in charge of frontier and general security from 1953.

Khachaturiyan, Aram Ilich, Armenian-born Russian composer (*Masquerade Suite*, 1944), b.1903, d.1978.

Khaki, first worn 1843, introduced by Colonel Sir Harry Burnett Lumsden, b.1821, d.1896, of the Queen's Own Corps of Scouts and Guides, became general in the 2nd Afghan War.

Khaki Election, Great Britain, won by Conservatives, 28 Sept. to 16 Oct. 1900.

Khartoum, capital of the Sudan, founded *c.*1823.

Khayyam, Omar, Persian poet (*The Rubaiyat*), lived in the 11th century.

Khedive of Egypt, the last, Abbas Hilmi II, deposed 1914.

Khmer Rouge, revolutionary Cambodian political movement, captured Phnom Penh 1975; leader Pol Pot ruled Cambodia (renamed Kamouchea) 1975–79, perpetrating mass killings ('Year Zero').

Khomeini, Ayatollah Ruhollah (Sayyid Ruhollah Moussari), Iranian Shi'ite Muslim leader (Imam of Iran 1979–89), b.c.1900, d.1989.

Khosru I, Persian ruler from 531, d.579.

Khosru II, Persian ruler from 591, murdered 628.

Khrushchev, Nikita Sergeyevich, Russian statesman, b.1894, d.1971.

Khufu (Cheops), Egyptian king. *fl.* *c.*2900 BC.

Kidd, Captain William, Scottish pirate, b.*c.*1645, hanged 1701.

Kiel canal, first opened 1784; second opened 21 June 1895.

Kiel mutiny, of the German Navy, World War I, 3 Nov. 1918.

Kierkegaard, Søren, Danish philosopher, b.1813, d.1855.

Kilimanjaro, highest African mountain (19,710 ft.) first climbed 1889 by the German geographer Hans Meyer, b.1858, d.1929.

Killiecrankie, Battle of, between the Jacobites and the Royal force, 27 July 1689.

Killigrew, Thomas, English playwright (*The Parson's Wedding*, 1637), b.1612, d.1683.

'Kilmainham Treaty', between Gladstone and Parnell, May 1882.

Kilogram, national standard established in Britain 1897.

Kindergarten, first American, opened by the American educationalist Elizabeth Peabody, b.1804, d.1894, at Boston 1860.

Kindergarten, first English, opened *c.*1850 by Johannes Ronge.

Kindergarten, first Froebel, started at Blankenburg, Switzerland, 1837–45, by the German educationalist Friedrich Wilhelm August Froebel, b.1782, d.1852.

Kinetic theory of gases, postulated 1859 by the Scottish physicist James Clerk Maxwell, b.1831, d.1879.

Kinetoscope, invented 1887 by the American inventor Thomas Alva Edison, b.1847, d.1931.

King, Henry, English divine and poet, b.1592, d.1669.

King, William Mackenzie, Canadian prime minister (1921–30, 1935–48), b.1874, d.1950.

King Charles the Martyr, anniversary of, commemorating his execution 1649, held 30 Jan.

King Edward VII Land, Antarctica, sighted 1842 by Sir James Clark Ross, b.1800, d.1862; identified 1902 by the English explorer Robert Scott, b.1868, d.1912.

King George V Dock, Glasgow, opened 10 July 1931.

King George V Dock, London, opened 1921.

King George V Land, Antarctica, discovered 1912–13 by the Australian explorer Sir Douglas Mawson, b.1882, d.1958.

King George's War, waged by Britain and France in North America 1745–54.

Kinglake, Alexander William, English traveller (*Eothen*, 1844) and historian, b.1809, d.1891.

King, Martin Luther, Jr., American Civil Rights leader, b.1929, assassinated 4 April 1968.

King Philip's War, waged 1675–76 by the American Indian chief Philip, killed 1676.

King, Stephen, American horror novelist (*The Shining,* 1977), b.1947.

King's College, Cambridge University, founded by King Henry VI, 1441.

King's College, London University, founded 1829; reincorporated 1882.

King's College, New York (now Columbia University), founded by grant of King George II, 1754.

Kingsley, Charles, English writer (*Westward Ho!* 1855), b.1819, d.1875.

Kingsley, Henry, English writer (*Ravenshoe,* 1861), b.1830, d.1876.

Kingsley, Mary, English traveller and writer (*Travels in West Africa*, 1897), b.1862, d.1900.

King's Police Medal, instituted by Royal Warrant 1909.

Kingsway, London, opened 18 Oct. 1905.

King William Island, Arctic, discovered 1831 by the Scottish explorer Sir James Clark Ross, b.1800, d.1862.

Kinsey, Alfred, American sexologist (the Kinsey Reports 1948, 1953), b.1894, d.1956.

Kinshasa, see **Léopoldville.**

Kipling, John Lockwood, British artist, b.1837, d.1911.

Kipling, Rudyard, British writer (*Kim*, 1911), b.1865, d.1936.

Kircher, Athanasius, German inventor of the magic lantern (1646), b.1601, d.1680.

Kiritimati, *see* **Christmas Island.**

'Kirke's Lambs', British soldiers led at the Battle of Sedgemoor (1685) by the English brigadier Percy Kirke, b.*c.*1646, d.1691.

Kissinger, Henry Alfred, American diplomat, foreign policy adviser and analyst (secretary of state 1973–77), b.1923.

Kit-Cat Club, London, anti-Jacobite dining club of writers, politicians, etc., existed roughly 1700–20.

Kitchener of Khartoum, Herbert, Viscount, British soldier, b.1850, drowned 1916.

Kléber, Jean Baptiste, French general, b.1755, assassinated 1800.

Klee, Paul, Swiss painter (*High Spirits*, 1939), b.1879, d.1940.

Klein, Calvin, American fashion designer, b.1942.

Kleist, Heinrich von, German poet and playwright (*Prinz Friedrich von Homburg*, 1811), b.1777, d.1811.

Klemperer, Otto, German conductor, b.1885, d.1973.

Klondike gold rush, gold discovered 1896; rush began 1897.

Klopstock, Friedrich Gottlieb, German poet (*Messias*, 1748–73), b.1724, d.1803.

Kneller, Sir Godfrey, German-born portrait painter, b.*c.*1648, d.1723.

Knight, Dame Laura (née Johnson), English painter, b.1877, d.1970.

Knight, William Angus, Scottish philosopher, b.1836, d.1916.

Knights Hospitallers of St John of Jerusalem, Order founded during the First Crusade, recognized by Papacy 1113.

Knights of Malta, Order of St John of Jerusalem, 1529–1798.

Knights of Rhodes, Order of St John of Jerusalem, 1309–1522.

Knights Templars, Order formed *c.*1118, recognized by Papacy 1128, abolished 1314.

Knights, Teutonic, Order formed 1190, recognized by Papacy 1191, went to Prussia *c.*1225.

Knitting Frame, Cotton's, invented 1864 by the merchant William Cotton, b.1786, d.1866.

Knossos Excavations, started 1900 by the English archaeologist Sir John Evans, b.1851, d.1941.

Knowles, James, English architect and founder (1877) of the *Nineteenth Century*, b.1831, d.1908.

Knowles, Sir James Sheridan, Irish-born playwright (*Virginius*, 1820), b.1784, d.1862.

Knox, John, Scottish religious reformer, b.*c.*1505, d.1572.

Knox, Ronald, English writer, b.1888, d.1957.

Knut II, the Great (Canute), king of Denmark and England, b.*c.*995, d.1035.

Knut III (Hardeknut), king of Denmark (1035–42) and England, d.1042.

Knut IV, St, king of Denmark (1080–86), killed 1086.

Knut V, king of Denmark (1147–57), assassinated 1157.

Knut VI, king of Denmark (1182–1202), b.1163, d.1202.

Koberger, Anton, German pioneer printer and publisher, b.*c.*1445, d.1513

Koch, Charles Henri Emmanuel, German traveller and naturalist, b.1809, d.1879.

Koch, Robert, German bacteriologist and discoverer 1882 of the TB bacillus, b.1843, d.1910.

'Kodak' folding cameras, first marketed 1898 by the American inventor George Eastman, b.1854, d.1932.

Kodály, Zoltán, Hungarian composer (*Háry János*, 1926), b.1882, d.1967.

Kodiak Island, Alaska, discovered 1764 by the Russian fur-trader Stephen Glotov.

Koestler, Arthur, Hungarian-born British author and journalist (*Darkness at Noon,* 1940), b.1905, committed suicide 1983.

Koh-I-Noor, Indian diamond, known since 1304; acquired by East India Company, and presented to British regalia 1850.

Kohl, Helmut, German politician (chancellor of West Germany 1982–90, of reunited Germany since 1990), b.1930.

Kokoschka, Oskar, Austrian painter, b.1886, d.1980.

Kollwitz, Käthe, German artist, b.1867, d.1945.

Königsmark, Otto Wilhelm, Freiherr von, German general, b.1639, d.1688.

Koninck, Laurent Guillaume de, Belgian palaeontologist, b.1809, d.1887.

Konrad von Würzburg, German poet (*Trojanerkrieg*, 1280–87), d.1287.

Koran, sacred book of Islam, written approximately 620 to 632.

Korda, Sir Alexander, Hungarian-born film producer, b.1893, d.1956.

Korea, occupied by Japan 1905 and formally annexed to that country 22 Aug. 1910; occupied and partitioned by USA and USSR 1945, becoming North Korea and South Korea in 1948.

Korean Truce, between the United Nations and North Korea, signed 27 July 1953.

Korean War, between the United Nations and North Korean and Chinese forces, June 1950 to June 1951.

Kosciuszko, Tadeusz, Polish leader b.1746, d.1817.

Kossuth, Lajos, Hungarian patriot, b.1802, d.1894.

Kotzebue, August Friedrich Ferdinand von, German playwright (*Adelheid von Wulfingen*, 1789), b.1761, killed 1819.

Koussevitsky, Sergei, Russian-born conductor, b.1874, d.1951.

Krafft-Ebing, Richard, Freiherr von, German expert in mental disorders, b.1840, d.1902.

Kreisler, Fritz, Austrian-born violinist, b.1875, d.1962.

Kreuger, Nils Edvard, Swedish painter, b.1858, d.1930.

Kreutzer, Rodolphe, French-born violinist, b.1766, d.1831.

Krishnamurti, Jiddu, Indian mystic, b.1895, d.1986.

Kronstadt, Russian naval base, founded 1710; scene of mutiny March 1921.

Kropotkin, Prince Peter, Russian scientist and anarchist (*Mutual Aid*, 1902), b.1842, d.1921.

Kruger, Stephanus Johannes Paulus, Boer leader and president of South Africa (1883–1900), b.1825, d.1904.

Krupp Works, founded 1810 at Essen, Germany, by Friedrich Krupp, b.1787, d.1826, and developed by his son Alfred Krupp, b.1812, d.1887.

Krusenstern, Adam Ivan, circumnavigator (1803–06) of the world, b.1770, d.1846.

Krylov, Ivan Andreievich, Russian writer of fables, b.1786, d.1844.

Krypton, inert gas, first obtained 1898 from the atmosphere by the British scientists Sir William Ramsay, b.1852, d.1916, and Morris William Travers, b.1872, d.1961.

Kubrik, Stanley, American film director (*Doctor Strangelove*, 1963), b.1928.

Ku Klux Klan, American secret society, founded 1865 at Polask, Tennessee; revived 1915 by William J. Simmons, and again in 1945 by Dr Samuel Green.
Kubelik, Jan, Czech violinist, b.1880, d.1940.
Kublai Khan, Mongolian emperor (1276–94), b.1216, d.1294.
Kulturkampf, Bismarck's struggle with Catholic Church in Germany 1871–87.
Kun, Béla, Communist leader in Hungary March–Aug. 1919, b.1886, disappeared in Russia after 1919.
Kundera, Milan, Czechoslovakian author (*The Book of Laughter and Forgetting,* 1980), b.1929.
Kung, Hans, Swiss Roman Catholic theologian (*Does God Exist?* 1978), b.1928.
Kuomintang, Chinese national republic party, founded at the beginning of 20th century.
Kuprin, Aleksandr, Russian novelist (*Yama*, *the Pit*, 1909), b.1870, d.1938.
Kuropatkin, Alexei Nikolaievich, Russian general, b.1848, d.1925.
Kurosawa, Akira, Japanese film director (*Ran,* 1985), b.1910.
Kut, Mesopotamia, World War I, captured by the British 1915; surrendered to the Turks 1916, retaken by the British 1917.
Kutuzov, Mikhael Ilarionovich, Russian diplomat, administrator and soldier, b.1743, d.1813.
Kuwait, Gulf state, became British protectorate 1899; recognized an independent under British protection 1914; complete independence 1961.
Kyd, Thomas, English playwright (*The Spanish Tragedy*, 1586), b.c.1558, d.1594.
Kynaston, Edward, English actor (possibly the last to take female parts), b.c.1640, d.1706.
Kyoto, capital of Japan until 1868.

L

Labé, Louise (La Belle Cordière), French poet (*Sonnets*, 1555), b.c.1525, d.1566.

Labiche, Eugène Marin, French playwright (*Le Voyage de M. Perrichon*, 1860), b.1815, d.1888.

Labienus, Titus, Roman tribune, killed 45.

Labor Day, USA and Canada, first Monday in Sept. Inaugurated 1882; officially adopted 1894.

Labouchère, Henry, English politician and journalist (founded *Truth*, 1877), b.1831, d.1912.

Labour Day, 1 May.

Labour Party, origins in the Labour Representation League, organized 1869, and the Labour Electoral Association, formed by the TUC in 1887; founded (as Labour Representation Committee) at a conference in London 27–28 Feb. 1900; present name adopted 1906; constitution adopted 1918.

La Bruyère, Jean de, French writer (*Characters*, 1688), b.1645, d.1696.

Labuan, Malay Archipelago, island off N.W. Borneo, ceded to Britain by the Sultan of Brunei 1846; part of Straits Settlements until 1946 when transferred to North Borneo.

La Calprenède, Gauthier de Costes de, French writer (*Cassandre*, 1642–50), b.1614, d.1663.

Laccadive, Minicoy and Amindivi Islands, *see* **Lakshadweep Islands.**

Lace-making, pillow, introduced 1561 into Germany by the German Barbara Uttman, b.1514, d.1575.

LaChaise, François de, father confessor to Louis XIV, b.1624, d.1709.

Lactantius Firmianus, early Christian Father, b.c.260, d.c.340.

'Ladies of Llangollen', Lady Eleanor Butler, b.1778, d.1829 and Sarah Ponsonby, b.1778, d.1831.

'Ladies' Peace', the Treaty of Cambrai, renewing the Treaty of Madrid, signed 1529.

Ladislaus I, St (Laszlo), king of Hungary (1077–95), b.1040, d.1095.

Ladislaus II, king of Hungary (1161), b.c.1134, d.1162.

Ladislaus III, king of Hungary (1204–05), b.1199, d.1205.

Ladislaus IV, king of Hungary (1272–90), b.1262, murdered 1290.

Ladislaus V, king of Hungary (1444–57), b.1440, d.1457.
Lady Day (Annunciation of the Virgin), 25 March.
Lady Margaret Hall, Oxford University, founded 1879.
Ladysmith, Siege of, Boer War, Oct. 1899, relieved 28 Feb. 1900.
Laetare Sunday, the fourth Sunday in Lent.
La Fayette, Marie Joseph Paul Yves Roch Gilbert du Motier, Marquis de, French political reformer, b.1757, d.1834.
La Fayette, Marie Madeleine, Comtesse de, French writer, b.1634, d.1693.
Laffitte, Jacques, French financier, b.1767, d.1844.
Laforgue, Jules, French poet (*Complaintes*, 1885), b.1860, d.1887.
La Follette, Robert, American senator, b.1855, d.1925.
La Fontaine, Jean de, French writer (*Fables*, 1668–90), b.1621, d.1695.
La Guardia, Fiorello, American lawyer and politician (reformist mayor of New York City 1933–45), b.1882, d.1947.
Lagerlöf, Selma, Swedish novelist (*Gösta Berling*, 1894), b.1858, d.1940.
Lagrange, Joseph Louis, Italian-born scientist, b.1736, d.1813.
Lakshadweep Islands, Indian Ocean, discovered by the Portuguese 1498; sequestrated by Britain 1877; now a territory of India.
Lalande, Joseph Jérome Lefrançais de, French astronomer, b.1732, d.1807.
Lalo, Édouard, French composer (*Symphonie espagnole*, 1875), b.1823, d.1892.
Lamarck, Jean Baptiste Pierre Antoine de Monet, Chevalier de, French naturalist, b.1744, d.1829.
Lamartine, Alphonse Marie Louis de, French writer (*Meditation*, 1820), b.1790, d.1869.
Lamb, Charles, English essayist (*Elia*, 1823), b.1775, d.1834.
Lamb, John, British pioneer in the development of gas turbine propulsion, b.1890, d.1958.
Lambert, Constant, English composer (*Rio Grande*, 1929), b.1905, d.1951.
Lambert, John, English Puritan general, b.1619, d.1684.
Lambeth Articles, concerning predestination and election, drawn up 1595 by John Whitgift, archbishop of Canterbury, b.*c.*1530, d.1604.
Lambeth Bridge, London, opened 1862, pulled down 1929, new bridge opened 1932.

Lambeth Conference, Anglican bishops' assembly, first convened 1867.

Lambeth Palace, origin uncertain, chapel built 1245–70, Water Tower built *c.*1430.

Lamennais, Fèlicité Robert de, French church reformer (*Paroles d'un croyant*, 1834), b.1782, d.1854.

Lammas Day, 1 Aug.

Lamond, Frederick, Scottish pianist, b.1868, d.1948.

La Motte-Fouqué, Friedrich, Freiherr de, German writer (*Undine*, 1811), b.1777, d.1843.

L'Amour, Louis, American writer of western novels (*Hondo*, 1953), b.1908, d.1988.

Lamp, electric, first public demonstration 1879 by the inventor Sir Joseph Swan, b.1828, d.1914.

Lampedusa, Giuseppi Tomasi Di, Italian writer (*The Leopard*, 1955–56), b.1896, d.1957.

Lancashire witch, the last, Mary Nutter, b.1856, d.1928.

Lancaster, Burt (Burton Stephen Lancaster), American film actor (*The Swimmer*, 1968), b.1913.

Lancaster, Duchy of, established 1265; attached to the Crown since 1399.

Lancers, form of quadrille, came into fashion in Britain *c.*1850.

Lancet, The, British medical journal, founded 1823 by the English surgeon Thomas Wakley, b.1795, d.1862.

Lancret, Nicolas, French painter (*Les cinq sens*), b.1660, d.1743.

Land, Edwin, American inventor of the Polaroid camera 1948, colour version 1963, b.1909, d.1991.

Land Registry, British, established 1862, reformed 1875; now operates under Land Registration Acts 1925–88.

Landor, Walter Savage, English writer (*Imaginary Conversation*, 1824–46), b.1775, d.1864.

Landowska, Wanda, Polish-born harpsichord player, b.1877, d.1959.

Landseer, Sir Edwin, English painter (*Suspense*, 1834), b.1804, d.1875.

Landus, pope 913–914.

Lane, Sir Hugh, Irish art collector, b.1875, drowned at sea 1915.

Lane Bequest, of modern paintings, bequeathed by Sir Hugh Lane, shared by Britain with Eire 1959.

Lanfranc, archbishop of Canterbury (1070–89), b.*c.*1005, d.1089.

Lang, Andrew, Scottish writer and translator (*Myth, Ritual and Religion*, 1887), b.1844, d.1912.

Lang, Fritz, German-born film director (*Metropolis,* 1927), b.1890, d.1976.

Lange, David, New Zealand politician (prime minister 1984–89), b.1942.

Langham, Simon, archbishop of Canterbury (1366–68), d.1376.

Langland, William, English poet (*Piers Plowman*, 1362), lived during the second half of the 14th century.

Langton, Stephen, archbishop of Canterbury (1207–28), b.*c.*1150, d.1228.

Langtry, Lillie ('The Jersey Lily'), actress, b.1852, d.1929.

Lanier, Sidney, American poet (*Florida*, 1875), b.1842, d.1881.

Lansbury, George, British socialist leader, b.1859, d.1940.

Lansdowne, William Petty Fitzmaurice, Marquess of, Irish-born secretary of state, b.1737, d.1805.

Lansky, Meyer, American Mafia figure, b.1902, d.1983.

Lanthanum, metallic element, discovered 1839 by Swedish scientist Karl Gustav Mosander, b.1797, d.1858.

Laos, French protectorate 1893, became independent sovereign state, within the French Union, 1949; became a republic in 1975.

Lâo-tse, Chinese founder of Taoism, b.*c.*604 BC.

La Paz, capital of Bolivia, founded 1548 by the 16th-century Spanish explorer Alfonso de Mendoza.

La Pérouse, Jean François de Galaup, Comte de, French navigator, b.1741, probably shipwrecked 1788.

Laplace, Pierre Simon, Marquis de, French astronomer, b.1749, d.1827.

Laporte, Pierre de, valet to Louis XIV and intriguer, b.1603, d.1650.

Larbaud, Valéry, French writer (*Enfantines*, 1918), b.1881, d.1957.

Lardner, Ring (Ringgold Wilmer Lardner), American humorous writer (*Gullible's Travels*, 1917), b.1885, d.1933.

Largillière, Nicolas de, French painter (*Mlle Duclos*), b.1656, d.1746.

Larkin, Philip, British poet, jazz critic and librarian (*High Windows,* 1974), b.1922, d.1985.

Laroche, Raymonde, Baronne de, French aviator, first woman in the world (1910) to qualify for a pilot's certificate.

La Rochefoucald, François de, French writer (*Maxims*, 1665), b.1613, d.1680.

Larousse, Pierre Athanase, French encyclopaedist, b.1817, d.1875.

Laryngoscope, use introduced 1861 by the American physician Louis Elsberg, b.1836, d.1885.

Laryngoscopy, study founded by the Bohemian scientist Johann Nepomuk Czermak, b.1828, d.1873.

La Salle, Robert Cavelier, Sieur de, French explorer and navigator (the Mississippi, 1682), b.1643, assassinated 1687.

Las Casas, Bartolomé de, Spanish prelate, b.1474, d.1566.

Lascaux caves, S.W. France, painted caves discovered by five boys from Montignac 1940.

Lasker, Emanuel, German chess player, b.1868, d.1941.

Laski, Harold, English politician and economist, b.1893, d.1950.

Lassalle, Ferdinand, German socialist (*System of Acquired Rights*, 1860), b.1825, killed 1864.

Lassie, collie dog film star, first appeared in *Lassie Come Home* 1943.

Lasso, Orlando di, Dutch composer (*Psalma Davidis poenitentiale*), b.c.1531, d.1594.

László, Philip, Hungarian painter, b.1869, d.1937.

Latent heat, nature defined *c.*1765 by the British scientist Joseph Black, b.1728, d.1799.

Lateran Councils, First, 18 March 1123 onwards; **Second,** April 1139; **Third,** March 1179; **Fourth,** 1215; **Fifth,** 3 May 1512 to 16 March 1517.

Lateran Treaty, between the Holy See and the kingdom of Italy, 1929.

Latimer, Hugh, English religious reformer, b.c.1485, burnt at the stake 1555.

La Tour, Maurice Quentin de, French artist (*Louis XV*), b.1704, d.1788.

Latrobe, Charles Joseph, lieutenant governor of Victoria, Australia, b.1801, d.1875.

Latterday Saints, Church of Jesus Christ of the (Mormons), founded 1827 by the American Joseph Smith, b.1805, d.1844.

Latvia, ruled by Russia 1795–1918; independence declared 1919; occupied by the Russians June 1940 and admitted to the Soviet Union Aug. 1940; gained independence from the former Soviet Union 21 Aug. 1991.

Latvian language, earliest known text dated 1585.

Laud, William, archbishop of Canterbury (1633–45), b.1573, beheaded 1645.

Laudanum, alcoholic tincture of opium, formula developed *c.*1660 by the English physician Thomas Sydenham, b.1624, d.1689.

Lauder, Sir Harry, Scottish comedian and singer, b.1870, d.1950.
Lauderdale, John Maitland, Duke of, Scottish statesman, b.1616, d.1682.
Laughing gas (nitrous oxide), discovered 1772 by the English scientist Joseph Priestley, b.1733, d.1804. First used 1844 as an anaesthetic in dentistry by the American dentist Horace Wells, b.1815, d.1848.
Laughton, Charles, English-born actor, b.1899, d.1962.
Laurel and Hardy, comedy duo of silent and talking pictures: Stan Laurel, b.1890, d.1965, Oliver Hardy, b.1892, d.1957.
Laurie, Annie (Mrs Alexander Ferguson), b.1682, d.1764.
Laurier, Sir Wilfrid, first French-Canadian premier of Canada (1896–1911), b.1841, d.1919.
Lausanne Pact, between the Allies and Germany, signed 1932.
Lausanne, Treaty of, concerning Turkey, signed 24 July 1923.
Lautrec, Henri Marie Raymond de Toulouse, French painter (*Attablés*), b.1864, d.1901.
Laval, Pierre, French statesman, b.1883 executed 1945.
La Vallière, Louise de, mistress of Louis XIV, b.1644, d.1710.
Lavater, Johann Kaspar, Swiss theologian and physiognomist, b.1741, d.1801.
Lavery, Sir John, Ulster painter, b.1856, d.1941.
Lavoisier, Antoine Laurent, French scientist, b.1743, guillotined 1794.
Law, John, Scottish controller-general of finance in France, b.1671, d.1729.
Law, William, English theologian (*Serious Call,* 1729), b.1686, d.1761.
Lawes, William, English composer ('Gather ye rosebuds while ye may'), b.1582, killed 1645.
Lawrence, anti-pope 498.
Lawrence, D(avid) H(erbert), English writer (*Lady Chatterley's Lover*, 1928), b.1885, d.1930.
Lawrence, Dr Ernest Orlando, American physicist, b.1901, d.1958.
Lawrence, John Laird Mair, Baron Lawrence, viceroy and governor-general of India (1864–69), b.1811, d.1879.
Lawrence, Sir Thomas, English painter (*Mrs Siddons*), b.1769, d.1830.
Lawrence, T(homas) E(dward) ('Lawrence of Arabia'), British explorer and writer (*Seven Pillars of Wisdom*, 1926), b.1888, d.1935.

Lawrence, Kansas, sacked by Quantrill Gang, 1863.

Layamon, English priest and historian (*The Brut*), lived in the late 12th and early 13th centuries.

Layard, Sir Austen Henry, archaeologist and diplomat, b.1817, d.1894.

LDV (Local Defence Volunteers), formed May 1940, became Home Guard July 1940; disbanded 1 Nov. 1944.

Leacock, Stephen, English-born Canadian humorist (*Nonsense Novels*, 1911), b.1869, d.1944.

League of Nations, founded 28 April 1919; superseded by the UN 8 April 1946.

Leaky, Louis Seymour Bazett, Anglo-Kenyan archaeologist and anthropologist, discoverer of early primate fossil remains in Olduvai Gorge, E. Africa, 1959, b.1903, d.1972.

Lean, David, British film director (*The Bridge on the River Kwai*, 1957), b.1908, d.1991.

Leaning Tower of Pisa, built 1174–1350.

Leap year, the system by which every fourth year comprises 366 days, the extra day being 29 Feb.

Lear, Edward, English artist and humorist (*Book of Nonsense*, 1846), b.1812, d.1888.

Leary, Timothy, American psychologist and experimental drugs guru, b.1920.

Lease-Lend, US aid to Britain programme, proposed by President Roosevelt 1940; put into action 1941; made reciprocal 1942.

Leather, artificial, first manufactured in Britain 1884.

Leather hose, for fire fighting, invented 1672.

Leavis, Frank Raymond, British literary scholar and critic (*The Great Tradition*, 1948), b.1895, d.1978.

Lebanon, part of the Ottoman Empire 1516–1919; under French mandatory rule 1920–41; independence proclaimed 1941; French withdrawal completed 1946; intermittent civil war between Christian and Muslim factions 1975–76; Israeli occupations 1978, 1980, 1982–85 in reprisal for Lebanon-based Palestinian attacks on Israeli border settlements; Lebanese government authority over rival militias restored 1990–92.

Leblanc, Nicolas, French chemist, b.1742, d.1806.

Le Brun, Charles, French painter (*La Famille de Darius*), b.1619, d.1690.

Le Carre, John (David John Moore Cornwell), British spy novelist (*The Spy Who Came in from the Cold*, 1963), b.1931.

Lecky, William Edward Hartpole, Irish historian, b.1838, d.1903.
Lecocq, Charles, French composer (*Giroflé-Girofla*, 1874), b.1832, d.1918.
Leconte de Lisle, Charles Marie, French poet (*Poèmes antiques*, 1852), b.1818, d.1894.
'Le Corbusier' (Charles Edouard Jeanneret), Swiss-born architect, b.1887, d.1965.
Lecouvreur, Adrienne, French actress, b.1692, d.1730.
Le Despenser, Hugh, Earl of Winchester, royal favourite, b.1262, hanged 1326.
Lee, Ann, English founder (1758) of the religious movement the Society of Shakers, b.1736, d.1784.
Lee, Nathaniel, English playwright (*The Rival Queens*, 1677), b.*c.*1653, d.1692.
Lee, Robert Edward, American Confederate general, b.1807, d.1870.
Lee, Sir Sidney, English editor of the *Dictionary of National Biography*, b.1859, d.1926.
Leech, John, English engraver, b.1817, d.1864.
Leeds University, England, founded 1874, granted university status 1904.
Leeuwenhoek, Anton van, Dutch microscopist, b.1632, d.1723.
Le Fanu, Sheridan, Irish writer (*In a Glass Darkly*, 1872), b.1814, d.1873.
Legal memory, in England, dates back to accession of Richard I, 1 Sept. 1189.
Le Gallienne, Richard, English poet (*English Poems*, 1892), b.1866, d.1947.
Legion of Honour (La Légion d'Honneur), created by the French Consular law of 19 May 1802.
Legitimacy, by marriage of parents, made legal in England 1926.
Lego®, construction toy using plastic bricks, developed in Denmark 1947.
Legros, Alphonse, French artist (*Ex voto*, 1861), b.1837, d.1911.
Lehár, Franz, Hungarian composer (*The Merry Widow*, 1905), b.1870, d.1948.
Lehmann, Beatrix, English actress, b.1903, d.1979.
Lehmann, John, English writer and editor, b.1907, d.1987.
Lehmann, Lilli, German operatic singer, b.1848, d.1929.
Lehmann, Lotte, German-born operatic singer, b.1888, d.1976.

Lehmann, Rosamund, English novelist (*Dusty Answer*, 1927), b.1903, d.1990.

Leibniz, Gottfried Wilhelm, German philosopher, b.1646, d.1716.

Leicester, Robert Dudley, Earl of, Elizabethan courtier, b.*c.*1531, d.1588.

Leicester University, England, founded 1918 as the Leicester, Leicestershire and Rutland College; became University College, Leicester, 1927; gained university status 1957.

Leif Ericsson, Icelandic discoverer of North America *c.*1000.

Leigh, Vivien (Vivien Hartley), English actress, b.1913, d.1967.

Leighton, Frederick, Lord, English painter (*Andromache*, 1888), b.1830, d.1896.

Leipzig University, Germany, founded 1409.

Lekeu, Guillaume, French composer (*Andromède*, 1891), b.1870, d.1894.

Leland, John, English antiquary (*Itinerary*, 1710–12), b.*c.*1506, d.1552.

Lely, Cornelis, Dutch statesman, engineer and planner of the Zuider Zee, b.1854, d.1929.

Lely, Sir Peter, German-born painter (*Nell Gwynn*), b.1618, d.1680.

Lemmon, Jack (John Uhler Lemmon III), American film actor (*The Apartment*, 1960), b.1925.

Lemon, Mark, English writer and editor *of Punch*, b.1809, d.1870.

Lemonnier, Pierre Charles, French astronomer, b.1715, d.1799.

Lenbach, Franz, German painter (*Bismarck*), b.1836, d.1904.

'Lenclos, Ninon de' (Anne Lenclos), French courtesan, b.1620, d.1705.

L'Enfant, Pierre Charles, French architect and town planner in the USA, b.1754, d.1825.

Le Moine, François, French painter (*Ruth et Boaz*, 1711), b.1688, committed suicide 1737.

Le Nain, The brothers, French painters: Antoine, b.1588, d.1648, Louis, b.1593, d.1648, and Mathieu, b.1607, d.1677.

Lenin, Nikolai (Vladimir Ilyich Ulianov), Russian Bolshevik leader, b.1870, d.1924.

Leningrad, former name for St Petersburg 1924–91 (previously St Petersburg 1703–1914, Petrograd 1914–1924) named after Lenin 1924.

Leningrad, Siege of, by the Germans, relieved after 16 months by the Russians 18 Jan. 1943.
Lennon, John, *see* **Beatles.**
Lennox, Charlotte, American-born writer (*The Female Quixote*, 1752), b.1720, d.1804.
'Leno, Dan' (George Galvin), English comedian, b.1861, d.1904.
Le Normand, Henri René, French playwright (*Le Lâche*, 1925), b.1882, d.1951.
Le Nôtre, André, French landscape architect (St James's Park, London), b.1613, d.1700.
Lens, first referred to by Meisner in 13th century.
Lent, period of 40 days of fasting preceding Easter.
Leo I, the Great, St, pope 440–461.
Leo II, St, pope 682–683.
Leo III, St, pope 795–816.
Leo IV, St, pope 847–855.
Leo V, pope 903.
Leo VI, pope 928.
Leo VII, pope 936–939.
Leo VIII, pope 963–964.
Leo IX (Bruno), pope 1049–54, b.1002, d.1054.
Leo X (Giovanni de Medici), pope 1513–21, b.1475, d.1521.
Leo XI (Alessandro de Medici), pope 1605, b.*c.*1535, d.1605.
Leo XII (Annibale della Genga), pope 1823–29, b.1760, d.1829.
Leo XIII (Gioacchino Pecci), pope 1878–1903, b.1810, d.1903.
León, Juan Ponce de, Spanish colonial administrator, b.1460, killed 1521.
León, Luis Ponce de, Spanish poet, b.*c.*1527, d.1591.
Leonardo da Vinci, Italian engineer and artist (*Mona Lisa*), b.1452, d.1519.
Leone, Sergio, Italian director of spaghetti westerns (*A Fistful of Dollars,* 1964), b.1921, d.1989.
Leopardi, Giacomo, Italian poet (*Operette Morali*, 1827), b.1798, d.1837.
Leopold I, Holy Roman emperor (1658–1705), b.1640, d.1705.
Leopold II, Holy Roman emperor (1790–92), b.1747, d.1792.
Leopold I, first king of the Belgians (1831–65), b.1790, d.1865.
Leopold II, king of the Belgians (1865–1909), b.1835, d.1909.
Leopold III, king of the Belgians (1934–51), b.1901, d.1983.
Léopoldville, now Kinshasa, capital of the former Belgian Congo, now Zaire; founded 1881 by the Welsh explorer Sir Henry Morton Stanley, b.1841, d.1904.

Lepanto, Naval Battle of, fought between the Holy League under Don John and the Turks, 7 Oct. 1571.

Lepidus, Marcus Aemilius, Roman triumvir, d.13.

Le Play, Pierre Guillaume Frédéric, French engineer and economist, b.1806, d.1882.

Leprosy, mentioned in India 1400 and in Egypt 1350 BC; bacillus discovered 1872 by the Norwegian physician Gerhard Hansen, b.1841, d.1912.

Lermontov, Mikhail Yurevich, Russian writer (*A Hero of Our Times*, 1839), b.1814, killed in a duel 1841.

Le Sage, Alain René, French writer (*Gil Blas*, 1715–35), b.1668, d.1747.

Leschetizky, Theodor, Polish-born pianist, b.1830, d.1915.

Lespinasse, Jeanne Julie Eléonore de, French writer (*Lettres*, 1809), b.1732, d.1776.

Lesseps, Ferdinand de, French canal builder, b.1805, d.1894.

Lessing, Doris, English writer (*Martha Quest*, 1952), b.1919.

Lessing, Gotthold Ephraim, German writer (*Laokoon*, 1766), b.1729, d.1781.

L'Estrange, Sir Roger, English pamphleteer, journalist and translator, b.1616, d.1704.

Le Sueur, Eustache, French painter (*Vie de St Bruno*, 1645–48), b.1617, d.1655.

Lesueur, Jean François, French composer (*Paul et Virginie*, 1794), b.1760, d.1837.

Letchworth, England's first garden city, founded 1903.

Letter Office, General, first established in England by Act of Parliament 1660.

Letters of Marque, licences granted to private persons to fit out armed ships in time of war, abolished by the Declaration of Paris, 1855.

Leukaemia, disease of the blood, treatment developed by the American physician Edward Gamaliel Janeway, b.1841, d.1911.

Levant Company, English trading venture, founded 1581; chartered 1592.

Le Vau, Louis, French architect, b.1612, d.1670.

Levellers, English republican and democratic group; appeared 1647, crushed by Cromwell 1649, disappeared after Restoration 1660.

Lever, Charles, Irish-born novelist (*Harry Lorrequer*, 1837), b.1806, d.1872.

Leverhulme, William Lever, Viscount, English manufacturer, b.1851, d.1925.

Leverrier, Urbain, French astronomer (predicted position of the planet Neptune 1846), b.1811, d.1877.

Levi, Primo, Italian author, survivor of Auschwitz (*The Periodic Table,* 1975), b.1919, d.1987.

Levi-Strauss, Claude, French anthropologist and founder of structuralism, b.1908.

Lewes, Battle of, between Henry III and barons, 1265.

Lewis, C(live) S(taples), English scholar and writer (*The Screwtape Letters*, 1942), b.1898, d.1963.

Lewis, Meriwether, American explorer of the far West, b.1774, committed suicide 1809.

Lewis, 'Monk' (Mathew Gregory Lewis), English writer (*The Monk*, 1796), b.1775, d.1818.

Lewis, Sinclair, American novelist (*Babbitt*, 1922), b.1885, d.1951.

Lewis, Percy Wyndham, English writer (*Childermass*) and painter, b.1884, d.1957.

Lewis machine gun, invented 1911 by the American Isaac Newton Lewis, b.1858, d.1931.

Lewisite, poison gas, invented 1916 by the American chemist Gilbert Newton Lewis, b.1875, d.1946.

Leyden jar, electric condenser first made 1746 by the Dutch scientist Pieter van Musschenbroek, b.1692, d.1761, and his pupil Cunaeus in Leyden; and simultaneously by the German divine Ewald von Kleist at Cammin in Pomerania.

Leyden University, Netherlands, founded 1575.

Liadov, Anatol Constantinovich, Russian composer (*Danse de l'Amazone*), b.1855, d.1914.

Liao dynasty, China, 907–1125.

Liberace (Wladziu Valentino Liberace), American pianist and entertainer, b.1919, d.1987.

Liberal Party, British origins in the Whigs (so named *c.*1679); present name used from *c.*1816, adopted officially during 1830s; merged with the Social Democratic Party to form the Social and Liberal Democratic Party in 1988.

Liberals, Spanish supporters of 1812 constitution; French opponents of 'Ultras' in 1815 and 1820–30; Italian opponents of Austrian rule after 1815; European supporters of 1848 revolts.

Liberia, West Africa, founded by freed slaves brought (1820) from the USA to Liberia on board the *Elizabeth* by American Colonization Society; became a Commonwealth 1838, declared independent republic 26 July 1847.

Liberius, pope 352–366.

Liberty Bell, Independence Hall, Philadelphia, hung 1753, replaced 1781, cracked 1835.

Library, first public, built in Rome by C. Asinius Pollio 39 BC; Vatican, begun by pope Nicolas V, 1447; Bodleian opened 1602; Advocates' Library, Edinburgh, founded 1682 (now National Library of Scotland); British Museum, founded 1753; Congress, established 1800; London, founded 1840; British Library established 1973.

Library Act, first British Public, passed 1850; after several amendments, superseded by the Act of 1919.

Library Association, American, established 1876.

Library Association of the United Kingdom, established 1877.

Libreville, capital of Gabon, founded 1843–48.

Libya, North Africa, conquered by Italians 1911–30; became an independent state 24 Dec. 1951; People's Republic 1969.

Lichfield Cathedral, England, constructed 13th–14th centuries.

Licinius, Roman emperor (307–323), b.c.250, executed 324.

Lick Observatory, Mt Hamilton, USA, founded 1876–88 by the legacy of James Lick, b.1796, d.1876.

Lie, Jonas, Norwegian novelist (*The Pilot and His Wife*, 1874), b.1833, d.1908.

Lie, Trygve Halvdan, Norwegian-born secretary general of the United Nations (1946–53), b.1896, d.1968.

Lie detector, principle stated and first apparatus constructed by the Italian criminologist Cesare Lombroso, b.1836, d.1909.

Lieber, Francis, German-born founder (1829–33) of the *Encyclopaedia Americana*, b.1800, d.1872.

Liebermann, Max, German painter (*Knöpflerinnen*), b.1848, d.1935.

Liebig, Justus Freiherr von, German chemist, b.1803, d.1873.

Liebknecht, Karl, German socialist leader, b.1871, killed 1919.

Liebknecht, Wilhelm, German socialist leader, b.1826, d.1900.

Liechtenstein, formed (as the Principality of Vaduz) 1342; enlarged to present size 1434; constituted as the Principality of Liechtenstein 1719; independent since 1866.

Liege Cathedral, Belgium, first cathedral destroyed 1794, second, constructed 10th century, rebuilt 13th century.

Lifeboat, first, designed by the English coach-builder Lionel Lukin 1785.

Lifeline, fired by mortar from shore to ship, invented 1807 by the English barrack-master George William Manby, b.1765, d.1854.

Life Magazine, American periodical founded 1936; folded in 1970, but later revived.

Lift, first hydraulic passenger, installed in New York 1857 by the American inventor Elisha Graves Otis, b.1811, d.1861; electric lifts developed in USA and Britain during 1880s.

Ligature, use in amputations, introduced by the French surgeon Ambroise Paré, b.*c*.1510, d.1590.

Light, composition of, discovered 1660 by Sir Isaac Newton, b.1642, d.1727.

Light, refraction of, law postulated 1621 by the Dutch scientist Willebrord Snell, b.1591, d.1626.

Light, velocity of, first calculated 1675 by Olaus Roemer, b.1644, d.1710; also measured by Jean Bernard Léon Foucault, b.1819, d.1868.

Light Brigade, Charge of the, Balaklava, 25 Oct. 1854.

Light year, distance (nearly 6 million million miles) travelled by light in one year.

Lightfoot, Joseph Barber, English theologian, b.1828, d.1889.

Lighthouse, **Pharos,** Alexandria, built *c*.280 BC; **Eddystone,** built 1698, 1708, 1759, 1879–81; **Bell Rock,** 1807–10; **Bishop Rock,** 1858.

Lightning conductor, principle discovered 1747 by the American statesman Benjamin Franklin, b.1706, d.1790.

Ligne, Charles Joseph, Prince de, field marshal, b.1735, d.1814.

Liguori, Alfonso Maria dei, St, Italian theologian, b.1696, d.1787.

Lilburne, John ('Freeborn John'), English pamphleteer and Leveller leader, b.*c*.1614, d.1657.

Liliencron, Detlev von, German writer (*Krieg und Frieden*, 1891), b.1844, d.1909.

Lilienthal, Otto, German engineer, b.1848, d.1896.

Liliuokalani, last queen of Hawaii (1891–93), b.1838, d.1917.

Lilliput, British periodical, founded 1937 by the Hungarian journalist Stefan Lorant, b.1901.

Lillo, George, English dramatist (*The London Merchant*, 1731), b.1693, d.1739.

Lilly, William, English astrologer, b.1602, d.1681.

Lima, Peru, founded *c.*1541 by the Spanish conquistador Francisco Pizarro, b.1478, d.1541.

Lime juice, made compulsory in the Royal Navy as a preventative of scurvy 1795. Its use introduced for this purpose by Sir Gilbert Blane, b.1749, d.1834.

Limelight (Drummond Light), invented by Sir Goldsworthy Gurney, b.1793, d.1875; introduced by Thomas Drummond, b.1797, d.1840.

Limitation of Armaments Conference, held at Washington 12 Nov. 1921 to 6 Feb. 1922.

Limousin, Léonard, French painter (*Marguérite de Valois*), b.*c.*1505, d.*c.*1577.

Linacre, Thomas, English founder 1518 of the (Royal) College of Physicians, b.*c.*1460, d.1524.

Lincoln, Abraham, 16th US president (1861–65), b.1809, assassinated 14 April 1865.

Lincoln Cathedral, England, construction began 1086, consecrated 1092.

Lincolnshire Insurrection, largely against religious and fiscal oppression, arose 1536, suppressed 1536–37.

Lind, Jenny (The 'Swedish Nightingale'), operatic singer, b.1820, d.1887.

Lindbergh, Charles, American aviator crossed the Atlantic 20–21 May 1927, b.1902, d.1974.

Lindisfarne (Holy Island), chosen as the site of his church and monastery by St Aidan 635.

Lindley, John, English botanist, b.1799, d.1865.

Lindsay, Lady Anne, Scottish poet (*Auld Robin Gray*, 1771), b.1750, d.1825.

Lindsay, Vachel, American poet (*The Congo*, 1914), b.1879, d.1931.

Line coordinates, geometry, introduced 1868–69 by the German mathematician and physician Julius Plücker, b.1801, d.1868.

Ling, Pehr Henrik, Swedish pioneer in gymnastics, b.1776, d.1839.

Lingard, John, English historian, b.1771, d.1851.

Linklater, Eric, British writer (*Poet's Pub*, 1929), b.1899, d.1974.

Linnaeus, Carl, Swedish botanist, b.1707, d.1778.

Linnean Society, London, founded 1788 by the botanist Sir James Edward Smith, b.1759, d.1828.

Linoleum, invented by the Englishman Frederick Walton, 1860.

Linotype, invented 1884 by the German-born Ottmar Mergenthaler, b.1854, d.1899. First made in England 1892.

Linton, Sir Richard, New Zealand-born founder of the Big Brother Movement (scheme for migration of boys from Britain to Australia), b.1879, d.1959.

Linus, St, pope 67–76.

Liotard, Jean Etienne, French painter (*Général Hérault*), b.1702, d.1789.

Lippi, Fra Lippo, Italian painter (*St Margaret*), b.c.1406, d.1469.

Lippershey, Hans, Dutch optician and inventor, 1608, of the telescope, d.1619.

Lippmann, Walter, American political commentator and writer, b.1889, d.1974.

Lipton, Sir Thomas, Scottish-born merchant and sportsman, b.1850, d.1931.

Liquefaction of gas, principle discovered 1878 by the French chemist Louis Paul Cailletet, b.1832, d.1913.

Lisbon earthquake (greatest of many suffered by the city), 1 Nov. 1755.

List, Friedrich, German economist, b.1789, committed suicide 1846.

Listener, The, first published 16 Jan. 1929, ceased publication 1991.

Lister, Joseph Lister, Baron, English surgeon, b.1827, d.1912.

Liszt, Franz, Hungarian-born composer (*Piano concertos*, 1857 and 1863), b.1811, d.1886.

Lithium, an alkali metal, discovered 1817 by the Swedish chemist Johann August Arfvedson, b.1792, d.1841.

Lithography, invented 1798 by the German inventor Alois Senefelder, b.1771, d.1834.

Lithuania, ruled by Russia 1795–1918; proclaimed an independent republic 16 Feb. 1918; occupied by the Russians and admitted to the Soviet Union 1940; became independent republic 10 Sept. 1991.

Lithuanian language, earliest known text dated 1547.

Litolff, Henry Charles, English pioneer 1851 in the publication of cheap editions of music, b.1818, d.1891.

Little Entente Permanent Council, founded on Czech-Yugoslav Treaty of 14 Aug. 1920; created 16 Feb. 1933; collapsed 1938.

Little Rock, Arkansas, USA, scene of racial conflict 1957.

Littleton, Sir Thomas, English jurist, b.1422, d.1481.

Littré, Maximilien Paul Emile, French compiler of a French dictionary, b.1801, d.1881.

Litvinov, Maksim Maksimovich, Russian diplomat, b.1876, d.1951.

Liutprand, Lombard divine and chronicler, b.c.921, d.972.

Liverpool, Robert Banks Jenkinson, Earl, British statesman (prime minister 1812–27), b.1770, d.1828.

Liverpool Cathedral, first stone laid 19 July 1904, consecrated 19 July 1924.

Liverpool University, civic inauguration 7 Nov. 1903.

Livery companies, London, see under individual names – *Skinners, Vintners, etc.*

Livia Drusilla, Roman empress, b.c.55 BC, d. AD 29.

Livingston, Edward, American statesman, b.1764, d.1836.

Livingston, Robert, Scottish-born administrator in New York, b.1654, d.1728.

Livingstone, David, Scottish explorer and missionary, b.1813, d.1873.

Livius Andronicus, Roman poet, lived in the 3rd century BC.

Livonia, ruled by Russia 1710–1918; absorbed into Latvia 1918.

Livy (Titus Livius), Roman historian, b.59 BC, d. AD 17.

Llandaff Cathedral, original building opened 1120; second, 18th century; third, built 1844–69.

'Llangollen, Ladies of', Lady Eleanor Butler, b.1778, d.1829, and Sarah Ponsonby, b.1778, d.1831.

Llewelyn I, prince of North Wales (1194–1229), d.1240.

Llewelyn II, prince of North Wales (1246–82), killed in battle 1282.

'Lloyd, Marie' (Matilda Alice Victoria Wood), English music-hall comedian, b.1870, d.1922.

Lloyd George, David, British statesman (prime minister 1916–22), b.1863, d.1945.

Lloyd's of London, first known allusion as Edward Lloyd's Coffee House, Tower St, London, Feb. 1688.

Lloyd's List and Shipping Gazette, London, founded 1734.

Lloyd's Register, of shipping, first prepared c.1764.

Lloyd Webber, Andrew, British composer of popular musicals (*Evita,* 1976), b.1948.

Loanda (or Luanda), capital of Angola, oldest extant European settlement in Africa, founded 1576.

Lobachevsky, Nikolai Ivanovich, Russian mathematician, b.1793, d.1856.

Lobel, Matthias de, French botanist and physician, lived early in the 17th century.

Locarno Pact, guaranteeing peace and frontiers in Europe, signed 16 Oct. 1925.

Loch Lomond, Scotland, first swum (22 miles) by Commander Gerald Forsberg, b.1912, in 1959.

Lochner, Stephen, German painter (*The Last Judgment*), b.*c.*1401, d.1451.

Locke, John, English philosopher (*Essay Concerning Human Understanding*, 1690), b.1632, d.1704.

Locke, Joseph, English civil engineer, b.1805, d.1860.

Lockerbie Disaster, terrorist bomb destroyed Pan Am flight 103 which crashed onto Scottish village killing 244 passengers, 15 crew and 11 on the ground, 21 Dec. 1988.

Lockhart, John Gibson, Scottish writer (*Ancient Spanish Ballads*, 1823), b.1794, d.1854.

Lockwood, James Booth, American Polar explorer, b.1852, d.1884.

Lockwood, Margaret, British actress (*The Lady Vanishes,* 1938), b.1916, d.1990.

Lockyer, Sir Joseph Norman, English astronomer, b.1836, d.1920.

Locomotives, early models constructed 1803 by the English engineer Richard Trevithick and 1814 by the English civil engineer George Stephenson, b.1781, d.1848.

Lodge, Sir Oliver, British physicist, b.1851, d.1940.

Lodge, Thomas, English writer (*Rosalynde*, 1590), b.*c.*1558, d.1625.

Loeb, James, American banker and philanthropist, b.1867, d.1933.

Loeb Classical Library, authoritative texts and translations, series founded by James Loeb, 1912.

Loeffler, Charles Martin, American composer (*A Pagan Poem*, 1909), b.1861, d.1935.

Loewe, Carl, German composer (*Erlkönig*), b.1796, d.1869.

Löffler, Friedrich, German bacteriologist, b.1852, d.1915.

Lofting, Hugh, English-born writer (*Dr Dolittle*, 1920), b.1896, d.1947.

Logan, Benjamin, American pioneer, b.c.1743, d.1802.

Logarithms, invented 1614 by the Scottish inventor John Napier, b.1550, d.1617.

Logic, study founded by the Greek philosopher Aristotle, b.384, d.322 BC.

Logical positivism, philosophical movement originating in Vienna in 1920s.

Logue, Cardinal Michael, archbishop of Armagh, b.1840, d.1924.

Lollards, English church reformers (followers of John Wyclif) after 1382, active during early 15th century.

Lombard, Peter, Italian theologian (*Sententiae*, 1145–50), b.c.1100, d.c.1160.

Lombard League, of cities in Lombardy, founded 1167.

Lombardo, Pietro, Italian sculptor, b.c.1435, d.1515.

Lombards, invaded Italy 568; conquered by Franks 774.

Lombroso, Cesare, Italian pioneer criminologist, b.1836, d.1909.

Lomonosov, Mikhail Vasilievich, Russian scientist and writer, b.1711, d.1765.

London, Jack (John Griffith), American novelist (*The Call of the Wild*, 1903), b.1876, d.1916.

London, Metropolitan Police Force set up 1829; London divided into postal districts 1858; Port of London Authority established 1909.

London, Declaration of, concerning maritime law, signed 1909.

London, Tower of, built mainly at the end of the 11th century, additions made in the late 17th century.

London Bridge, Old, built by Peter, cvhaplain of St Mary's Colechurch, 1176–1209.

London Bridge, New, constructed 1824–31 by Sir John Rennie, b.1794, d.1874.

London Company, formed to colonize part of Virginia, chartered 1606.

London County Hall, foundation stone laid 9 March 1912.

Londonderry, Edith Helen, Marchioness of, founder and director of the Women's Legion, first to be created (1917) a DBE (military), b.1879, d.1959.

London Gazette, founded 1665.

London Irish Volunteer Rifles, now the only Irish territorial infantry regiment in Britain, formed 25 Nov. 1859.

London Library, London subscription library, founded 1840, opened 1841.

London Naval Conference, concerning war at sea, held 1908–09.

London Naval Treaty, ratified 1930.

London Oratory, established 1849 by the English theologian and poet Frederick William Faber, b.1814, d.1863.

London-Paris daily air service, inaugurated 25 Aug. 1919.

London-Paris phone service, opened 1891.

London Symphony Orchestra, first concert given 9 June 1904.

London Salvage Corps, founded 1866.

London University, founded 1828, chartered 1836.

Long, Huey, US Senator and governor of Louisiana, b.1893, shot 1935.

Long, John Luther, American writer (*Madame Butterfly*, 1898), b.1861, d.1927.

Longchamp, William of, bishop of Ely and statesman, d.1197.

Longfellow, Henry Wadsworth, American poet (*Hiawatha*, 1855), b.1807, d.1882.

Longhi, Pietro, Italian painter (*Exhibition of a Rhinoceros*), b.1702, d.1785.

Longinus, Greek philosopher, b.*c*.213, beheaded 273.

Long Island, first settled *c*.1640; annexed to New York 1664.

Longman, Thomas, English publisher, b.1699, d.1755.

Longomontanus, Christian Sorensen, Dutch astronomer, b.1562, d.1647.

Long Parliament, called 1640, purged 1648, expelled 1653, recalled 1659, dissolved 1660.

Longueuil, Charles le Moyne, Sieur de, French pioneer in Canada, b.1626, d.1685.

Longus, Greek writer in 4th or 5th century (*Daphnis and Chloë*).

Longworth, Nicholas, American pioneer in viticulture, b.1782, d.1863.

Lönnrot, Elias, Finnish collector of folk material, b.1802, d.1884.

Löns, Hermann, German writer (*Mein grunes Buch*), b.1866, killed in battle 1914.

Lonsdale Boxing Belt, founded 1909 by the English sportsman Lord Lonsdale, b.1857, d.1944.

Loomis, Mahlon, American radio pioneer, b.1826, d.1886.

Loop, first aeronautic, performed 27 Aug. 1913, by the Russian pilot Peter Nesterov.

Lope de Vega, Spanish playwright (*Pedro en Madrid*), b.1562, d.1635.

Lopez, Carlos Antonio, president of Paraguay (1844–62), b.1790, d.1862.

Lopez, Francisco Solano, president of Paraguay (1862–70), b.1827, killed in battle 1870.

Lorca, Federico García, Spanish writer (*Bodas de sangre*, 1933), b.1899, shot 1936.

Lord Howe Island, S. Pacific, discovered by Lt H. L. Ball 1778.

Lord Mayor of London, office traditionally held to have been founded 1189.

Lord Mayor's Show, London, first held 1215, first organized, Sir Christopher Drape's pageant 1566.

Lords, House of, absolute power of veto abolished by Act of Parliament 1911.

Lords Appellants, group of English nobles, held power 1388–97.

Lords Ordainers, group of English nobles, held power 1310–16.

Loren, Sophia (Sofia Scicolone), Italian film actress (*The Millionairess*, 1961), b.1934.

Lorentz, Hendrik Antoon, Dutch physicist, b.1853, d.1928.

Lorenz, Adolf, Austrian surgeon, b.1854, d.1946.

Lorenzetti, Ambrogio, Italian painter, b. before 1319, d. after 1347.

Lorenzetti, Pietro, Italian painter, born before 1320, died after 1345.

Lorenzo di Pietro, Italian artist, b.c.1412, d.1480.

Loreto, Italy, reputed site of the house of the Virgin Mary, miraculously deposited in 1295.

Lorimer, George Horace, American writer (*Letters from a Self-made Merchant*, 1902), b.1868, d.1937.

Loring, William Wing, American military commander and adviser, b.1818, d.1886.

Lorne, John Douglas Sutherland Campbell, Marquess of, governor general of Canada (1878–83), b.1845, d.1914.

Lorraine, ruled by France 1766–1870, by Germany 1871–1918, by France 1918–40, by Germany 1940–44, by France since 1944.

Lorraine, Claude, French painter (*Liber veritatis*), b.c.1600, d.1682.

Lorre, Peter, Hungarian-born film actor (*The Maltese Falcon*, 1941), b.1904, d.1964.

Lorris, Guillaume de, French poet (part of the *Roman de la Rose*), lived in the first half of the 13th century.

Lortzing, Albert, German composer (*Der Wildschütz*, 1842), b.1801, d.1851.

Los Angeles, California, founded 1781.

Lothair I, Holy Roman emperor (817–855), b.795, d.855.

Lothair II, Holy Roman emperor (1075–1137), b.c.1070, d.1137.

Lothair III, king of France (954–986), b.941, d.986.

Lotharingia, created by Treaty of Verdun, 843.

'Loti, Pierre' (Julian Viaud), French writer (*Pécheur d' Islande*, 1886), b.1850, d.1923.

Lotto, Lorenzo, Italian painter (*St Jerome*), b.c.1480, d.1556.

Lotze, Rudolf Hermann, German philosopher, b.1817, d.1881.

Loudon, John Claudius, Scottish horticulturist, b.1783, d.1843.

Louis I, emperor and king of France, b.778, d.840.

Louis II, king of France (877–879), b.846, d.879.

Louis III, king of France (879–882), b.c.863, d.882.

Louis IV, king of France (936–954), b.921, d.954.

Louis V, king of France (986–987), b.967, d.987.

Louis VI, king of France (1108–37), b.1081, d.1137.

Louis VII, king of France (1137–80), b.c.1121, d.1180.

Louis VIII, king of France (1223–26), b.1187, d.1226.

Louis IX (St Louis), king of France, b.1214, reigned 1226–70, d.1270. Canonized 1297.

Louis X, king of France (1314–16), b.1289, d.1316.

Louis XI, king of France (1461–83), b.1423, d.1483.

Louis XII, king of France (1499–1515), b.1462, d.1515.

Louis XIII, king of France (1610–43), b.1601, d.1643.

Louis XIV, king of France (1643–1715), b.1638, d.1715.

Louis XV, king of France (1715–74), b.1710, d.1774.

Louis XVI, king of France (1774–92), b.1754, guillotined 1793.

Louis XVII, titular king of France (1793–95), b.1785, said to have died 1795.

Louis XVIII, king of France (1814–24), b.1755, d.1824.

Louis Ferdinand, prince of Prussia, b.1772, killed in battle 1806.

Louisiana, USA, first settled 1699; admitted to the Union 1812.

Louisiana Purchase, from France, of territory west of the Mississippi, completed by the USA 1803.

Louis Napoleon (Napoleon III), emperor of the French (1852–70), b.1808, d.1873.

Louis Philippe, king of France (1830–48), b.1773, d.1850.

Lourdes, first visions of Bernadette Soubirous at, 1858. Festival of Our Lady at, celebrated 11 Feb.

Loutherbourg, Philip James, French-born artist, b.1740, d.1812.

Louvre, Paris, designed 1546–78 by the French architect, Pierre Lescot, b.*c.*1510, d.1578.

Louÿs, Pierre, French writer (*Aphrodite*, 1896), b.1870, d.1925.

Lovejoy, Owen, American abolitionist, b.1811, d.1864.

Lovelace, Richard, Cavalier poet (*Lucasta*, 1649), b.1618, d.1658.

Loveless, George, British trade union pioneer ('Tolpuddle martyr' 1834), b.1792, d.1874.

Lover, Samuel, Irish novelist (*Rory O'More*, 1836), b.1797, d.1868.

Low, Sir David, New Zealand-born cartoonist, b.1891, d.1963.

Low, Juliette Gordon, founder of the Girl Scouts in America, b.1860, d.1927.

Low, Sampson, English publisher, b.1797, d.1886.

Low Sunday, first Sunday after Easter.

Lowe, Sir Hudson, Irish-born governor of St Helena (1815–21), b.1769, d.1844.

Lowell, Amy, American poet, b.1874, d.1925.

Lowell, James Russell, American writer (*Biglow Papers*, 1848 and 1867), b.1819, d.1891.

Lowell Observatory, Arizona, founded 1894 by the American astronomer Percival Lowell, b.1855, d.1916.

Lowestoft, Naval battle of, between the English and the Dutch, 3 June 1665.

Lowie, Robert Heinrich, Austrian-born American anthropologist, b.1883, d.1957.

Lowndes, William Thomas, English bibliographer, b.*c.*1798, d.1843.

Lowry, Malcolm, British novelist (*Under the Volcano,* 1947), b.1909, d.1957.

Loyola, Ignatius, St, Spanish founder 1534 of the Society of Jesus, b.1491, d.1556.

Loyola University, Chicago, founded as St Ignatius College 1870; established with present status and title 1907.

Lubbock, Sir John, Baron Avebury, English writer and naturalist, b.1834, d.1913.

Lubin, David, American merchant and founder of the International Institute of Agriculture, b.1849, d.1919.

Lubitsch, Ernst, German film director, b.1892, d.1947.

Lucan, Marcus Annaeus, Roman poet (*Pharsalia*), b.39, committed suicide 65.

Lucaris, Cyril, Greek theologian, b.1572, d.1637.

Lucas, Edward Verrall, English writer (*Over Bemerton's*, 1908), b.1868, d.1938.
Lucas, Frank Laurence, English writer (*Poems,* 1935), b.1894, d.1967.
Lucas, George, American film director and producer (*Star Wars,* 1977), b.1944.
Lucas van Leyden, Dutch painter (*The Last Judgment*), b.*c.*1494, d.1533.
Luce, Henry Robinson, American publisher, b.1898, d.1967.
Lucian, Greek writer (*Dialogues*), b.*c.*120, d.180.
Lucifer matches, invented 1827 by the English chemist John Walker, b.*c.*1781, d.1859.
Lucius I, St, pope 253–254.
Lucius II (Gherardo Caccianemici dal Orso), pope 1144–45.
Lucius III (Ubaldo Allucingoli), pope 1181–85.
Lucknow residency, defended by the Duke of Cornwall's Light Infantry, 1857.
Lucrece *or* **Lucretia**, victim of Tarquinius Superbus, committed suicide 510 BC.
Lucretius, Roman poet (*De Rerum Natura*), b.*c.*96, d.*c.*55 BC.
Lucullus, Roman general, b.*c.*110, d.57 BC.
Lucy, St, martyred *c.*305.
Lucy, Sir Thomas, prototype of Shakespeare's 'Justice Shallow', b.1532, d.1600.
Luddites, English machine wreckers, active 1810–18.
Ludendorff, Erich von, German general, b.1865, d.1937.
Ludlow, Edmund, English Puritan soldier and regicide, b.*c.*1617, d.1692.
Ludwig, Emil, German writer (*Napoleon*, 1924), b.1881, d.1948.
Ludwig I, king of Bavaria (1825–48), b.1786, d.1868.
Ludwig II, king of Bavaria (1864–86), b.1845, d.1886.
Ludwig III, king of Bavaria (1913–18), b.1845, d.1921.
Lugard, Frederick John Dealtry Lugard, Baron, pioneer administrator in East Africa, b.1858, d.1945.
Luini, Bernardino, Italian painter (*Madonna*), b.*c.*1481, d.1532.
Lull, Ramón, Catalan mystic, b.*c.*1236, d.1315.
Lully, Jean-Baptiste, Italian-born composer (*Alceste*, 1674), b.1632, d.1687.
Lumet, Sidney, American film and TV director (*Serpico,* 1974), b.1924.
Lumière, Auguste, French pioneer in cinematography, b.1862, d.1954.

Lumière, Louis, French pioneer in cinematography, b.1864, d.1948.

Lundy, Benjamin, American abolitionist, b.1789, d.1839.

Luneville, Peace of, between France and Austria, signed 1801.

Lunik I, Russian lunar rocket, launched 11 Oct. 1958.

Lunik II, Russian lunar rocket, hit the moon 10.00 hrs BST, 13 Sept. 1959.

Lusaka, former capital of Northern Rhodesia, now Zambia, 1964.

Lusitania, Atlantic passenger liner, launched 7 June 1906; torpedoed by the Germans 7 May 1915.

Lutecium, rare earth metal discovered independently 1907 by the Austrian chemist Baron von Welsbach, b.1858, d.1929, and 1906 by Georges Urbain.

Luther, Martin, German church reformer, b.1483, excommunicated 1521, d.1546.

Lutheran Church, organized 1522.

Luthuli, Albert John, South African political and civil rights leader; 1960 Nobel peace prize, b.1898, d.1967.

Luttrell Psalter, illuminated manuscript in the British Museum, dated *c.*1340.

Lutyens, Sir Edwin Landseer, English architect, b.1869, d.1944.

Lützen, Battle of, between the Swedes and the Imperialists in the Thirty Years' War, 16 Nov. 1632.

Lützow, Adolf, Freiherr von, German military leader, b.1782, d.1834.

Luxembourg, grand duchy, created by the Congress of Vienna, 1814–15; neutrality guarantied 1817; constitution granted 1868 and revised 1919 and 1948.

Luxembourg, Palace of, Paris, built 1615–20.

Luxemburg, Rosa, German socialist leader, b.1870, killed 1919.

Luxorius, Roman epigrammatist, *fl.* early 6th century.

Luynes, Charles d'Albert, Duc de, constable of France, b.1578, d.1621.

Lvov, Alexis von, composer of the Russian national anthem ('God save the Czar', 1833), b.1798, d.1870.

'Lyall, Edna' (Ada Ellen Bayly), English novelist (*Donovan*, 1882), b.1857, d.1903.

Lyautey, Louis Hubert Gonsalve, French commissary-general in Morocco (1912–25), b.1854, d.1934.

Lycurgus, Spartan reformer believed to have lived in the 7th or 8th century BC.

Lydekker, Richard, English naturalist, b.1849, d.1915.
Lydgate, John, English poet (*Troy Book*, 1412–20), b.*c.*1370, d.*c.*1451.
Lyell, Sir Charles, Scottish geologist, b.1797, d.1875.
Lyly, John, English writer (*Euphues*, 1578), b.*c.*1554, d.1606.
Lyman, Theodore, American naturalist, b.1833, d.1897.
Lynching, term believed to derive from the American military leader Charles Lynch, b.1736, d.1796.
Lyndhurst, John Singleton Copley, Baron, statesman, b.1772, d.1863.
Lyndsay, Sir David, Scottish poet (*The Three Estaits*, 1540), b.1490, d.1555.
Lyon, Mary, American advocate of advanced education for women, b.1797, d.1849.
Lyon, Nathaniel, American military commander, b.1818, killed in battle 1861.
Lyons, France, founded 43 BC by Lucius Plancus.
Lyons, Ecumenical Councils of, first: 1245; second: 1274.
Lyons, Joseph Aloysius, Australian statesman (prime minister 1932–39), b.1879, d.1939.
Lysander, Spartan commander, *fl.* end of the 5th and beginning of the 4th century BC.
Lysenko, Trofim Denisovich, Russian scientist, b.1898, d.1976.
Lysimachus, Greek general, b.*c.*355, killed in battle 281 BC.
Lysippus, Greek sculptor, lived in the 4th century BC.
Lysistratus, Greek sculptor, lived in the 4th century BC.
Lyte, Henry Francis, British hymn-writer (*Abide with me*, 1833), b.1793, d.1847.
Lytle, William Haines, American poet, b.1826, killed in battle 1863.
Lyttleton, George, 1st Baron, English politician and writer, b.1709, d.1773.
Lytton, Bulwer, Lord Lytton, English novelist (*The Last Days of Pompeii*, 1834), b.1803, d.1873.
Lytton, Edward Robert Bulwer, Earl Lytton, viceroy of India (1876–80) and writer, b.1831, d.1891.

M

M1, London-Birmingham motorway, main section officially opened 2 Nov. 1959.

'Maartens, Maarten' (Joost Marius William van der Poerten-Schwartz), Dutch-born novelist (*God's Fool*, 1893), b.1858, d.1915.

Maastricht, Treaty of, provides timetable for European political, economic and monetary union, ratified July 1993.

Mabillon, Jean, French monk and writer, b.1632, d.1707.

Mabinogion, Welsh epic collection, compiled 14th-15th centuries.

Mabuse, Jan de, Flemish painter (*Madonna and Child*), b.c.1470, d.c.1533.

Macadamized roads, invented 1816 by the Scottish surveyor John Loudon Macadam, b.1756, d.1836.

McAdoo, William Gibbs, American politician, b.1863, d.1941.

Macao, China, first settled by the Portuguese 1557; Portuguese suzerainty recognized by China by treaty of 1887; attained partial autonomy 1976; sovereignty to pass to China 1999.

MacArthur, Douglas, American general, b.1880, d.1964.

McArthur, John, English pioneer in New South Wales, b.1767, d.1834.

Macaulay, Dame Rose, English novelist (*Potterism*, 1920), b.1887, d.1958.

Macaulay, Thomas Babington, Lord, historian (*History of England*, 1849–61), b.1800, d.1859.

Macbeth, king of the Scots (1040–54), killed in battle 1057.

Maccabees, Jewish leaders from *c*.170 BC and rulers until 63 BC.

McCarthy, Joseph Raymond, American lawyer and politician (prominent as a demagogue 1950–54), b.1909, d.1957.

McCarthy, Justin, Irish politician and historian, b.1830, d.1912.

McClellan, George Brinton, American general, b.1826, d.1885.

McClintock, Admiral Sir Francis Leopold, Irish-born explorer, b.1819, d.1907.

McClure, Sir Robert John le Mesurier, British navigator, b.1807, d.1873.

McCook, Alexander McDowell, American general, b.1831, d.1903.

McCormack, Count John, Irish tenor, b.1884, d.1945.

McCormick, Cyrus Hall, American inventor 1831 of the reaper, b.1809, d.1984.

McCoy, Sir Frederick, Irish-born palaeontologist, b.1823, d.1899.
MacCunn, Hamish, Scottish composer (*Cior Mhor*, 1887), b.1868, d.1916.
MacDiarmid, Hugh (Christopher Murray Grieve), Scottish poet (*A Drunk Man Looks at a Thistle,* 1926), b.1892, d.1978.
Macdonald, Flora, Scottish rescuer 1746 of the Young Pretender, b.1722, d.1790.
MacDonald, George, Scottish writer (*At the Back of the North Wind*, 1871), b.1824, d.1905.
MacDonald, James Ramsay, British statesman (prime minister (1924, 1929–35), b.1866, d.1937.
Macdonough, Thomas, American naval officer, b.1786, d.1825.
McDougall, William, English-born psychologist (*Introduction to Social Psychology*, 1908), b.1871, d.1938.
MacDowell, Edward Alexander, American composer (*Sea Pieces*, 1898), b.1861, d.1908.
Macedonians, ruled Greece 338–306 BC.
MacEwen, Sir William, Scottish surgeon, b.1848, d.1924.
McGill University, Montreal, chartered 1821, opened 1829. Named after the Scottish benefactor James McGill, b.1744, d.1813.
McGillivray, Alexander, American Indian chief, b.*c.*1739, d.1793.
Macgregor, Robert ('Rob Roy'), Scottish rebel, b.1671, d.1734.
Machaut, Guillaume de, French poet, b.*c.*1300, d.1377.
Machen, Arthur, English writer (*The Great Return*, 1915), b.1863, d.1947.
Machiavelli, Niccolò di Bernardo dei, Italian political reformer (*The Prince*, 1532), b.1469, d.1527.
Machine gun, models made by Drummond 1626, Palmer 1663, Puckle 1718, Gatling 1862, Nordenfeldt 1873, Hotchkiss 1878, Maxim 1884.
Macintosh, Charles, Scottish chemist and inventor (1823) of waterproofs, b.1766, d.1843.
McKay, Charles, Scottish singer (*Cheer, Boys, Cheer*), b.1814, d.1889.
McKaye, Steele, American playwright (*Hazel Kirke*, 1880), b.1842, d.1894.
Macke, August, German painter (*Franz Marc*), b.1887, killed 1914.
Mackensen, August von, German field-marshal, b.1849, d.1945.

Mackenzie, Sir Compton, British novelist (*Sinister Street*, 1913–14), b.1883, d.1972.

Mackenzie, Henry, Scottish writer (*The Man of Feeling*, 1771), b.1745, d.1831.

Mackenzie, William Lyon, Canadian politician and lawyer, b.1795, d.1861.

McKinley, Mt, Alaska, first climbed 1913 by the American missionary Hudson Stock, b.1863, d.1920.

McKinley, William, 25th US president (1897–1901), b.1843, assassinated 1901.

Mackintosh, Charles Rennie, Scottish architect and designer, b.1868, d.1928.

Mackintosh, Sir James, Scottish historian and lawyer, b.1765, d.1832.

Macklin, Charles, British actor, b.c.1697, d.1797.

'Maclaren, Ian' (John Watson), Scottish novelist (*Beside the Bonnie Brier Bush*, 1894), b.1850, d.1907.

McLean, Sir Donald, New Zealand statesman, b.1820, d.1877.

Macleish, Archibald, American poet (*Conquistador*, 1932), b.1892, d.1982.

'Macleod, Fiona' (William Sharp), Scottish novelist (*The Immortal Hour*, 1900), b.1855, d.1905.

Maclise, Daniel, Irish-born painter (*The Death of Nelson*, 1857–66), b.1806, d.1870.

McLoughlin, John, American fur trader and explorer, b.1784, d.1857.

Maclure, William, American geologist, b.1763, d.1840.

McMahon Line, delineating the N. E. frontier of India, agreed by British, Chinese and Tibetan representatives at the 1914 Simla Conference. Named after the British representative Sir Henry McMahon, b.1862, d.1949.

Macmanus, Terence Bellew, Irish patriot, b.c.1823, d.1860.

McMaster, John Bach, American historian, b.1852, d.1932.

Macmillan, Daniel, Scottish publisher, b.1813, d.1857.

Macmillan, Harold, 1st Earl of Stockton, British statesman (prime minister 1957–63), b.1894, d.1986.

McMillan, Margaret, American-born pioneer in British school clinics, b.1860, d.1931.

McMillan, Rachel, American-born pioneer in British nursery school work, b.1859, d.1917.

MacNaghten Rules, legal definition of insanity, formulated after the trial for murder of Daniel MacNaghten, 1843.

Macon, Nathaniel, American statesman, b.*c.*1757, d.1837.

Maconchy, Dame Elizabeth, English composer (*Great Agrippa*, 1935), b.1907.

Maconochie, Captain Alexander, Scottish geographer and prison reformer, first secretary of the Royal Geographical Society, b.1787, d.1860.

McPherson, Aimée Semple, American evangelist, b.1890, d.1944.

Macpherson, James, Scottish 'editor' of Ossian, b.1736, d.1796.

Macpherson, Samuel Charters, Scottish administrator in India, b.1806, d.1860.

Macready, William Charles, English actor, b.1793, d.1873.

Macrinus, Roman emperor (217–218), b.164, killed 218.

MacSwiney, Terence James, Irish patriot, b.1880, starved himself to death in prison 1920.

McTaggart, John McTaggart Ellis, English philosopher, b.1866, d.1925.

MacVeagh, Wayne, American lawyer and diplomat, b.1833, d.1917.

Macy, Mrs Anne Sullivan American teacher of Helen Keller, b.1866, d.1936.

Madagascar, discovered by the Portuguese navigator Diego Diaz 1500; annexed by France 1895; became autonomous 1958 and fully independent 1960.

Madame Tussaud's Waxworks, London, founded by the Swiss showperson Mme Marie Tussaud (1760–1850); new building opened 1928.

Madariaga, Don Salvador de, Spanish-born writer (*Don Quixote; A Psychological Study*, 1934), b.1886, d.1978.

Madden, Sir Frederic, English antiquary and palaeographer, b.1801, d.1873.

Madeira Islands, discovered 1418 by pupils of Prince Henry the Navigator, b.1394, d.1460.

Madeira Pet, British-owned ship, made first voyage (51 days) from Liverpool to Chicago, arriving 14 July 1857.

Madeleine, Paris, construction begun 1764, completed 1842.

Madison, James, 4th US president (1809–17), b.1751, d.1836.

Madoc, reputed Welsh discoverer of America, lived in the second half of 12th century.

Mad Parliament, held in Oxford 1256.

Madras State, India, trading begun by the British 1611; brought under British rule by 1801; reorganized and made smaller 1956 and 1960; renamed Tamil Nandu 1968.

Madrid University, Spain, founded 1508.

Maecenas, Gaius Cilnius, Roman statesman and patron of letters, b.c.70, d.8 BC.

Maes, Nicolas, Dutch painter (*The Card Players*), b.1632, d.1693.

Maeterlinck, Maurice, Belgian writer (*The Blue Bird*, 1909), b.1862, d.1949.

Mafeking, Cape Province, besieged by the Boers 12 Oct. 1899; relieved by the British 17 May 1900.

Magdalen College, Oxford University, founded 1458 by William of Waynefletc, b.1395, d.1486.

Magdalene College, Cambridge University, founded by Thomas, Baron Audley of Walden 1542.

Magellan, Ferdinand (Ferñao Magalhães), Portuguese navigator, whose ship first circumnavigated the world (1519–22), b.c.1480, killed 1521.

Magdeburg hemispheres, demonstrating air pressure, invented 1654 by the German scientist Otto von Guericke, b.1602, d.1686.

Magendie, François, French scientist, b.1783, d.1855.

Magenta, Battle of, between the Italian and the Austrians, 4 June 1859.

Magic lantern, invented 1646 by the German scientist Athanasius Kircher, b.1601, d.1680.

Maginn, William, Irish writer (*Homeric Ballads*, 1849), b.1793, d.1842.

Maginot Line, French defence system, construction began 1928, handed over to the Germans 1940.

Magistrate, first British stipendiary, Henry Fielding, appointed 1748; first British woman, Miss Emily Duncan, appointed 26 May 1913.

Magliabechi, Antonio, Italian librarian, b.1633, d.1714.

Magna Charta, sealed by King John at Runnymede, 15 June 1215.

Magnesium, discovered 1808 by the English chemist Sir Humphry Davy, b.1778, d.1829.

Magnetic clutch, eliminating spring action, invented 1900 by the American engineer Bion Joseph Arnold, b.1861, d.1942.

Magnetic compass, used by Chinese before 1200; variations of the, discovered 1622 by the English scientist Edmund Gunter, b.1581, d.1626.

Magnetic pole, North, located 1831 by Sir James Clark Ross, b.1800, d.1862.

Magnetic pole, South, reached by the Shackleton Expedition, 16 Jan. 1909.

Magnetism, defined 1600 by the English physician, William Gilbert, b.1540, d.1603.

Magnetism by electricity, achieved 1820 by the French physicist Dominique François Arago, b.1786, d.1853.

Magnus I, the Good, king of Norway and Denmark (1035–47), b.1024, d.1047.

Magnus II, king of Norway (1067–69), d.1069.

Magnus III, king of Norway (1093–1103), d.1103.

Magnus IV, king of Norway (1130–35), d.1135.

Magnus V, king of Norway (1162–84), killed in battle 1184.

Magnus VI, king of Norway (1263–80), b.1238, d.1280.

Magnus VII, king of Norway (1319–43), b.1316, d.1374.

Magritte, René, Belgian painter, b.1898, d.1967.

Magsaysay, Ramón, Philippines statesman, b.1907, d.1957.

'Mahabharata', Indian epic, composed about the 6th century BC.

Mahan, Alfred Thayer, American naval historian, b.1840, d.1914.

'Mahdi, The', name applied to several Muslim leaders, especially the Sudanese rebel, Mohammed Ahmed, b.*c.*1843, rose against Anglo-Egyptian government, d.1885.

Mahler, Gustav, Bohemian composer (*Symphonies*, 1891–1913), b.1860, d.1911.

Mahmud I, sultan of Turkey (1730–54), b.1696, d.1754.

Mahmud II, sultan of Turkey (1808–39), b.1785, d.1839.

Mahommed *or* **Mahomet**, *see* **Mohammed**.

Maiden Castle, Dorset, developed in the Iron Age, turned into a camp 250 BC destroyed *c.*AD 70; excavated 1934.

Mail Coaches, first ran between Bristol and London, 1784.

Mailer, Norman, American novelist (*The Naked and the Dead*, 1948), b.1923.

Maillol, Aristide, French sculptor, b.1861, d.1944.

Maimonides (Moses ben Maimon), Jewish theologian (*Mishna Torah*), b.1135, d.1204.

Maine, Sir Henry James Sumner, English jurist and historian, b.1822, d.1888.

Maine, US battleship, blown up in Havana Harbour 1898.

Maine, USA, first successful settlement 1623, admitted to the Union 1820.

Maintenon, Françoise d'Aubigné, Mme, de, wife of Louis XIV, b.1635, d.1719.

Maitland, Frederick William, English jurist, b.1850, d.1906.

Maitland, William, Scottish statesman, b.*c.*1528, d.1575.

Major, John, British statesman (prime minister since 1990), b.1943.

Majorca (Mallorca), conquered by James I of Aragon, 1229.

Majorian, Roman emperor (457–461), d.461.

Makarios III, Cypriot archbishop and statesman (president 1960–74, 1974–77), b.1913, d.1977.

Malacca, settled by the Portuguese 1511, came under British rule 1824; incorporated in the Malayan Union 1946.

Malachy, St, b.*c.*1094, d.1148.

Malamud, Bernard, Jewish American author (*The Natural*, 1952), b.1914, d.1986.

Malaria parasite, discovered 1895–98 by the Indian-born physician Sir Ronald Ross, b.1857, d.1932.

Malatesta, Enrico, Italian anarchist, b.1853, d.1932.

Malawi (formerly Nyasaland), constituted 1891 as the British Central Africa Protectorate; federated with Southern and Northern Rhodesia 1953; became an independent republic 6 July 1964.

Malawi, Lake (formerly Lake Nyasa), discovered 1859 by the Scottish explorer David Livingstone, b.1813, d.1873.

Malaya, Straits Settlements formed 1826; Federation of Malaya formed 1895, occupied by Japanese 1942–45, became a sovereign member state of the British Commonwealth 1957; joined Malaysia in 1963.

Malcolm I, king of the Scots, 942–954.

Malcolm II, king of the Scots, 1005–34.

Malcolm III, king of the Scots (1054–93), killed 1093.

Malcolm IV, king of the Scots (1153–65), b.*c.*1141, d.1165.

Malcolm X (Malcolm Little), American black nationalist leader, b.1925, assassinated Feb. 1965.

Malcontents, Treaty of the, signed with the Prince of Parma, 19 May 1579.

Maldives, Indian Ocean, came under British protection 1887; became independent 1965, and a republic in 1968.

Maldon, Battle of, between the Danes and the East Saxons, 991.

Mâle, Emile, French art critic and historian (*L'An Mil*), b.1862, d.1954.

Malebranche, Nicolas, French philosopher, b.1638, d.1715.

Malesherbes, Chrétien Guillaume de Lamoignon, French statesman, b.1721, guillotined 1794.
Malherbe, François de, French poet (*Larmes de St Pierre* 1587), b.1555, d.1628.
Mali, conquered by French 1898 and incorporated (as French Sudan) into French West Africa; gained independence 1960.
Malinowski, Bronislaw, Polish-born anthropologist, b.1884, d.1942.
Malipiero, Francesco, Italian composer (*I Corvi di San Marco*, 1932), b.1882, d.1973.
Mallarmé, Stéphane, French poet (*L'Après-midi d'un faune*, 1876), b.1842, d.1898.
Malle, Louis, French film director (*Au Revoir, Les Enfants*, 1988), b.1932.
Mallet, David, Scottish poet (*William and Margaret*, 1723), b.*c.*1705, d.1765.
Mallorca, *see* **Majorca**.
Malmö, Treaty of, between Gustavus Vasa and the Danes, signed 1523.
Malone, Edmond, Irish literary critic, b.1741, d.1812.
Malory, Sir Thomas, English writer (*Le Morte Darthur*, printed 1485), d.*c.*1471.
Malpighi, Marcello, Italian biologist, b.1628, d.1694.
Malplaquet, Battle of, between the Allies and the French, 11 Sept. 1709.
Malraux, André, French writer (*La Condition humaine*, 1933), b.1901, d.1976.
Malta, ruled by Knights of St John of Jerusalem (1530–1798); conquered from French by English 1800; annexed to the British Crown by the Treaty of Paris 1814. Awarded the George Cross by King George VI, 15 April 1942. Became independent in 1964, and a republic in 1974.
Malta, Knights of, Order of St John of Jerusalem, 1529–1798.
Malthus, Thomas Robert, English economist and population expert (*Essay on the Principle of Population*, 1798), b.1766, d.1834.
Malvern Hill, Battle of, American Civil War, 1 July 1862.
Malvern Festival, of English drama, instituted 1928.
Mamluks, ruled Egypt 1250–1517, Iraq 1749–1831.

Man, Isle of, ceded to Scotland 1266; came under English government 1290; ruled by Stanley family 1405–1651, 1660–1736; by Duke of Atholl 1736–66; Crown colony 1766–1866; home rule since 1866.

Manmade fibres, industry established *c.*1885 by the French scientist Hilaire, Comte de Chardonnet, b.1839, d.1924.

Manasseh ben Israel, Portuguese-born Jewish scholar, who successfully interceded with Cromwell for the readmission of Jews to England, b.1604, d.1657.

Manchester Guardian, founded 1821, changed its name to *The Guardian* 1959.

Manchester November Handicap, first run 1876.

Manchester-Liverpool Railway, opened 15 Sept. 1830.

Manchester Ship Canal, construction begun 1887; opened 1894.

Manchester University, founded 1846 as Owens College by the English philanthropist John Owens, b.1790, d.1846; first session formally opened 6 Oct. 1903.

Manchu dynasty, China, 1644–1912.

Mandela, Nelson, African nationalist leader, b.1918.

Mandelstam, Osip, Russian poet (*Karmen,* 1913), b.1891, d.1938.

Mandeville, Bernard de, Dutch-born physician and writer (*A Fable of the Bees*, 1714), b.1670, d.1733.

Manet, Édouard, French painter (*Olympia*, 1865), b.1832, d.1883.

Manetho, Egyptian historian, lived in the 4th century BC.

Manfred, king of Sicily (1255–66), b.*c.*1232, killed in battle 1266.

Manganese, metallic chemical element, isolated by J. G. Gahn 1774.

Manganese steel, discovered 1885 by the British metallurgist Sir Robert Abbott Hadfield, b.1859, d.1940.

Manhattan Bridge, NY, construction began 1901; officially opened 1909.

Manhattan Island, bought (1626) from the Indians by Peter Minuit, b.*c.*1580, d.1638.

Manhattan Project, codename for the top secret US programme to develop the atomic bomb during World War II.

Mani, Persian founder of Manichaeism, b.*c.*215, crucified *c.*276.

Manila Conference, on South East Asia defence, held 6–8 Sept. 1954.

Manilius, Roman poet in 1st century.

Manin, Daniele, Italian statesman, b.1804, d.1857.

Manitoba, organized as the Red River Settlement 1812, admitted to the Dominion of Canada 1870.

Manley, Mary de la Riviere, English writer (*Secret Memoirs*, 1709), b.*c.*1663, d.1724.

Manley, Norman, Jamaican statesman, b.1893.

Manlius, Titus, Roman statesman, *fl.* 363–340 BC.

Mann, Heinrich, German novelist (*Professor Unrat*, 1904), b.1871, d.1950.

Mann, Thomas, German novelist (*Buddenbrooks*, 1901), b.1875, d.1955.

Mann Act (White Slave Act), brought into being 1910 by the American politician James Robert Mann, b.1856, d.1922.

Manning, Cardinal Henry Edward, English convert (6 April 1851) to Catholicism, b.1808, d.1892.

Manning, Olivia, British author (*Fortunes of War* series 1960–80), b.1908, d.1980.

Mannyng, Robert, English poet (*Handlyng Synne*), b.*c.*1264, d.*c.*1340.

Manoel I, king of Portugal (1495–1521), b.1469, d.1521.

Manoel II, king of Portugal (1908–10), b.1889, d.1932.

Mansard, François Nicolas, French architect, b.1598, d.1666.

Mansard, Jules Hardouin, French architect, b.1645, d.1708.

'Mansfield, Katherine' (Katherine Beauchamp), New Zealand short-story writer (*The Dove's Nest*, 1923), b.1888, d.1923.

Mansfield College, Oxford University (formerly Spring Hill College, Birmingham), refounded at Oxford 1886.

Manship, Paul, American sculptor, b.1885, d.1966.

Mansion House, London, designed 1739 by the English architect George Dance, b.1700, d.1768.

Manson, Charles, American mass murderer, b.1934.

Mansur, Caliph, founder (762) of Baghdad, d.775.

Mantegna, Andrea, Italian painter (*St Euphemia*), b.1431, d.1506.

Mantell, Gideon Algernon, English geologist, b.1790, d.1852.

Manu, Laws of, Brahman code, composed before 3rd century BC.

Manuel I (Commenus), Byzantine emperor (1143–80), b.*c.*1120, d.1180.

Manuel II (Palaeologus), Byzantine emperor (1391–1425), b.1350, d.1425.

Manutius, Aldus, Venetian printer, b.1449, d.1515.

Manzoni, Alessandro, Italian writer (*I Promessi sposi*, 1825–27), b.1785, d.1873.

Maori Wars, New Zealand, began 1860, ended 1870.

Mao Tse Tung, Chinese communist leader and founder of the People's Republic of China, b.1893, d.1976.

Map, Walter, Welsh writer (*De nugis curialium*), b.c.1138, d.1209.

Mapplethorpe, Robert, American photographer, b.1946, d.1989.

Mapungubwe, Zimbabwe, ruins of remarkable buildings erected 12th to 16th centuries.

Mar, John, Earl of, Jacobite leader, b.1675, d.1732.

Marat, Jean Paul, French revolutionary leader, b.1743, assassinated 1793.

Marathon, Battle of, between Greeks and Persians, 29 Sept. 490 BC.

Marbeck, John, English composer and organist, b.1523, d.1585.

Marble Arch, London, built 1828; re-erected at Cumberland Gate, Hyde Park, 1851.

Marbling, printing process came into use in England late in the 17th century.

Marburg Colloquy, Protestant conference, held 1529.

Marc Antony (Marcus Antonius), Roman leader, b.c.83, committed suicide 30 BC.

Marc, Franz, German painter (*La Tour des chevaux bleux*), b.1880, killed in battle 1916.

Marcellinus, St, pope 296–308.

Marcellus, St, pope 308–309.

Marcellus II, pope 1555.

March, Roger de Mortimer, Earl of, statesman, b.c.1287, hanged 1330.

March, Roger de Mortimer, Earl of, lieutenant of Ireland, b.1374, killed in battle 1398.

Marchmont, Patrick Hume, Earl of, statesman, b.1641, d.1724.

Marcian (Martianus Capella), 5th century North African writer.

Marcion of Sinope, shipowner and founder of the sect of Marcionites, b.c.100, d.c.165.

Marco Polo, Italian explorer, b.1254, d.1324.

Marconi, Guglielmo, Italian radio pioneer, b.1874, d.1937.

Marconi Transatlantic Wireless Service, inaugurated 1907.

Marcus Aurelius, Roman emperor (161–180), author of the *Meditations*, b.121, d.180.

Marcuse, Herbert, German-born political philosopher and critic, b.1898, d.1979.

Mardi Gras, the last day of carnival, celebrated on Shrove Tuesday.
Marengo, Battle of, between Napoleon and the Austrians, 4 June 1800.
Margaret, queen of Navarre, and writer (*The Heptameron*, 1558), b.1492, d.1690.
Margaret, St, queen of Scotland, b.*c.*1045, d.*c.*1093.
Margaret, Mary Alacoque, St, French visionary (Sacred Heart 1673–75), b.1647, d.1690.
Margaret, Maid of Norway, b.1283, drowned 1290.
Margaret Tudor, queen of Scotland, b.1489, d.1541.
Margarine, invented by the French chemist Hippolyte Mège-Mouriés, b.1817, d.1880.
Marggraf, Andreas, German chemist, b.1709, d.1782.
Maria I, queen of Portugal (1777–86), b.1734, d.1816.
Maria Theresa, Austrian empress, b.1717, d.1780.
Mariana Islands, Pacific, passed into US trusteeship 1947; except Guam, which was ceded by Spain to the USA 1898.
Marianus Scotus, Irish historian, b.1028, d.1082.
Marie Amélie, queen of France, b.1782, d.1866.
Marie Antoinette, queen of France, b.1755, guillotined 1793.
Marie Byrd Land, Antarctica, discovered 1929 by the American admiral Richard Evelyn Byrd, b.1888, d.1957.
Marie Leszczynska, queen of France, b.1703, d.1768.
Mariette, Auguste Ferdinand François, French Egyptologist, b.1821, d.1881.
Marignan, Battle of, between the French and the Swiss, 13–14 Sept. 1515.
Marine steam turbines, first installed in the *Turbinia* 1894.
Marini, Marino, Italian sculptor, b.1901, d.1980.
Marinus I, pope 882–884.
Marinus II, pope 942–946.
'Mario, Giuseppe' (Giovanni de Candia), Italian operatic singer, b.1810, d.1883.
Mariotte, Edme, French physician, b.*c.*1620, d.1684.
Maris, William, Dutch painter (principally landscapes and animals), b.1844, d.1910.
Marischal College, Aberdeen, founded 1593 by George Keith, Earl Marischal, b.*c.*1553, d.1623.
Marists, Catholic orders, Fathers founded 1816, Brothers founded 1817, Sisters founded 1834.
Maritain, Jacques, French philosopher, b.1882, d.1973.

Marius, Caius, Roman consul, b.*c.*155, d.86 BC.
Marivaux, Pierre Carlet de, French writer (*L'Amour et la Verité*, 1720), b.1688, d.1763.
Mark, St, pope 336–337.
Markham, Sir Clements Robert, English geographer and historian, b.1830, d.1916.
Markham, Gervase, English scholar and agricultural reformer, b.*c.*1568, d.1637.
Markova, Alicia, English dancer, b.1910.
Marlborough, John Churchill, Duke of, victor (1704) at Blenheim, b.1650,
Marlborough, Sarah, Duchess of, b.1660, d.1744.
Marley, Bob, Jamaican reggae singer, b.1945, d.1981.
Marlowe, Christopher, English poet and dramatist (*Doctor Faustus*, 1588), b.1564, killed 1593.
Marmont, August Viesse de, Duc de Raguse, marshal of France, b.1774, d.1852.
Marmontel, Jean François, French writer (*Aristomène*, 1749), b.1723, d.1799.
Marne, Battle of the, World War I, 6–12 Sept. 1914.
Maronites, Christian heretical sect, appeared in the Lebanon *c.*681, reconciled to Rome 1182; massacre by Druses 1860.
'Marprelate, Martin', unidentified writer of Puritan pamphlets issued 1588–89.
Marquesas Islands, French Polynesia, formally annexed by France 1842.
Marquette, Jacques, French missionary and explorer in America, b.1637, d.1675.
Marquis, Don, American humorous writer (*Archy and Mehitabel*, 1927), b.1878, d.1937.
Marriages, clandestine, abolished in England 1754; non-religious, made legal 1836.
Married Women's Property Act, Britain, became law 1883.
Marryat, Frederick, English sailor and novelist (*Mr Midshipman Easy*, 1836), b.1792, d.1848.
Mars, 'canals' observed 1877 by the Italian astronomer Giovanni Schiaparelli, b.1835, d.1910.
Marsalis, Wynton, American jazz trumpeter and composer, b.1961.
'Marseillaise, La', composed and written 1792 by the French Claude Joseph Rouget de l'Isle, b.1760, d.1836.

Marsh, James, English pioneer in electromagnetism, b.1794, d.1846.

Marshal, William, Earl of Pembroke, regent of England, d.1219.

Marshall Islands, Pacific, passed into US trusteeship 1947–87.

Marshall Plan, for European post-war recovery, devised 1947 by the American General George Catlett Marshall, b.1880, d.1959.

Marshalsea Prison, London, established by King Edward II's reign; abolished 1849.

Marsilius of Padua, Italian writer (*Defensor Pacis*, 1324), lived in the 2nd half of the 13th and the 1st half of the 14th centuries.

Marston, John, English playwright (*Antonio and Mellida*, 1602), b.*c.*1575, d.1634.

Marston Moor, Battle of, between the Parliamentarians and the Royalists 2 July 1644.

Martello towers, English coastal defences, built at the turn of the 18th century.

Martha's Vineyard, Mass., discovered 1602 by the English navigator Captain Bartholomew Gosnold, d.1607.

Marti, José Maria, Cuban patriot, b.1853, killed in battle 1895.

Martial, Latin poet (*Epigrams*), b.*c.*40, d.104.

Martin, St, bishop of Tours, b.*c.*316, d.397.

Martin, John, English painter (*Belshazzar's Feast*, 1821), b.1789, d.1854.

Martin I, St, pope 649–653, d.655.

Martin II, Martin III (non-existent; numbering confused with Popes Marinus I and II).

Martin IV (Simon Monpitié de Brion), pope 1281–85, b.*c.*1210, d.1285.

Martin V (Otto Colonna), pope 1417–31, d.1431.

Martin du Gard, Roger, French writer (*Les Thibault*, 1922–40), b.1881, d.1958.

Martineau, Harriet, English writer (*Feats on the Fjord*, 1841), b.1802, d.1876.

Martini, Padre (Giambattista Martini), Italian composer, b.1706, d.1784.

Martinique, discovered 1502 by Christopher Columbus; colonized by the French from 1625.

Martinmas, Feast of St Martin, celebrated 11th Nov.

Martinu, Bohuslav, Czech composer (*The Judgment of Paris*, 1935), b.1890, d.1959.

Martyn, Henry, English missionary, b.1781, d.1812.

Marvell, Andrew, English poet (*Appleton House*), b.1621, d.1678.
Marx Brothers, American comedy team (*Duck Soup*, 1933): Chico (Leonard), b.1887, d.1961; Harpo (Adolph), b.1888, d.1964; Groucho (Julius Henry), b.1901, d.1979; Zeppo (Herbert), b.1901, d.1979.
Marx, Karl, German socialist (*Das Kapital*, 1867–83), b.1818, d.1883.
Mary, Queen of Scots, b.1542, beheaded 1587.
Mary, Queen, wife of King George V, b.1867, d.1953.
Mary I, queen of England (1553–58), b.1516, d.1558.
Mary II, queen of England, Scotland and Ireland, b.1662, d.1694.
Mary Celeste, derelict ship, found 5 Dec. 1872.
Mary of Modena, queen of King James II, b.1658, d.1718.
Maryland, USA, first settled 1634, one of the 13 original states of the Union.
Maryland University, Baltimore, founded 1807.
Marylebone Cricket Club, founded 1787; first match 1788; present ground opened 1814.
Masaccio (Tommaso di Ser Giovanni di Mone), Italian painter (*Madonna and Child*), b.1401, d.c.1428.
Masaniello (Tommaso Aniello), Italian patriot, b.1623, murdered 1647.
Masaryk, Jan, Czech statesman, b.1886, d.1948.
Masaryk, Thomas Garrigue, Czech president (1918–35), b.1850, d.1937.
Mascagni, Pietro, Italian composer (*Cavalleria rusticana*, 1890), b.1863, d.1945.
Masefield, John, English poet (*The Everlasting Mercy*, 1911), b.1878; Poet Laureate from 1930, d.1967.
Masham, Abigail, Lady Masham, court favourite, d.1734.
Maskelyne, John Nevil, English conjuror, b.1839, d.1917.
Masolino, Italian painter (*Madonna*), b.c.1383, d.c.1447.
Mason, John, English founder 1631 of New Hampshire, USA, b.1586, d.1635.
Mason, Lowell, American composer (*From Greenland's Icy Mountains*), b.1792, d.1872.
Mason-Dixon Line, boundary between Pennsylvania and Maryland (and so between free and slave regions), fixed 1763–67.
Maspero, Gaston, French Egyptologist, b.1846, d.1916.
Massachusetts, USA, first settled 1620; one of the 13 original states of the Union.

Massachusetts Bay Company, granted territory 1628 by the Council of New England; grant ratified by Royal Charter 1629.

Massachusetts Institute of Technology, founded Boston 1859; moved to Cambridge, Mass., 1915.

Masséna, Marshal André, Italian-born French army leader, b.1756, d.1817.

Massenet, Jules, French composer (*Manon Lescaut*, 1884), b.1842, d.1912.

Massey, Vincent, first Canadian governor-general of Canada (1952–59), b.1887, d.1967.

Massinger, Philip, English dramatist (*The City Madam*, 1632), b.1583, d.1640.

Masson, David, Scottish historian, b.1822, d.1907.

Master Gunner of England, office last held (from 1709) by Colonel James Pendlebury, d.*c.*1758.

Master of the King's Musick, title originated *c.*1625; first Master, Nicholas Lanier, b.1588, d.1666.

Masters, Edgar Lee, American poet (*Spoon River Anthology*, 1915), b.1869, d.1950.

Mastoid, operation first successfully performed in 1774 by the French surgeon Jean Louis Petit.

Masurian Lakes, Battles of the, World War I, between the German and the Russians, 1914–15.

Masurium (technetium), chemical element, discovered 1925 by I. and W. Noddack. Confirmed by C. Perrier and E. Segré 1937.

Mata Hari (Margarete Gertrude Zelle), Dutch spy, b.1876, shot 1917.

Matapan, Battle of, World War II, 28 March 1941.

Matches, book, invented 1892 by the American attorney John Pusey.

Matches, friction, wooden, invented 1827 by the English chemist John Walker, b.*c.*1781, d.1859.

Matches, safety, invented 1855 by the Swedish inventor Johan Edvard Lundström.

Mather, Cotton, American witch-hunting writer (*Memorable Providences Relating to Witchcraft*, 1685), b.1663, d.1728.

Mather, Increase, American president of Harvard College, b.1639, d.1723.

Mathews, Charles James, English actor and playwright, b.1803, d.1878.

Matilda, queen of England, d.1083.

Matisse, Henri, French painter (*Odalisque*, 1910), b.1869, d.1954.

Matsys, Quentin, Flemish painter (*Burial of Christ*), b.*c.*1466, d.1530.

Matterhorn, Swiss-Italian frontier, first climbed 1865 by the English mountaineer Edward Whymper, b.1840, d.1911.

Matthay, Tobias, English musician, b.1858, d.1945.

Matthew, Tobie, archbishop of York (1606–28), b.1546, d.1628.

Matthew of Paris, English historian (*Chronica majora*), d.1259.

Matthias, Holy Roman emperor (1612–19), b.1557, d.1619.

Matthias Corvinus, king of Hungary (1458–90), b.1440, d.1490.

Maturin, Charles Robert, Irish writer (*Melmoth*, 1820), b.1782, d.1824.

Maud, wife of King Henry I of England, b.1080, d.1118.

Maugham, William Somerset, British writer (*Of Human Bondage*, 1916), b.1874, d.1965.

Mau Mau, nationalist rebel movement in Kenya 1952–57.

Maundy Thursday, commemoration on the Thursday before Easter of Christ's washing the Apostles' feet.

Maupassant, Guy de, French writer (*Boule de suif*, 1880), b.1850, d.1893.

Maupertuis, Pierre Louis, French mathematician, b.1698, d.1759.

Maurepas, Jean Frédéric Phélipeaux, Comte de, French statesman, b.1701, d.1781.

Mauretania, Atlantic passenger liner, launched 20 Sept. 1906.

Mauriac, François, French novelist (*Le Baiser aux Lépreux*, 1922), b.1885, d.1970.

Maurice, Byzantine emperor (582–602), b.*c.*540, assassinated 602.

Mauritania, West African republic, French protectorate from 1903, colony from 1920; gained full independence 1960.

Mauritius, settled by the Dutch 1638–1710; taken by the French 1715, and British 1810; independent member of the Commonwealth since 1968.

Maurois, André (Emile Herzog), French writer (*Vie de Disraeli*, 1927), b.1885, d.1967.

Maurras, Charles, French writer (*Les Amants de Venise*, 1902), b.1868, d.1952.

Maury, Jean Siffrein, French cardinal and political writer, b.1746, d.1817.

Mauve, Anton, Dutch painter (*Watering Horses*), b.1838, d.1888.

Mauveine, first synthetic organic dye, discovered 1856 by the English chemist Sir William Henry Perkin, b.1838, d.1907.

Mawson, Professor Sir Douglas, Antarctic explorer, b.1882, d.1958.
Maxentius, Roman emperor (306–312), drowned 312.
Maxim machine gun, invented 1884 by the American-born inventor Sir Hiram Stevens Maxim, b.1840, d.1916.
Maximian, Roman emperor (286–305), committed suicide 310.
Maximilian, Austrian-born emperor of Mexico (1864–67), b.1832, shot 1867.
Maximilian I, king of Bavaria (1806–25), b.1756, d.1825.
Maximilian II, king of Bavaria (1848–64), b.1811, d.1864.
Maximilian I, Holy Roman emperor (1493–1519), b.1459, d.1519.
Maximilian II, Holy Roman emperor (1564–76), b.1527, d.1576.
Maximin, Roman emperor (235–238), murdered 238.
Maximin, Roman emperor (308–313), d.313.
Maximus, St, the Confessor, b.*c.*580, d.662.
Maximus, Roman emperor (383–388), executed 388.
Maxton, James, Scottish socialist, b.1885, d.1946.
Maxwell, James Clerk, Scottish physicist, b.1831, d.1879.
Maxwell, Robert Ian (Jan Ludwig Hoch), Czech-born publishing tycoon and corrupt businessman, b.1923, d.1992.
May, Phil, humorous artist, b.1864, d.1903.
May, Thomas, English writer (*History of the Long Parliament*, 1647), b.1595, d.1650.
Mayakovsky, Vladimir Vladimirovich, Russian poet, b.1894, committed suicide 1930.
Mayan empire, Mexico, flourished 3rd to 15th centuries AD.
May Day, day of celebration connected with vegetation and labour.
Mayenne, Charles de Lorraine, Duc de, French king-maker, b.1554, d.1611.
Mayer, Joseph, English antiquary and philanthropist, b.1803, d.1886.
Mayer, Louis Burt, Russian-born American film mogul, head of MGM, b.1885, d.1957.
Mayerling Tragedy, in which the Crown Prince Rudolf of Austria and Mary Vetsera committed suicide 30 Jan. 1889.
Mayflower Pilgrims, set sail from Plymouth for New England 6 Sept. 1620; arrived Plymouth Rock, Massachusetts, 16 Dec. 1620 (OS).
Mayhew, Henry, English writer on social subjects (particularly London), b.1812, d.1887.
Maynooth, Irish seminary for Catholic priesthood, founded 1795.

Mayor, first English woman, Elizabeth Garrett Anderson, b.1836, d.1917, elected mayor of Aldeburgh 1908.

Mayow, John, English physiologist, b.1640, d.1679.

Mazarin, Jules, Cardinal, Italian-born French statesman (Regent 1642–61), b.1602, d.1661.

Mazarine, public library of Paris, opened 1643; absorbed by the Bibliothèque Nationale 1930.

Mazeppa, Ivan Stepanovich, Cossack leader, b.*c.*1644, d.1709.

Mazzini, Giuseppe, Italian leader, b.1805, d.1872.

MCC (Marylebone Cricket Club), founded 1787; first match 1788; present ground opened 1814.

Mead, Richard, English Royal physician, b.1673, d.1754.

Meagher, Thomas Francis, Irish patriot, b.1823, drowned 1867.

Meal Tub Plot, 1679, conceived by the English adventurer Thomas Dangerfield, b.1650, d.1685.

Mecca, Muslim holy city, captured by Mohammed 630; by Ibn Sa'ud 1924.

Mechnikov, Ilya, *see* **Metchnikoff, Elie.**

Mecklenburg Declaration, of American independence, made 1775.

Medal, first English, struck by King Charles I, 1643. The first medal given to all ranks: King George II's 1745–46.

Medawar, Sir Peter, British immunologist, Nobel prize (with Burnet) 1960, b.1915, d.1987.

Medical inspection of schoolchildren, first British, held at Bradford 1899.

Medical profession, British, opened 1876 to women by the efforts of the English physician and mathematician Sophia Louisa Jex-Blake, b.1840, d.1912.

Medici family, ruled Florence 1434–94, 1512–27, 1530–1737.

Medici, Catherine de', queen of France and regent (1560–72), b.1519, d.1589.

Medici, Cosimo de', Florentine leader, b.1389, d.1464.

Medici, Ferdinand de', grand duke of Tuscany (1587–1609), b.1549, d.1609.

Medici, Giovanni de', Italian military commander, b.1498, mortally wounded 1526.

Medici, Lorenzo de', the Magnificent, Florentine leader, b.1449, d.1492.

Medici, Maria de', queen of France (regent 1610–17), b.1573, d.1642.

Medina, Arabian city, home of Mohammed after *hegira* 622.

Medina-Sidonia, Alonso Pérez de Guzman el Bueno, Duke of, Spanish Armada commander, b.1550, d.1615.
Medtner, Nikolai, Russian-born composer (*Märchen*), b.1880, d.1951.
Meer, Jan van der, Dutch painter (*The Astronomer*), b.1628, d.1691.
Meerut, place of outbreak of Indian Mutiny, 10 May 1857.
Mège-Mouriés, Hippolyte, French chemist and inventor 1869 of margarine, b.1817, d.1880.
Mèhul, Étienne Nicolas, French composer (*Joseph*, 1807), b.1763, d.1817.
Meilhac, Henri, French playwright (with Halévy, *Barbe-Bleue*, 1866), b.1831, d.1897.
Meillet, Antoine, French philologist, b.1866, d.1936.
Meir, Golda (Golda Mabovitz), Israeli politician (prime minister 1969–74), b.1898, d.1978.
Meissonier, Jean Ernest, French painter (*Napoleon with His Staff*), b.1815, d.1891.
Melanchthon, Philipp (Schwartzerd), German religious reformer, b.1497, d.1560.
Melba, Dame Nellie (Helen Porter Mitchell), Australian singer, b.1861, d.1931.
Melbourne, William Lamb, Viscount, British statesman (prime minister 1834–41), b.1779, d.1848.
Melbourne University, Victoria, Australia, founded 1854; opened 1855.
Melchett, Alfred Moritz Mond, Baron, English industrialist, b.1868, d.1930.
Melchiades, St, pope 311–314.
Melchior, Lauritz, Danish operatic singer, b.1890, d.1973.
Melkites, name given to orthodox Christians after 451, and again to Catholics after 1724, in the Levant.
Mellon, Andrew William, American financier, b.1855, d.1937.
'Melmoth, Sebastian' (Oscar Wilde), Irish writer, b.1856, d.1900.
Melrose Abbey, Scotland, founded by King David I, 1136.
Melville, Herman, American novelist (*Moby Dick*, 1852), b.1819, d.1891.
Melville, James, Scottish reformer, b.1556, d.1614.
Member of parliament, first woman, Lady Astor, took her seat in the House of Commons 1 Dec. 1919.
Memling, Hans, Flemish painter (*The Marriage of St Catherine*), b.*c.*1435, d.*c.*1494.

Memorial Day (Decoration Day), USA, 30 May; first observed 1869.

Menai suspension bridge, built 1818–26 by the Scottish engineer Thomas Telford, b.1757, d.1834.

Menander, Greek playwright (*Diskolos*), b.342, d.*c*.291 BC.

Mencius, Chinese philosopher, b.372, d.*c*.289 BC.

Mencken, Henry Louis, first editor (1924–33) of the *American Mercury*, b.1880, d.1956.

Mendel, Gregor, Austrian monk and pioneer student of heredity, b.1822, d.1884.

'Mendele Moichersforim' (Shalom Abramovich), Yiddish writer, b.1835, d.1917.

Mendeleyev, Dmitri Ivanovich, Russian chemist, b.1834, d.1907.

Mendelian Principles of Heredity, postulated 1865 by the Austrian scientist and monk Gregor Johann Mendel, b.1822, d.1884.

Mendelsohn, Erich, German-born architect, b.1887, d.1953.

Mendelssohn, Felix, German composer (*Fingal's Cave*, 1830), b.1809, d.1847.

Mendelssohn, Moses, German Jewish philosopher, b.1729, d.1786.

Mendès, Catulle, French poet (*Philomela*, 1864), b.1841, killed in an accident 1909.

Mendès-France, Pierre, French statesman (prime minister 1954–55), b.1907, d.1982.

Mendoza, Antonio de, Spanish poet (*La Celestina*), b.*c*.1590, d.1644.

Menelik I, emperor of Ethiopia, son of Solomon and Sheba, lived in 13th century BC.

Menelik II, emperor of Ethiopia (1889–1913), b.1844, d.1913.

Menendez Pidal, Ramón, Spanish philologist, b.1869, d.1968.

Mengs, Anton Raffael, German painter (*Mount Parnassus*, 1861), b.1728, d.1779.

Menin Gate, Belgium, memorial to the British who fell in the Ypres salient, World War I; unveiled 1927.

Menken, Adah Isaacs, American actress, b.1835, d.1868.

Mennonites, religious movement, originating among Anabaptists 1525, founded 1537 by the Dutch religious leader Menno Simons, b.1492, d.1559.

Menorca (Minorca), captured by British 1708, returned to Spain 1802.

Menotti, Gian-Carlo, Italian-born composer (*The Medium*, 1946), b.1911.

Menpes, Mortimer, Australian-born painter (*Head of Cecil Rhodes*), b.1859, d.1938.

Mensheviks, minority fraction of Russian Social-Democrat Party at Congress in Brussels and London, 1903; expelled from Party by Bolsheviks in 1912.

Menshikov, Prince Aleksandr Danilovich, Russian statesman, b.1672, d.1729.

Menton, elected by plebiscite to be annexed to France 1860.

Menuhin, Sir Yehudi, American-born violinist, b.1916.

Menzies, Sir Robert, Australian statesman (prime minister 1939–41, 1949–66), b.1894, d.1978.

Merbecke, John, English composer and organist, b.1523, d.1585.

Mercator, Gerardus, Flemish geographer (first world map 1538; first atlas published 1595), b.1512, d.1594.

Mercer, John, English chemist and inventor 1850 of mercerising, b.1791, d.1866.

Mercers' Company, London livery company, first recorded reference 1172; chartered 1393.

Merchant Taylors Company, London livery company, origins uncertain; first chartered by King Edward III, 1327; again chartered by King Henry VII, 1503.

Merciless Parliament, which condemned friends of Richard II to death, Feb.-May 1388.

Mercury, planet, transit first observed 1631 by the French scientist Pierre Gassendi, b.1592, d.1655.

Mercury vapour lamp, invented 1901 by the American scientist Peter Cooper-Hewitt, b.1861, d.1921.

Meredith, George, English writer (*The Egoist*, 1879), b.1828, d.1909.

'Meredith, Owen' (Edward Robert Bulwer Lytton, Earl Lytton), English poet (*The Wanderer*, 1857), b.1831, d.1891.

Merezhkovsky, Dmitri Sergeivich, Russian writer (*Leonardo da Vinci*, 1901), b.1865, d.1941.

Mergenthaler, Ottmar, German-born inventor of Linotype, b.1854, d.1899.

Meridian, first measured 1735–36 by the Frenchmen Charles Marie la Condamine, b.1701, d.1774, and Pierre Louis Moreau de Maupertuis, b.1698, d.1759.

Merimée, Prosper, French novelist (*Carmen*, 1845), b.1803, d.1870.

Merit, Order of, Great Britain, founded 1902.

Mermaid Theatre, first English theatre opened in the City of London since The Restoration, opened 1959.

Merovingian Dynasty, ruled France 481–751.

Mersen, Treaty of, dividing the kingdom of Lothair II between Charles the Bald and Louis the German, signed 8 Aug. 870.

Mersey Tunnel, Liverpool-Birkenhead, construction began 1925; opened 1934.

Merton, Walter de, bishop of Rochester (1274–77), d.1277.

Merton College, Oxford University, founded 1264–74 by Walter de Merton.

Meryon, Charles, French engraver (*La Vieille Morgue*), b.1821, d.1868.

Mesmerism, founded 1776 by the German physician Friedrich Franz Mesmer, b.1734, d.1815.

Mesozoic Era, Earth history, between 70 and 200 million years ago.

Messager, André, French composer (*Véronique*, 1898), b.1853, d.1929.

Messalina, Valeria, Roman empress, executed 48.

Messiaen, Olivier, French composer (*L'Ascension*, 1933), b.1908, d.1992.

Mestrovic, Ivan, Yugoslav sculptor, b.1883, d.1962.

Metaphysical Society, London, founded 1869 by the English architect Sir James Knowles, b.1831, d.1908.

Metastasio, Pietro, Italian writer (*Olimpiade*, 1733), b.1698, d.1782.

Metaurus, Battle of, between the Romans and the Carthaginians, 207 BC.

Metcalf, John ('Blind Jack of Knaresborough'), English horse dealer and racer, athlete, soldier, road and bridge builder, b.1717, d.1810.

Metchnikoff, Elie, Russian-born bacteriologist (Nobel prize 1908), b.1845, d.1916.

Metellus Macedonicus, Quintus Caecilius, Roman praetor, d.115 BC.

Meteors, Leonid, great shower recorded 12 Nov. 1833

Meteorological Office, London, founded 1850 by the English meteorologist James Glaisher, b.1809, d.1903.

Methodism, John Wesley, b.1703, d.1791, founded the first Methodist association May 1738. First General Conference of Methodists 1744. The Methodist Church of Great Britain and Ireland, uniting the Wesleyan, Primitive and United Methodist Churches, founded 20 Sept. 1932.

Methodists, Primitive, Methodist sect, appeared 1811.

Methodists, United, group of Methodist sects, merged 1857, joined by other sects 1907.

Methuen Treaty, concerning British trade with Portugal, negotiated 1703 by the British statesman and diplomat John Methuen, b.*c.*1650, d.1706.

Metre, national standard, established in Britain 1897.

Metric system, introduced and legally adopted in France 1 Aug. 1793; new standards adopted 1889.

Metronome, invented 1812 by the mechanician Winkel of Amsterdam.

Metropolitan District Railway, London, opened 24 Dec. 1868 between Mansion House and S. Kensington.

Metropolitan drainage system, London, planned and carried out 1855–65 by the English engineer Sir Joseph William Bazalgette, b.1819, d.1891.

Metropolitan Museum of Art, New York, opened 1871.

Metropolitan Opera Company, New York, founded as Abbey's Italian Opera Company 1883.

Metropolitan Opera House, New York, opened 22 Oct. 1883; gold curtain installed 1905.

Metropolitan Police, London, established 1829.

Metropolitan Railway, London, opened 10 Jan. 1863 between Paddington and Farringdon Street; electrified between Baker Street and Harrow 1904; Paris, opened 1900.

Metropolite, The, London's oldest music hall, opened 1861; renamed London's Irish Music Hall 1959.

Metsu, Gabriel, Dutch painter (*The Music Lesson*), b.1629, d.1667.

Metternich, Clemens, Prince, Austrian diplomat and statesman, b.1773, d.1859.

Metz, Siege of, Franco-Prussian War, 27 Aug. to Oct. 1870.

Meulen, Adams Frans van der, Flemish painter (*Nancy and Arras*), b.1632, d.1690.

Meung, Jean de, French writer (part of the *Roman de la Rose*), b.*c.*1250, d.*c.*1305.

Mexican War, between the USA and Mexico, 1846–48.

Mexico, conquered by the Spanish 1520; Spanish viceroyalty 1535–1821; war of independence 1810–21; period of national formation 1810–1910; social revolution 1911–21.
Meyer, George W., American composer (*For Me and My Girl*), b.1884, d.1959.
Meyerbeer, Giacomo (Jakob Beer), German-born composer (*The Huguenots*, 1836), b.1791, d.1864.
Meyerhof, Otto, German physiologist, b.1884, d.1951.
Meyerling Tragedy, *see* **Mayerling Tragedy**.
Meynell, Alice, English writer (*The Children*, 1896), b.1847, d.1922.
Meyrink, Gustav, Austrian writer (*The Golem*, 1915), b.1868, d.1932.
Mezzotint process, invented 1642 by the Dutch-born engraver Ludwig von Siegen, b.c.1609, d.1680.
Miami, University of, Florida, founded 1925; opened 1926.
Michael, Sir John, British field marshal, b.1804, d.1886.
Michael I, Byzantine emperor (811–813), d.845.
Michael II, Byzantine emperor (820–829), d.829.
Michael III, Byzantine emperor (842–867), assassinated 867.
Michael IV, Byzantine emperor (1034–41), d.1041.
Michael V, Byzantine emperor (1041–42).
Michael VI, Byzantine emperor (1056–57).
Michael VII, Byzantine emperor (1071–78).
Michael VIII, Byzantine emperor (1260–82), b.1234, d.1282.
Michael, tsar of Russia (1613–45), b.1596, d.1645.
Michael, king of Romania (1927–30), b.1921.
Michaelis, Johann David, German theologian, b.1717, d.1791.
Michaelmas (Feast of St Michael the Archangel), celebrated 29 Sept.
Michaud, Joseph François, French historian (*Biographie Universelle*, 1811–28), b.1767, d.1839.
Michelangelo, Italian artist (*Pietà*), b.1475, d.1564.
Michelet, Jules, French historian, b.1798, d.1874.
Michelozzi, Michelozzo, Italian artist, b.1396, d.1472.
Michelson, Albert Abraham, American scientist, b.1852, d.1931.
Michigan, USA, first settled 1668; admitted to the Union 1837.
Michigan University, Ann Arbor, founded 1839; opened 1841.
Mickiewicz, Adam, Polish poet (*Konrad Wallenrod*, 1827), b.1798, d.1855.

Microbes, as agents of disease, postulated 1546 by the Italian physician Fracastoro, b.1483, d.1553.
Microphone, invented 1877 by the German-born inventor Emile Berliner, b.1851, d.1929; and 1878 by the American inventor David Edward Hughes, b.1831, d.1900.
Microscope, traditionally invented by the Dutch opticians Johann and Zacharias Janssen *c.*1590; used by Galileo 1610 and Hooke 1665.
Microwave telecommunication system, first publicly demonstrated 1931; first commercial service 1934.
Middle Ages, in W. Europe, roughly 5th century to 15th century; in E. Europe 330–1453; in Arab world 622–1517.
Middle English, in use from the 12th century to *c.*1500.
Middleton, Conyers, English scholar (*Life of Cicero*, 1741), b.1683, d.1750.
Middleton, Thomas, English playwright (*A Game of Chesse*, 1624), b.*c.*1570, d.1627.
Midrash, Rabbinical commentary or the Holy Scriptures, compiled 1st to 12th centuries.
Midsummer Day (Feast of the Nativity of St John the Baptist), 24 June; summer solstice, 21 or 22 June.
Midsummer Night: 23 June.
Midway, Battle of, World War II, between the Americans and the Japanese, 5–6 June 1942.
Midwinter, winter solstice, 21 or 22 Dec.
Mieris, Frans van, Dutch painter (*The Lute Player*), b.1635, d.1681.
Miës van der Rohe, Ludwig, German-born architect, b.1886, d.1969.
Mignard, Pierre, French painter (*Le Printemps*), b.1612, d.1695.
Migne, Jacques Paul, French theologian (*De la Liberté*), b.1800, d.1875.
Mignet, François Auguste Marie, French historian (*Charles-Quint*, 1854), b.1796, d.1884.
Migraine, described by Aretaeus of Cappadocia in *c.*131.
Milan Cathedral, Italy, constructed 1386–1813; consecrated 1577.
Milan Decree, extending ban on British goods, issued by Napoleon 1807.
Mildenhall Treasure, Roman silver tableware, discovered near Mildenhall, Suffolk, 1942–43.
Mile, British Statute, established by law 1593.

Milhaud, Darius, French composer (*David*, 1954), b.1892, d.1974.
Military Cross, Great Britain, instituted 1 Jan. 1915.
Milk, evaporated, process invented 1856 by the American Gail Borden, b.1801, d.1874.
Milky Way, constitution discovered by the German-born astronomer Sir William Herschel, b.1738, d.1822.
Mill, James, British philosopher, b.1773, d.1836.
Mill, John Stuart, English philosopher (*On Liberty*, 1859), b.1806, d.1873.
Millais, Sir John, English painter (*Eve of St Agnes*, 1862), b.1829, d.1896.
Millay, Edna St Vincent, American writer (*Poems*, 1929), b.1892, d.1950.
Millenium, period of 1,000 years, particularly that of Christ's reign in person on Earth.
Miller, Arthur, American playwright (*Death of a Salesman*, 1949), b.1915.
Miller, Glen, American jazz trombonist, arranger and bandleader, b.1904, died in plane crash 1944.
Miller, Henry, American writer (*Tropic of Cancer*, 1931), b.1891, d.1980.
Miller, Joe, English comedian, b.1684, d.1738.
Millerand, Alexandre, French statesman, b.1859, d.1943.
Millet, Jean François, French painter (*The Gleaners*, 1857), b.1814, d.1875.
Milligan, Spike (Terence Alan), British humourist ('The Goon Show', 1949–60), b.1918.
Millikan, Robert Andrews, American scientist, b.1868, d.1953.
Mills, George, British shipbuilder, b.1808, d.1881.
Milman, Henry Hart, dean of St Paul's and historian, b.1791, d.1868.
Milne, Alan Alexander, Scottish writer (*Winnie the Pooh*, 1926), b.1882, d.1956.
Milner, Alfred, Lord, colonial secretary (1919–21), b.1854, d.1925.
Miltiades, Greek general, d.489 BC.
Milton, John, English pamphleteer (*Areopagitica*, 1644) and poet (*Paradise Lost*, 1667), b.1608, d.1674.
Milwaukee, Wisconsin, founded by the French-American fur-trader Solomon Laurent Juneau, b.1793, d.1856.
Milyukov, Paul Nikdayevich, Russian politician and historian, b.1859, d.1943.

Mindanao, World War II, reconquered by the Americans 23 June 1945.
Minden, Battle of, between the English and the French, 1 Aug. 1759.
Mines, explosive, first used by Russians at Kronstadt between 1853 and 1856.
Ming Dynasty, China, 1368–1644.
Ministries, *see under significant word of title:* **Agriculture**, etc.
Minnesota, USA, organized as a Territory 1849; granted statehood 1858.
Minoan Age, Crete, dating from the late Neolithic age to 1200 BC.
Minoan Civilization, discovered 1900 by the English archaeologist Sir John Evans, b.1851, d.1941.
Minoan Script B, Mycenaean Greek, first deciphered 1952 by the English architect Michael Ventris, b.1922, d.1956.
Minorca, *see* **Menorca.**
Mint, The Royal, London, origins uncertain; first recorded mention 1229.
Minto, Gilbert John Elliot-Murray-Kynynmond, Earl of, governor general of Canada (1898–1904) and viceroy of India (1905–10), b.1845, d.1914.
Minuit, Peter, purchaser 1626 of Manhattan Island, b.*c.*1580, d.1638.
Miocene Epoch, Earth history, 35 million years ago.
Mirabeau, Honoré Gabriel Riquetti, Comte de, French political writer, b.1749, d.1791.
Miracle Plays, originated in France; first played in England about the beginning of the 14th century and continued into the 16th century.
Mirage of Hastings, occurred July 1798.
Miró, Joan, Spanish painter (*The Horse*), b.1893, d.1983.
Mishima, Yukio (Hiraoka Kimitake), Japanese writer (*Sea of Fertility,* 1965–70), b.1925, committed ritual suicide 1970.
Missionary Ridge, Battle of, American Civil War, 24–25 Nov. 1863.
Mississippi River, navigated 1682 by Robert Cavelier, Sieur de La Salle, b.1643, assassinated 1687.
Mississippi Scheme, inaugurated as the 'Western Company' 1717 by the Scottish financier John Law, b.1671, d.1729.
Missouri, USA, first settled 1735; made a Territory 1812; admitted to the Union 1821.
Mistral, Frédéric, Provençal poet (*Mirèio*, 1859), b.1830, d.1914.

'Mistral, Gabriela' (Lucila Gedoy Alcayaga), Chilean poetess (*Tala*, 1938), b.1889, d.1957.

MIT (Massachusetts Institute of Technology), founded Boston 1859, moved to Cambridge, Mass., 1915.

Mitchel, John, Irish patriot, b.1818, d.1875.

Mitchell, Sir Thomas Livingston, Australian explorer, b.1792, d.1855.

Mitchum, Robert, American film actor (*The Night of the Hunter*, 1955), b.1917.

Mitford, Mary Russell, English writer (*Our Village*, 1824–32), b.1787, d.1855.

Mithridates I, satrap of Pontus 402–363 BC.

Mithridates II, king of Pontus, d.302 BC.

Mithridates III, king of Pontus 302–266 BC.

Mithridates IV, king of Pontus, d.c.222 BC.

Mithridates V, king of Pontus 222–184 BC.

Mithridates VI, king of Pontus, assassinated 123 BC.

Mithridates VII, king of Pontus (122–63 BC), b.c.131, d.63 BC.

Mitscherlich, Eilhard, German scientist, b.1794, d.1863.

Mitterrand, François Maurice Marie, French statesman (president since 1981), b.1916.

Mivart, St George Jackson, English biologist, b.1827, d.1900.

Moabite Stone, discovered at Dibon by the German missionary F. Klein, 1868.

Modern face, type design, introduced c.1788 by the English bookseller John Bell, b.1745, d.1831.

Modigliani, Amadeo, Italian-born artist (*Woman with Cigarette*, 1911), b.1884, d.1920.

Modjeska, Helena, Polish actress, b.1844, d.1909.

Moe, Jörgen Engebretsen, Norwegian poet, b.1813, d.1882.

Moeran, Ernest John, English composer (*Rhapsody*, 1924), b.1894, d.1950.

Moguls, ruled India 1525–1707.

Mohammed, the Prophet, founder c.610 of Islam, b.c.570, d.632.

Mohammed I, Ottoman emperor (1413–21), b.1387, d.1421.

Mohammed II, sultan of Turkey (1451–81), b.1430, d.1481.

Mohammed III, sultan of Turkey (1595–1603), b.1566, d.1603.

Mohammed IV, sultan of Turkey (1648–87), b.1638, d.1692.

Mohammed V, sultan of Turkey (1909–18), b.1844, d.1918.

Mohammed VI, sultan of Turkey (1918–22), b.1861, d.1926.

Mohammed Ali, viceroy of Egypt (1805–49), b.1769, d.1849.

Mohl, Hugo von, German botanist, b.1805, d.1872.

Mohr, Charles Theodor, German-born botanist, b.1824, d.1901.

Moir, David Macbeth, Scottish physician and writer, b.1798, d.1851.

Moiseiwitsch, Benno, Russian-born pianist, b.1890, d.1963.

Moissan, Henri, French scientist, b.1852, d.1907.

Moivre, Abraham de, French-born mathematician, b.1667, d.1754.

Moldavia, *see* **Moldova.**

Moldova (formerly Moldavia), formed 1940 from land ceded by Romania to the Soviet Union and from parts of Ukraine; independence declared from former USSR Aug. 1991.

Molesworth, Mrs (Mary Louisa Stewart), British writer (*Robin Redbreast*, 1892), b.1839, d.1921.

Molière, Jean Baptiste Poquelin, French playwright (*Le Malade Imaginaire*, 1673), b.1622, d.1673.

Molinism, Jesuit reconciliation of predestination and free will, postulated in his *Concordia* (1588) by Luis de Molina, b.1535, d.1600.

Molinos, Miguel de, Spanish founder (in his *Guida Spirituale*, 1675) of the Quietist movement, b.1640, condemned by Inquisition 1687, d.1697.

Mollison, James Allan, British aviator, b.1906, d.1959.

Molly Maguires, Irish-American secret labour organization, flourished in Pennsylvania *c.*1865–75; also Irish secret society of the 1840s.

Molnar, Ferenc, Hungarian writer (*Liliom*, 1909), b.1878, d.1952.

Molotov, Vyacheslav Mikhailovich Skryabin, Bolshevik leader, b.1890, d.1986.

Moltke, Helmut, Graf von, German field marshal, b.1800, d.1891.

Molybdenum, metal discovered 1778 by the Swedish chemist Carl Wilhelm Scheele, b.1742, d.1786.

Mommsen, Theodor, German historian, b.1817, d.1903.

Mompou, Federico, Spanish composer (*Dialogues*, 1923), b.1893, d.1987.

Monaco, independence recognized by Savoy 1489, by France 1512, by Papacy and Spain 1524; alliance with France since 1641; constitutional monarchy established 1911; reign of Prince Rainier since 1949.

Monasteries, English, dissolved 1536–39.

Monastery, first Christian, founded *c.*315 by the Egyptian Pachomius on an island in the Nile.

Monck, George, Duke of Albemarle, English soldier, Cromwellian governor of Scotland (1654–60) and restorer of Charles II, b.1608, d.1670.

Mond, Ludwig, German-born chemist and businessman, b.1839, d.1909.

Monet, Claude, French artist (*Waterloo Bridge*), b.1840, d.1926.

Monge, Gaspard, Comte de Péluse, French mathematician, b.1746, d.1818.

Mongolia, recognized Chinese suzerainty in 1636 (Inner) and 1688 (Outer); Soviet-controlled Mongolian People's Republic established 1924; achieved independence 1945; new democratic constitution adopted 1992.

Mongols, invaded China 1210, Transoxiana 1219, Caucasia 1221, Persia 1222, Russia 1224, Central Europe 1241, Mesopotamia 1258. Ruled China 1280–1368; Persia 1225–1386; Russia 1242–1380.

Monk, Maria, fraudulent exposer of convent life, b.*c.*1817, d.1850.

Monk, Thelonius, American jazz pianist and composer, b.1917, d.1982.

Monkey gland, transplantation for rejuvenation introduced by the Russian-born surgeon Serge Voronov, b.1866, d.1951.

Monmouth, Battle of, New Jersey, American War of Independence, 28 June 1778.

Monmouth's Rebellion, led 11 June to 6 July 1685 by James, Duke of Monmouth, b.1649, beheaded 1685.

Monocacy, Battle of, American Civil War, 8 July 1864.

Monophysitism, Christian heresy, condemned at Council of Chalcedon 451.

Monotheletism, Christian heresy similar to monophysitism, condemned at Council of Constantinople 680.

Monotype, invented 1887 by the American inventor Tolbert Lanston, b.1844, d.1913.

Monroe, James, 5th US president (1817–25), b.1758, d.1831.

Monroe Doctrine, concerning American foreign policy, announced by President James Monroe 1823.

Monroe, Marilyn (Norma Jean Mortenson *or* Baker), American film star (*Gentlemen Prefer Blondes,* 1953), b.1926, d.1962.

Mons, Retreat from, World War I, Aug. 1914.

Mont Blanc, first climbed June 1786 by the French mountaineer Jacques Balmat, b.1762, d.1834.

Mont Blanc Tunnel, construction began 1959; completed 1961.

Mont Cenis Pass, between France and Italy, completed 1806; tunnel opened 1871.

Mont Saint Michel, France, monastery founded by Aubert, bishop of Avranches 708.

Montagna, Bartolommeo, Italian painter (*Presentation of Christ in the Temple*), b.c.1450, d.1523.

Montagu, Lady Mary Wortley, English writer and traveller, b.1689, d.1762.

Montague, Charles Edward, English writer (*Fiery Particles*), b.1867, d.1928.

Montaigne, Michel Eyquem de, French essayist, b.1533, d.1592.

Montalembert, Marc René, Marquis de, French engineer and soldier, b.1714, d.1800.

Montana, USA, first settled 1809; made a Territory 1864; admitted to the Union 1889.

Montanism, Christian heresy, prominent in Asia Minor; in 2nd century.

Montcalm, Louis Joseph, Marquis de, French general, b.1712, mortally wounded in battle 1759.

Montefiore, Sir Moses Haim, Italian-born champion of Jewish freedom, b.1784, d.1885.

Montemayor, Jorge de, Spanish poet (*La Diana Enamorada*, c. 1550), b.c.1520, assassinated 1561.

Montenegro, independent since 14th century; monarchy since 1910; occupied by Austrians 1916–18; part of the former Yugoslavia 1919–91.

Montespan, Françoise Athénaïs, Mme de, mistress of Louis XIV, b.1641, d.1707.

Montesquieu, Charles de Secondat, Baron de la Brède et de, French writer (*Lettres Persanes*, 1721), b.1689, d.1755.

Montessori method, in education, founded *c.*1909 by the Italian educationalist Maria Montessori, b.1870, d.1952.

Monteverdi, Claudio, Italian composer (*Orfeo*, 1608), b.1567, d.1643.

Monteux, Pierre, French conductor, b.1875, d.1964.

'Montez, Lola' (Marie Dolores Eliza Rosanna Gilbert), adventuress, b.1818, d.1861.

Montezuma I, Aztec emperor (1436–64), b.1390, d.1464.

Montezuma II, last Aztec emperor (1502–20), b.*c.*1480, killed 1520.

Montfort, Simon de, English crusader and baronial leader, b.*c.*1208, killed in battle 1265.

Montfort, Simon de, English soldier and rebel, b.1240, d.1271.

Montgolfier, Joseph Michel, French balloonist, b.1740, d.1810.

Montgomerie, Alexander, Scottish poet (*The Cherry and the Slae*), b.*c.*1556, d.*c.*1610.

Montgomery, Bernard Law Montgomery, Viscount, British soldier; appointed field marshal 1944, b.1887, d.1976.

Month, in astronomy, 29.53 days; in calendar 28, 29, 30 or 31 days; in law, 28 days.

Montholon, Charles Tristan, Comte de, French general, b.1783, d.1853.

Monticelli, Adolphe, French painter (*Baigneuses*), b.1824, d.1886.

Montmorency, Anne, Duc de, French statesman and soldier, b.1493, d.1567.

Montpensier, Anne Marie Louise d'Orléans, Duchesse de ('Grande Mademoiselle'), b.1627, d.1693.

Montreal, Canada, founded 1642.

Montreal University, founded 1876; opened 1878.

Montrose, James Graham, Marquis of, Royalist supporter, b.1612, hanged 1650.

Moody, Richard Clement, first governor (1841–49) of the Falkland Islands, b.1813, d.1887.

Moody, Dwight Lyman, American revivalist, b.1837, d.1899.

Moon alphabet, for the blind, invented 1845 by the English Dr William Moon, b.1818, d.1894.

Moon, Sun Myung, South Korean founder of the Unification Church ('Moonies') in 1954, b.1920.

Moorcroft, William, English veterinary surgeon and explorer, b.1765, d.1825.

Moore, Brian, Irish-born novelist (*Black Robe*, 1985), b.1921.

Moore, George, Irish writer (*Esther Waters*, 1894), b.1852, d.1933.

Moore, Henry, English sculptor (*Madonna*), b.1898, d.1986.

Moore, Sir John, Scottish soldier, b.1761, died of wounds 1809.

Moore, Thomas, Irish poet (*Lalla Rookh*, 1817), b.1779, d.1852.

Moraes Barros, Prudente de, president of Brazil (1894–98), b.1841, d.1902.

Morality plays, played mainly in the 15th and 16th centuries.

Moral Rearmament, religious movement founded 1921 by the American religious leader Frank Buchman, b.1878, d.1961.

Moran, Edward, English-born painter (*Outward Bound*), b.1829, d.1901.

Morand, Paul, French novelist (*Fermé la Nuit*, 1922), b.1888, d.1975.

Moravian Brethren, Christian sect, appeared 1457 among followers of Hus, regathered 1722, began mission work 1732.

Moravian Church in America, founded 1739 by Bishop August Gottlieb Spangenberg, b.1704, d.1792.

More, Hannah, English writer (*Coelebs in Search of a Wife*, 1809), b.1745, d.1833.

More, Paul Elmer, American writer (*Pages from an Oxford Diary*, 1937), b.1864, d.1937.

More, Sir Thomas, Lord Chancellor (1529–32) and writer (*Utopia*, 1516), b.1478, beheaded 1535.

Moreau, Gustave, French painter ((*Oedipe et le Sphinx*, 1868), b.1826, d.1898.

Morgan, Charles, English novelist (*Portrait in a Mirror*, 1929), b.1894, d.1958.

Morgan, John Pierpont, American financier, b.1837, d.1913.

Morgan, Sir Henry, Welsh buccaneer, b.*c.*1635, d.1688.

Morgan, William de, English writer (*Joseph Vance*, 1906), b.1839, d.1917.

Morgenthau, Henry, German-born financier, b.1856, d.1946.

Morier, James, British traveller and writer (*Hajji Baba*, 1824), b.*c.*1780, d.1849.

Mörike, Eduard Friedrich, German poet, b.1804, d.1875.

Morison, James, Scottish founder 1843 of the Evangelical Union, b.1816, d.1893.

Morisot, Berthe, French painter (*Le Berceau*, 1873), b.1841, d.1895.

Morland, George, English painter (*The Angler's Repast*), b.1763, d.1804.

Morley, Henry, English writer and editor, b.1822, d.1894.

Morley, John, Viscount Morley, English statesman and writer (*Edmund Burke*, 1867), b.1838, d.1923.

Mormon movement, founded 1827 in Fayette, N.Y., by the American religious leader Joseph Smith, b.1805, murdered 1844.

Mornay, Philippe de (Duplessis-Mornay), 'the Pope of the Huguenots', b.1549, d.1623.

Moro, Antonio, Flemish painter (*Mary Tudor*), b.*c.*1520, d.*c.*1576.

Morocco, arrival of the first Arabs under Okbar ben Nafi' 682; first invasion of Spain under Ibn Tariq 711; dynastic governments 788 to 1911; French protectorate 1912–56; independence 2 March 1956.

Moroni, Giambattista, Italian painter (*Ludovico di Terzi*), b.*c.*1525, d.1578.

Morris, Gouverneur, American diplomat and statesman, b.1752, d.1816.

Morris, William, English artist and writer (*News from Nowhere*, 1891), b.1834, d.1896. Founded the Kelmscott Press 1891–98.

Morris dancing, revived in England as a result of Cecil Sharp's first seeing Morris dancing under the leadership of William Kimber, b.1873, at Headington, Oxford, 26 Dec. 1899.

Morrow, Dwight Whitney, American financier, b.1873, d.1931.

Morse, Henry, English Jesuit missionary in England, b.1595, executed 1645.

Morse code, invented *c.*1832 by the American inventor Samuel Finley Breese Morse, b.1791, d.1872.

Mortar, developed 1756 by the English architect John Smeaton, b.1724, d.1792.

Mortimer, Edmund, Earl of March, lieutenant of Ireland, b.1391, d.1425.

Mortimer, Roger, Earl of March, royal adviser, b.*c.*1287, hanged 1330.

Morton, Cardinal John, archbishop of Canterbury (1486–1500), b.*c.*1420, d.1500.

Morton, Thomas, Scottish shipwright and inventor, b.1781, d.1832.

Moscheles, Ignaz, Austrian pianist and composer, b.1794, d.1870.

Moschus, Greek poet of Syracuse, lived in 2nd century BC.

Moscow, Russian capital, burnt and pillaged by the Mongols 1382; taken and burnt by the French Sept. 1812; battle of Moscow 5–7 Sept. 1812.

Moscow Conference, World War II, 9–21 Nov. 1944.

Moseley, Henry Gwyn Jeffreys, British physicist, b.1887, killed in battle 1915.

'Moses, Grandma' (Mrs Anna Mary Robertson Moses), American primitive painter, b.1860, d.1961.

Moslem League, founded in India 1906.

Mosley, Sir Oswald, British political leader, b.1896, d.1980; Conservative, Independent and Labour MP (1918–31), founded New Party 1931, British Union of Fascists 1932, British Union Movement 1948.

Moszkowski, Moritz, German-born pianist and composer (*Spanish Dances*), b.1854, d.1925.

Mother's Day, 2nd Sun. in May (USA); 2nd Sun. in March (UK).

Motherwell, William, Scottish poet (*Jeannie Morrison*, 1832), b.1797, d.1835.

Motion, planetary, Kepler's Laws of, 1609 and 1619.

Motley, John Lothrop, American diplomat and historian (*The Rise of the Dutch Republic*, 1856), b.1814, d.1877.

Motorcar, invented 1890–95.

Motor scooter, first, invented 1919 by Greville Bradshaw.

Motor cycle, three-wheeled model built 1884 by Edward Butler; two-wheeled model built in Paris 1900 by the Werner Frères.

Mott, Lucretia, American anti-slavery worker, b.1793, d.1880.

Mountbatten of Burma, Louis Mountbatten, Earl, British sailor and administrator, b.1900, d.1979.

'Mounties', Royal Canadian Mounted Police, formed as the North-West Mounted Police 1873; assumed present title 1920.

Mount Palomar, California, site of observatory selected 1934, observatory opened 1949.

Mount Wilson Observatory, California, opened 1904.

Moussorgsky, Modest, Russian composer (*Boris Godunov*, 1874), b.1839, d.1881.

Mowbray, Thomas, **Duke of Norfolk**, warden of the Scottish Marches, b.*c.*1366, d.1399.

Mozambique (formerly Portuguese East Africa), discovered by Vasco da Gama's fleet 1498; first colonized 1505; created an overseas territory of Portugal 1951; became an independent republic 1975.

Mozart, Wolfgang Amadeus, German composer (*Don Giovanni*, 1787), b.1756, d.1791.

Mubarak, Hosni, Egyptian politician (president since 1981), b.1928.

Mudie, Charles Edward, founder of Mudie's library (1842–1937), b.1818, d.1890.

Mugabe, Robert, Zimbabwean politician (president since 1980), b.1924.

Muggeridge, Malcolm, British journalist, writer and TV personality, b.1903, d.1990.

Muggletonians, religious sect, founded *c.*1651 by the English journeyman tailors Lodowicke Muggleton, b.1609, d.1698, and John Reeve, b.1608, d.1658.

Mühlenberg, Heinrich Melchior, German-born pioneer of American Lutheranism, b.1711, d.1787.

Mukden, Battle of, between Russians and Japanese, fought Feb.–March 1905.

'Mulberry', artificial harbour used at Arromanches, Normandy, in 1944.

Muldoon, Robert David, New Zealand statesman (prime minister 1974–84), b.1921.

Mullan, John, American soldier and surveyor, b.1830, d.1909.

Müller, Fritz, German naturalist, b.1827, d.1897.

Müller, Wilhelm, German poet, b.1794, d.1827.

Mulock, Dinah Maria (Mrs Craik), English writer (*John Halifax, Gentleman*, 1857), b.1826, d.1887.

Mulready, William, Irish painter, b.1786, d.1863.

Mulroney, Martin Brian, Canadian statesman (prime minister 1984–93), b.1939.

Mumbles Railway, Swansea, Britain's oldest passenger railway, first recorded journey 1807; closed 1 Jan. 1960.

Mumford, Lewis, American writer (*The Culture of Cities*, 1938), b.1895, d.1990.

Munch, Edvard, Norwegian painter, b.1863, d.1944.

Münchhausen, Karl Friedrich Hieronymus, Baron von, German cavalry officer, b.1720, d.1797.

Munday, Anthony, English writer and spy, b.1553, d.1633.

Munich Pact, determining the fate of Sudetenland, made 29 Sept. 1938.

Munich Putsch, unsuccessfully attempted by Hitler, 8 Nov. 1923.

Munkácsy, Michael, Hungarian painter (*The Blind Milton*, 1878), b.1844, d.1900.

Munnings, Sir Alfred, English painter (*The Prince of Wales on Forest Witch*, 1921), b.1878, d.1959.

Munro, Hector Hugh ('Saki'), British writer (*Chronicles of Clovis*, 1911), b.1870, killed in battle 1916.

Munro, Sir Thomas, governor of Madras, b.1761, d.1827.

Münster, Treaty of, concluding 30 Years' War, 1649.

Murad I, Turkish sultan (1350–89), b.1319, assassinated 1389.

Murad II, Turkish sultan (1421–51), d.1451.

Murad III, Turkish sultan (1574–96), d.1596.

Murad IV, Turkish sultan (1623–40), b.*c.*1611, d.1640

Murad V, Turkish sultan (1876), b.1840, d.1904.
Murasaki, Lady, Japanese novelist (*Tale of Genji*), lived in the 10th century.
Murat, Achille, Prince, French writer (*Letters of a United States Citizen*, 1830), b.1801, d.1841.
Murat, Joachim, French soldier and king of Naples, b.1767, shot 1815.
Murchison, Sir Roderick Impey, Scottish geologist, b.1792, d.1871.
Murdoch, Dame Iris, Anglo-Irish writer (*The Sea, The Sea*, 1978), b.1919.
Murdoch, (Keith) Rupert, Australian-born American publishing and media tycoon, b.1931.
Murdock, William, Scottish engineer and inventor, 1792 of coal-gas lighting, b.1754, d.1839.
Murfreesboro, Battle of, American Civil War, 31 Dec. 1862 to 2 Jan. 1863.
Murger, Henri, French novelist (*Scènes de la vie de Bohème*, 1848), b.1822, d.1861.
Murillo, Bartolomé, Spanish painter (*Vision of St Anthony*), b.1617, d.1682.
Murmansk, Russian port on the Kola peninsula, founded 1915.
Murphy, Jeremiah Daniel, Irish boy linguist, b.1806, d.1824.
Murray, Gilbert, Australian-born classical scholar, b.1866, d.1957.
Murray, Sir James, British editor of the *Oxford English Dictionary* (1879–1928), b.1837, d.1915.
Murray, Sir John, Canadian oceanographer, b.1841, d.1914.
Murray, John, Scottish publisher, and founder 1809 of the *Quarterly Review*, b.1778, d.1843.
Murry, John Middleton, English critic (*Aspects of Literature*, 1920), b.1889, d.1957.
Museums Association, London, founded 1889.
Museum of Modern Art, New York, established 1929.
Music printing, first complete collection of part-songs printed from movable type issued *c.*1498 by Ottaviano dei Petrucci, b.1466, d.1539.
Musil, Robert, Austrian writer (*The Man Without Qualities*, 1930–42), b.1880, d.1942.
Muslim Era, began 16 July 622.
Musset, Alfred de, French playwright (*Les Nuits*, 1835–36), b.1810, d.1857.

Mussolini, Benito, Italian dictator, b.1883; founded Fascist movement 1919; came to power 1923; fell and was arrested 1943; rescued by the Germans 1943; executed 1945.

Mussorgsky, *see* **Moussorgsky.**

Mustafa Kemal (Kemal Atatürk), Turkish soldier and statesman (prime minister 1923–38), b.1880, d.1938.

Mustapha I, Turkish sultan (1617–18, 1622–23), b.1591, strangled 1639.

Mustapha II, Turkish sultan (1695–1703), b.1664, d.1703.

Mustapha III, Turkish sultan (1757–74), b.1717, d.1774.

Mustapha IV, Turkish sultan (1807–08), b.1779, put to death, 1808.

Mustard gas, first used by the Germans in World War I, July 1917.

Mutation, biological variation, study first developed 1901 by the Dutch botanist Hugo de Vries, b.1848, d.1935.

Mutiny, *Bounty* 1789, Nore 1797, *Danaë* 1800, Indian 1857–58, Curragh 1914.

Muybridge, Eadweard, English pioneer in the study of human and animal movement, b.1830, d.1904.

Muzaffar-ed-Din, shah of Persia (1896–1907), b.1853, d.1907.

Muziano, Girolamo, Italian painter (*St Jerome*), b.1530, d.1590.

Myddleton, Sir Hugh, English builder of 'New River', b.*c.*1560, d.1631.

Myers, Frederick William Henry, English writer, and joint-founder 1882 of the Society for Psychical Research, b.1843, d.1901.

My Lai Massacre, slaughter of South Vietnamese women and children by American soldiers in the hamlet of My Lai during the Vietnam War, 16 May 1968.

Mytens, Daniel, Dutch painter (*Duke of Hamilton*, 1629), b.*c.*1590, d.*c.*1647.

Myxomatosis, first used to destroy rabbits in Australia 1950; in Britain 1952.

N

Nabokov, Vladimir Vladimirovich, Russian-born writer (*Lolita*, 1955), b.1899, d.1977.

Nabonassar, Era of (Babylonian chronology), began 26 Feb. 747 BC.

Nabonidus, king of Babylonia, d.*c*.539 BC.

Nachtigal, Gustav, German explorer, b.1834, d.1885.

Nagasaki, Japan, bombed by the Allies' second atomic bomb Aug. 1945.

Nagy, Imre, Hungarian Communist leader, b.1895, executed 1958.

Naidu, Sarajini, Indian politician, b.1879, d.1949.

Naipaul, Vidiadhar Surajprasad, British Trinidad-born writer of Indian descent (*A House for Mr Biswas,* 1961), b.1932.

Nairne, Caroline, Baroness Nairne, Scottish ballad writer (*Charlie is My Darling*), b.1766, d.1845.

Namier, Lewis, Polish-born historian, b.1888, d.1960.

Nanak, Indian religious leader, founder of the Sikh religion, b.1469, d.1538.

Nancy, Battle of, between the Duke of Lorraine and Charles the Bold, 5 Jan. 1477.

Nanga Parbat, Himalayas, climbed by a German Austrian expedition 3 July 1953.

Nansen, Fridtjof, Norwegian explorer, b.1861, expedition to Greenland 1888, d.1930.

Nantes, Edict of, granting tolerance to French Protestants, signed by Henry IV, 1598; revoked by Louis XIV, 1685.

Napier, Sir Charles, naval strategist and politician, b.1786, d.1860.

Napier, John, Scottish inventor 1614 of logarithms, b.1550, d.1617.

Napier, Sir William, Irish-born historian of the Peninsular War, b.1785, d.1860.

Naples, ruled by Normans 1139–94, by Angevins 1265–1382, by Aragonese 1442–1501, by Spain 1503–1707, by Austria 1707–34, by Bourbons 1734–99, 1815–60.

Napoleon II, king of Rome, duke of Reichstadt, b.1811, d.1832.

Napoleon III, French president (1848–51) and emperor (1852–70), b.1808, d.1873.

Napoleon Buonaparte, emperor of France, b.1769; consul 1799; emperor 1804; king of Italy 1805; abdicated 1814; at Elba 1814–15; defeated at Waterloo and banished to St Helena 1815; d.1821.

Napoleonic Wars, waged between the Allies and the French 1799 to 1815.

Narses, Byzantine general, b.*c.*478, d.*c.* 573.

Narvik, Norway, scene of unsuccessful Allied expedition, World War II, 28 May–9 June 1940.

NASA (National Aeronautics and Space Administration), US government agency which coordinates the US space programme, founded 1958.

Naseby, Battle of, between Parliamentarians and Royalists, 14 June 1645.

Nash, 'Beau' (Richard Nash), master of ceremonies at Bath, b.1674, d.1762.

Nash, John, English architect, b.1752, d.1835.

Nash, Paul, English painter, b.1889, d.1946.

Nashe, Thomas, English writer (*Pierce Penilesse*, 1592), b.1567, d.1601.

Nasmyth, James, Scottish engineer, b.1808, d.1890.

Nasr-ed-Nir, shah of Persia (1848–96), b.*c.*1831, assassinated 1896.

Nasser, Gamal Abdul, Egyptian ruler 1954–70 (president 1956–70) b.1918, d.1970.

Natal, annexed to Cape Colony 1844; made a British colony 1856; merged in the Union of South Africa 1910.

Nathan's, theatrical costumiers, established in London 1790.

Nation, The, British periodical, founded 1907; absorbed into the *New Statesman* 1931.

Nation, Carry, American temperance advocate, b.1846, d.1911.

National Assembly, of France, formed 1789; renamed Constituent Assembly 1789; replaced by the Legislative Assembly 1791.

National Debt, began definitely 1694.

National Farmer's Union, London, founded 10 Dec. 1908.

National Gallery, London, founded 1824.

National Guard, USA, founded 1903.

National Health Service, Great Britain, came into effect 5 July 1948.

National Park, Britain's first, started by a gift of 300 acres near Snowdon 1935.

National Physical Laboratory, Great Britain, founded 1899.
National Playing Fields Association, Great Britain, granted charter 3 Jan. 1933.
National Portrait Gallery, London, founded 1857; opened 1859.
National Rifle Association of America, powerful pro-gun lobby established in 1871.
National Savings Movement, Great Britain, founded 1916.
National Socialism, Germany, founded 1919.
National Socialist German Workers Party (Nazis), founded by Adolf Hitler 1919.
National Socialist Party, Germany, founded 1843.
National Society for the Prevention of Cruelty to Children, London, founded 1884.
National Sporting Club, Great Britain, founded 1891.
National Theatre, *see* **Royal National Theatre.**
National Trust, for places of historic interest or natural beauty, Great Britain, founded 1895.
National Trust for Scotland, for places of historic interest or natural beauty, founded 1931.
National University of Ireland, Dublin, came into being 31 Oct. 1909. Previously Royal University of Ireland, founded 1882, superseding the Queen's University in Ireland, founded 1849.
Nationalisation of the Bank of England, 1946.
NATO (North Atlantic Treaty Organization), mutual defence pact between 13 European nations and the USA, signed 4 April 1949.
Nattier, Jean Marc, French painter (*Portrait a Lady of in Blue*), b.1685, d.1766.
Nature, British periodical, began publication 1869 under the editorship of Sir Joseph Norman Lockyer, b.1836, d.1920.
Nature Conservancy, Great Britain, set up 1949.
Naundorff, Karl Wilhelm, pretender to the throne of France, d.1845.
'Nautical Almanac', British, first published 1767.
Nautilus, USS, first atomic-powered submarine, launched Jan. 1954.
Naval Architects, Institution of, London, founded 1860.
Naval Limitation Conference, Washington, DC, held 1921–22.
Navarino, Battle of, between the Allied and Egyptian fleets, 20 Oct. 1827.
Navarrete, Battle of, between the Black Prince and Spanish rebels, 13 April 1367.
Navratilova, Martina, Czech-born US tennis champion, b.1956.

Nayler, James, English Quaker, b.c.1617, d.1660.

Nazianzen, St Gregory, b.c.330, d.390.

Nazis, German National Socialists, movement founded 1919.

NBC (National Broadcasting Company), American radio and TV network (one of the 'Big Three' with CBS and ABC), established 1926.

Neal, Daniel, English historian of New England, b.1678, d.1743.

Neale, John Mason, English hymn-writer (*Jerusalem the Golden*, 1865), b.1818, d.1866.

Neander, Johnson August Wilhelm, German theologian, b.1780, d.1850.

Neanderthal Man, remains discovered near Dusseldorf 1856.

Nebraska, USA, discovered by Francisco Vasquez de Coronado 1541; sold to the USA by France 1803; first settled 1847; admitted to the Union 1867.

Nebraska University, Lincoln, founded 1867; opened 1871.

Nebuchadnezzar, Babylonian king 605–562 BC.

Nebula, in Andromeda, described by the Arab astronomer Al Sufi before 1000.

Necker, Jacques, French statesman and financier, b.1732, d.1804.

Needle and Thread Ceremony, Queen's College, Oxford University, 1 Jan. each year.

Negus, hot, sweet wine and water, invented 1704 by the English soldier Colonel Francis Negus, b.c.1665, d.1732.

Nehru, Pandit Jawaharlal, Indian statesman (prime minister 1947–64), b.1889, d.1964.

Nekrasov, Nikolai Alekseievich, Russian poet, b.1821, d.1877.

Nelson, Horatio, Lord, English sailor, b.1758, killed in action 1805.

Nemours, Louis, Duc de, French soldier, b.1814, d.1896.

Nennius, Welsh writer (*Historia Britonum*), lived in the 8th century.

Neodymium, metallic element, discovered 1885 by the Austrian chemist Baron von Welsbach, b.1858, d.1929.

Neon, gaseous element, discovered 1898 by the Scottish scientist Sir William Ramsay, b.1852, d.1916.

Nepal, independent kingdom, conquered by the Gurkhas 1768; constitutional monarchy since 1951.

Nepomuk, St John of, national hero of Bohemia, killed 1393.

Nepos, Cornelius, Roman biographer, b.c.100, d.c.25 BC.

Nepos, Julius, Roman emperor (474–475), d.480.

Neptune, planet, position predicted 1845 by the English astronomer John Couch Adams, b.1819, d.1892, and 1846 by the French astronomer Urbain Leverrier, b.1811, d.1877; observed 23 Sept. 1846 by the German astronomer Johann Gottfried Galle, b.1812, d.1910.

Neri, St Filippo, b.1515, d.1595.

Nernst, Walther, German physicist, b.1864, d.1941.

Nero, Roman emperor (54–68), b.37, committed suicide 68.

Neruda, Jan, Czech writer (*Mala Strana*, 1878), b.1834, d.1891.

Nerva, Roman emperor (96–98), b.*c.*30, d.98.

Nerval, Gérard de (Gérard Labrunie), French writer (*Voyage en Orient*, 1848–50), b.1808, d.1855.

Nesbit, Edith, English children's writer (*The Treasure Seekers*, 1899), b.1858, d.1924.

Nesselrode, Karl Robert, Count, Russian statesman, b.1780, d.1862.

Nestorian Church, Middle Eastern religious movement dating from the deposition 431 of Nestorius, Patriarch of Constantinople (428–431), d.*c.*451.

Netherlands, The, revolt against Spain (1572–1609), war with Spain (1621–48); republic 1650–72, 1702–47; French domination 1795–1813; restored as an independent monarchy 1814; Belgian provinces seceded 1830; new constitution granted 1848, revised constitution granted 1917.

Neuhof, Theodor, Baron von, German king of Corsica (1736–43), b.1686, d.1756.

Neuilly, Treaty of, between the Allies and Bulgaria, signed 1919.

Neumann, Alfred, German writer (*Alfred de Musset*, 1925), b.1895, d.1952.

Neutrons, nuclear particles, discovered 1932 by the English scientist Sir James Chadwick, b.1891, d.1974.

Nevada, USA, first settled 1849; created a Territory 1861; admitted to the Union 1864.

Nevada University, Reno, founded 1873; opened 1874.

Neville, George, archbishop of York and chancellor of England, b.*c.*1433, d.1476.

Neville's Cross, Battle of, between the Northern Levies and the Scottish armies, 17 Oct. 1346.

Nevin, Ethelbert Woodbridge, American composer (*Narcissus*, 1891), b.1862, d.1901.

Nevinson, Henry Woodd, English journalist, b.1856, d.1941.

New Amsterdam, early name of New York City until 1664.

Newberry Library, Chicago, founded by the will of the American financier Walter Loomis Newberry, b.1804, d.1868.

Newbolt, Sir Henry, English writer (*Drake's Drum*, 1914), b.1862, d.1938.

New Caledonia, South Pacific, discovered by Captain James Cook 1774; annexed by France 1853.

Newcastle, William Cavendish, Duke of, Royalist supporter, b.1592, d.1676.

New College, Oxford University founded 1379 by William of Wykeham, b.1324, d.1404.

Newcomen, Thomas, English engineer and inventor, b.1663, d.1729.

New Daily, The, British newspaper, founded 1960.

New Deal, USA, President Roosevelt's legislative policy 1933 onwards.

New Delhi, Indian capital, construction began 1911; opened officially 10 Feb. 1931.

Newdigate Prize, Oxford University, for English verse, endowed 1805 by Sir Roger Newdigate, b.1719, d.1806.

New England Confederation, formed 1643; dissolved 1684.

New Forest, England, named by William the Conqueror 1079; scheduled as a National Park 1877.

Newfoundland, discovered by John Cabot 1497; annexed by England 1583; constituted a Dominion 1917; created a Province of Canada 1949.

Newgate, London prison, rebuilt 1770–83 by the English architect George Dance the younger, b.1741, d.1825; demolished 1902–03.

New Guinea, *see* **Papua New Guinea.**

New Hampshire, USA, first settled 1623; entered the Union 1788.

New Hebrides, *see* **Vanuatu.**

New Jersey, USA, first settled in the early 17th century; entered the Union 1787.

Newman, Ernest, English music critic (*The Life of Richard Wagner*, 1933–37), b.1868, d.1959.

Newman, John Henry, English religious leader and writer (*Apologia Pro Vita Sua*, 1864), b.1801, converted to Catholicism 1845, became cardinal 1879, d.1890.

Newman, Paul, American film star (*Cool Hand Luke,* 1967), b.1925.

Newmarch, Mrs Rosa, English music critic (*Promenade Concert Notes*), b.1857, d.1940.

Newmarket, English racing centre, first developed as such by King Charles I.

New Mexico, USA, first settled 1598; annexed to New Spain 1771; made a Territory 1850; admitted to the Union 1912.

Newnes, Sir George, English newspaper and magazine publisher, b.1851, d.1910.

New Orleans, Louisiana, founded *c.*1718 by the French Canadian explorer Jean Baptiste le Mayne, Sieur de Bienville, b.1680, d.1768.

Newport, Rhode Island, USA, first settled 1639.

'New River', London, built between 1609 and 1613 by the English goldsmith Sir Hugh Myddleton, b.*c.*1560, d.1631.

News Chronicle, formed by amalgamation of the *Daily News* and the *Daily Chronicle* 1930. Incorporated in the *Daily Mail* 1960.

Newsfilms, introduced 1911 by the French photographer Charles Pathé, b.1873, d.1957.

News of the World, founded 1 Oct. 1843.

New South Wales, Australia, declared British by Cook on 23 Aug. 1770; first free settlers arrived 1793.

Newspaper, first British daily, the *Daily Courant*, began 11 March 1702.

Newspaper advertisement duty, abolished in Britain 1853.

Newspaper stamp tax, introduced in Britain 1712; abolished 1855.

Newspapers, first printed on a train (the *Grand Trunk Herald*), produced by the American inventor Thomas Alva Edison, b.1847, d.1931.

New Statesman, British periodical, founded 1913; absorbed *The Nation* 1931; now called *New Statesman and Society*.

New Stone Age, six to eight thousand years ago.

New Style, British calendar (Gregorian), introduced Sept. 1752.

Newton, Huey, American black activist, co-founder of the Black Panther Party, b.1942, assassinated 1989.

Newton, Sir Isaac, English scientist (*Principia*, 1687), b.1642, d.1727.

Newton, Thomas, English divine, b.1704, d.1782.

New Year's Day, 1 Jan.

New York City, founded as New Amsterdam 1626.

New Yorker, The, American literary magazine founded in 1925 by editor Harold Ross, b.1892, d.1951.

New York Herald Tribune, American newspaper, founded as *The New York Tribune* 1841 by the American editor Horace Greeley, b.1811, d.1872.

New York Public Library, founded 1895.

New York State, USA, first settled by the Dutch 1614; came under English rule 1664; entered the Union 1788.

New York Times**,** American newspaper, founded 1851 by the American editor and politician Henry Jarvis Raymond, b.1820, d.1869, called the *New York Daily Times* 1851–57.

New York University, founded 1831.

New Zealand, discovered 925 by the Polynesian explorer Kupe; rediscovered 1642 by the Dutch navigator Abel Janszoon Tasman, b.1603, d.1659; declared a dominion 1907; national day, 6 Feb., celebrating the signing with the Maoris of the Treaty of Waitangi 1840.

Nexö, Martin Andersen, Danish novelist (*Ditte*, 1917–21), b.1869, d.1954.

Ney, Michel, Duc d'Elchingen, Prince de la Moskova, marshal of France, b.1769, shot 1815.

Niagara Falls, first crossed on a tightrope 1859 by the French acrobat Charles Blondin, b.1824, d.1897.

Nibelungenlied, German epic poem, compiled *c.*1160.

Nicaea, First Council of, ecumenical council, convened 325.

Nicaea, Second Council of, ecumenical council, convened 787.

Nicaragua, colonized by the Spanish from 1520s; achieved independence from Spain 1821; became an independent republic 1838; guerilla war led by Augusto Cesar Sandino against American occupation 1927–33; Anastasio Somoza assumed presidency 1936, followed by his sons; 1979 Somoza dynasty overthrown by Sandinista Liberation Front; Sandinistas lost parliamentary majority in free elections 1990.

Niccoli, Niccolò, Italian humanist and book collector, b.1364, d.1437.

Nice (Nizza), elected by plebiscite to be annexed to France 1860.

Nicene Creed, believed to be fundamentally the work of St Cyril of Jerusalem, b.*c.*315, d.386; promulgated at Nicaea 325.

Nicephorus, St, b.190, martyred 258.

Nicephorus I, Byzantine emperor (802–811), killed in battle 811.

Nicephorus II (Phocas), Byzantine emperor (963–969), b.*c.*912, assassinated 969.

Nicephorus III (Botaniates), Byzantine emperor 1097–81.

Nicholas I, St, pope 858–867, d.867.

Nicholas II (Gerard), pope 1059–61.
Nicholas III (Giovanni Guetano Orsini), pope 1277–80, d.1280.
Nicholas IV (Girolamo Masci), pope 1288–93, d.1293.
Nicholas IV (Pietro Rainalducci), anti-pope 1328–30, d.1333.
Nicholas V (Tomaso Parentucelli), pope 1447–55, b.1398, d.1455.
Nicholas I, emperor of Russia (1825–55), b.1796, d.1855.
Nicholas II, emperor of Russia (1894–1919), b.1868, murdered 1919.
Nicholson, Jack, American film star and director (*One Flew Over the Cuckoo's Nest,* 1975), b.1937.
Nicholson, John, Irish-born general in India, b.1812, died of wounds 1857.
Nicholson, Sir William, English artist (*W. E. Henley*), b.1872, d.1949.
Nicias, Peace of, effected 421 BC by the Greek statesman Nicias executed 413 BC.
Nickel, discovered 1754 by the Swedish scientist Baron Cronstedt, b.1722, d.1765.
Nickel carbonyl, a gas, discovered 1899 by the German-born chemist Ludwig Mond, b.1839, d.1909.
Nicklaus, Jack William, US champion golfer, b.1940.
Nicobar Islands, Bay of Bengal, annexed by Britain 1869; centrally administered by the government of India from 1956 to date.
Nicol prism, polarisation of light, invented 1828 by the Scottish physicist William Nicol, b.c.1768, d.1851.
Nicolai, Otto, German composer (*The Merry Wives of Windsor*, 1849), b.1810, d.1849.
Nicolls, Richard, first English governor (1664–67) of New York, b.1624, killed 1672.
Nicot, Jean, French diplomat, introduced tobacco into France, b.c.1530, d.1600.
Niebuhr, Reinhold, American theologian, b.1892, d.1971.
Niepce, Nicéphore, French physician and pioneer in photography, b.1765, d.1833.
Nietzsche, Friedrich, German philosopher (*Also Sprach Zarathustra*, 1883–85), b.1844, d.1900.
Niger, navigated by Mungo Park 1795.
Niger, West Africa, made a French colony 1922; became fully independent republic 1960.
Nigeria, former British colony, achieved independence within the Commonwealth 1960.

'Night of the Long Knives', Nazi purge in Germany, 30 June 1934.

Nightingale, Florence, English pioneer in the training of nurses, b.1820, d.1910.

Nightingale Training School, first British training school for nurses, founded by Florence Nightingale at St Thomas's Hospital, London, 1860.

Nihilism, Russian revolutionary movement, founded *c.*1860.

Nijinsky, Vladimir, Russian dancer, b.1892, d.1950.

Nikisch, Artur, Hungarian conductor, b.1855, d.1922.

Nile, Source of the, discovered 1862 by the English explorer John Hanning Speke, b.1827, d.1864 and Colonel James Augustus Grant, b.1827, d.1892.

Nile, Battle of the (Battle of Aboukir Bay), between the British and the French 1 Aug. 1798.

Nile Bridge, Cairo, built by the British engineer Sir William Arrol, b.1839, d.1913.

Nine Lessons and Nine Carols, festival held at King's College Chapel, Cambridge, each year on Christmas Eve.

Nineveh, Assyrian capital, excavated 1845–47 by the archaeologist and diplomat Sir Austen Henry Layard, b.1817, d.1894.

Ninian, St, b.*c.*360, d.432.

'Ninon de Lenclos' (Anne Lenclos), French courtesan, b.1620, d.1705.

Niobium (columbium), chemical element, isolated 1801 by the English chemist Charles Hatchett, b.c.1765, d.1847.

Nitrogen, discovered 1772 by the Scottish physician Daniel Rutherford, b.1749, d.1819.

Nitrogen trichloride, discovered 1811 by the French scientist Pierre Louis Dulon, b.1785, d.1838.

Nitroglycerine, manufacture perfected *c.*1860 by the Swedish chemist Alfred Nobel, b.1833, d.1896.

Nitrous oxide, first used 1844 as an anaesthetic in dentistry by the American dentist Horace Wells, b.1815, d.1848.

Nitroprussides, discovered 1841, by the Scottish chemist Lord Playfair, b.1818, d.1898.

Nixon, Richard Milhous, 37th US president (1969–74), resigned 1974, b.1913.

Noailles, Adrien Maurice, Duc de, French soldier, b.1678, d.1766.

Nobel, Alfred, Swedish chemist and philanthropist, b.1833, d.1896.

Nobel Peace Prize, founded by Alfred Nobel 1895.
Nobile, Umberto, Italian explorer, b.1885, d.1978.
Noguchi, Hideyo, Japanese bacteriologist, b.1876, d.1928.
Nollekens, Joseph, British sculptor (*King George III*), b.1737, d.1823.
Non-Euclidean geometry, founded 1829 by the Russian mathematician Nicholas Lobachevsky, b.1793, d.1856.
Nonjurors, British clergymen who refused to take the oath of allegiance 1689–1805.
No Plays, Japanese traditional plays dating from 15th century.
Nordenskjöld, Otto, Swedish explorer and scholar, b.1869, d.1928.
Norfolk, Hugh Bigod, Earl of, Crusader, d. about 1177.
Norfolk Island, South Pacific, discovered by Captain James Cook 1774; settled 1856; made an external territory of Australia 1913.
Norham, Peace of, between Scotland and England, held 1209.
Norman, Conolly, Irish alienist and reformer, b.1853, d.1908.
Norman, Montagu Collet, Baron Norman, governor of the Bank of England (1920–44), b.1871, d.1950.
Norman Conquest, of England, by William the Conqueror 1066.
Normandy, founded 911.
Normandy, Alphonse René le Mire de, French-born chemist and inventor 1851, of a distiller for sea water, b.1809, d.1864.
Normandy Offensive, World War II, began 6 June 1944.
Norris, Frank, American novelist (*The Pit*, 1903), b.1870, d.1902.
Norroy King of Arms, post established in the 13th century.
'North, Christopher' (John Wilson), Scottish writer (*Recreations*, 1842), b.1785, d.1854.
North, Frederick, Earl of Guildford, British statesman (prime minister 1770–82), b.1732, d.1792.
North, Sir Thomas, English translator (Plutarch's *Lives*, 1579), b.*c.*1525, d.*c.*1601.
Northampton, Treaty of, recognising the independence of Scotland, signed 1328.
North Atlantic Treaty, signed at Washington, DC, 4 April 1949; amended in London by protocol 17 Oct. 1951.
North Carolina, USA, first settled 1585; permanently settled 1663; entered the Union 1789.
North Channel, between Scotland and Northern Ireland, swum 1947 for the first time, by Tom Blower of Nottingham.
Northcliffe, Alfred Charles William Harmsworth, Viscount, Irish-born newspaper owner, b.1865, d.1922.

Northcote, Henry Stafford Northcote, Baron, governor-general (1903–07) of Australia, b.1846, d.1911.

North Dakota, USA, first settled 1766; formed part of the Dakota Territory 1861; admitted to the Union 1889.

Northeast Passage, navigated 1878–79 by the Swedish explorer Nils Adolf Erik Nordenskiöld, b.1832, d.1901.

Northern Ireland, administration by separate parliament and executive government established by the Government of Ireland Act, 1920; 1969–70 violence between Protestant and Catholic communities erupted, British troops eventually stationed to prevent bloodshed, provoking terrorist campaign from IRA, Northern Irish parliament suspended 1972 and replaced by Direct Rule from London.

Northern Territory, Australia, formerly part of New South Wales, annexed to South Australia 1863; placed under the control of a Commonwealth Administrator 1931; now an administrative division of N. central Australia.

Northern Underground Line, London, opened 1904 as the Great Northern and City Railway.

Northern Wei Dynasty, China, 386

North Pole, first reached 6 April 1909 by the American explorer Robert Edwin Peary, b.1856, d.1920; first flown over 1926 by the American aviator Richard E. Byrd, b.1888, d.1957; atomic-powered *Nautilus*, first submarine to reach it underwater, 1958; first successful dogsled expedition 1968–69; first person to reach it alone by dogsled, Japanese Naomi Uemura, 1978.

North Staffordshire, **University College of,** Keele, founded 1949.

Northumberland, Henry Percy, Earl of, marshal of England, b.1342, killed in battle 1408.

Northumberland, Thomas Percy, Earl of, rebel, b.1528, beheaded 1572.

Northwest Frontier Province, N. Pakistan, part of British India 1901–47.

Northwest Mounted Police, Canada, formed 1873; renamed the Royal Canadian Mounted Police, 1920.

Northwest Passage, discovered 1850–54 by the British navigator Sir Robert John le Mesurier McClure, b.1807, d.1873.

Northwest Ordinance, for the government of US Western territories, passed 1787.

Northwest Territories, Canada, administered by a commissioner since 1952.

Northwestern University, Illinois, founded 1851.
Norton, Thomas, English poet (with Sackville, *Gorboduc*, 1561), b.1532, d.1584.
Norway, united with Sweden 1319–55, with Denmark 1380–89, with Sweden and Denmark 1389–1450, with Denmark 1450–1814, with Sweden 1814–1905; independent kingdom since 1905; German occupation 1940–45.
Norwich, granted first charter by King Henry II, 1158.
Norwich Cathedral, constructed 1096 to *c.* 1150.
Nostradamus, French astrologer (*Centuries*, 1555), b.1503, d.1566.
Notke, Bernt, German artist (*St George and the Dragon*, 1489), b.*c.* 1440, d.1509.
Notre Dame de Paris, constructed 1163–82.
Nottingham, Charles Howard, Earl of, Lord High Admiral, b.1536, d.1624.
Nottingham University, opened as University College 1881; achieved university status 1948.
Nova Scotia, first settled by the French in the early century; ceded to Britain 1713; became a province of Canada 1867.
'Novalis' (Friedrich von Hardenberg), German poet (*Hymnen an die Nacht*, 1798–1800), b.1772, d.1801.
Novatian, anti-pope 251.
Novello, Ivor, British actor and composer, b.1893, d.1951.
Novello, Vincent, English music publisher, b.1781, d.1861.
Noverre, Jean-Georges, French pioneer ballet-master at the Opéra-Comique, b.1727, d.1810.
Novi, Battle of, between the Allies and the French, 15 Aug. 1799.
Noyes, Alfred, English poet (*Drake*, 1908), b.1880, d.1958.
Noyes, John Humphrey, American founder 1848 of the Oneida Community, b.1811, d.1886.
Noyon, Treaty of, between France and Spain, signed 1516.
Nuclear disintegration, in nitrogen atoms, first observed by Rutherford in 1919.
Nuclear fission, in uranium atoms, first observed by Hahn and Strassman in 1939.
Nuclear reactor, first American, built at Chicago University Dec. 1942 by the Italian atomic physicist Enrico Fermi, b.1901, d.1954.
Nuclear reactor, first British, built at Harwell 1947.
Nuffield, William Richard Morris, 1st Viscount, motor manufacturer and philanthropist, b.1877, d.1963.

Nuffield College, Oxford University, founded 1937.
Nuffield Foundation, formed 1943.
Nunez, Alvar, Spanish navigator and discoverer 1528 of Florida, d.1564.
Nunez, Pedro, Spanish painter (*Philip* IV), b.1601, d.1654.
Nuremberg, War Crimes Tribunal, World War II, held Nov. 1945–Oct. 1946.
Nureyev, Rudolph, Russian-born ballet dancer, choreographer and director, b.1938, d.1993.
Nuri-es-Said, Iraqi general and prime minister of the Arab Federation, b.1888, assassinated 1958.
Nurses, training of, organised by the English pioneer Florence Nightingale, b.1820, d.1910.
Nuttall, Enos, first archbishop of the West Indies, b.1842, d.1916.
Nutter, Mary, the last Lancashire witch, b.1856, d.1928
Nyasa, Lake, *see* **Malawi, Lake.**
Nyasaland, *see* **Malawi.**
Nylon, discovered 1927 by research workers of the American firm Du Pont de Nemours.
Nylon shirts, first introduced in the USA 1939.
Nymphenburg, Bavarian chateau, constructed 1664; porcelain manufactured since 1747.
Nyon Conference, on the suppression of Mediterranean submarine piracy, held 1937.

O

Oak Apple Day, 29 May, celebrating the Restoration of King Charles II, 1660.
'Oaks, The', Epsom, first run 1779.
Oates, Titus, English conspirator (1678), b.1649, d.1705.
Oath of Strasbourg, sworn between Charles the Bold and Louis the German against Lothair 1842.
Oath of the Tennis Court, French Revolution, 20 June 1789.
Oberammergau, Germany, scene of the decennial presentation of the Passion Play since 1634.
Oberlin, Johann Friedrich, German reformer, b.1740, d.1826.
O'Brien, Conor Cruise, Irish diplomat, journalist, writer and critic, b.1917.
O'Brien, William Smith, Irish patriot, b.1803, d.1864.
Observer*, *The, British newspaper, began publication 1791.
O'Casey, Sean, Irish-born dramatist (*Juno and the Paycock*, 1924), b.1884, d.1964.
Occleve, Thomas, English poet (*De Regimine Principum*), b.*c.*1369, d.*c.*1450.
Ockham, William of, English-born philosopher, b.*c.*1280, d.*c.*1349.
O'Clery, Michael, Irish historian (*Annals of the Four Masters*, 1632–36), b.1575, d.1643.
O'Connell, Daniel, Irish nationalist leader, b.1775, d.1847.
O'Connor, Roderic, Irish king, b.1116, d.1198.
Octavia, wife of Marc Antony, d.11 BC.
Octavian (Augustus), first Roman emperor (27 BC–AD 14), b.63 BC, d. AD 14.
Octavia, wife of the Roman Emperor Nero, killed 62 BC.
October Revolution, Russia, 7 Nov. 1917 (New Style).
Oddfellows, Independent Order of, temperance society, founded in Manchester 1810; in the USA 1819.
Odo de Clugny, St, pioneer in the development of musical theory, d.942.
Odovacar, Scirian king of Italy (476–493), killed 493.
Odyssey, Greek epic, attributed to Homer, believed to have lived in the 11th, 10th or 9th century BC.
Oecolampadius, Johannes, German religious reformer, b.1482, d.1531.

OEEC (Organization for European Economic Cooperation), set up 16 April 1948.
Oersted, Hans Christian, Danish pioneer in electromagnetism, b.1777, d.1851.
Offa's Dyke, Welsh border defence, constructed 779 by Offa, king of Mercia, b.747, d.796.
Offenbach, Jacques (Jakdo Levy Eberst), German-born composer (*Tales of Hoffman*, 1881), b.1819, d.1880.
O'Flaherty, Liam, Irish novelist (*The Informer*, 1925), b.1897, d.1984.
Oglethorpe, James Edward, English founder (1732) of Georgia, USA, b.1696, d.1785.
'O Henry', *see* **Porter, William Sydney.**
O'Higgins, Bernardo, Chilean leader, b.1776, d.1842.
Ohio, USA, first settled 1788; entered the Union 1803.
Ohio Company, English colonizing organization, chartered 1749.
Ohm's Law, of electrical resistance, pronounced 1827 by the German physicist George Simon Ohm, b.1787, d.1854. His law of sound vibrations: 1843.
Ohnet, Georges, French writer (*Serge Panine*, 1881), b.1848, d.1918.
Ohthere, Norse explorer, lived in the 9th century.
Oil, distilled from coal and shale 1847–50 by the Scottish chemist James Young, b.1811, d.1883.
Oil, struck 1859 in Pennsylvania (first known drilling in the world) by the American oil prospector Colonel Edwin Laurentine Drake, b.1819, d.1880.
Oil drilling, rotary method first adopted in Texas *c.*1900.
Oil lighting, first used for London streets 1681.
Oil tanker, prototype (*The Gluckauf*) built on Tyneside 1886.
Oil tanker, first 100,000 dead weight tonnage, built 1958.
Oil tanker, world's first gas turbine powered, the British GTS *Auris*, made maiden voyage 1959.
Oil well, first, drilled at Titusville, Pennsylvania, 1859.
Oireachtas, National Parliament of the Irish Republic, founded 1937.
Oistrakh, David, Russian violinist, b.1908, d.1974.
Oistrakh, Igor, Russian violinist, b.1931.
Okapi, first noted 1878 by the Russian-born explorer Wilhelm Junker, b.1840, d.1892.
O'Keefe, Georgia, American artist, b.1887, d.1986.
Okhotsk, East Siberia, founded 1649.

Okinawa, Battle of, World War II, 1 April–22 June 1945.
Oklahoma, USA, first settled 1887; created a Territory 1890; admitted to the Union 1907.
Olaf I, king of Norway (995–1000), b.969, drowned 1000.
Olaf II, St, king of Norway (1016–29), b.995, killed in battle 1030.
Olaf III, king of Norway (1067–93), d.1093.
Olaf IV, king of Norway (1103–16), d.1116.
Olaf V, king of Norway (1381–87), d.1387.
Olav V, king of Norway (1957–91), b.1903, d.1991.
Olbers, Heinrich Wilhelm Mathias, German astronomer, b.1758, d.1840.
Old Age Pensions Act, Great Britain, came into force 1 Jan. 1909.
Old Catholics, religious movement formed 1870–71.
'Old Pretender, The' (James Francis Edward Stewart), b.1688, d.1766.
Old Style, British calendar (Julian), superseded by New Style 1752.
Old Vic, London theatre, built 1818, assumed its present role 1914.
Oldcastle, Sir John, English leader of the Lollards, hung 1417.
Oldenbarneveldt, John van, Dutch statesman, b.1547, executed 1619.
Oldys, William, English antiquary, b.1696, d.1761.
Oleic acid, fat-forming acid, discovered 1815 by the French scientist Michel Eugene Chevreul, b.1786, d.1889.
Olga, St, d.*c*.969.
Oligocene Epoch, Earth history, 45 million years ago.
Oliphant, Laurence, South African-born writer and journalist, b.1829, d.1888.
Olivares, Gaspar, Spanish statesman, b.1587, d.1645.
Oliver, Isaac, French-born miniature painter (*James I*), b.*c*.1556, d.1617.
Olivier, Sir Laurence, **Baron Olivier of Brighton**, English actor, b.1907, d.1989.
Olmsted, Denison, American scientist, b.1791, d.1859.
Olympiad, ancient Greek 4-year period, calculated by the Olympian games.
Olympias, mother of Alexander the Great, killed 316 BC.
Olympic Era, began 1 July 776 BC.
Olympic Cup, instituted 1906 by Baron Pierre de Coubertin, b.1863, d.1937.

Olympic Games, ancient, held 776 BC to AD 394.

Olympic Games, idea of revival introduced 1892 by Baron Pierre de Coubertin, b.1863, d.1937.

Olympic Games, modern, 1st Athens, Greece 1896; 2nd Paris, France 1900; 3rd St Louis, USA 1904; 4th London, England 1908; 5th Stockholm, Sweden 1912; 6th Berlin, Germany 1916 (cancelled); 7th Antwerp, Belgium 1920; 8th Paris, France 1924; 9th Amsterdam, Netherlands 1928; 10th Los Angeles, USA 1932; 11th Berlin, Germany 1936; 12th Tokyo, Japan, and Helsinki, Finland 1940 (cancelled.); 13th London, England 1944 (cancelled); 14th London, England 1948; 15th Helsinki, Finland 1952; 16th Melbourne, Australia 1956 (equestrian sports at Stockholm); 17th Rome, Italy 1960; 18th Tokyo, Japan 1964; 19th Mexico City, Mexico 1968; 20th Munich, Germany 1972; 21st Montreal, Canada 1976; 22nd Moscow, USSR 1980 (boycotted); 23rd Los Angeles, USA 1984 (boycotted); 24th Seoul, South Korea 1988; 25th Barcelona, Spain 1992; 26th Atlanta, USA 1996.

Olympic Winter Games, official, 1st Chamonix, France 1924; 2nd St Moritz, Switzerland 1928; 3rd Lake Placid, USA 1932; 4th Garmisch-Partenkirchen, Germany 1936; 5th St Moritz, Switzerland 1948; 6th Oslo, Norway 1952; 7th Cortina d'Ampezzo, Italy 1956; 8th Squaw Valley, USA 1960; 9th Innsbruck, Austria 1964; 10th Grenoble, France 1968; 11th Sapporo, Japan 1972; 12th Innsbruck, Austria 1976; 13th Lake Placid, USA 1980; 14th Sarajevo, Yugoslavia 1984; 15th Calgary, Canada 1988; 16th Albertville, France 1992; 17th Lillehammer, Norway 1996.

Olympic Winter Games, unofficial, first London 1908; second Antwerp 1920).

O'Mahony, John, Irish patriot, b.1816, d.1877.

Oman, Sir Charles, historian, b.1860, d.1946.

Omar, second of the Mahommedan Caliphs, b.*c.*581, assassinated 644.

Omar Khayyam, Persian poet (*Rubaiyat*), lived in the 11th century.

Omar Pasha, Turkish soldier and statesman, b.1806, d.1871.

O'Meara, Barry Edward, Napoleon's surgeon at St Helena, b.1786, d.1836.

Ompteda, Georg von, German novelist (*Herzeloyde*, 1905), b.1863, d.1931.

Onassis, Aristotle Socrates, Argentine ship-owner, b.1906, d.1975.

Oneida Community, NY, founded 1848 by the American reformer John Humphrey Noyes, b.1811, d.1886.

O'Neill, Eugene, American playwright (*Strange Interlude*, 1928), b.1888, d.1953.

O'Neill, Peggy, American socialite, b.*c.*1796, d.1879.

Ontario, Canada, settled by the French; British territory from 1763; organized as Upper Canada 1791; made a province of Canada 1867.

OPEC, see **Organization of Petroleum Exporting Countries**.

Open-hearth method, of making Bessemer steel invented *c.*1866 by the electrical engineers Sir William Siemens, b.1823, d.1883, and Ernst Werner von Siemens, b.1816, d.1892.

Opera, first real, *La Dafne* (1597) by Rinuccini and Peri.

Operation Desert Shield, military operation by US and UN allies in Kuwait to deter further Iraq attacks on Kuwait after the Iraqi invasion of Kuwait Aug. 1990.

Operation Desert Storm, massive air bombardment of Iraqi forces in Kuwait by US and allies during the Persian Gulf War Jan. 1991.

Operation Overlord, codename for the Allied invasion of Normandy, 6 June 1944.

Ophthalmoscope, invented 1851 by the German scientist Hermann von Helmholtz, b.1821, d.1894.

Opie, Amelia Alderson, English writer (*Father and Daughter*, 1801), b.1769, d.1853.

Opie, John, English painter (*The Assassination of Rizzio*, 1787), b.1761, d.1807.

Opium War, China, between Britain and China, waged 1840–42.

Oppenheimer, Julius Robert, American nuclear physicist, 'father of the atomic bomb', b.1904, d.1967.

Orange, **William I, Prince of** (William the Silent), b.1533, d.1584.

Orange, William II, Prince of, b.1626, d.1650.

Orange, William III, Prince of (William IV, king of England), b.1650, d.1702.

Orange Free State, South Africa, first settled *c.*1810; proclaimed British Territory 1848; independence recognized 1854; finally created a Province of the Union of South Africa 1910.

Orangemen, Irish Protestant association, formed by 1795.

Oratorians, religious order, founded I575 by St Filippo Neri, b.1515, d.1595.

Oratorio, first, deemed to have been composed 1600 by the Italian composer Emilio del Cavalieri, b.*c.*1550, d.1602.

Oratory, The, Birmingham, founded 1847.

Oratory, The (Brompton Oratory), London, founded 1850.

Orcagna, Italian artist (*Life of the Virgin*), b.*c.*1308, d.1368.

Orchardson, Sir William, Scottish painter (*Napoleon on board the* Bellerophon, 1880), b.1832, d.1910.

Ordericus Vitalis, English historian, b.1075, d.*c.*1143.

Ordinance of 1787, for the government of US western territories.

Ordnance Survey, of Great Britain, set up 1791.

Ordovician Period, Earth history, 420 million years ago.

Oregon, USA, first settled *c.*1830; made a Territory 1848; admitted to the Union 1859.

Oregon University, founded 1876.

Oregon Trail, Missouri to Oregon, first travelled 1811.

Orff, Carl, German composer (*Carmina Burana*, 1937), b.1895, d.1982.

Orford, Robert Walpole, Earl of, English statesman, b.1676, d.1745.

Organization for Economic Cooperation and Development (OECD), international organization based in Paris, succeeded OEEC 1960.

Organization for European Economic Cooperation (OEEC), established 1848; superseded by OECD 1960.

Organization of American States, formed 1948.

Organization of Petroleum Exporting Countries (OPEC), established 1961 to co-ordinate petroleum supply policies and prices.

Orgetorix, leader of the Helvetii against Julius Caesar, d.*c.*60 BC.

Oriel College, Oxford University, founded by King Edward II 1326.

Origen, Alexandrean theologian, b.185, d.254.

Orinoco, South American river, discovered 1498 by Christopher Columbus; first explored by the Spaniard Diego de Ordaz 1531–32.

Orissa, India, conquered by the British 1803; constituted a separate Province 1936; the independent princely states merged with the State of Orissa 1949.

Orkneys, passed (by default) from Danish to Scottish ownership 1468; formally annexed to the Scottish crown 1471.

Orlando, Vittorio Emanuele, Italian statesman, b.1860, d.1952.
Orleanists, French political party, arose *c.*1790; ceased to exist *c.*1874
Orleans, relieved by Jeanne d'Arc 1429.
Orléans, Charles, Duc d', French poet, b.1391, d.1465.
Orléans, Henri, Prince d', explorer, b.1867, d.1901.
Orley, Bernard, Flemish painter (*Charles V*), b.*c.*1488, d.1541.
Orlov, Aleksei Feodorovich, Prince, Russian statesman, b.1787, d.1862.
Ormonde, Sir James ('Black James'), Lord Treasurer of Ireland, killed 1497.
Orm *or* **Ormin**, English poet (*Ormulum*), *fl.* 13th century.
Orosius, Spanish historian (*Historia adversus Paganos*), lived in the late 4th and early 5th centuries.
Orozco, José Clemente, Mexican painter, b.1883, d.1949.
Orpen, Sir William, Irish painter (*In the Wicklow Mountains*), b.1878, d.1931.
Orrery, Roger Boyle, Earl of, statesman and soldier, b.1621, d.1679.
Orsini, Felice, Italian patriot, b.1819; unsuccessful attempt on the life of Napoleon III, 1858; executed 1858.
Ortega Saavedra, Daniel, Nicaraguan guerrilla and political leader (president 1981–90), b.1945.
Ortega y Gasset, José, Spanish writer (*La Rebelión de las Masas*, 1930), b.1883, d.1955.
Orthodox Eastern Church, finally separated from the Western Church 1054.
Orton, Arthur, English pretender to the Tichbourne title, b.1834, d.1898.
Orton, Joe (Kingsley Orton), British playwright (*Entertaining Mr Sloane*, 1964), b.1933, d.1967.
Orwell, George (Eric Blair), British political writer (*Animal Farm*, 1945), b.1903, d.1950.
Osborne, Dorothy, **Lady Temple,** wife of Sir William Temple, b.1628, d.1699, b.1627, d.1695.
Osborne, John, English actor and playwright (*Look Back in Anger*, 1956), b.1929.
Oscar I, king of Sweden and Norway (1844–59), b.1799, d.1859.
Oscar II, king of Sweden (1872–1907) and Norway (1872–1905), b.1829, d.1907.
Oscillograph, first devised (ondograph) by Hospitalier in 1903.
Osiander, Andreas, German religious reformer, b.1498, d.1552.

Osler, Sir William, Canadian professor of medicine, b.1848, d.1919.
Oslo, Convention of, electing the Norwegian King Magnus king of Sweden, 1319.
Osman Pasha, Turkish field-marshal, b.1832, d.1900.
Osmium, metallic element, discovered 1803 by the English chemist Smithson Tennant, b.1761, d.1815.
'Ossian' (James Macpherson), Scottish poet, b.1736, d.1796.
Ossory, Cearbhall, Lord of, king of Dublin (875), d.888.
Ostend Manifesto, concerning the future of Cuba, drawn up 1854 (but was implemented).
Osteopathy, founded 1874 by the American surgeon Andrew Taylor Still, b.1828, d.1917.
Ostrog Bible, first Russian Bible (printed in Church Slavonic), published by order of Konstantin, Prince of Ostrog, 1580–81.
Ostwald Process, for the preparation of nitric acid, invented 1900 by the German scientist Wilhelm Ostwald, b.1853, d.1932.
Oswald, Lee Harvey, b.1939, presumed assassin of US president J. F. Kennedy 22 Nov. 1963, killed by Jack Ruby 24 Nov. while in police custody.
Oswald, St, king of the Northumbrians, b.c.605, killed in battle 642.
Oswald, St, archbishop of York (972–992), d.992.
Otago, New Zealand province, shore stations established 1832; first officially organized band of settlers landed 1848.
Otho, Roman emperor (69), b.32, committed suicide 69.
Otis, Elisha Graves, American inventor (particularly of lift machinery), b.1811, d.1861.
Ottawa, Canada, founded 1827 as Bytown by the English engineer John By, b.1781, d.1836.
Ottawa Conference, Imperial Economic Conference held 21 July–20 Aug. 1932.
Otto I, the Great, Holy Roman emperor (962–973), b.912, d.973.
Otto II, Holy Roman emperor (973–983), b.955, d.983.
Otto III, Holy Roman emperor (996–1002), b.980, d.1002.
Otto IV, Holy Roman emperor (1209–18), b.c.1182, d.1218.
Otto I, king of Greece (1832–62), b.1815, d.1867.
Ottocar I, king of Bohemia (1198–1230), d.1230.
Ottocar II, king of Bohemia (1253–78), b.c.1230, killed in battle 1278.
Ottoman Empire, began 1288; ended 1923 when Turkey became a republic.

Otway, Thomas, English playwright (*Venice Preserved*, 1682), b.1652, d.1685.
Ouchy, Treaty of, by which Turkey recognized Italian sovereignty in Tripoli, signed 19 Oct. 1912.
Oudenarde, Battle of, between British and French, 11 July 1708.
'Ouida' (Marie Louise de la Ramée), English novelist (*Under Two Flags*, 1867), b.1839, d.1908.
Outlawry, abolished in Britain 1879.
Outram, Benjamin, English civil engineer, b.1764, d.1805.
Outward Bound Mountain School, Eskdale, opened 1950.
Outward Bound Sea School, Aberdovey, opened autumn 1941.
Ovaries, human, nature discovered 1672 by the Dutch naturalist Jan Swammerdam, b.1637, d.1680.
Overbeck, Johann Friedrich, German painter (*Pietà*, 1846), b.1789, d.1869.
Overbury, Sir Thomas, English courtier and writer (*Characters*), b.1581, poisoned 1613.
Overland mail, USA, from the Mississippi River to California, authorized by Act of Congress 1857; inaugurated 15 Sept. 1858.
Overland telegraph line, completed from Darwin to Adelaide, 1872.
Ovid (Publius Ovidius Naso), Latin poet (*Metamorphoses*), b.43 BC, d. AD 17.
Owen, Sir Richard, English naturalist, b.1804, d.1892.
Owen, Robert, English social reformer, b.1771, d.1858.
Owen, Wilfred, British poet and war hero ('Anthem for Doomed Youth'), b.1893, d.1918.
Owen Falls Dam, Jinja, Uganda, opened 1954.
Owen Glendower (Owain Glyndwr), Welsh rebel leader, b.*c.*1350, d.*c.*1416.
Owens College, now Manchester University, founded 1846 (opened 1851) by the bequest of the English merchant John Owens, b.1790, d.1846.
Oxenstierna, Count Axel Gustafsson, chancellor of Sweden, b.1583, d.1654.
OXFAM (Oxford Committee for Famine Relief), charitable Thirld World relief agency founded 1942.
Oxford, Edward de Vere, Earl of, English poet (to whom Shakespeare's works have been attributed), b.1550, d.1604.
Oxford, Robert de Vere, Earl of, court favourite, b.1362, d.1392.

Oxford and Cambridge Boat Race, first held 10 June 1829. First broadcast 2 April 1927.

Oxford English Dictionary (New English Dictionary), published 1884–1928; updated at regular intervals ever since.

Oxford Group, religious movement founded 1921 by the American evangelist Frank Buchman, b.1878, d.1961; first so named 1929.

Oxford India paper, first made at the OUP's Wolvercote Mill 1875; copied from an Indian paper brought to Oxford 1841.

Oxford Movement, launched by the English divine John Keble, b.1792, d.1866, on 14 July 1833.

Oxford tracts (*Tracts for the Times*), issued in defence of the Church of England as a Divine institution 1833 onwards.

Oxford Union Society, founded 1625.

Oxford University, in existence before 1200; granted charter by King Henry III, 1248; incorporated by Queen Elizabeth I, 1570; religious tests abolished 1871; Rhodes Scholarships founded 1902; women admitted to degrees 1920.

Oxford University Observatory, founded 1873.

Oxford University Press, founded 1585.

Oxygen, isolated 1773 by the Swedish scientist Karl Scheele, b.1742, d.1786; 1774 by the English scientist Joseph Priestley, b.1733, d.1804.

Oxyhydrogen blowpipe, invented 1801 by the American chemist Robert Hare, b.1781, d.1858.

Ozone, discovered 1840 by the German scientist Christian Friedrich Schönbein, b.1799, d.1868.

P

Pablos, Juan, Italian-born first printer in the western hemisphere, d.*c.*1561.
Pachmann, Vladimir de, Russian pianist, b.1848, d.1953.
Pachomius, St, pioneer of coenobitic monasticism, b.*c.*292, d.*c.*346.
Pacific, War of the, between Chile and Peru and Bolivia, 1879 to 1884.
Pacific Cable, completed at Suva 31 Oct. 1902.
Pacific Ocean, first sighted Sept. 1513 by the Spanish navigator Basco Nuñez de Balboa, b.*c.*1475, d.*c.*1517.
Packard, Alpheus Spring, American scientist, b.1839, d.1905.
Paderewski, Ignace Jan, president of Poland (1940–41), and pianist and composer, b.1860, d.1941.
Padua, University of, founded 1222.
Paganini, Nicolò, Italian violinist, b.1782, d.1840.
Paget, Sir James, English surgeon, b.1814, d.1899.
Paget, William, Baron Paget, statesman and diplomat, b.1505, d.1563.
Pahang, Peninsular Malaysia state, entered into treaty relations with Britain 1874–95; agreed with three other states to form a federation 1895; federal council of these states constituted 1909.
Pahlavi, Mohammed Reza, shah of Persia (1941–79), b.1919, d.1980.
Pahlavi, Reza Shah, ruler of Persia from 1921 and shah (1925–41), b.1877, d.1944.
Paine, Thomas, English-born radical (*The Rights of Man,* 1791–92), b.1737, d.1809.
Painlevé, Paul, French statesman and pioneer in aviation, b.1863, d.1933.
Painter, William, English translator (*Palace of Pleasure,* 1566–67), b.*c.*1540, d.1594.
Pakistan, established as a dominion and separated from India 1947, as East Pakistan and West Pakistan; proclaimed an Islamic republic 1956; East Pakistan gained independence as Bangladesh 1971.
Palafox y Melzi, José de, duke of Saragossa, b.1780, d.1847.
Palaeocene Epoch, Earth history, 70 million years ago.
Palaeozoic Era, Earth history, between 200 and 520 million years ago.

Palestine, conquered from Turks by British 1917–18; British mandate proclaimed 1922, ended 1948; partitioned between Jordan and new state of Israel 14 May 1948.

Palestine Liberation Organization (PLO), formed 1964 to bring about an independent state of Palestine.

Palestrina, Giovanni Pierluigi da, Italian composer, b.1525, d.1594.

Paley, William, English philosopher and theologian, b.1743, d.1805.

Palgrave, Francis Turner, English compiler of *The Golden Treasury* (1861), b.1824, d.1897.

Palissy, Bernard, French potter (invented Palissy Ware c.1545), b.1509, d.1580.

Palladio, Andrea, Italian architect, b.1518, d.1580.

Palladium, metallic element, discovered 1803 by the English scientist William Hyde Wollaston, b.1766, d.1828.

Pallavicino, Pietro Sforza, Italian cardinal and writer, b.1607, d.1667.

Palma, Jacopo, Italian painter (*Epiphany*), b.c.1480, d.1528.

Palmer, Edward Henry, English expert in Middle East languages and politics, b.1840, murdered 1882.

Palmer, George, English biscuit manufacturer, b.1818, d.1897.

Palmer, Samuel, English painter, b.1805, d.1881.

Palmer, William, English murderer, b.1824, hanged 1856.

Palmerston, Henry John Temple, Viscount, British statesman (prime minister 1855–58, 1859–65), b.1784, d.1865.

Palmgren, Selim, Finnish composer (*Peter Schlemihl*), b.1878, d.1951.

Palm Sunday, Sun. before Easter.

Palomar, Mt, California, site of observatory selected 1934; observatory opened 1949.

Panama, proclaimed an independent republic 1903; new constitution adopted 1946.

Panama Canal, preliminary work 1881–89; construction began again 1904; opened 15 Aug. 1914.

Panama Canal Zone, treaty defining government and use signed by USA and Panama 18 Nov. 1903; zone disestablished October 1979.

Pan-American Union, Washington, DC, founded 1890.

Panchatantra, Sanskrit collection of fables, assembled c.5th century.

Panchen Lama, deputy temporal and spiritual leader of Tibet, office dating from 1640.

Pancras, St, b.290, martyred 304.

Pandulf, Italian-born bishop of Norwich and Papal legate, d.1226.

Paneth, Professor Friedrich Adolf, Austrian scientist, b.1887, d.1958.

Pan-German League (*Alldeutschen Verband*), German nationalist organization, founded 1891, superseded by nationalist parties after 1918.

Panizzi, Sir Anthony, Italian-born librarian of the British Museum (1856–66), b.1797, d.1879.

Pankhurst, Mrs Emmeline, English suffragette leader, b.1858, d.1928.

Pankhurst, Dame Christabel, English suffragette leader, b.1880, d.1958.

Pantheon, Rome, built by Agrippa *c.*25 BC; rebuilt *c.*120 by Hadrian; transformed into a Christian church 609.

Panthéon, Paris, designed by the French architect Jacques Germain Soufflot, b.1709, d.1780; built 1754–80 as a church; secularized 1789.

Pantomimes, introduced into England by the English dancing-master John Weaver, b.1673, d.1760.

Paoli, Pascal, Corsican patriot, b.1725, d.1807.

Papadopoulos, George, military ruler of Greece (1967–73), b.1919.

Papagos, Alexander, Greek soldier, b.1883, d.1955.

Papal States, finally incorporated with the Italian kingdom 1859–60 and 1870.

Papandreou, Andreas, Greek politician (premier 1981–89), b.1919.

Papandreou, George, Greek politician (premier 1944–45, 1964–65), b.1888, d.1968.

Papen, Franz von, German statesman (chancellor, 1932, vice chancellor 1933–34), b.1879, d.1969.

Paper, traditionally invented by the Chinese Tsai-Lun 105.

Papini, Giovanni, Italian writer (*Storia di Cristo*, 1921), b.1881, d.1956.

Papinian, Roman jurist, killed 212.

Papua New Guinea, New Guinea first sighted by Spanish and Portuguse navigators in the 16th century; 1884 British protectorate established over southern area (Papua) and Germany took possession of the northern area (New Guinea); German areas came under Australian control 1914, and remained under Australian supervision 1921–70; self-government established over the whole territory Dec. 1973; complete independence Sept. 1975.

Paracelsus (Theophrastus Bombastus von Hohenheim), Swiss physician, b.1493, d.1541.

Parachutes, believed to have been invented 1785 by the French balloonist Jean Pierre Blanchard, b.1753, d.1809; first used 1802 by the Frenchman André Garnevin, b.1769, d.1823.

Paraffin, discovered 1830 by the German inventor Baron von Reichenbach, b.1788, d.1869.

Paraffin industry, originated in England 1856 by the Scottish chemist James Young, b.1811, d.1883.

Paraguay, declared independent of Spanish rule 1811.

Paratroops, first developed by the Russians *c.*1925; first used in war by the Germans in 1940.

Parcel post, inland, began in Britain 1883.

Parchment, traditionally invented by Eumenes II of Pergamon in the 2nd century BC.

Paré, Ambroise, French surgeon, b.1510, d.1590.

Pareto, Vilfredo, Italian economist and sociologist, b.1848, d.1923.

Paris, Matthew, English historian (*Chronica Majora*), d.1259.

Paris, Treaty of, adjusting the claims of King Henry III of England, ratified Dec. 1259; ending the Seven Years' War 1763; ending War of American Independence 1783; ending the Napoleonic Wars 1814 and 1815; ending Crimean War 1856.

Paris, University of, founded 1120.

Paris Observatory, founded 1667–1771.

Paris Peace Accords, ceasefire agreement intended to end the Vietnam War, signed by N. Vietnam, S. Vietnam and USA, 27 Jan. 1973.

Park, Mungo, Scottish explorer (explored Niger 1796), b.1771, d.*c.*1805.

Parker, Charlie 'Bird', jazz alto saxophonist, b.1920, d.1955.

Parker, Matthew, archbishop of Canterbury (1559–75), d. 1575.

Parker, Richard, leader of the mutineers (1797) at the Nore, b.*c.*1767, hanged 1797.

Parkes, Alexander, English scientist and inventor (1855) of celluloid, b.1813, d.1890.

Parkhurst, John, bishop of Norwich (1560–75), b.*c.*1512, d.1575.

Parking meters, first introduced in Britain in Westminster 1958.

Parkman, Francis, American historian, b.1823, d.1893.
'Parley, Peter', pseudonym adopted by both the English writers William Martin, b.1801, d.1867, and George Mogridge, b.1787, d.1854.
Parliament, first called as advisory body by King John in 1213.
Parliament, Addled, held 1614.
Parliament, Cavalier, held 1660 to 1678.
Parliament, Long, held 1640 to 1653, 1659 to 1660.
Parliament, Mad, held in Oxford 1256.
Parliament, Merciless, which condemned friends of Richard II to death, 1388.
Parliament, Rump, held 1648 to 1653, and 1659.
Parliament, Short, held 1640.
Parliament of Dunces, reign of King Henry IV, met at Coventry 1404.
Parmenides, Greek philosopher, lived in the 6th and 5th centuries BC.
Parmigianino, Francesco, Italian painter (*St Jerome*), b.1503, d.1540.
Parnell, Charles Stewart, Irish nationalist leader, b.1846, divorce case 1889, d.1891.
Parr, Catherine, queen of Henry VIII, b.1512, d.1548.
Parr, Thomas ('Old Parr'), probably the longest-lived Englishman, b.*c.*1483, d.1635.
Parry, Sir Charles Hubert Hastings, English composer (*De Profundis,* 1891), b.1848, d.1918.
Parsees, Indian followers of Zoroaster, b.*c.*659, d.*c.*582 BC.
Parsons, Elizabeth, the 'Cock Lane ghost', b.1749, d.1807.
Parsons, Robert, Jesuit missionary in England, b.1546, d.1610.
Parthenogenesis, first recognized by the Greek philosopher Aristotle, b.384, d.322 BC.
Parthenon, Athens, rebuilt by Pericles *c.*447–436 BC; wrecked by an explosion 1687.
Parthian Empire, in existence 227 BC to AD 224.
Parton, James, English-born writer (*Aaron Burr*, 1857), b.1822, d.1891.
Partridge, John, English astrologer, b.1644, d.1715.
Pascal, Blaise, French philosopher, scientist and theologian (*Lettres Provinciales*, 1656–57), b.1623, d.1662.
Paschal I, St, pope 817–824, d.824.
Paschal II (Ronieri), pope 1099–1118, d.1118.
Paschal III (Guido), anti-pope 1164–68.

Pasquier, Etienne, French writer (*Recherches de la France*, 1560–1615), b.1529, d.1615.

Passchendaele, Battle of, Belgium, World War I, 28 Sept. 1918.

Passion Play, Oberammergau, Germany, acted every 10 years since 1634.

Passover (*Peisach*), Jewish feast, begins on evening of the 14th day of Nisan.

Passy, Frédéric, French economist, b.1822, d.1912.

Pasternak, Boris, Russian poet and novelist (*Dr Zhivago*, 1957), b.1890, d.1960.

Pasteur, Louis, French scientist, b.1822, d.1895.

Paston, John, English country gentleman, b.1421, d.1466.

Pastor, Ludwig, Freiherr von, German historian of the popes, b.1854, d.1928.

Patent, world's first, granted in Venice to the German printer John of Speyer 1469.

Pater, Walter Horatio, English writer and critic (*Marius the Epicurean*, 1885), b.1839, d.1894.

Paterson, Mrs Emma Anne, first woman admitted (1875) to the Trade Union Congress, b.1848, d.1886.

Pathé, Charles, French pioneer film producer (*The Dancing Years*), b.1873, d.1957.

Pathé News Reel, founded by the French photographer Charles Pathé 1911.

Pathology, modern practice founded by Rudolf Virchow, b.1821, d.1902.

Patmore, Coventry, English writer (*The Angel in the House*, 1854–62), b.1823, d.1896.

Patrick, St, b.c.372, d.c.463; **Order of,** founded by George III in 1783.

Patti, Adelina, operatic singer, b.1843, d.1919.

Pattinson, Hugh Lee, English metallurgical chemist and inventor, b.1796, d.1858.

Patton, George Smith, American World War II general, b.1885, d.1945.

Paul, St, the Apostle, beheaded c.67.

'Paul, Jean' (Johann Paul Friedrich Richter), German humorous writer (*Hesperus*, 1795), b.1763, d.1825.

Paul I, tsar of Russia (1799–1801), b.1754, murdered 1801.

Paul I, St, pope 757–767, d.767.

Paul II (Pietro Barbo), pope 1464–71, b.1417, d.1471.

Paul III (Alessandro Farnese), pope 1534–49, b.1468, d.1549.

Paul IV (Giovanni Pietro Caraffa), pope 1555–59, b.1476, d.1559.
Paul V (Camillo Borghese), pope 1605–21, b.1552, d.1621.
Paul of the Cross, St, Italian founder (1720–25) of the Passionists, b.1694, d.1775.
Paul the Deacon, Italian historian, lived in the 8th century.
Pauli, Professor Wolfgang, Austrian physicist, b.1900, d.1958.
Paulinus, Roman bishop of York, d.644.
Paulus Lucius Aemilius, Roman general, b.*c.*229, d.160 BC.
Pausanias, Spartan military commander, d.*c.*470 BC.
Pausanias, Greek traveller and writer (*Description of Greece*), lived in the 2nd century.
Pavarotti, Luciano, Italian tenor, b.1935.
Pavlov, Ivan Petrovich, Russian scientist, b.1849, d.1936.
Pavlova, Anna, Russian dancer, b.1885, d.1931.
Paxton, Sir Joseph, English designer (1850) of the Crystal Palace, b.1801, d.1865.
PAYE (Pay As You Earn), British income-tax system, introduced 1944.
Payne, John Howard, American writer (*Home, Sweet Home*, 1823), b.1791, d.1852.
Pazzi Assassination, of Giuliano de' Medici 26 April 1478.
Peabody, Elizabeth Palmer, American pioneer in kindergarten provision, b.1804, d.1894.
Peabody, George, American merchant and philanthropist, b.1795, d.1869.
Peace, Charles, English murderer, b.*c.*1832, hanged 1879.
Peace Congress, First International, held in London 1843.
Peace Corps, US agency established by President J. F. Kennedy 1961 to provide volunteers to work in Third World countries.
Peace Pledge, initiated 1934 by the Rev. Dick Sheppard, d.1937.
Peacock, Thomas Love, English writer (*Headlong Hall*, 1816), b.1785, d.1866.
Peake, Mervyn Laurence, British writer and artist (*Gormenghast Trilogy,* 1946–59), b.1911, d.1968.
Peale, Charles Willson, American painter (*George Washington*, 1772), b.1741, d.1826.
Pearl Harbour attack, World War II, made by the Japanese on the Honolulu naval base 7 Dec. 1941.
Pearse, Pádraic, Irish nationalist leader, b.1879, shot 1916.
Pearson, Sir Arthur, English newspaper owner and philanthropist (founded *Pearson's Weekly*, 1890), b.1866, d.1921.

Pearson, John, English theologian (*Exposition of the Creed*, 1659), b.1613, d.1686.

Pearson, Lester Bowles, Canadian statesman (prime minister 1963–68), b.1897, d.1972.

Pearson, William, English astronomer, b.1767, d.1847.

Peary, Robert, American explorer in the Arctic, b.1856, d.1920.

Peasants' Revolt, led by the English rebel Wat Tyler 1381.

Peasants' War, South Germany, 1525.

Peck, Francis, English antiquary (*Desiderata Curiosa*, 1732–35), b.1692, d.1743.

Peckham, John, archbishop of Canterbury (1279–92), d.1292.

Pecock, Reginald, Welsh theologian (*Book of Faith*, 1466), b.*c.*1395, d.*c.*1460.

Peculiar People, religious movement, founded in London 1838 by John Banyard.

Pedal bicycle, first, built 1838 by Kirkpatrick Macmillan.

Pedro the Cruel, king of Castile and Leon (1350–69), b.1334, killed in combat 1369.

Pedro I, emperor of Brazil (1822–31), b.1798, d.1834.

Pedro II, emperor of Brazil (1831–89), b.1825, d.1891.

Peel, Sir Robert, British statesman (prime minister 1834, 1841–45) and reorganizer (1829) of London's police force, b.1788, d.1850.

Peele, George, English writer (*David and Bethsabe*, 1599), b.*c.*1558, d.*c.*1597.

Peep-of-Day Boys, Irish Protestant secret society, flourishing at the end of the 18th century.

Péguy, Charles, French writer (*Jeanne d'Arc*, 1897), b.1873, d.1914.

Peine Forte et Dure, used in England as late as 1741.

Peirce, Benjamin, American scientist, b.1809, d.1880.

Peisistratus, Greek statesman, b.*c.*605, d.527 BC.

Peking Man, early Pleistocene period remains discovered near Peking 1927.

Pelagius I, pope 555–561, d.561.

Pelagius II, pope 579–590, d.590.

Pelagius, British theologian, b.*c.*360, d.*c.*420.

Pelé (Edson Arantes do Nascimento), Brazilian football player, b.1940.

Pellegrini, Carlo, Italian-born caricaturist ('Ape' in *Vanity Fair*), b.1839, d.1889.

Pelletier, Pierre Joseph, French chemist, b.1788, d.1842.

Pelopidas, Greek statesman and general, killed in battle 364 BC.
Peloponnesian League, organized by Sparta *c.*550 BC; ended in the 4th century BC.
Peloponnesian War, between Sparta and Athens, 431 to 404 BC.
Peltier effect, heat properties of electric currents, discovered 1834 by the French scientist Jean Charles Athanase Peltier, b.1785, d.1845.
Pembroke, Mary Herbert, Countess of, patroness of poets, b.1561, d.1621.
Pembroke, William Herbert, Earl of, governor of Calais, b.*c.*1501, d.1570.
Pembroke College, Cambridge University, founded as the Hall or House of Valence-Mary by Mary de St Paul, widow of the Earl of Pembroke, 1347.
Pembroke College, Oxford University, founded 1624; previously known as Broadgates Hall.
PEN, International, London, world association of writers, founded 1921.
Penang, state of Peninsula Malaysia consisting of the island of Penang (formerly Prince of Wales' Island) and the province of Wellesley; first British settlement in the Malay Peninsula, ceded by the Sultan of Kedah to the East India Company 1786, Province Wellesley being added 1800; incorporated with Malacca and Singapore 1826 under a single government; known as the Straits Settlements 1867–1946.
Pencils, possibly invented much earlier, but certainly in use by the mid-16th century.
Pendleton, Edmund, Federalist Party leader in Virginia, b.1721, d.1803.
Pendulum, isochronism observed 1582 and time-keeping mechanism devised 1641 by Galileo Galilei; pendulum clocks constructed 1649 by Vincenzio Galilei, and 1658 by the Dutch scientist Christiaan Huygens (who described the principles in his *Horologium Oscillatorium*, 1673), b.1629, d.1695; compensated pendulum constructed 1722 by the English mechanician George Graham, b.1675, d.1751.
Penicillin, discovered 1928 by Sir Alexander Fleming, b.1881, d.1955.
Peninsular War, between the Allies and Napoleon, 1808 to 1814.
Penn, William, English Quaker, founder (1682) of Pennsylvania, b.1644, d.1718.
Pennell, Joseph, American artist, b.1860, d.1926.

Penney, William George, British physicist, creator of the British atomic bomb (1952), b.1909, d.1991.

Pen nibs, steel, manufacture perfected 1829 by the English industrialists Sir Josiah Mason, b.1795, d.1881, and Joseph Gillott, b.1797, d.1873.

Pennsylvania, USA, first settled 1682; ratified US Constitution 1787.

Pennsylvania University, Philadelphia, founded 1740.

Penny postage, invented 1837 and put into effect 1840 by Sir Rowland Hill, b.1795, d.1879.

Penrose, Francis Cranmer, English archaeologist and astronomer, b.1817, d.1903.

Pentecost, Christian feast of the Holy Spirit, celebrated on Whit-Sunday.

Pepin I, Frankish ruler, d.640.

Pepin II, Frankish ruler, d.714.

Pepin III, king of the Franks (751–768), d.768.

Pepper, John Henry, English illusionist ('Pepper's Ghost'), b.1821, d.1900.

Pepsin, first described 1836 by the German physiologist Theodor Schwann, b.1810, d.1882.

Pepusch, Dr John Christopher, German-born composer (*The Beggar's Opera*, 1728), b.1667, d.1752.

Pepys, Samuel, English statesman and diarist (1660–69), b.1633, d.1703.

Perak, state of peninsula Malaysia; entered into treaty relations 1874–95 with Britain; agreed 1895 with three other Malay states to form a federation; federal council of these states formed 1909.

Perceval, Spencer, prime minister of Great Britain (1809–12), b.1762, assassinated 1812.

Percier, Charles, French architect, b.1764, d.1838.

Percussion cap, gunmaking, introduced into the British Army 1842.

Percussion lock, gunmaking, invented 1805 by the Scottish minister the Rev. Alexander John Forsyth, b.1768, d.1843.

Percy, Sir Henry ('Hotspur'), b.1364, killed in battle 1403.

Percy, John, English physician and metallurgist, b.1817, d.1889.

Percy, Lord, of Newcastle, pioneer in English education, b.1887, d.1958.

Perdiccas, regent of the Macedonian Empire (323–321 BC), assassinated 321 BC.

Perdita (Mary Robinson), English actress and mistress of Prince of Wales, b.1758, d.1800.

Peres, Shimon, Israeli politician (prime minister 1984–86), b.1923.

Peretz, Isaac, Yiddish writer, b.1852, d.1915.

Pérez de Ayala, Ramón, Spanish writer (*Belarmino y Apolonio* 1921), b.1881, d.1962.

Pérez de Cuellar, Javier, Peruvian diplomat and UN secretary general (1982–92), b.1920.

Pérez Galdos, Benito, Spanish (*Gloria*, 1877), b.1843, d.1920.

Pergolesi, Giovanni Battista, Italian composer (*La Serva Padrona*, 1733), b.1710, d.1736.

Pericles, Greek statesman, b.*c.*492 BC.

Perim, island off Aden, permanently occupied by the British 1857.

Periodic law, relating to chemical elements, developed 1869 from a paper published 1864 of the English chemist John Newlands, b.1837, d.1898, by the Russian chemist Dmitri Ivanovich Mendeleieff, b.1834, d.1907.

Periwig, use general in W. Europe approximately 1660–1800.

Perkin, Sir William Henry, English chemist and discoverer (1856) of mauveine, b.1838, d.1907.

Perkins, Loftus, English engineer and pioneer in refrigeration, b.1834, d.1891.

Perkins, William, English theologian (*Armilla Aurea*, 1590), b.1558, d.1602.

Perlman, Itzhak, Israeli-born concert violinist, b.1945.

Permanent Court of Arbitration, The Hague, established 1899.

Permanganate acid, first obtained 1830 by the German chemist Eilhard Mitscherlich, b.1794, d.1863.

Permian Period, Earth history, 220 million years ago.

Péron, Eva Duarte de ('Evita'), Argentinian political figure, first wife of Juan Péron, b.1919, d.1952.

Perón, Juan Domingo, ruler of Argentina (1946–55), b.1895, d.1974.

Perrault, Charles, French collector of fairy tales (*Contes de ma Mère l'Oie*, 1697), b.1628, d.1703.

Perrers, Alice, royal mistress, d.1400.

Perret, Auguste, French architect and pioneer in the use of modern concrete construction, b.1874, d.1954.

Perronet, Edward, English hymn-writer (*All Hail the Power of Jesu's Name*, 1780), b.1721, d.1792.

Perronneau, Jean Baptiste, French painter, b.1715, d.1783.
Perrot, Sir John, Lord Deputy of Ireland (1584–88), b.*c.*1527, d.1592.
Perry, John, English traveller and canal builder, b.1670, d.1732.
Perry, Stephen Joseph, English astronomer, b.1833, d.1889.
Pershing, John Joseph, American general, b.1860, d.1948.
Persia, *see* **Iran.**
Persian Gulf States, *see* **Bahrain, Kuwait, Qatar.**
Persian Gulf War, between Iraq and allied coalition sponsored by the UN, Jan.–March 1991; triggered by the Iraqi invasion of Kuwait 2 Aug. 1990.
Persian Wars, with the Greek city-states, 500–449 BC.
Persigny, Jean Gilbert Victor Fialin, Duc de, French diplomat and statesman, b.1808, d.1872.
Persius, Latin writer (*Satires*) b.34, d.62.
Perthes, Justus, German publisher, b.1749, d.1816.
Pertinax, Roman emperor (193), b.126, assassinated 193.
Peru, declared an independent republic 1821.
Perugino (Pietro Vannucci), Italian painter (*The Assumption*), b.1446, d.1524.
Peruzzi, Baldassare, Italian architect, b.1481, d.1536.
Pervigilium Veneris, anonymous Latin poem written probably in the 2nd century.
Pestalozzi, Johann Heinrich, Swiss educationalist (opened his first orphan school 1798), b.1746, d.1827.
Pétain, Marshal Henri Philippe, French soldier and statesman (prime minister 1940–44), b.1856, d.1951.
Peter, St, the Apostle, crucified *c.*67
Peter I, the Great, tsar of Russia (1689–1725), b.1672, d.1725.
Peter I Land, Antarctic island, discovered 1821 by the Russian Admiral von Bellingshausen; annexed by Norway 1929–31.
Peter II, tsar of Russia (1728–30), b.1715, d.1730.
Peter III, tsar of Russia (1762), b.1728, murdered 1762.
Peterborough, Charles Mordaunt, Earl of, admiral and diplomat, b.1658, d.1735.
Peterborough Cathedral, England, present building begun 1117; consecrated 1238.
Peterhouse, Cambridge, founded by Hugh de Balsham, bishop of Ely, 1284.
Peter Lombard, Italian theologian (*Sententiae*, 1145–50), b.*c.*1100, d.*c.*1160.

Peterloo, massacre at reform meeting at St Peter's Field, Manchester 16 Aug. 1819.

Petermann, August Heinrich, German cartographer, b.1822, committed suicide 1878.

Peter Martyr, St, Italian inquisitor, killed 1252.

Peter Martyr, Italian Protestant leader, b.1500, d.1555.

Peters, Carl Friedrich, German music publisher, b.1779, d.1827.

Peter's Pence, annual English offering to the pope, first sent 787; abolished 1534.

Petersen, Wilhelm, Greek-born composer (*Grosse Messe*, 1930), b.1890, d.1957.

Peter the Hermit, French Crusader, d.*c.* 1115.

Peter the Wild Boy, b.*c.* 1712, d.1785.

Petipa, Marius, French dancer and choreographer, b.1822, d.1910.

Petition of Right, submitted by the House of Commons to King Charles I and accepted by him 1628.

Petitioners, political group (connected with Whigs), became prominent 1680.

Petit Trianon, Versailles, constructed 1762–68 by the French architect Jacques Ange Gabriel, b.*c.* 1698, d.1782.

Petöfi, Sandor, Hungarian national poet, b.1823, killed in battle 1849.

Petra, ruins of Nabataean and Graeco-Roman settlements in the present territory of Jordan, built mainly 6th century BC to 3rd century AD.

Petrarch (Francesco Petrarca), Italian poet (*Rime in Vita e Morte*), b.1304, d.1374.

Petre, Edward, English Jesuit missionary to England, b.1631, d.1699.

Petrie, Sir William Flinders, English archaeologist, b.1853, d.1942.

Petrified Forest, Arizona, established as a national monument 1906.

Petrol engine, first constructed 1883 by the German engineer Gottlieb Daimler, b.1834, d.1900.

Petroleum, first transported in the brig *Elizabeth Watts* from the USA to Europe, arriving at the Port of London 1861.

Petroleum flashpoint, apparatus for its determination (the Abel close-test instrument) invented *c.* 1879 by the English chemist Sir Frederick Augustus Abel, b.1827, d.1902.

Petronius 'Arbiter', Roman writer (*The Satyricon*), committed suicide *c.*66.

Petrucci, Ottaviano dei, Italian pioneer music printer, b.1466, d.1539.

Petty, Sir William, English economist, b.1623, d.1687.

Petunia, double, first grown (in France) *c.*1855.

Pfister, Albrecht, German pioneer printer, b.*c.*1420, d.*c.*1470.

Phalaris, tyrant of Acragas, b.*c.*570, killed *c.*554 BC.

Pharmaceutical Society of Great Britain, founded 1841, incorporated by Royal Charter 1843.

Pharnaces I, first king of Pontus 190–156 BC.

Pharnaces II, king of Pontus, killed 47 BC.

Pharos, near Alexandria, site of the world-famous lighthouse built *c.*280 BC, and demolished in the 14th century.

Phelps, Samuel, English actor-manager, b.1804, d.1878.

Phelps, Thomas, English astronomer, b.1694, d. after 1776.

Phidias, Greek sculptor, b.*c.*490, d.*c.*432 BC.

Philadelphia, Pennsylvania, founded under a patent from King Charles II, 1681.

Philby, 'Kim' (Harold Adrian Russell), British spy, defected to the Soviet Union 1963, b.1911, d.1988.

Philemon, Greek playwright (*The Treasure*), b.*c.*360, d.263 BC.

Philidor, François André Danican, French chess champion, b.1726, d.1795.

Philip, anti-pope 768.

Philip I, possibly mythical early king of Macedonia.

Philip II, king of Macedonia, father of Alexander the Great, b.*c.*382, assassinated 336 BC.

Philip III, king of Macedonia (323–317 BC), assassinated 317 BC.

Philip IV, king of Macedonia (297–296 BC).

Philip V, king of Macedonia (220–179 BC), d.179 BC.

Philip I, king of France (1059–1108), b.1052, d.1108.

Philip II, king of France (1180–1223), b.1165, d.1223.

Philip III, the Bold, king of France (1270–85), b.1245, d.1285.

Philip IV, the Fair, king of France (1285–1314), b.1268, d.1314.

Philip V, the Tall, king of France (1317–22), b.*c.*1294, d.1322.

Philip VI, king of France (1328–50), b.1293, d.1350.

Philip I, the Handsome, king of Spain (1506), b.1478, d.1506.

Philip II, king of Spain (1556–98), b.1527, d.1598.

Philip III, king of Spain (1598–1621), b.1578, d.1621.

Philip IV, king of Spain (1621–65), b.1605, d.1665.

Philip V, king of Spain (1700–46), b.1683, d.1746.

Philip Neri, St, b.1515, d.1595.

'Philippe Egalité' (Louis-Philippe, Duc d'Orléans), b.1747, guillotined 1793.

Philippi, Battle of, between Octavius and Antony and the Senate party, 42 BC.

Philippines, discovered by the Portuguese navigator Ferdinand Magellan 1521; ceded by Spain to the USA. 1898; became an independent republic 1946.

Philippines, Naval Battle of the, World War II, 23–25 Oct. 1944.

Philips, John, English poet (*Cyder*, 1708), b.1676, d.1709.

Philips, Richard, governor of Nova Scotia (1720–49), b.1661, d.1751.

Phillipps, Sir Thomas, English book and MSS. collector, b.1792, d.1872.

Phillpotts, Eden, Indian-born writer (*The Girl and the Faun*, 1916), b.1862, d.1960.

Philo Judaeus, Jewish philosopher of Alexandria, b.*c.*15 BC, d.*c.*AD 50.

Philopoemen, Greek general, b.*c.*253, executed 184 BC.

Phipps, Charles John, English theatre architect, b.1835, d.1897.

'Phiz' (Hablot Knight Browne), English artist and illustrator, b.1815, d.1882.

Phlogiston theory, propounded 1731 by the German scientist Georg Ernst Stahl, b.1660, d.1734.

Phocion, Greek statesman and general, b.*c.*402, d.317 BC.

Phoenix Park Murders, Dublin, the murder of Lord Frederick Cavendish and Thomas Henry Burke by Irish patriots 6 May 1882.

'Phoney War', at beginning of World War II, Oct. 1939–March 1940.

Phonograph, first sound recording machine, invented 1876 by the American inventor Thomas Alva Edison, b.1847, d.1931.

Phosphorus, discovered 1669 by the German alchemist Henning Brandt.

Photius, patriarch of Constantinople, b.*c.*820, d.891.

Photochromolithography, process invented 1868 by the British photolithographer William Griggs, b.1832, d.1911.

Photoelectric property of selenium, first observed 1875 by the English scientist Willoughby Smith, b.1828, d.1891.

Photoengraving, invented in France 1827.

Photograph, earliest surviving, taken 1835 by William Fox Talbot, b.1800, d.1877.

Photographer, the first, the English inventor Thomas Wedgwood, b.1771, d.1805.

Photographic roll film, invented 1884 by the American inventor George Eastman, b.1854, d.1932.

Photography, principle discovered 1823 by the French physician Joseph Nicéphore Niepce, b.1765, d.1833.

Photography, colour, invented 1907 by the French inventor Auguste Lumière, b.1862, d.1954.

Photogravure, invented 1895 by the Czech-born manufacturer Karl Klietsch (Karel Klic), b.1841, d.1926.

Phraates I, king of Parthia 175–170 BC.

Phraates II, king of Parthia (138–127 BC), killed 127 BC.

Phraates III, king of Parthia (70–57 BC), murdered 57 BC.

Phraates IV, king of Parthia (37 BC-AD 2), murdered AD 2.

Phraates V, king of Parthia (2–5), killed 5.

Phrenology, study founded by the German physician Franz Joseph Gall, b.1758, d.1828.

Phthisis, bacillus discovered 1890 by the German bacteriologist Robert Koch, b.1843, d.1910.

Physick, Philip Synge, American pioneer surgeon, b.1768, d.1837.

Piaf, Edith (Giovanna Gassion), French singer, nicknamed 'Little Sparrow', b.1915, d.1963.

Piaget, Jean, Swiss child psychologist, b.1896, d.1980.

Pianoforte, first practical model invented c.1710 by the Italian harpsichord-maker Bartolommeo Cristofori, b.1655, d.1731.

Piatigorsky, Gregor, Russian-born cellist, b.1903, d.1976.

Piazzi, Giuseppe, Italian astronomer, b.1746, d.1826.

Picard, Jean, French astronomer, b.1620, d.1682.

Picasso, Pablo, Catalan artist (*Guernica*, 1937), b.1881, d.1973.

Piccadilly Circus, London, new underground station opened 1928; first lit by electricity 1932.

Piccard, Auguste, Belgian physicist and explorer of the stratosphere and the bathysphere, b.1884, d.1962.

Piccolomini, Prince Octavio, military commander who brought to an end the Thirty Years' War, b.1599, d.1656.

Pickens, Andrew, American soldier and politician, b.1739, d.1817.

Pickering, John, leader in the Pilgrimage of Grace (1536), executed 1537.

Pickering, Timothy, American statesman, b.1745, d.1829.
Pickering, William, British publisher who introduced cloth bindings, b.1796, d.1854.
Pickford, Mary (Gladys Mary Smith), American film star, b.1893, d.1979.
'Pickle the Spy', *see* **Alastair Macdonell.**
Pico della Mirandola, Count Giovanni, Italian philosopher (*Heptaplus*, 1490), b.1463, d.1494.
Picric acid (trinitrophenol), known since 1771; effective use dates from 1885 when Turpin patented its use as a charge for shells.
Picture Post, British periodical, published 1938–58.
Pierce, Franklin, 14th US president (1853–57), b.1804, d.1869.
Pierné, Gabriel, French composer (*La Croisade des enfants*, 1902), b.1863, d.1937.
Piero della Francesca, Italian painter (*The Baptism of Christ*), b.c.1415, d.1492.
Piero di Cosimo, Italian painter (*Death of Procris*), b.1462, d.c.1521.
Pierrot, role created by the French actor Jean Gaspard Debureau, b.1796, d.1846.
Pietermaritzburg, capital of Natal province, South Africa, founded 1839.
Pig iron, process of production improved 1709 by the English ironmaster Abraham Darby, b.1677, d.1717.
Pigalle, Jean Baptiste, French sculptor (*Love and Friendship*), b.1714, d.1785.
Piggot, Lester, British champion jockey, b.1935.
Pike, Zebulon Montgomery, American soldier and explorer, b.1779, killed in battle 1813.
Pilate, Pontius, Roman procurator in Judea 26–36.
Pilgrim Fathers, set sail in the *Mayflower* from Plymouth 6 Sept. 1620; arrived Plymouth Rock, Massachusetts, 16 Dec. 1620 (OS).
Pilgrim Trust, established 1930 by the American philanthropist Edward Stephen Harkness, b.1874, d.1940.
Pilgrimage of Grace, 1536, Yorkshire insurrection led by the English attorney Robert Aske, executed 1537.
Pill, the, oral contraceptive, first became widely available 1961.
Pilsudski, Józef, Polish statesman (premier 1926–28, 1930–35), b.1867, d.1935.
Piltdown Skull, discovered 1912; exposed as a fraud 1955.
Pinchbeck, alloy of copper and zinc, invented 1732 by the English clockmaker Christopher Pinchbeck, b.1670, d.1732.

Pinckney, Charles Cotesworth, American statesman and diplomat, b.1746, d.1825.

Pindar, Greek poet (*Odes*), b.c.522, d.443 BC.

'Pindar, Peter' (John Wolcot), English writer (*The Lousiad*, 1785), b.1738, d.1819.

Pinero, Sir Arthur, English playwright (*The Second Mrs Tanqueray*, 1893), b.1855, d.1934.

Pinkerton Detective Agency, USA, founded *c.*1852 by the American detective Allan Pinkerton, b.1819, d.1884.

Pinkie, Battle of, between the English and the Scots, 10 Sept. 1547.

Pinochet, Augusto, Chilian military leader (1973–89), head of the junta that overthrew Allende in 1973, b.1915.

Pinter, Harold (Harold Da Pinta), British playwright and screenwriter (*Betrayal*, 1978, 1982), b.1930.

Pinturicchio, Bernardino, Italian painter (*Dispute of St Catherine*), b.1454, d.1513.

Pinza, Ezio, Italian opera singer, b.1892, d.1957.

Pinzon, Martin Alonso, Spanish navigator, b.c.1440, d.1493.

Pinzon, Vicente Yañez, Spanish navigator, b.c.1460, d.c.1524.

Piozzi, Mrs Hester Lynch (Mrs Thrale), friend of Dr Samuel Johnson, b.1741, d.1821.

Pipe Rolls, of English Exchequer, annual rolls introduced 1110 by Roger, bishop of Salisbury; discontinued 1834.

Piper, John, English painter and designer for opera and ballet, b.1903, d.1992.

Pirandello, Luigi, Italian playwright (*Six Characters in Search of an Author*, 1921), b.1867, d.1936.

Piranesi, Giambattista, Italian artist (*Carceri d' Invenzione*), b.1720, d.1778.

Pisa, Council of, assembled 25 March to unite Christendom under a new pope, dissolved 7 Aug. 1409.

Pisa, Leaning Tower of, *see* **Leaning Tower of Pisa.**

Pisa, University of, founded 1343 by the Florentine leader Lorenzo de' Medici, b.1449, d.1492.

Pisanello, Vittore, Italian artist (*The Miraculous Stag Appearing to St Eustace*), b.c.1380, d.1456.

Pisano, Andrea, Italian sculptor, b.c.1290, d.1348.

Pisistratus, Greek statesman, b.c.605, d.527 BC.

Piso Caesoninus, Lucius Calpurnius, Roman statesman, d.c.40 BC.

Pissarro, Camille, French painter (*Paysanne Assise*), b.1830, d.1903.
Pissarro, Lucien, French-born painter (*Chrysanthèmes*), b.1863, d.1944.
Pistols, first manufactured by Camillo Vetelli, *c.*1540.
Piston, Walter, American composer (*Violin concerto*, 1939), b.1894, d.1976.
Pistrucci, Benedetto, Italian-born gem engraver and medallist, b.1784, d.1855.
Pitcairn Island, Pacific Ocean, discovered 1767 by the English navigator Philip Carteret, d.1796; settled by mutineers from the *Bounty* 1790.
Pitman, Sir Isaac, English shorthand pioneer, b.1813, d.1897.
Pitt, William ('the Elder'), Earl of Chatham, British statesman (prime minister 1756–57, 1766–67), b.1708, d.1778.
Pitt, William ('The Younger'), British statesman (prime minister 1783–1801, 1804–05), b.1759, d.1806.
Pius I, St, pope 141–154.
Pius II (Aeneas Silvius), pope 1458–64, b.1405, d.1464.
Pius III (Francesco Nanni-Todeschini-Piccolomini), pope 1503, b.1439, d.1503.
Pius IV (Giovanni Angelo Medici), pope 1559–65, b.1499, d.1565.
Pius V, St (Michele Ghislieri), pope 1566–72, b.1504, d.1572.
Pius VI (Giovanni Angelo Braschi), pope 1775–99, b.1717, d.1799.
Pius VII (Luigi Barnaba Chiaramonti), pope 1800–23, b.1740, d.1823.
Pius VIII (Francesco Xaviero Castiglioni), pope 1829–30, b.1761, d.1830.
Pius IX (Giovanni Maria Mastai-Ferretti), pope 1846–78, b.1792, d.1878.
Pius X, St, (Giuseppe Sarto), pope 1903–14, b.1835, d.1914.
Pius XI (Achille Ratti), pope 1922–39, b.1857, d.1939.
Pius XII (Eugenio Pacelli), pope 1939–58, b.1876, d.1958.
Pizarro, Francisco, Spanish *conquistador* of Peru, b.*c.*1478, assassinated 1541.
Pizarro, Gonzalo, Spanish *conquistador*, executed 1548.
Place, Francis, English radical reformer, b.1771, d.1854.
Plague, bacillus discovered 1894 independently by the Swiss scientist, Alexander Emile John Yersin, b.1863, d.1943, and the Japanese doctor Shibasaburo Kitasato, b.1856, d.1931; last pandemic 1894–1901.
Plague of London (The Great Plague), 1664–65.

Planck, Max, German physicist (formulated quantum theory 1900), b.1858, d.1947.

Planetary motion, Kepler's laws of, 1609, 1609 and 1619.

Plankton, term introduced 1886 by Henson.

Planquette, Robert, French composer (*Les Cloches de Corneville*, 1877), b.1848, d.1903.

Plantin, Christopher, French printer, b.1514, d.1589.

Plassey, Battle of, between Lord Clive and Indian rebel forces 23 June 1757.

Platform scales, invented 1831 by the American engineer Thaddeus Fairbanks, b.1796, d.1886.

Plath, Sylvia, American poet and writer (*The Bell Jar*, 1961), b.1932, committed suicide 1962.

Platinite, alloy, discovered by the French scientist Charles Edouard Guillaume, b.1861, d.1938.

Platinum, found in Spain at least as early as 1538; discovered in England 1741 by the English chemist William Brownrigg, b.1711, d.1800.

Plato, Greek philosopher (*The Republic*), b.c.427, d.347 BC.

Platt Amendment, American measure concerning Cuba, framed 1901 by the American politician Orville Hitchcock Platt, b.1827, d.1905. Abolished 1934.

Plautus, Roman playwright (*Amphitruo*), b.c.254, d.184 BC.

Playfair, Sir Nigel, English actor-manager, b.1874, d.1934.

Playfair, William Henry, Scottish architect, b.1789, d.1857.

Playford, John, English music publisher, b.1623, d.1686.

Pléiade, The, French literary movement, launched 1549.

Pleistocene Epoch, The Great Ice Age, between 20,000 and one million years ago.

Plekhanov, Georgi Valentinovich, Russian socialist leader, b.1857, d.1918.

Plesiosaurus, remains first discovered 1821 by the English fossil collector Mary Anning, b.1799, d.1847.

Plimsoll Line, limit to which a ship may be loaded, brought into force 1876 by the efforts of the coal merchant and politician Samuel Plimsoll, b.1824, d.1898.

Pliny, the Elder, Latin writer (*Historia Naturalis*, 77), b.23, d.79.

Pliny, the Younger, Latin writer (*Epistles*), b.62, d.114.

Pliocene Epoch, Earth history, 15 million years ago.

Plotinus, Egypt-born philosopher, b.205, d.270.

Plücker, Julius, German scientist, b.1801, d.1868.

Plumptre, Edward Hayes, English theologian and classical scholar, b.1821, d.1891.

Plunkett, Sir Horace, Irish statesman and pioneer in agricultural cooperation, b.1854, d.1932.

Plural voting, discontinued in Britain by Act of Parliament 1948.

Plutarch, Greek philosopher and historian, b.50, d.*c.*120.

Pluto, planet, discovered 1930 by the American astronomer Clyde William Tombaugh, b.1906.

Pluto, Channel underwater oil pipeline ('Pipeline Under The Ocean'), first in action 12 Aug. 1944; proposed by the British engineer Arthur Clifford Hartley, b.1889, d.1960.

Plutonium, transuranic element, produced in the USA 1940.

Plymouth breakwater, constructed 1811–41 by the Scottish civil engineer John Rennie, b.1761, d.1821.

Plymouth Brethren, religious movement, founded 1830 by the Rev. John Nelson Darby, b.1800, d.1882.

Plymouth Colony, Massachusetts, first settled permanently by the Pilgrim Fathers 1620.

Pneumatic tyre, invented 1845 by the Scottish engineer Robert William Thomson, b.1822, d.1873; perfected 1888 by the Scottish inventor John Boyd Dunlop, b.1840, d.1921.

Pocahontas, American Indian chieftain's daughter and wife of John Rolfe m.1595–1622, b.1595, brought to England 1616, d.1617.

Pococke, Edward, English orientalist, b.1604, d.1691.

Poe, Edgar Allan, American writer (*The Gold Bug*, 1843), b.1809, d.1849.

Pogany, Willy, Hungarian-born painter and illustrator, b.1882, d.1955.

Poggendorff, Johann Christian, German scientist, b.1796, d.1877.

Poggio, Gian Francesco, Italian scholar and writer (*Facetiae*), b.1380, d.1459.

Poincaré, Raymond, French statesman, b.1860, d.1934.

Poindexter, George, American politician, b.1879, d.1953.

Point Pleasant, Battle of, between the Virginia militia and the Indians, 10 Oct. 1774.

Poison gas, first used in World War I by the Germans 22 April 1915; first used by the British 25 Sept. 1915.

Poissy, Colloquy of, to reconcile French Catholics and Protestants, held 1561.

Poitier, Sidney, black American film star (*In the Heat of the Night*, 1967), b.1924.
Poitiers, Battle of, between the English and the French 19 Sept. 1356.
Poland, independent kingdom since 1025; first partition (Prussia, Russia and Austria) 1772–93; second (Prussia and Russia) 1793–95; third (Prussia, Russia and Austria) 1795–1918; independent republic 1919–39; German occupation 1939–44; communist regime 1947–89; democratic constitution adopted 1989.
Polarization of heat, discovered 1837 by the Scottish scientist James David Forbes, b.1809, d.1868.
Polarization of light, discovered by the Dutch scientist Christiaan Huygens, b.1629, d.1695. Experiments on polarization carried out 1845 by the English scientist Michael Faraday, b.1791, d.1867.
Polders, arable land, created in the Zuyder Zee; first undertaken on a large scale 1930.
Pole, Margaret, Countess of Salisbury, b.1473, beheaded 1541.
Pole, Cardinal Reginald, archbishop of Canterbury, b.1500, d.1558.
Police, London, reorganized 1829 by the English statesman Sir Robert Peel, b.1788, d.1850.
Polignac, Prince Jules de, French diplomat and statesman, b.1780, d.1847.
Poliomyelitis, vaccine discovered 1934 by the American bacteriologist William Hallock Park, b.1863, d.1939; Salk vaccine developed 1954 by the American scientist Jonas Edward Salk, b.1914.
Polish Succession, War of the, concerning the succession to the throne of Poland, 1733–35.
Politian (Angelo Ambrogini), Italian scholar and poet (*La Giostra*), b.1454, d.1494.
Polk, James Knox, 11th US president (1845–49), b.1795, d.1849.
Poll tax, first levied in England 1380; abolished 1689; revived April 1990 (as Community Charge), re-abolished 1992.
Pollajuolo, Antonio, Italian artist, b.*c*.1432, d.1498.
Pollard, Alfred Frederick, English historian, b.1869, d.1948.
Pollitt, Harry, English Communist leader, b.1890, d.1960.
Pollock, Sir Frederick, English jurist, b.1845, d.1937.
Pollock, Jackson, American abstract painter, b.1912, d.1956.
Polo, Marco, Italian explorer, b.1254, d.1324.
Polonium, radio-active element, discovered 1898 by the French scientists Pierre and Marie Curie.

Pol Pot (Saloth Sar), Cambodian politician, head of the Khmer Rouge which ruled Cambodia 1975–79.

Polybius, Greek historian, b.*c.*205, d.123 BC.

Polycarp, St, bishop of Smyrna, martyred 155.

Polycrates, tyrant of Samos, crucified 522 BC.

Polyglot Bible, Complutensian, first polyglot Bible, prepared 1514–22.

Polythene, discovered by Imperial Chemical Industries chemists 1933.

Pombal, Sebastião José de Carvalho e Mello, Marquess of, Portuguese statesman, b.1699, d.1782.

Pompadour, Mme de, mistress of Louis XV, b.1721, d.1764.

Pompeii, Italy, devastated by the eruptions of Mt Vesuvius 63 and 79; ruins discovered 1748.

Pompey, Roman statesman, b.106, murdered 48 BC.

Pompidou, George, French politician (president 1969–74), b.1911, d.1974.

Ponce de Léon, Juan, Spanish colonial administrator, b.1460, killed 1521.

Ponce de Léon, Luis, Spanish poet, b.*c.*1527, d.1591.

Pond, John, English astronomer, b.1767, d.1836.

Pondicherry, India, settled by the French 1674; administration transferred to the government of India 1954; made a Union Territory in 1962.

Pons, Lily, French operatic singer, b.1904, d.1976.

Pontiac's Rebellion, 1763–64, led by the American Indian chief Pontiac, b.*c.*1720, reputed murdered 1769.

Pontian, St, pope 230–235.

Pontius Pilate, Roman procurator of Judea 26–36.

Pontormo, Jacopo, Italian painter (*The Deposition*), b.1494, d.1556.

Pony Express, USA, began 1860, ended 1861.

Poole, William Frederick, American bibliographer and historian, b.1821, d.1894.

Poor Clares, Order of Franciscan nuns organized by St Clare, b.*c.*1193, d.1253.

Poor Law System, begun in Britain 1601, reformed 1834, abolished 1929.

Poore, Richard, English bishop and builder of Salisbury Cathedral, d.1237.

Pope, Alexander, English poet (*The Rape of the Lock*, 1714), b.1698, d.1744.

Pope, Sir Thomas, privy councillor and philanthropist, b.*c.*1507, d.1559.

'Popish Plot', to murder King Charles II, invented 1678 by Titus Oates, b.1649, d.1705; agitation 1678–81.

Poppaea Sabina, wife of Nero, killed by Nero 65.

Popper, Sir Karl Raimund, Austrian-born British philosopher, b.1902.

Popular Front, policy of co-operation of left-wing parties against Fascism, between 1933 and 1939.

Porcelain, printing on, first achieved in Liverpool and Worcester 1756–57; introduced into France 1789 by Christopher Potter, d.1817.

Pordenone, Giovanni Antonio, Italian painter (*Le Mariage de Ste Catherine*), b.*c.*1483, d.1539.

Porphyry, Greek philosopher, b.233, d.*c.*304

Porson, Richard, English classical scholar, b.1759, d.1808.

Port Elizabeth, South Africa, founded 1820.

Port radar system, world's first, opened at Gladstone Dock, Liverpool, 30 July 1948.

Port Royal, French abbey near Paris, founded 1204; transferred to Paris 1626; suppressed 1704.

Port Said, Egypt, founded 1859.

Porta, Giovanni Battista della, Italian sculptor, b.1542, d.1597.

Porteous Riots, Edinburgh, occasioned at a public execution by the hasty action of the captain of the City Guard, John Porteous, hanged by the mob 1736.

Porter, Cole, American composer (*Anything Goes*, 1934), b.1893, d.1964.

Porter, William Sydney ('O Henry'), American writer (*The Gentle Grafter*, 1908), b.1862, d.1910.

Portland, Maine, first settled 1633; assumed present name 1786.

Portland, Oregon, founded 1845; chartered 1851.

Portland cement, invented 1824 by the English stonemason Joseph Aspdin, b.1779, d.1855.

Portland vase, Roman glass funerary urn now in British Museum, probably made in the 1st century BC; bought 1770 by Sir William Hamilton, lent by the Duke of Portland to the British Museum (smashed 1845).

Porto Rico,*see* **Puerto Rico.**

Portsmouth, England, granted a charter by King Richard I, 1194.

Portsmouth, Treaty of, ending the Russo-Japanese war (1904–05), signed 5 Sept. 1905.

Portugal, declared an independent monarchy 1143; ruled by Spain 1581–1640; Bragança monarchy 1640–1910; proclaimed a republic 1910; ruled by prime minister Dr Salazar 1932–68; military coup 1974; constitutional reform and democratization 1982–89.

Portuguese East Africa, *see* **Mozambique.**

Portuguese Guinea, *see* **Guinea-Bissau.**

Portuguese India, former Portuguese overseas province, discovered 1498 by the Portuguese navigator Vasco da Gama; first colonized 1505; status changed to overseas territory 1951; annexed by India 1961.

Portuguese Timor, former Portuguese overseas province, first colonized 1586; created an independent province 1896; overseas territory 1951; annexed by Indonesia 1975.

Portuguese West Africa, *see* **Angola.**

Positivism, philosophical system, developed 1822 by the French philosopher Auguste Comte, b.1798, d.1857.

Positrons, positive particles, discovered 1932 by the American scientist Carl David Anderson, b.1905, d.1991.

Post, Wiley, American pioneer aviator, b.1899, died in an air crash 1935.

Post Office Savings Bank, system introduced in Britain 1861.

Postage stamps, adhesive, first used in Britain 6 May 1840.

Postage stamps, hand-struck, first used in Britain 1661.

Postal orders, first used in Britain 1 Jan. 1881.

Postcards, stamped, introduced in Britain 1870.

Postcards, with adhesive stamps, use permitted in Britain from 1894.

Potassium, discovered 1807 by the English chemist Sir Humphry Davy, b.1778, d.1829.

Potato famine, in Ireland, 1845 to 1849.

Potatoes, introduced into England 1587 by Sir Walter Raleigh, b.1552, d.1618.

Potemkin, Gregory Alexandrovich, Russian statesman, b.1739, d.1791.

Potgieter, Everhardes Johannes, Dutch poet (*Florence*, 1868), b.1808, d.1875.

Potsdam Agreement, World War II, 17 July to 2 Aug. 1945.

Pott, Percivall, English pioneer in modern surgery, b.1714, d.1788.

Potter, Beatrix, English writer and illustrator of children's books (*Jemima Puddleduck*), b.1866, d.1943.

Potter, Dennis, British film and TV writer and novelist (*Pennies from Heaven*, 1978), b.1935.

Potter, Sir Thomas, joint-founder of the *Manchester Guardian*, b.1773, d.1845.

Poulenc, Francis, French composer (*Mouvement perpetuel*), b.1899, d.1963.

Pound, Ezra Loomis, American-born poet (*Cantos*, 1925 onwards), b.1885, d.1972.

Pound, Imperial standard weight established in Britain 1844.

Pourtalès, Louis François de, Swiss-born naturalist, b.1824, d.1880.

Poussin, Nicolas, French painter (*Venus and Adonis*), b.1594, d.1665.

Powell, Anthony, British novelist (*A Dance to the Music of Time*, 12 vols, 1951–75), b.1905.

Powell, Humphrey, English printer who established (1551) Ireland's first printing press at Dublin, lived until after 1556.

Powell, Michael, British film director, writer and producer (*The Thief of Baghdad*, 1946), b.1905, d.1990.

Powell, Vavasour, Welsh itinerant preacher, b.1617, d.1670.

Power loom, Cartwright's, invented 1785 by Edmund Cartwright, b.1743, d.1823.

Powys, John Cowper, English writer (*A Glastonbury Romance*, 1933), b.1872, d.1963.

Powys, Llewellyn, English author (*Apples be Ripe*, 1930), b.1884, d.1939.

Powys, Theodore Francis, English novelist (*Mr Tasker's Gods*, 1925), b.1875, d.1953.

Poynings' Law, regulating Irish government, passed 1495 by Sir Edward Poynings, Lord Deputy of Ireland, b.1459, d.1521.

Prado, Spain, national museum of paintings and sculpture, founded 1819.

Praed, Winthrop Mackworth, English poet (*Molly Mog*), b.1802, d.1839.

Pragmatism, idea introduced 1878 by the American scientist Charles Sanders Peirce, b.1839, d.1914.

Prague, Czech capital, in existence by 600.

Prague, Treaty of, ending the war between Austria and Prussia, signed 23 Aug. 1866.

Prague University, founded by the Emperor Charles IV, 1348.

Praseodymium, rare earth element, discovered 1885 by the Austrian chemist Baron von Welsbach, b.1858, d.1929.

Pratt, Charles, Earl Camden, Lord Chancellor, b.1714, d.1794.
Pratt, Silas Gamaliel, American composer (*Zenobia*, 1882), b.1846, d.1916.
Pratt Institute, New York, founded 1887.
Pratt Institute, Pittsburg, founded by Silas Gamaliel Pratt 1906.
Praxiteles, Greek sculptor, b.*c.*390, d.*c.*332 BC.
Prayer Book, *see* **Book of Common Prayer.**
Pre-Cambrian Period, Earth history, more than 520 million years ago.
Prefabricated house, first, a toll house created on the West Bromwich to Birmingham highway *c.*1830; dismantled 1926.
Premium Bonds, first issued in Britain 1956.
Premonstratensian Canons, founded 1120 by St Norbert, b.*c.*1080, d.1134.
Pre-Raphaelites, English art movement, flourished in the mid-19th century.
Presbyterianism, modern founder John Calvin, b.1509, d.1564; introduced to Scotland 1559–60 by John Knox, b.*c.*1505, d.1572; established again 1638–41, established finally 1690.
Prescott, William Hickling, American historian (*The Conquest of Mexico*, 1843), b.1796, d.1859.
Presley, Elvis Aaron, American popular singer, b.1935, d.1977.
Press Association, London, founded 1868.
Pressburg, Treaty of, between France and Austria, signed 26 Dec. 1805.
Prester John, mythical medieval monarch of Asia.
Prestonpans, Battle of, between the Jacobites and government forces 21 Sept. 1745.
Pretoria, capital of the Union of South Africa, founded 1855.
Pretorius, Andries Wilhelmus Jacobus, founder of the Transvaal, b.1799, d.1853 .
Prevost, Sir George, governor-general of Canada (1811–16), b.1767, d.1816.
Prévost, Marcel, French novelist (*Les Demi-vièrges*, 1894), b.1862, d.1941.
Prévost, The Abbé (Antoine François Prévost d'Exiles), French novelist (*Manon Lescaut*, 1731), b.1697, d.1763.
Price, Hugh, founder (1571) of Jesus College, Oxford, b.*c.*1495, d.1574.
Pride's Purge, of the Long Parliament, carried out 1648 by the Parliamentary general Thomas Pride, d.1658.

Prideaux, Humphrey, English theologian and scholar, b.1648, d.1724.

Priestley, John Boynton, English writer (*The Good Companions*, 1929), b.1894, d.1984.

Priestley, Joseph, English scientist, b.1733, d.1804.

Primaticcio, Francesco, Italian painter (*Diane de Poitiers*), b.1504, d.1570.

Prime minister, office introduced in Britain 1721–42, but not legally recognized until 1905.

Primitive Methodists, movement founded 1811 by the English Methodist Hugh Bourne, b.1772, d.1852.

Primrose League, British Conservative organization, founded in 1883 by Lord Randolph Churchill, b.1849, d.1894.

Prince, Thomas, English governor of Massachusetts, b.1600, d.1673.

Prince Edward Island, Canada, discovered 1534 by the French navigator Jacques Cartier, b.1491, d.1557.

Princeton, New Jersey, first settled 1696.

Princeton, Battle of, American War of Independence, 3 Jan. 1777.

Principe, former Portuguese overseas territory, discovered by the Portuguese 1471; part of São Tomé and Principe.

Printer's device, first known example printed in Fust and Schoeffer's Mainz Psalter, 1484.

Printing, known in China and Japan by 8th century, movable type invented 1041; invented (in Europe) at Mainz c.1440; movable type used by Gutenberg in 1454; steam press (1810) and cylinder press (1811) invented by the German inventor Friedrich Koenig, b.1774, d.1833.

Printing offices, provincial, suppressed by order of the Star Chamber 23 June 1585.

Prior, Matthew, English poet (*To a Child of Quality*), b.1664, d.1721.

Priscian, Roman grammarian, lived in the late 5th and early 6th centuries.

Priscillian, Spanish theologian, burnt at the stake 385.

Prisons, first used in England for punishment during 16th century.

Privy councillor, first woman, Miss Margaret Bondfield (1873–1953), appointed 1929.

Prize fight, last held in England, between Sayers and Heenan 17 April 1860.

Probabilities, theory of, modern approach founded by the French philosopher Blaise Pascal, b.1623, d.1662.
Probus, Roman emperor (276–282), killed 282.
Proclus, Greek philosopher, b.*c.*410, d.485.
Procopius, Byzantine historian, d.*c.*562.
Proctor, Richard Anthony, English astronomer, b.1837, d.1888.
Profumo Affair, resignation of Tory cabinet minister John Profumo, b.1915, d.1992, for affair with call girl Christine Keeler (who was also involved with a Russian diplomat), 1963.
Prohibition, came into effect nationally in the USA 17 Jan. 1920; repealed 1933.
Prokofiev, Sergei Sergeievich, Russian composer (*Peter and the Wolf*, 1936), b.1891, d.1953.
Promenade Concerts, London, founded 1895 by the English composer and conductor Sir Henry Wood, b.1869, d.1944.
Prontosil, sulphonamide drug, curative powers discovered 1935 by the German bacteriologist Gerhard Domagk, b.1895
Propertius, Latin poet (*Cynthia*, 25 BC), b.*c.*48, d.*c.*14 BC.
Protagoras, Greek philosopher, lived in the 5th century BC.
Proterozoic Era, earth history, more than 520 million years ago.
Protestant Episcopal Church, USA, founded 1789.
Protogenes, Greek painter, lived in the late 4th century BC.
Proton, unit of positive charge, the hydrogen nucleus of the atom, identified 1912 by the New Zealand-born scientist Lord Rutherford, b.1871, d.1937.
Protoplasm, discovered in the 18th century; first so named 1846 by the German botanist Hugo von Mohl, b.1805, d.1872.
Protozoa, unicellular animals, discovered 1674 by the Dutch scientist Antony van Leeuwenhoek, b.1632, d.1723.
Proudhon, Pierre Joseph, French social reformer, b.1809, d.1865.
Proust, Marcel, French novelist (*A la recherche du temps perdu*, 1913–27), b.1871, d.1922.
Prout, Ebenezer, English music theorist (*Harmony*, 1889), b.1835, d.1909.
Proxima Centauri, star nearest to the Earth, discovered 1916 by the Scottish astronomer Robert T. A. Innes, b.1861, d.1933.
Prudentius, Aurelius Clemens, Spanish poet (*Contra Symmachum*), b.348, d.410.
Prud'hon, Pierre Paul, French painter (*L'Assomption*, 1816), b.1758, d.1823.
Prussia, kingdom 1701–1918.

Prussian blue, discovered by the German scientist Johann Konrad Dippel, b.1673, d.1734.

Prussic acid, discovered 1782 by the Swedish chemist Karl Scheele, b.1742, d.1786.

Prynne, William, Puritan champion and pamphleteer, b.1600, d.1669.

Pryor, Roger Atkinson, New York Supreme Court judge and Confederate general, b.1828, d.1919.

'Psalmanazar, George', French-born imposter, b.*c.*1679, d.1763.

Psychoanalysis, study founded by the Austrian psychoanalyst Sigmund Freud, b.1856, d.1939.

Ptolemy, Claudius, Alexandrian geographer, lived in the 2nd century.

Ptolemy I (Soter), king of Egypt (323–285 BC), d.283 BC.

Ptolemy II (Philadelphus), king of Egypt (285–*c.*246 BC), d.*c.*246 BC.

Ptolemy III (Euergetes), king of Egypt (*c.*246–*c.*222 BC), d.*c.*222 BC.

Ptolemy IV (Philopator), king of Egypt (221–204 BC), d.204 BC.

Ptolemy V (Epiphanes), king of Egypt (204–181 BC), d.181 BC.

Ptolemy VI (Philometor), king of Egypt (181–145 BC), killed in battle 145 BC.

Ptolemy VII (Physcon), king of Egypt (145–117 BC), d.117 BC.

Ptolemy VIII (Lathyros), king of Egypt (117–107, 89–81 BC), d.81 BC.

Ptolemy IX (Alexander), king of Egypt 107–89 BC), killed *c.*89 BC.

Ptolemy X, (Alexander II), king of Egypt (80 BC), killed 80 BC.

Ptolemy XI (Auletes), king of Egypt (80–58, 55–51 BC), d.51 BC.

Ptolemy XII, king of Egypt (51–*c.*47 BC), drowned *c.*47 BC.

Ptolemy XIII, king of Egypt (47–44 BC), killed 44 BC.

Ptolemy XIV (Caesarion), king of Egypt (47–30 BC), b.47, murdered 30 BC.

Public Libraries Act, first, permitting the establishment of English public libraries, passed 1850.

Public Safety, Committee of, French Revolution, established 1793.

Public Trustee Office, London, opened 1908.

Publishers' cloth, introduced into Britain 1820 by the British publisher William Pickering, b.1796, d.1854.

Puccini, Giacomo, Italian composer (*Tosca*, 1900), b.1858, d.1924.

Puddling furnace, invented 1784 by the British iron-master Henry Cort, b.1740, d.1800.

Puerto Rico (formerly Porto Rico), discovered by Christopher Columbus 1493; ceded by Spain to the USA 1898.

'Puffing Billy', pioneer locomotive, invented 1813 by the inventor William Hedley, b.1779, d.1843.

Puget, Pierre, French artist (*Milo of Crotona*, 1683), b.1622, d.1694.

Pulaski, Count Casimir, Polish soldier in Washington's army, b.1748, died of wounds 1779.

Pulcheria, Byzantine empress (450–453), b.399, d.453.

Pulitzer Prizes, for American writing, founded 1917 through the philanthropy of the Hungarian-born newspaper owner Joseph Pulitzer, b.1847, d.1912.

Pullman sleeping car, invented 1864 by the American financier George Mortimer Pullman, b.1831, d.1897.

Pultava, Battle of, between the Russians and the Swedes 8 July 1709.

Pumping engine, atmospheric, invented *c.*1708 by the English engineer Thomas Newcomen, b.1663, d.1729.

Punch, British periodical, founded 17 July 1841 by the English engraver Ebenezer Landells, b.1808, d.1850, and the English writer Mark Lemon, b.1809, d.1870.

Punch and Judy, puppet play, origins (probably Italian) uncertain; introduced into England via France in the 17th century.

Punic War, First, between Rome and Carthage, 264 to 241 BC.

Punic War, Second, between Rome and Carthage, 218 to 201 BC.

Punic War, Third, between Rome and Carthage, 149 to 146 BC.

Punjab, India, annexed by Britain 1849; constituted an autonomous province 1937; partitioned between India and Pakistan 1947.

Purcell, Henry, English composer (*Dido and Aeneas*, 1689), b.*c.*1658, d.1695.

Purchas, Samuel, English compiler (*Purchas, His Pilgrimage*, 1613), b.*c.*1575, d.1626.

Purdue University, Lafayette, Indiana, founded 1874.

Purim, Jewish festival, celebrated 14th and 15th days of Adar.

Pusey, Edward Bouverie, English theologian, b.1800, d.1882.

Pushkin, Alexander Sergeievich, Russian writer (*Ruslan and Ludmilla*, 1820), b.1799, killed in a duel 1837.

Putnam, Frederick Ward, American anthropologist, b.1839, d.1915.

Putnam, George Palmer, American publisher, b.1814, d.1872.

Puvis de Chavannes, Pierre, French painter (*St Geneviève*), b.1824, d.1898.

Pu Yi, Henry, last emperor of China (1908–12), first emperor of Manchukuo (1934–45), b.1905, d.1967.

Pygmies, African, first discovered 1870 by the German ethnologist Georg August Schweinfurth, b.1836, d.1925.

Pym, John, English, Puritan leader, b.1584, d.1643.

Pynson, Richard, French-born pioneer printer in England, d.1530.

Pyramids, Battle of the, between Napoleon and the Mamelukes, 21 July 1798

Pyrenees, Peace of the, ending war between France and Spain, Nov. 1659.

Pyridine, organic base, discovered 1851 by the Scottish chemist Thomas Anderson, b.1819, d.1874.

Pyroscope, invented by the Scottish mathematician Sir John Leslie, b.1766, d.1832.

Pyrrho of Elis, Greek philosopher, b.c.360, d.270 BC.

Pyrrhus, Greek king, b.c.318, d.272 BC.

Pyruvic acid, organic acid, first obtained 1835 by the Swedish chemist Baron Berzelius, b.1779, d.1848.

Pythagoras, Greek philosopher and mathematician, b.c.582, d.500 BC.

Q

Qaddafi, Muammer el-, Libyan revolutionary leader (since 1969), b.1942.
Qatar, Persian Gulf State, became a British protectorate 1916; declared independence 1971.
Quadragesima, the forty days of Lent; sometimes restricted to the first Sunday in Lent.
Quadrant, reflecting, invented 1731 by the English mathematician John Hadley, b.1682, d.1744.
Quadrille, first introduced into Britain 1815.
Quadruple Alliance, of the Allies against Napoleon, 1814–15.
Quadruple Treaty, guaranteeing the constitutional monarchies of Spain and Portugal, signed by France and Britain 1834.
Quakers (Society of Friends), founded 1647 by the English shoemaker George Fox, b.1624, d.1690; first Quaker MP elected 1833.
Quant, Mary, British fashion designer, b.1934.
Quantitive analysis, theory developed 1754 by the British scientist Joseph Black, b.1728, d.1799.
Quantum theory, formulated 1900 by the German physicist Max Planck, b.1858, d.1947.
Quare, Daniel, English clockmaker and inventor 1687 of repeating watches, b.1648, d.1724.
Quark, subatomic (smallest elementary) particle, existence first suggested by Murray Gell-Mann and George Zweig 1964.
Quarles, Francis, English poet (*Emblems*, 1635), b.1592, d.1644.
Quarter days, in England and Ireland, 25 March, 24 June, 29 Sept., 25 Dec.; in Scotland, 2 Feb., 15 May, 1 Aug., 11 Nov.
Quarter Sessions, British court of record, held 4 times a year by Statute since 1363.
Quarterly Review, began publication 1809; first editor: William Gifford, b.1756, d.1826; publisher: John Murray, b.1778, d.1843.
Quaternary Period, the last million years of Earth history.
Quaternions, vector analysis, invented 1852 by the Scottish mathematician, Sir William Rowan Hamilton, b.1805, d.1865.
Quatre Bras, Battle of, between the British and the French, 16 June 1815.
Quebec, Canada, founded 3 July 1608 by the French navigator Samuel de Champlain, b.1557, d.1635.
Quebec Act, concerning the government and territory of the Province of Quebec, 1774.

Quebec Conference, World War II, held 11–24 Aug. 1943.

Queen Alexandra's Day, first held 26 June 1912. The emblem was then an artificial rose.

Queen Anne's Bounty, ecclesiastical fund, founded in England 1703.

Queen Elizabeth, Atlantic passenger liner, launched 27 Sept. 1938.

'Queen, Ellery' (Frederic Dannay and Manfred B. Lee), American detective fiction writers (*The Roman Hat Mystery,* 1929); *Ellery Queen Mystery Magazine* began 1941.

Queen Mary, Atlantic passenger liner, launched 26 Sept. 1934.

Queen Mary Land, Antarctica, discovered 1912 by the English Captain John King Davis, b.1884.

Queen Maud Land, Antarctica, placed under Norwegian sovereignty 1939.

Queensberry Rules, for glove-fighting, initiated 1867 by Lord Queensberry, b.1844, d.1900.

Queens' College, Cambridge University, founded 1448 by Queen Margaret of Anjou; refounded by Elizabeth Widville, consort of King Edward IV, 1465.

Queen's College, The, Oxford University, founded by Robert de Eglesfield 1340–41.

Queensland, Australia, formed into separate colony 1859.

Queen's University, Belfast, came into being 1909. Previously Queen's College, Belfast.

Quetta, city in W. central Pakistan, founded 1876.

Quetta Earthquake, 31 May 1935.

Quevedo, Francisco Gomez de, Spanish writer (*Sueños*, 1627), b.1580, d.1645.

Quiberon Bay, Battle of, between English and French fleets 20 Nov. 1759.

Quietism, contemplative mystical movement, founded 1675 by the Spanish theologian Miguel de Molinos, b.1640, d.1697.

Quiller-Couch, Sir Arthur ('Q'), English writer (*Troy Town*, 1888), b.1863, d.1944.

Quilter, Roger, English composer (*Where the Rainbow Ends*, 1911), b.1877, d.1953.

Quin, James, London-born Irish actor, b.1693, d.1766.

Quincey, Thomas de, English writer (*Confessions of an Opium-eater*, 1821), b.1785, d.1859.

Quinet, Edgar, French historian, b.1803, d.1875.

Quinine, discovered 1820 by the French scientists Pierre Joseph Pelletier, b.1788, d.1842, and Joseph Bienaimé Caventou, b.1795, d.1877.

Quinquagesima, the 50 days immediately preceding Easter; or the Sunday before Ash Wednesday.

Quintana, Manuel José, Spanish writer (*Pelayo*, 1805), b.1772, d.1857.

Quintilian, Roman orator (*Institutio Oratoria*), b.*c*.35, d.95.

Quirinal Palace, Rome, designed 1574 by the Italian architect Domenico Fontana, b.1543, d.1607.

Quisling, Vidkun, Norwegian puppet premier (1942–45) and traitor, b.1887, executed 1945.

Quito, capital of Ecuador, annexed by the Spaniards 1533, created a city 1541.

Quiz programme, first, broadcast in Canada 15 May 1935.

Quiz programme, first British, the Inter-Regional Spelling Competition (later Regional Round) broadcast 25 Nov. 1937.

Qumran, Palestinian village, site of Dead Sea Scrolls, found by shepherd 1947.

Quorn Hunt, predominantly Leicestershire, county first hunted 1698–1753 by Thomas Boothby; first Master Hugo Meynell from 1753 to 1800.

R

R 101, British dirigible, first trials 14 Oct. 1929; flew the Atlantic 30 July 1930; crashed at Beauvais 5 Oct. 1930.

Raabe, Peter, German music historian (*Franz Liszt,* 1931), b.1872, d.1945.

Rabbi ben Ezra (Abraham ben Meir ibn Ezra), Spanish Jewish scholar, b.*c.*1092, d.1167.

Rabbinical Bible, first published 1516–17 by the Christian printer Daniel Bomberg, d.1549.

Rabelais, François, French writer (*Gargantua, c.*1532), b.1483, d.1553.

Rabies, effective treatment developed 1885 by the French scientist Louis Pasteur, b.1822, d.1895.

Rabin, Yitzhak, Israeli politician (prime minister 1974–77), b.1922.

Rachel, Elisa (Elisa Rachel Félix), Swiss-born actress, b.1821, d.1858.

Rachmaninoff, Sergei, Russian-born composer (*Rhapsody on a theme by Paganini*), b.1873, d.1943.

Racine, Jean, French playwright (*Phèdre,* 1677), b.1639, d.1699.

Rackham, Arthur, English artist and illustrator, b.1867, d.1939.

Radar, first practical demonstration made 1935 by a team led by the British scientist Sir Robert Watson-Watt, b.1892, d.1973.

Radcliffe, Anne, English novelist (*The Mysteries of Udolpho,* 1794), b.1764, d.1823.

Radcliffe Observatory, Oxford University, founded 1771, through the benefaction of the executors of the English physician John Radcliffe, b.1650, d.1714.

Radek, Karl (Karl Sobelsohn), Russian Bolshevik leader, b.1885, d.*c.*1939.

Radetzky, Josef, Count of Radetz, Austrian field-marshal, b.1766, d.1858.

Radiation, theory developed 1900 by the German physicist Max Planck, b.1858, d.1947; and also 1896 by the German physicist Wilhelm Wien, b.1864, d.1938.

Radioactivity, discovered 1896 by the French scientist Antoine Henri Becquerel, b.1852, d.1908.

Radiometer, invented 1873–76 by the English scientist Sir William Crookes, b.1832, d.1919.

Radio photographs, first transmitted from Britain to the USA 1924.

Radio signals, first detected 1888; first sent across the Atlantic (Cornwall to Newfoundland) 1901 by the Italian inventor Guglielmo Marconi, b.1874, d.1937.

Radiotelephone service, first, initiated 1927.

Radio Times, British periodical, first published 28 Sept. 1923.

Radio tuning, selective, basic principles of the method defined 1898 by the British physicist Sir Oliver Lodge, b.1851, d.1940.

Radio waves, discovered 1888 by the German physicist Heinrich Rudolf Hertz, b.1857, d.1894; theory developed 1868 by the Scottish physicist James Clerk Maxwell, b.1831, d.1879.

Radisson, Pierre Esprit, French explorer, b.*c.*1632, d.*c.*1710.

Radium, discovered 1898 by the French scientist Pierre Curie, b.1859, d.1906; isolated 1902 by Mme Curie.

Radon, radioactive element, discovered 1900 by the German scientist F. E. Dorn.

Raeburn, Sir Henry, Scottish painter (*The Macnab*), *b.*1756, d.1823.

Raemaekers, Louis, Dutch cartoonist, b.1869, d.1956.

RAF (Royal Air Force), established 1918.

Raff, Joseph Joachim, Swiss-born composer (*Im Walde*), b.1822, d.1882.

Raffles, Sir Stamford, British founder (1819) of Singapore, b.1781, d.1826.

Raglan, Fitzroy James Henry Somerset, Baron, commanded the British troops at the Crimea, b.1788, d.1855.

Rahere, founder 1123 of St Bartholomew's Hospital, London, d.1144.

Raikes, Robert, English founder (1780) of Sunday schools, b.1735, d.1811.

Railway, mining railways in use in Europe in 16th century; first public railway (Wandsworth to Croydon) opened 1803; first recorded journey (Mumbles) 1807; first public steam (Stockton to Darlington) opened 1825; first public electric (City and South London) opened 1890.

Railway letter stamps, first issued in Britain 1891.

Railway ticket dating machine, first, invented 1837 by the British inventor Thomas Edmondson, b.1792, d.1851.

Raimondi, Marcantonio, Italian engraver, b.*c.*1480, d.*c.*1534.

Raines Law, 1896, relating to liquor sales in New York State, framed by the American politician John Raines, b.1840, d.1909.

Rainier, Prince, of Monaco, b.1923; m. Grace Kelly 19 April 1956.

Rákóczy, Francis II, prince of Transylvania, b.1676, d.1735.

Raleigh, Sir Walter, English mariner and explorer, b.1552, beheaded 1618.

Ramadan, Islamic month (depending on moon) of fasting during the day.

Raman Effect, physics, discovered 1928 by Sir Chandrasekhara Venkata Raman, b.1888, d.1970.

Rambouillet, Catherine de Vivonne, Marquise de, French patron of men of letters, b.1588, d.1665.

Rameau, Jean Philippe, French composer (*Dardanus,* 1739), b.1683, d.1764.

Rameses I, king of Egypt (about 1315–1314 BC), d.c.1314 BC.

Rameses II, king of Egypt (about 1292–1225 BC), d.c.1225 BC.

Rameses III, king of Egypt (about 1198–1167 BC), d.c.1167 BC.

Ramillies, Battle of, between the British and the French, 23 May 1706.

Ramsay, Allan, Scottish poet (*The Gentle Shepherd,* 1725), b.1686, d.1758.

Ramsay, Sir William, Scottish scientist, b.1852, d.1916.

Ramsden, Jesse, English instrument maker, b.1735, d.1800.

Ramus, Petrus (Pierre de la Ramée), French philosopher, b.1515, killed 1572.

Ramuz, Charles Ferdinand, Swiss novelist, b.1878, d.1947.

Ranavalona III, last queen of Madagascar (1883–1916), b.1861, d.1916.

Randall, John, English, shipbuilder, b.1755, d.1802.

Randolph, Sir Thomas, Earl of Moray, regent of Scotland, d.1332.

Randolph, Thomas, English writer (*Amyntas,* 1638), b.1605, d.1635.

Randolph, William, English founder (1693) of William and Mary College, Virginia, b.1650, d.1711.

Ranelagh, London pleasure gardens, opened to the public 1742; closed 1803.

Ranjit Singh, Sikh ruler (1799–1838).

Ranjitsinhji, Prince, Indian cricketer, b.1872, d.1933.

Ranke, Leopold von, German historian, b.1795, d.1886.

Rankin, Thomas, Scottish Methodist reformer, b.1738, d.1810.

Rankine, William John Macquorn, Scottish civil engineer and molecular physicist, b.1820, d.1872.

Rapallo, Treaties of, settling the frontiers between Yugoslavia and Italy, signed 1920; between Germany and Russia, signed 1922.

Raphael, Italian painter *(St Catherine)*, b.1483, d.1520.

Rapin du Thoyras, Paul de, French historian, b.1661, d.1725.

Rappard, Professor William, Swiss political scientist, b.1883, d.1958.

Rasmussen, Knud Johan Victor, Danish Polar explorer, b.1879, d.1933.

Raspe, Rudolf Eric, German-born writer (*Baron Munchhausen*, 1785), b.1737, d.1794.

Rasputin (Grigori Yefimovich Novych), Russian court intriguer, b.1871, assassinated 15 Dec. 1916.

Ratcliffe, Samuel Kerkham, English journalist, b.1868, d.1958.

Ratdolt, Erhard, German pioneer printer b.*c.*1443, d.*c.*1528.

Rathbone, William, English founder (1859) of the District Nurse movement, b.1819, d.1902.

Rathenau, Walter, German statesman, b.1867, assassinated 1922.

Rationing, food, in Britain, World War I, 1916–18; World War II, began 8 Jan. 1940, ended 1953. In Germany, World War II, began 27 Aug. 1939.

Rationing, 'points', World War II, began in Britain 1 Dec. 1941.

Rattigan, Sir Terence, British playwright (*The Winslow Boy,* 1935), b.1892, d.1967.

Rauschenberg, Robert, American painter, b.1925.

Ravel, Maurice, French composer (*Tombeau de Couperin,* 1917), b.1875, d.1937.

Ravenna, chief residence of the Roman emperors 404–476, and of Byzantine exarchs 540–751; ceded to Papacy 756; recovered from Venetians 1509.

Rawalpindi, Treaty of, concluding the 3rd Afghan War, signed 8 Aug. 1919.

Rawlins, Thomas, English medallist and playwright, b.*c.*1620, d.1670.

Rawlinson, Sir Henry Crewicke, English Assyriologist, b.1810, d.1895.

Rawsthorne, Alan, English composer (*Cortège,* 1945), b.1905, d.1971.

Ray, John, English naturalist, b.1627, d.1705.

Ray, Man, American artist and photographer, b.1890, d.1976.

Rayleigh, John William Strutt, Baron, English scientist, b.1842, d.1919.

Raymond I, count of Toulouse 852–864.

Raymond II, count of Toulouse 918–924.

Raymond III, count of Toulouse 924–950.

Raymond IV, count of Toulouse (1093–1105) and crusader, d.1105.

Raymond V, count of Toulouse 1148–94.

Raymond VI, count of Toulouse (1194–1222), d.1222.

Raymond VII, count of Toulouse (1222–49), d.1249.

Raymond le Gros (Raymond Fitzgerald), English ruler of Ireland, d.c.1182.

Rayon, first successfully manufactured 1889 by the French chemist Hilaire, Comte de Chardonnet, b.1839, d.1924.

Razor, Safety, invented 1901 by the American manufacturer King Camp Gillette, b.1855, d.1932.

Read, Sir Herbert, English poet and critic, b.1893, d.1968.

Reade, Charles, English novelist (*The Cloister and the Hearth,* 1861), b.1814, d.1884.

Reader's Digest, American periodical began in 1922 by DeWitt Wallace.

Reade's kettledrum, condenser for the microscope, invented 1861 by the chemist Joseph Bancroft Reade, b.1801, d.1870.

Reading, Rufus Isaacs, Marquess of, British lawyer and viceroy of India (1921–26), b.1860, d.1935.

Reading University, founded 1892 as the University Extension College; university status 1926.

Reagan, John Henninger, American statesman, b.1818, d.1905.

Reagan, Ronald Wilson, American film actor and 40th president of the US (1981–89), b.1911.

Real Academia Español, founded at Madrid July 1713.

Reaper, invented 1826 by the Scottish inventor Patrick Bell, b.1799, d.1869. First practical machine invented 1831 by the American Cyrus Hall McCormick, b.1809, d.1884.

Réaumur scale, temperature, invented by the French scientist René Antoine Ferchault de Réaumur, b.1683, d.1757.

Rebecca Riots, Wales, 1839 and 1843.

Recamier, Mme, French leader of society, b.1777, d.1849.

Rechabites, Independent Order of, temperance society founded at Salford 1835.

Recife, Brazil, founded 1536.

Reclus, Jean-Jacques, French geographer and anarchist, b.1830, d.1905.

Record Office, first British local, established at Bedford 1923.

Records, Public, first brought under the superintendence of the Master of the Rolls in Britain by Act of Parliament 1838.

Redding, Otis, American soul singer ('Sittin' on the Dock of the Bay', 1967), b.1941, killed in plane crash 1967.

Red Cross, International, founded at Geneva 1864.

Redford, Robert, American film actor and director (*The Natural,* 1984), b.1937.

Redgrave, Sir Michael, British film and stage actor (*The Lady Vanishes,* 1938), b.1905, d.1985.

Redgrave, Vanessa, British film and stage actress, b.1937.

'Red Sunday', Russian revolt, took place at St Petersburg 22 Jan. 1905.

Redmond, John Edward, Irish patriot, b.1856, d.1918.

Redouté, Pierre Joseph, French botanical artist, b.1759, d.1840.

Reed, Talbot Baines, English writer of books for boys, b.1852, d.1903.

Reed, Walter, American bacteriologist, b.1851, d.1902.

Reflex and voluntary action, distinguished 1833–37 by the English physiologist Marshall Hall, b.1790, d.1857.

Reformation, started 1517 by the German reformer Martin Luther, b.1483, d.1546.

Reformatory, first British, opened at Redhill 1850.

Refraction, Double, theory made public 1810 by the French physicist Etienne Louis Malus, b.1775, d.1812.

Refraction of light, law postulated 1621 by the Dutch scientist Willebrord Snell, b.1591, d.1626.

Refrigerated railway waggons, first used in the USA 1877.

Refrigerator, invented 1867 by the French inventor Charles Tellier, b.1828, d.1913.

Regency period, approximately 1810 to 1830.

Reger, Max, German composer (*Sinfonietta*), b.1873, d.1916.

Regiomontanus (Johannes Müller), German astronomer, b.1436, d.1476.

Regional broadcasting, in Britain, began with the opening of the transmitting station at Brookmans Park 21 Oct. 1929.

Registered trademark, first, the Red Badge of Messrs Bass & Co.'s Pale Ale, created 1855.

Registrar-General, first British, Thomas Henry Lister (appointed 1836), b.1800, d.1842.

Registration, of births, marriages and deaths, instituted in Britain by Thomas Cromwell, b.c.1485, beheaded 1540; made compulsory 1837.

Regnault, Henri, French painter (*Salome,* 1870), b.1843, killed in battle 1871.

Régnier, Mathurin, French satirical writer (*Macette*), b.1573, d.1613.

Regulus, Marcus Atilius, Roman hero, lived in the 3rd century BC.

Rehan, Ada, Irish-born actress, b.1860, d.1916.

Reichenbach, Hans, German born exponent of the philosophy of science, b.1891, d.1953.

Reichstadt, Napoléon Francis Joseph Charles, Duc de (Napoleon II), b.1811, d.1832.

Reichstag, German parliament, reconstituted 1867–71; building burnt 27 Feb. 1933; trial began at Leipzig 21 Sept. 1933.

Reid, Sir William, governor of the Bermudas (1839–46), b.1791, d.1858.

Reign of Terror, French Revolution, 1793–94.

Reinach, Salomon, French archaeologist (*Apollo,* 1902–03), b.1858, d.1932.

Reinhardt, Max, Austrian pioneer of the Modern Theatre, b.1873, d.1943.

Réjane, Gabrielle, French actress, b.1857, d.1920.

Relativity, **Special Theory of,** propounded 1905; **General Theory of,** propounded 1916: both by the German-born scientist Albert Einstein, b.1879, d.1955.

Relief map, earliest (of Peru), prepared for the 9th Inca, d.1191.

Remarque, Erich Maria, German-born novelist (*All Quiet on the Western Front,* 1929), b.1898, d.1970.

Rembrandt Harmens van Rijn, Dutch painter (*Woman Taken in Adultery,* 1644), b.1606, d.1669.

Remington, Frederick, American artist, b.1861, d.1909.

Remonstrance, Grand, parliamentary indictment of Charles I, Nov. 1641.

Remonstrants, Dutch religious movement, founded 1609.

Rémusat, Charles François Marie, Comte de, French writer and politician, b.1797, d.1875.

Renaissance, of Italian art, between 14th and 16th centuries.

Renan, Ernest, French theologian (*La Vie de Jesus,* 1863), b.1823, d.1892.

Reni, Guido, Italian painter (*Deeds of Hercules,* 1617–21), b.1575, d.1642.
Rennie, John, Scottish civil engineer, b.1761, d.1821.
Renoir, Jean, French-born American film director (*La Grande Illusion,* 1937), b.1894, d.1979.
Renoir, Pierre Auguste, French painter (*Les Grands Boulevards*), b.1841, d.1919.
Renwick, James, Scottish Covenanter, b.1662, executed 1688.
Reparations, German, after World War I, paid 1921–31.
Repeating watch, invented 1687 by the English clockmaker Daniel Quare, b.1648, d.1724.
Repington, Cardinal Philip, bishop of Lincoln, d.1424.
Repplier, Agnes, American essayist (*To Think of Tea,* 1932), b.1858, d.1950.
Republic, French, First 1793–1804, Second 1848–52, Third 1875–1940, Fourth 1946–58, Fifth since 1958; English 1649–60; Spanish 1873–74, 1931–39; Portuguese since 1910; Italian since 1946; German 1918–33, 1949 to date.
Republican Party, USA, present-day party formed 1854.
Respighi, Ottorino, Italian composer (*La Boutique Fantasque,* 1919), b.1879, d.1936.
Restif de la Bretonne, Nicolas Edmé, French writer (*Monsieur Nicolas,* 1794–97), b.1734, d.1806.
Restoration, English, of King Charles II, 29 May 1660.
Restoration, French, of King Louis XVIII, 1814.
Reszke, Jean de, Polish operatic singer, b.1850, d.1925.
Retarded potentials, relativity theory, made public 1867 by the German scientist Ludwig Lorenz, b.1829, d.1891.
Retreat from Mons, World War I, Aug. 1914.
Retz, Jean François Paul de, Cardinal de, abbot of St Denis and politician, b.1614, d.1679.
Reuchlin, Johann, German scholar and pioneer in Hebrew grammar, b.1455, d.1522.
Reunion, Indian Ocean, discovered 1507 by the Portuguese navigator Diego Fernandes Pereira; formally annexed by France 1643; an overseas department of France since 1946.
Reuter, Paul Julius (Josephat), Baron de, German-born pioneer in the speedy transmission of news, b.1821, d.1899.
Reuters, press agency, founded by the German-born Paul Julius Reuter 1849.
Revere, Paul, American revolutionary, b.1735, d.1818.
Revised Version of the Bible, completed 1884.

Rexists, Belgian Fascist party, founded 1935 by Léon Degrelle.

Reykjavik, Iceland capital, founded *c.*875.

Reymont, Wladislaw Stanislaw, Polish novelist (*The Promised Land,* 1898), b.1868, d.1925.

Reynolds, George Nugent, Irish poet (*Kathleen O'More,* 1800), b.*c.*1770, d.1802.

Reynolds, Sir Joshua, English painter (*Nelly O'Brien*), b.1723, d.1792.

Rhankaves, Alexandres, Greek statesman, b.1810, d.1892.

Rhee, Syngman (Li Sung-man), ruler of South Korea (1948–60), b.1875, d.1965.

Rheims Cathedral, construction began 1210, mostly completed by 1298; west front erected in the 14th century.

Rheinberger, Josef, Liechtenstein composer of organ sonatas, b.1839, d.1901.

Rhenium, metallic element, discovered 1925.

Rhine, Confederation of the, of German states, formed by Napoleon 1806; collapsed 1813.

Rhineland, occupied by French 1792–1813; by Allies 1918–30; taken over by Hitler 7 March 1936.

Rhode Island, USA, first settled 1636; entered the Union 1790.

Rhodes, Cecil John, Central African pioneer, b.1853, d.1902.

Rhodes, Colossus of, statue built *c.*285 BC; destroyed by an earthquake 224 BC.

Rhodes, Island of, seized by the Knights Hospitallers 1309; ceded to the Turks 1522; seized by the Italians 1912; ceded to Greece 1947.

Rhodes Scholarships, for the education at Oxford of overseas students, set up 1902 by the will of Cecil John Rhodes, b.1853, d.1902.

Rhodesia, *see* **Zimbabwe.**

Rhodesia, Northern, *see* **Zambia.**

Rhodesia, Southern, *see* **Zimbabwe.**

Rhodesia and Nyasaland, Federation of, consisting of Northern Rhodesia, Southern Rhodesia and Nyasaland 1953–63.

Rhodesia University, multi-racial, foundation stone laid 1953.

Rhodium, metallic element, discovered 1803 by the English scientist William Hyde Wollaston, b.1766, d.1828.

Rhondda, Margaret Haig Thomas, Viscountess, founder and editor (1920–58) of *Time and Tide,* b.1883, d.1958.

Ribauit, Jean, French navigator and pioneer colonist in North America, b.*c.*1520, killed 1565.

Ribbentrop, Joachim von, German Nazi leader, b.1893, hanged 1946.

Ribbing machine, for stocking manufacture, invented 1759 by the English manufacturer Jedediah Strutt, b.1726, d.1797.

Ribera, Jusepe de, Spanish-born painter (*St Sebastian*), b.1591, d.1652.

Ricardo, David (Israel), English economist (*Principles of Political Economy*, 1817), b.1772, d.1823.

Ricci, Matteo, Italian missionary in China, b.1552, d.1610.

Rice, Elmer (Elmer Reizenstein), American playwright (*Counsellor-at-law,* 1931), b.1892, d.1967.

Rich, Richard, English traveller and writer (*Newes from Virginia,* 1610), *fl.* late 16th and early 17th centuries.

Richard I, **Coeur de Lion**, Crusader and king of England (1189–99), b.1157, killed in battle 1199.

Richard II, king of England (1377–99), b.1367, murdered 1400.

Richard III, king of England (1483–85), b.1452, killed in battle 1485.

Richard de Bury, English divine and book collector (*Philobiblon*), b.1281, d.1345.

Richard of Cirencester, English historian (*Speculum Historiale*), d.c.1401.

Richard of Devizes, English historian of the late 12th century.

Richards, Alfred Bate, English writer and first editor (1855) of the *Daily Telegraph, b.*1820, d.1876.

Richards, Frank, English writer (the 'Billy Bunter' series for boys), b.1875, d.1961.

Richardson, Dorothy, English novelist (*Pilgrimage*), b.1873, d.1957.

Richardson, Jonathan, English painter (*Matthew Prior*), b.1665, d.1745.

Richardson, Sir Ralph David, British actor (*The Fallen Idol,* 1948), b.1902, d.1983.

Richardson, Samuel, English novelist (*Pamela,* 1740), b.1689, d.1761.

Richelieu, Cardinal Armand Jean du Plessis, Duc de, French statesman, b.1585, d.1642.

Richemont, Henri Louis Victor Hébert, Comte de, Pretender to the throne of France, d.1853.

Richepin, Jean, French writer (*Monsieur Scapin,* 1886), b.1845, d.1926.

Richmond, George, English painter (*William Wilberforce*), b.1809, d.1896.

Richter, Ernst Friedrich, German composer and writer on harmony, b.1808, d.1879.

Richter, Hans, Hungarian-born conductor (particularly of Wagner's works), b.1843, d.1916.

Richthofen, Manfred, Freiherr von, German aviator in World War I, b.1892, d.1918.

Ricordi, Giovanni, Italian music publisher, b.1785, d.1853.

Riddell, George Allardice, Baron, newspaper proprietor, b.1865, d.1934.

Ridley, Nicholas, bishop of London, b.*c.*1500, burnt at the stake 1555.

Ridolfo, Roberto di, Italian intriguer in England, b.1531, d.1612.

Ridpath, George, Scottish writer and journalist, d.1726.

Riefenstahl, Leni, German film director and Nazi propagandist (*Triumph of the Will,* 1934), b.1902.

Riemann, Hugo, German music historian, b.1849, d.1919.

Riemenschneider, Tilman, German sculptor (*Adam and Eve*), b.*c.*1468, d.1531.

Rienzi, Cola di, Italian reformer, b.*c.*1313, murdered 1354.

Rifle, Enfield, invented by the Frenchman Claude Minié, b.1814, d.1879; Lee-Enfield introduced in Britain 1895; the Belgian FN. 30 adopted by Britain 19 Jan. 1954.

Riga, Latvian capital, founded 1200.

Rigaud, Hyacinthe, French painter (*Louis XIV*), b.1659, d.1743.

Rigaud, Stephen Peter, English mathematician and astronomer, b.1774, d.1839.

Rights, Declaration (Feb.) and Bill (Oct.) of, 1689.

Rights of Man, Declaration of, issued by the French Constituent Assembly 1789.

Rijeka-Susak (formerly Fiume), seized by d'Annunzio 1919; ruled by Italy 1924–47; part of Croatia since 1947.

Riley, James Whitcomb, American poet (*Love Lyrics,* 1899), b.1853, d.1916.

Riley, John, English painter to the Court, b.1646, d.1691.

Rilke, Rainer Maria, German poet (*Duinese Elegies,* 1923), b.1875, d.1926.

Rimbaud, Arthur, French poet (*Les Illuminations,* 1886), b.1854, d.1891.

Rimini, Francesca da, Italian heroine, wife of Giovanni Malatesta and mistress of Paolo il Bello, murdered c.1285.

Rimmer, William, English-born artist (*A Dying Centaur*), b.1816, d.1879.

Rimsky-Korsakov, Nikolai Andreievich, Russian composer (*Le Coq d'Or*, 1910), b.1844, d.1908.

Rinehart, William Henry, American sculptor, b.1825, d.1874.

Ring, wedding, changed from right to left hand in English Prayer Book of 1549, and in *Rituale Romanum* of 1614.

Rio de Janeiro, capital of Brazil, site believed to have been discovered by the Portuguese navigator André Gonçalves 1502.

Rio de Oro, former region of W. Africa comprising south of Spanish Sahara (now Western Sahara); annexed by Spain 1885.

Ripley, Thomas, English architect, b.*c.*1683, d.1758.

Ripon, George Frederick Samuel Robinson, Marquess of, statesman, b.1827, d.1909.

Risorgimento, movement for Italian unity in 19th century.

Ritchie, Charles Thomas, Baron Ritchie, British statesman, b.1838, d.1906.

Ritschl, Albrecht, German theologian, b.1822, d.1889.

Ritson, Joseph, English antiquary (*Bibliographia Poetica,* 1802), b.1752, d.1803.

Rittenhouse, David, American astronomer, b.1732, d.1796.

Ritter, Hermann, German inventor (1876) of the viola alta, b.1849, d.1926.

Rivera, Diego, Mexican painter of murals, b.1886, d.1957.

River Plate, Battle of the, between British cruisers and the German *Graf Spee,* Dec. 1939.

Rivers, Richard Woodville, Earl, High Constable of England, executed 1469.

Rizzio, David, Italian secretary to Mary Queen of Scots, b.*c.*1533, murdered 1566.

Ro, artificial language produced 1919 by the American Foster.

Robbia, Luca della, Italian sculptor, b.*c.*1400, d.1482.

Robert I, king of France (922–923), killed in battle 923.

Robert II, king of France (996–1031), d.1031.

Robert I, king of Scotland (1306–29), b.1274, d.1329.

Robert II, king of Scotland (1371–90), b.1316, d.1390.

Robert III, king of Scotland (1390–1406), b.*c.*1340, d.1406.

Robert of Gloucester, English historian, probably lived in the 13th and 14th centuries.

Robert the Bruce, king of Scotland (1306–29), b.1274, d.1329.

Robert Gordon's College, Aberdeen, founded 1729; became Robert Gordon Institute of Technology, then The Robert Gordon University 1992.

Roberts, Frederick Sleigh, Earl, commander-in-chief India (1885–93), b.1832, d.1914.

Roberts, Richard, Welsh inventor, b.1789, d.1864.

Robertson, James, Scottish governor of New York, b.*c.*1720, d.1788.

Robertson, Sir John, Australian statesman, b.1816, d.1891.

Robertson, Thomas William, English playwright (*Caste*, 1867), b.1829, d.1871.

Robeson, Paul, American negro singer, b.1898, d.1976.

Robespierre, Maximilien Marie Isidore, French Revolutionary leader, b.1758, guillotined 1794.

Robin Hood, legendary English hero, may have lived *c.*1200, or possibly a century later.

Robinson, Edward G. (Emmanuel Goldenberg), Romanian-born American film actor (*Little Caesar*, 1930), b.1893, d.1973.

Robinson, Henry Crabb, English diarist, b.1775, d.1867.

Robinson, Mary ('Perdita'), English actress and mistress of Prince of Wales, b.1758, d.1800.

Rob Roy (Robert Macgregor), Scottish outlaw, b.1671, d.1734.

Robsart, Amy, wife of Robert Dudley, Earl of Leicester, b.*c.*1532, d.1560.

Robson, Dame Flora, English actress, b.1902, d.1984.

Rochambeau, Jean Baptiste Donatien de Vimeur, Comte de, French soldier in Washington's army, b.1725, d.1807.

Rochdale canal, constructed (opened 1804) by the Scottish civil engineer John Rennie, b.1761, d.1821.

Rochester, John Wilmot, Earl of, poet (*Poems on Several Occasions*, 1680), b.1647, d.1680.

Rock drill, invented 1871 by the American inventor Simon Ingersoll, b.1818, d.1894.

Rockall Island, Outer Hebrides, first British landing 1810; formally annexed by the Royal Navy 1955.

Rockefeller Foundation, established 1913 through the philanthropy of the American financier John Davison Rockefeller, b.1839, d.1937.

Rocker, Rudolf, German-born anarchist leader, b.1873, d.1958.

'Rocket, The', first successful high-speed locomotive, built 1829 by George Stephenson, b.1781, d.1848, and Robert Stephenson, b.1803, d.1859.

Rockingham, Charles Watson Wentworth, Marquess of, prime minister (1765–66, 1782), b.1730, d.1782.
Rocroi, Battle of, between the French and the Spaniards, 19 May 1643.
Roderick, king of Connaught and last high king of Ireland, d.1198.
Rodgers, Richard, American composer (with Oscar Hammerstein, *Oklahoma*,1943), b.1902, d.1979.
Rodin, Auguste, French sculptor (*Le Baiser,* 1898), b.1840, d.1917.
Rodney, Admiral George Brydges, b.1719, d.1792.
Rodrigues, Indian Ocean, discovered by the Portuguese 1645; formally ceded to Britain 1814.
Roebling, John Augustus, German-born civil engineer, b.1806, d.1869.
Rogation Days, the three days before Ascension Day.
Roger I, of Sicily, b.1031, d.1101.
Roger II, king of Sicily (1112–54), b.1093, d.1154.
Roger the Great, bishop of Salisbury (1102–39), d.1139.
Roger de Wendover, English historian (*Flores Historiarum*), d.1236.
Rogers, Samuel, English poet (*Italy,* 1822–28), b.1763, d.1855.
Rogers, Will, American humorist, b.1879, died in an air crash 1935.
Rogers, William, English educationalist, b.1819, d.1896.
Roget's Thesaurus, compiled 1852 by the English scholar Peter Mark Roget, b.1779, d.1869.
Roland, Chanson de, French version of the Roland epic dating from the 11th century; Roland traditionally died fighting on 15 Aug. 778.
Rolfe, Frederick ('Baron Corvo'), English novelist (*Hadrian the Seventh*, 1904), b.1860, d.1913.
Rolfe, John, English colonist in Virginia, b.1585, d.1622.
Rolland, Romain, French writer (*Jean Christophe,* 1904), b.1866, d.1944.
Rolle, Richard, English writer (*The Pricke of Conscience*), b.*c.*1290, d.1349.
Rollo, Sir William, Royalist soldier, executed 1645.
Rolvaag, Ole Edvart, Norwegian-born novelist, b.1876, d.1931.
'Romains, Jules' (Louis Farigoule), French writer (*Les Hommes du bon volonté,* 1932–46), b.1885, d.1972.
Roman era, began 21 April 753 BC.

Roman type, first used in England by the French-born printer Richard Pynson, d.1530.

Romanes Lectures, Oxford University, founded 1891 by the Canadian-born scientist George John Romanes, b.1848, d.1894.

Romania, Wallachia and Moldavia united 1856; principality 1866–81; monarchy 1881–1947; communist regime 1948–89; new constitution and multi-party democracy introduced 1991.

Romanus, pope 897.

Romanus I, Byzantine emperor (919–944), d.948.

Romanus II, Byzantine emperor (959–963), d.963.

Romanus III, Byzantine emperor (1028–34), d.1034.

Romanus IV, Byzantine emperor (1068–71), d.1071.

Romberg, Sigmund, Hungarian composer (*The Student Prince*, 1924), b.1887, d.1951.

Rome, traditional date of foundation 21 April 753 BC.

Rome, University of, founded 1244.

Romer, Carl Ferdinand von, German geologist, b.1818, d.1891.

Römer, Olaus, Danish astronomer (calculated velocity of light in 1675), b.1644, d.1710.

Romilly, Sir Samuel, English legal reformer, b.1757, committed suicide 1818.

Romney, George, English painter (*Lady Hamilton*), b.1734, d.1802.

Romulus Augustulus, Roman emperor (last in West) 475–476.

Ronald, Sir Landon, English conductor, b.1873, d.1938.

Ronsard, Pierre de, French poet (*Hymne de la France*, 1549), b.1524, d.1585.

Röntgen Rays, discovered c.1895 by the German scientist Wilhelm von Röntgen, b.1845, d.1923.

Rooftop landing, first successfully made in Paris 1913 by the French aviator Jules Vedrines, b.1881, d.1919.

Roosevelt, Mrs Eleanor, b.1884, d.1962.

Roosevelt, Franklin Delano, 32nd US president (1933–45), b.1882, d.1945.

Roosevelt, Theodore, 26th US President (1901–09), b.1858, d.1919.

Root, Elihu, American statesman, b.1845, d.1937.

Roper, Margaret, scholar and daughter of Sir Thomas More, b.1505, d.1544.

Rops, Félicien, Belgian artist (*Buveuse d'absinthe*, 1865), b.1833, d.1898.

Rorschach test, devised in 1942 by the Swiss psychiatrist Hermann Rorschach, b.1884, d.1922.

Rosa, Carl, German-born founder of the Carl Rosa Opera Company, b.1843, d.1889.

Rosa, Salvator, Italian painter (*Death of Socrates*), b.1615, d.1673.

'Rosamund, Fair' (Rosamund Clifford), mistress of King Henry II, d.*c.*1176.

Rosaniline, red dye, discovered 1858 by the German scientist August Wilhelm von Hofmann, b.1818, d.1892.

Roscius Gallus, Quintus, Roman actor, b.*c.*126, d.62 BC.

Roscoe, William, English writer (*Lorenzo de' Medici,* 1796), b.1753, d.1831.

Rose of Lima, St, first canonized saint in the New World, b.1586, d.1617.

Rosebery, Archibald Philip Primrose, Earl of, prime minister (1894–96) and Liberal leader, b.1847, d.1929.

Rosegger, Peter, Austrian writer (*Mann und Weib,* 1879), b.1843, d.1918.

Rosenberg, Isaac, English poet, b.1890, killed 1918.

Roses, Wars of the, between the houses of Lancaster and York, 1455–85.

Rosetta Stone, deciphered 1821–28 by the French Orientalist Jean François Champollion, b.1790, d.1832.

Rosh ha-Shanah (Feast of the Trumpets), the Jewish New Year, 1st day of Tishri.

Rosicrucians, occult society in 17th century, revived in 18th century and several times since.

Ross, Sir James Clark, Scottish explorer, b.1800, d.1862.

Ross, Sir John, Scottish explorer, b.1777, d.18S6.

Ross, Sir Ronald, Indian-born pioneer in the cure of malaria, b.1857, d.1932.

Rosse, William Parsons, Earl of, astronomer, b.1800, d.1867.

Rossellino, Antonio, Italian sculptor, b.1427, d.*c.*1479.

Rossetti, Christina Georgina, English poet (*Goblin Market,* 1862), b.1830 d.1894.

Rossetti, Dante Gabriel, English painter (*Dante's Dream*) and poet, b.1828, d.1882.

Rossi, Charles, English sculptor (*James Wyatt*), b.1762, d.1839.

Rossini, Gioacchino, Italian composer (*The Barber of Seville,* 1816), b.1792, d.1868.

Rostand, Edmond, French playwright (*Cyrano de Bergerac*, 1897), b.1868, d.1918.

Rosyth, Scotland, naval base, construction begun 1909.

Rotary International, founded USA 1905; Britain 1914.

Rotary printing press, invented 1846 by the American inventor Richard March Hoe, b.1812, d.1886.

Roth, Philip, American novelist (*Portnoy's Complaint,* 1969), b.1933.

Rothamsted experimental station, world's first agricultural experimental station, founded 1843 by the English agriculturist Sir John Bennet Lawes, b.1814, d.1900.

Rothenstein, Sir John, director of the Tate Gallery 1938–64, b.1901.

Rothenstein, Sir William, English painter (*T. E. Lawrence*), b.1872, d.1945.

Rotherhithe-Stepney tunnel, London, opened 12 June 1908.

Rothermere, Harold Sidney Harmsworth, Viscount, British newspaper publisher, b.1868, d.1940.

Rothschild, Meyer Amshel, German financier, b.1743, d.1812.

Rouault, Georges, French painter (*Henri Lebasçue*), b.1871, d.1958.

Roubillac, Louis François, French-born sculptor (*Handel,* 1738), b.1695, d.1762.

Rouen, Siege of, by King Henry V of England, 1418–19.

Rouen Cathedral, construction began 1206.

Rouget de l'Isle, Claude Joseph, French composer of the *Marseillaise* (1792), b.1760, d.1836.

Roundheads, nickname of Parliamentary Supporters during the English Civil War period of the mid-17th century.

Rousseau, Henri, French painter (*La Chasse au tigre*), b.1844, d.1910.

Rousseau, Jean Jacques, Swiss-born writer (*Du Contrat social,* 1762), b.1712, d.1778.

Routledge, George, English publisher, b.1812, d.1888.

Rouvray, Battle of (Battle of the Herrings), between the English and the French, 1429.

Roux, Pierre Paul Emile, French bacteriologist, b.1853, d.1933.

Rover Scouts, movement formed in Britain 1919.

Rowan, Archibald Hamilton, United Irishman, b.1751, d.1834.

Rowe, Nicholas, English writer (*Tamerlane,* 1702), b.1674, d.1718.

Rowlandson, Thomas, English artist (*Dance of Death*, 1814–16), b.1756, d.1827.

Rowley, William, English playwright (*A Woman Never Vext*, 1632), b.*c.*1585, d.*c.*1642.

Rowley Poems, '15th-century poems' written 1765 onwards by the English poet Thomas Chatterton, b.1752, committed suicide 1770.

Rowntree, Joseph, English Quaker educationist, b.1801, d.1859.

Rowton Houses, poor men's hotels in London, founded 1892 onwards by the philanthropist Baron Rowton, b.1838, d.1903.

Roxana, wife of Alexander the Great, killed 311 BC.

Roy, Rob (Robert Macgregor), Scottish rebel, b.1671, d.1734.

Royal Academy of Arts, London, founded 1768.

Royal Aeronautical Society, founded 1866 as the Aeronautical Society of Great Britain; present name since 1919.

Royal Air Force, formed 1918.

Royal Albert Hall, London, opened by Queen Victoria, 29 March 1871.

Royal and Ancient Golf Club of St Andrews, founded 1754.

Royal Astronomical Society, London, founded 1820, chartered 1831.

Royal Automobile Club, founded 1897.

Royal Canadian Mounted Police, founded as the North-West Mounted Police 1873; assumed present title 1920.

Royal College of Physicians, London, founded 1518.

Royal College of Surgeons, London, founded 1800.

Royal Dutch Petroleum Company, established at The Hague 16 June 1890.

Royal Exchange, London, founded 1566–71 by the English financier Sir Thomas Gresham, b.1519, d.1579.

Royal Flying Corps, approved by King George V as title for the aeronautical branch of the Armed Forces 1912; superseded by R.A.F. in 1918.

Royal George, The, sank at Portsmouth 1782.

Royal Hospital, Chelsea, built 1682–92 by the English architect Sir Christopher Wren, b.1632, d.1723; opened 1694.

Royal Hunt Cup, Ascot, first run 1843.

Royal Institute of International Affairs, London, founded 1920.

Royal Institution of Great Britain, London, founded 1799.

Royal London Homeopathic Hospital, founded 1849 by Dr Frederick Hervey Foster Quin, b.1799, d.1878.

Royal Marine Corps, constituted 1664 as the Duke of York and Albany's Maritime Regiment of Foot.

Royal Marriage Act, passed 1772.

Royal Military Academy, Sandhurst (combining Sandhurst and Woolwich), came into being 2 April 1946.

Royal National Theatre, established as National Theatre in 1962 with Sir Laurence Olivier as director; 'Royal' added to name in 1988.

Royal Naval Reserve, formed in Britain under the Royal Naval Reserve (Volunteers) Act of 1859.

Royal Oak, torpedoed by the Germans in World War II, 14 Oct. 1939.

Royal Observatory, Greenwich, founded 1675.

Royal Opera House, Covent Garden, London, opened 15 May 1858. Preceded by two other opera houses, both destroyed by fire

Royal Shakespeare Company, founded 1960.

Royal Society for the Prevention of Cruelty to Animals, London, founded 1824.

Royal Society of Arts, London, founded 1754.

Royal Society of British Artists, London, founded 1823.

Royal Society of London, organized 1660; constituted by Royal Charter 1662.

Royal Society of Painters in Watercolours, London, founded 1804.

Royce, Josiah, American philosopher, b.1855, d.1916.

Royden, Maude, English leader of the women's movement and preacher, b.1876, d.1956.

Ruadri, king of Connaught and last high king of Ireland, d.1198.

Ruanda-Urundi, former territory of central Africa, ceded 1919 to Belgium as a mandatory of the League of Nations; trusteeship territory by United Nations' agreement 1946; divided into the independent states of Rwanda and Burundi 1962.

Rubber, synthetic, first produced 1891 by the English chemist, Sir William Tilden, b.1842, d.1926.

Rubber, vulcanization of, patented by the English merchant Thomas Hancock, b.1786, d.1865; pioneered 1839 by the American manufacturer Charles Goodyear, b.1800, d.1860.

Rubber factory, first, built 1819 in London by the English merchant Thomas Hancock, b.1786, d.1865.

Rubber tree, first cultivated at the Royal Botanic Gardens, Kew; introduced by Sir Henry Wickham, b.1846, d.1928, into the Far East c.1885.

Rubbra, Edmund, English composer and conductor, b.1901, d.1986.

Rubens, Peter Paul, Flemish painter (*The Descent from the Cross,* 1614), b.1577, d.1640.

Rubidium, chemical element, discovered by the German scientists Bunsen, b.1791, d.1860, and Gustav Robert Kirchhoff, b.1824, d.1887.

Rubinstein, Anton, Russian pianist and composer (*Dmitri Donskoi,* 1851), b.1829, d.1894.

Rubinstein, Nikolai, Russian pianist, b.1835, d.1881.

Ruby, Jack (Jacob Rubinstein), nightclub owner and assassin of Lee Harvey Oswald (assassin of J.F. Kennedy), b.1911, d.1967.

Rude, François, French sculptor (*Jeanne d'Arc,* 1852), b.1784, d.1855.

Rudolf I, German king (1273–91), b.1218, d.1291.

Rudolf II, Holy Roman emperor (1576–1612), b.1552, d.1612.

Rueda, Lope de, Spanish playwright (*Medora*), b.*c.*1510, d.*c.*1565.

Rufinus, Tyrannius, Italian theologian, b.*c.*342, d.410.

Rugby football, started by William Webb Ellis of Rugby School 1823; legalized 1846.

Rugby league, seceded from Rugby Union 1895 as Northern Union; adopted present name 1922.

Rugby union, British, founded 1871.

Ruhmkorff, Heinrich Daniel, German physicist, b.1803, d.1877.

Rule Britannia, first published 1740; words by the Scottish poet James Thomson, b.1700, d.1748; music by the English composer Thomas Arne, b.1710, d.1778.

Rumania, *see* **Romania**.

Rumelia, Eastern, ruled by Bulgaria since 1878.

Rumford, Benjamin Thompson, Count von, American-born scientist, b.1753, d.1814.

Rump Parliament, England, 6 Dec. 1648 to 20 April 1653, and 1659.

Runcie, Robert, archbishop of Canterbury (1979–90), b.1921.

Runciman, Walter, **Baron Runciman,** British shipowner, b.1847, d.1937.

Rupert, German king (1400–10), b.1352, d.1410.

Rupert of the Rhine, Prince, b.1619, d.1682.

Rush, Benjamin, American physician and abolitionist, b.1745, d.1813.

Rush-Bagot Convention, providing for an unarmed frontier between the USA and Canada, signed 1817.

Rushdie, Salman, British author (*Midnight's Children,* 1981), persecuted by *fatwa* (order to kill) from Islamic fundamentalist leader Ayatollah Khomeni for supposedly blasphemous content of his novel *Satanic Verses* (1988), b.1947.

Rushworth, John, English surgeon and promoter of dispensaries, b.1669, d.1736.

Ruskin, John, English art critic and writer (*The Stones of Venice,* 1851–53), b.1819, d.1900.

Russell, Bertrand, English philosopher (*History of Western Philosophy*, 1946), b.1872, d.1970.

Russell, George ('AE'), Irish writer, b.1867, d.1935.

Russell, Lord John, 3rd Earl Russell, British statesman (prime minister 1846–52, 1865–66), b.1792, d.1878.

Russell, John Scott, Scottish naval architect (the *Great Eastern*), b.1808, d.1882.

Russell, William Howard, British war correspondent, b.1820, d.1907.

Russia, Mongol domination 1242–1368, Muscovite ascendancy 1328–1613; Romanov Empire 1613–1917; revolutionary period 1917–22; largest constituent of the USSR 1922–91.

Russian Navy, founded by Count Feodor Apraksin, b.1671, d.1728.

Russian Revolutions, abortive revolution, Jan.-Oct. 1905; February Revolution, 8–14 March 1917; October Revolution, 7 Nov. 1917; Civil War, 1917–22; USSR formed Dec. 1922.

Russo-Japanese War, began 1904; ended 1905.

Russo-Turkish Wars, 1696; 1768–74; 1787–91; 1806–12; 1828–29; 1853–55; 1877–78.

Rutebeuf, French troubadour, lived in the 13th century.

Rutgers University, New Jersey, USA, founded as Queen's College 1766; became Rutger's College 1825.

Ruth, 'Babe' (George Herman Ruth), American champion baseball player, b.1895, d.1948.

Ruthenium, metallic element, discovered 1845 by the German chemist Karl Ernst Claus, b.1796, d.1864.

Rutherford, Daniel, Scottish physician and discoverer (1772) of Nitrogen, b.1749, d.1819.

Rutherford, Ernest, Baron, New Zealand-born scientist, b.1871, d.1937

Rutherford, Mark (William Hale White), English writer (*The Revolution in Tanner's Lane*, 1887), b.1831, d.1913.

Rutherford, Samuel, Scottish Covenanter, b.*c.*1600, d.1661.

Ruthven, Raid of, 1582, named after one of the conspirators William Ruthven, Baron Ruthven, b.*c.*1541, beheaded 1584.

Ruwenzori, Mt, Tanzania, first climbed by the Duke of the Abruzzi 1906.

Ruysbroek, Johannes, Dutch mystical writer (*De Vera Contemplatione*), b.1293, d.1381.

Ruysdael, Jakob, Dutch painter (*Dutch Dunes*), b.1628, d.1682.

Ruyter, Michael Adriaanszoon de, Dutch admiral, b.1607, d.1676.

Rye House Plot, conspiracy of Whigs to assassinate King Charles 11, April 1683.

Rylands Library, John, Manchester, founded 1899 by his widow in memory of John Rylands, b.1801, d.1888.

Rymer, Thomas, English archaeologist and compiler (*Foedera*, 1704–35), b.1641, d.1713.

Rysbrack, John Michael, Flemish sculptor (*John Howard*), b.*c.*1693, d.1770.

Ryswick, Treaty of, ending the war between France and the Allies, signed Sept. 1697.

S

Saarland, placed under the control of the League of Nations 1919; reverted to Germany 1935; administered by France 1945–57; returned to Germany 1957–59.

Saar Offensive, World War II, 9–30 Sept. 1939.

Saarinen, Eliel, Finnish-born architect and town planner, b.1873, d.1950.

Sabata, Victor de, Italian conductor and composer (*Gethsemani,* 1925), b.1892, d.1967.

Sabatier, Louis Auguste, French theologian, b.1837, d.1901.

Sabatini, Rafael, Italian writer (*Scaramouche,* 1921), b.1875, d.1950.

Sabbath, Jewish day of rest, seventh day of week; Christian day of rest, first day of week (Lord's Day) since 4th century.

Sabinian, pope 604–607.

Saccharin, discovered 1879 by the American scientist Ira Remsen, b.1846, d.1927, and C. Fahlberg.

Sacheverell, Henry, English clergyman and pamphleteer, b.c.1674, d.1724.

Sachs, Hans, German writer of *Meisterlieder*, b.1494, d.1576.

Sackville, Charles, Earl of Dorset, English poet, b.1638, d.1706.

Sackville, Thomas, Earl of Dorset, English playwright (with Norton, *Gorboduc*, 1561), b.1536, d.1608.

Sackville-West, Victoria, English writer (*All Passion Spent,* 1931), b.1892, d.1962.

Sadat, Anwar el-, Egyptian politician (president 1970–81), b.1918, assassinated 1981.

Sade, Donatien Alphonse François, Marquis de, French writer (*Justine,* 1791), b.1740, d.1814.

Sadi, Persian poet (*Gulistan,* 1258), b.c.1184, d.1292.

Sadleir, Michael, English publisher and writer (*Fanny by Gaslight,* 1940) b.1888, d.1957.

Sadler's Wells, London theatre, opened in 1765; reconstructed 1879; closed 1916; reopened 1931.

Sadowa, Battle of (Königgrätz), between Austrians and Persians, 3 July 1866.

Safety bicycle, invented 1874 by the English inventor H. J. Lawson at Brighton.

Safety lamp, miner's, invented 1815 by the English scientist Sir Humphry Davy, b.1778, d.1829.

Safety razor, invented 1901 by the American manufacturer King Camp Gillette, b.1855, d.1932.

Sagan, Carl, American astronomer and sci-fi novelist, b.1934.

Sagan, Françoise (Françoise Quoirez), French writer (*Bonjour tristesse,* 1956), b.1935.

Sahagun, Bernardino de, Spanish missionary and historian of Mexico, b.*c.*1499, d.1590.

Sailors' Rests, founded by the English philanthropist Agnes Elizabeth Weston, b.1840, d.1918.

St Albans Abbey, England, original church built 303; construction of bbey begun 1077; abbey consecrated 1115.

St Andrews University, Scotland, founded by Bishop Wardlaw 1411.

St Andrews Cathedral, Scotland, built 1159–1318.

St Andrew's Day, 30 Nov.

St Anne's College, Oxford University, founded 1879.

St Anthony's College, Oxford University, founded 1950.

St Bartholomew, Massacre of, slaughter of Huguenots in Paris, 24 Aug.–17 Sept. 1572.

St Benet's Hall, Oxford University, founded 1947.

St Catharine's College, Cambridge University, founded by Robert Woodlark, Provost of King's College, 1473.

St Catherine's Society, Oxford University, founded 1868.

St Cyr, French military training school, founded 1686.

St David's Cathedral, Wales, constructed 1176–98.

St David's Day, 1 March.

St Dunstan's, Regent's Park, London, home for blinded soldiers and sailors founded 1915 by the English newspaper owner and philanthropist Sir Arthur Pearson, b.1866, d.1921.

Ste-Beuve, Charles Augustin, French writer and critic (*Causeries du Lundi*, 1863–70), b.1804, d.1869.

Ste-Chapelle, Paris, constructed 1245–48.

St Edmund Hall, Oxford University, reputed to have been founded 1226.

St Évremond, Charles, French soldier and poet, b.*c.*1613, d.1703.

St Exupéry, Antoine de, French writer (*Vol de nuit,* 1931) and aviator, b.1900, killed in battle 1944.

St George's Day, 23 April.

St Gaudens, Augustus, American sculptor (*Abraham Lincoln,* 1887), b.1848, d.1907.

St-Germain, Treaty of, settling with Austria, signed 10 Sept. 1919.

St Gotthard Pass, carriage road constructed 1820–30.

St Gotthard Tunnel, construction began 1872; completed 1880; railway opened 1882.

St Helena, South Atlantic, discovered by the Portuguese navigator João de Nova 1502; formally annexed by the British East India Company 1661; Crown Colony since 1834.

St Hilda's College, Oxford University, founded 1893.

St James's Gazette, the British newspaper, founded 1880, absorbed into the *Evening Standard* 1905.

St James's Palace, London, built by King Henry VIII, 1532–33.

St John, Henry, Viscount Bolingbroke, statesman, b.1678, d.1751.

St John's College, Cambridge University, founded by Lady Margaret, Countess of Richmond and Derby, 1511.

St John's College, Oxford University, founded 1555 by Alderman Sir Thomas White, b.1492, d.1567.

St Just, Louis de, French Revolutionary leader, b.1767, guillotined 1794.

St Katharine's Dock, Port of London, built by the Scottish engineer Thomas Telford, b.1757, d.1834, between 1826 and 1829.

St Kitts-Nevis, British West Indies, discovered by Christopher Columbus 1493; ceded to the British 1713; with Anguilla formed British colony 1882–1967; British Associated State 1967–83; Anguilla separated 1983; gained full independence 1983.

St Laurent, Louis Stephen, Canadian statesman (prime minister 1948–57), b.1882, d.1973.

Saint Laurent, Yves, French fashion designer, b.1936.

St Lawrence River, North America, explored 1535–36 by the French navigator Jacques Cartier, b.1491, d.1557.

St Lawrence Seaway Project, officially launched 1954; opened to deep-draught merchant shipping 25 April 1959; officially opened 26 June 1959.

St Leger, Doncaster, first run 1776.

St Lucia, British West Indies, believed to have been discovered 1502 by Christopher Columbus; ceded to Britain by France 1814; gained self-government as British Associated State 1967; full independence within the Commonwealth 1979.

St Mark's, Venice, reconstructed 1437–52 by the Italian Michelozzo, b.1396, d.1472.

St Martin-in-the-Fields, London, built 1722–26 by the Scottish architect James Gibbs, b.1682, d.1754.
St Mary Redcliffe, Bristol, built 1325–1475.
St Patrick's Cathedral, New York, constructed 1858–79.
St Patrick's Day, March 17.
St Paul's Cathedral, London, constructed 1675–1710 by Sir Christopher Wren, b.1632, d.1723.
St Peter's, Rome, constructed 1445–1626.
St Peter's Hall, Oxford University, founded 1929.
St Pierre, Charles, French writer and reformer, b.1658, d.1743.
St Pierre, Jacques Henri Bernardin de, French writer (*Paul et Virginie,* 1787), b.1737, d.1814.
St Saëns, Camille, French composer (*Samson and Delilah,* 1877), b.1835, d.1921.
Saintsbury, George, English literary historian and critic, b.1845, d.1933.
Saint-Simon, Claude Henri, Comte de, French political reformer, b.1760, d. 1825.
Saint-Simon, Louis de Rouvroy, Duc de, French writer (*Memoirs,* 1752), b.1675, d.1755.
St Swithin's Day, 15 July.
St Valentine's Day (Old Candlemas), 14 Feb.
St Valentine's Day Massacre, machine-gunnning of 'Bugs' Moran's gang members by henchmen of Al Capone in a Chicago garage, 14 Feb. 1927.
St Vincent, John Jervis, Earl of, Admiral of the Fleet, b.1735, d.1823.
St Vincent, British West Indies, believed to have been discovered by Christopher Columbus 1498; ceded to Britain by France 1783; with the Grendines, formed a British Associated State 1969–79; gained full independence 1979.
Sakharov, Andrei Dmitrievich, Soviet nuclear physicist and political dissident, 1975 Nobel peace prize, b.1921, d.1989.
Saki, *see* **Munro, Hector Hugh.**
Saladin, sultan of Egypt and soldier, b.1137, d.1193.
Salazar, Antonio de Oliveira, Portuguese dictator 1932–68, b.1889, d.1970.
Sale, George, English translator (1734) of the Koran, b.*c.*1697, d.1736.
Salicylic acid, discovered 1838 by the Italian chemist Rafaelle Piria, b.1815, d.1865.

Salinas (Serrano), Pedro, Spanish poet and literary critic (*Jorge Manrique,* 1947), b.1891, d.1951.

Salinger, Jerome David, American author (*A Catcher in the Rye,* 1951), b.1916.

Salisbury, John de Montacute, Earl of, diplomat and soldier, b.*c.*1350, beheaded 1400.

Salisbury, Robert Arthur Talbot Gascoyne-Cecil, Marquess of, British statesman (prime minister 1885–92, 1895–1902), b.1830, d.1903.

Salisbury Cathedral, England, construction began 1220; consecrated 1258.

Saliva, digestive action of, discovered by the Italian scientist Lazaro Spallanzani, b.1729, d.1799.

Salk vaccine, against poliomyelitis, developed 1954 by the American scientist Jonas Edward Salk, b.1914

Sallust, Roman historian, b.86, d.34 BC.

Salmasius, Claudius (Claude de Saumaise), French scholar, b.1588, d.1653.

Salomon, Dr Erich, German pioneer in the use of the miniature camera and in candid-camera technique, b.1886, probably killed at Auschwitz 1944.

SALT (Strategic Arms Limitation Talks), between US and USSR, Salt I signed 26 May 1972; Salt II signed 18 June 1979.

Salt, Sir Titus, English wool manufacturer, b.1803, d.1876.

Salt Lake City, Utah, USA, founded 1847.

Salten, Felix, Austrian writer (*Bambi*, 1923), b.1869, d.1945.

Salters Company, London livery company, origins uncertain; chartered by King Edward III, 1377.

Saltykov, Mikhail (Evgrafovich Shchedrin), Russian writer (*Fables,* 1885), b.1826, d.1889.

Salvador, El, colonized by Spanish 1524; became independent 1841; became a republic 1856; 12-year civil war between government and leftist rebels ended 1992.

Salvarsan, a drug curing syphilis, discovered 1908 by the German bacteriologist Paul Ehrlich, b.1854, d.1915.

Salvation Army, religious movement, founded 1865 in London by General William Booth, b.1829, d.1912.

Salvator Rosa, Italian painter (*Death of Socrates*), b.1615, d.1673.

Salyut, first orbital space station (USSR), launched April 1971.

Salzburg Festival, in honour of Mozart, founded 1877.

Samarium, metallic element, discovered 1879 by the French scientist Paul Emile Lecoq de Boisbaudran, b.1838, d.1912.

Samoa, American, discovered 1722; created neutral territory 1889; ceded to the USA 1899–1904 and 1925.
Samoa, Western, mandated to New Zealand 1919; achieved full independence 1962.
Samuel, Herbert, **1st Viscount Samuel,** British statesman, b.1870, d.1963.
Sancho I, king of Portugal (1185–1211), d.1211.
Sancho II, king of Portugal (1223–48), b.*c.*1210, d.1248.
Sanctuary, Right of, abolished in England 1623–24.
Sand, George (Armandine Dupin), French writer (*Lélia,* 1833), b.1804, d.1876.
Sandburg, Carl, American poet (*Cornhuskers,* 1918), b.1878, d.1967.
Sandby, Paul, English artist, b.1725, d.1809.
Sandhurst Royal Military College, founded 1799 by the Duke of York; occupied present site 1812.
Sandino, Augusto Cesar, Nicaraguan rebel leader (inspiration of the Sandinista rebels in the 1970s), b.1893, d.1934.
Sandow, Eugene, strong man and wrestler, b.1867, d.1925.
Sandringham House, Norfolk, British royal residence, purchased by King Edward VII, 1861; rebuilt 1871.
Sand River Convention, recognising the establishment of the independent South African Republic (The Transvaal), signed by Britain 17 Jan. 1852.
Sandwich, Edward Montagu, Earl of, admiral, b.1625, killed in battle 1672
Sandwich Islands, *see* **Hawaii.**
Sandys, Sir Edwin, organizer of the colony of Virginia, b.1561, d.1629.
Sandys, George, English poet (*Hymn to my Redeemer)* and translator, b.1578, d.1644.
San Francisco Conference, World War II, held 25 April–26 June 1945.
San Francisco Earthquake, took place 18–19 April 1906.
Sangallo, Antonio di, Italian architect, b.*c.*1485, d.1546.
Sanger, Frederick, British biochemist, awarded Nobel prize for chemistry 1958 and 1977, b.1918.
Sanger, 'Lord' George, English circus manager, b.1825, murdered 1911.
Sanger, John, English circus manager, b.1816, d.1889.
Sankey, Ira David, American hymn-writer, b.1840, d.1908.

San Marino, world's smallest republic; founded 9th to 10th centuries; independence recognized by the Papacy 1631; under Italian protection since 1860.

San Martin, José de, South American liberator, b.1778, d.1850.

San Nicandro, Italy, place of Judaic sect, led by Donato Manduzio, b.1885, converted 1930, d.1948.

San Quentin, California, state prison opened 1852.

Sansovino, Jacopo, Italian sculptor and architect, b.1486, d.1570.

Santa Anna, Antonio López de, Mexican statesman and soldier, b.1795, d.1876.

Santa Claus (St Nicholas), bishop of Myra in Lycia, *fl.* 11th century

Santa Fe Trail, USA-Mexican trading route, mainly used 1822 to 1861.

Santa Sophia, Istanbul, built 532–537 on the site of two previous churches; converted into a mosque 1453.

Santayana, George, Spanish-born philosopher and writer, b.1863, d.1952.

Santillana, Iñigo Lopez de Mendoza, Marquis of, Spanish poet (*Comedieta de Ponza*), b.1398, d.1458.

Santos-Dumont, Alberto, Brazil-born pioneer aviator, b.1873, d.1932.

São Paulo, Brazil, founded by the Portuguese 1554.

São Tomé, Portuguese colony from 1521; gained independence 1974.

Sappho, Greek poetess, lived in the 6th century BC.

Sarajevo, capital of Bosnia-Herzegavina; scene of the murder of the Archduke Franz Ferdinand 28 June 1914; 1991–93 besieged by Serbian forces after disintegration of the former Yugoslavia.

Sarasate, Pablo de, Spanish violinist, b 1844, d.1908.

Saratoga, Battle of, between the Americans and the British, 17 Oct. 1777.

Sardinia, ruled by Spain 1592–1713; ruled by Savoy from 1720; became part of Italy 1861.

Sardou, Victorien, French playwright (*Madame Sans Gene,* 1893), b.1831, d.1908.

Sargent, John, Italian-born painter of American descent (*Suggia*), b.1856, d.1925.

Sargent, Sir Malcolm, English conductor, b.1895, d.1967.

Sargon I, king of Babylonia, lived in the 39th century BC.

Sargon II, king of Assyria (722–705 BC), murdered 705 BC.

Sarmiento, Domingo Faustino, president of Argentina (1868–74), b.1811, d.1888.

Saroyan, William, American writer (*The Daring Young Man on the Flying Trapeze,* 1934), b.1908, d.1981.

Sarto, Andrea del, Italian painter (*Birth of the Virgin,* 1514), b.1486, d.1531.

Sartre, Jean Paul, French writer (*Les Mains Sales,* 1948), b.1905, d.1980.

Saskatchewan, Canada, created a separate province 1905.

Sassanids, ruled Persia 226–651.

Sassoon, Siegfried, English writer (*Memoirs of a Fox-hunting Man,* 1928), b.1886, d.1967.

Satellite, first American (Explorer I), successfully launched from Cape Canaveral, Florida, 31 Jan. 1958; first Russian (Sputnik I), successfully launched 4 Oct. 1957; second Russian, 3 Nov. 1957.

Satie, Erik, French composer (*Gymnopédies,* 1888), b.1866, d.1925.

Saturn, rings described 1655 by the Dutch astronomer Christiaan Huygens, b.1629, d.1695.

Saud, Ibn, king of Saudi Arabia (1926–53), b.c.1880, d.1953.

Saudi Arabia, formally proclaimed a kingdom 1932.

Saumarez, James Saumarez, Baron de, British admiral, b.1757, d.1836.

Saussure, Horace Benedict de, Swiss physicist and Alpinist, b.1740, d.1799.

Savage, Edward, American artist (*The Washington Family*), b.1761, d.1817.

Savage, Richard, English poet (*The Wanderer,* 1729), b.c.1697, d.1743.

***Savannah*,** first steam-propelled ship, crossed the Atlantic 1819.

Savak, Persian secret police under the shah, disbanded 1977.

Savary, Anne Jean Marie René, Duke of Rovigo, French general and diplomat, b.1774, d.1833.

Savery, Thomas, English military engineer and inventor, b.c.1650, d.1715.

Savigny, Friedrich Karl von, German jurist (*Das Recht des Besitzes,* 1803), b.1779, d.1861.

Savile, Sir Henry, English classical scholar and philanthropist, b.1549, d.1622.

Savings bank, first examples established by Priscilla Wakefield at Rotherham 1804, and by Henry Duncan at Ruthwell, Scotland, 1810.

Savoy, elected by plebiscite to be annexed to France 1860; dukes of Savoy ruled Sardinia from 1720 and Italy from 1860–1946.

Savonarola, Girolamo, Italian reformer, b.1452, excommunicated 1497, executed 1498.

Saxaphone, invented 1846 by the Belgian musical instrument-maker Adolphe Sax, b.1814, d.1894.

Saxe, Maurice, Comte, marshal of France, b.1696, d.1750.

Saxhorn, invented 1843–45 by the Belgian musical instrument-maker Adolphe Sax, b.1814, d.1894.

Saxo-Grammaticus, Danish historian, b.*c.*1150, d.*c.*1205.

Saxton, Christopher, English map designer, lived in the late 16th century.

Sayers, Tom, English pugilist, b.1826, d.1865.

Scaliger, Joseph Justus, French scholar and critic, b.1540, d.1600.

Scaliger, Julius Caesar, Italian-born philosopher and scientist, b.1484, d.1558.

Scapa Flow, Scotland, scene of the scuttling of the German battleships, 23 June 1919.

Scarlatti, Alessandro, Italian composer, b.1659, d.1725.

Scarlatti, Domenico, Italian composer, b.1685, d.1757.

Scarron, Paul, French writer (and husband of Mme de Maintenon), b.1610, d.1660.

Schacht, Hjalmar, German statesman and banker, b.1877, d.1970.

Schadow, Johann Gottfried, German sculptor (*Frederick the Great*), b.1764, d.1850.

Scharnhorst, German battleship, sunk by the British Navy off North Cape 26 Dec. 1943.

Scharnhorst, Gerhard Johann David von, German general, b.1755, d.1813.

Scharwenka, Xaver, German composer (*Meisterschule des Klavierspiels*), b.1850, d.1924.

Scheele, Carl Wilhelm, Swedish chemist, b.1742, d.1786.

Scheer, Admiral Reinhard, German naval chief, b.1863, d.1928.

Scheffer, Ary, Dutch-born painter (*Mignon,* 1836), b.1795, d.1858.

Schelling, Friedrich Wilhelm Joseph von, German philosopher, b.1775, d.1854.

Scherer, Wilhelm, German historian of language and literature, b.1841, d.1886.

Schiaparelli, Giovanni, Italian astronomer, b.1835, d.1910.

Schick test, for immunity from diphtheria, discovered 1913 by the Hungarian-born scientist Bela Schick, b.1877, d.1967.
Schiele, Egon, Austrian expressionist painter, b.1890, d.1918.
Schiller, Friedrich von, German writer (*Die Räuber,* 1782), b.1759, d.1805.
Schirmer, Gustav, German-born music publisher, b.1829, d.1893.
Schism, Great, between Western and Eastern Churches, complete 1054.
Schism, Papal, 1378–1417.
Schism of Photius, from which arose *c.*880 the Eastern Orthodox Church, occasioned by the actions of the Patriarch Photius, b.*c.*820, d*c.*891.
Schlegel, August, German critic and writer, b.1767, d.1829.
Schlegel, Friedrich, German poet, b.1772, d.1829.
Schleswig-Holstein, N.W. German state, under Danish rule 1460–1864, under Prussian rule from 1864.
Schlieffen, Alfred, Graf von, German soldier and strategist, b.1833, d.1913.
Schliemann, Heinrich, German excavator of Troy, b.1822, d.1890.
Schmidt, Helmut, German politician (chancellor of West Germany 1974–82), b.1918.
Schnabel, Artur, Austrian-born pianist, b.1882, d.1951.
Schnitger, Arp, German organ-builder, b.1648, d.1720.
Schnitzer, Eduard (Emin Pasha), German-born doctor and administrator in Turkey, Egypt and Central Africa, b.1840, d.1892.
Schnitzler, Arthur, Austrian writer (*Professor Bernhardi,* 1912), b.1862, d.1931.
Scholes, Percy, English musicologist, b.1877, d.1958.
Schoenberg, Arnold, Viennese-born composer, b.1874, d.1951.
Schomberg, Frederick Herman Schomberg, Duke of, German-born C.-in-C. of British forces in Ireland (1689–90), b.1615, killed in battle 1690.
Schomburgk, Richard, German-born botanist in Australia, b.1811, d.1890.
Schönberg, Arnold, Austrian-born composer (*Pierrot Lunaire,* 1912), b.1874, d.1951.
Schopenhauer, Arthur, German philosopher (*The World as Will and Idea*, 1819), b.1788, d.1860.
Schott, Bernhard, German music publisher, d.1817.

Schreiner, Olive, South African writer (*Story of an African Farm*, 1883), b.1859, d.1922.

Schrödringer, Erwin, Austrian-born scientist, b.1887, awarded the Nobel prize for physics 1933, d.1961.

Schubert, Franz, German composer (*Erlkönig*, 1815), b.1797, d.1828.

Schumann, Clara (*née* Wieck), German pianist, b.1819, d.1896.

Schumann, Elizabeth, German-born operatic singer, b.1891, d.1952.

Schumann, Robert, German composer (*Carnaval*, 1834–35), b.1810, d.1856.

Schuyler, General Philip John, American Revolutionary leader, b.1733 d.1804.

Schwann, Theodor, German physiologist, b.1810, d.1882.

Schwarzenburg, Felix, Austrian statesman, b.1800, d.1852.

Schweitzer, Dr Albert, Alsatian musician, theologian and medical missionary, b.1875, d.1965.

Sciascia, Leonardo, Italian novelist (*Salt in the Wound*, 1956), b.1921, d.1989.

Scientist, term first introduced 1840 by the Master of Trinity College, Cambridge, William Whewell.

Scientology, Church of, quasi-religious movement founded 1952 by L. Ron Hubbard.

'Scinde Dawk', first Indian postage stamp, issued 1 July 1852.

Scipio Africanus, Roman general, b.c.236, d.183 BC.

Scipio Africanus, the younger, Roman general, b.185, d.129 BC.

Scipio, Quintus Caecilius Metellus Pius, Roman consul and colonial administrator, committed suicide 46 BC.

Scopas, Greek sculptor, lived in the 4th century BC.

Scopes trial, of local teacher accused of teaching Darwinian theories in Dayton, Tennessee, held 1925.

Scoresby, William, English navigator in Arctic regions, b.1760, d.1829.

Scorsese, Martin, American film director (*Taxi Driver*, 1976), b.1942.

Scot, Michael, Scottish astronomer and alchemist, b.c.1175, d.c.1234.

Scotland, crown united with that of England 1603; kingdoms united 1707.

Scotland Yard, New, designed 1891 by the Scottish architect Richard Norman Shaw, b.1831, d.1912.

Scott, Charles Prestwich, English editor (of *Manchester Guardian,* 1872–1929) and politician, b.1846, d.1932.
Scott, Cyril, English composer (*Oboe Concerto,* 1948), b.1879, d.1970.
Scott, Robert Falcon, Antarctic explorer, b.1868, d.1912.
Scott, Sir Peter Markham, British naturalist, writer and TV wildlife presenter, b.1909, d.1989.
Scott, Sir Walter, Scottish poet and novelist (*Waverley,* 1814), b.1771, d.1832.
Scottish Labour Party, founded 1888 by the Scottish socialist Keir Hardie, b.1856, d.1915.
Scotus, Duns, Scottish philosopher, b.*c.*1266, d.1308.
Screw propeller, invented 1836 by the English inventor Sir Francis Pettit Smith, b.1808, d.1874.
Screw threads, standardized 1841 by the English mechanical engineer Sir Joseph Whitworth, b.1803, d.1887.
Scriabin, Alexander Nikolaievich, Russian composer (*Poème Satanique*), b.1872, d.1915.
Scribe, Eugène, French playwright (*Valérie,* 1822), b.1791, d.1861.
Scribner, Charles, American publisher, b.1821, d.1871.
Scripps, Edward Wyllis, American newspaper publisher, b.1854, d.1926.
Scroggs, Sir William, Lord Chief Justice of England, b.*c.*1623, d.1683.
Scrope, Richard le, archbishop of York (1398–1405), b.*c.*1350, executed 1405.
Scudéry, Madeleine de, French writer (*Clélie,* 1654–61), b.1607, d.1701.
Scurvy, fruit juice first used against, in 1601 by Sir James Lancaster, d.1620.
Scuttling, of German Grand Fleet 21 June 1919; of *Graf Spee,* 17 Dec. 1939.
Seaplane, first invented 1911 by the American aviation pioneer and inventor Glenn Hammond Curtiss, b.1878, d.1930.
Searchlights, pioneer model invented 1763 by the Liverpool dock-master William Hutchison, b.1715, d.1801.
Sea Scouts, movement started in Britain 1908.
Sea Serpent, sighted in the South Atlantic by the crew of H.M. corvette *Daedalus* 1848.
Seaton, Edward Cator, English promoter of vaccination, b.1815, d.1880.

Seaweed propagation, method discovered 1886 by the French botanists Edouard Bornet, b.1828, d.1911, and Gustave Adolphe Thuret, b.1817, d.1875.

Sebastian, king of Portugal (1557–78), b.1554, killed in battle 1578.

Sebastiano del Piombo, Italian painter (*Raising of Lazarus*), b.*c.*1485, d.1547.

Secularism, founded 1846 by the English co-operator George Jacob Holyoake, b.1817, d.1906.

Sedan, Battle of, between the Germans and the French, 1 Sep. 1870; German break-through at, May 1940.

Seddon, Frederick Henry, English murderer, b.1870, hanged 1912.

Sedgemoor, Battle of, between King James II and the Duke of Monmouth 6 July 1685.

Sedgwick, Rev. Adam, English geologist, b.1785, d.1873.

Sedgwick, Robert, major-general of Massachusetts forces, d.1656.

Sedley, Sir Charles, English writer (*Bellamira,* 1687), b.*c.*1639, d.1701.

Seed drill, invented 1731 by the English agricultural writer Jethro Tull, b.1674, d.1741.

Seed Testing, scientific method originated 1869 by the German plant physiologist Friedrich Nobbe, b.1830, d.1922.

Seeley, Sir John Robert, English writer (*Ecce Homo,* 1865), b.1834, d.1895.

Segovia, Andrès, Spanish guitarist, b.1893, d.1987.

Seiber, Mátyás, composer (*Ulysses,* 1949), b.1905, d.1960.

Seguier, William, English artist and first Keeper of the National Gallery, b.1771, d.1843.

Seismograph, earth tremor reader, invented by the Chinese Chang Heng 132.

Sejanus, Lucius Aelius, Roman prefect, murdered 31.

Selborne, Roundell Palmer, Earl of, Lord Chancellor, b.1812, d.1895.

Selby, William, English-born organist and composer, b.1738, d.1798.

Selden, John, English jurist (*Table Talk,* 1689), b.1584, d.1654.

Selenium, discovered 1817 by the Swedish chemist Baron Berzelius, b.1779, d.1848.

Selenous acid, first obtained 1827 by the German chemist Eilhard Mitscherlich, b.1794, d.1863.

Seleucid dynasty, ruled Syria 312–64 BC.
Seleucid era, began 1 Sept. 311 BC.
Seleucus I, Middle Eastern ruler, b.c.356, assassinated 281 BC.
Seleucus II, Middle Eastern ruler (246–227 BC), d.227 BC.
Seleucus III, Middle Eastern ruler (227–223 BC), assassinated 223 BC.
Seleucus IV, Middle Eastern ruler (187–176 BC), assassinated 176 BC.
Seleucus V, Middle Eastern ruler (126 BC), assassinated 126 BC.
Seleucus VI, Middle Eastern ruler (9695 BC), assassinated 95 BC.
Self-starter, for cars, developed 1911 by the inventor Charles Franklin Kettering, b.1876, d.1958.
Selfridge's, Oxford Street department store, London, opened 15 March 1909. Founded by the American merchant Gordon Selfridge, b.1858, d.1947.
Selim I, sultan of Turkey (1512–21), b.1465, d.1521.
Selim II, sultan of Turkey (1566–74), b.1524, d.1574.
Selim III, sultan of Turkey (1789–1808), b.1762, strangled 1808.
Seljuk *or* **Jalalian era**, began 15 March 1079.
Selkirk, Alexander, the real 'Robinson Crusoe', b.1676, d.1721.
Sellers, Peter, British comedy actor and entertainer (*The Ladykillers,* 1955), b.1925, d.1980.
Selous, Frederick Courteney, English explorer, b.1851, killed 1917.
Selwyn, George Augustus, first bishop of New Zealand (1842–67), b.1809, d.1878.
Selwyn College, Cambridge University, founded in memory of Bishop George Augustus Selwyn 1882.
Semaphore signalling, pioneered 1666 by Lord Worcester; developed 1792 by Claude Chappé and 1796 by Lord George Murray; perfected 1803 by Admiral Home Riggs Popham.
Semmelweiss, Ignatz Philipp, Hungarian discoverer of antisepsis, b.1816, d.1865.
Semmering Pass, the Alps, railway constructed 1848–54.
Sempill, Robert, Scottish poet (*Life and Death of Habbie Simpson,* 1640), b.c.1595, d.c.1665.
Senancour, Étienne Pivert de, French writer (*Obermann,* 1804), b.1770, d.1846.
Seneca, Roman orator, b.c.54 BC, d. AD 39.
Seneca, Roman philosopher, b.c.4 BC, committed suicide AD 65.
Senefelder, Alois, German inventor 1798 of lithography, b.1771, d.1834.

Senior, Nassau William, English economist, b.1790, d.1864.
Senlac, Battle of (Battle of Hastings), between the Normans and the English Oct. 1066.
Sennacherib, king of Assyria (705–681 BC), murdered 681 BC.
Sensory and motor nerves, distinguished 1807 by Sir Charles Bell, b.1774, d.1842.
Septuagint, Greek version of the Old Testament believed to have been made 270 BC.
Sequoyah, American Indian leader of the Cherokee nation, b.*c.*1770, d.1843.
Serapeum, ruins of, discovered 1850 by the French Egyptologist Auguste Ferdinand François Mariette, b.1821, d.1881.
Serbia, ruled by Turks 1459–1829; occupied by Austrians 1915–18; republic of the former Yugoslavia 1918–91.
Serfs, emancipated in Prussia 1807; liberated from Imperial Russian domination 1861.
Sergius I, St, pope 687–701.
Sergius II, pope 844–847.
Sergius III, pope 904–911.
Sergius IV, pope 1009–12.
Sertorius, Quintus, Roman general and administrator in Spain, assassinated 72 BC.
Servetus, Michael (Miguel Serveto), Spanish theologian, b.1511, burnt at the stake 1553.
Service, Robert William, English-born writer (*Songs of a Sourdough,* 1907), b.1876, d.1958.
Servile Wars, Sicily 103–101 BC; Italy 73–71 BC.
Sesostris I, king of Egypt (1980–1933 BC), d.1933 BC.
Sesostris II, king of Egypt (1906–1887 BC), d.1887 BC.
Sesostris III, king of Egypt (1887–1849 BC), d.1849 BC.
Sesshu, Toyo, Japanese painter, b.1421, d.1507.
Sessions, Roger, American composer (*Montezuma,* 1947), b.1896, d.1985.
Seti I, king of Egypt (1313–1292 BC), d.1292 BC.
Seti II, king of Egypt (1209–05 BC), d.1205 BC.
Settle, Elkanah, English poet and playwright (*The Empress of Morocco,* 1671), b.1648, d.1724.
Seurat, Georges, French pointilliste painter (*Une Baignade,* 1884), b.1859, d.1891.
Seven Days' Battles, near Richmond, Virginia, American Civil War, 26 June to 2 July 1862.
Seven Sleepers of Ephesus, allegedly slept from 247 to 447.

Seven Weeks' War, between Prussia and Austria (and her allies), 1866.

Seven Years' War, between Prussia (and England) and the Allies, 1756–63.

Seventeen year locust, a cicada whose development from egg to adult needs 17 years.

Sévérac, Déodat de, French composer (*Le Parc aux cerfs*), b.1873, d.1921.

Severinus, pope 640.

Severn, Joseph, English painter (*Spectre Ship*), b.1793, d.1879.

Severn tunnel, England, construction begun 1873; completed 1886.

Severus, Roman emperor (193–211), b.146, died in Britain 211.

Severus, Roman emperor (306–307), d.307.

Sévigné, Marquise de, French writer (*Lettres*), b.1626, d.1696.

Seward, Anna ('The Swan of Litchfield'), English poet and letter-writer, b.1747, d.1809.

Sewell, Anna, English writer (*Black Beauty,* 1877), b.1820, d.1878.

Sewing machine, models patented by Charles Weisenthal 1755, and Thomas Saint 1790; Thimonnier produced a machine 1830; models patented by Newton and Archbold 1841; Singer used Howe's needle for his model 1850.

Sextant, invented 1731 by the Englishman John Hadley, b.1682, d.1744.

Seychelles, Indian Ocean, probably discovered by the Portuguese *c.*1500; annexed by France 1744; ceded to Britain 1814; became an independent republic within the Commonwealth 1976.

Seymour, Edward, Earl of Hertford and Duke of Somerset (The Protector), b.*c.*1506, beheaded 1552.

Seymour of Sudeley, Thomas Seymour, Baron, Lord High Admiral, b.*c.*1508, executed 1549.

Sforza, Francesco, Duke of Milan, b.1401, d.1466.

Shackleton, Sir Ernest, Antarctic explorer, b.1874, d.1922.

Shadwell, Thomas, English writer (*Bury Fair,* 1689), b.*c.*1642, d.1692.

Shaftesbury, Anthony Ashley Cooper, 1st Earl of, English politician, b.1621, d.1683.

Shaftesbury, Anthony Ashley Cooper, 3rd Earl of, English philosopher, b.1671, d.1713.

Shaftesbury, Antony Ashley Cooper, 7th Earl of, English philanthropist, b.1801, d.1885.

Shah Jehan, Mogul emperor of Delhi (1627–58), and builder of the Taj Mahal, d.1666.

Shakers, Society of, religious movement, seceded from Quakers 1747 under James and Jane Wardley; first settlement in America founded 1776 by Ann Lee, b.1736, d.1784.

Shakespeare, William, English dramatist, b.1564, d.1616.

Shakespeare Memorial Theatre, new building opened at Stratford-on-Avon 23 April 1932.

Shang Yin dynasty, China, 1766 to 1122 BC.

Sharp, Cecil James, English collector of English folk songs and dances, b.1859, d.1924.

Sharp, Granville, English anti-slavery pioneer, b.1735, d.1813.

Sharp, William ('Fiona Macleod') Scottish novelist (*The Immortal Hour*, 1900), b.1855, d.1905.

Sharpeville Massacre, shooting by South African police of anti-apartheid marchers protesting against Pass Laws, 70 killed, 190 injured, 21 March 1960.

Shaw, George Bernard, Irish-born playwright (*Man and Superman*, 1903), b.1856, d.1950.

Shaw, Martin, English composer (*Mr Pepys,* 1926), b.1876, d.1958.

Shaw, Richard Norman, Scottish architect, b.1831, d.1912.

Shearer, Moira, Scottish ballerina, b.1926.

Shee, Sir Martin Archer, Irish painter (*Prospero and Miranda*), b.1770, d.1850.

Shee, Sir William, first British Roman Catholic judge since the Revolution, b.1804, d.1868.

Sheffield University, founded 1879 as Firth College by the English manufacturer Mark Firth, b.1819, d.1880; constituted a university college 1897; achieved university status 1905.

Sheldonian Theatre, Oxford, built 1669 by the archbishop of Canterbury, Gilbert Sheldon, b.1598, d.1677.

Shelley, Mary Wollstonecraft, English writer (*Frankenstein,* 1818), b.1797, d.1851.

Shelley, Percy Bysshe, English poet (*Queen Mab,* 1813), b.1792, drowned at sea 1822.

Shenstone, William, English poet (*The Schoolmistress,* 1742), b.1714, d.1763.

Sheppard, Jack, English highwayman, b.1702, hanged 1724.

Sheratone, Thomas, English cabinetmaker, b.1751, d.1806.

Sheridan, Richard Brinsley, Irish playwright (*School for Scandal,* 1776), b.1751, d.1816.

Sherman, General William Tecumseh, American general (march to the sea, Nov.–Dec. 1864), b.1820, d.1891.

Sherriff, Robert Cedric, English-born dramatist (*Journey's End,* 1928), b.1896, d.1975.

Sherrington, Sir Charles, British physiologist, b.1859, d.1952.

Sherwood, Robert Emmet, American playwright (*The Petrified Forest*), b.1896, d.1955.

Shi'a, Islamic religious movement, founded *c.*658.

Shiloh, Battle of, American Civil War, 6–7th April 1862.

Shinwell, Lord Emanuel ('Manny'), British Labour politician, b.1884, d.1986.

Ship, first gas-turbine propelled (HMS *Grey Goose*), fitted with two Rolls-Royce RM 60 engines 1955; first guided-missile (HMS *Girdle Ness*), commissioned 1956; first ocean-going iron (*The Great Britain*), built 1843 by the British engineer Isambard Brunel, b.1806, d.1859; first steam-propelled (*Savannah*), crossed the Atlantic 1819; first turbine-propelled (*Turbinia*), invented 1897 by the British engineer, Sir Charles Parsons, b.1854, d.1931.

Ship Money, first levied in England 1007. Also levied, without parliament's consent, by King Charles I, 1634–36.

Shipton, Mother, English witch and prophet, reputed to have been born *c.*1487 as Ursula Southill, and to have died 1561.

Shirley, Sir Anthony, English adventurer, b.1565, d.*c.*1635.

Shirley, James, English playwright (*The Traitor,* 1631), b.1596, d.1666.

Sholem Aleichem, *see* **Aleichem, Sholem**.

Shore, Jane, mistress of King Edward IV, d.*c.*1527.

Shorthand, first, with signs, invented 1588 by the Englishman Dr Timothy Bright, b.1551, d.1615.

Shorthouse, Joseph Henry, English novelist (*John Inglesant,* 1881), b.1834, d.1903.

Shostakovich, Dmitri, Russian composer (*Lady Macbeth of Mzensk* 1934), b.1906, d.1975.

Shrewsbury, Treaty of, recognising Llewelyn II's overlordship of Wales, signed 1265.

Shrove Tuesday, first day of Lent, and the day before Ash Wednesday.

Shute, Nevil (Nevil Shute Norway), novelist (*A Town Like Alice,* 1949), b.1899, d.1960.

SI units (Système International d'Unités), accepted standard of scientific units (metre (m), kilogram (kg), second (s), ampere (A), kelvin (K), mole (mol) and candela (cd)), first proposed 1960.

Siam, *see* **Thailand.**

Sibelius, Jean, Finnish composer (*Finlandia,* 1899), b.1865, d.1957.

Siberch, John, of Siegburg, set up the first printing press in Cambridge 1521.

Sicilian Vespers, massacre of French residents in Sicily, 31 March 1282.

Sicily, autonomous region of Italy, conquered by Arabs in 8th century, by Normans in 11th century; ruled by Aragonese 1301–1713, by Bourbons 1735–1860.

Sickert, Walter Richard, German-born painter (*Victor Lecour,* 1922), b.1860, d.1942.

Siddons, Mrs Sarah, English actress, b.1755, d.1831.

Sidgwick, Henry, English philosopher and champion of women's rights, b.1838, d.1900.

Sidmouth, Henry Addington, Viscount, statesman, b.1757, d.1844.

Sidney, Algernon, English democrat, b.1622, executed 1683.

Sidney, Sir Philip, English writer (*Defence of Poesie,* 1591) and soldier, b.1554, killed 1586.

Sidney Sussex College, Cambridge University, founded under the will of the Lady Frances Sidney, Countess Dowager of Sussex, 1596.

Siebold, Philipp Franz von, German ethnographer and naturalist (particularly with regard to Japan), b.1796, d.1866.

Siegen, Ludwig von, Dutch-born engraver and inventor (1642) of the mezzotint process, b.c.1609, d.1680.

Siemens, Ernst Werner von, German electrical engineer, b.1816, d.1892.

Siemens, Sir William, German-born electrical engineer, b.1823, d.1883.

Siena, University of, founded 1247.

Sienkiewicz, Henryk, Polish novelist (*Quo Vadis?* 1896), b.1846, d.1916.

Sierra Leone, earliest English settlement 1787; British colony 1808–1960; gained independence within the Commonwealth 1961; declared a republic 1971.

Sièyes, Emmanuel Joseph, French statesman, b.1748, d.1836.

Sigebert, king of the Franks, assassinated 575.

Sigismund, Holy Roman emperor (1433–37), b.1368, d.1437.
Sigismund I, king of Poland (1506-1548), b.1467, d.1548.
Sigismund II, king of Poland (1548–72), b.1520, d.1572.
Sigismund III, king of Poland (1587–1632), b.1566, d.1632.
Sign language, for deaf and dumb people, developed 1765 by the French priest Charles Michel, Abbé de l'Epée, b.1712, d.1789.
Signac, Paul, French painter (*Le Pont des Arts,* 1914), b.1863, d.1935.
Signorelli, Luca, Italian painter (*Eternal Destiny of Man*), b.*c.*1442, d.1523.
Sigurdsson, Jón, Icelandic statesman, b.1811, d.1879.
Sihanouk, Prince Norodom, Cambodian politician (king 1941–55, prime minister and head of state 1960–70), b.1922.
Sikh religion, founded by the Indian religious leader Nanak, b.1459, d.1538.
Sikh Wars, India, between the British and the Sikhs, 1845–46, 1848–49.
Sikkim, under British control 1861–1947; became Indian protectorate1950, and state in 1975.
Sikorsky, Igor Ivan, Russian-born inventor of the helicopter, b.1889, d.1972.
Silesia, a Bohemian fief 1335–1740; Prussian 1740–1871; German 1871–1945; Polish since 1945.
Silesian Wars, between Prussia and Austria, 1740–42, 1744–45 and 1756–62.
Silicones, study developed 1899–1941 by the English chemist Frederick S. Kipping, b.1863, d.1949; practical applications discovered 1941 by J. F. Hyde.
Silk, traditionally invented 2640 BC; silkworms brought to Constantinople *c.*AD 550; first silk mill in USA established 1839.
Silk, artificial, made 1883 by the English chemist Sir Joseph Wilson Swan, b.1828, d.1914. Industry founded *c.*1885 by the French scientist Hilaire, Comte de Chardonnet, b.1839, d.1924.
Silurian Period, Earth history, 350 million years ago.
'Silurist, The' (Henry Vaughan), poet, b.1622, d.1695.
Silverius, St, pope 536–537.
Silvester I, St, pope 314–336.
Silvester II (Gerbert), pope 999–1003.
Silvester III, pope 1045.
Silvester IV, anti-pope 1105.
Silvestrians, monastic order founded by St Silvester, d.1267.

Simenon, Georges, Belgian novelist, creator of 'Inspector Maigret', b.1903, d.1989.

Simeon I, tsar of Bulgaria, reigned 893–927.

Simeon Stylites, St, b.387, d.459.

Simhath Torah (Rejoicing of the Law), Jewish holiday, 23rd day of Tishri.

Simnel, Lambert, pretender, b.*c.*1475, died after 1525.

Simon, Sir John, British public health pioneer, b.1816, d.1904.

Simon, John, Viscount, British lawyer and statesman, b.1873, d.1954.

Simon de Montfort, English baronial leader, b.*c.*1208, killed in battle 1265.

Simplicius, pope 468–483.

Simplon Pass, over the Alps, built 1800–07; tunnel built 1898–1906.

Simpson, Maxwell, British chemist, b.1815, d.1902.

Simson, William, Scottish painter (*Solway Moss-Sunset,* 1831), b.1800, d.1847.

Sinatra, Frank (Francis Albert), American popular singer and film actor, b.1915.

Sinclair, Upton, American novelist (*Boston,* 1928), b.1878, d.1968.

Sind War, between British and Baluchi forces, March 1843.

Sinding, Christian, Norwegian composer (*Rustle of Spring*), b.1856, d.1941.

Singapore, founded 1819 by the British administrator Sir Stamford Raffles, b.1781, d.1826, held by Japanese 1942–1945; independent state within the Commonwealth since 1959; part of the Federation of Malaysia from 1963; became independent republic 1965.

Singer, Isaac Bashevis, Yiddish writer (*Shosha,* 1978), 1978 Nobel prize for literature, b.1904.

Sinigaglia, Leone, Italian composer (*Danze Piemontese*), b.1868, d.1944.

Sinn Fein, political party, founded 1905 by the Irish patriot Arthur Griffith, b.1872, d.1922.

Siphon, principle discovered 1577 by the Scottish mathematician William Welwood, died after 1622.

Sirisius, St, pope 384–399.

Sisinnius, pope 708.

Sisley, Alfred, French painter (*Le Canal du Loing*), b.1839, d.1899.

Sismondi, Jean Charles Leonard de, Swiss-born economist and historian, b.1773, d.1842.
Sitting Bull, American Indian chief, b.*c.*1837, killed 1890.
Sitwell, Dame Edith, English writer (*Bath,* 1932), b.1887, d.1964.
Sitwell, Sir Osbert, English writer (*Miracle on Sinai,* 1933), b.1892, d.1969.
Sitwell, Sacheverell, English writer (*Southern Baroque Art,* 1924), b.1897, d.1988.
Siward the Strong, earl of Northumberland, d.1055.
Six Day War, between Israel and Arab coalition, ended 10 June 1967.
Six-shooter, automatic, invented 1836 by the American inventor Samuel Colt, b.1814, d.1862.
Sixtus I, St, pope 115–125.
Sixtus II, St, pope 257–258, martyred 258.
Sixtus III, St, pope 432–440.
Sixtus IV (Francesco della Rovere), pope 1471–84, b.1414, d.1484.
Sixtus V (Felice Peretti), pope 1585–90, b.1521, d.1590.
Skanderbeg (Iskander Bey or George Castriota), Albanian leader, b.*c.*1403, d.1468.
Skeat, Walter William, English philologist, b.1835, d.1912.
Skelton, John, English poet (*Phyllyp Sparowe,* 1542–46), b.*c.*1460, d.1529.
Skinners Company, London livery company, founded in the 12th century; first charter granted by King Edward III, 1327.
Skyscraper, first, erected in Chicago 1884–85; designed by the American architect William Le Baron Jenney, b.1832, d.1907.
Skywriting, in England, first done 1922 over Epsom Downs by the British aviator J. C. Savage.
Slater, Oscar, German-born victim of wrongful imprisonment (1909–28) for murder, b.*c.*1872, d.1948.
Slave trade, British, abolished 1805–07.
Slavery, declared illegal in Britain 1772; abolished in British possessions 1834; in French possessions 1848; in the USA 1863.
Slaves, first negro, introduced into an English colony, landed at Virginia 1620.
Sleeping cars, railway, invented *c.*1864 by the American financier George Mortimer Pullman, b.1831, d.1897.
Slimming, by the elimination of starch in diet, made popular by the English undertaker William Banting, b.1797, d.1878.
Sloane, Sir Hans, Irish-born physician, b.1660, d.1753.
Sluter, Claus, Dutch sculptor (*Well of Moses*), d.1406.

Smallpox, eradicated by World Health Organization 1980.
Smart, Christopher, English poet (*Song to David,* 1763), b.1722, d.1771.
Smeaton, John, English civil engineer and designer 1759 of the Eddystone Lighthouse, b.1724, d.1792.
Smedley, Francis Edward, English novelist (*Frank Fairlegh,* 1850), b.1818, d.1864.
Smetana, Bedrich, Bohemian composer (*The Bartered Bride,* 1866), b.1824, d.1884.
Smiles, Samuel, Scottish writer (*Selfhelp,* 1859), b.1812, d.1904.
Smirke, Sir Robert, English architect (The British Museum), b.1781, d.1867.
Smith, Adam, Scottish economist (*The Wealth of Nations,* 1776), b.1723, d.1790.
Smith, Bernard, German-born, organ builder, b.*c.*1630, d.1708.
Smith, Bessie, American blues singer, 'Empress of the Blues', b.1898, d.1937.
Smith, Sir Francis Pettit, English inventor, b.1808, d.1874.
Smith, George Joseph, English murderer (The Brides in the Bath), b.1872, hanged 1915.
Smith, Joseph, American founder 1827 of the Mormon Church, b.1805, murdered 1844.
Smith, Dame Maggie, British film and stage actress (*The Prime of Miss Jean Brodie,* 1967), b.1934.
Smith, Sydney, British divine, journalist and wit, b.1771, d.1845.
Smith, William, 'father of British geology', b.1769, d.1839.
Smithsonian Institution, Washington, DC, established 1846, through the endowment of the French-born scientist James Smithson, b.1765, d.1829.
Smolensk, Battle of, between the French and the Russians 16–17 Aug. 1812.
Smollett, Tobias, Scottish novelist (*Roderick Random,* 1748), b.1721, d.1771.
Smuts, Jan Christiaan, South African statesman (prime minister 1919–24, 1939–48), b.1870, d.1950.
Smybert, John, Scottish-born artist (*Bishop Berkeley and his Family,* 1731), b.1688, d.1751.
Smyth, Dame Ethel, English composer (*The Wreckers,* 1909), b.1858, d.1944.
Snow, Sir Charles Percy, English scientist and writer (*The Masters,* 1951), b.1905, d.1980.
Snow, John, British anaesthetist, b.1813, d.1858.

Snowden, Philip, Viscount Snowden, British statesman, b.1864, d.1937.
Snowdonia, first British national park, founded by gift of 300 acres near Snowdon to the National Trust 21 Jan. 1935.
Snyders, Frans, Flemish painter (*Stag-Hunt*), b.1579, d.1657.
Soane, Sir John, English architect, b.1753, d.1837.
Soap opera, originated in Chicago *c.*1928.
Soap tax, imposed in England 1712; abolished 1853.
Sobieski, John (John III), king of Poland (1674–96), b.1624, d.1696.
Social Democrat Party (SDP), British political party founded in 1981 by 'gang of four' defectors from the Labour Party: David Owen, Shirley Williams, Roy Jenkins and William Rodgers; dissolved 1988 and merged with the Liberals to form the Social and Liberal Democratic Party.
Social insurance, first begun in Germany 1883; begun in Britain 1911; Beveridge Report on Social Security 1942; system reorganized 1946.
Socialist parties, founded: Germany 1869; France (several) 1870s and 1880s; Portugal 1875; Denmark 1878; Spain 1879; Belgium 1885; Holland and Switzerland 1888; Sweden 1889; Norway 1890; Italy 1892; Russia 1898; Finland 1899. In England, Labour Representation Committe formed 1900, became Labour Party of Great Britain 1906.
Society for the Prevention of Cruelty to Animals, Royal, founded London 1824.
Society for the Prevention of Cruelty to Children, USA, founded 1874 by the American lawyer Elbridge Thomas Gerry, b.1837, d.1927.
Society for the Prevention of Cruelty to Children, National, founded London 1884.
Society for Promoting Christian Knowledge, founded 1698 by the English philanthropist Dr Thomas Bray, b.1656, d.1730.
Society for Propagating the Gospel in Foreign Parts, London, founded 1701.
Society for Psychical Research, London, founded 1882.
Society of Antiquaries, London, founded 1707, reconstituted 1717, granted Royal Charter 1751.
Society of Antiquaries of Scotland, founded 1780.
Society of Friends (Quakers), founded 1647 by the George Fox, b.1624, d.1690.

Society of Indexers, London, founded by G. Norman Knight 1957.

Society Islands, Polynesia, discovered 1607 by the Portuguese explorer Pedro Fernandez de Queiros, b.1560, d.1614; became French protectorate 1843 and colony 1880.

Socotra, island in the Indian Ocean, part of S. Yemen; ceded to Britain 1878 and formally annexed 1886.

Socrates, Greek philosopher, b.*c.*470, condemned to death 399 BC.

Soddy, Frederick, English scientist, b.1877, d.1956.

Sodium, discovered 1807 by the English scientist Sir Humphry Davy, b.1778, d.1829.

Sodoma, Giovanni, Italian painter (*Christ Scourged*), b.1477, d.1549.

Sol-fa, tonic, invented *c.*1845 by the English musician Sarah Ann Glover, b.1785, d.1867.

Solar compass, invented 1836 by the American William Austin Burt, b.1792, d.1858.

Solar parallax, deduced 1639 by the English astronomer Jeremiah Horrocks, b.*c.*1617, d.1641.

Solar year, length determined by the Greek astronomer Hipparchus, *fl.* 160–125 BC.

Solferino, Battle of, between the French and the Sardinians and Austrians, 24 June 1859.

Solidarity (*Solidarnosc*), Polish trade union, formed 22 Sept. 1980 by Lech Walesa who headed the popular campaign for democratic reform which led to free elections in 1989; Walesa elected president in Dec. 1990.

Solid fuel injection principle, invented 1890 by the English engineer Herbert Ackroyd-Stuart.

Solomon Islands, independent state and member of the Commonwealth; discovered 1568 by the Spanish navigator Alvaro de Mendana; British protectorate established 1893–99.

Solon, Greek statesman, b.*c.*640, d.*c.*558 BC.

Solti, George, Hungarian-born British conductor, b.1912.

Solstice, summer, longest day, 21 or 22 June, according to the year; **winter,** shortest day, 21 or 22 Dec., according to the year.

Solvay process, ammonia process for making sodium carbonate, invented 1863 by the Belgian industrial chamist Ernest Solvay, b.1838, d.1922.

Solzhenitsyn, Alexander Isayevich, Russian dissident writer (*The Gulag Archipelago,* 1973–75), b.1918.

Somalia, Italian protectorate 1899–1941; British military administration 1941–49; UN trusteeship 1950–60; united with former British Somaliland to form an independent republic 1960.

Somaliland, British, *see* **British Somaliland.**

Somaliland, French, *see* **Djibouti.**

Somaliland, Italian, *see* **Somalia.**

Somers, Sir George, English discoverer 1609 of the Bermudas, b.1554, d.1610.

Somerset, Edward Seymour, Duke of (The Protector), b.*c.*1506, beheaded 1552.

Somerset, Robert Carr, Earl of, Scottish politician, b.*c.*1590, d.1645.

Somerville, Mary, British scientist, b.1780, d.1872.

Somerville, William, English poet (*The Chase,* 1735), b.1675, d.1742.

Somerville College, Oxford University, founded 1879.

Somme, Battle of the, World War I, 24–25 Sept. 1914 and July-Oct. 1916.

Sondheim, Stephen, American composer and lyricist (*A Little Night Music,* 1973), b.1930.

Sontag, Susan, American writer and critic (*Illness as Metaphor,* 1978), b.1933.

Sontius, River, scene of the battle between Theodoric, king of the Ostrogoths and Odoacer 15 March 496.

Sophia, electress of Hanover, b.1630, d.1714.

Sophia Alekseievna, regent of Russia (1682–89), b.1657, d.1704.

Sophia Charlotte, queen of Prussia, b.1668, d.1705.

Sophia Dorothea, electress of Hanover, b.1666, d.1726.

Sophocles, Greek playwright ((*Oedipus Coloneus*), b.*c.*496, d.*c.*405 BC.

Sophonisba, queen of Numidia, lived in the 3rd century BC.

Sopwith, Sir Thomas Octave, British pioneer aviator, b.1888, d.1989.

Sorabji, Cornelia, Indian barrister, b.1866, d.1954.

Sorbonne, Paris, founded 1253 by the French priest Robert de Sorbon, b.1201, d.1274.

Sordello, Italian troubadour, lived in the 13th century, b.*c.*1422.

Sorel, Agnes, mistress of King Charles VII of France, d.1450.

Sorel, Georges, French political theorist (*Reflexions sur la Violence,* 1908), b.1847, d.1922.

Sorolla y Bastida, Joaquin, Spanish painter (*King Alfonso*), b.1863, d.1923.

SOS, international distress call signal, adopted by the International Radiotelegraph Conference 1912.

Sotheby's, London auction rooms, founded by Samuel Baker 1744.

Soufflot, Jacques Germaine, French architect, b.1709, d.1780.

Soult, Nicolas Jean de Dieu, statesman and marshal of France, b.1769, d.1851.

Sousa, John Philip, American composer (*El Capitan,* 1896), b.1854, d.1932.

Sound recording, first done by machine 1876 (Edison's phonograph); first gramophone disk made 1887 by Berliner.

South, Sir James, English astronomer, b.1785, d.1867.

South, Robert, English court preacher, b.1634, d.1716.

South Africa, Union of, came into being 31 May 1910; achieved independence 1961.

Southampton, Henry Wriothesley, Earl of, patron of William Shakespeare, b.1573, d.1624.

Southampton, Thomas Wriothesley, Earl of, statesman, b.1505, d.1550.

Southampton University, founded 1902; achieved university status 1952.

South Carolina, discovered 1497 by John Cabot; settled permanently 1670; re-admitted to the Union 1868.

Southcott, Joanna, English self-styled prophet, b.1750, d.1814.

South Dakota, first reached 1743 by the French family Vérendrye; admitted to the Union 1889.

Southeast Asia Collective Defence Treaty, signed at Manila 8 Sept. 1954.

Southerne, Thomas, Irish-born playwright (*Oroonoko,* 1696), b.1660, d.1746.

Southey, Robert, English poet (*Joan of Arc,* 1796), b.1774, d.1843.

South Pole, first reached 14 Dec. 1911 by the Norwegian explorer Roald Amundsen, b.1872, d.1928.

South Sea Bubble, South Sea Company incorporated 1711; financial collapse 1720; fraud exposed 1721.

Southwell, Robert, English poet and Jesuit martyr, b.*c.*1561, hanged 1595.

Southwood, Julius Salter Elias, Viscount, British newspaper publisher, b.1873, d.1946.

Souvestre, Emile, French novelist (*Derniers Bretons,* 1835–37), b.1806, d.1854.

Soweto (Southwest Township), racially segrated urban area S.W. of Johannesburg, South Africa.

Soyer, Alexis, Reform Club chef, b.1809, d.1858.

Space shuttle, first re-usable manned spacecraft (US), launched 12 April 1981.

Space-time concept, first mooted by the Dutch scientist Hendrik Antoon Lorentz, b.1853, d.1928.

Spain, Muslim invasion 711; last Muslims expelled 1492; ruled by Hapsburgs 1516–1700, by Bourbons 1700–1808, 1814–70, 1874–1931; republics 1873–74, 1931–39; dictatorship of Primo de Rivera 1923–30; Franco regime 1939–75; King Juan Carlos acceded to the thone Nov. 1975; new democratic constitution 1977–78.

Spanish Armada, assembled 1587; defeated by the English 29 July 1588.

Spanish Civil War, began 16 July 1936; ended 31 March 1939.

Spartacus, leader of the Roman slaves, killed in battle 71 BC.

Speaker of the House of Commons, post instituted 1377.

Specific gravity, principle discovered by the Greek scientist Archimedes, b.287, d.212 BC.

Spectacles, known in Europe in 14th century.

Spectator, The, British periodical, first, 1711–12, edited by the English writer Joseph Addison, b.1672, d.1719 and Sir Richard Steele, b.1672, d.1729; British periodical, second, founded 1828 by Robert Rintoul, b.1787, d.1858.

Spectrograph, invented 1919 by the English experimental physicist Francis William Aston, b.1877, d.1945.

Spectroheliograph, for photographing the sun, invented 1910 by the American astronomer George Ellery Hale, b.1868, d.1938.

Spectrum, of sunlight, discovered 1666 by Sir Isaac Newton, b.1642, d.1727.

Spectrum analysis, originated 1859 by the German scientist Robert Wilhelm Bunsen, b.1811, d.1899, and Gustav Robert Kirchhoff, b.1824, d.1887.

Spee, Maximilian, Graf von, German naval commander, b.1861, died in a naval battle 1914.

Speed, John, English map-maker, b.*c.*1552, d.1629.

Speke, John Hanning, English discoverer 1862 of the source of the Nile, b.1827, d.1864.

Spellman, Cardinal Francis J., archbishop of New York (1939–67), b.1889, d.1967.

Spence, Sir Basil, British architect (Coventry Cathedral, 1951–62), b.1907, d.1976.

Spencer, Herbert, English philosopher (*Man versus the State,* 1884), b.1820, d.1903.

Spencer, Sir Stanley, English painter (*Resurrection, Cookham,* 1922–27), b.1891, d.1959.

Spender, Stephen, English poet, b.1909.

Spengler, Oswald, German philosopher (*The Decline of the West,* 1918–22), b.1891, d.1936.

Spenser, Edmund, English poet (*The Faerie Queene,* 1589–96), b.*c.*1552, d.1599.

Sperry, Elmer Ambrose, American inventor, b.1860, d.1930.

Spielberg, Stephen, American film director and producer (*Jurassic Park,* 1993), b.1947.

Spin, aeronautic, first voluntary, performed 1915 by English pilot J. C. Brooke; first scientifically investigated 1917 by English physicist F. A. Lindemann.

Spinello Aretino, Italian painter (*Madonna and Saints,* 1391), d.*c.*1410.

Spinning frame, Arkwright's, invented 1768 by the English inventor Sir Richard Arkwright, b.1732, d.1792.

Spinoza, Benedict (Baruch Despinoza), Dutch philosopher (*Ethics*), b.1632, d.1677.

Spiral nebulae, discovery publicly announced 1850 by the astronomer the Earl of Rosse, b.1800, d.1867.

Spiritualism, modern, began at Hydeville, USA, in 1847–48.

Spitfires, last fly-past over London commemorating the Battle of Britain, Sunday, 20 Sept. 1959.

Spithead, British Fleet mutiny at, 16 April 1797.

Spock, Benjamin, American paediatrician, psychiatrist and political activist (*The Common Sense Book of Baby and Child Care,* 1946), b.1903.

Spode, Josiah, English potter, b.1754, d.1827.

Spohr, Ludwig, German composer and violinist, b.1784, d.1859.

Spoonerisms, originated by the English don the Rev. William Archibald Spooner, b.1844, d.1930.

Spottiswoode, John, archbishop of St Andrews, b.1565, d.1639.

Spotsylvania Courthouse, Battle of, American Civil War, 8–21 May 1864.

Spring, *c.*21 March to 21 June in the northern hemisphere.

Spurgeon, Charles Haddon, English Baptist leader, b.1834, d.1892.

Spurs, Battle of the, between the English and the French, 16 Aug. 1513.
Sputnik, series of Russian earth satellites, first launched 4 Oct. 1957.
Spyri, Johanna, Swiss writer (*Heidi*), b.1827, d.1901.
Squarcione, Francesco, Italian painter (*Madonna with Child*), b.1394, d.1474.
Squire, Sir John, English writer, b.1884, d.1958.
Sri Lanka, formerly Ceylon; a British colony from1802; gained independence in 1948; became a republic within the Commonwealth 1972, and renamed Democratic Socialist Republic of Sri Lanka.
SSAFA (Soldiers', Sailors' and Airmen's Families Association), London, founded 1885; incorporated by Royal Charter 1926.
Staël, Mme de, French writer (*Delphine,* 1802), b.1766, d.1817.
Stafford, Edward, **Duke of Buckingham,** Lord High Constable, b.1478, beheaded 1521.
Stafford, Henry, **Duke of Buckingham,** politician, b.*c.*1454, beheaded 1483.
Stahl, Georg Ernst, German propounder (1731) of the phlogiston theory, b.1660, d.1734.
Stainer, Sir John, English composer (*The Crucifixion,* 1887), b.1840, d.1901.
Stainless steel, invented 1916 by the Englishman Harry Brearley at Sheffield.
Stair, John Dalrymple, Earl of, soldier and diplomat, b.1673, d.1747.
Stalin, Joseph (Joseph Vissarionovich Dzhugashvili), Soviet dictator, b.1879, d.1953.
Stamp Act, passed 1764; repealed 1766.
Stamp booklets, first used in Britain 1904.
Stamp duty, introduced in England 1694.
Stamped envelopes, first British, designed by the Irish artist William Mulready, b.1786, d.1863; issued 1840.
Standard Oil Company, founded 1870 by the American financier John Davison Rockefeller, b.1839, d.1937.
Standard, Battle of the, between the English and the Scottish 22 Aug. 1138.
Standish, Myles, English colonizer of New Plymouth, b.1584, d.1656.
Stanford, Sir Charles Villiers, Irish composer (*The Canterbury Pilgrims*, 1884), b.1852, d.1924.

Stanford University, California, founded 1891 through an endowment from the American railway builder Leland Stanford, b.1824, d.1893.

Stanhope, Lady Hester, English traveller, b.1776, d.1839.

Stanhope, Philip Dormer, Earl of Chesterfield, statesman, b.1694, d.1773.

Stanislaus I, king of Poland (1705–09, 1733), b.1677, d.1766.

Stanislaus II, king of Poland (1764–95), b.1732, d.1798.

Stanislavski, Constantin Sergeivich, Russian actor and producer, b.1863, d.1938.

Stanley, Sir Henry Morton, Welsh explorer, b.1841, d.1904. Meeting with David Livingstone, b.1813, d.1873, 10 Nov. 1871.

Stanley, John, English organist and composer (*Zimri*, 1760), b.1713, d.1786.

Stannary Parliament, Cornwall, last held at Truro 1752.

Stanton, Mrs Elizabeth Cady, American champion of women's rights, b.1815, d.1902.

Star, The, British newspaper, founded 1888; absorbed by the *Evening News*, 1960.

Star Chamber, English prerogative court inaugurated in the 14th century; abolished by the Long Parliament 1641.

Stark, James, English painter (*The Valley of the Yare*), b.1794, d.1859.

Stark effect, polarization of light, discovered 1913 by the German physicist Johannes Stark, b.1874, d.1957.

Stationers' Company, London, livery company incorporated 1557; charter confirmed by Queen Elizabeth I, 1559; monopoly ended 1842.

Statius, Latin poet (*Silvae*), d.96.

Statue of Liberty, New York harbour, designed 1876 by the French sculptor Frédéric Auguste Bartholdi, b.1834, d.1904; unveiled 28 Oct. 1886.

Staunton, Howard, English chess player, b.1810, d.1874.

Stavisky, Alexandre, French swindler, b.1886, d.1934.

Stead, William Thomas, English editor and reformer, b.1849, drowned at sea 1912.

Steamboat, first, the *Charlotte Dundas* built 1801 by the British engineer William Syminton, b.1763, d.1831; first practical, invented 1787 by the American inventor John Fitch, b.1743, d.1798.

Steam engine, invented 1698 by the English military engineer Captain Thomas Savery, b.*c.*1650, d.1715.

Steam hammer, invented 1839 by the Scottish engineer James Nasmyth, b.1808, d.1890.
Steam plough, invented 1850–60 by the English engineer John Fowler, b.1826, d.1864.
Steam pumping engine, invented 1705 by the English mechanic Thomas Newcowen, b.1663, d.1729; perfected 1767 by the Scottish engineer James Watt, b.1736, d.1819.
Steam turbine, driving high-speed electric generator, invented 1884 by Sir Charles Parsons, b.1854, d.1931.
Stearin, fat formed from glycerine and stearic acid, discovered by the French scientist Michel Eugène Chevreul, b.1786, d.1889.
Steel, cast by the crucible process, invented *c.*1750 by the English clockmaker Benjamin Huntsman, b.1704, d.1776.
Steel rails, first made *c.*1858 by the British engineer Sir John Brown, b.1816, d.1896.
Steele, Sir Richard, Irish-born writer (*The Spectator,* 1711–12), b.1672, d.1729.
Steen, Jan, Dutch painter (*Music master*), b.1626, d.1679.
Steer, Philip Wilson, English painter (*Chepstow Castle*), b.1860, d.1942.
Stein, Sir Aurel, Hungarian-born archaeologist in Asia, b.1862, d.1943.
Stein, Gertrude, American writer (*The Autobiography of Alice B. Toklas*, 1933), b.1872, d.1946.
Steinbeck, John, American author (*The Grapes of Wrath,* 1939), Nobel prize for literature 1962, b.1902, d.1968.
Steiner, Rudolf, Hungarian-born philosopher and educationist, b.1861, d.1925.
Steinitz, William, German-born chess champion, b.1836, d.1900.
Steinmetz. Charles Proteus, German-born electrical engineer, b.1865, d.1923.
Steinway G., Sons, piano manufacturers, firm founded Brunswick *c.*1825; New York 1853; London 1875; Hamburg 1880.
Stellar parallax, study developed and advanced by the German astronomer Wilhelm Struve, b.1793, d.1864.
Stendhal (Marie Henri Beyle), French novelist (*Le Rouge et le Noir,* 1831), b.1783, d.1842.
Steno, Nicolaus, Danish scientist, b.1631, d.1686.
Stephen, St, king of Hungary (1001–38), b.*c.*977, d.1038.
Stephen I, St, pope 254–257.
Stephen II, pope 752.

Stephen III, pope 752–757.
Stephen IV, pope 768–772.
Stephen V, pope 816–817.
Stephen VI, pope 885–891.
Stephen VII, pope 896–897, murdered 897.
Stephen VIII, pope 928–931.
Stephen IX, pope 939–942.
Stephen X (Frederick), pope 1057–58.
Stephen, king of England (1135–54), b.*c.*1097, d.1154.
Stephen I, king of Hungary (998–1038), b.977, d.1038.
Stephen II, king of Hungary (1114–31), b.1100, d.1131.
Stephen III, king of Hungary (1161–73).
Stephen IV, king of Hungary (1162), d.1166.
Stephen V, king of Hungary (1270–72), b.1239, d.1272.
Stephen, Sir James Fitzjames, English jurist and writer, b.1829, d.1894.
Stephen, Sir Leslie, English writer (editor of the *Dictionary of National Biography*), b.1832, d.1904.
Stephen the Great, prince of Moldavia, b.1431, d.1504.
Stephen Harding, St, founder of the Cistercian Order, d.1134.
Stephens, Alexander Hamilton, American statesman, b.1812, d.1883.
Stephens, George, English runic archaeologist, b.1813, d.1895.
Stephens, James, Irish writer (*The Crock of Gold,* 1912), b.1882, d.1950.
Stephenson, George, English civil engineer and inventor, b.1781, d.1848.
Stephenson, Robert, English civil engineer, b.1803, d.1859.
Stepniak, Sergei (Sergei Mikhailovich Kravchinski), Russian revolutionary emigre and writer, b.1852, d.1895.
Stereochemistry, study initiated 1874 by the Dutch scientist Jacobus Hendricus van't Hoff, b.1852, d.1911.
Stereoscope, invented *c.*1838 by the English scientist Sir Charles Wheatstone, b.1802, d.1875.
Stereotype process, invented 1725 by the Scottish inventor William Ged, b.1690, d.1749.
Sterling, John, Scottish writer (*The Election,* 1841), b.1806, d.1844.
Sterling, taken off the British gold standard 20 Sept. 1931.
Sterne, Laurence, Irish-born writer (*Tristram Shandy,* 1760–67), b.1713, d.1768.

Stethoscope, invented by the French physician René Théophile Hyacinthe Läennec, b.1781, d.1826.
Stetson hats, manufactured by the American industrialist John Batterson Stetson, b.1830, d.1906.
Steuben, Frederick William, Baron von, German-born soldier in American service, b.1730, d.1794.
Stevens, Alfred, English painter and sculptor (Wellington monument, 1856–92), b.1818, d.1875.
Stevens, Henry, American bibliographer, London, b.1819, d.1886.
Stevens, John, American inventor 1813 of the ironclad, b.1749, d.1838.
Stevenson, Adlai, American politician, b.1900, d.1968.
Stevenson, David, Scottish civil engineer, b.1815, d.1886.
Stevenson, Robert, Scottish engineer, b.1772, d.1850.
Stevenson, Robert Louis, Scottish writer (*Treasure Island*, 1883), b.1850, d.1894.
Stevenson, Thomas, Scottish engineer and meteorologist, b.1818, d.1887.
Stewart, Balfour, Scottish meteorologist, b.1828, d.1887.
Stewart, Dugald, Scottish philosopher, b.1753, d.1828.
Stewart, Robert, Duke of Albany, regent of Scotland, b.c.1340, d.1420.
Stiegel, Henry William, American pioneer glass manufacturer, b.1729, d.1785.
Stieler, Adolf, German cartographer, b.1775, d.1836.
Stifter, Adalbert, Bohemian-born writer (*Studien,* 1844–51), b.1805, d.1868.
Stigand, archbishop of Canterbury, d.I072.
Stilicho, Flavius, Roman general, assassinated 408.
Still, Andrew Taylor, American founder (1874) of osteopathy, b.1828, d.1917.
Stillingfleet, Edward, bishop of Worcester (1689–99), b.1635, d.1699.
Stirling, James, Scottish mathematician, b.1692, d.1770.
Stirling, James Hutchison, Scottish philosopher, b.1820, d.1909.
Stirner, Max (Kaspar Schmidt), German anarchist (*The Ego and His Own*), b.1806, d.1856.
Stockhausen, Karlheinz, German composer, b.1928.
Stockmar, Christian Friedrich, Baron von, adviser to Queen Victoria, b.1787, d.1863.
Stockton, Frank R., American novelist and short-story writer (*The Lady or the Tiger?* 1884), b.1834, d.1902.

Stoicism, philosophical system founded in the 4th century BC. by Zeno of Citium, b.340, d.270 BC.

Stoker, Bram, Irish writer (*Dracula,* 1897), b.1847, d.1912.

Stokes, Sir George Gabriel, Irish-born physicist, b.1819, d.1903.

Stokes, Margaret McNair, Irish archaeologist, b.1832, d.1900.

Stokowski, Leopold, English-born conductor, b.1882, d.1977.

Stolberg, Friedrich Leopold, Graf zu, German poet (*Timoleon,* 1784), b.1750, d.1819.

Stolypin, Piotr Arkadevich, Russian statesman, b.1863, assassinated 1911.

Stone, Lucy, American champion of women's rights and abolitionist, b.1818, d.1893.

Stone, Nicholas, English architect, b.1586, d.1647.

Stone Age, Old, between ten thousand and one million years ago; **Middle,** between 4,500 and 10,000 years ago; **New,** between 4,000 and 4,500 years ago.

Stopes, Dr Marie, English pioneer in family planning, b.1880, d.1958.

Stoppard, Tom, Czech-born British playwright (*Rosencrantz and Guidenstern are Dead,* 1966), b.1937.

Storm, Theodor, German writer (*Gedichte,* 1852), b.1817, d.1888.

Storting, Norwegian parliament, founded 1814.

Stoss, Veit, German sculptor (*Annunciation*), b.1438, d.1533.

Stothard, Thomas, English painter (*The Canterbury Pilgrims*), b.1755, d.1834.

Stow, John, English antiquary (*Survey of London,* 1598), b.1525, d.1605.

Stowe, Mrs Harriet Beecher, American writer (*Uncle Tom's Cabin,* 1851–52), b.1811, d.1896.

Stowe Collection of manuscripts, now in the British Museum, collected by the English antiquary Thomas Astle, b.1735, d.1803.

Strabo, Greek geographer, b.c.64 BC, d.c.AD 22.

Strachey, John St Loe, English editor of *The Spectator* (1896–1925), b.1860, d.1927.

Strachey, Lytton, English writer (*Eminent Victorians,* 1918), b.1880, d.1932.

Stradella, Alessandro, Italian composer (*Esther*), b.c.1645, murdered 1682.

Stradivari, Antonio, Italian violin-maker, b.1644, d.1737.

Strafford, Thomas Wentworth, Earl of, British statesman, b.1593, executed 1641.

Strang, William, British artist (*Rudyard Kipling*), b.1859, d.1921.

Strange, Sir Robert, Scottish engraver, b.1721, d.1792.
Straparola, Giovanni Francesco, Italian writer (*Piacevoli notti*, 1550–54), b.*c*.1495, d.*c*.1557.
Strasbourg, ceded to France under the Treaty of Ryswyck 1697.
Stratford, John de, archbishop of Canterbury (1333–48), d.1348.
Strathcona and Mount Royal, Donald Alexander Smith, Baron, Scottish-born statesman in Canada, b.1820, d.1914.
Straus, Oskar, Austrian composer (*The Chocolate Soldier,* 1908), b.1870, d.1954.
Strauss, Johann, Austrian composer (*Die Fledermaus,* 1874), b.1825, d.1899.
Strauss, Richard, German composer (*Der Rosenkavalier,* 1911), b.1864, d.1949.
Stravinsky, Igor, Russian-born composer (*The Fire Bird,* 1910), b.1882, d.1971.
Street, George Edmund, English architect, b.1824, d.1881.
Street lighting, in England, first oil 1681; first gas *c*.1812; first electricity *c*.1880.
Streptomycin, first isolated 1943 by the Russian-born scientist Selman Abraham Waksman, b.1888, awarded Nobel Prize 1952, d.1973.
Stresemann, Gustav, German statesman, b.1878, d.1929.
Stretcher bearers, introduced *c*.1792 by the Baron Pierre François Percy, b.1754, d.1825.
Stribling, Thomas Sigismund, American novelist (*The Store,* 1932), b.1881, d.1965.
Strickland, Agnes, English historian (*Lives of the Queens of England,* 1840–48), b.1796, d.1874.
Strijdom, Johannes Gerhardus, prime minister (1954–58) of the Union of South Africa, b.1893, d.1958.
Strike, General, in Britain, 3 –13 May 1926.
Strindberg, Johan August, Swedish playwright (*Miss Julie,* 1888), b.1849, d.1912.
Strip cartoons, originated by the German artist Wilhelm Busch, b.1832, d.1908.
Stroheim, Erich von, film actor, b.1886, d.1957.
Strongbow, Richard, Earl of Pembroke and Strigul (Richard de Clare), d.1176.
Strontium, metallic element, discovered 1808 by the English chemist Sir Humphry Davy, b.1778, d.1829.
Struensee, Johann Friedrich, German-born statesman in Denmark, b.1731, executed 1772.

Strutt, Joseph, English antiquary, b.1749, d.1802.

Struve, Friedrich Georg Wilhelm, German astronomer, b.1793, d.1864.

Struve, Peter Berngardovich, Russian writer and politician, b.1870, d.1944.

Strychnine, discovered 1818 by the French chemists Pierre Joseph Pelletier, b.1788, d.1842, and Joseph Bienaimé Caventou, b.1795, d.1877.

Strype, John, English historian (*Cranmer,* 1694), b.1643, d.1737.

'Stuart, La belle' (Frances Teresa Stuart, Duchess of Richmond and Lennox), mistress of Charles II, b.1647, d.1702.

Stuart, John, Earl of Bute, statesman, b.1713, d.1792.

Stuart, John McDouall, Scottish explorer, first (1860) to reach the centre of Australia, b.1815, d.1866.

Stubbs, George, English painter (*Mares and Foals*), b.1724, d.1806.

Stubbs, Henry, English writer (*The Commonwealth of Oceana,* 1660), b.1632, d.1676.

Stukeley, William, English antiquary, b.1687, d.1765.

Sturdee, Sir, Frederick Charles Doveton, Admiral of the Fleet, b.1859, d.1925.

Sture, Sten, regent of Sweden and founder of the University of Uppsala, b.*c.*1440, d.1503.

Sturge, Joseph, English reformer and philanthropist, b.1793, d.1859.

Sturluson, Snorri, Icelandic historian (*Heimskringla*), b.1179, killed 1241.

Sturt, Charles, English explorer of Australia, b.1795, d.1869.

Stuyvesant, Peter, Dutch governor of New Amsterdam (now New York), b.*c.*1602, d.1682.

Stylites, Simeon, St, d.*c.*459.

Suarez, Francisco de, Spanish theologian, b.1548, d.1617.

Submachine gun, invented 1921 by the American inventors John Taliaferro Thompson, b.1860, d.1940, and John N. Blish.

Submarine, first navigable, invented 1620 by the Dutch scientist Cornelis Jacobszoon Drebbel, b.1572, d.1633; first British model launched at Barrow 2 Oct. 1901; first atomic-powered, US submarine *Nautilus,* launched 21 Jan. 1954.

Submarine telephone system, first long-distance, laid across the Atlantic 1956.

Submarine warfare, World War I, declared by Germany 4 Feb. 1915.

Sucre, Antonio José de, South American liberator and president of Bolivia (1826–28), b.1795, assassinated 1830.

Sudan, achieved self-government 1953; independence as a democratic republic proclaimed 1956.

Sudermann, Hermann, German playwright (*Die Ehre,* 1888), b.1857, d.1928.

Sue, Eugène, French novelist (*Le Juif errant,* 1844–1845), b.1804, d.1857.

Suetonius, Roman historian, b.75, d.160.

Suez Canal, Egypt, concession granted 1855 to French engineer Ferdinand de Lesseps, b.1805, d.1894; construction begun April 1859; opened 17 Nov. 1869; British occupation of Canal Zone 1882; convention signed 1888; British evacuated Zone 1955; canal nationalized by Egyptian Government July 1956; British and French invasion of Zone Nov. 1956; forces withdrawn Dec. 1956.

Suffren St Tropez, Pierre André de, French admiral, b.1729, d.1788.

Sugar, grape, discovered 1799 by the French scientist Joseph Louis Proust, b.1754, d.1826.

Sugar in beet, discovered 1747 by the German physicist Andreas Sigismund Marggraf, b.1709, d.1782.

Suger, French statesman, b.*c.*1081, d.1151.

Suggia, Mme Guilhermina, Spanish cellist, b.1888, d.1950.

Sui dynasty, China, 581–618.

Suicides, buried at crossroads transfixed by a stake until 1834.

Sukkoth (Feast of Tabernacles), Jewish holiday 15th day of Tishri.

Sulawesi (also Celebes), island in E. Indonesia.

Suleiman, sultan of Adrianople 1402–10.

Suleiman I, sultan of Turkey (1520–66), b.1494, d.1566.

Suleiman II, sultan of Turkey (1687–91), b.1641, d.1691.

Sulfanilamide, first synthesized 1908 by the German scientist P. Gelmo.

Sulla, Lucius Cornelius, Roman statesman and soldier, b.138, d.78 BC.

Sullivan, Sir Arthur, English composer (*The Mikado,* 1885), b.1842, d.1900.

Sullivan, Sir Edward, Lord Chancellor of Ireland (1883–85), b.1822, d.1885.

Sully, Maximilien de Béthune, Duc de, French statesman, b.1560, d.1641.

Sully-Prudhomme, René François Armand, French poet (*L'Idéal,* 1865), b.1839, d.1907.

Sulphonamide drugs, first produced 1935 (Prontosil) and 1938 (M & B).

Sumatra, Indonesia, settled *c.*1510 by the Portuguese; taken over by the Dutch *c.*1596 onwards; included in the independent Republic of Indonesia, established 1949.

Summer, 21 June to 21 Sept., in the northern hemisphere.

Summer solstice, *see* **Solstice.**

Summer Time, British, introduced 21 May 1916; made permanent institution by House of Commons vote 17 July 1925.

Sumner, John Bird, archbishop of Canterbury (1848–62), b.1780, d.1862.

Sumter, Fort, Battle of, American Civil War, 12–14 April 1861.

Sun, distance from earth, first reliably calculated 1673 by Cassius and Riches; rotation first observed 1610 by Galileo.

Sun spots, discovered by Joannes Fabricius, b.1587, d.1615.

Sun Yat-Sen, Chinese revolutionary leader, b.1867, d.1925.

Sunday schools, founded in Gloucester 1780 by the English publisher and reformer Robert Raikes, b.1735, d.1811.

Sunday Times, The, British newspaper, founded 1822.

Sung dynasty, China 960–1279.

Superconductivity, of metals, discovered 1911 by the Dutch scientist Heike Kamerlingh Onnes.

Superman, comic strip hero, first appeared in print 1938.

Suppé, Franz von, Austrian-born composer (*Poet and Peasant*), b.1819, d.1895.

Supremacy, Acts of, separating the Anglican from the Catholic Church, signed by Henry VIII in 1534 and by Queen Elizabeth in 1559.

Surgeons' Company, London, founded 1746.

Surgical instruments, steam sterilization of, introduced 1886 by the German scientist Ernst von Bergmann, b.1836, d.1907.

Surinam (formerly Netherlands Guiana), first settled by the English 1630; ceded to the Netherlands 1667; became self-governing 1954 and fully independent 1975.

Surrealism, art movement, manifesto issued 1924 by the French poet André Breton, b.1896, d.1966.

Surrey, Henry Howard, Earl of, English poet and soldier, b.*c.*1517, beheaded 1547.

Surtees, Robert Smith, English novelist (*Handley Cross,* 1843), b.1803, d.1864.

Suso, Heinrich, German mystic (*Das Büchlein der Wahrheit*, *c.*1329), b.1300, d.1366.

Sussex, Thomas Radclyffe, Earl of, Lord Lieutenant of Ireland (1560–64), b.*c.*1526, d.1583.

Suttee (*Sati*), compulsory or voluntary widow-sacrifice, made illegal in India 1829.

Sutter, John Augustus, American pioneer, b.1803, d.1880.

Sutton, Thomas, English founder (1611) of Charterhouse School, b.1532, d.1611.

Sutton Hoo, Suffolk, ship-burial treasure discovered 1939.

Suvorov, Aleksandr Vasilievich, Russian field marshal, b.1729, d.1800.

Svalbard Archipelago, Norwegian sovereignty recognized 1920; officially incorporated in Norway 1925.

Svendsen, Johan, Norwegian composer (*Norwegian Rhapsody*) and violinist, b.1840, d.1911.

Sverdrup, Otto, Norwegian explorer in the Arctic, b.1855, d.1930.

Sverrir, king of Norway (1177–1202), d.1202.

Svevo, Italo (Ettore Schmitz), Italian writer, b.1864, d.1928.

Swabian League, The Great, formed by Frederick III, 1488; disintegrated 1534.

Swammerdam, Jan, Dutch scientist, b.1637, d.1680.

Swan, Sir Joseph Wilson, English pioneer in electric lighting and photography, b.1828, d.1914.

'Swan of Lichfield, The', *see* **Anna Seward.**

Swanson, Gloria, American film star (*Sunset Boulevard*, 1950), b.1899, d.1983.

SWAPO (South West Africa People's Organization), founded 1959 to oppose South Africa's rule; won majority in 1989 elections in Nambia.

Swarthmore College, Pennsylvania, founded by the Society of Friends 1864.

Swaziland, protected by the South African Republic 1894–99; administered by the governor of the Transvaal 1903–07; administered by a British High Commissioner from1907; gained independence 1968.

Sweden, Christian since *c.*1000; ruled by Vasas 1521–1810, by Bernadottes since 1810.

Swedenborg, Emanuel, Swedish theologian (*Heavenly Arcana*, 1749–56), b.1688, d.1772.

Swedenborgian Church, organized 1788 by Robert Hindmarsh, b.1759, d.1835.

'Swedish Nightingale', *see* **Jenny Lind.**

Sweelinck, Jan, Dutch organist and composer (*Cantationes Sacrae*), b.1562, d.1621.

Sweet, Henry, English philologist, b.1845, d.1912.

Swete, Henry Barclay, British theologian, b.1835, d.1917.

Sweynheym, Conrad, pioneer German printer in Italy, lived in the 15th century.

Swift, Jonathan, Irish divine and writer (*Gulliver's Travels*, 1726), b.1667, d.1745.

Swinburne, Algernon Charles, English poet (*Atalanta in Calydon*, 1865), b.1837, d.1909.

Swithin, St, bishop of Winchester, d.862.

Swithin's Day, St, 15 July.

Switzerland, state formed 1291–1798; unified Helvetic Republic established 1798; present area and neutrality achieved 1815.

Sydenham, Thomas, English physician and medical pioneer, b.1624, d.1689.

Sydney, New South Wales, founded 1788.

Sydney Harbour Bridge, officially opened 19 March 1932.

'Sylva, Carmen' (Elizabeth, queen of Rumania), b.1843, d.1916.

Sylvester I, St, pope 313–335, d.335.

Sylvester II, pope 999–1003, d.1003.

Sylvester, Joshua, English writer and translator (mainly from the French), b.1563, d.1618.

Symbolism, artistic and literary movement, originated in Paris 1886–89.

Symington, William, British marine engineer, b.1763, d.1831.

Symmachus, St, pope 498–514.

Symonds, John Addington, English writer and translator, b.1840, d.1893.

Symons, George James, English meteorologist, b.1838, d.1900.

Syndicalism, revolutionary doctrine formulated by Fernand Pelloutier, b.1867, d.1901.

Synge, John Millington, Irish playwright (*The Playboy of the Western World*, 1907), b.1871, d.1909.

Synod of the clergy, first held in England at Hertford 673.

Synthetic geometry, theory developed by the Swiss mathematician Jakob Steiner, b.1796, d.1863.

Synthetic oil production, initiated 1850 by the Scottish scientist James Young, b.1811, d.1883.

Syphilis, bacillus discovered 1905 by the German scientists Erich Hoffman, b.1868, d.1959, and Fritz Schaudinn; curative drug

'Salvarsan' discovered 1908 by the German bacteriologist Paul Ehrlich, b.1854, d.1915.

Syracuse University, New York State, founded 1849; moved to present site 1870.

Syria, ruled by Turks 1517–1918; under French mandate 1920–41; became independent 1944; joined Egypt in the United Arab Republic 1958–61; government dominated by the Arab Socialist Renaissance (Ba'ath) Party; president Hafez el-Assad has held power since 1970.

Széchenyi, Count Stephen, Hungarian statesman, b.1791, committed suicide 1860.

Szymanowski, Karol, Polish composer (*Symphonie Concertante*, 1933), b.1883, d.1937.

T

Tabari, Abu Ja'far, Arab historian, b.839, d.*c.*923.

Tabernacles, Feast of (Sukkoth), Jewish holiday, 15th day of Tishri.

Table turning, in Spiritualist seances, began in the USA 1848, reached Europe 1852.

Tabora, capital of Western Province, Tanzania, founded by Arab slave and ivory traders *c.*1820.

Tabriz, capital of Azerbaijan Province, Iran, reputed to have been founded by Zobeidah, wife of Harun-el-Rashid, 791.

Tacitus, Roman emperor (275–276), d.276.

Tacitus, Cornelius, Roman historian, b.*c.*55, d.*c.*116.

Tacoma Narrows, American suspension bridge, collapsed after construction 1940.

Taddeo di Bartolo, Sienese painter, b.*c.*1362, d.*c.*1422.

Tadema, Sir, Lawrence Alma-, Dutch-born painter, b.1836, d.1912.

Taffeta, in its earliest form, introduced into England in the 14th century.

Taft, William Howard, 27th US president (1909–13), b.1857, d.1930.

Taganrog, Sea of Azov port, founded 1769 on the site of a fortress erected by Peter the Great, 1698.

Taglioni, Maria, Italian ballerina, b.1804, d.1884.

Tagore, Rabindranath, Indian poet and philosopher (*Gitanjali*, 1912), b.1861, d.1941.

Tahirites, ruling family in Khorassan, Persia 813–872.

Tahiti, largest of the French Society Islands, discovered 1767 by the English naval captain Samuel Wallis, b.1728, d.1804.

Taillefer, 11th-century bard, struck the first blow at the Battle of Hastings, 1066.

Taine, Hippolyte, French historian, b.1828, d.1893.

Tait, Archibald Campbell, archbishop of Canterbury (1869–82), b.1811, d.1882.

Taiwan (formerly Formosa), ceded to Japan by China 1895; seized by Chiang Kai-shek 1945 and held after evacuation of Chinese mainland in 1949.

Taj Mahal, Agra, India, mausoleum built (1632) by the Emperor Shah Jehan (d.1666) for his favourite wife Mumtaz Mahal

Tajikistan, former Soviet Socialist Republic (admitted to the USSR 1929), declared independence from the Soviet Union 6 Sept. 1991.

Talana Hill, near Dundee, north Natal, scene of the first Battle of the Boer War 20 Oct. 1899.

Talavera, Battle of, between the English and the French 27–28 July 1809.

Talbot, William Henry Fox, English pioneer in photography, b.1800, d.1877. Invented instantaneous photography 1851.

Taliesin, Welsh bard, reputed to have lived in the 6th century.

'Talkies', first shown in commercial cinemas 1928.

Talking books, for the blind, first sponsored 1934 by the American lawyer Robert Forsythe Irwin, b.1892.

Tallage, special tax on English towns, first levied in the reign of King Henry I, ceased with the 1332 levy, formally abolished 1340.

Tallahassee, capital of Florida, reputed to have been founded by the Spaniards 1638.

Talleyrand-Périgord, Charles Maurice de, French diplomat and statesman, b.1754, d.1838.

Tallien, Jean Lambert, French Revolutionary leader, b.1769, d.1820.

Tallinn, Estonia, founded by Waldemar II of Denmark 1219.

Tallis, Thomas, English composer (*Song of Forty Parts*), b.c.1505, d.1585.

Talmud, Rabbinical thesaurus, recension completed during the 5th century; first complete edition published 1520–23 by the Christian printer Daniel Bomberg, d.1549.

Tamar Bridge, linking Devon and Cornwall, completed 1961.

Tamerlane, Tartar conqueror, b.*c.*1336, d.1405.

Tammany Hall, New York political organization, founded *c.*1789. Tammany Hall Scandal took place 1870.

Tancred, crusader, b.*c.*1078, d.1112.

Tandy, James Napper, United Irishman, b.1740, d.1803.

T'Ang dynasty, China 618–906.

Tanganyika, former E. African state; German territory 1884–1914; conquered by British forces 1914–18; mandated territory of the League of Nations 1920–46; United Nations trusteeship 1946; gained inependence 1961; united with Zanzibar 1964 as the United Republic of Tanzania.

Tanganyika, Lake, discovered 1858 by the English explorers Burton, b.1821, d.1890, and John Hanning Speke, b.1827, d.1864.

Tangier, ruled by Portugal 1471–1662, England 1662–84, Morocco 1684–1904; international zone created 1923, terminated 1956; made summer capital of Morroco and free port 1962.

Tank Corps, British Army, formation authorized 28 July 1917.

Tanks, tested and so-named 29 Jan. 1916, first used by the British Army on the Somme 15 Sept. 1916.

Tannenberg, Battle of, between Teutonic Order and Poles 1410; and between the Germans and the Russians 26–31 Aug. 1914.

Tanner, Thomas, English antiquary (*Notitia Monastica,* 1695), b.1674, d.1735.

Tannhauser, German minnesinger, lived in the 13th century.

Tantalum, metallic element, discovered 1802 by A. G. Ekeberg.

Tanzania, E. African republic, formed by the union of Tanganyika and Zanzibar 1964.

Taoism, religious movement, thought to have been founded by the Chinese sage Lâo-tsze, who lived in the late 7th and early 6th centuries BC.

Tarkington, Booth, American writer (*Penrod,* 1914), b.1869, d.1946.

Tarleton, Sir Banastre, English general in the American War of Independence, b.1754, d.1833.

Tarlton, Richard, English actor, d.1588.

Tarquin (Lucius Tarquinius Superbus), Roman king, b.534, d.510 bc.

Tartini, Giuseppe, Italian violinist and composer (*Trillo del Diavolo*), b.1692, d.1770.

Tasman, Abel Janszoon, Dutch navigator, b.c.1603, d.c.1659.

Tasmania, discovered 1642 by the Dutch navigator Abel Janszoon Tasman, b.c.1603, d.c.1659.

Tassili rock paintings, Sahara, discovered by the Camel Corps officer Lieutenant Brenans 1933.

Tasso, Torquato, Italian poet (*La Gerusalemme Liberata,* 1576), b.1544, d.1595.

Tata, Jamsetji Nasarwanji, Indian pioneer industrialist and philanthropist, b.1839, d.1904.

Tate, Sir Henry, English manufacturer and philanthropist, b.1819, d.1899.

Tate, Nathum, Irish-born poet laureate (*Panacea,* 1700), b.1652, d.1715.

Tate Gallery, London, officially opened 21 July 1897; founded by the English manufacturer Sir Henry Tate, b.1819, d.1899; re-assumed its original name 1932.

Tatham, Charles Heathcote, British architect, b.1772, d.1842.
Tati, Jacques (Jacques Tatischeff), French comedy actor and film maker (*Jour de Fête,* 1949), b.1908, d.1982.
Tatler, The, 1709–11, edited by the Irish-born writer Sir Richard Steele, b.1672, d.1729.
Tattersall's, London horse auction and sporting centre, founded 1776 by the English horse-auctioneer Richard Tattersall, b.1724, d.1795.
Tatum, Art, American jazz pianist, b.1909, d.1956.
Tauber, Richard, Austrian-born operatic singer, b.1892, d.1948.
Tauchnitz, Karl Christoph Traugott, German publisher and printer, b.1761, d.1836.
Taussig, Frank William, American economist, b.1859, d.1940.
Taverner, John, English composer of masses and motets, b.*c.*1495, d.1545.
Tavernier, Jean Baptiste, French traveller and merchant in the East, b.1605, d.1689.
Taxi cabs, first official recognition of their existence shown in the draft of proposed cab regulations for London, issued by the Home Secretary 21 Jan. 1907.
Tay Bridge, Scotland, opened 1887.
Taylor, Alan John Percival, British historian (*The Origins of the Second World War,* 1961), b.1906, d.1990.
Taylor, Alfred Swaine, English medical jurist (*The Principles and Practice of Medical Jurisprudence,* 1865), b.1806, d.1880.
Taylor, Elizabeth, American film star (*Cat on a Hot Tin Roof,* 1958), b.1932.
Taylor, Jeremy, English theologian (*Holy Living,* 1650, and *Holy Dying,* 1651), b.1613, d.1667.
Taylor, John ('The Water-Poet'), English writer (*The Pennyles Pilgrimage,* 1618), b.1580, d.1653.
Taylor, Zachary, 12th US president (1849–50), b.1784, d.1850.
Tchaikovsky, Piotr Ilyich, Russian composer (*Eugen Onegin,* 1879), b.1840, d.1893.
Tea, traditionally invented 2737 BC by the Chinese emperor Shen Nung; reached Holland 1610; first recorded reference in Britain 1658; Indian tea reached Britain 1839.
Teach, Edward ('Blackbeard'), English pirate, killed 1718.
Technetium (Masurium), discovered 1925 by I. and W. Noddack. Confirmed by C. Perrier and E. Segré of the University of California, 1937.
Tecumseh, American Indian Chief, b.1768, killed in battle 1813.

Tedder, Arthur William, Baron, marshal of the Royal Air Force, b.1890, d.1967.

Te Deum, the 'Ambrosian Chant', probably composed in the 5th century.

Teheran Conference, World War II, between the Allied statesmen Roosevelt, Stalin and Churchill 28 Nov. to Dec. 1943.

Teixeira, Pedro, Portuguese explorer in South America, d.1640.

Tel-Aviv, Israel, coastal city, founded 1909, capital since 1948.

Telegraph, invented 1832 by the American inventor Samuel Morse, b.1791, d.1872.

Telegraph, ocular, invented 1792 by the French engineer Claude Chappe, b.1763, d.1805.

Telegraph cable, first laid across English Channel 1851; first Atlantic, laid 1857.

Telegraph line, first practical, patented 1837 by the English inventors Sir William Fothergill Cooke, b.1806, d.1879, and Sir Charles Wheatstone, b.1802, d.1875; first, set up between Washington and Baltimore 1844 by the American inventor Samuel Morse, b.1791, d.1872; monopoly granted to Post Office 1869.

Telemann, George Philipp, German composer (*Der Tag des Gerichts*), b.1681, d.1767.

Telepathy, first so named 1882 by the English writer Frederick William Henry Myers, b.1843, d.1901.

Telephone, invented 1860 by Reis; patented 1876 by the Scottish-born inventor Alexander Graham Bell, b.1847, d.1922.

Telephone exchange, first commercial exchange in US 1878.

Telephone service, first automatic, inaugurated in London 1927.

Telescope, traditionally invented by Roger Bacon in the 13th century; model presented 2 Oct. 1608 to Dutch General Estates by the optician Hans Lippershym, d.1619.

Telesphorus, St, pope 125–136.

Teletext, broadcast system for displaying information on a TV which is continuously updated, Ceefax® (BBC) and Oracle® (ITV) first introduced 1973.

Television, first demonstrated 1926 by the Scottish inventor John Logie Baird, b.1888, d.1946; **colour**, first publicly demonstrated in Glasgow 1927; the two-colour system demonstrated 1944 by the Scottish inventor John Logie Baird, b.1888, d.1946; **commercial**, began in Britain 1955; **satellite**, began in the UK 1989.

Television broadcast, first BBC experimental, 1929; first BBC experimental programme broadcast 1932; first satellite broadcast 1962 (via Telestar).

Telford, Thomas, Scottish engineer, b.1757, d.1834.

Tell, William, mythical Swiss patriot of 13th century.

Teller, Edward, Hungarian-born American nuclear physicist, designer of the H-bomb, b.1908.

Tellier, Charles, French inventor 1867 of the refrigerator, b.1828, d.1913.

Tellurium, white metal-element, discovered by Reichenstein 1782.

Telstar I & II, the first privately-owned communications satellites, launched 1962–65.

Tempest, Marie, English actress, b.1864, d.1942.

Templars, Order of the Knights, founded *c.*1118, ended 1314.

Temple, Jerusalem, first destroyed by Nebuchadnezzar 586 BC; second built 516 BC, destroyed by Titus AD 70.

Temple, Shirley, Amercan child film star (*Curly Top,* 1935), later US diplomat, b.1928.

Temple, Sir William, statesman and writer, b.1628, d.1699.

Temple Bar, Fleet Street, London, built 1672 by Sir Christopher Wren, b.1632, d.1723; re-erected at Theobalds Park, Essex, 1878.

Teniers, David, the elder, Flemish painter (*Temptation of St Anthony*), b.1582, d.1649.

Teniers, David, the younger, Flemish painter (*The Prodigal Son*), b.1610, d.1690.

Tenison, Thomas, archbishop of Canterbury (1694–1715), b.1636, d.1715.

Tennant, Smithson, English chemist and discoverer (1804) of iridium, b.1761, d.1815.

Tennessee, USA, first settled 1757; admitted to the Union 1796.

Tennessee University, USA, founded at Knoxville 1794.

Tennessee Valley Authority, USA, established 1933.

Tenniel, Sir John, English illustrator of Lewis Carroll's *Alice's Adventures in Wonderland* (1865), b.1820, d.1914.

Tennis, Lawn, origins in outdoor real tennis, played in France in 18th century. Invented as 'sphairistike' by Major Wingfield in 1874, and Lawn Tennis Association formed 1888.

Tennis, Royal, played in France in 11th century; played in England by Henry VII as early as 1497.

Tennis Court Oath, French Revolution, 20 June 1789.

Tennyson, Lord Alfred, English poet (*In Memoriam*, 1850), b.1809, d.1892.

Terbium, metallic element, discovered by the Swedish chemist Karl Gustav Mosander, b.1797, d.1858.

Ter Borch, Gerard, Dutch painter (*Guitar Lesson*), b.1617, d.1681.

Terence, Roman playwright (*Phormio*), b.c. 185, d.c. 159 BC.

Teresa, Mother (Agnes Gonxha Bojaxhiu), Roman Catholic missionary, founded new order Missionaries of Charity in Calcutta 1950, Nobel peace prize 1979, b.1910.

Teresa, St (Teresa de Cepeda y Ahumada), b.1515, d.1582.

Terpander, 'Father of Greek music', lived in the 7th century BC.

Territorial Army, inaugurated at Buckingham Palace 1907. Yeomanry and Volunteer Force units transferred to the newly constructed Territorial Force 1958.

Terry, Dame Ellen, English actress, b.1848, d.1928.

Terry, Sir Richard, English composer of church music, b.1865, d.1938.

Tertiary Period, Earth history between 1 and 70 million years ago.

Tertullian, Roman theologian (*Apologeticus,* 197), b.c. 155, d.c. 220.

Teschen, The Peace of, averting war between Austria and Prussia, signed 13 May 1779.

Test Act, British measure against Catholic office-holding, 1673; extended to peers 1678; repealed 1828–29.

Test-tube baby, first (Louise Brown), born in London 1978.

Tet offensive, major Vietcong offensive against towns and cities in South Vietnam 30 Jan. 1968 (Vietnamese New Year 'Tet').

Tetrazzini, Luisa, Italian operatic singer, b.1871, d.1940.

Tetzel, Johann, German ecclesiastic, b.1455, d.1519.

Teutoburg Forest, Battle of the, between the Cherusei and the Romans AD 9.

Teutonic Knights, military order of Crusaders, founded 1189–91.

Tewfik Pasha, Khedive of Egypt, b.1852, d.1892.

Texas, USA, proclaimed a republic 1836; admitted to the Union 1845.

Texas Rangers, mounted military police, formed 1836.

Texas University, Austin, founded 1883.

Textile Institute, Manchester, founded 1910.

TGV (Trains à Grande Vitesse), French high-speed train, first introduced 27 Sept. 1981 between Paris-Lyon.

Thackeray, William Makepeace, Indian-born novelist (*Vanity Fair,* 1847–48), b.1811, d.1863.
Thailand, former name Siam (until 1939 and 1945–49), absolute monarchy until 1932; constitutional monarchy from 1932.
Thales, Greek statesman and philosopher, b.*c.*624, d.*c.*548 BC.
Thalidomide, sedative drug used in pregnancy 1957–61, found to cause severe birth defects 1962 and removed from the market.
Thallium, metallic element, discovered 1861 by the English scientist Sir William Crookes, b.1832, d.1919.
Thames, river steamboat service inaugurated 1905.
Thames Tunnel, constructed 1825–43 by the French-born engineer Sir Marc Isambard Brunel, b.1769, d.1849.
Thanksgiving Day, USA, commemorating the 1623 harvest, celebrated the 4th Thurs. in Nov.. First national Thanksgiving Day 26 Nov. 1789.
Thatcher, Margaret Hilda, first woman prime minister of the UK (1979–90), b.1925.
Thayer's Law of Camouflage, defined 1910 by the American painter Abbott Henderson Thayer, b.1849, d.1921.
Theatre, first permanent English, opened in London 1576.
Theatre, first television, opened at Brighton 1953.
Theatre footlights, first used in Britain 1672.
Theatre-in-the-round, first used in cinematography by Grimion Samson at the Paris Exhibition 1900.
Theatre lighting, first gas, 1803 (Lyceum, London); first electric, 1846 (Opera, Paris).
Theatres, English, closed by the Puritans 1642; reopened 1660.
Thelwall, John, English reformer, b.1764, d.1834.
Themistocles, Greek general, b.*c.*525, d.459 BC.
Theobald, archbishop of Canterbury, d.1161.
Theocritus, Greek poet, b.before 300, d. after 270 BC.
Theodora, Byzantine empress, d.548.
Theodore, anti-pope 687.
Theodore I, pope 642–649.
Theodore II, pope 897–898.
Theodore I, tsar of Russia (1584–98), b.1557, d.1598.
Theodore II, tsar of Russia (1605), b.1589, murdered 1605.
Theodore III, tsar of Russia (1676–82), b.1661, d.1682.
Theodore of Mopsuestia, Syrian theologian, b.*c.*350, d.*c.*428.
Theodore of Tarsus, archbishop of Canterbury (668–690), b.602, d.690.
Theodoret, Syrian theologian, b.393, d.458.

Theodoric, anti-pope 1100.
Theodoric, king of the Ostrogoths (493–526), b.*c.*454, d.526.
Theodosius I, Byzantine emperor (379–395), b.*c.*346, d.395.
Theodosius II, Byzantine emperor (408–450), b.401, d.450.
Theodosius III, Byzantine emperor (716–717).
Theognis, Greek poet, lived in the 6th and 5th centuries BC.
Theophrastus, Greek philosopher, b.*c.*371 d.*c.*287, BC.
Theosophical Society, founded in the USA 1875 by the Russian-born Mme Helena Blavatsky, b.1831, d.1891; in Britain by the English leader Annie Besant, b.1847, d.1933.
Theresa of Avila, St, b.1515, d.1582.
Thérèse of Lisieux, St (Little Flower of Jesus), b.1873, d.1897.
Thermidor, French Revolutionary calendar month of July-Aug.
Thermionic emission, observed 1883 by the American scientist Thomas Alva Edison, b.1847, d.1931.
Thermionic valve, diode developed 1900 by Fleming; triode developed 1907 by Lee de Forest; tetrode developed 1916 by von Schottky.
Thermionics, study developed by the English physicist Sir Owen Willans Richardson, b.1879, d.1959.
Thermochemistry, study developed by the German scientist Germain Henri Hess, b.1802, d.1850.
Thermodynamics, study founded by the German scientist Rudolf Julius Emanuel Clausius, b.1822, d.1888.
Thermoelectricity, discovered 1821 by the German physicist Thomas Seebeck, b.1770, d.1831.
Thermopylae, Battle of, between Greeks and Persians 480 BC.
Thibaut IV, king of Navarre and troubadour, b.1201, d.1253.
Thicknesse, Philip, English soldier and writer, b.1719, d.1792.
Thierry, Augustin, French historian, b.1795, d.1856.
Thiers, Adolphe, French statesman, b.1797, d.1877.
Thimonnier, Barthélemy, French tailor and inventor (1830) of a sewing machine, b.1793, d.1859.
Third-class travel, British Railways, abolished 3 June 1956.
Third Republic, France 1871–1940.
Thirkell, Angela, English writer (*Love Among the Ruins,* 1948), b.1890, d.1961.
Thirty-nine Articles, of the Church of England, agreed by Convocation 1563; enforced by Parliament 1571; revised 1604.
Thirty Years War, religious wars in Germany 1618–48.
Thistle, Order of the, founded by James III of Scotland *c.*1480; revived in 1687 and 1703.

Thistlewood, Arthur, English conspirator and murderer, b.1770, hanged 1820.

Thomas, Ambroise, French composer (*Mignon,* 1866), b.1811, d.1896.

Thomas, Dylan, Welsh writer (*Under Milk Wood,* 1954), b.1914, d.1953.

Thomas Aquinas, St, Italian philosopher and theologian (*Summa Theologiae*), b.1227, d.1274.

Thomas à Becket, St, archbishop of Canterbury (1162–70), b.*c.*1118, martyred 1170.

Thomas à Kempis, German theologian (*The Imitation of Christ*), b.*c.*1397, d.1471.

Thomas Cook's, travel agents, founded 1841 by the English pioneer Thomas Cook, b.1808, d.1892.

Thomas of Erceldoune ('Thomas the Rhymer'), Scottish prophet and writer, lived in the 13th century.

Thomason, George, English bookseller and collector of contemporary pamphlets, d.1666.

Thompson, David, English-born explorer in Canada, b.1770, d.1857.

Thompson, Edith, English murderess, b.1893, hanged 1922.

Thompson, Francis, English poet (*The Hound of Heaven,* 1893), b.1859, d.1907.

Thompson, John Taliaferro, American inventor 1921 of the submachine ('Tommy') gun, b.1860, d.1940.

Thomson, Elihu, English-born engineer, b.1853, d.1937.

Thomson, James, Scottish poet (*The Seasons,* 1726–30), b.1700, d.1748.

Thomson, Sir Joseph John, English scientist (postulated existence of electrons, 1893), b.1856, d.1940.

Thomson, Robert William, Scottish engineer and inventor 1845 of pneumatic tyres, b.1822, d.1873.

Thomson, Virgil, American composer (*Four Saints in Three Acts,* 1934), b.1896, d.1989.

Thoreau, Henry David, American writer (*Walden,* 1854), b.1817, d.1862.

Thoresby, John, statesman and archbishop of York (1351–73), d.1373.

Thoresby, Ralph, English antiquary, b.1658, d.1725.

Thorium, radioactive element, discovered 1828 by the Swedish chemist Baron Jöns Jakob Berzelius, b.1779, d.1848.

Thorndike, Dame Sybil, English actress, b.1882, d.1976.

Thornton, William, British-born architect (1793–1827) of the US Capitol, d.1827.

Thornton, Robert, English antiquary, b.1623, d.1678.

Thorvaldsen, Bertel, Danish sculptor, b.1770, d.1844.

Thothmes I, king of Egypt 1557–1501 BC.

Thothmes II, king of Egypt 1501 BC.

Thothmes III, king of Egypt 1501–1447 BC.

Thothmes IV, king of Egypt 1420–1411 BC.

Thou, Jacques Auguste de, French historian, b.1553, d.1617.

Thrale, Mrs Hester Lynch (Mrs Piozzi), friend of Dr Samuel Johnson, b.1741, d.1821.

Thrasybulus, Greek statesman, killed *c.*390 BC.

Three Choirs Festival, annual West Country festival, founded 1724

Three-Mile Island accident, nuclear power plant in Pennsylvania that went critical and threatened to explode 28 March–27 April1979.

Threshing machine, first, invented 1784 by the Scottish millwright Andrew Meikle, b.1719, d.1811.

Throckmorton, Sir Nicholas, English diplomat, b.1515, d.1571.

Thucydides, Greek historian of the Peloponnesian War, b.*c.*460, d.*c.*398 BC.

Thulium, a metal of the rare earths, discovered 1879 by Per Teodor Cleve.

Thurber, James, American humorous artist and writer (*The Middle-aged Man on The Flying Trapeze*), b.1894, d.1961.

Thurloe, John, English statesman, b.1616, d.1668.

Thurlow, Edward Thurlow, Baron, Lord Chancellor, b.1731, d.1806.

Thurstan, archbishop of York, d.1140.

Tiananmen Square, central square in Beijing, site of massacre of student pro-democracy protestors by Chinese troops, 3–4 June 1989.

Tiberius, Roman emperor (AD 14–37), b.42 BC, d. AD 37.

Tibullus, Albius, Roman poet, b.*c.*54, d.18 BC.

Tichborne, Chidiock, English conspirator, b.*c.*1558, executed 1586.

Tichborne Claimant, The, the Australian butcher, Arthur Orton, b.1834; claimed Tichborne inheritance 1871–72; tried for perjury 1873–74; imprisoned 1874–84; d.1898.

Tickell, Thomas, English poet (*Colin and Lucy*), b.1686, d.1740.

Ticker-tape machine, invented by the American inventors, Thomas Alva Edison, b.1847, d.1931, and Franklin Leonard Pope, b.1840, d.1895.

Tieck, Ludwig, German novelist (*Magelone,* 1796), b.1773, d.1853.

Tiepolo, Giovanni Battista, Italian painter (*St Catherine of Siena*), b.*c.*1694, d.1769.

Tiffany, Charles Lewis, American jeweller, b.1812, d.1902.

Tigranes, king of Armenia (96–55 BC), b.140, d.55 BC.

Tillett, Benjamin, English labour leader, b.1860, d.1943.

Tillotson, John, archbishop of Canterbury (1691–94), b.1630, d.1694.

Tilly, Johann Tserklaes, Count of, Imperial general, b.1559, killed 1632.

Tilsit, Treaty of, between Napoleon and Russia, 1807.

Timaeus, Greek philosopher, lived in the 5th and 4th centuries.

Time and Tide, British periodical, founded 1920 by Lady Rhondda, b.1883, d.1958.

Times, The, founded London 1785 by the English merchant John Walter, b.1739, d.1812; present name since 1788.

Timoleon, Greek statesman, b.*c.*410, d.*c.*337 BC.

Timon of Athens, lived in the 5th century, BC.

Tindal, Mathew, English theologian, b.1653, d.1733.

Tintoretto (Jacopo Robusti), Italian painter (*The Miracle of St Mark*), b.1518, d.1594.

Tippecanoe, Battle of, between the Americans and the Indians, 7 Nov. 1811.

Tippett, Michael, English composer (*The Midsummer Marriage,* 1955), b.1905.

Tippoo Sahib, sultan of Mysore, b.1749, killed in battle 1799.

Tiptoft, John, Earl of Worcester, 'the Butcher of England', b.*c.*1427, executed 1470.

Tirpitz, German warship, destroyed by the British Navy in World War II, 12 Nov. 1944.

'Tirso de Molina' (Gabriel Téllez), Spanish playwright (*El Burlador de Sevilla,* 1630), b.1571, d.1648.

Tisserand, François Félix, French astronomer, b.1845, d.1896.

Tissue culture, devised 1907 by the American biologist Ross Harrison, b.1870, d.1959.

Titanic, Atlantic passenger liner, sank on her maiden voyage 15 April 1912; wreckage located 500 miles south of Newfoundland Sept. 1985, and explored July 1986.

Titanium, under the name Menachinite, discovered 1791 by the English scientist the Rev. William Gregor, b.1761, d.1817. Called Titanium 1795.

TitBits, British periodical, founded 1881 by George Newnes, b.1851, d.1910.

Titian (Tiziano Vercelli), Italian painter (*Sacred-and Profane Love*), b.c.1486, d.1576.

Tito, Marshal Josip Broz Yugoslav statesman (prime minister 1945–53, president 1953–80), b.1892, d.1980.

Titus, Roman emperor (79–81), b.40, d.81.

Tobacco, brought from America to Europe in 16th century; introduced 1560 into France by the French ambassador to Portugal, Jean Nicot, b.1530, d.1600.

Tobacco pipe, Indian, brought by Ralph Lane, first governor of Virginia, to Sir Walter Raleigh 1586.

Tobruk, World War II, taken by the British 22 Jan. 1941; recaptured after an eight months siege by Rommel 21 June 1942.

Tocqueville, Alexis de, French politician and writer (*Ancien Régime et la Revolution,* 1856), b.1805, d.1859.

Togo, Heihachito, Japanese naval pioneer, b.1847, d.1934.

Togoland, surrendered by Germany to the British and French 1914; divided into British Togoland and French Togoland by the League of Nations 1922; British Togoland joind Ghana 1957; French Togoland became independent as Togo 1960.

Toleration, religious, granted to German rulers by the Peace of Augsburg 1555; in Transylvania by John Sigismund 1568; in France by Edict of Nantes 1598; in England by the Act of Toleration 1639.

Tolkein, John Ronald Revel, British fantasy novelist and literary scholar (*The Lord of the Rings,* 1954–55), b.1892, d.1973.

Toller, Ernst, German playwright, b.1893, committed suicide 1939.

Tolstoy, Count Leo, Russian writer (*War and Peace,* 1864–68), b.1828, d.1910.

Tomato, brought from South America to Europe in 16th century.

Tomkins, Thomas, British calligrapher (*The Beauties of Writing,* 1777), b.1743, d.1816.

Tommasini, Vincenzo, Italian composer (*Medea,* 1906), b.1878, d.1950.

Tommy gun, invented 1921 by the American inventors John Taliaferro Thompson, b.1860, d.1940, and John N. Blish.

Tompion, Thomas, English clockmaker, b.1639, d.1713.

Tom Thumb, (General Charles Sherwood Stratton), American dwarf, b.1838, d.1883.

'Tom Thumb, The', first railway engine built 1830 in the USA, constructed by the American inventor Peter Cooper, b.1791, d.1883.

Tone, Wolfe, United Irishman, b.1763, committed suicide 1798.

Tonga, South Pacific, discovered by the Dutch 1616, and by Abel Janszoon Tasman 1643; proclaimed a British Protectorate 1900; gained independence 1970.

Tonic sol-fa system, invented *c.*1845 by the English musician Sarah Ann Glover, b.1785, d.1867.

Tonson, Jacob, English publisher, b.*c.*1656, d.1736.

Tonti, Henri de, Italian-born explorer in North America, b.*c.*1650, d.1704.

Tontine, annuity system, introduced *c.*1653 by the Italian banker Lorenzo Tonti, b.*c.*1633, d.*c.*1689.

Tooke, John Horne, English politician and writer (*The Diversions of Purley*, 1786–98), b.1736, d.1812.

Toplady, Augustus Montague, English divine and hymn-writer (*Rock of Ages*, 1775), b.1740, d.1778.

Tories, British political group, first so named 1679.

Toronto University, Canada, founded 1827.

Torpedo, motor, invented by the American engineer Herschel Clifford Parker, b.1867.

Torpedo, Submarine, invented 1866 by the English engineer Robert Whitehead, b.1823, d.1905.

Torquemada, Tomás de, leader (1483) of the Spanish Inquisition, b.1420, d.1498.

Torrens, Sir Robert Richard, Irish-born statesman in Australia, b.1814, d.1884.

Torricelli, Evangelista, Italian inventor of the barometer, b.1608, d.1647.

Torrigiano, Pietro, Italian sculptor (*Henry VII's Tomb*), b.1472, d.1522.

Toscanini, Arturo, Italian conductor, b.1867, d.1957.

Tosti, Sir Francesco Paolo, singing master to the British royal family and composer, b.1846, d.1916.

Tostig, earl of the Northumbrians, killed 1066.

Tottel, Richard, English publisher (*Miscellany,* 1557), d.1594.

Toulon, scene of the sabotaging of the French Fleet in World War II, 27 Nov. 1942.

Toulouse-Lautrec, Henri de, French painter, b.1864, d.1901.

Tourneur, Cyril, English playwright (*The Atheist's Tragedy*, *c.*1611), b.*c.*1575, d.1626.

Tourniquet, invented in the Thirty Years War by the German surgeon Fabriz von Hilden, b.1560, d.1634.

Tourniquet, screw, invented by the French surgeon Jean Louis Petit, b.1674, d.1750.

Tours, Battle of, between Charles Martel and the Saracens, 732.

Toussaint l'Ouverture, François Dominique, governor-general of Santo Domingo (now Haiti), born a slave *c.*1743, d.1803.

Tovey, Sir Donald, English musicologist, b.1875, d.1940.

Townshend, Charles Townshend, Viscount, British statesman and agricultural pioneer, b.1674, d.1738.

Toynbee, Arnold Joseph, British historian (A *Study of History*, 1934–54), b.1889, d.1975.

Toynbee Hall, London, founded 1885 as a memorial to the British social reformer Arnold Toynbee, b.1852, d.1883.

Trachoma, main cause of blindness, virus first isolated by the Chinese scientist F. F. T'ang 1957.

***Tracts for the Times*,** Oxford Group tracts issued in defence of the Church of England as a divine institution 1833 to 1841.

Tracy, Spencer, American film and stage actor (*Captains Courageous*, 1937), b.1900, d.1967.

Trades Union Congress, Great Britain, formed 1868.

Trafalgar, Battle of, between Lord Nelson and the French and Spanish fleets, 21 Oct. 1805.

Traherne, Thomas, English poet, b.*c.*1637, d.1674.

Trajan, Roman emperor (98–117), b.*c.*54, d.117.

Tramway, first, opened in New York 26 Nov. 1832; first introduced into England by G. F. Train 1860; first English electrified tramway, Leeds 1891; last tram in London ran 6 July 1952.

Transandine railway tunnel, between Chile and Argentine, opened 1910.

Transatlantic cable, first laid 1858.

Transatlantic flight, first non-stop solo flight (Long Island to Paris) made 20–21 May 1927 by the American aviator Charles Augustus Lindbergh, b.1902. First woman Transatlantic flier, Amelia Earhart, b.1898, flew Newfoundland to Wales 18 June 1928.

Transatlantic cable signal, first, received 14 Dec. 1901 at St John's, Newfoundland, by the Italian radio pioneer Guglielmo Marconi, b.1874, d.1937.

Transatlantic telephone cables, between the United Kingdom, Canada and the USA inaugurated 1956.

Transcendental Club, formed in USA 1836.

Transistors, first demonstrated by scientists of the Bell Telephone Laboratories 1948.

Trans-Siberian railway, construction begun 1891, completed 1906.

Transvaal, colonized by the Boers after 1836; independence recognized by Britain 1852; annexed by Britain 1877; independence restored 1881; reconquered 1902; joined South Africa 1910.

Transvaal gold-bearing lode, discovered 1883.

Transverse-propelled ship, first (the *Oriana*), launched 1959.

Transylvania, ruled by Austria 1698–1848, 1849–67; by Hungary 1867–1920; by Rumania 1920–40, and since 1947.

Trappist Order, founded 1664 by Armand de Rancé, b.1626, d.1700.

Trasimeno, Battle of Lake, between Hannibal and the Romans, 217 BC.

Trebizond, Black Sea port, founded 756 BC (as Trapezoz); site of Empire of Comneni 1204–1461; captured by Turks 1461 and renamed Trabzon.

Tree, Sir Herbert Beerbohm, English actor-manager, b.1853, d.1917.

Treitschke, Heinrich von, German historian, b.1834, d.1896.

Trelawny, Edward John, English writer, b.1792, d.1881.

Trelawny, Sir Jonathan, bishop of Winchester (1707–21), b.1650, d.1721.

Trent, Council of, Catholic ecumenical council, held 1545 to 1563.

Trevisa, John of, English writer and translator, b.1326, d.1412.

Trevithick, Richard, English engineer, b.1771, d.1833.

Trianon, Treaty of, between Hungary and the Allies, signed 4 June 1920.

Triassic Period, Earth history, 195 million years ago.

Trieste, ruled by Austria 1382–1918, by Italy 1918–45; free territory 1942–54; partitioned by Italy and Yugoslavia 1954.

Trinity College, Cambridge University, founded by King Henry VIII 1546.

Trinity College, Oxford University, founded 1555 by Sir Thomas Pope, d.1559.

Trinity Hall, Cambridge University, founded by William Bateman, bishop of Norwich, 1350.

Trinity House, London, origins in the medieval Guild of Mariners, developing into the Corporation of Trinity House of Deptford Strond which was granted its first Charter by King Henry VIII, 1514.

Triode valve (audion), invented 1906 by the American inventor Lee de Forest, b.1873, d.1961.

Triple Alliances, in Europe, 1668, 1717, 1820, 1827, 1881, 1882.

Tristan da Cunha, group of Atlantic islands, discovered March 1506 by the Portuguese navigator Tristão da Cunha, b.*c.*1460, d.*c.*1540; settled 1810, annexed by Britain 1816.

Trolleybus, first used in England 1909.

Trollope, Anthony, English novelist (*Barchester Towers,* 1857), b.1815, d.1882.

Trollope, Mrs Frances, English writer (*Domestic Manners of the Americans*, 1832), b.1780, d.1863.

Trotsky, Leon (Lev Davidovich Bronstein), Russian Revolutionary leader, b.1877, exiled 1929, assassinated 1940.

Troy, destroyed *c.*1200 BC; site at Hissarbik discovered 1801 by the English arhaeologist Sir William Gell, b.1777, d.1836; excavations carried out by the German archaeologist Heinrich Schliemann, b.1822, d.1890.

Troy ounce, for precious metals and stones, legalized in Britain 1853.

Truck Act, prohibiting payment in kind, passed by Parliament 1831.

Trudeau, Pierre Elliott, Canadian statesman (prime minister 1968–79, 1980–84), b.1919.

Truffaut, François, French film director and critic (*Day for Night,* 1973), b.1932, d.1984.

Truman, Harry S., 33rd US president (1945–53), b.1884, d.1972.

Trumbull, John, American painter, b.1756, d.1843.

Trunk call dialling, first introduced in Britain at Bristol, 5 Sept. 1959.

Truth, founded 1877 and edited by the English scholar Henry Labouchere, b.1831, d.1912; ceased publication 1957.

Tsushima, Naval battle of, between the Japanese and Russian fleets, 27 May 1905.

Tuberculosis, bacillus discovered 1882 by the German bacteriologist Robert Koch, b.1843, d.1910.

TUC *see* **Trades Union Congress.**

Tucuman, Congress of, declared the independence of Argentina 9 July 1816.

Tuke, Sir Brian, 'Master of the Postes', d.1545.

Tulane University, New Orleans, founded 1834.

Tull, Jethro, English agricultural pioneer and inventor of the seed drill 1731, b.1674, d.1741.

Tungsten, metallic element, discovered 1781 by the Swedish chemist Carl Wilhelm Scheele, b.1742, d.1786; isolated 1783 by the Spanish chemist Fauste d'Elhuyar, b.1755, d.1833; ductile, discovered 1906 by the American scientist William David Collidge, b.1873.

Tuning fork, said to have been invented 1711 by the English trumpeter and lutenist John Shore, d.1752.

Tunney, Gene (James Joseph Tunney), American ex-world heavyweight champion, b.1897, d.1978.

Tunstall, Cuthbert, Master of the Rolls and bishop of Durham (1530–59), b.1474, d.1559.

Turbine, first reaction, built 1839; steam, invented 1884 by the British engineer Sir Charles Parsons, b.1854, d.1931.

Turbojet, first (the De Havilland Comet), entered airline service 1958.

Turboprop airliner, first (the Bristol Britannia), entered scheduled service 1 Feb. 1957.

Turboprop engine, first (the Rolls-Royce Dart), 1947.

Turenne, Henri de la Tour d'Auvergne, Vicomte de, French soldier, b.1611, killed in battle 1675.

Turgenev, Ivan Sergeievich, Russian novelist (*A Sportsman's Sketches,* 1846), b.1818, d.1883.

Turgot, bishop of St Andrews, d.1115.

Turgot, Anne Robert Jacques, French statesman, b.1727, d.1781.

Turina, Joaquin, Spanish composer (*Sinfonia Sevillana*), b.1882, d.1949.

Turing, Alan Mathison, British mathematician, conceived the *Turing Machine* and other important theoretical contributions to early computer science, b.1912, committed suicide 1954.

Turks, rebelled against Avars 552, defeated Byzantine army 1071, defeated by Mongols 1243; Ottomans crossed Dardanelles 1345, defeated Serbs at Kossovo 1389, defeated by Timur 1402, captured Constantinople 1453. Ottoman Empire collapsed 1922 and republic of Turkey proclaimed 1923.

Turner, Joseph Mallord William, English painter (*The Grand Canal, Venice*), b.1775, d.1851.

Turner, Thomas, English potter who introduced (1780) the willow pattern, b.1749, d.1809.

Turpin, Dick, English highwayman, b.1705, hanged 1739.

Tussaud's, Mme, London waxworks, opened 1835 by the Swiss-born showperson Mme Marie Tussaud, b.1760, d.1850.

Tutankhamun, tomb of, discovered 1922.

Tutu, Desmond, South African Anglican archbishop and anti-apartheid campaigner, Nobel peace prize 1984, b.1931.

Twain, Mark (Samuel Langhorne Clemens), American writer (*Tom Sawyer*, 1876), b.1835, d.1910.

Twelfth Night (Old Christmas Day or, The Feast of the Three Kings), celebrated on night of 5 Jan.

Two Thousand Guineas, Newmarket, first run 1809.

Tycho Brahe, Danish astronomer, b.1546, d.1601.

Tyler, John, 10th US president (1841–45), b.1790, d.1862.

Tyler, Wat, English rebel leader, killed 1381.

Tynan, Kenneth, British theatre critic and writer, b.1920, d.1980.

Tyndale, William, English translator of the Bible, b.c.1494, strangled and burnt at the stake 1536.

Tyndall, John, Irish-born scientist, b.1820, d.1893.

Typewriter, model constructed 1873 by Sholes and Glidden; first modern version (Underwood) constructed 1898 by F. X. Wagner.

Typhoid fever, bacillus described by Eberth 1880.

Typhus, bacillus described by Ricketts 1910.

Tyres, *see* **Pneumatic Tyres.**

Tyrrell, Anthony, English spy, b.1552, d.c.1610.

Tzetzes, John, Byzantine scholar, b.c.1110, d.1180.

U

Ubaldini, Petruccio, Italian-born writer and illuminator, b.*c.*1524, d.*c.*1600.

Uberweg, Friedrich, German philosopher, b.1826, d.1871.

Uccello, Paolo, Italian artist (*Deluge, c.*1445), b.*c.*1396, d.1475.

Udall, Nicholas, English playwright (*Ralph Roister Doister, c.*1553), b.1505, d.1556.

UFO (Unidentified Flying Object), first 'noticed' by the American Kenneth Arnold June 1947.

Uganda, British Protectorate 1894–96; gained independence 1962; became republic 1967.

Ugolino da Siena, Italian painter, lived in the 14th century.

Uhde, Fritz von, German painter, b.1848, d.1911.

Ukraine, former Soviet Socialist Republic, declared independence Dec.1991.

Ulfilas, translator of the Bible into Gothic, b.*c.*311, d.383.

Ulloa, Francisco de, Spanish navigator of the Californian coast, d.*c.*1540.

Ulpianus, Roman jurist, killed *c.*228.

Ulster, former kingdom in Northern Ireland divided 1921 into Northern Ireland (Antrim, Armagh, Down, Fermanagh, Londonderry and Tyrone) and the Republic of Ireland (Cavan, Donegal and Monaghan).

Umberto I, king of Italy (1878–1900), b.1844, assassinated 1900.

Umberto II, king of Italy (1946), b.1904, d.1983.

Unamuno, Miguel de, Spanish writer, b.1864, d.1937.

Underground railroad, system by which negro slaves were enabled to escape through the northern states of America, 1825 onwards.

Underground railway, first opened in London 1863 (Metropolitan Railway); first electric line opened 1890 (City & South London Railway).

Undset, Sigrid, Norwegian novelist (*Kristin Lavransdatter*), b.1882, d.1949.

UNESCO (United Nations Educational, Scientific and Cultural Organization), established 4 Nov. 1946.

UNICEF (United Nations Children's Fund), established 1946.

Unidentified Flying Objects, *see* **UFO.**

Uniformity, Acts of, 1549, 1552, 1559, 1662.

Union, Act of, between England and Scotland 1707; between Britain and Ireland 1800.

Union, Decree of (*Laetentur caeli*), uniting the Latin and Greek churches, issued 6 July 1439.

Union of Soviet Socialist Republics, formed 1922 from Russian empire and other Soviet republics in the Baltic created after 1917 revolution; Soviet empire enlarged 1924–45; 1985 new policies of *perestroika* (reorganization) and *glasnost* (openness) introduced by president Mikhail Gorbachev; Baltic and other constituent republics pressed for independence; 19 Aug. 1991 hardliners attempted military coup to restore communist authority; 29 Aug. communist party banned by Russian president Boris Yeltsin; formation of the Commonwealth of Independent States (CIS) 8 Dec. 1991; Gorbachev resigned as Soviet president and USSR ceased to exist 26 Dec. 1991.

Union Pacific Railway, USA, built mainly 1862–1869.

United Boys' Brigade of America, founded 1887.

United Church of Christ, formed in the USA through the union of the General Council of the Congregational Christian Churches with the Evangelical and Reformed Church 1957.

United Kingdom (Great Britain), formed 1801.

United Nations, formed 1942; organization set up 1945.

United States of America, declared independence 1776; constitution established 1787.

Universal Postal Union, founded at Bern 9 Oct. 1875.

University College, London University, opened 1828.

University College, Oxford University, once believed to have been founded 872; in existence by 1170.

UNO, *see* **United Nations**.

Updike, John (Hoyer), American novelist and critic (*Rabbit Run,* 1960), b.1932.

Uranus, planet discovered 13 March 1781 by the German-born astronomer William Herschel, b.1738, d.1822.

Urfey, Thomas d', English playwright (*The Comical History of Don Quixote,* 1694–1696), b.*c.*1653, d.1723.

Urien, British prince, lived in the 6th century.

Urquhart, Sir Thomas, Scottish writer and translator, b.*c.*1611, d.1660.

Urquiza, Justo José de, president of Argentina (1854–1860), b.1800, assassinated 1870.

Ursinus, Zacharias, German theologian who, with Caspar Olevianus, b.1536, d.1587, published (1563) the Heidelburg Catechism, b.1536, d.1583.

Ursuline Order, of nuns, founded 1535.

Uruguay, independence established 1828.

Ussher, James, archbishop of Armagh and writer, b.1581, d.1656.

USSR, *see* **Union of Soviet Socialist Republics.**

Ustinov, Peter Alexander, British actor, director, playwright and author (*Topkapi*, 1964), b.1921.

Utah, USA, settled 1847; organized as a Territory 1850; admitted to the Union 1896.

Utah University, Salt Lake City, founded 1850; reopened under present name 1867.

Utamaro, Kitagawa, Japanese artist, b.753, d.1806.

U Thant, Burmese diplomat (secretary general of the UN 1962–71), b.1909, d.1974.

Utrillo, Maurice, French painter, b.1883, d.1955.

Uttman, Barbara, German woman who introduced (1561) pillow lace-making into Germany, b.1514, d.1575.

U-2 incident, shooting down of US military spy plane by Soviet missiles over Russia, 1 May 1960; pilot Gary Powers was exchanged for a Soviet agent two years later.

V

Vaccination, against smallpox, pioneered by Lady Mary Wortley Montagu, b.1689, d.1762; revived 1796 by Edward Jenner, b.1749, d.1823.
Vacuum flask, invented by the Scottish scientist Sir James Dewar, b.1842, d.1923.
Vaihinger, Hans, German philosopher, b.1852, d.1933.
Valdivia, Pedro de, Spanish conquistador in Chile, killed 1554.
Valency, double, isomerism, study developed 1893 by the Swiss chemist Alfred Werner, b.1866, d.1919.
Valens, Byzantine emperor (364–378), killed in battle 378.
Valentine, pope 827.
Valentine, St, martyred c.270
St Valentine's Day, 14 Feb.
Valentinian I, Roman emperor (364–375), b.321, d.375.
Valentinian II, Roman emperor (375–392), b.371, d.392.
Valentinian III, Roman emperor (425–455), d.419, assassinated 455.
Valentino, Rudolph, film actor (especially in silent movies), b.1895, d.1926.
Valera, Eamon de, Irish statesman (prime minister 1927–48, 1951–54, 1957–59; president 1959–73), b.1882, d.1975.
Valerian, Roman emperor, 253–260.
Valéry, Paul, French writer, b.1871, d.1945.
Valle-Inclán, Ramón del, Spanish novelist, b.1870, d.1936
Vallet, Edouard, Swiss painter (*Sunday in the Valais*, 1919), b.1876, d.1929.
Valois dynasty, ruled France 1328–1589.
Vallotton, Félix, Swiss painter (*The Rape of Europa*, 1908), b.1865, d.1925.
Valparaiso, Chile, founded 1536.
Van Buren, Martin, 8th US president (1837–41), b.1782, d.1862.
Van Der Meer, Jan, Dutch painter, b.1628, d.1691.
Van Doren, Carl, American writer, b.1885, d.1950.
Van Gogh, Vincent, Dutch painter (*Sunflowers*), b.1853, committed suicide 1890.
Van Dyck, Sir Anthony, Flemish-born painter (*Charles I*), b.1599, d.1641.
Van Loon, Hendrick, American writer (*Story of Mankind*, 1921), b.1882, d.1944.

Vanadium, metallic element, discovered by Sefström 1830.
Vanbrugh, Sir John, English playwright and architect, b.1664, d.1726.
Vancouver, George, British navigator b.1758, d.1798.
Vandals, crossed Rhine 406; entered Spain 409; crossed to Africa 429; sacked Rome 455; defeated by Belisarius 533.
Vanderbilt, Cornelius, American financier, b.1794, d.1877.
Vanderbilt University, Tennessee, founded 1872.
Vane, Sir Henry, statesman, b.1613, executed 1662.
Vanhomrigh, Esther, Dean Swift's 'Vanessa', b.1690, d.1723.
Vanuatu (formerly New Hebrides), South Pacific, discovered by the Portuguese navigator Pedro Fernandez de Queiras, b.*c.*1560, d.1614.
Vargas Llosa, Mario, Peruvian novelist (*The Time of the Hero,* 1963), and politician, b.1936.
Varro, Marcus Terentius, Roman writer, b.116, d.27 BC.
Vasco da Gama, Portuguese explorer and navigator, b.*c.*1460, d.*c.*1525.
Vascular surgery, initiated by the French surgeon Alexis Carrel, b.1873, d.1945.
Vatican, papal residence since 1377.
Vatican Council, Catholic general council, held 1869–70.
Vaughan, Henry ('The Silurist'), Welsh poet, b.1622, d.1695.
Vaughan, William, colonizer of Newfoundland, b.1577, d.1641.
Vaughan Williams, Ralph, English composer (*Hugh the Drover,* 1911–14), b.1872, d.1958.
Vauxhall Gardens, open from *c.*1661 to 1859.
Veblen, Thorstein, American sociologist, b.1857, d.1929.
VE Day, Victory in Europe, 8 May 1945.
Veidt, Conrad, film actor, b.1894, d.1943.
Velazquez, Diego Rodriquez de Silva, Spanish painter (*The Rokeby Venus*), b.1599, d.1660.
Venezuela, independence proclaimed 1811, secured 1830.
Venice, independent republic under rule of doges 697–1797; ruled by Austria 1797–1805, 1815–48, 1849–66.
Venizelos, Eleutherios, Greek statesman, b.1864, d.1936.
Verdi, Giuseppe, Italian composer (*Rigoletto,* 1851), b.1813, d.1901.
Verdun, Battle of, between Germans and French, Feb.-April 1916
Vere, Edward de, Earl of Oxford, poet, b.1550, d.1604.

Vereeniging, Treaty of, between English and Boers, signed 1902.

Verhaeren, Emile, Belgian poet, b.1855, d.1916.

Verlaine, Paul, French poet, b.1844, d.1896.

Vermeer, Jan, Dutch painter, b.1632, d.1675.

Vermont, USA, first settled 1724; admitted to the Union 1791.

Veronese (Paolo Caliari), Italian painter, b.1528, d.1588.

Versailles, Treaty of, signed 28 June 1919.

Vertue, George, English engraver, b.1684, d.1756.

Vespasian, Roman emperor (69–79), b.11, d.79.

Vespucci, Amerigo, Italian explorer, b.1451, d.1512.

Vestris, Mme (Lucia Elizabeth Mathews), actress, b.1797, d.1856.

Veto, abolished in Polish Diet 1791; last used by British sovereigns 1707; established in UN Security Council 1945.

Vianney, Jean Marie (The Curé d'Ars), French priest, b.1787 d.1859.

Viceroy, title of British colonial ruler of India 1858–1947.

Vico, Giambattista, Italian writer, b.1668, d.1744.

Vichy, place of French government 1940–47.

Victoria, queen, b.1819, d.1901.

Victoria and Albert Museum, London, opened 18 May 1852.

Victoria Cross, premier British decoration for valour, founded by Queen Victoria 1856.

Victorian Order, Royal, founded by Queen Victoria 1896.

Vidal, Gore, American novelist, essayist and critic (*Burr*, 1974), b.1925.

Video recorders, first domestic system (Sony Betamax) introduced 1975.

Vidocq, François Eugène, French criminal and detective, b.1775, d.1857.

Vienna, besieged by Turks 1529 and 1683.

Vienna, Congress of, 1814–15.

Vietnam, socialist republic in S.E. Asia; conquered by France 1858–84, and incorporated as part of French Indochina (with Laos, Cambodia and Annam); occupied by Japanese 1940–45; French authority restored 1945, but Vietminh resistance led to defeat of French 1954; country partitioned at Geneva conference 1954 between North Vietnam and South (Republic of) Vietnam; war between North and South escalated 1956–65; US troops supported the South 1965–73; Paris Peace Accords 1973 ended US involvement, but further fighting led to the defeat of the South in March 1975; united socialist republic established 1976.

Vietnam War, *see* **Vietnam.**

Vieuxtemps, Henri, Belgian violinist and composer, b.1820, d.1881.

Vigfússon, Gudbrandur, Icelandic scholar, b.1828, d.1889.

Vigny, Alfred de, French writer, b.1797, d.1863.

Villa-Lobos, Heitor, Brazilian composer (*Vidapura,* 1918), b.1887, d.1959.

Villa Pancho, Mexican rebel leader, b.*c.*1878, d.1923.

Villiers, Barbara, Countess of Castlemaine, Duchess of Cleveland, b.1641, d.1709.

Villiers, George, Duke of Buckingham, English courtier, b.1592, assassinated 1628.

Villiers, George, Duke of Buckingham, courtier and statesman, b.1628, d.1687.

Villon, François, French criminal and poet, b.1431, disappeared 1463.

Vinegar Bible, so-called for its 'Parable of the Vinegar' (i.e. Vineyard), published 1717.

Vintners Company, London livery company, origins uncertain; first recorded reference 1321; Letters Patent granted 1363; first charter 1437.

Violin playing, first made the subject of formal tuition 1730 by the Italian violinist Francesco Geminiani, b.1687, d.1762.

Virchow, Rudolf, German founder of the science of modern pathology, b.1821, d.1902.

Virgil (Publius Vergilius Maro), Roman, poet (*Aeneid*), b.70, d.19 BC.

Virginia, USA, first settled 1607, entered the Union 1788.

Viroids, isolated 1971.

Viruses, existence of, discovered 1897 by Martinus Beijerinck, Dutch botanist.

Visconti, Luchino, Italian film director (*Death in Venice,* 1971), b.1906, d.1976.

Vitalis, Ordericus, English historian, b.1075, d.*c.*1143.

Vitruvius (Marcus Vitruvius Pollio), Roman architect in 1st century BC.

Vivaldi, Antonio, Italian composer (*La Stravaganza*), b.*c.*1676, d.1741.

Vivisection, law regulating passed 1876.

Vodka, manufacture of, prohibited in Russia 1914–25.

Volta, Alessandro, Italian physicist, b.1745, d.1827.

Voltaire, François Marie Arouet de, French writer (*Candide*, 1759), b.1694, d.1778.

Volunteers of America, founded by Generals Ballington Booth and Maud Ballington Booth 1896.

Vonnegut, Kurt, Jr, American author (*Slaughter-house Five*, 1969), b.1922.

Von Neumann, John, German mathematician, b.1903, d.1957.

Von Stroheim, Erich, film actor, b.1886, d.1957.

Vortigern, British leader, lived in the 5th century.

Vostok I, first manned space flight (USSR), 12 April 1961, crewed by Yuri Gagarin; Vostok 6 carried the first woman into space, Valentina V. Tereshkova, 16–19 June 1963.

Vulcanization of rubber, patented 1843 by the English merchant Thomas Hancock, b.1786, d.1865.

Vulgate, Latin translation of Bible, made 382–405 by St Jerome.

W

Waals, Johannes Diderik van der, Dutch scientist and Nobel prize winner, b.1837, d.1923.

Wadham College, Oxford University, founded 1612 by bequest of Nicholas Wadham, d.1609.

Wafd, Egyptian political party, formed 1919.

Wagner, Cosima, wife of Richard Wagner, b.1837, d.1930.

Wagner, Richard, German composer (*Lohengrin*, 1848), b.1813, d.1883.

Wagram, Battle of, between Napoleon and the Austrians 5–6 July 1809.

Wain, John, English novelist (*Hurry on Down*, 1953), b.1925.

Wainewright, Thomas Griffiths, the English poisoner and artist, b.1794, d.1852.

Waitangi, Treaty of, signed with the Maoris in New Zealand, 6 Feb. 1840.

Waksman, Dr Selman Abraham, Russian-born discoverer 1943 of streptomycin, b.1888, awarded Nobel prize 1952, d.1978.

Walburga, St, b.*c.*710, d.*c.*777.

Waldenses, Christian heretic sect, founded during 12th century by Peter Walds of Lyon.

Waldteufel, Emil, French composer of dance music (*Estudiantina*), b.1837, d.1915.

Wales, finally subdued by England 1284 (rebelled 1400–10); united with England 1536–47; first archbishop of (the bishop of St Asaph), enthroned 1 June 1920.

Walesa, Lech, Polish trade union leader and politician, b.1943, founder of Solidarity 'free trade union' and president of Poland (since 1990).

Walker, George, governor of Londonderry, b.1618, killed in battle 1690.

Walkinshaw, Clementina, mistress of the Young Pretender, b.*c.*1726, d.1802.

Wall Game, held at Eton College on St Andrew's Day, 30. Nov.

Wall, Max (Maxwell George Lorimer), British comedian, b.1908, d.1990.

Wall Street Journal, American financial broadsheet, established 1889.

Wallace, Alfred Russel, English naturalist, b.1823, d.1913.

Wallace, Lew, American writer (*Ben Hur*, 1880), b.1827, d.1905.

Wallace, Sir William, Scottish leader, b.c.1274, executed 1305.

Wallace Collection, The, London, bequeathed by the widow of Sir Richard Wallace, b.1818, d.1890, opened 1900.

Wallenstein, Albrecht von, Bohemian soldier, b.1583, assassinated 1634.

Waller, Edmund, English poet and politician, b.1606, d.1687.

Waller, Sir William, soldier and politician, b.c.1597, d.1668.

Wallis, John, English mathematician, b.1616, d.1703.

Wallis, Samuel, English naval captain and discoverer (1767) of Tahiti, b.1728, d.1804.

Walpole, Horace, Earl of Oxford, English writer (*The Castle of Otranto*, 1764), b.1717, d.1797.

Walpole, Hugh, New Zealand-born novelist (*Rogue Herries*, 1930), b.1884, d.1941.

Walpole, Robert, Earl of Oxford, British statesman (virtual prime minister 1721–42), b.1676, d.1745.

Walpurga, St, English abbess of Heidenheim, d.c.779.

Walsh, John, English publisher of music, d.1736.

Walsingham, Sir Francis, British statesman, b.c.1530, d.1590.

Walsingham, Thomas, English historian (*Chronica Majora*), d.c.1422.

Walter, Bruno (Bruno Walter Schlesinger), German-born conductor, b.1876, d.1962.

Walter, John, English merchant and founder 1785 of *The Times*, b.1739, d.1812.

Walther von der Vogelweide, German minnesinger and poet (*The Palestine Song*), d.c.1230.

Walton, Izaak, English writer (*The Compleat Angler*, 1653), b.1593, d.1683.

Walton, Sir William, English composer (*Façade*, 1922), b.1902, d.1983.

Wan Li period, China, 1573–1619.

Warbeck, Perkin, French-born pretender, b.1474, executed 1499.

Warburg Institute, University of London, founded by Professor Aby Warburg, b.1866, d.1929.

Warburton, William, bishop of Gloucester (1759–79), b.1698, d.1779.

Ward, Mrs Humphry (Mary Augusta Ward), Tasmanian-born novelist (*Robert Elsmere*, 1888), b.1851, d.1920.

Warham, William, archbishop of Canterbury (1504–32), b.c.1450, d.1532.

Warhol, Andy (Andrew Warhola), American pop artist, b.1927, d.1987.

Warlock, Peter (Philip Heseltine), English composer (*The Curlew*), b.1894, d.1930.

Warner, Sylvia Townsend, English writer (*Lolly Willowes,* 1926), b.1893, d.1978.

Warren Commission, 1963 tribunal investigating the assassination (Nov. 1961) of US President John F. Kennedy, headed by Chief Justice Earl Warren, b.1891, d.1974.

Warren, Robert Penn, American author (*All the King's Men,* 1946), b.1905, d.1989.

'Warwick the Kingmaker' (Richard Neville, Earl of Warwick), b.1428, killed 1471.

Washington, Booker Taliaferro, black American educationist, b.*c.*1859, d.1915.

Washington, George, 1st US president (1789–97), b.1732, d.1799.

Washington DC, capital of USA, founded 1791.

Washington, USA, created a Territory 1853; admitted to the Union 1889.

Washington, Treaty of, between the USA and Great Britain, signed 1871.

Wassermann, August von, German scientist and inventor 1906 of the Wassermann Test, b.1866, d.1925.

Wassermann, Jakob, novelist (*Christian Wahnschaffe,* 1919), b.1873, d.1933.

Water, first analysed 1783 by the French chemist Antoine Laurent Lavoisier, b.1743, d.1794.

Water closets, invented 1596 by the English poet Sir John Harington, b.1561, d.1612.

'Water Poet, The', (John Taylor), English writer (*The Pennyles Pilgrimage,* 1618), b.1580, d.1653.

Watergate, Washington headquarters of the US Democratic Party, burgled by operatives of the Nixon White House 17 June 1972; their discovery and subsequent White House cover-up led to Nixon's resignation in Aug. 1974.

Waterloo, Battle of, 18 June 1815.

Waterloo Bridge, London, old bridge built by the Scottish engineer John Rennie, b.1761, d.1821. New bridge opened to vehicles 1942; formally opened 1945.

Watermarks, in paper, first known example made *c.*1282.

Waterproof clothing, invented 1823 by the Scottish chemist Charles Macintosh, b.1766, d.1843.

Watson, George Lennox, British yacht designer, b.1851, d.1904.

Watson, Richard, bishop of Llandaff and scientist, b.1737, d.1816.

Watt, James, Scottish engineer and inventor, b.1736, d.1819.

Watt, Robert, Scottish physician and bibliographer, b.1774, d.1819.

Watteau, Antoine, French painter (*The Embarkation for Cythera*, 1717), b.1684, d.1721.

Watts, Sir George Frederick, English painter (*Paolo and Francesca*, 1848), b.1817, d.1904.

Watts, Isaac, English hymn-writer (*Jesus Shall Reign*), b.1674, d.1748.

Waugh, Evelyn, English writer (*Brideshead Revisited*, 1945), b.1903, d.1966.

Wave mechanics, defined 1923 by the French scientist Prince Louis de Broglie, b.1892, d.1987.

Wavell, Archibald Percival Wavell, Earl, viceroy of India (1943–47), b.1883, killed 1953.

Wayne, John (Marian Michael Morrison, 'The Duke'), American film star (*She Wore a Yellow Ribbon*, 1949), b.1907, d.1979.

Waynflete, William of, bishop of Winchester and founder 1458 of Magdalen College, Oxford, b.*c.*1395, d.1486.

Weather map, first drawn 1820 by the German astronomer and physicist Heinrich Wilhelm Brandes, b.1777, d.1834.

Weather prediction, study founded by the French scientist Jean Baptiste Pierre Antoine de Monet, Chevalier de Lamarck, b.1744, d.1829.

Webb, Beatrice, b.1858, d.1943, and **Sidney**, b.1859, d.1947, British sociologists, m. 1892.

Weber, Carl Maria, German composer (*Der Freischütz*, 1821), b.1786, d.1826.

Weber, Max, German social scientist (*The Protestant Ethic and the Spirit of Capitalism*, 1904–05), b.1864, d.1920.

Webern, Anton von, Austrian composer (*Passacaglia*, 1908), b.1883, d.1945.

Webster, John, English playwright (*The White Devil*, 1612), b.*c.*1580, d.*c.*1625.

Webster, Noah, American dictionary maker (first published 1806), b.1758, d.1843.

Wedekind, Frank, German writer, b.1864, d.1918.

Wedgwood, Josiah, English potter, b.1730, d.1795

Week, the seven days from midnight on Saturday to midnight the following Saturday; adopted in Roman Empire from Jewish custom *c.*500.

Wei dynasty, China, 368 to 557.

Weight reduction, by the elimination of starch in diet, popularized by the English undertaker, William Banting, b.1797, d.1878.

Weill, Kurt, composer (*Die Dreigroschenopfer*, 1928), b.1900, d.1950.

Weimar Republic, Germany 1918–33.

Weingartner, Felix, conductor, b.1863, d.1942.

Weishaupt, Adam, German philosopher and founder 1776 of the Illuminati, b.1748, d.1830.

Weizmann, Dr Chaim, Polish-born scientist, Zionist leader and first president of Israel, b.1874, d.1952.

Welles, Orson, American film director, producer, screenwriter and actor (*Citizen Kane,* 1941), b.1915, d.1985.

Wellington, Arthur Wellesley, Duke of, British soldier and statesman, b.1769, d.1852.

Wells, Herbert George, English writer (*Kipps*, 1905), b.1866, d.1946.

Wells, Fargo & Co., American express company, founded 1852.

Welsbach mantle, invented by the Austrian chemist Baron von Welsbach, b.1858, d.1929.

Welsh literature, recorded before 600.

Welwyn Garden City, built 1920

Wembley Exhibition (British Empire Exhibition), Wembley, opened 23 April, closed 1 Nov. 1924.

Wentworth, William Charles, Australian pioneer, b.1793, d.1872.

Werfel, Franz, Austrian writer, b.1890, d.1945.

Werner, Alfred, Swiss chemist who developed (1893) the study of double valency, b.1866, d.1919.

Wesker, Arnold, English playwright (*Roots,* 1959), b.1932.

Wesley, Charles, English hymn-writer (*Jesu, Lover of My Soul*), b.1707, d.1788.

Wesley, John, founder (1738) of Methodism, b.1703, d.1791.

West Bank, former Jordanian territory west of the river Jordan occupied by Israel 1967.

West, Benjamin, American painter (*The Death of General Wolfe*, 1771), b.1738, d.1820.

West, Mae, American comedy actress of stage and film (*I'm No Angel,* 1933), b.1892, d.1980.

West, Rebecca (Cicely Fairfield), English writer (*The Meaning of Treason*, 1949), b.1892, d.1983.

West Virginia, USA, separated from Virginia 1861, admitted to the Union 1863.

Western Australia, founded 1829; reached overland 1875 on third attempt (1875–76) by the Australian explorer Ernest Giles, b.1835, d.1897.

Westminster Abbey (Collegiat Church of St Peter), built 1056–1745; consecrated 1065.

Westminster Assembly, religious body, sat 1643–49.

Westminster Cathedral, England, opened 1903; consecrated 1910.

Westminster Gazette, The, British newspaper, founded 1892; absorbed into *The Daily News* 1928.

Westminster, Statute of, regulating British Commonwealth relations, passed 1931

Westphalia, kingdom of, existed 1807–14.

Westphalia, Peace of, ending the Thirty Years War, signed 1648.

Wetterhorn, 12,162 ft. peak near Grindelwald, first climbed by the Swiss guides Bannholzer and Jaun 1844.

Weyden, Rogier van der, Flemish painter (*The Last Judgment*), b.c.1400, d.1464.

Weyprecht, Karl, German discoverer 1873 of Franz Josef Land in the Arctic, b.1838, d.1881.

Whaling Commission, International, set up 1946.

Wharton, Henry, English scholar, b.1664, d.1695.

Wheatstone bridge, invented by the English scientist Sir Charles Wheatstone, b.1802, d.1875.

Whigs, British political group, first so named 1679; split 1791.

Whistler, James McNeill, American-born painter (*Portrait of My Mother*), b.1834, d.1903.

Whiston, Joseph, London bookseller, d.1780.

Whitaker's Almanack, founded 1868 by the English publisher Joseph Whitaker, b.1820, d.1895.

Whitby, Synod of, held 664.

White, Gilbert, English naturalist (*The Natural History and Antiquities of Selbourne*, 1789), b.1720, d.1793.

White, William Hale ('Mark Rutherford'), English writer (*Catherine Furze*, 1893), b.1831, d.1913.

White Lotus Day, commemorating the death of the founder of the Theosophical Society, Mme Blavatsky, b.183, d.1891.

White Russia, Soviet republic declared 1919.

White Ship, The, sank with Prince William 1120.
Whitehead, Alfred North, British philosopher, b.1861, d.1947.
Whitefield, George, English Calvinist Methodist, b.1714, d.1740.
Whitehead, Robert, English inventor and torpedo manufacturer, b.1823, d.1905.
Whiteman, Paul, American jazz conductor, b.1891, d.1967.
Whitlam, Edward Gough, Australian statesman (prime minister 1972–75), b.1916.
Whitley Councils, concerning British labour conditions, largely founded 1917 by John Henry Whitley, Speaker of the House of Commons, b.1866, d.1935.
Whitman, Walt, American poet (*Leaves of Grass*, 1855), b.1819, d.1892.
Whitsunday (Pentecost), seventh Sunday after Easter.
Whittingham, Charles, English printer, b.1767, d.1840.
Whittington, Dick, Lord Mayor of London (1397), b.*c.*1358, d.1423.
Whittle, Sir Frank, English pioneer in jet propulsion, b.1907.
Whitworth, Sir Joseph, English mechanical engineer who standardized (1841) screw threads, b.1803, d.1887.
Whymper, Edward, English climber (1865) of the Matterhorn, b.1840, d.1911.
Whyte-Melville, George John, Scottish writer, b.1821, d.1878.
Wickham, Sir Henry, pioneer rubber planter, b.1846, d.1928.
Widor, Charles Marie, French composer (*Symphonie Romaine*), b.1844, d.1937.
Wien, Wilhelm, German physicist and exponent of the theory of radiation, b.1864, d.1938.
Wieniawski, Henri, Polish violinist and composer (*Légende*), b.1835, d.1880.
Wilberforce, Samuel, English divine, b.1805, d.1873.
Wilberforce, William, English suppressor of slavery, b.1759, d.1833.
Wild, Jonathan, English receiver and informer, b.*c.*1682, hanged 1725.
Wilde, Oscar, Irish-born wit and writer (*The Importance of being Earnest*, 1895), b.1856, d.1900.
Wilder, Billy, American film director, producer and screenwriter (*Double Indemnity*, 1944), b.1906.
Wilder, Thornton, American author and playwright (*The Bridge of San Luis Rey,* 1927), b.1897, d.1975.
Wilfrid, St, English divine, b.634, d.710.

Wilhelm, Karl Friedrich, German composer (*Die Wacht am Rhein*, 1854), b.1815, d.1873.
Wilhelmina, queen of the Netherlands (1890–1948), b.1880, d.1962.
Wilhelmshaven, first German military port, opened officially 17 June 1869.
Wilkes, John, English politician, b.1727, d.1797.
Wilkins, Sir Hubert, Australian explorer, b.1888, d.1958.
William I, king of Prussia and emperor of Germany, b.1797, succeeded his brother 1861, proclaimed emperor 1871, d.1888.
William II, emperor of Germany, b.1859, succeeded 1888, abdicated 1918, d.1942.
William II Land, Antarctica, discovered 1903 by the German explorer Erich von Drygalski, b.1865, d.1949.
William IV, king of Great Britain and Ireland (1830–37), b.1765, d.1837.
William and Mary, College of, Williamsburg, Virginia, founded 1693 by the English colonist William Randolf, b.1650, d.1711.
William of Malmesbury, English historian, b.*c.*1095, d.1143.
William of Ockham, English philosopher, d.*c.*1349.
William of Orange (William III), king of England, Scotland and Ireland (1689–1702), b.1650, d.1702.
William of Wykeham, bishop of Winchester and founder (1379) of New College, Oxford, and 1382 of Winchester College, b.1324, d.1404.
William Rufus (William II), king of England (1087–1100), b.*c.*1056, shot 1100.
William the Conqueror (William I), b.*c.*1027, conquered England 1066, d.1087.
William the Lyon, king of Scotland (1165–1214), b.1143, d.1214.
William the Silent, Prince of Orange, b.1533, killed 1584.
Williams, Sir George, founder (1844) of the YMCA, London, b.1821, d.1905.
Williams, Ralph Vaughan, English composer (*Hugh the Drover*, 1911–14), b.1872, d.1958.
Williams, Tennessee (Thomas Lanier Williams), American writer (*A Streetcar Named Desire*, 1947), b.1912, d.1983.
Williams, Walter, last surviving veteran (Confederate) of the American Civil War, b.1843, d.1960.
Willow pattern, introduced 1780 by the English potter Thomas Turner, b.1745, d.1809.
Wilson, 'Beau' (Edward), London man about town, killed 1694.

Wilson, Sir Angus, English writer (*Hemlock and After*, 1952), b.1913, d.1991.

Wilson, Harold, Baron, British statesman (prime minister 1964–70, 1974–76), b.1916.

Wilson, John, English lutenist and composer, b.1595, d.1673.

Wilson, John ('Christopher North'), Scottish writer (*Recreations*, 1842), b.1785, d.1854.

Wilson, Woodrow, 28th US president (1913–21), b.1856, d.1924.

Wilson Cloud Chamber, invented 1911 by the Scottish scientist Charles Thomson Rees Wilson, b.1869, Nobel prize, 1927, d.1959.

Wilson's Fourteen Points, announced by President Wilson 8 Jan., accepted by Germany 27 Oct. 1918.

Wilton carpet, introduced into Britain from the USA *c.*1878.

Winchester Cathedral, England, constructed *c.*1079 to 1093.

Windmill, first mentioned in Persia in 7th century; first mentioned in England in 1191.

Windsor, adopted by the British royal family as the family title 17 July 1917.

Wingate, Orde Charles, British soldier, b.1903, killed 1944.

Winslow, Edward, English governor of Plymouth Colony, b.1595, d.1655.

Winstanley, Gerrard, English communist, active 1648–52.

Winterhalter, Franz Xaver, German-born painter (*The Prince Consort*), b.1806, d.1873.

Winthrop, John, English governor of Massachusetts, b.1588, d.1649.

Winthrop, John, English governor of Connecticut, b.1606, d.1676.

Wireless telegraphy, brought into being 1895 by the Italian inventor Guglielmo Marconi, b.1874, d.1937.

Wisconsin, USA, first settled 1670; created a Territory 1836; admitted to the Union 1848.

Wiseman, Cardinal Nicholas, first archbishop of Westminster, b.1802, d.1865.

Witchcraft, last trial for (of Jane Wenham, d.1730) in England 1712; last in Scotland 1722; statutes against witchcraft repealed 1736.

Wittelsbach dynasty, ruled Bavaria 1180–1918.

Wittgenstein, Ludwig, Austrian-born philosopher, b.1889, d.1951.

Wodehouse, Sir Pelham Grenville, British comic novelist (*Right Ho, Jeeves,* 1934), b.1881, d.1975.

Woffington, Peg, Irish-born actress, b.c.1714, d.1760.

Wolcot, John ('Peter Pindar'), English writer (*The Lousiad*, 1785), b.1738, d.1819.

Wolf, Hugo, Austrian composer (*Der Corregidor*, 1896), b.1860, d.1903.

'Wolf of Badenoch, The', Alexander Stewart, Earl of Buchan and Lord of Badenoch, b.c.1343, d.c.1405.

Wolfe, James, English general, b.1727, killed 1759.

Wolf-Ferrari, Ermanno, Italian-born composer (*I Gioielli della Madonna*, 1911), b.1876, d.1948.

Wollstonecraft, Mary, English social reformer (*Vindication of the Rights of Women*, 1792), b.1759, d.1797.

Wolsey, Cardinal Thomas, English divine and statesman, b.c.1475, d.1530.

Women's Legion, voluntary British wartime organization of drivers founded by the Marchioness of Londonderry, b.1879, d.1959.

Women's suffrage, New Zealand 1893, Australia 1902, Finland 1907, Norway 1913, Britain 1918–28, USA 1920, France 1944, Italy 1945.

Wood, Anthony à, English antiquary, b.1632, d.1695.

Wood, Sir Henry, English conductor and composer, b.1869, d.1944.

Woolf, Virginia, English writer (*Mrs Dalloway,* 1925), b.1882, d.1941.

Worcester, Battle of, between Parliamentary and Royalist forces, 3 Sept. 1651.

Worcester Cathedral, built 1084–89; burnt 1202; restored 1218.

Worcester porcelain, manufactured since 1781.

Worde, Wynkyn de, Alsace-born pioneer printer in England, d.c.1534.

Wordsworth, Dorothy, English writer, b.1771, d.1855.

Wordsworth, William, English poet (*The Prelude,* 1805), b.1770, d.1850.

Work, Henry Clay, American composer (*Marching Through Georgia*), b.1832, d.1884.

Worker-priest movement, French, instituted 1943, banned by the Vatican 1959.

World Association of Girl Guides and Girl Scouts, formed in London 1928.

World Bank (International Bank for Reconstruction and Development), to encourage investment in the Third World, established 1945.

World Council of Churches, constituted 23 Aug. 1948.
World Cup, soccer, 1930 Montevideo, Uruguay (winner Uruguay); 1934 Rome, Italy (winner Italy); 1938 Paris, France (winner Italy); 1950 Rio de Janeiro, Brazil (winner Uruguay); 1954 Berne, Switzerland (winner W. Germany); 1958 Stockholm, Sweden (winner Brazil); 1962 Santiago, Chile (winner Brazil); 1966 London, England (winner England); 1970 Mexico City, Mexico (winner Brazil); 1974 Munich, W. Germany (winner W. Germany); 1978 Buenos Aires, Argentina (winner Argentina); 1982 Madrid, Spain (winner Italy); 1986 Mexico City, Mexico (winner Argentina); 1990 Rome, Italy (winner W. Germany); 1992 USA.
World Health Organization, constitution drawn up 1946; confirmed as a specialized agency of the United Nations 1948.
World War I, 28 July 1914 to 11 Nov. 1918.
World War II, 1 Sept. 1939 to 15 Aug. 1945.
Worms, Diet of, called to condemn Luther 1521.
Worth, Charles Frederick, English-born dressmaker, b.1825, d.1895.
Wotton, Sir Henry, diplomat and writer, b.1568, d.1639.
Wren, Sir Christopher, English architect (St Paul's Cathedral, 1675–1711), b.1632, d.1723.
Wright, Frank Lloyd, American architect, b.1869, d.1959.
Wright, Orville, American pioneer aviator, b.1871, d.1948.
Wright, Wilbur, American pioneer aviator, b.1867, d.1912. Orville and Wilbur Wright flew their first plane 17 Dec. 1903.
Wulfstan, St, bishop of Worcester, b.*c.* 1012, d.1095.
Wulfstan, archbishop of York, d.1023.
Wyatt, Sir Thomas, English lyric poet, b.1503, d.1542.
Wyatt, Sir Thomas, English rebel, b.*c.* 1521, executed 1554.
Wycherley, William, English playwright (*The Country Wife*, 1675), b.*c.* 1640, d.1715.
Wyclif, John, English religious reformer, b.*c.* 1320, d.1384. His version of the Bible (the early version) completed *c.* 1382–84; the later version completed *c.* 1388.
Wykeham, William of, bishop of Winchester, and founder (1379) of New College, Oxford, and 1382 of Winchester College, b.1324, d.1404.
Wynkyn de Worde, Alsace-born pioneer printer in England, d.*c.* 1534.
Wyoming, USA, first settled 1834; Territory 1868; admitted to the Union 1890.

Xenon, element, discovered 1898 by Ramsay and Travers.
Xenophon, Greek writer (*Anabasis*), b.c.430, d.355 BC.
X-rays, discovered 1895 by the German scientist Wilhelm von Rontgen, b.1845, d.1923.
Xerography, basic principles discovered in 1938 by the American inventor Chester Floyd Carlson, b.1906, d.1968.
XYZ Mission, to arrange Franco-American treaty, 1798.

Y

Yale, Elihu, American administrator, b.1648, d.1721.

Yale locks, invented by the American inventor Linus Yale, b.1821, d.1868.

Yale University, Connecticut, founded as school 1701; first called Yale College 1716; chartered 1745; Yale University since 1887.

Yalta, Conference of, Feb. 1945.

Yamamoto, Gombei, Japanese prime minister (1913–14, 1923), b.1852, d.1933.

Yard, imperial standard, length established in Britain 1844.

Yarrow, Sir Albert Fernandez, English engineer and inventor, b.1842, d.1932.

Year of confusion, first of the Julian Calendar and including 80 extra days, 46 BC.

Yeardley, Sir George, governor of Virginia, b.*c.*1580, d.1627.

Yeats, William Butler, Irish writer, b.1865, d.1939.

Yellow Book, The, English quarterly literary journal in which appeared many outstanding contributions by late 19th-century writers and artists, published 1894 to 1897.

Yellow fever, cause discovered 1900 by the American bacteriologist Walter Reed, b.1851, d.1902.

Yellowstone National Park, first American national park to be designated, 1872.

Yeltsin, Boris Nikolayevich, Russian politician, b.1931, president of the Russian Fedearation since the dissolution of the Soviet Union in 1991.

Yevtushenko, Yevgeny Aleksandrovich, Russian poet (*Babi Yar,* 1961), b.1933.

Yiddish language, earliest known document dated 1396.

Yokohama, Japanese port, first opened to foreign trade through the intervention of Commodore Perry, 1859.

Yom Kippur War, *see* **Arab-Israeli Wars.**

Yonge, Charlotte Mary, English writer (*The Heir of Redclyffe*, 1853), b.1823, d.1901.

York Minster, present structure erected mainly 1291–1345, with important addition in the middle of the 15th century.

Yorktown, Virginia, Siege of, in which Cornwallis surrendered to Washington 1781.

Yosemite National Park, California, designated 1890.

Youmans, Vincent, American composer (*No, No Nanette*, 1924), b.1898, d.1946.

Young, Arthur, English agricultural administrator and writer, b.1741, d.1820.

Young, Brigham, American Mormon leader, b.1801, d.1877.

Young, Edward, English poet (*Night Thoughts*, 1742), b.1683, d.1765.

Young, James, Scottish chemist and founder 1856 of the paraffin industry, b.1811, d.1883.

Young, Thomas, English scientist, b.1773, d.1829.

Young Italy, nationalist group, founded 1831 by Giuseppe Mazzini, b.1805, d.1872.

Young Men's Christian Association, founded in London 1844 by Sir George Williams, b.1821, d.1905.

Young Women's Christian Association, founded in London by Lady Kinnaird, b.1816, d.1888.

Youth Hostels Association, founded 1930.

Ypres, First Battle of, World War I, 19 Oct.–22 Nov. 1914.

Ypres, Second Battle of, World War I, 22 April–25 May 1915.

Ypres, Third Battle of, World War I, July–Aug. 1917.

Ysaÿe, Eugène, Belgian violinist and conductor, b.1858, d.1931.

Ytterbium, chemical element, discovered 1878 by the French scientist Jean Charles Gallisard de Marignac, b.1817, d.1894.

Yttrium, chemical element, discovered by the scientist Johan Gadolin 1794.

Yüan dynasty, China, 1280–1368.

Yugoslavia, kingdom proclaimed 1 Dec. 1918; constitution established 1921 monarchist dictatorship 1929–41; Communist regime 1945–1980; in 1991 the constituent republics of Slovenia, Croatia and Bosnia Hezogovnia declared independence and fierce fighting errupted between Serbs, Croatians and Muslims.

Yule, Sir Henry, Scottish administrator in India, b.1820, d.1889.

Yuletide, the Christmas festival.

Yung Chêng period, China 1723–35.

Yung Lo period, China 1403–24.

Z

Zachary, St, pope 741–752.

Zagreb University, Croatia, founded 1669.

Zaharoff, Sir Basil, Turkish-born cosmopolitan financier and armaments manufacturer, of Greek descent and British nationality, b.1849, d.1936.

Zambia, administered by the British South Africa Company by 1900; unified as Northern Rhodesia 1911; made a British protectorate 1924; part of Federation of Rhodesia and Nyasaland 1953–63; gained independence within the Commonwealth 1964.

Zamenhof, Lazarus Ludovic, Polish inventor (1887) of Esperanto, b.1859, d.1917.

Zandonai, Riccardo, Italian composer (*Francesca da Rimini*, 1914), b.1883, d.1944.

Zangwill, Israel, English Jewish novelist (*Children of the Ghetto*, 1892), b.1864, d.1926.

Zanzibar, first visited by the English 1591; united with Pemba under one sovereign, Seyyid Said bin Sultan 1822; placed under British protection by the sultan and formally declared a British protectorate 1890; constitutional government established 1891; slavery abolished by the sultan 1897; new constitution granted 1956; became independent within the Commonwealth 1963, and a republic 1964; joined Tanganyika to form United Republic of Tanzania 1964.

Zapata, Emiliano, Mexican revolutionary leader, b.c.1879, murdered 1919.

Zapf, Hermann, German type designer, b.1910

Zarubin, Georgi, Soviet Deputy Foreign Minister, b.1900, d.1958.

Zeebrugge Raid, World War I, 22 April 1918.

Zeeman, Pieter, Dutch scientist (discovered the Zeeman effect 1896) and Nobel prize winner (1902), b.1865, d.1943.

Zeiss, Carl, German optical instrument manufacturer and founder of the firm of that name, b.1816, d.1888.

Zemstvos, Russian provincial assemblies formed 13 Jan. 1864.

Zen Buddhism, founded *c.*520 when Bodhi-Dharma (480–528) went to China.

Zeno, Roman emperor (474–491) at Constantinople, d.491.

Zeno of Citium, Greek philosopher, b.340, committed suicide 270 BC.

Zeno of Elea, Greek philosopher, b.*c.*490, d.*c.*430 BC.

Zenobia, queen of Palmyra, d.*c.*285.
Zeppelins, invented 1900 by the German Count Ferdinand von Zeppelin, b.1838, d.1917. Zeppelin L21 destroyed at Cuffley 3 Sept. 1916; L33 in Essex 24 Sept. 1916.
Zero, absolute, approximately achieved 1921 at Leyden University's physical laboratory.
Zetkin, Klara, German communist leader, b.1857, d.1933.
Zeuss, Johann Kaspar, German pioneer (1853) in the study of Celtic philology, b.1806, d.1856.
Zhukov, Georgi Konstantinovich, Soviet field marshal, b.1896, d.1974.
Zhukovskii, Vassily Andreievich, Russian poet, b.1783, d.1852.
Ziegfeld, Florenz, American producer of the Ziegfeld Follies (from 1917), b.1869, d.1932.
Zimbabwe, formerly Southern Rhodesia (until 1964) and Rhodesia (1964–79), British colony founded by British South Africa Company 1890; joined with former Northern Rhodesia and former Nyasaland to form Federation of Rhodesia and Nyasaland 1953–63; Ian Smith prime minister 1964–79 (declared unilateral independence from Britain 1965); proclaimed a republic 1970; gained independence 1980.
Zimbalist, Efrem, Russian-born violinist, b.1889, d.1985.
Zimisces, John, Byzantine emperor (969–976), b.*c.*925, d.976.
Zincography, illustration process, invented in Paris 1850.
Zingarelli, Nicola Antonio, Italian composer (*Giulietta e Romeo*, 1769), b.1752, d.1837.
Zinoviev Letter, forged instructions for Communist uprising in Great Britain, published Oct. 1924. Supposedly written by Grigori Zinoviev, Russian revolutionary leader, b.1883, shot 1936.
Zinzendorf, Nikolaus Ludwig, German leader of the Moravian Community, b.1700, d.1760.
Zionist Congress, first world, held at Basle 1897.
Zionist Movement, founded 1897 by Theodor Herzl, b.1860, d.1904.
Zirconia, mineral discovered 1789 by the German chemist Martin Heinrich Klaproth, b.1743, d.1817.
Zirconium, chemical element, isolated 1824 by the Swedish chemist Baron Berzelius, b.1779, d.1848.
Zizka, John, Hussite leader, b.*c.* 1370, d.1424.
Zoë, Byzantine empress (1028–50), d.1050.
Zoega, Georg, Danish-born archaeologist, b.1755, d.1809.
Zoffany, John, English-born painter, b.1725, d.1810.

Zog (Ahmed Beg Zogu), king of Albania (1928–39), b.1895, d.1961.
Zola, Emile, French novelist (*Thérèse Raquin,* 1866), b.1840, d.1902.
Zollverein, German Customs Union, formed 1834.
Zomba, city in S. Malawi, founded *c.*1880; capital of Malawi since 1971.
Zoological Society, London, founded 1826 by Sir Stamford Raffles, b.1781, d.1826.
Zorn, Anders, Swedish artist, b.1860, d.1920.
Zoroaster (Zarathustra), Persian religious leader and founder of Zoroastrianism, b.*c.*659, d.*c.*582 BC.
Zorrilla, José, Spanish poet (*Don Juan Tenorio,* 1844), b.1817, d.1893.
Zosimus, Greek historian active mid 5th century.
Zosimus, St, pope 417–418.
Zsigmondy, Richard, Austrian pioneer in the development of colloid chemistry, b.1865, d.1929.
Zucchi, Antonio Pietro, Italian painter, b.1726, d.1795.
Zuckerman, Sir Solly, South African-born anatomist, b.1904, d.1984.
Zuckmayer, Carl, German playwright (*Der Hauptmann von Köpenick,* 1931), b.1896, d.1977.
Zuider Zee, the Netherlands, reclamation of inundated land planned 1891 by the Dutch engineer and statesman Dr C. Lely, b.1854, d.1929; inaugurated 1 May 1919; last gap closed 28 May 1932; repaired 1945.
Zukor, Adolph, Hungarian-born film industry pioneer, b.1873, d.1976.
Zuloaga, Ignacio, Spanish painter, b.1870, d.1945.
Zululand, first war 1879; second 1906. Zululand annexed to Natal 30 Dec. 1897.
Zumalacárregui, Tomás, Spanish general, b.1788, d.1835.
Zurbaran, Francisco de, Spanish painter (*Apotheosis of St Thomas Aquinas*), b.1598, d.1662.
Zutphen, Siege of, Sept. 1586.
Zweig, Arnold, German novelist (*Sergeant Grischa,* 1927), b.1887, d.1968.
Zweig, Stefan, Austrian writer, b.1881, committed suicide 1942.
Zwingli, Huldreich, Swiss religious reformer, b.1484, killed 1531.
Zymose, yeast-cell fermenting agent, discovered 1903 by the German scientist Eduard Buchner, b.1860, d.1917.

EXCEPTIONALLY GIFTED CHILDREN

Exceptionally Gifted Children examines the origin, development and school histories of 15 Australian children who are among the most remarkably gifted young people ever to be identified and studied in any country. Covering the first ten years of a longitudinal research project which will trace the children through to adulthood, the book examines in detail the children's early lives and influences, their families and personal characteristics. More importantly, it explores the school experiences of these remarkable children, the opportunities offered, and more often denied, to them and the effects of their early school life on their educational and social development – how the normal school environment can affect exceptionally gifted children's self-esteem, self-concept, motivation, capacity to find and form friendships, and the children's own attitudes towards their unusual abilities and achievements.

Miraca U.M. Gross is Senior Lecturer in Gifted Education at the University of New South Wales, Australia.

EXCEPTIONALLY GIFTED CHILDREN

Miraca U.M. Gross

London and New York

To John

First published 1993
by Routledge
11 New Fetter Lane, London EC4P 4EE

Simultaneously published in the USA and Canada
by Routledge
29 West 35th Street, New York, NY 10001

Reprinted 1993

Typeset in Baskerville by Michael Mepham, Frome, Somerset
Printed and bound in Great Britain by
Mackays of Chatham PLC, Chatham, Kent

British Library Cataloguing in Publication Data
A catalogue record for this book is available
from the British Library.

Library of Congress Cataloging in Publication Data
Gross, Miraca U.M. Exceptionally gifted children / by
Miraca U.M. Gross.
p. cm.
Includes bibliographical references and index.
1. Gifted children—Education—Australia—Case studies.
I. Title
LC3999.4.G76 1993 92–23118
CIP

ISBN 0–415–06416–3 (Hbk)
ISBN 0–415–06417–1 (Pbk)

CONTENTS

FIGURES AND TABLES

FIGURES

TABLES

1

THE SCOPE OF THE PROBLEM

In the ordinary elementary school situation, children of IQ 140 waste half their time. Those above IQ 170 waste practically all their time. With little to do, how can these children develop powers of sustained effort, respect for the task, or habits of steady work?

(Hollingworth, 1942, p. 299)

Hadley Bond, aged 22 months, was out for a walk with his mother. Although it was late autumn in the southern Australian city where they lived, the sun was still warm, and Hadley was becoming weary. His steps began to falter. Holly, his mother, checked her watch and found that they had been out for rather longer than she had intended. 'My goodness, Hadley,' she said, 'can you guess how long we've been walking?' 'About 26½ minutes, I think,' said Hadley – and he was right!

Hadley was the third son born to Holly and Robert Bond. Adrian, aged 8 at Hadley's birth, and John, aged almost 6, were intelligent, quick-witted children, perceptive, intellectually curious and academically successful at school. The family quickly realized, however, that Hadley's abilities went far beyond anything they could have imagined. He was a child of truly phenomenal mathematical ability. By 18 months of age he was already fascinated by the maths drill programs which John and Adrian had used on the family's home computer. He delighted in simple addition problems. He would squat on the floor working out the answer to a question with plastic beads and then joyously type it into the computer, laughing with delight when the response was verified. He had taught himself to read before the age of 18 months and by his second birthday he had his own library of small books which he read with great enjoyment.

By the time Hadley turned 5 he had, with the help of the computer, taught himself to add, subtract, multiply and divide. He was fascinated by maths problems and enjoyed developing his own. He had the reading and comprehension skills of an 8-year-old and avidly read everything he could get his hands on. He passionately wanted to go to school where, he believed, his learning would progress even more speedily and he would have access to all the wonderful books in the school library which his older brothers had described to him.

Unhappily, Hadley missed the cut-off date for school entry by a mere two weeks; however, in acknowledgement of his remarkable abilities in maths and reading, the state Education Department decided to allow him 'visiting rights' in the reception class of a school in his neighbourhood. For legal reasons, Holly was required to accompany him as he was underage and so could not be formally enrolled.

Holly was appalled by the simplistic and undemanding curriculum presented to her son. Despite having admitted Hadley to the class on the basis of his phenomenal abilities, the school was unwilling to adapt the curriculum to his needs. Hadley, who had taught himself addition and subtraction at the age of 3, was forced to sit quietly with the rest of the class while the teacher introduced the numbers 1 to 10. He was not permitted to do anything that could not be undertaken by the other children. Far from gaining access to a new and entrancing world of literature, he was taken, with the other 5-year-olds, through introductory exercises in reading readiness.

Hadley's IQ on the *Stanford-Binet Intelligence Scale L-M* is 178. At the age of 5 years 6 months, he had a mental age of 9 years 9 months. He was bright enough, and intellectually mature enough, to know that there was something far wrong with the way he was being treated. He was bored, frustrated and resentful. Before the end of the first week he was protesting quietly but firmly to his parents that he was learning nothing at school and did not want to return. He had learned more, and had been given more intellectual freedom, in pre-school. Concerned that such a negative experience, if it continued, might leave their son with a lasting dislike for school, Holly and Robert decided to concede to Hadley's wishes. Hadley became Australia's youngest dropout, after a school experience of barely two weeks.

Of course, Hadley's story does not end there. A few months later, at the 'legal' age for school entry, his parents enrolled him at a different state school which promptly recognized his remarkable abilities by allowing him to enter at Grade 1, rather than Reception level, an immediate grade-skip of 12 months. The full story of Hadley's progress through school is told in this book.

When Ian Baker was 1 year old he would 'help' his mother with the washing, counting his nappies as she dropped them into the washing machine. His reading skills developed almost as early as his numerical ability, and by age 2 he would entertain himself for hours playing music from his much loved collection of elderly 45 r.p.m. records and audio casettes. He had taught himself to select his favourites by reading the labels.

By 3 years 6 months Ian was reading small books and at pre-school, which he entered at age 4, he enjoyed helping the teacher by reading aloud to the rest of the class while she prepared for the next lesson. When he realized that the other children could not see the illustrations, he developed the technique of holding the book upside down so that his classmates, seated round him, could see the pictures and follow the story as he pointed to the words. He was a vibrant, energetic child, enthralled by new knowledge and propelled by a compulsion to learn everything he could about everything that crossed his path.

Australian children enter pre-school at age 4 and formal schooling at age 5, around the same age as British children and 12 months earlier than their American counterparts. By the time Ian entered school he was reading, with keen pleasure and full comprehension, E.B. White's *Charlotte's Web*. Difficulties arose, however, in the first few weeks. Although Sally Baker, Ian's mother, had tentatively mentioned to the reception class teacher that Ian was already an avid and fluent reader, the teacher was reluctant to believe her. The situation was complicated by the fact that Ian had long since passed through the stage of needing to 'sound out' words and now read silently and absorbedly; his teacher, even when she did notice him reading, assumed that he was simply looking at the pictures. In consequence, she insisted that Ian work through the reading readiness exercises with the rest of the children. As for maths, which had been a joy and an obsession for Ian since he turned 4, by which age he had already mastered addition and subtraction of numbers up to 1,000 – maths in the Reception class was limited to the recognition of the numbers 1 to 10.

Ian and Hadley, 1,000 miles apart, had virtually identical introductions to the world of school. The first lesson the two boys learned was that school would teach them nothing which they had not taught themselves at least two years previously; the second was that they had absolutely nothing in common with the other children in their classes. Ian in particular found the social isolation hard to take. His reading capacity, his interests, the games he wanted to play at break and lunch, the television programmes he preferred, were all radically different from those of the other 5-year-olds. Before long he was disliked, resented and rejected by his classmates. Being a lad of spirit, and furious with the school's refusal to let him learn, Ian returned the resentment in full measure.

Ian had never been an easy child to live with. His parents, Brock and Sally, had noticed from his early years that when he was bored or frustrated he could become quite aggressive towards other children, especially his brother, Bill, who was three years younger. Ian made no secret of his extreme dislike of school, but his parents were not at first aware of the seriousness of the situation. This occurred some eight months into the school year, when the vice-principal and Ian's teacher requested that the Bakers visit the school for an interview. In this meeting, Brock and Sally were informed that Ian was uncontrollable in class, that he was displaying bouts of alarming physical violence towards other students, and that the school wanted to refer him to a special school for behaviourally disturbed children, attached to the psychiatric branch of a large children's hospital. As part of the referral procedure, Ian would be psychometrically assessed by the region's educational psychologist.

By a happy chance, the psychologist had a particular interest in gifted children, and chose to test Ian on the *Stanford-Binet L-M* rather than on a test with a lower ceiling. Ian's IQ was assessed as at least 170, and tests of reading achievement established that he had the reading and comprehension skills of a 12-year-old.

The psychologist explained to the staff of Ian's school that he was not behaviourally disturbed. His hostility and aggression arose out of his desperate loneliness, bewilderment and intellectual frustration. Ian's progress through school is described in depth in Chapter 8. As will be told, his first few years of schooling were a saga of educational misjudgment. Despite his tested abilities and achievement, he was required to work in lockstep progression, with age-peers, through the curriculum of the grade in which he was enrolled. At the age of 9 years 11 months, for the purposes of the present study, Ian took the *Scholastic Aptitude Test–Mathematics (SAT–M)*, a standardized test of maths achievement taken by American 17- and 18-year-olds wishing to enter university. The average score varies from year to year, but is usually around 500. Ian, seven years younger than the students for whom the test is designed, made the remarkable score of 560! Despite this, his teacher insisted that he undertake the Grade 4 maths curriculum with the other 9-year-olds.

During his Grade 4 year, Brock and Sally decided to have Ian's cognitive abilities reassessed. Accordingly, at the age of 9 years 3 months, Ian was assessed firstly on the *Wechsler Intelligence Scale for Children (WISC–R)* and subsequently on the *Stanford-Binet*, the scale on which he had first been tested at age 5. Ian ceilinged out on the *WISC–R*, scoring scaled scores of 19 on all subscales of both the verbal and performance subtests. On the *Stanford-Binet* Ian, in the words of the psychologist's report, 'sailed through all the items through to the highest level of all, Superior Adult Three. Here he did start to fail on some items but nevertheless his IQ came off the top of this scale also'. Ian scored a mental age of 18 years 6 months, exactly twice his chronological age and thus a ratio IQ of 200. In addition, the psychologist administered standardized achievement tests of reading and spelling; in both, Ian scored at adult level.

Children scoring at IQ 180 or above appear in the population at a ratio of fewer than one in 1 million. Requiring Ian to undertake all his school work with age-peers of average ability was rather like requiring a child of average intelligence to spend six hours a day, five days a week, interacting solely with children who were profoundly intellectually handicapped.

The psychologist was appalled to hear that a child of such exceptional talent was being required to plod through a lockstep curriculum with other Grade 4 students. She expressed her concern strongly in her written report.

> I was somewhat concerned to hear from Ian and his parents that he has been doing Grade 4 maths along with his classmates. We clearly have here a boy who has extreme talent in the maths area... I would strongly suggest that Ian most clearly needs acceleration in his maths programme. He is likely to be become quite bored and frustrated by maths at his own age level and it seems to be a real waste of true talent.
>
> Over the years Ian's parents and teachers have had occasional bouts of difficult behaviour from Ian. He certainly is not a subtle sort of child... His parents have found, as is true with many other gifted and talented children, that when Ian becomes bored, and does not have his 'fix' of intellectual activity, it is then that the difficult behaviour begins... It is important to remember that his behaviour only deteriorates to unacceptable levels when he is signalling that he is bored and is not getting the intellectual stimulation he needs by legitimate means.
>
> It needs to be remembered that for Ian to be intellectually stimulated, the activities presented to him need to be of a particularly high level. He certainly will not be challenged by the types of problems and puzzles which generally interest children of his age. Certainly, working with the Binet, he could dismiss such questions without a second thought, and they obviously hold no interest for him, nor any satisfaction when he has solved them.'

In response to Brock and Sally's pleading that Ian be given some sort of extension or enrichment work to keep his mind alive, the school principal stated frankly that it would be 'political suicide' for her to establish any differentiated programme for the intellectually gifted students in her school. Two years later, a letter from Sally to the Director-General of Education of the State drew the response that 'all children have gifts and talents' and that 'a policy which treats gifted and talented children as a discrete group is likely to be rigid and divisive in its application'.

Christopher Otway has been rather more fortunate. Like Ian Baker, he is a child of quite remarkable intellectual ability. At the age of 11 he achieved a mental age of 22 years on the *Stanford-Binet*, and a ratio IQ of 200. At 11 years 4 months his score on the *SAT–M* was an astonishing 710 – more than two standard deviations above the mean for this test normed on students six years his senior. Fewer than 4 per cent of college-bound 18-year-olds could expect to gain such a score.

From his earliest years Chris displayed prodigious abilities in both maths and language. Like Hadley and Ian, he taught himself to read before his second birthday and by age 4 he was reading children's encyclopaedias and had acquired a range and level of general knowledge that most teachers would be happy to encounter in fifth or sixth Grade students. His maths ability was equally remarkable. By the time he entered pre-school at the usual age of 4 he was capable of working, in maths, at Grade 4 level.

In contrast to the débâcle which greeted Hadley's and Ian's entry into formal schooling, the principal and teachers of Chris's primary school recognized, within days of his enrolment, that this was a child who would need a radically different educational programme if he were to fulfil his astonishing potential. This school, and the larger school which he subsequently attended, designed for Chris an individualized programme which incorporated, at various points in his schooling, grade-skipping; subject acceleration in his areas of major strength; general in-class enrichment; a pull-out enrichment programme in English, creative thinking and problem solving; and participation in a cluster group programme for gifted students arranged by a local teacher training college.

The combination of acceleration and enrichment has permitted Chris to work at something approaching his own pace, while broadening his knowledge base by taking on a much wider range of subjects than is usually permitted or practicable. In October 1991, aged 14 years 11 months, Chris took university entrance examinations in mathematics, physics, chemistry and economics, gaining an average mark of 98 per cent. At the end of 1992 he will repeat these exams – but this time in legal studies, accounting, Australian studies, English and biology. He will complete his final grade of high school just before his sixteenth birthday, having undertaken a remarkable range of subjects from which he can choose those which he will study at university.

This book is the story of 15 remarkable children. They have been selected, to have their stories told, from a larger group of 40, each equally remarkable, each equally at risk because they differ, quite radically and in many ways, from the great majority of children in our schools.

In special education – the education of children with special needs – each field employs specific terminologies which are used both to indicate the degree to which a child differs from the norm for his or her age-peers, and, by association, to suggest techniques which educators might use to assist the child to attain his or her educational potential. Teachers of the intellectually disabled, for example, recognize mild, moderate, severe and profound levels of intellectual disability, and the level and type of intervention prescribed for the child are dictated by the degree of severity of the condition.

Educators working with deaf students recognize four levels of hearing impairment – again termed mild, moderate, severe and profound. A child with a mild hearing impairment can cope quite happily with the regular classroom as long as his teacher is made aware of his impairment and is prepared to make certain adjustments to her teaching style. The child with moderate hearing impairment usually requires medical intervention – the prescription of a hearing aid specifically tailored to her needs – as well as a supportive group of classmates and a sensitive and flexible teacher who will provide special speech and language assistance. However, children who have severe or profound degrees of hearing impairment require much more than sound amplification and general assistance. These children must also be trained in combinations of lipreading, cued speech, signing and fingerspelling, and both the curriculum and the teaching methodologies used in the classes in which they are placed must be adapted to their special needs. Where these children are integrated into the regular classroom both the teacher and the classmates of the profoundly deaf student must be prepared to learn to speak his or her language; as educators we acknowledge that it is important for the hearing impaired child's academic and social development that he or she should be assisted to develop warm and supportive relationships with other students.

Teachers of hearing impaired and intellectually handicapped children have avoided the temptation to treat their clientele as if they were a homogeneous group. No one would seriously suggest that a profoundly retarded child should be expected to master the curriculum that would be presented to a student with a mild intellectual impairment. Until comparatively recently, however, teachers and psychologists working with intellectually gifted students have been trapped in precisely this mind-set. We have developed identification strategies, designed curricula, and established special programmes based on the assumption that what works for a moderately gifted student will also work for the extremely gifted. Fortunately, this perception is breaking down, at least in North America and Europe, if not yet in Australia. We are beginning to acknowledge the need to recognize degrees, as well as types, of giftedness (Tannenbaum, 1983; Webb, Meckstroth and Tolan, 1983; Janos and Robinson, 1985).

Giftedness is much more than intellectual precocity. As early as 1961 DeHaan and Havighurst proposed six domains in which students might excel; these were intellectual ability, creative thinking, scientific ability, social leadership, mechanical skills, and talent in the fine arts. In subsequent years a multiplicity of definitions has arisen, all emphasizing multiple talents but, in the majority of cases, also acknowledging the importance of intellectual giftedness as one domain or subcategory (Marland, 1972; Tannenbaum, 1983: Gagné, 1985, 1991a; Feldhusen and Hoover, 1986). It would be simplistic to define intellectual giftedness solely in terms of IQ scores; nonetheless the intelligence quotient is a useful index of the relationship (and in the case of the gifted child, the discrepancy) between mental age and chronological age. A moderately gifted 9-year-old with a mental age of 12 and thus an IQ of approximately 133 is 'out of synch' by a matter of three years before he has even passed through elementary school; however, his exceptionally gifted age-mate with a mental age of 15 and an IQ of approximately 167 looks across a chasm of six years from the age at which he is capable of reasoning to the grade level in which he is likely to be placed on the basis of his chronological age. The IQ can assist us to understand the fundamental differences in mental processing between moderately and extremely gifted students.

Silverman (1989, p. 71) has defined the highly gifted as 'those whose advancement is significantly beyond the norm of the gifted'. By 'advancement', she implies aptitude or potential, rather than performance; research on the school performance of the highly gifted suggests that the majority of these children are required to work, in the regular classroom, at levels several years below their tested achievement (Hollingworth, 1926, 1942: Pringle, 1970: Painter, 1976). Silverman suggests that any child who scores three standard deviations above the mean on an individual test of reasoning ability should be termed highly gifted; that is, children of IQ 145 or above.

The present study, however, is concerned with two subsets of the highly gifted: children who are exceptionally or profoundly gifted. The term 'exceptionally gifted' refers to children who score in the IQ range 160–179 (Kline and Meckstroth, 1985), while 'profoundly gifted' refers to those very rare individuals who score at or above IQ 180 (Webb, Meckstroth and Tolan, 1983).

Just as the properties of the normal curve of distribution dictate that there will be many more students of average ability than gifted students, so the moderately gifted will outnumber the highly gifted, and the highly gifted will considerably outnumber the exceptionally and profoundly gifted. Moderately gifted students of IQ 125 appear in the population at a ratio of approximately 1 in 20. Highly gifted students of IQ 145 are approximately 1 in 1,000. Fewer than 9 children in 100,000 could be classed as exceptionally gifted with IQ scores of 160+, while fewer than 1 in 1 million are profoundly gifted. Over the last 60 years a number of researchers in gifted education have proposed that the number of children who score in the extremely high ranges of IQ may somewhat exceed the theoretical expectations derived from the normal curve (Terman, 1926; Burt, 1968; Robinson, 1981; Silverman, 1989; Gross, 1989a); however, even the most generous over-prediction would affirm that exceptionally and profoundly gifted children comprise a tiny minority, even among the gifted.

Because moderately gifted students so greatly outnumber their highly, exceptionally and profoundly gifted counterparts, the identification procedures we recommend and the programmes we develop for gifted students are generally based on the characteristics, learning styles and needs of the moderately gifted. Particularly in Australia, there are very few programmes directed specifically to the needs of the highly gifted. Yet researchers have noted profound differences between moderately gifted and exceptionally gifted students on almost every cognitive and affective variable studied to this date. In terms of intellectual capacity alone, the profoundly gifted child of IQ 190 differs from moderately gifted classmates of IQ 130 to the same degree that the latter differ from intellectually handicapped children of IQ 70. If they are to come anywhere near to maximizing their remarkable intellectual or academic potential, exceptionally and profoundly gifted children require an educational programme which differs significantly in structure, pace and content from that which might be offered to the moderately gifted.

A pull-out programme offering what Stanley (1979) terms 'relevant academic enrichment' for a few hours each week might be an excellent interventive response to the needs of a Grade 4 student who is capable of Grade 6 maths; however, enrichment taken by itself would be an inadequate and inappropriate response to students such as Hadley, Ian and Christopher who, while still at elementary school, displayed achievement in maths and language more usually found among students preparing for university entrance.

The developmental histories and school experiences of Hadley, Ian, Chris and 12 other exceptionally and profoundly gifted young people are narrated and evaluated in this book. Unfortunately, Hollingworth's assertion (1942), which begins this chapter, that extremely gifted children in the regular classroom waste practically all their time, is borne out by the experiences of the majority of the children in this study. Only a small minority of the subject children have enjoyed educational programmes which have been thoughtfully planned and appropriate responses to their intellectual, academic and social needs.

THE CHILDREN

I am Scottish by birth, and my education and initial teacher training took place in Edinburgh, as did my first two years of teaching. I emigrated to Australia in the late 1960s and spent a further 20 years with the South Australian Education Department, teaching in state (government) primary schools. For 12 of these years I taught academically gifted children in a variety of special settings, including cluster groupings, pull-out programmes and full-time self-contained classes.

In February 1978 the South Australian Association for Gifted and Talented Children (SAAGTC) was constituted in the state capital, Adelaide, and I became one of the founding committee members and, in 1980, Association President, a position I held for six years. SAAGTC is an extremely active organization of teachers, parents, psychologists and other community members with an interest in the education and welfare of intellectually gifted children. By 1983 the Association had established a highly successful network of five programmes for gifted and talented children from the Adelaide metropolitan and near-country regions. Four of the programmes operate on Saturday afternoons, using the facilities of a large school a short distance from the city centre; the fifth programme, for students aged 13–18, operated, at that time, in the early evenings, using the facilities and teaching staff of the University of Adelaide.

Children who attend the SAAGTC programmes are referred to the Association by teachers, psychologists or parents on the basis of unusually high intellectual or academic ability. During the seven years from 1978 to 1985 six children with IQ scores of more than 160 were referred to the students' programmes. I was especially intrigued by these children. In both their academic and social development they seemed quite different not only from their age-peers but from other more moderately gifted children who also attended the programmes. Academically they were quite remarkable, and excelled even in the accelerated and enriched curriculum we were offering. Socially, some were confident and outgoing from their first weeks in the programme, while others seemed hesitant and unsure of the other children, and took some time to find their feet; but almost all of them, once they had gained in self-confidence and were sure of their acceptance, interacted with the other children with a maturity, sensitivity and instinctive courtesy that one would scarcely expect from young people many years their senior. Yet, in the majority of cases, their parents reported that at school they were often deeply unhappy and socially rejected.

In 1985 the South Australian Education Department awarded me a full salaried scholarship to study overseas for my Masters degree in Gifted Education, and in June that year I entered Purdue University in Indiana, to work with Distinguished Professor John F. Feldhusen at the Gifted Education Resource Institute. Feldhusen and the outstanding team of scholars in gifted education, psychological and educational measurement, research methodology and curriculum who became my graduate committee encouraged my interest in extremely gifted students, and when, having gained my Masters, I decided to enter Ph.D. study at Purdue I had no difficulty in choosing my field of doctoral research. I had, for some years, been informally observing the academic and social development of the six South Australian IQ 160+ students with the permission and support of their parents, and I decided that my Ph.D. work would be an expansion of this.

In 1987 I was awarded the Hollingworth Award for Research in the Psychology and Education of the Gifted, for a proposal to formalize and expand the study into a series of longitudinal, comparative case studies of the academic, social and emotional development of between 10 and 15 children scoring at IQ 160+ in the eastern states of Australia, following each child through to the end of his or her secondary education. This international research award, sponsored annually by Intertel, had previously been won only by American educators and researchers, and the resulting publicity in the Australian media resulted in several referrals, by psychologists and teachers, of children whom they believed might meet the entrance criteria. In addition, the study was publicized through the *Bulletin of the Australian Psychological Society* and through other education agencies in the various states.

By the end of 1987, 28 children had been identified for the study, and by the end of 1991 there were 40. In 1989 I completed my Ph.D. dissertation, which was an in-depth study of the academic, social and emotional development of 15 of these children, and it is these 15 who are the subject of this book. The study will continue until 2001, when the youngest of the 40 children will graduate from secondary school.

The procedure by which the study was publicized, the methodology and procedures employed and the procedures by which the 15 children reported here were selected from the larger group of 40, are described in Chapter 3. For the moment, let me simply say that the 15 children you will meet in these pages have scored at or above IQ 160 on the *Stanford-Binet Intelligence Scale (L-M)*, that they were aged between 5 and 13 during the years 1988–9 when the majority of the data were collected, and that they live, and are being educated, in the eastern states of Australia.

This brief introduction will not attempt an in-depth portrayal of the early development, family background, academic achievements, recreational interests, school progress, or psychosocial development of the 15 children. Subsequent chapters address each of these issues in depth, and a composite portrait will be created of each child as the narrative progresses. Rather, this chapter will provide a brief introduction to each child in order to set the scene for the more comprehensive analysis which will be possible through reading the text as a whole.

It is important to note that the names of the children and their families are pseudonyms selected by the families themselves.

Adam

Adam Murphy is 10 years old. Although the middle child in his family, he has been treated more as a first-born; there is a 14-year gap between Adam and his older sister, Anne. His younger sister, Mary, has just turned 8.

For most of Adam's life he lived in a beautiful but isolated region of his state, and attended country schools. He and his parents, Edward and Georgina, love country life. His education, however, has been an on-going problem. Adam taught himself to read at 18 months of age, and by the time he entered school was reading at Grade 4 level. With a few exceptions, Adam's teachers have been unable to cope with his self-acceleration; in Grade 2, despite having been assessed as having a reading age of 12 years, he was presented, in class, with readers and other texts at Grade 2 level.

Eventually, the Murphys sold up and moved to the capital city of their state, where they believed they would have a better chance of finding a school which would respond to Adam's intellectual and social needs. The new school has tried to accommodate Adam's needs, but his teachers find it difficult to cope with a young boy who is undeniably brilliant but who, after years of imposed academic underachievement, now seems to show only spasmodic interest in learning.

Adam was tested on the *Stanford-Binet Intelligence Scale* at the age of 5 years 7 months and obtained an IQ score of 162.

Adrian

Adrian Seng, aged 16, is the eldest of three boys; his brothers Colin and Edmund are aged 14 and 13 respectively. All three boys are remarkably gifted; at the age of 9 years 7 months Edmund recorded a mental age of 17 years 5 months on the *Slosson Intelligence Test* – a ratio IQ of 182. Adrian is a pleasant, well-adjusted, good-humoured young man, whose modesty, good nature and cheerful personality have won him a wide circle of friends.

Adrian, whose parents are Chinese, born and educated in Hong Kong, is the most profoundly gifted of the 40 children in this study. He taught himself to read before the age of 2 and by 3 he had the reading, writing and mathematical abilities of a 6-year-old. At age 3½ he could multiply two-digit numbers by two-digit numbers in his head. By 5, the usual age for school entry in his state, he had completed, in home study, the first six years of the elementary schools maths curriculum.

At the age of 6 years he was assessed on the Stanford-Binet and was found to have a mental age of 14 – a ratio IQ of more than 220.

Adrian's parents were fortunate in finding schools whose staffs were insightful enough and flexible enough to provide, for this profoundly gifted young boy, a radically different educational programme. The elementary and high schools worked together to design a programme of concurrent enrolment incorporating both grade-skipping and subject acceleration combined with curriculum compacting and enrichment. Adrian's special programme has satisfied his intellectual, social and emotional needs. He is the only child of the 15 who believes that he has been permitted to work, at school, at the level of which he is capable. When he completed his elementary education he attended high school for some subjects, university for others. His programme is described in depth in later chapters. Suffice it to say that Adrian took the *Scholastic Aptitude Test–Mathematics (SAT–M)* at 8 years 10 months and made the phenomenal score of 760. He gained his Bachelor of Science degree shortly after his fifteenth birthday.

Alice

Alice Marlow is 11 years old. She is blonde, fair-complexioned, quiet and graceful; underneath, she has a strength and firmness that belie her delicate appearance. Her brother Henry is 14, and they have a step-sister, Alana, aged 22, who lives in the United States but with whom the two younger children have a warm and loving relationship. Douglas Marlow, Alice's father, is managing director of a large and successful business in one of Australia's major cities; her mother, Bianca, is a co-director of the company.

Alice is the only child of the 15 who was not visibly reading before entry to school. However, the development and expansion of her reading skills in the first few months of school were so remarkable that her mother now believes it is possible that she was, indeed, reading before entry but keeping it to herself. She is now an avid reader who possesses a keen and lively sense of humour and delights in puns and word-play. She is a talented horsewoman, and sings in a prestigious girls' choir.

Alice's school has permitted her a grade-skip of one year, and this has lessened the boredom and dissatisfaction with school which she felt previously. She still feels, however, that she could work at a much higher level in class if more challenging tasks were offered to her. At the age of 6 years 10 months she obtained an IQ score of 167 on the *Stanford-Binet*.

Anastasia

Anastasia Short, aged 11, is an only child. With her parents, Alison, who is Indian by birth, and Tony, who is Australian, she lives in a pleasant, leafy suburb of a large city. Three years ago Tony completed the restoration of their 80-year-old house; it is an exquisite job undertaken with keen enthusiasm but with a meticulous care for detail.

Both these qualities are evident in Anastasia. She has inherited her mother's dark eyes, luxuriant hair, and luminous complexion, and although not conceited about her physical attractiveness, she likes to take care of her appearance and ensure that she is well presented. When an idea or a task arouses her interest she throws herself into the project with tremendous enthusiasm and takes great pride in her work. She is multi-talented: as well as having exceptional academic abilities, she is an excellent pianist, a talented singer, and a superb actress, and everything is done with flair and elan.

At the age of 6 years 3 months Anastasia was assessed on the *Stanford-Binet*. She scored at the ceiling of the test. Calculation of a ratio IQ, however, places her IQ at 173. Anastasia is not working in school at a level indicated either by her intellectual potential or by her scores on standardized tests of achievement. She is lonely, socially rejected by her age-peers, and deeply unhappy.

Cassandra

Cassandra (Sandy) Lins is 14 years old; her brother Mike is 16. Both Sandy's parents are physicians; Livia, who is Hungarian by birth, works in general practice; Keith, who was born in England of Australian and Irish parents, is a specialist in child neurology.

Cassandra has a remarkable gift for language. Her stories and poetry could well have been written by an adult with a rich and mature vocabulary, and a sensitive ear for phrasing. She is an exceptionally talented pianist, and has displayed such aptitude for swimming that she was invited to train for the state squad in her age group. (She gently refused.) She displays high levels of achievement on standardized tests of language, maths and spelling. However, the only accommodation Sandy's school has made for her academic needs has been a pull-out programme in maths, music and creative thinking. She is a gentle, warm-hearted girl who is sincerely liked by her teachers and classmates; she is the class member to whom others turn for comfort or support in times of trouble. She admits, however, to moderating her academic achievements for peer acceptance.

At 9 years 11 months Cassandra obtained an IQ score of 167 on the *Stanford-Binet*.

Christopher

Christopher Otway, aged 15, and his younger brother Jonathon, aged 13, are both subjects of this study. The family background of the two boys will be briefly outlined in the description of Jonathon, later in this chapter.

As was described earlier, Christopher obtained a mental age of 22 years on the *Stanford-Binet* at the chronological age of 11 years. As the psychologist who tested him pointed out, this meant that he had passed virtually every item on the test, right up to Superior Adult Three. He scored at the ceiling of the test; however, a ratio calculation gives him an IQ of 200. To extend the testing further, the psychologist administered the *Wechsler Adult Intelligence Scale (WAIS–R)*. Here Christopher performed at the absolute maximum on abstract reasoning and arithmetic, placing him in the 'very superior' range even compared to adults.

The psychologist's assessment includes some interesting analyses of Christopher's styles of processing information.

> [Christopher] works at trying to put every piece of information or every problem which he had to solve into some sort of category. Perhaps at his level of intellectual activity this is the most efficient way of handling the multitude of information and ideas which he handles each day. I also observed (as have his parents) that Christopher is one of the few people who truly seems to be able to handle information in parallel. For instance, when he was working on quite a difficult question on the assessment, and was obviously thinking and talking on that particular problem, he suddenly interrupted himself to produce the solution to a previous problem which he felt he could improve on.

Christopher's achievements in maths and language are quite remarkable. At the age of 11 years 4 months he achieved the phenomenal score of 710 on the *Scholastic Aptitude Test–Mathematics (SAT–M)* and 580 on the *Scholastic Aptitude Test–Verbal (SAT–V)*. He is fortunate in that his school has provided him with a programme of grade-skipping, subject acceleration and enrichment designed to meet both his academic and social needs.

Fred

Fred Campbell is the oldest of two children; his sister Penny is 14. Fred is currently aged 15. Fred's school has combined grade-skipping, subject acceleration and extension in their sincere efforts to foster his exceptional abilities in maths and science. He entered Grade 10, in high school, two weeks after his thirteenth birthday, and will enter university in February 1993, less than two months after he turns 16. He plans to take a B.Sc. degree with specialization in maths and physics, a course to which he is well suited, as he topped his state in the selection tests for the Australian Physics Olympiad.

Fred taught himself to read before his third birthday and his remarkable numeracy skills developed shortly afterwards. His advancement in maths and language was largely ignored by his elementary school and he was bored, frustrated and socially rejected by age-peers. The remarkable level of his academic achievement came to light when, at the age of 12 years 1 month he scored 640 on the *SAT–M* and 500 on the *SAT–V*.

Fred is a slight, dark-haired lad whose face lights up with pleasure when he is addressed on one of his particular interests. He has a breadth of general knowledge that is quite remarkable in one so young. At the age of 11 years 1 month he obtained an IQ score of 163 on the *Stanford-Binet*.

Hadley

Hadley Bond's experiences in his first two weeks of schooling were described at the start of this chapter. At the present time Adrian, his eldest brother, is 18 years of age, John is almost 16, and Hadley himself is a small, freckled, wiry child of 10. Physically and intellectually he abounds with energy; his agility and skill in sport, in which he takes a passionate interest, are matched by an intellectual agility which is expressed in a boundless curiosity coupled with quite remarkable levels of academic achievement.

Hadley was reading at 18 months of age and could do simple addition and subtraction before the age of 2 years. At the age of 7 years 7 months he had the reading and spelling abilities of a 12-year-old and at 7 years 9 months he scored at the 78th percentile for American Year 8 students on the *Cooperative Achievement Test–Mathematics*. Hadley's elementary school provided him with a programme of radical acceleration and he entered Grade 7, the first year of high school in his state, at age 9. He loves school, excels academically, and is one of the most popular members of his class.

At 8 years 3 months Hadley obtained a mental age of 14 years 8 months on the *Stanford-Binet*, and thus a ratio IQ of 178.

Ian

Ian Baker is 13 years old; his brother Bill is three years younger. At the age of 2 Ian announced to a family friend, 'You know, my father is a mathematician and my mother is a physiotherapist', and this quiet insistence on accuracy and precision has remained with him throughout his elementary school career.

As described earlier in this chapter, Ian has a phenomenal gift for mathematics. He was reading and counting before the age of 2. At the age of 5 years 11 months he was assessed as having the reading accuracy and comprehension skills of a child six years his senior. At the age of 9 years 11 months he scored 560 on the *SAT–M*. Ian's chief passion in life, however, is cartography, and this will be explored in some depth in later chapters.

At the age of 9 years 3 months, Ian obtained a mental age on the *Stanford-Binet* of 18 years 6 months, scoring at the ceiling of the test. A ratio calculation places his IQ score at 200.

For most of his school career Ian was required to work, in class, at the level of his age-peers. It is only in the last two years that he has been permitted an educational programme that comes anywhere near to meeting his academic and social needs.

Jade

Jade Vincent, aged almost 11, is the eldest of four children; her siblings Kaye, Nicholas and Mark are aged 9, 7 and 5 respectively. Michael, Jade's father, is a self-employed builder. Caroline, her mother, was working as a credit manager until Mark's birth; she now works from home running her own small business, an agency for children's entertainers.

Jade has her mother's verve, energy and enthusiasm. In her earlier years she was like a humming bird, darting about joyously, seeking information from every source she could find. She spoke her first word at five months of age, was talking in sentences before her first birthday, and was walking around by herself at ten months. By the time she went to school she was a fluent and avid reader. Unfortunately, much of her school experience has been deeply unhappy.

Jade was assessed on the *Stanford-Binet* at the age of 5 years 2 months and obtained a mental age of 9 years 0 months. This score was at the ceiling of the test; however, a ratio IQ calculation places her IQ at 174.

Jonathon

Jonathon Otway, aged 13, is the younger brother of Christopher, who has been described earlier in this chapter. Jonathon is an attractive, outgoing boy with a wide, rather mischievous, grin. He has inherited the keen wit and dry humour of his father, David, who is personnel manager for a large industrial corporation. His mother, Elizabeth, is a pharmacist working both in a hospital and in a retail outlet. They are a close and supportive family, who visibly enjoy each other's company.

In contrast to the intellectual intensity of his elder brother, Jonathon has a much more relaxed attitude to life and learning. This has tended to mask his keen intelligence; for some years Jonathon's teachers tended to take him at face value. He is actually an extremely gifted young man. At the age of 8 years 4 months, Jonathon obtained a mental age of 14 years 2 months on the *Stanford-Binet*. A ratio calculation places his IQ at 170.

The psychologist who tested Jonathon commented on his well-developed sense of humour:

> Jonathon's verbal responses [were] of exceptionally high quality. He is a very fluent and articulate sort of child, who has highly developed abstract reasoning skills. It was also obvious that Jonathon has a well-developed sense of humour, too, and often he handled test items on two levels. Firstly he would answer the test question exactly

as it was given at a very high level, but then he would give me a supplementary and much more humorous answer or interpretation of the item which he had just completed.

Richard

Richard McLeod, currently aged 15, is the eldest of three boys; his brothers Tom and Alexander are aged 13 and 7 respectively. All three children are highly intelligent; Tom's IQ score on the *Slosson Intelligence Test* is 155. Alasdair, Richard's father, holds a Ph. D. in computing control systems and works as a computer consultant. Ursula, his mother, is a former elementary school teacher who now manages a small business selling data storage products.

Richard's early maths development was quite phenomenal. At the age of 4 he amazed a professor of mathematics at a major Australian university by doing arithmetic mentally in binary, octal and hexadecimal. 'It was as natural to him as the decimal system,' says Ursula, simply. At the age of 12 years 6 months Richard made the remarkable score of 780 – almost three standard deviations above the mean – on the *SAT–M*.

Richard is a young man of many talents. He is a gifted musician and composer, and has won two state-wide elementary school chess championships. During the seven years of his elementary schooling Richard attended four different schools. None was able to offer him a programme designed to respond to his exceptional mathematical abilities while allowing him access to other children who share his abilities and interests.

At the age of 10 years 11 months Richard achieved a mental age of 18 years 4 months on the *Stanford-Binet*, and thus an IQ score of 160.

Rick

Rick Ward has just turned 10. His younger sister Tiffany is 8. They take their blond hair, blue eyes and fair complexions from their Australian mother, Jan, rather than their Italian father, Tony. Rick is an enthusiastic, outgoing and affectionate child whose love of learning was evident from his earliest years. He was reading before the age of 3 and his remarkable mathematical abilities developed at such a rate that at 6 years 6 months of age he scored at the 68th per centile for 9-year-olds on the *Nottingham Number Test*.

Changes of school policy and practice regarding acceleration and extension of highly able students have caused considerable disruption to Rick's school progress. He is working, in class, at a level well below his tested achievement in reading, maths and spelling.

Rick was tested on the *Stanford-Binet* at the age of 3 years 11 months and obtained a mental age of 6 years 6 months and an IQ of 162.

Roshni

Roshni Singh is almost 9 years old. She is the eldest of four children; her brothers Harjeet, Roshan and Harpal are 6, 4 and 1½ years old, respectively. Sarah, Roshni's mother, is Australian. Juspreet, her father, is Indian, of the Sikh religion, and was born in Singapore. Roshni is a delicately beautiful child, with dark, expressive eyes which are alive with intelligence. She is intensely aware of her identity as a 'Punjabi person' and her adherence to the Sikh faith.

Roshni was reading before the age of 3, and by 4 was writing letters to her relatives in Singapore on the family's personal computer. At 5 years 5 months of age she scored at the 84th percentile for 8-year-olds on the *Leicester Number Test*. She has a boundless enthusiasm for learning and a seemingly endless supply of energy.

Roshni was permitted to grade-skip to be with children closer to her mental and emotional age. At the age of 6 years 4 months she was in Grade 3, working with 8- and 9-year-olds. She thoroughly enjoyed the intellectual and social companionship of the older students, and was one of the most popular children in her class.

Roshni was assessed on the *Stanford-Binet* at the age of 2 years 9 months and obtained an IQ score of 162.

Rufus

Rufus Street is 15 years of age. He is an only child and lives with his parents, Daniel, a psychologist employed in government service, and Rachel, who manages the accounts department of a legal office, in a large Australian city.

Rufus' remarkable abilities in maths, reading and writing were identified at an early age. He has an outstanding sensitivity to language, and his poetry and story writing show a maturity far beyond his years. He is a quick-witted lad with an excellent sense of humour, wide-ranging interests and a zest for learning.

Rufus was tested on the *Stanford-Binet* at the age of 5 years 4 months. His IQ score of 168 was at the ceiling of the test for his age; unfortunately, as the psychologist testing him did not record full details on the test report, it is not possible to make a fuller analysis of his performance.

EXCEPTIONALLY AND PROFOUNDLY GIFTED CHILDREN: THE PREVIOUS RESEARCH

Someone has said that genius is of necessity solitary, since the population is so sparse at the higher levels of mental ability. However, adult genius is mobile, and can seek out its kind. It is in the

> case of the child with extraordinarily high IQ that the social problem is most acute. If the IQ is 180, the intellectual level at six is almost on a par with the average eleven-year-old, and at ten or eleven is not far from that of the average high school graduate. Physical development, on the other hand, is not likely to be accelerated more than 10 per cent, and social development probably not more than 20 or 30 per cent. The inevitable result is that the child of 180 IQ has one of the most difficult problems of social adjustment that any human being is ever called upon to meet.
>
> (Burks, Jensen and Terman, 1930, p. 264)

More than 60 years ago one of the earliest and greatest researchers on the cognitive and affective development of the gifted warned that extraordinarily gifted students were children at risk. Subsequent research on the psychosocial development of the exceptionally and profoundly gifted suggested that the social development of these children is somewhat more accelerated than is implied by Terman and his colleagues (Hollingworth, 1942; DeHaan and Havighurst, 1961; Barbe, 1964). Nonetheless, Terman's basic premise stands: social maturity and social adjustment are not the same thing, and children scoring in the highest ranges of intelligence are too infrequent to find many congenial companions.

Children of exceptional intellectual potential are an understudied and underserved population. It has been assumed, for too long, that the academic and social needs of the extremely gifted will be met by placing them in educational programmes designed for moderately gifted students. Indeed, the majority of educators and psychologists working with gifted children are quite unaware of how greatly the intellectual and emotional development of the exceptionally gifted differs from that of moderately gifted age-peers.

In a comprehensive review of the research on the psychosocial development of the intellectually gifted, Janos and Robinson (1985) indicated that research findings regarding favourable personal and social adjustment emanate from studies of moderately gifted, rather than highly gifted, children. Janos and Robinson claimed that although the special problems of the extremely gifted demand urgent investigation, 'the research devoted to exploring them pales in comparison with that devoted to virtually any other maladaptive set of behaviours' (Janos and Robinson, 1985, p. 182).

Why is so little known about extremely gifted children? Feldman (1979) contended that the principal reason why the most extreme forms of intellectual giftedness have been so little studied was Terman's early belief that an IQ of 140 or above constituted 'genius'; he further claimed that this served to concentrate the attention of early researchers on the more moderate levels of giftedness, and called attention away from the highly precocious. Leta Hollingworth, however, argued that exceptionally gifted students are not studied because, as a group, they do not disrupt the smooth functioning of the school or the community. 'Society attends to that which is socially annoying. The school attends to those who give it trouble' (Hollingworth, 1931, p. 3). Unlike other groups of exceptional students, the blind, the intellectually disabled or the autistic, the difficulties encountered by exceptionally gifted students are not immediately apparent and, because the extremely gifted tend to internalize their problems (Hollingworth, 1942), they generally cause little disruption to the school. Exceptionally gifted children such as Ian Baker, whose boredom and frustration erupt in physical aggression towards their classmates, are the exception rather than the rule.

It is surprising that very highly gifted students do not rebel more frequently against the inappropriate educational provision which is generally made for them. Studies have repeatedly found that the great majority of highly gifted students are required to work, in class, at levels several years below their tested achievement (Hollingworth, 1926; Kincaid, 1969; Painter, 1976). Underachievement may be imposed on the exceptionally gifted child through the constraints of an inappropriate and undemanding educational programme or, as often happens, the child may deliberately underachieve in an attempt to seek peer-group acceptance (Pringle, 1970). Extremely gifted children are likely to have problems of educational adaptation early in their school careers (Hollingworth, 1942). The problems of serious academic underachievement are compounded by the unlikelihood of their finding congenial companionship in a heterogeneous class setting where their extraordinary intellectual abilities, the way they view the world, their tendency to think in abstract principles rather than concrete examples, their levels of moral reasoning and even their play interests are so conspicuously different from those of their age-peers (Hollingworth, 1942).

In her numerous papers and presentations, Hollingworth repeatedly argued that educators and psychologists have an obligation to study, as well as serve, the exceptionally gifted (Hollingworth, 1926, 1931, 1942). Despite this, well-designed longitudinal studies which trace the academic, social and emotional development of these children are extremely rare.

The most thorough and comprehensive examination of the characteristics of intellectually gifted children has certainly been that of Terman and his colleagues. The longitudinal research reported in five volumes under the general title *Genetic Studies of Genius* (Terman, 1925; Cox, 1926; Burks, Jensen and Terman, 1930; Terman and Oden, 1947, 1959) derived from an initial study of 1,528 children, the majority of whom scored at or above IQ 140 on the *Stanford-Binet Intelligence Scale*, and follow-up studies undertaken as these children progressed through adolescence and adulthood. The initial study (Terman, 1925) made an exhaustive analysis of the subjects' racial and social origin, the composition of their families, their early development and physical health, their special abilities, school progress and educational history, their reading interests, hobbies and play interests, and their traits of character and personality.

In the third and fourth volumes of the study, *The Promise of Youth*, and *The Gifted Child Grows Up*, Terman and his colleagues reported on a secondary study of those subjects within the gifted group who scored at or above IQ 170. No significant differences were found between the exceptionally gifted and the total group on measures of early development, health, age at marriage, fertility, or rate of marriage or divorce. The exceptionally gifted group, however, learned to read significantly earlier than did their moderately gifted age-peers, they were more often accelerated through school and a greater proportion of them went on to college (Terman and Oden, 1947). Interestingly, Terman noted that there was no appreciable difference between the high school grades attained by the high group and the total group; indeed around 25 per cent of the extremely gifted men had college records that were only fair to poor (Terman and Oden, 1947).

In the 1930 follow-up, when the mean age of the gifted group was 14 years, 60 per cent of the extremely gifted boys and 73 per cent of the extremely gifted girls were reported by their teachers and parents as being definitely solitary or 'poor mixers'. Terman pointed out, however, that this did not imply that these children were disliked or even unappreciated by their schoolmates; the majority of the extremely gifted group had been elected by their classmates to various class offices within the previous few years. Terman suggested, indeed, that the children of IQ 170–180 were 'loners' from preference rather than as a result of social rejection; in his view it was when the child's IQ approached 180 that the problems of salience and social isolation became severe (Burks, Jensen and Terman, 1930).

Hughes and Converse (1962), however, summarized the misgivings of several critics regarding certain methodological weaknesses in the selection procedures employed by Terman. To be tested for inclusion in the study, children had firstly to be nominated by their class teacher. Teachers are notoriously poor at identifying intellectual talent in children without the support of objective assessment procedures (Pegnato and Birch, 1959; Baldwin, 1962; Gear, 1976) and teachers in the schools canvassed by Terman may well have ignored highly gifted children from low-status racial and socio-economic groups, as well as highly gifted children who were underachieving. As will be discussed in Chapter 5, the oriental schools which the majority of Chinese students attended were not canvassed for possible participants. Hughes and Converse claimed that the children eventually included in the gifted group represented less than one-fifth the number of children of IQ 140+ theoretically present in the population surveyed. The gifted group studied by Terman was, in other words, comprised of intellectually gifted children fortunate enough to be so identified by their schools.

An additional concern arises from the fact that a substantial number of Terman's gifted group had been academically accelerated. Of the 35 children of IQ 170+ reported by Burks, Jensen and Terman in the 1930 follow-up study, only two had not been grade-skipped! The generally positive academic and social adjustment reported for this group may not have characterized children of similar levels of ability whose talents were not recognized by their teachers and who consequently were not selected for participation in the study.

A follow-up study by Feldman (1984), which compared 26 members of Terman's gifted sample whose IQ scores were 180 and above with a control group of 26 individuals selected at random from the total gifted group, found that while for the men the level of distinction attained in careers was somewhat greater for the IQ 180+ group, this was true for only a few of the subjects, not for the group overall. Tannenbaum (1986), however, pointed out that even if only four of the 19 males of IQ 180 achieved high levels of distinction in their careers, this is still a considerably greater proportion than one would expect to find in the general population.

Undoubtedly the most significant and influential research in the field of *exceptional* intellectual potential has been that undertaken by Leta Stetter Hollingworth. Hollingworth's interest in the extremely gifted was sparked by her association with 'Child E', a boy of IQ 187 whose academic and social progress she followed until her death in 1939 (Hollingworth, Garrison and Burke, 1917, 1922; Hollingworth, 1926, 1942). *Children Above IQ 180*, published posthumously in 1942, analysed then current and previous conceptions of intellectual giftedness, described 19 children of IQ 180 and above reported by previous researchers, and described in remarkable detail the intellectual, academic and social development of 12 New York children of IQ 180 and above whom Hollingworth herself had studied over the 23 years from 1916 till her untimely death from cancer at 53.

Hollingworth was fascinated by the differences she found in the cognitive and affective development of moderately gifted and extremely gifted children. She defined the IQ range 125–155 as 'socially optimal intelligence' (Hollingworth, 1926). She found that children scoring within this range were well-balanced, self-confident and outgoing individuals who were able to win the confidence and friendship of age-peers. She claimed, however, that above the level of IQ 160 the difference between the exceptionally gifted child and his or her age-mates is so great that it leads to special problems of development which are correlated with social isolation, and that these difficulties appear particularly acute between the ages of 4 and 9 (Hollingworth, 1931). It follows that for the optimization of these children's extraordinary potential, their remarkable intellectual gifts should be identified and fostered as early as possible before patterns of underachievement or social isolation become established.

In 1922 Hollingworth proposed and oversaw an educational experiment designed to discover whether, under conditions of equal educational opportunity, moderately gifted and highly gifted children would attain different levels of scholastic achievement. Two special opportunity classes for gifted children were established at Public School 165 in New York, for an experimental period of three years, Group A housing 26 children of IQ 150–183, and Group B housing an equivalent number of children of IQ 134–154. The two classes were taught under identical conditions (Hollingworth and Cobb, 1928), each being taught by a team of no fewer than seven teachers, including Hollingworth herself. The enrichment and extra-curricular opportunities offered were the same for both classes, and the curriculum was differentiated within each class to enable each student to progress according to his or her capacity. Hollingworth reported that even under these conditions of equal educational opportunity the achievement of the exceptionally gifted children was consistently superior to that of the moderately gifted. 'Children of the age herein studied (7–9) cannot be equalized in achievement by the equalization of opportunity' (Hollingworth and Cobb, 1928, p. 32). This finding is extremely important given the emphasis placed on 'equal educational outcomes' by a number of Australian education systems.

Hollingworth's conclusion stands in striking contrast to Terman's finding that the school achievement of his subjects of IQ 170 did not differ significantly from that of the total group, and suggests that further research is required on the scholastic achievement of extremely gifted children in the regular classroom compared with the achievement of equally gifted children in special educational settings. Little research of this nature has been undertaken.

The second of Hollingworth's major educational experiments was the establishment of an enriched and accelerated curriculum for gifted learners at the newly formed Speyer School, Public School 500. The school, established in February 1936, contained seven full-time classes of slow-learning children (IQ 75–90) and two full-time 'Terman classes' of gifted children. The minimum IQ of students in the Terman classes was around 130 and the median IQ over the five-year period of the classes' existence varied between 140 and 145. This chapter commenced with Hollingworth's famous statement that 'in the ordinary elementary school situation, children of IQ 140 waste half their time. Those above IQ 170 waste practically all of their time' (Hollingworth, 1942, p. 299). In accordance with these views, the Terman classes of the Speyer School were established as an experiment in accelerated enrichment, based on the premise that students of IQ 130 'need, on the average, about one half of their time in the elementary school for mastering the standard curriculum set up for "all the children"' (Hollingworth, 1942, p. 310). Half the school day was devoted to prescribed elementary school subjects, in which the students were accelerated through the regular curriculum, and the remaining half to enrichment activities, preparing the students for entry to Year 9 of senior high school at age 13 (Hollingworth, 1942, p. 314). Ninety pupils attended the Terman classes during the five years of the Speyer School's existence.

Three studies have compared the family, academic and social characteristics of moderately gifted and exceptionally gifted children. Gallagher (1958), comparing the friendship patterns of gifted children scoring below and above IQ 165, noted that the exceptionally gifted tended to have greater problems of social acceptance than did children scoring between IQ 150 and 164. DeHaan and Havighurst (1961) examined the differences between what they termed 'second-order' (IQ 125–160) and 'first-order' (IQ 160+) gifted children. They believed that the second-order gifted child achieves good social adjustment because he has sufficient intelligence to overcome minor social difficulties, but is not 'different' enough to induce the severe problems of salience encountered by the exceptionally gifted student. Barbe (1964), comparing moderately gifted children (IQ 120–134) with highly and exceptionally gifted age-peers (IQ 148–174) found little difference in the emotional adjustment of the two groups, with the exception of a significant difference in 'freedom from nervous habits' in favour of the moderately gifted (Barbe, 1964, p. 66). These studies, however, were of short duration; no attempt was made to trace the emotional development of the subjects through their school careers.

A number of single-subject case studies have reported on children of truly phenomenal levels of intellectual ability. Langenbeck (1915) described a young girl who at age 5 had a mental age of 11 years (and thus a ratio IQ of over 200), and an oral vocabulary of almost 7,000 words. Goldberg (1934) made a clinical study of 'K', of IQ 196, who at 3½ years of age could calculate on which day of the week any given date would fall. Terman and Fenton (1921) reported on 'Betty Ford', a remarkably gifted child author who by age 7 had compiled a personal anthology of almost 200 stories and poems. However, with the exception of 'Betty Ford', who appeared in a subsequent report on seven highly gifted juvenile writers (Burks, Jensen and Terman, 1930), the published findings on these children were limited to the single report.

Longitudinal studies of exceptionally gifted children such as Audrey Grost's account of the academic and emotional development of her profoundly gifted son (Grost, 1970) and my own on-going study of the radical acceleration programme of young mathematics prodigy Terence Tao (Gross, 1986, 1988) are comparatively rare. Some of the best known studies are retrospective, written when the children have attained adulthood, or even after the subject's death (Montour, 1976; Bergman, 1979). It is important that studies of the psychosocial development of exceptionally gifted children, which may differ radically from that of age-peers, be written *in current time*, that is, at the time when the young subjects are actually experiencing the upbringing, the school programmes, the social relationships and the other influences that contribute to their overall development.

During the last 30 years a small number of studies has examined the social and emotional development of groups of exceptionally and profoundly gifted children in current time. Gallagher and Crowder (1957) investigated a group of 36 highly gifted students in primary school, and found that one quarter of them had considerable emotional difficulties. Selig (1959) studied the personality structure of 27 New York elementary school students of mean IQ 180, as revealed by the Rorshach technique, to test a hypothesis of association between emotional instability and exceptional intellectual giftedness. In this group the incidence of emotional/social maladjustment was five times the estimated incidence among school children generally. Sheldon (1959) found that 15 of his sample of 28 children of IQ 170+ reported feelings of isolation and rejection, but concluded that an extremely high IQ is not in itself a sufficient cause for perceptions of isolation; he believed that the negative self-perceptions of his subjects arose in part from factors in the dynamic roles played by the school and family.

A significant contribution to the research on extremely gifted students was made in the early 1980s by Paul Janos, who compared the psychosocial development of 32 children aged 6–9 with IQs in excess of 164, with that of 49 age-peers of moderately superior intellectual ability (Janos, 1983). Although the exceptionally gifted were generally rated higher in terms of their academic performance, they were more isolated than their age peers, had greater problems of social development, and, in the case of a substantial minority, seemed to lack the motivation to develop their intellectual talents. Janos emphasized, however, that the social isolation experienced by these children was not the clinical isolation of emotional disturbance, but was caused by the absence of a suitable peer group with whom to relate. There are virtually no points of common experience and common interest between a 6-year-old with a mental age of 6 and a 6-year-old with a mental age of 12. Hollingworth would have applauded Janos' conclusion: she herself emphasized that when exceptionally gifted children who have been rejected by age-peers are removed from the inappropriate grade-placement, and are permitted to work and play with intellectual peers, the loneliness and social isolation disappear and the child is accepted as a valued classmate and friend (Hollingworth, 1942).

These studies are extremely valuable; however, they examined the psychosocial development of extremely gifted children during only one period of their school lives, rather than tracing their social and emotional growth or deterioration through childhood and adolescence.

Flack (1983) conducted comparative case studies of the development, interests and attitudes of 10 Indiana students aged 12–15 who had participated in the 1982 Midwest Talent Search and had made composite scores of between 1,250 and 1,360 on the *Scholastic Aptitude Tests–Verbal and Mathematics*. Flack investigated the early development of the children, their school and leisure-time interests, the children's perceptions of their school experiences, their family relationships, their goals, aspirations and career interests, and their social relationships with classmates. Data gathering procedures, however, were limited to a single questionnaire and a single interview of 1½–2 hours' duration with each parent and subject child. Standardized achievement tests other than the *SAT* were not employed, and schools' or teachers' perceptions of the children's scholastic performance were not acquired. Flack reported that 'the thrust of this initial study was to ascertain and report the perceptions that students and their parents had of the educational process, not the perceptions schools and teachers had of the students' (Flack, 1983, p. 45).

In his book *Nature's Gambit* Feldman (1986) gives a fascinating account of six highly unusual children whom he terms 'prodigies' – children who are 'unique in having an extremely specialized gift that is expressed only under very specific, culturally evolved, environmental conditions' (Feldman, 1986, p. 9). Feldman emphasizes that prodigies do not exhibit extraordinary performance across a wide range of activities; rather, they are 'the most precociously specialized specialist that we know about' (p. 10). In this the prodigy differs very significantly from the exceptionally gifted subjects reported by Terman and Hollingworth, or indeed the children of the present study – 'the high IQ individual (who) possesses generalized intellectual abilities that seem to permit high levels of functioning in a wide range of environments' (Feldman, 1986, p. 9). Feldman discusses the influence of peer relationships, motivation and family support on the development of the prodigy's specific talent; not surprisingly, however, he does not examine the psychological correlates of extreme intellectual precocity.

Of the studies reported above, only those of Terman and Hollingworth followed the exceptionally gifted students from an early age and recorded their academic, social and emotional progress through childhood and adolescence. There is an urgent need for further observation of the academic, social and emotional development of students whose extraordinary intellectual potential should qualify them to make significant contributions to the societies in which they live, provided that their youthful potential is permitted to flower into adult productivity. Silverman and Kearney are engaged in longitudinal studies of American children of IQ 170+ in Colorado and Maine (Silverman and Waters, 1987; Silverman and Kearney, 1989; Silverman, Gross and Kearney, 1991). The present study, the first few years of which are the focus of this book, will trace the intellectual, academic, social and emotional development of 40 exceptionally and profoundly gifted Australian elementary school children through their childhood and adolescence until each child has graduated from high school.

As will become clear, the school histories of the 15 children who are reported here differ very widely. The schools attended by some of the children have made thoughtfully planned and carefully monitored responses to their intellectual, academic and social needs. The programmes offered to others have been textbook examples of educational mismanagement.

The efficacy or inadequacy of the schooling experienced by these Australian children has depended almost entirely on three factors: firstly, the extent to which their teachers and school administrators have been able to recognize and respond to individual differences in children, and in particular the characteristics and needs of the intellectually gifted; secondly, the willingness or reluctance of their schools to employ those interventive procedures which research has shown to be particularly effective with exceptionally and profoundly gifted students; and lastly, but most importantly, the degree to which the principal and staff of the child's school have been prepared to withstand the extremely egalitarian ethos which pervades much of the Australian education system.

2

GIFTED EDUCATION IN AUSTRALIA

Democracy demands that all of its citizens begin the race even. Egalitarianism insists that they all finish even.

(Price, 1970, p. 34)

The previous chapter introduced 15 children of truly remarkable intellectual and academic potential, and gave an overview of some of the educational and psychological research which has contributed to our knowledge of how extremely gifted children learn, develop and view the world. The children are living in Australia. The previous research has been undertaken in North America, Europe and Asia and there is very little empirical research on gifted and talented children in Australia. There has been no other longitudinal Australian study of the exceptionally gifted.

Educational programmes and educational research arise where they are valued and supported. We do, in Australia, have some fine programmes for gifted students, such as Melbourne's University High School and the Selective High Schools and Opportunity Classes in New South Wales; these programmes, however, are continually under attack from those politicians, community groups and teachers' industrial unions to whom they represent an ideologically unacceptable premise: that gifted children differ, from their age-peers, in their capacity to learn, and need differentiated educational provision if they are to achieve at the level of which they are capable. Some sound research has been undertaken by Australian educators and psychologists with genuine knowledge and interest in the gifted, but generally research in gifted education in Australia is poorly funded and the results are not adequately disseminated. In any case, Australian teachers, unlike their counterparts in North America, have traditionally shown little interest in accessing the research literature in their fields. Perhaps reading the peer review journals savours too greatly of 'intellectualism'.

Australia has little chance of developing first-rate programmes for gifted and talented students until we rid ourselves of our national intolerance of people whom we deride as 'intellectuals'. Historian Katherine West has noted that while Australia allows itself national heroes in sport and, to a certain degree, in big business, we have never allowed ourselves intellectual heroes. In this respect, we differ totally from many European countries where some intellectuals are household names.

'In Australia, by contrast,' writes West, 'intellectual superiority is not a source of national pride. Instead, it invokes feelings of personal inferiority among those who fear that they will be shown up in a society whose dominant national mythology is that people are and should be equal' (West, 1987, p. 15).

As West points out, it is time we redesigned the kind of equality we really need in Australian education: not equal outcomes but equal opportunity to fulfil people's different educational potential. Brian Start, John Smyth Professor of Education at the University of Melbourne, states succinctly that all children have an equal right to develop maximally; the equal right to develop, however, should not be confused with a right to equal development. This mistake, claims Start, is basic in the arguments of those espousing the 'equality of outcomes' ideology (Start, 1986b, p. 831).

Nonetheless, as will be shown in this and subsequent chapters, the push for 'equality of educational outcomes' has occupied the attention of a good many Australian politicians, educational bureaucrats and teacher union leaders for much of the 1980s and early 1990s. As the principles of the 'equality of outcomes' movement are violated most visibly by the achievements of those academically gifted students who have been permitted to fulfil their potential, it is logical that much of the effort of this movement is directed towards the suppression of programmes for gifted children and the imposition of policies and practices designed to 'level down' the intellectually superior and achieve, where possible, parity of educational attainment.

One approach to achieving equality of educational outcomes is to require that all children, regardless of their capacity to learn, should undertake the same curriculum, at the same time, at the same pace, and to the degree that it can be controlled, in classes which contain as wide a range of intellectual ability as can be managed by the average teacher. Research has shown that ability grouping produces substantial academic gains for gifted children (Kulik, 1985, 1992; Kulik and Kulik 1982, 1984a, 1991; Vaughn, Feldhusen and Asher, 1991; Rogers, 1992); therefore proponents of equality of outcomes argue strongly that gifted students must be educated in mixed-ability classes.

To defend this approach, however, politicians and bureaucrats responsible for the allocation of educational resources must claim that a child's innate capacity to learn has little influence on his or her ultimate academic success. It is no coincidence that in Victoria, one of the states most committed to equality of educational outcomes, the former Minister of Education Joan Kirner, should have announced, in 1989, that her vision for the future of Victorian education meant recognizing that the major determinants of achievement are social class, race and gender, rather than individual attributes such as diligence, potential or ability (Sheridan, 1989).

An alternative rationale is to pretend that intellectual differences among children do not exist in the first place. This argument is favoured by the 'equal outcomes' proponents in a number of Australian states but it is, of course, riskier and requires the use of carefully selected terminology if reality is to be effectively denied. Not even the most militantly left-wing unionist would suggest that all children are to some degree intellectually disabled but that some have been able to overcome their disabilities through effective parenting and education. A more seductive argument is that all children are potentially gifted and with an equitable distribution of social and material resources all could achieve excellence.

Acceptance of this principle leads naturally to a socio-political stance whereby any suggestion that a specific group of gifted students needs extra assistance can be dismissed as not only irrelevant but doubly elitist. If all are gifted, there is no need for strategies to identify gifted and talented students. There is no need for special provisions for the gifted, except in such cases where, as with students whose gift lies in sport or music, it is deemed more economically viable to congregate resources, and children, at a central point. There is certainly no need for teachers to have special training; if all are gifted, a generalist pre-service teacher education course will equip the young teacher to foster the gifts of all the students in his or her class.

Charles Boag, a reporter with *The Bulletin*, a widely read Australian journal of political and social comment, put it in a nutshell.

> Neglect is only part of the story. A large part of the problem is dramatically Australian; if servicing the gifted and talented is anti-egalitarian, simply redefine 'gifted and talented' to include most or all children (all-ability schools) and Eureka! you are educating the gifted and talented.
>
> (Boag, 1990, p. 48)

It was this philosophy that enabled the Director-General of Education of Ian Baker's state to tell Sally Baker that 'all children have gifts and talents' and that it was 'the responsibility of all schools to develop organisational and classroom practices which benefit all children and enable their gifts and talents to be recognised and fostered'.

INTERNATIONALLY RECOGNIZED DEFINITIONS OF GIFTEDNESS AND TALENT

Overseas experts in gifted education, visiting Australia to speak at conferences or examine our educational provisions, are often bemused by the degree to which international research in gifted education has been, and is, ignored by Australian teachers working with gifted children or by bureaucrats responsible for the development of educational policy. There seems to be a particular lack of awareness, and lack of interest, in the models and definitions of giftedness which have evolved over the last 15 years and which influence the ways educators in other countries now think about the cognitive and affective development of gifted students.

To place in context the development of theory since the late 1970s, it is necessary to go back a little further.

A number of modern researchers, both in Australia and overseas, have suggested that in the first half of this century giftedness was viewed only as high intellectual capacity. This is over-simplistic and misleading. As early as 1926 Leta Hollingworth reported on what she defined as 'special talents': areas of outstanding potential or performance which seemed independent of general intelligence. Only a few years later Terman and his colleagues (Burks, Jensen and Terman, 1930) were reporting on the prevalence of special abilities identified among children in the gifted group, and advocating that schools should take care to identify and foster these abilities.

DeHaan and Havighurst

One of the earliest structured definitions of multiple talents was developed by DeHaan and Havighurst in 1961. As was briefly indicated in Chapter 1, these researchers proposed six 'domains of excellence' in which children could display unusually high capacity; these were intellectual ability; creative thinking; scientific ability; social leadership; mechanical skills; and talent in the fine arts. As Tannenbaum has pointed out (Tannenbaum, 1983) the only significant difference between the DeHaan and Havighurst list and the Marland definition which followed 11 years later is that the earlier one is much more explicit about the meaning of each domain.

The Marland definition

In 1972 the United States Office of Education, under Commissioner Sidney P. Marland, published the results of a two-year study into the status of educational services for gifted students in American schools. The report suggested that the considerable majority of gifted students at that time received no special assistance to develop their abilities, and that there was an alarming incidence of academic underachievement among the nation's ablest young people. This led both to an upsurge of interest in, and concern for, the needs of gifted children, and to the development of a new, multi-faceted definition of giftedness which has influenced educators of the gifted worldwide. What is seldom recognized is how much the Marland definition owes to DeHaan and Havighurst.

> Gifted and talented children are those identified by professionally qualified persons, who by virtue of outstanding abilities are capable of high performance. These are children who require differentiated educational programmes and services beyond those normally provided by the regular school programme in order to realise their contribution to self and society.
>
> Children capable of high performance include those with demonstrated achievement and/or potential ability in any of the following areas:
>
> 1. General intellectual ability
> 2. Specific academic aptitude
> 3. Creative or productive thinking
> 4. Leadership ability
> 5. Visual and performing arts
> 6. Psychomotor ability
>
> (Marland, 1972, p. 10)

The Marland Report went on to say that for the utilization of these identification criteria it could be assumed that gifted and talented children encompassed a minimum of 3–5 per cent of the population.

In 1978 the US Congress revised Marland's definition to read:

> [Gifted and talented students are] children, and wherever applicable, youth who are identified at the pre-school, elementary or secondary level as possessing demonstrated or potential abilities that give evidence of high performance capability in areas such as intellectual, creative, specific academic or leadership ability or in the performing and visual arts, and who by reason thereof require services or activities not ordinarily provided by the school.
>
> (US Congress, Educational Amendment of 1978 [P.L. 95–561, IXA])

The 1978 revision omitted the domain of psychomotor ability through a belief that many psychomotor talents, such as dance, could be accommodated within the category of performing arts, and through a concern that a number of schools were using grant money intended for the development of gifted programmes to support existing sports and athletic programmes, claiming that in this way they were fostering the talents of students in Category 6. The revised version, however, retained three important emphases:

— gifted students were not only those who were already demonstrating high level performance; they were those with the potential to achieve, as well as those who were achieving. This opened the way for the recognition of, and development of programmes for, the underachieving gifted child;
— giftedness, as Terman and Hollingworth had signalled, and as DeHaan and Havighurst had overtly stated, should be seen as multi-faceted and encompassing affective elements, such as social leadership, as well as cognitive and creative skills;
— it was not enough to identify the gifted and talented; the school must respond by providing services outside of and beyond those which would be offered in the normal school programme.

Renzulli's 'three-ring' definition

In 1978 Joseph Renzulli developed a theoretical model of giftedness which was to have considerable influence both in North America and in Australia. Renzulli's 'three-ring' definition proposed that giftedness is an interaction among three basic clusters of human traits – above average, but not necessarily superior, general ability, high levels of task commitment, and high levels of creativity. 'Gifted and talented children are those possessing or capable of developing this composite set of traits and applying them to any potentially valuable area of human performance' (Renzulli, 1978, p. 261).

We can begin to see how succeeding models of giftedness were built each upon the other. Like DeHaan and Havighurst 17 years previously, and Marland in 1972, Renzulli recognized that giftedness could be sited in the creative and socio-affective, as well as the cognitive, domains. What was new about Renzulli's definition, however, was the requirement that the three traits be interactively present before a child could be acknowledged as gifted. Within the Renzulli model the child 'earns the right' to special services by displaying the above average ability, task commitment and creativity which Renzulli states are 'the necessary ingredients' of giftedness (Renzulli and Smith, 1980, p. 10).

Since the mid-1980s Renzulli's definition, and the identification and programme models predicated on it, have been subject to increasingly rigorous criticism in the international journals of gifted education (Jellen, 1983; Kontos *et al.*, 1983; Gagné, 1985, 1991b; Borland, 1989; Jarrell and Borland, 1990). Renzulli's theories still have many adherents, but there is a growing concern that his model does not allow for the underachieving gifted child; as will be discussed in subsequent chapters, American, British and Australian research reveals that the majority of academically gifted students underachieve significantly in the regular classroom and many are seriously demotivated by the time they have passed through the first few years of elementary school. These children can hardly be described as 'task-committed'. Furthermore, as far back as 1962 Getzels and Jackson found that above an IQ threshhold of 120 (the top 10 per cent of the population) there is virtually no correlation between intelligence and creativity; they are quite different constructs. The requirement that a child must be both academically able *and* highly creative before we acknowledge her as gifted is somewhat analogous to defining as physically gifted only those students who display talent in both athletics and music on the grounds that both require psychomotor skill.

A major weakness of the three models described above is that none of the definitions recognizes the importance of the home and school environment in dictating the degree, and perhaps the direction, in which a gifted child's abilities may be fostered.

Tannenbaum's psychosocial definition

A model which both addresses the relationships between potential and achievement – 'the links between promise and fulfilment' (Tannenbaum, 1983, p. 95) – and clearly identifies the role of the environment, is that of Abraham Tannenbaum. Tannenbaum points out that many young people who consume knowledge speedily and efficiently in their early years fail to develop as producers of ideas as they develop. Tannenbaum's psychosocial definition of giftedness gently probes the moral and ethical issues of contribution as against consumership.

> Keeping in mind that developed talent exists only in adults, a proposed definition of giftedness in children is the potential for becoming critically acclaimed performers or exemplary producers of ideas in spheres of activity which enhance the moral, physical, emotional, social, intellectual or aesthetic life of the community.
>
> (Tannenbaum, 1983, p. 86)

Tannenbaum holds that children who have the potential for succeeding as gifted adults not only require the general and specific abilities mentioned in some of the earlier definitions of giftedness, but also must have facilitative personality attributes and some 'special encounters with the environment' to foster the emergence of talent. The five internal and external variables that 'mesh into excellence' are illustrated by a starfishlike design with giftedness produced by the overlap of all five factors.

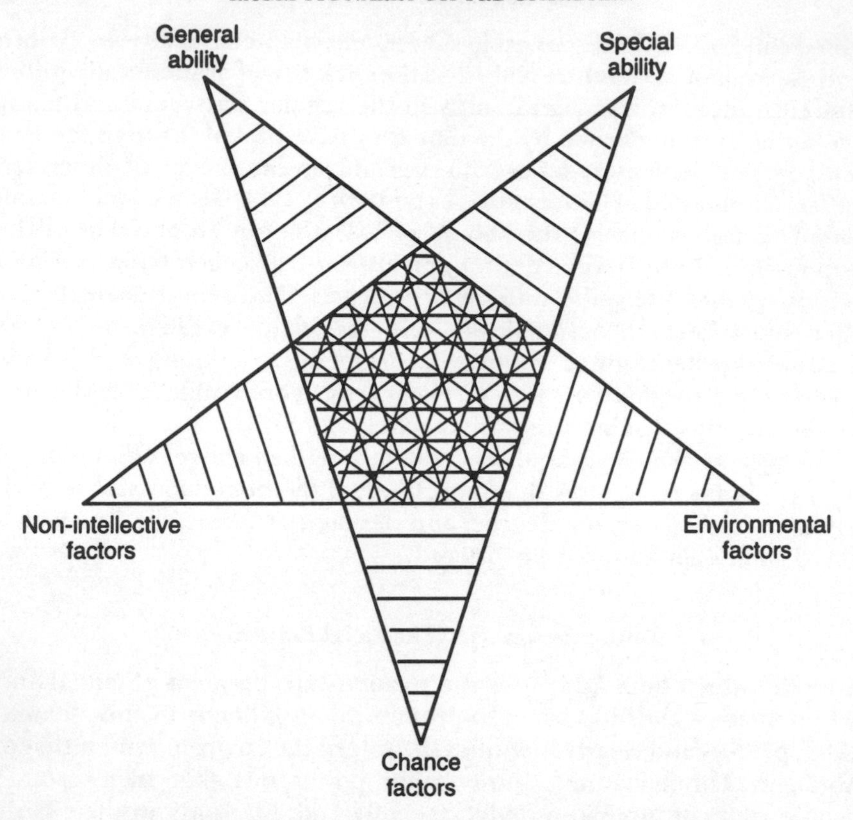

Figure 2.1 The five factors that 'mesh' into excellence. Tannenbaum's psychosocial model of giftedness (Tannenbaum, 1983)

General ability

Tannenbaum points out that the 'G' factor, or testable general intelligence, features to some degree in all talent areas. He adds, however, that different levels of intellectual ability are required for various kinds of accomplishment. Very high levels of abstract reasoning ability may be required for certain activities – certain areas of academic study, for example – while somewhat lesser degrees may be required for other activities.

Special ability

For an individual to emerge as gifted, his or her reasoning ability must be anchored in some specific area of performance. As well as the capacity to think well, gifted people must have special capacities and affinities for particular kinds of work. Some special abilities can be identified in children in the very early years; others do not become apparent until much later in childhood.

Non-intellective factors

Ability alone will not produce outstanding accomplishment. Tannenbaum points out that this requires a confluence of various non-intellective facilitators such as motivation, a secure self-concept, the capacity to stay on task, 'the willingness to sacrifice short-term satisfactions for the sake of long-term accomplishment' (Tannenbaum, 1983, p. 88), sound mental health, the desire to show and share one's talent, and many others.

Environmental factors

Tannenbaum identifies many environmental influences which dictate not only the degree to which the child's ability will be permitted to develop but even the kinds of talent that a society is willing to honour (or tolerate?) and the amount of investment that the society is willing to make in the cultivation of these talents. These environmental influences include not only the child's family, peer group, school and community, but also the economic, legal, social and political institutions of the country in which the child is being brought up and educated.

Chance factors

The influence of chance can be crucial to the emergence of an individual's talent, yet it has not been addressed by previous researchers. Chance factors are those entirely unpredictable events in a person's life which can be critical in permitting exceptional potential to be recognized or encouraged. It may be that the child finds exactly the right teacher at exactly the right stage of his or her talent development. It may be, on the other hand, that the job market in a young person's area of talent unexpectedly closes up, so that there is no opportunity for her to fulfil her promise. As Tannenbaum points out, 'The unexpected can originate anywhere, in the economy, the social milieu, the workplace, the family, and even within the body itself when there is a sudden change in a person's health status that can affect a career' (Tannenbaum, 1983, p. 208).

While earlier definitions were, in the main, listings of the traits or constituents of giftedness, Tannenbaum's model reveals the complex and subtle interweaving of the individual's general and special abilities with personalogical and environmental variables, moderated by random factors which can assist or hinder the translation of promise into fulfilment.

Gagné's differentiated model of giftedness and talent

The model of Françoys Gagné, developed in 1985, provides a diagrammatic representation of the link between promise and fulfilment, or potential and performance, but sets the factors of personality and environment in a somewhat different relationship to those of aptitude or ability, than does Tannenbaum.

Gagné argues that the terms *giftedness* and *talent* should not be used synonymously, and he proposes a most useful distinction: 'Giftedness corresponds to competence which is distinctly above average in one or more domains of ability. Talent refers to performance which is distinctly above average in one or more fields of human performance' (Gagné, 1985, p. 108).

A student can be gifted – that is, possess aptitude, or competence, or potential significantly beyond what we would expect for his or her age – in any one of several domains of human ability or, for that matter, in all of them. Gagné suggests four major domains: intellectual, creative, socio-affective and sensori-motor. In his 1985 and 1991(b) publications, he leaves the door open for the identification or differentiation of other general domains of ability by including a fifth domain labelled, simply, 'other'. Psychomotor ability is, correctly in this writer's view, subsumed within the sensorimotor domain.

Unlike Renzulli, Gagné separates the domains of intellectual and creative ability; it is not necessary, under this definition, for a child to possess high potential in both these domains before he or she may be acknowledged as gifted.

The gifted student may become talented – that is, demonstrate superior performance or achievement, in any one, or many, of a multiplicity of talent fields. Gagné emphasizes that specific talents may develop from the intertwining of abilities from several different domains. In music, for example, the skilled composer-performer may draw on abilities from the cognitive, creative, socio-affective and sensori-motor domains. He further demonstrates that excellence in many fields of performance, for example computer science, requires the interweaving of several quite different talents.

In the centre of his model Gagné places a catalytic cluster of personalogical and environmental variables which can either facilitate or impede the translation of giftedness into talent. At the centre of this cluster, and directly linking potential and performance, is motivation. Motivation, in this model, is not a 'necessary ingredient' of giftedness, but the development of motivation is a necessary condition for the emergence of talent. The cluster of personalogical variables – the child's attitudes, interests, and so much more – and environmental variables such as the

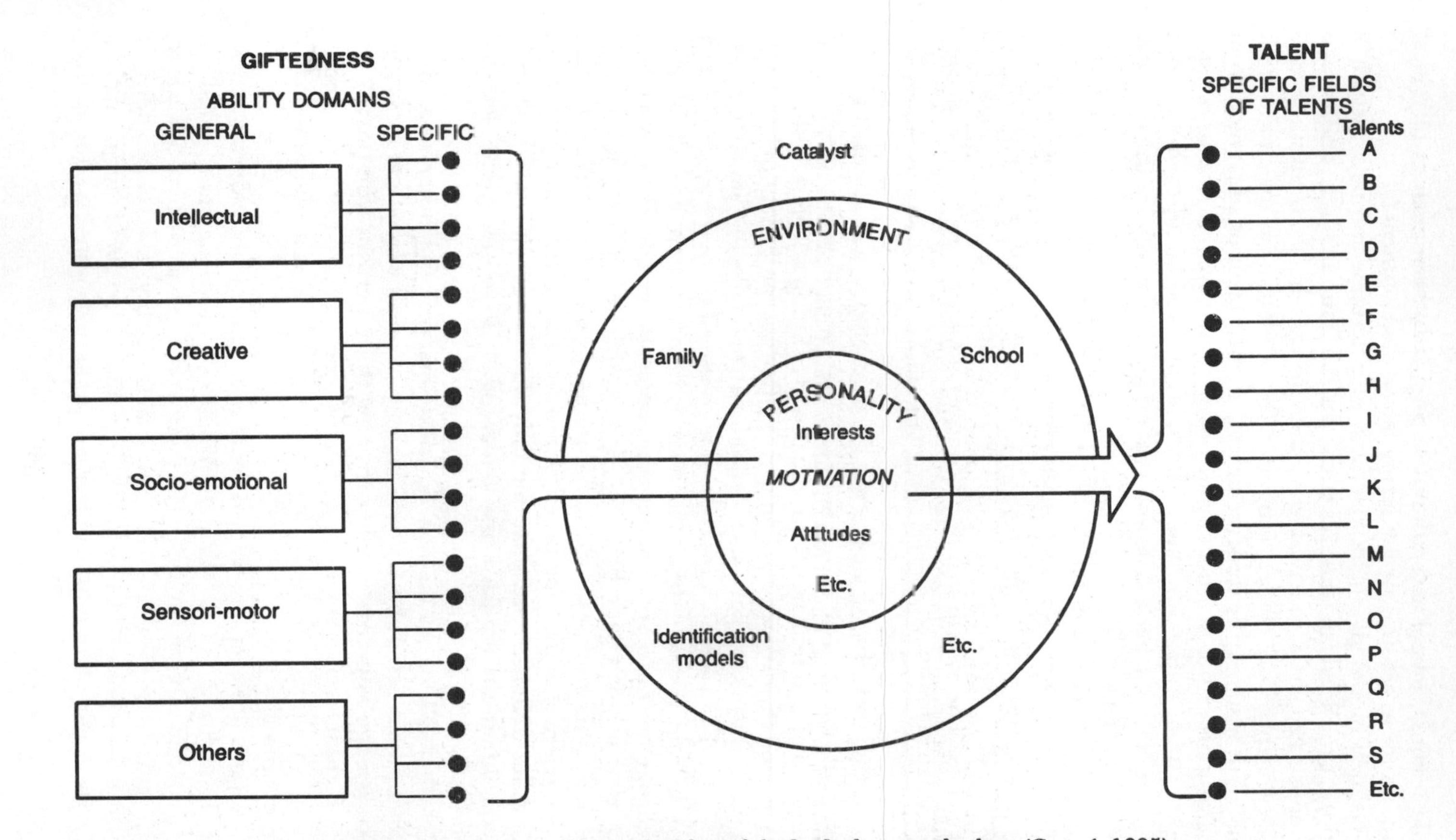

Figure 2.2 Graphic representation of Gagné's differentiated model of giftedness and talent (Gagné, 1985)

child's family, school and cultural setting, is likewise seen as of critical importance in assisting or hindering talent development.

Gagné's model gives us a definition of giftedness and talent which is solidly grounded in the research on human abilities, and which demonstrates, in a practical way, the linkages between aptitude and achievement. This model recognizes the student who may have high ability but who may be underachieving, demotivated or prevented from realizing his or her potential by environmental, psychological or physiological circumstances. In other words, a child can be gifted but not yet talented. The teacher's task, and challenge, is to recognize the gift, and foster the talent.

An education system which adopts the Gagné definition commits itself to identifying high potential in students – real potential, not imagined potential proposed for political reasons! – and creating an educational and social environment which will develop that potential into high performance. The system is not, by contrast, looking only for the already motivated achiever.

The majority of Australian states have developed definitions of giftedness and talent. No state, however, has adopted the psychosocial definition of Tannenbaum. Only the Board of Studies of New South Wales has utilized the differentiated model of giftedness and talent proposed by Gagné. For the most part, state definitions are politicians' amalgamations of Marland and Renzulli which, although useful in their way, are 20 and 14 years old respectively as this book is being written, and do little to challenge our perceptions about the relationships between potential and performance, or what schools can do to translate aptitude into achievement. Furthermore, as Borland has pointed out, the Renzulli definition is not really adequate for practical purposes and 'the consequences of using this definition are such that only those children who are already succeeding in the regular classroom are likely to receive special services' (Borland, 1989, p. 15).

Neither Tannenbaum nor the developers of the other models of giftedness discussed above would suggest for one moment that we should acknowledge as gifted (or talented) only those persons who possess the very highest levels of intellectual, creative, socio-affective or psychomotor ability; or those who make the most significant contributions to the common weal.

Neither, however, are we looking at the majority of children when we use the terms 'gifted' or 'talented'. Whether we are examining giftedness in academic subjects, in the performing arts, in sport or in social leadership, giftedness or talent refers to exceptionality: a level of ability or performance possessed or achieved by a small minority of the population. The claim that all or most children are potentially gifted is educationally and psychologically untenable and indicates a philosophical confusion between the concept of gifts and the concept of individual strengths.

STRENGTHS

Every child, regardless of his or her level of general ability, has an area of individual strength: something that stands out as the high point relative to his or her other abilities. For Margaret, a child whose language skills are several years below her chronological age, the capacity to work, in maths, at the level of her classmates, may be a much valued strength.

Some years ago I taught a Grade 4 class which contained 'Jamie' (not his real name), a delightful but slow learning 10-year-old whose maths achievement was at the average level for first graders and whose skills in reading and spelling were what one would generally expect in second grade. Jamie's relative strengths lay in the psychomotor domain, but even here his development was delayed. His gross and small motor coordination were around the average for third-grade children. The other children in my class were extremely supportive of Jamie in schoolyard games, and made sure that he had his fair share of successes when they played team games such as the ever-present football. No one, however, including Jamie himself, would have suggested that he was 'gifted' in sport. If I had tried to persuade myself that he was, on the grounds that every child must possess a gift or a talent, I would have had to claim that all 30 children in my class were gifted in sport, as every one of the other 29 had considerably more ability in this field than Jamie. This would have led to some pretty strange looks in the staffroom.

Every child has individual strengths and weaknesses, and it is the responsibility of the caring and professional teacher to identify and foster the strengths, and identify and remediate the weaknesses. In some children, a small minority, their weaknesses are of such an order that they require specific and differentiated help within special education, but the individual weaknesses of most children fall well within the normal distribution of abilities. We do not suggest that every child has areas of disability. For some children, again a small minority, their strengths are of such an order that we can justifiably call them gifts, but we should not suggest that all children are gifted.

Nonetheless, the confusion between gifts and strengths, and the insistence of a vocal minority of Australian educators that all children have gifts and talents, has severely hampered the education of gifted students in Australia.

CONFLICTING VIEWS OF GIFTEDNESS

I believe that philosophically, morally, politically, and educationally the

> *approach must be that all* children have gifts and talents which need to be identified, valued and fostered.
>
> (Colanero, 1985, p. 46)

> *Giftedness is not something that children have all the time or do not have at all.*
>
> (Giles, November 1986, in Hansard, p. 1774)

> *This school has a policy and philosophy that recognises that all children have gifts and talents.*
>
> (Uraidla Primary School, in Creed, 1986, p. 117)

These three quotations represent the views of a curriculum adviser, a senior executive and a primary school from the Education Department of South Australia. The first quotation is taken from an invited paper presented in 1984 at the Australian National Workshop on Gifted and Talented Children from Populations with Special Needs. This workshop, funded by the Australian Commonwealth Schools Commission, gathered together in the federal capital, Canberra, a specially selected group of educators from every state in Australia. The workshop was designed

> to bring together people with a knowledge of the needs of girls and other special populations as they relate to the education of gifted and talented children... It was hoped that the group's deliberations would broaden the parameters of giftedness and highlight significant areas for possible future initiatives within Australia.
>
> (Braggett, 1985, p. 1)

The last two decades have seen, in most Western nations, a broadening of the conceptions of giftedness, from the view of giftedness simply as high intelligence to a concern for identifying and fostering a wide range of talents and abilities (Goldberg, 1981; Tannenbaum, 1983, 1986; Gagné, 1985, 1991a; Feldhusen and Baska, 1989). However, while other nations have been moving, during the last few years, towards an awareness of *levels* of giftedness, and the associated requirement for differentiated levels of provision for the gifted (Heller, 1989; Feldhusen, 1989), Australia has been moving towards a view of giftedness as universal. In Australia 'the parameters of giftedness' have not only broadened; they have been stretched to a point which the majority of educators and psychologists working internationally in the field would consider to be quite untenable.

In 1988, Abraham Tannenbaum, speaking at a conference organized by the South Australian Association for Gifted and Talented Children, commented that he had noted with concern the emergent view, among a small but vocal minority of Australian educators, that all children, including the intellectually disabled, possess gifts and talents. Tannenbaum vigorously refuted this premise.

> Unfortunately, there are still some people who adopt a pseudo scientific belief that the human mind consists of many discrete abilities, and that if you break down these independent abilities and keep on breaking them down, you will eventually reach a point where there are more special aptitudes than there are people walking the face of the earth. And the logical conclusion and absurdity that arises from this belief is the idea that if there are many more aptitudes around than people, then surely each human being must have a chance of possessing at least one superior aptitude. Sadly, however, this is not so. God was not a democrat when She distributed abilities.
>
> (Tannenbaum, 1988)

The confusion between gifts and strengths has already been discussed. In the early and mid-1980s a number of Australian states, led by South Australia, began to use the term 'children with gifts and talents' in place of 'gifted and talented children'. It is important to note that the change was much more than semantic; it was motivated by socio-political, rather than purely educational, concerns and indicated what Braggett, as early as 1981, identified as 'a strong egalitarian thrust' (Braggett, 1984, p. 3). It is possible to distinguish radical differences in the ideological, political and philosophical approaches of those states and school systems which have adopted the 'gifts and talents' terminology and those which speak of 'gifted and talented children'.

Schools and systems which adopt the 'gifts and talents' approach focus on developing what they call 'the gifts and talents of all children'. Gifts and talents are seen as synonymous with children's strengths and interests rather than areas of above average potential or performance. Generally these schools and systems advocate a very moderate degree of curriculum differentiation through lateral enrichment within the regular classroom, and discourage or actively prohibit acceleration or ability grouping. Within this framework, the identification of children who possess unusual academic or intellectual potential is discouraged or seen as elitist and socially divisive. Charles Boag quotes the reaction of a senior executive from the Education Department of Tasmania: 'Helping the gifted overlooks and devalues the excellence that is inherent in everyone' (Boag, 1990, p. 49).

The gifts and talents approach arose, initially, out of a laudable desire to encourage a broader, more flexible conception of giftedness; however, it lent itself too readily as a tool for the 'equality of outcomes' movement and educators with special interest in the gifted have begun to suggest that it has done us a great disservice in engendering a neglect of the needs of intellectually and academically gifted students and, in particular, the needs of children of exceptional intellectual potential.

> Few people, if any, can object to the move to provide for a wider range of gifts and talents... It is essential to look after the more able students and not to concentrate on the highest achievers alone. Nevertheless, I question whether, in our zeal to broaden our educational base, we are sometimes beginning to neglect the highest group once again. I am convinced that this is already apparent in some schools. We should remember that outstanding potential does exist, and it behooves us as educators to search it out and make extraordinary provision for it when it is required.
>
> (Braggett, 1986(b), p. 26)

Schools and systems which use the term 'gifted and talented children' generally acknowledge that all children have relative strengths and particular interests, and require both enrichment and extension, but incorporate the belief that there are children in our schools whose relative strengths, when compared with age-peers, are of such an order that they can truly be termed gifted. Following the lead of Marland, it is generally agreed that this group comprises at least 5 per cent of the population: in other words most classrooms would have at least one gifted student. These schools and systems are more likely to attempt some form of systematized identification of at least some types of giftedness, and generally permit various forms of ability grouping and acceleration, or even the establishment of special classes and selective schools with funding and organizational support.

The view that every child has gifts and talents has been firmly refuted by a cross-party committee of the Australian Senate, which spent two years in the latter half of the 1980s investigating Australian provisions for gifted and talented children.

> Children can generally do one thing better than they can do other things. This does not indicate, however, that these children are gifted in the one particular area where their performance is higher than in other areas. The criterion against which talent should be judged is the performance level of their age peers.
>
> (Commonwealth of Australia, 1988, p. 1)

Nevertheless, not all educational bureaucrats would agree with the Senate Report. Ann Morrow, the former Chief Executive in Victoria, was reported as claiming that 'a third to a half' of students in her state could be viewed as 'especially gifted or talented' (Boag, 1990, p. 49). Jim Giles, the then Director of Studies in South Australia, told the Senate Committee that 'every child at some point in his or her development may exhibit gifts and/or talents' (Hansard, 1988, p. 1,782) and then suggested to the Chairman of the Senate Committee that the title of the committee's investigation should be changed from 'The Education of Gifted and

Talented Children' to 'An Inquiry into Education to Foster the Gifts and Talents of Children' (p. 1,808). As late as April 1991, the *Canberra Times* reported the President of the State Association for Gifted and Talented Children as saying that his organization was considering a name change to Association Fostering Gifts and Talents in Children, in the hope that it would 'modify society's stigma against us' (Hobson, 1991, p. 8).

Braggett (1986b) has outlined the major difficulties confronting the proponents of gifted education in Australia. These include the egalitarian belief that provision should not be made for able students because of the more pressing needs of other more visibly disadvantaged groups, a lack of educational commitment to the concept of providing effectively for individual differences, the lack of awareness among Australian teachers of the specific needs of gifted and talented children, and 'an educational philosophy in which social factors are sometimes considered to be more important than other factors' (Braggett, 1986b, p. 15). It is significant that in the quotation from the Proceedings of the National Workshop that began this section, Colanero (1985) stated firstly that education for the gifted is a moral issue, a philosophical concern, and a political question; only latterly did she acknowledge it as an educational issue.

THE INFLUENCE OF EGALITARIANISM

The extreme egalitarianism which characterizes Australian society has its origins in the country's beginnings, in the late eighteenth century, as a British penal colony established to hold convicts sentenced to transportation. Society was split into two distinct and antithetic classes, the aristocracy and landed gentry whose role was to govern and administer the new colony, and the convicts who were leased to the gentry as bond servants, were forbidden to own property, and whose lot, in many cases, was little better than that of slaves. From this immediate separation of interests there developed an intense class hatred, coupled with an extreme resentment against any privilege inherited rather than acquired by 'honest labour' (Ward, 1958). This resentment of inherited wealth and inherited power has carried over into a very real hostility toward high intellectual ability, which is covertly viewed by many Australians as an inherited, and therefore unmerited, passport to wealth and status through success in school and access to higher-level employment.

This equation of intellectual giftedness with social and economic privilege, and the consequent distrust and resentment of the intellectually gifted, has had significant effects on the development of gifted education in Australia. Co-existing with the national resistance to anything which can be construed as 'elitism' is a genuine fear that if, one fosters the individual talents of a student, one will do him a disservice through setting him apart from his peers. Ronald Conway, in his book *The Great Australian*

Stupor discusses the national intolerance of intellectuals and comments drily that 'by the Second World War there were few things other than economic injustice, adultery or a 'smart alec' which could arouse the passions of the average citizen' (Conway, 1971, p. 50).

In 1978 and 1980 the Australian Commonwealth Schools Commission brought to Australia Dr Miriam Goldberg, Professor of Psychology and Education at Teachers College, Columbia University. Goldberg's brief was to examine, evaluate and report on the state of Australia's provisions for gifted and talented students at that time. Goldberg found that a major deterrent to the provision of differentiated curriculum for the gifted was the conviction, among educators and laymen alike, that the ability to 'get along' with everyone was of major importance, and the fear that 'any school procedures which single children out as more able than the generality might jeopardize their sense of identity with, and acceptance by, the common man' (Goldberg, 1981, p. 8).

Goldberg had hit on an important truth about Australian educational values. Professor David Cohen of Macquarie University in Sydney spoke for many Australian educators when, twelve years after Goldberg's first visit, he claimed that 'The really important things in education cannot be measured, weighed or counted. I'm referring to things like self-esteem, like being physically fit, *like getting along well with other people* [author's emphasis], like having well-balanced emotional development' (Kusko, 1990, p. 67).

Coupled with this belief that a sense of community is a quality to be valued even over intellectual strength, and strengthened by the aforementioned distrust of academic ability, is the peculiarly Australian urge to 'cut down the tall poppies'. Australian dramatist Joanna Murray-Smith, then aged 27, was asked, in a media interview on her return from overseas, whether she felt that her contemporaries resented the fact that she is visibly successful.

> I am aware that in this country, for some reason, particularly in creative fields, peers are actually much more mean-spirited about other people's success... In Europe and even in America, the notion of one of your peers being successful creates the response: 'Isn't that terrific, because their success is going to make things easier for me.'
> I think the mean spirit is a very destructive and depressing aspect of working in Australia.
>
> (Fraser, 1989, p. 102)

Russell Ward, in his study *The Australian Legend*, views this levelling attitude in which Australians seem to have a need 'to reduce everyone, in fact, to the same level as themselves' (Ward, 1958, p. 75) as another aspect of Australian egalitarianism. Combined with the genuine Australian concern for the underdog, and the desire to 'equalize upwards' by assisting those disadvantaged by intellectual, physical or social handicaps, there is a strong impulse to 'level down' by hindering the advancement of those 'unfairly' endowed with high intellectual or academic potential. It is not surprising that the movement for 'equality of educational outcomes' found such fertile soil in which to plant the seeds of egaliterianism.

Like most Western democracies, Australia allocates considerable funding to programmes designed to give intellectually, socially and economically disadvantaged children access to a quality education. The need for such compensatory programmes is undeniable. Goldberg, however, in 1978 and 1980 noted a swell of feeling among Australian teachers that the most talented teachers should be placed at the service of average and below average students to ensure 'some common level of attainment' (Goldberg, 1981, p. 9). This disturbed her; she had seen it before and could recognize the context.

In her report, *Issues in the Education of Gifted and Talented Children in Australia and the United States* (Goldberg, 1981), Goldberg warned Australians of the events of the early 1960s in America, when educators such as Tumin (1963) argued forcefully that high intellectual or academic achievement did not arise from superior ability or potential but merely reflected fortunate social and environmental circumstances. Using this as a rationale, Tumin called for the disestablishment of such programmes for able students as then existed, on the grounds that they were perpetuating social injustice.

As early as 1961, Goldberg reminded us, Gardner had warned Americans of the danger of substituting 'equality of educational outcomes' for 'equality of educational opportunity'. 'The great advantage of the conception of equality of opportunity is that it candidly recognizes differences in achievement' (Gardner, 1961, p. 21). Goldberg now warned Australians that educators who espouse the 'equality of outcomes' philosophy often oppose special provision for the gifted, as such programmes conflict with their goal of universal levelling. She could see the strong and disturbing similarities between Australia at the beginning of the 1980s and America 20 years earlier.

Goldberg's report had a mixed reception. As a teacher at that time working in South Australia, I can remember the hostility and resentment with which it was greeted by some of our educational bureaucrats and even some educators working with the gifted and talented. 'Unnecessarily alarmist,' they said. 'Things won't go that far.'

In 1983, a mere two years after the publication of Goldberg's report, the Ministry of Education of the state of Victoria changed the wording of its education policy from 'equality of opportunity for all students' to 'equality of outcomes' (Victorian Ministry of Education, 1983). Four years later, the Commonwealth Schools Commission, in its policy on secondary education and youth, advised that 'instead of focussing exclusively on work tasks which differentiate between students and emphasize their differences, schools should also provide a balance of work tasks in which all students can participate as equals... This approach is summed up in the slogan 'equality of outcomes" (Commonwealth Schools Commission, 1987, p. 30). The provision of work tasks in which 'all students can participate as equals' demands that the tasks be set at a level where all can succeed. This was, in fact, a call for a minimal competency curriculum.

The synthesis of views and values discussed above has created a social climate which, remarkably, has permitted even senior executives of Australian education systems to decry gifted education programmes which exist within their own state systems. In 1984, Joan Kirner, then a Member of the Legislative Council and subsequently Victoria's Minister for Education and State Premier, felt able to make the remarkable assertion that 'gifted programmes' are the means whereby a ruling class stays dominant both in education and in the shaping of Australia's political economy (Kirner, 1984). Victoria's excellent University High School acceleration programme was even then receiving plaudits from educators involved in gifted education across Australia.

As Goldberg would no doubt have noted, Kirner's assertion echoes the arguments used by Tumin in 1963 to encourage the disbandment of programmes for gifted students.

As indicated earlier in this chapter, Kirner, in 1989, stated that her 'vision for the future' meant 'striving for equal outcomes for all students' and recognizing that the major determinants of achievement were 'social class, race and gender, rather than individual attributes such as diligence, potential or ability'. It is little wonder that an Australian education commentator at this time noted, in bemusement, that Victoria appeared to have 'an education minister whose views (were) fossilised in the 60s' (Sheridan, 1989, p. 26).

In 1986, Rodney Cavalier, then Minister for Education in the state of New South Wales, appended a preamble to his government's response to the nationwide inquiry by the Australian Senate into the educational needs of gifted children, claiming that the educational advantages of his state's Selective High Schools were 'largely illusionary' and stating that the major part of the Senate Committee's investigations were 'the ultimate exercise in the futile' and would 'enjoy irrelevance ab initio' (Cavalier, 1986, p. 1,270).

In 1990 Victoria's Chief Education Executive Ann Morrow, interviewed in the *Bulletin* report by Charles Boag, was reported as saying that she would not want to subject her own children to the 'pressure' experienced by students attending the University High School programme. Students interviewed by Boag refuted any suggestion of pressure and were vocal in their praise of the social and academic benefits of the programme.

Senior ministerial and government executives are normally extremely cautious in their public pronouncements regarding programmes under their jurisdiction which are paid for from the public purse; the fact that these highly experienced executives felt free to levy such strong political and social criticism suggests that gifted education may have been seen as a legitimate, or perhaps more importantly, defenceless, target.

PROGRAMMES AND PROVISIONS FOR THE GIFTED

It is not intended that this book should undertake a comprehensive analysis of the type and quality of Australian provisions for the gifted. Persons interested in a review of Australian policies, practices and attitudes during the 1980s are referred to the *1988 Report of the Senate Select Committee on the Education of Gifted and Talented Children* (Commonwealth of Australia, 1988). It should be noted, however, that in Australia, the broadening of the conceptions of giftedness over the last ten years has resulted in a considerable diversity of approach from state to state. Western Australia, for example, conducts a state-wide Talent Search each year to identify gifted children for special academic programmes in secondary school. New South Wales and the Northern Territory have a limited number of full-time self-contained classes for children of high academic potential; New South Wales also has 21 selective high schools for academically gifted and able students. Several states have cluster grouped programmes. Victoria has the aforementioned programme at University High School in Melbourne, which permits special self-contained classes of gifted students to accelerate through the six years of the secondary school curriculum in four years. Unfortunately, no other Victorian school has such a programme, so this excellent provision is limited to an intake of 25 children each year.

In South Australia the state Education Department has established four Special Interest Music Centres and one Special Interest Language Centre which provide special programmes for students with specific aptitudes in music and language. At elementary school level, a special programme has been established within Ascot Primary School in Adelaide, for a specially selected group of 13 children aged 8–12 who show outstanding promise in gymnastics. Children are selected for entry through tests of their gymnastic ability, and the school reduces their academic programme by one hour each day to facilitate their gymnastics training, which also continues before and after school each day and for a number of hours on the weekend.

Interestingly, the then Director of Studies within the South Australian Education Department informed the Senate Inquiry that the Special Interest Music Centres were established on economic, rather than pedagogical, grounds: ‘the only reason we have them is the practical reason again that to teach music to children who have gifts and talents in all schools is very expensive' (Hansard, 1986, p. 1,795). The stance adopted by the South Australian Education Department, that 'every child at some point in his or her development may exhibit gifts and/or talents' (Hansard, 1986, p. 1,782) leads naturally to the requirement that these gifts and talents should be addressed within the regular classroom.

The wording of the Education Department's policy changed, in 1987, from 'fostering gifts and talents *among* children' (South Australian Education Department, 1983), to 'fostering the gifts and talents *of* children' (South Australian Education Department, 1987), a subtle but significant change. As we have discussed, and as the Senate Select Committee pointed out (Commonwealth of Australia, 1988), this approach confuses 'gifts and talents' with children's personal strengths and students' 'gifts' or 'talents' are not compared with the achievements of age-peers; thus within this philosophy Jamie, in Grade 4, who was achieving in sport at Grade 3 level, would indeed be viewed as having a 'gift' for sport since his achievement level in other areas was lower still.

A number of state government education systems discourage their schools from grouping children by ability. A consultant with the Victorian Education Department explained some years ago why she counselled teachers to keep gifted children in the regular classroom: 'I used to withdraw the (gifted) children and have special sessions for them. But the Ministry's equal access policy meant that people who couldn't keep up but who wanted to come couldn't be turned away. It works better this way' (*Gifted Children's Taskforce*, 1987).

In 1985 the Australian Commonwealth Schools Commission invited the education systems throughout Australia to submit for publication descriptions of exemplary programmes for gifted children within their schools.

> The aim of the project was to provide comprehensive and accurate information to people involved or interested in the education of gifted and talented children. The specific objective is to document exemplary programmes currently being run, or recently run, in each State and Territory.
>
> (Creed, 1986, p. i)

One of the government schools whose programmes for gifted children were published as models of exemplary practice had developed, in the late 1970s, a pull-out programme for children talented in mathematics and language. However, according to the descriptor of current practice, 'it was realized that this solely academic spiralling [*sic*] was not catering for other talents' and 'the school philosophy was then revised to cater for all talents in the classroom routine' (Creed, 1986, p. 117).

The programme descriptor opens with the statement that 'this school has a policy and philosophy that recognizes that all children have gifts and talents' (Creed, 1986, p. 117). As the school concerned is a state primary school in South Australia, it is perhaps not surprising that it should have adopted this stance. Disturbingly, however, the statement of the aims and objectives of the programme continues with the following disclaimer: 'It is not the school's intention to exploit each gift or talent to its highest degree in the short time available, but to make the students aware of their own potentials so they may recognize them and, *at a later time*, use them to their best advantage' (Creed, 1986, p. 118).

The school's assumption that optimization of talent equates with exploitation gives cause for concern. More disturbing, however, is the school's assertion that optimization of student potential is not one of its educational aims. Australian children spend a minimum of seven years of their lives in elementary school; yet this school states that in this period, 'the short time available', its responsibilities are limited to making the students aware of their potential; the onus for developing that potential *at a later time* [author's emphasis] is laid on the elementary school child!

The programme outline contains the remarkable assertion that 'the formal curriculum, maths, language, spelling, etc., provides for automatic or regular extension of gifts and talents during subject times', and continues by stating that the 'information curriculum' is supplemented by electives such as music, art and computer studies, and 'by using students in all areas of the school's daily programme, from bin duty through to photocopying and assisting with materials orders' (Creed, 1986, p. 119). In Australian schools 'bin duty' means emptying the rubbish bins! The programme description does not enlarge on how this activity contributes to the fostering of gifts and talents.

The descriptor closes with an explanation of the school's decision to disband the pull-out programme which catered for specific talents through ability grouping. 'We felt this disrupted class management, created a specific group... and was of benefit to specific rather than to all students' (Creed, 1986, p. 122). On these criteria, schools should not withdraw children from the classroom for orchestra rehearsals, sports practice or remedial assistance!

Australian educators have developed, over the last few years, some excellent programmes for gifted and talented students, and descriptions of some of these are included in Creed's text. That the editors should have included the programme described above as a model of 'exemplary practice' is a testimony to the pervasive influence of the educational lobby which maintains that every child is gifted.

TEACHER EDUCATION AND RESEARCH

One of the major difficulties confronting Australian schools wishing to make special provision for children of high intellectual potential is that Australian teachers receive virtually no training, at either pre-service or in-service level, in how to identify and foster academic or intellectual talent. Two studies a decade apart (Start, John and Strange, 1975; Start, 1985) surveyed every Australian tertiary institution which offered teacher education programmes. Each was contacted with a questionnaire relating to their teacher education offerings in four areas: mentally, physically or emotionally handicapped children, migrant children, socio-economically deprived children, and gifted and talented children.

The situation regarding teacher preparation in gifted education was twice as positive in the mid-1980s as it had been in the mid-1970s. Nevertheless, in 1984, for every hour on teaching the gifted, student teachers had been exposed to 18 to 24 hours on teaching the disadvantaged. Furthermore, sessions on gifted education usually comprised one single-hour lecture in a general course, or elective units of three to six lectures. Whereas every institution had at least one compulsory unit or course on one or other form of disadvantage, no institution in Australia had a compulsory unit on gifted. One college replied to the survey saying that its students could consider the intellectually able as one topic in a comprehensive course, and approximately one lecture would be devoted to the area. The name of the course was 'Controversies in Education' (Start, 1985).

Currently, only a very small minority of tertiary institutions provide full semester courses on the education of able children at undergraduate or graduate level. In most states there is a complete absence of provision for specialist study in the field. Only two Australian universities, the University of New South Wales, in Sydney, and the University of Melbourne, in Victoria, offer full, on-campus, specialist programmes in gifted education at all levels of graduate study, led by educators who themselves have academic qualifications in this field. By contrast, in 1985–1986, almost 140 universities in the United States offered on-campus graduate programmes specifically for teachers of gifted children (Congressional Record, 1987).

As a result, the considerable majority of teachers running special programmes for gifted children in Australian schools have had no training in this field of education. Even more seriously, the majority of support teachers and consultants whose brief is to advise schools on the development of programmes and curricula for the gifted have had no access to pre-service or in-service courses in gifted education.

While a growing number of Australian academics are becoming aware of the educational needs of gifted children and the necessity to educate teachers to identify and foster academic talent, others labour under the same false impressions as the majority of teachers in schools. The head of primary teaching at a Melbourne teacher training institution claimed, in

1986, that gifted and talented children were coping well in schools and were achieving all they needed to.

> In my experience, those who are academically talented get more attention from the teachers and they don't need special treatment. I've never seen them neglected. I'm not particularly anxious to see resources put into this area of education because the school community should reflect the general community, not small parts of it alone.
>
> (Stephens, 1986, p. 2)

Yet Australian research refutes the claim that teachers give more attention to the academically talented. Whereas American and British studies indicate that in these countries teachers make more academic contacts with children who are perceived as high achievers, Leder (1987, 1988) has found that Australian teachers give significantly more attention and feedback to low achievers. Leder further established that even where able students in Australia are asked more challenging questions, they are not given sufficient wait time to enable them to respond at a level of complexity commensurate with the challenge of the question (Leder, 1988).

The then Director of Services in the New South Wales Education Department claimed, at an education conference in 1986, that gifted children were in danger of becoming pompous, undisciplined and incapable of communicating with the less talented if they were 'separated off' [*sic*] into a 'hothouse environment' such as a selective school (Susskind, 1986, p. 4). A professor of education at Monash University in Victoria is reported as claiming that gifted children who are placed in special programmes become socially inept and have no understanding of the handicapped and people of lesser abilities.

> 'What the gifted really learn (in acceleration programmes) is that "We're special and we're entitled to more than other people and we need a special school and special teachers". They become overambitious and they learn that they belong only if they are better than other people', Professor Balson said.
>
> (Daley, 1992, p. 2)

Research over many years in North America has shown that, far from creating arrogance or self-aggrandisement, grouping of gifted students has resulted in the children gaining in self-respect, a more realistic appraisal of their abilities, and a tolerance and respect for others (Hollingworth, 1942; Marland, 1972; Clark, 1983). Both the teachers and the parents of the children in Melbourne's University High School acceleration programme strongly reject Balson's assertions that the children become over-competitive, self-centred or socially inept.

A media report on the New South Wales' government's decision to implement, for the first time, a programme of accelerated progression for gifted students, quoted an academic from one of that state's universities as saying that grade-skipping could involve 'serious risks' as children who are permitted to accelerate may be physically abused by the children in the classes they move into as well as the students they leave behind (Totaro, 1990). I know of not one research study which substantiates this assertion. Rather, as later chapters will discuss, the empirical research on acceleration over the last 40 years has established that no social or emotional damage results from well-run, thoughtfully planned acceleration programmes (Daurio, 1979; Pollins, 1983; Southern and Jones, 1991).

Well-designed empirical studies in the education and psychology of the gifted are urgently needed in Australia. The development of defensible programmes for the gifted is hampered by the parlous state of Australian research in this field. A Commonwealth Schools Commission Seminar on the education of gifted and talented students in 1981 found that 'The paucity of Australian research and the absence of any real attempt to harness and interpret overseas research ... means that hypotheses are being stated and programmes are being developed within a data base vacuum' (Commonwealth Schools Commission, 1981, p. 47). The Senate Committee investigating gifted education in 1986–1988 found that little had changed.

Given the lack of teacher education and research on the needs and characteristics of the gifted, the low level of teacher awareness of these needs, and the prevailing social climate in which intellectual talent is decried and distrusted, it is not surprising that the reactions of a majority of Australian teachers towards the gifted range from apathy to overt hostility. An informal survey of teachers entering post-graduate education courses at an Australian teacher training institution found that in answer to the question, 'Who wants to have a gifted child in their classroom?' the overwhelming response was 'a shudder and descriptive adjectives of the 'beastly brat' category, plus some unfriendly anecdotal material' (Mares, 1986).

AUSTRALIAN TEACHERS UNIONS

Similar levels of misinformation and hostility are evident both in the curriculum policies and in the public pronouncements of the Australian teachers' industrial unions. Experimental programmes for gifted students involving alternative class structures such as full-time self-contained gifted classes, pull-out programmes, and acceleration come under vehement and closely organized attack from the unions. The trade union movement is a much more powerful economic, political and social force in Australia than in the United States and Britain and the threat of industrial intervention by teacher unionists is a very real deterrent to the establishment or implementation of special programmes for the gifted.

The Victorian teachers' unions have strongly opposed the continuation of the acceleration programme for gifted students at Melbourne's University High School, and continue to voice their opposition. The then Deputy President of the Victorian Secondary Teachers' Association claimed in 1986 that the acceleration programme was not a model for anything useful in Victorian schooling and that it was not likely to assist students in any way (Baker, 1986). In 1988, Clark, an officer of the Victorian Teachers' Federation, asserted on national television:

> We will oppose any extension of current gifted children's programmes in this state. We opposed the acceleration programme that's happening at University High School, and we opposed the selection of children for schools with specialized programmes. We will continue to do that, and we will do so vigorously.
>
> (Australian Broadcasting Commission, 1988)

Foggo, representing the National Teachers' Union, stated on the same programme, 'We just cannot give money to these children at the expense of the majority of children. It would be extremely elitist to do so' (Australian Broadcasting Commission, 1988). Two years later Foggo told Charles Boag: 'We're not anti the gifted and talented – just the allocation of resources to them' (Boag, 1990, p. 49).

The South Australian Institute of Teachers, addressing the issue of curriculum for the gifted, also rejected 'the redirecting of educational resources to groups in society who are already educationally privileged' (South Australian Institute of Teachers, 1985). The policy of the Victorian Teachers' Union on 'Children with Special Interests and Talents' states that when students are accelerated, 'serious social and emotional adjustments often occur in the short term and, more frequently, in the long term' (Victorian Teachers' Union, 1986, p. 90). As will be shown later, both assertions are contradicted by many years of educational and psychological research (Daurio, 1979; Robinson, 1983; Pollins, 1983).

In 1988 the Senate Select Committee on the Education of Gifted and Talented Children, which had spent the two previous years visiting each state in Australia and examining educational provisions for the gifted, brought out its report. This was a cross-party committee representing every major political party in Australia; yet – unusually for such a committee – it presented a unanimous report with not a single party, or a single member, dissenting from any point. The Senators had been deeply disturbed by what they had seen. In the first chapter of their report (Commonwealth of Australia, 1988) they wrote that gifted children were arguably among the most disadvantaged of educationally disadvantaged groups in Australian schools.

The Senate Committee made nine recommendations to the Federal Government. These included:

— that pre-service teacher training courses should include sufficient information about gifted children to make student teachers aware of the needs of these children and familiarize them with appropriate identification strategies and teaching techniques;
— that the professional development of teachers with special concern for girls, Aborigines and children from disadvantaged groups should include input on the identification and education of gifted children from these populations;
— that videotapes and associated curriculum materials be prepared to assist gifted children in geographically isolated conditions;
— that a national centre for research into the education of gifted children be established in an Australian university and be financially supported by the Federal Government during its establishment phase.

On the release of the Senate Report the Australian Teachers' Federation wrote to all state branches asking that they should not support the recommendations as the money to implement them would have to be drawn from existing sources (Start, 1991).

By contrast, in the following year the State Government of New South Wales created eight new selective high schools for highly able and gifted children, bringing its total number to 21. The funds to provide these special programmes were not, of course, withdrawn from that state's excellent programmes for the intellectually, physically or economically disadvantaged.

The Federal Government, incidentally, took over a year to respond to the Senate Report, which it did by stating that everything that was necessary for the education of gifted students was already being done, and that in any case the ultimate responsibility lay with the individual states.

As Brian Start of the University of Melbourne has written: 'Among deprived groups in Australia, gifted and talented children are unique. They alone face concerted action to prevent their full development by the very agencies in our society to whom the development of our nation's youth is entrusted' (Start, 1986a, p. 10).

ELITISM?

Australian educators have developed some excellent programmes for gifted and talented children. The 'gifted movement' within Australia is small but growing; small clusters of dedicated teachers, academics and parents persevere in their endeavours to improve the lot of able students in the face of community and government apathy and hostility. Each state has an association of parents and teachers concerned for the education and welfare of the gifted, and a National Association was established in 1985. However, the enthusiasm and dedication of volunteer groups and dedicated individuals is not enough in the absence of widespread teacher education, research and public awareness. After their two years of investigation into the education of gifted and talented children, the Senate Committee was forced to conclude, 'Most Australian schools do not appear to make any provision for the education of gifted children' (Commonwealth of Australia, 1988, p. 82).

In a study of social class in the United States, Fussell commented: 'Pushed far enough, class envy results in revenge egalitarianism' (Fussell, 1983, p. 102). In Australia, the education of gifted and talented children has always been seen as a social issue rather than an educational concern. It was an awareness of the dangers attendant on this misconception that prompted a former Minister for Education, The Honourable Kym Beazley Snr, in his keynote address to Australia's First National Conference on the Education of Gifted and Talented Children, to remind his audience that '"elitism" [is] a word properly applied to aristocratic and economic privilege, not to the recognition of special abilities, or the respect due to a child in school' (Beazley, 1984, p. 12). Perhaps the 'revenge egalitarianism' that militates against the full development of high intellectual potential in Australia is an inevitable result of this confusion of issues.

Beazley closed his presentation by acknowledging, with regret, the potency of the term 'elitism' as a deterrent to the establishment of programmes for the intellectually gifted.

> I fear the power of the word 'elitism' may lead to a refusal to see that schools and classrooms need to adjust to meet the needs and special problems of all children... Swift-learning, talented and highly creative children constitute a group whose needs *must* be met.
>
> (Beazley, 1984, p. 14)

'Elitism', in Australia, is a strongly pejorative term, especially when used in connection with the fostering of intellectual talent. As indicated earlier, Foggo, representing the National Teachers' Union, stated on national television that to commit public funds to the education of the gifted would be 'extremely elitist' (Australian Broadcasting Commission, 1988). By contrast, the terms 'elite' and 'elitist' take on radically different connotations when used in reference to the fostering of sporting talent.

In March 1989, two months before the Federal Government responded to the Senate Committee's report on the gifted and talented, a House of Representatives Committee completed a report on the status of sports funding and administration in Australia, under the title *Going for*

Gold. The thrust for this investigation came, in part, out of a certain disappointment, among Australians, in Australia's performance at the Seoul Olympics the previous year. Within weeks the Federal Government responded by committing 51.7 million dollars to provide assistance and encouragement grants for 'elite' athletes, with an additional 15.6 million dollars to support the hiring and training of first-class coaches to ensure that Australian athletes could command a more favourable position in future international competitions (Bruer, 1989). In 1989 the population of Australia was less than 17 million; this was an astonishing commitment of four dollars per head of population from a nation in recession. The dedication of these funds to the training of young people gifted in the psychomotor domain drew not a murmur of protest from the teacher unions. Nor did they express concern that the funds might have to be drawn from other sources.

Going for Gold (Commonwealth of Australia, 1989), uses the terms 'elite sport' and 'elite athletes' quite unabashedly throughout. In Australia, 'elitism' in fostering the talents of her most able sportsmen and women is not only applauded, but funded from the public purse; 'elitism' in discovering and fostering the intellectual talent of her most able youth arouses vigorous protest from politicians and educators alike.

As Cahill (1989) has commented, 'Gifted individuals have already taken us to the moon. They will be the ones who, if given the support and opportunity they deserve, will lead us into the twenty-first century.'

The study reported in this book will follow the social and emotional development, and the educational progress, of a group of exceptionally and profoundly gifted children undertaking their elementary and secondary schooling in Australia in the last two decades of the twentieth century and the first few years of the twenty-first. The social and political attitudes which have influenced the education of gifted and talented children in the 1980s have had a direct and deleterious effect on the educational provisions offered to the majority of the children in this study.

3

METHODOLOGY AND PROCEDURES OF THE STUDY

> *Multiple case studies are a demanding undertaking, but they have tremendous power to advance knowledge in the field of gifted education. The multiple case-study method of developing and testing theory is particularly powerful in areas where methods based on sampling logic are difficult or impossible to use because of the rarity of the phemonena.*
>
> (Moon, 1991, p. 165)

As Sidney Moon, the author of the above passage, would agree, there are few phenomena rarer in education and psychology than exceptionally and profoundly gifted children. This is doubtless why previous research on extreme intellectual precocity in children has comprised, in the main, isolated case studies of individual students (McElwee, 1934; Goldberg, 1934; Witty and Coomer, 1955).

Multiple-case studies, comparing the educational and psychological development of a number of young people, such as Roe's retrospective studies of the lives of eminent biologists, physicists and anthropologists, (Roe, 1951a, 1951b, 1953) are rare indeed. Furthermore, the research on extremely gifted students has generally concentrated on the children's intellective and academic characteristics rather than tracing their overall development within a social and academic setting. Little attempt has been made to understand or analyse the influences of upbringing or education on the child's personal or intellective growth.

Unfortunately some of the best known studies of the childhood and adolescence of highly gifted young people are retrospective, written when the children have already attained adulthood (as with the studies by Roe, mentioned above) or even after the subject's death, as with Montour's biography of child prodigy William James Sidis (Montour, 1976) and her subsequent comparison of the childhood and upbringing of Sidis with that of another remarkably gifted child, Norbert Weiner (Montour, 1977).

Retrospective studies of atypical development can be extremely useful. Ideally, however, studies of the academic and social development of profoundly gifted young people should be written *in current time*, that is, at the time when the young subjects are actually experiencing the upbringing, the school programmes, the social relationships and other influences that contribute to their overall development. In this way, events and situations which impact on the child's development can be observed as they occur rather than through the filter of an unintentionally biased or selective memory. The changing influences of family, school and society can be observed as they occur and can be analysed and discussed with the child himself and with others involved in his academic and personal growth. The young subject can describe his feelings, impressions or desires with an immediacy that is not possible from the more removed perspective of adulthood.

It is especially important, in cases of exceptional or profound intellectual giftedness, where the child's psycho-social development may differ radically from that of his age-peers, that the child's feelings and perceptions of the world should be recorded at the time when they are influencing his thoughts and actions, rather than related in later years, blurred or altered by his adult recollections.

The case study method is a sound approach for developing specific knowledge about exceptional giftedness. It enables the researcher to observe and describe intensively the particular and idiosyncratic features of an individual child's development (Foster, 1986). It provides a holistic view of the person being studied (Frey, 1978) and allows the researcher to develop and validate theories which are grounded in direct observation of an individual's behaviour and development. Indeed, close observation of the child in natural settings, the analysis of subjective factors such as his or her feelings, views and needs, and the use of a wide range of observation procedures, all of which are characteristic of good case study research, enable a more comprehensive observation of an individual than is possible with any other research methodology (Merriam, 1988).

CHARACTERISTICS OF CASE STUDY RESEARCH

There are four characteristics which are generally regarded as essential properties of good qualitative case study research: the studies should be particularistic, descriptive, heuristic and inductive (Merriam, 1988).

Case studies are 'particularistic' in that they focus on a particular individual, event or situation. The case study may, for example, present a holistic view of the ways in which an individual or group of children confronts specific problems. They are 'descriptive' in that the end product is a rich, interpretive description of the child or situation under investigation. The focus of the study should be broad, embracing as many variables as possible and tracing their interactions, often within a longitudinal framework (Asher, 1976). Rather than being limited by the standardized reporting mechanisms which characterize scientific inquiry, case studies 'use prose and literary techniques to describe, elicit images, and analyze situations' (Wilson, 1979, p. 448).

Case studies are essentially 'heuristic', enhancing the reader's understanding of the situation or individual under investigation. They can reveal previously unobserved relationships, leading to new perceptions about the phenomenon being studied. Lastly, case studies generally rely on 'inductive' reasoning. The researcher beginning a case study may have a tentative working hypothesis, but his or her expectations and perceptions are revised as the findings of the study are analysed and evaluated. 'Discovery of new relationships, concepts and understanding, rather than verification of predetermined hypotheses, characterizes qualitative case studies' (Merriam, 1988, p. 13).

Since case study inquiry is particularly suited to the development and elaboration of theory rather than to theory verification, it is particularly suited to the present study. The longitudinal comparative case studies which comprise this research are breaking new ground. The parlous state of Australian research on the gifted and talented means that very little is known about intellectually able students in that country (Commonwealth Schools Commission, 1981; Commonwealth of Australia, 1988) and this is the first research study on the exceptionally gifted (children above IQ 160) undertaken anywhere in Australasia. Quite simply, when this study began there existed no data bank on extremely gifted Australian children from which theory could be developed for validation!

MULTIPLE-CASE STUDIES

The study employs a wide range of observation techniques, which will be discussed more fully later in this chapter. The data-gathering procedures are both qualitative and quantitative and include tests of general ability, standardized tests of achievement in several academic subject areas, inventories of self-esteem and moral development, questionnaires completed by parents of the subject children, interviews with the children and their parents, school records, diaries, letters and other documentation.

Yin (1984) discussed the use of single-case methodologies in multiple-case studies. He advised that multiple-case research should be addressed as one would address multiple experiments – that is, following a replication logic. Within this framework each case is treated as if it were a 'whole' study, in which evidence is sought and analysed from a variety of sources. Each case (in this study each of the 15 children) is subjected to similar observation procedures and the data collection and analyses employed in the first case are replicated for each case in the study. Both the individual cases and the multiple-case results should be the focus of a summary report.

The strength of the multiple-case replication study lies in its usefulness for comparative case studies of small numbers of subjects. By comparing the results of several cases, one can increase the generalizability of each finding, while simultaneously identifying conditions under which that finding is likely to occur (Miles and Huberman, 1984). The multiple-case replication study is not, however, suitable for use with large numbers of cases; Yin (1984) warned that this would require extensive resources and time beyond the means of a single, independent researcher.

ADVANTAGES AND DISADVANTAGES OF CASE STUDY RESEARCH

Case study inquiry certainly has its limitations! Comprehensive, well-conducted case studies are extremely time-consuming and, in investigations such as the present study, in which subjects are scattered over an extremely large geographic area, they can also be extremely costly. Yin maintained that 'the demands of a case study on [the investigator's] intellect, ego and emotions are far greater than those of any other research strategy' (Yin, 1984, p. 56).

The success and value of qualitative case studies are largely dictated by the sensitivity and integrity of the investigator (Merriam, 1988). Researchers are the primary instrument of data collection and analysis; if they do not maintain an unbiased perspective they could simply select from the mass of available data that which supported their existing perceptions. For many years social scientists were wary of case study methodology, as indeed they were suspicious of any research design which was not based on direct experimentation, and the reliability, validity and generalizability of case study research were sometimes called into question. Scholars are now much more aware of the value of the well-designed case study as a powerful qualitative research strategy; nonetheless, the investigator who selects this methodology must pay explicit attention to these issues. The procedures which have been used in this study to increase the reliability and validity of research findings are discussed below.

The strengths and advantages of case study research far outweigh its limitations. Yin (1984) maintained that the unique strength of the case study is its ability to present a holistic view of an individual or event through the variety of evidence it can employ – observations, interviews, documents and artifacts. Anchored in real-life situations, as in this study, the case study is particularly valuable for exploratory research in the social sciences. It can be employed in cases where it is not feasible, or desirable, to manipulate the potential causes of behaviour (Merriam, 1988). It can provide a richly descriptive, illuminative picture of a complex social situation. It is ideally suited to the investigation and description of events or individuals characterized by their rarity, such as exceptionally or profoundly gifted children (Foster, 1986).

As mentioned earlier, when this study commenced the existing research on exceptionally and profoundly gifted children had been conducted overseas and was limited to a small number of studies, the majority of which were short term rather than longitudinal, and conducted retrospectively rather than in current time. There was no information bank on extremely gifted children in Australia.

Participants in Australia's first National Seminar on the Education of Gifted and Talented Children had already noted, with concern, that in gifted education in Australia 'hypotheses are being stated and programmes are being developed within a data base vacuum' (Commonwealth Schools Commission, 1981, p. 47). I had no wish to contribute to this phenomenon! Given that virtually nothing was known about the academic or social development of extremely gifted Australian children, it seemed pointless to develop ungrounded theory just for the sake of theorizing. It seemed more practical to use the findings of the previous overseas studies as a guide to the questions that might be asked, and the issues that might be investigated, within the present study. At a later time, when a substantial amount of data had been gathered about the extremely gifted children in this study, this data could be used to formulate theory which could provide a starting point for future research. Equally importantly, of course, the results of the present study could be used to advise schools on the development of appropriate individualized programmes for exceptionally and profoundly gifted children. That point has now been reached.

Accordingly, my selection of research questions which would guide my investigations in this study was influenced by the findings of the few overseas researchers who had undertaken significant studies on extremely gifted children, my familiarity with the Australian educational and social contexts and my knowledge of the six exceptionally gifted South Australian children whom I had studied informally for several years.

THE RESEARCH QUESTIONS

1 *Early development*

Do any patterns appear in the early speech or motor development of the subjects? What is the health status of the subjects: do the conditions of myopia, left-handedness or allergies characterize the sample to a significant degree? How do the subjects compare with the general population in height and weight both at birth and at the present time?

2 *Socio-educational status of subject's family*

What is the highest educational level attained by the subject's parents and grandparents? What are or were the estimated intellectual levels of the parents and grandparents? What occupations characterize the immediate family members? What socio-economic levels characterize the subject's immediate family?

3 *Siblings*
What is the intellectual status of the subject's siblings? Does any pattern of birth order characterize the subjects?

4 *Gender and race distribution*
What is the gender distribution in the sample? What is the racial distribution? What is the country of origin of the parents and grandparents? Is there an over-representation of Asian children in the sample, when compared with the Asian population of Australia?

5 *Early reading*
At what age did the subjects learn to read? How much parental assistance (if any) did they receive? What other conditions seemed to facilitate their learning to read?

6 *Leisure-time activities*
What are the preferred reading interests of the subjects? What are their play interests and leisure-time activities?

7 *Educational intervention*
What educational accommodation have teachers/schools made for these children who entered school already reading? What forms of educational intervention (e.g. acceleration or other special placement) have the subjects experienced?

8 *Mentorships*
To what degree have mentors or adults other than parents helped in the development of specific talents in the subjects?

9 *Underachievement*
To what extent, if any, do subjects appear to be working below their ability levels in school? How much of this is imposed by the teacher or school and how much is deliberate underachievement?

10 *Social difficulties at school*
Have any of the subjects experienced hostility from classmates or teachers towards their intellectual capabilities? If so, has this had any effect on their academic performance, or their relationships with others? Is there any difference in the ease of social adjustment between subjects who have had special educational provision made for them and those who have not?

11 *Social and emotional development*
Do the parents and teachers of the subjects view them as emotionally stable and self-controlled? Are there differences in their academic and social self-esteem? Do subjects display any tendency towards social isolation? If so, is this isolation sought by the child or is it imposed by

peer rejection? What types of children do they select as preferred companions?

12 *Moral development*

What are the subjects' levels of moral development?

IDENTIFICATION OF SUBJECTS

Three criteria were set for identification and selection of the subjects of this study: (1) an IQ score of 160 or above on the *Stanford-Binet Intelligence Scale L-M*; (2) a chronological age of between 5 and 13 during the years 1988–1989, the period in which much of the early data was collected for the majority of the children; and (3) residence in Australia during the child's years of elementary schooling.

As related earlier, before the formal commencement of this study, six children with IQ scores in excess of 160 had been referred by psychologists or teachers to the students' programmes of the South Australian Association for Gifted and Talented Children (SAAGTC). Moreover, I had been informally observing the academic and social development of these children with the permission and support of their parents. The small research grant, but even more so the recognition, which came with the Hollingworth Award for Research in 1987 enabled me to expand the study into a series of longitudinal, comparative case studies of the academic, social and emotional development of children scoring at IQ 160+ in the Eastern states of Australia.

My initial intention was to limit the study to between 10 and 15 subjects. To increase the number from the six already identified to the desired 10–15, the study was publicized through the following channels:

— in the *Bulletin of the Australian Psychological Society*;

— in the newsletters of the Gifted Children's Associations in each state and in the newsletter of the National Australian of which I was then, coincidentally, editor;

— through letters to universities and Colleges of Advanced Education known to be offering teacher education courses on gifted or able learners;

— through letters to psychologists both in private practice and in government and private education systems, who were known to have a particular interest in gifted and talented children;

— through informal contact with colleagues throughout the subject states who run gifted programmes in schools.

Unlike Britain and the United States, Australia is not a test-oriented society. Generally, Australian schools do not administer IQ or general ability tests as part of their regular student assessment procedures; thus many schools are unaware that they have, within their population, students who have the potential to score at extraordinarily high levels on tests of intelligence, or who may already have done so on tests administered by private psychologists. As was the case with Hollingworth's study of IQ 180+ children, subjects were referred to this study by individual psychologists, and by teachers and parents who heard of the study through the procedures listed above and believed that they knew of children who were exceptionally gifted. The actual testing procedures through which IQs were established are described later in this chapter.

The above procedures, and the media publicity which resulted from the Hollingworth Award, drew considerable attention to the study among Australian educators and psychologists with special interest in the gifted. By January 1989, 31 children in the appropriate age and IQ range had been referred to the study from the eastern states of Australia: South Australia (18), Victoria (6), Australian Capital Territory (3), New South Wales (3) and Tasmania (1). This came as a very great surprise to me; I had not anticipated that so many children would have been successfully identified from this population which is characterized by its very scarcity.

The initial years of the study were to be the focus of my Ph.D. dissertation. Now I had more than twice as many subjects as had been anticipated! As discussed earlier, the multiple-case replication design, viewed to be the most effective for longitudinal comparative case studies, loses much of its effectiveness if so many cases are included that the characteristic and unique features of the individual subjects are lost. To avoid this possible blurring of focus, I decided that for the purposes of the dissertation study, 15 subjects would be selected from the 31 for intensive investigation. This strategy would adhere to the conditions described in the Hollingworth Award proposal and would permit a detailed and comprehensive analysis of the smaller, but still representative, sample during the first two years of the study.

I first considered random selection as a sampling method but rejected it as inappropriate to this particular study. The sample of 31 students included three children whose intellective capacities are of such an order that they cannot be fully measured even by the *Stanford-Binet L-M*. As was shown in Chapter 1, Ian at age 9 years 3 months achieved a mental age on the *Stanford-Binet L-M* of 18 years 6 months, Christopher at age 11 years achieved a mental age of 22 years, and Adrian at age 6 years 1 month achieved a mental age of 14 years 3 months. If ratio IQ scores were computed (mental age divided by chronological age multiplied by 100) these three children would obtain IQ scores of 200 or above.

These children are undoubtedly among the most profoundly gifted students who have ever passed through the Australian school systems, and it was decided that it would be ethically indefensible to exclude any of the three from this intensive phase of the study. Furthermore, the parents of several of the 31 subjects had kept full and detailed records, from infancy, of various aspects of their children's development. It was believed that these records, including detailed accounts of the children's unusually accelerated speech and motor development, and of their school history, would be invaluable to the study. Accordingly, it was decided to select for the dissertation study a group of 15 children which would include the three profoundly gifted subjects described above together with the children for whom the most comprehensive and detailed records were available, but which would still approximate the geographic and gender balance of the sample as a whole.

The resulting sample of 15 subjects includes 10 males and 5 females from South Australia (9 of the 18 subjects available), Victoria (4 of the 6 subjects available), and the Australian Capital Territory (2 of the 3 subjects available). The over-representation of South Australian subjects in the total sample probably arises from the greater visibility of the study in this state which was my home state for the earlier years of the study, when most of the subjects were identified. There is no evidence that it reflects an over-representation of children of IQ 160+ in the state itself! Since January 1989 a further nine children have been identified for the study, and the majority of these come from the states of Victoria and New South Wales. These children were obviously not available to be included in the first phase of the study; it was a matter, therefore, of selecting 15 from 31.

The IQ, age and sex of the 15 children selected for the dissertation

Table 3.1 IQ, age and sex of 15 selected subjects

Child	*Sex*	*IQ*	*Age at 1/1/89*
Rufus	Male	168	11 yrs 7 mths
Ian	Male	175+	9 yrs 8 mths
Jade	Female	174	7 yrs 0 mths
Christopher	Male	175+	12 yrs 0 mths
Jonathon	Male	170	9 yrs 4 mths
Fred	Male	163	11 yrs 11 mths
Cassandra	Female	167	11 yrs 0 mths
Alice	Female	167	8 yrs 0 mths
Hadley	Male	175+	7 yrs 4 mths
Adam	Male	163	7 yrs 3 mths
Rick	Male	162	6 yrs 3 mths
Roshni	Female	162	5 yrs 3 mths
Anastasia	Female	173	7 yrs 5 mths
Richard	Male	160	11 yrs 8 mths
Adrian	Male	175+	13 yrs 5 mths

study, and subsequently for this book, are shown in Table 3.1. It is important to note that the names used to denote subjects of this study, and family members of subjects, are pseudonyms selected by the subject families themselves.

The IQ range of the group of 15 children selected for this study is 160–175+, with a median of 168. The IQ range of the group of 16 subjects not selected is 160–175+, with a median of 166. (It is inappropriate to report mean IQs for the two samples because accurate IQs cannot be calculated for six children because of the ceiling effects of the *Stanford-Binet*.) Children for whom accurate IQs cannot be calculated beyond 175 because of these ceiling effects are recorded as IQ 175+.

Australian children with IQs of 160+ do not form a large subject pool. Australia itself in 1989 had a population of only 16 million persons, including, according to the most recent records available (Australian Bureau of Statistics, 1988c), 1.7 million children in the age range covered by this study. The normal distribution, which predicts that children scoring at and above an IQ of 160 on the *Stanford-Binet L-M* would present at a ratio of only 1:10,000 in the population, suggests that there are unlikely to be more than 170 such children in the entire country. As the five Eastern states from which the total sample is drawn contain 75 per cent of the Australian population, one would expect to find, in this population, no more than 128 children of IQ 160+. It is surprising, therefore, that in the absence of widespread testing, this study has identified no less than 31 per cent of the theoretical population of children testing at IQ 160+ in the five subject states.

However, as was briefly discussed in Chapter 1, researchers over the last 60 years have repeatedly found that the number of children identified in the IQ range 160 and above far exceeds the theoretical expectations derived from the normal curve of distribution (Terman, 1925; Burt, 1968; Feldman, 1984; Robinson, 1981; Silverman, 1989). It may be that the 40 children now identified represent a smaller proportion of Australian children of IQ 160+ than is predicted by the statistical tables.

TESTS OF INTELLECTIVE CAPACITY

Children participating in this study have achieved an IQ score of 160 or above on the *Stanford-Binet Intelligence Scale L-M*. The *Stanford-Binet* is generally regarded as the best single available measure of general intellective ability (Martinson, 1974; Stanley, 1977–1978) and the most reliable method of determining very high levels of intellective ability (Hagen, 1980; Silverman, 1992). It was found necessary to retest, using the *Stanford-Binet*, the small number of subjects who had been tested previously with other individualized tests of intelligence such as the *Wechsler Intelligence Scale for Children–Revised (WISC–R)* or group tests, because of the systematic depression of IQ scores at the high end of the scale on these instruments because of ceiling effects. Several children whose scores on the *WISC–R* were in the high 140s and lower 150s scored in excess of 160 on the *Stanford-Binet*, including one girl whose full-scale *WISC–R* score was 147 but whose score on the *Stanford-Binet* was 175+.

It was decided not to use the most recent version of the *Stanford-Binet*, the *Revision IV*, as this test, published in the United States in 1986, was not then widely in use in Australia. The large majority of the children identified for this study were tested with the *Stanford-Binet L-M* before 1987, when the *Revision IV* first became available in Australia. In addition, the two versions of the test are quite dissimilar, scores on the two versions are not easily comparable for children in the upper ranges of intelligence, and a number of researchers over the last few years have begun to express concern about the doubtful appropriateness of the *Revision IV* for use with intellectually gifted children.

The new test appears to generate significantly lower scores for the whole gifted range. The *Revision IV Manual* itself reports that mean composite scores for a group of 82 gifted children (average age 7 years 4 months) were 135 on the *L-M* version but only 121 on the *Revision IV* (Thorndike, Hagen and Sattler, 1986). Robinson (1992) reported that the mean IQ of linguistically precocious toddlers aged 30 months was 138 with a standard deviation of 9.6 when tested on the *Stanford-Binet L-M* but only 125 on the *Revision IV*. Kitano and De Leon (1988) reported that the *Revision IV* identifies fewer pre-school-age children as achieving IQ scores of 1.5 standard deviations above the mean than did the earlier *L-M* version. Thus it appears that even moderately gifted children are less likely to be identified through use of the *Revision IV* than would have been identified by using its predecessor.

An additional problem in the construction of the *Revision IV* is that, among other changes, it eliminates the mental age, which in the *L-M* version could be used to calculate a ratio IQ for exceptionally and profoundly gifted children such as Ian, Adrian, Christopher and Hadley whose scores went beyond the range of norms in the manual. Psychologists such as Silverman and Kearney (1989) who have a particular interest in the highly and exceptionally gifted, are now recommending that in cases where a child obtains three subtest scores at or near the ceiling of any current instrument, he or she should be tested on the *Stanford-Binet L-M* and ratio IQ scores computed for any child who scores beyond the test norms.

In a number of cases where potential subjects were referred to the study by classroom teachers and parents, the *Slosson Intelligence Test* (Slosson, 1985) was used as a screening test prior to administration of the *Stanford-Binet L-M*. The *Slosson* is a brief individual test of intelligence designed to be used by relatively untrained examiners as well as qualified professionals. It is an adaptation of items from the *Stanford-Binet* and was modelled on the *Stanford-Binet* as a parent test. Only one reliability coefficient is reported in the manual (a stability coefficient of 0.97 over a period of two months obtained on 139 individuals), but validity coefficients using the *Stanford-Binet* as a criterion are impressive, with nine studies showing correlations of 0.90 and above. Himelstein recommended the *Slosson* as a screening device. 'The *SIT* appears to be valuable as a quick screening device. Since inexperienced testers can administer this instrument quickly and accurately it has much to recommend it as a preliminary screening procedure' (Himelstein, 1972, p. 425).

The *Slosson* proved highly efficient as a predictor of extremely high scores on the *Stanford-Binet*: of 18 children scoring at or above IQ 157 on the *Slosson*, 16 (88.9 per cent) scored at or above IQ 160 on the *Stanford-Binet L-M*. To enable some degree of comparison between the IQ of subject children and their siblings, siblings were tested on either the *Stanford-Binet L-M* or the *Slosson Intelligence Test* during the first six months of 1989.

STANDARDIZED TESTS OF ACHIEVEMENT

The children took standardized tests of achievement in reading, spelling and mathematics, three academic subject areas which are regarded as of particular importance in Australian elementary schools. Their tested levels of achievement were then compared with the levels of work which the subjects were required or permitted to undertake in class, in order to judge the degree of 'fit' between the subjects' demonstrated achievement and the programmes provided for them by their schools.

I have listed below the various tests which were used in the study, and my reasons for selecting them. Full details of the populations on which the tests were standardized, and the reliability and validity of the various instruments can be found in my Ph.D. dissertation (Gross, 1989a) and, of course in the manuals of the tests themselves.

Because many standardized tests of achievement are constructed for grade-level performance, the teacher or researcher who wishes to assess the performance of gifted students frequently encounters the problem of 'ceiling effects': the test is much too easy for the children being tested, the whole group scores at the top of the scale and the observer cannot discriminate between the achievement levels of the individuals in the group. This, of course, is also the reason why, in a mixed-ability class, the performance of a highly gifted child on a standardized test (or a teacher-made test!) may seem no more outstanding than that of the bright or moderately gifted child. If the teacher of Christopher, at age 11, had tested his reading ability on the Neale Analysis of Reading, he would have presented as having reading accuracy and comprehension ages of 12 years 11 months – as no doubt would several other students in his class. The test 'ceilings out' at this level. There would be no way of the teacher knowing, from this performance, that at home Christopher was reading *Jane Eyre* and *Tess of the D'Urbervilles*.

One solution to the problem of ceiling effect is to employ off-level testing. This entails using a test which is standardized on an age group some years older than the gifted child you wish to test. It is unlikely, with this procedure, that the gifted child will reach the ceiling of the more advanced test, and a more accurate impression can be gained of his or her achievement level on the variable being tested. Off-level testing has been employed with all achievement testing undertaken in this study.

The Neale Analysis of Reading Ability

The *Neale Analysis of Reading Ability* (Neale, 1966) was administered to assess the children's levels of achievement in reading. This test is widely used by Australian teachers and psychologists to assess the reading achievement of elementary school children. Developed in Britain, with a standardization sample of British school children, it is suitable for use in Australia because the age/grade equivalents are similar for the two countries. An even newer version has been published since the testing described below was completed.

The *Neale Analysis*, which was normed on a standardization sample of children aged 6–11, contains three subtests, designed to assess reading accuracy, reading comprehension and speed (rate) of reading. Unfortunately, as this test has a ceiling of age 13 years on all three subtests, it proved of limited value for children in this study whose chronological ages were 9 years or over. Children who scored at or near the ceiling of this test were subsequently tested with the *Scholastic Aptitude Test–Verbal* (College Board, 1986).

Westwood Test of Spelling

The *Westwood Test of Spelling* (Westwood, 1979), sometimes called the South Australian Spelling Test, was administered to assess the children's level of achievement in spelling. This test, normed on a standardization sample of 23,000 students aged 6–15, is widely used throughout Australia. Because the ceiling of this test (15 years 6 months) is higher than that of many other tests created for use with elementary school students, it was able to measure the spelling achievement of the majority of subjects 11 years old and younger.

Cooperative Achievement Test: Arithmetic

Standardized testing of students' achievement in mathematics is undertaken in Australia even less frequently than testing of their verbal capacities. It proved difficult to find an appropriate test of mathematics achievement, standardized on an Australian population, which possessed good psychometric properties and a sufficiently high ceiling for the children in this study. Accordingly, the *Cooperative Achievement Test–Arithmetic* (Educational Testing Service, 1964) was employed for this purpose. This test, standardized on a sample of junior high school students in the United States, was designed to test the arithmetic achievement of children in US Grades 7–9. Because children in Australia enter school at age 5 or 5½ rather than age 6 or 6½ as in the United States, and because the Australian school year is generally 41 weeks in length rather than the 35–36 weeks common in the United States, it was anticipated that the test could be used to assess the achievement of children of average ability in Australian Grades 5–7. It was further anticipated that, because of the accelerated mathematics development of many of the children in this study, the test would assess the arithmetic achievement of all but the youngest subjects and those who were above the age of 10 and extraordinarily gifted in mathematics. The test proved successful for this purpose. Children above the age of 10 who scored beyond the ceiling of the test were subsequently tested on the *Scholastic Aptitude Test–Mathematics* (College Board, 1986).

The Leicester Number Test

The arithmetic achievement of the youngest subjects in the study, the 5- and 6-year-olds, was assessed using the *Leicester Number Test*. This test, standardized on a sample of 557 7-year-olds and 422 8-year-olds in the city of Leicester, England, was designed to assess the arithmetic achievement of children in the first two years of English primary schooling.

The Nottingham Number Test

The Leicester Number Test, although standardized on children 7 and 8 years of age, proved inadequate to assess fully the arithmetic achievement of some of the 5- and 6-year-olds, who scored at the ceiling of the test. These children were further tested using the *Nottingham Number Test*. This test was standardized on 472 9-year-olds and 483 10-year-olds in the third and fourth year of schooling in Nottingham, England.

Scholastic Aptitude Tests – Mathematical and Verbal

The College Board's *Scholastic Aptitude Tests–Mathematical and Verbal (SAT–M and SAT–V)* (College Board, 1986) are used by the Studies of Mathematically Precocious and Verbally Gifted Youth at Johns Hopkins University (SMPY and SVGY) to identify 10- to 14-year-olds who have extraordinary mathematical and verbal abilities. Julian Stanley, Director of the SMPY project, has frequently discussed the problem of using grade-level standardized achievement tests in the identification and assessment of students who are unusually gifted mathematically (Stanley, Keating and Fox, 1974; Stanley, 1977–78; Benbow and Stanley, 1983). Too many students reach the ceilings of such tests and, as a consequence, the tests fail to discriminate among students of exceptional mathematics ability. Accordingly, the SMPY and SVGY programmes employ the *SAT–M* and *SAT–V* which are standardized on a sample of United States high-school juniors and seniors.

The use of the *SAT–M* and *SAT–V* in this study was highly successful in measuring the mathematics and verbal achievement of students aged 10 and over. No student reached the ceiling of the *SAT–V* and a ceiling effect operated for only two students on the *SAT–M*.

TESTS OF PERSONALITY

Coopersmith Self-Esteem Inventory

It is generally accepted that the self-esteem of gifted children is significantly associated with personal satisfaction and efficient social and academic functioning (Purkey, 1970; Dean, 1977; Feldhusen and Hoover, 1986) and that children's self-concept is strongly influenced by their perceptions of what other people think of them (Tannenbaum, 1983). Previous studies of exceptionally gifted children have noted that they tend to have greater problems of social acceptance than do their moderately gifted peers (Gallagher, 1958; DeHaan and Havighurst, 1961). The *Coopersmith Self-Esteem Inventory* (Coopersmith, 1981) was used to measure subjects' self-esteem in social relationships, relationships with family and in their academic work.

The *Self-Esteem Inventory* (*SEI*) was designed to measure evaluative attitudes towards the self in social, academic, family and personal areas of experience. The School Form of the *SEI*, used in this study, yields a total score for overall self-esteem as well as separate scores for four subscales: general self; social self-peers; home-parents; and school-academic. The subscales allow for variance in perception of self-esteem in different areas.

All children aged 7 years old and over completed the *SEI*.

Defining Issues Test

Previous researchers studying exceptionally and profoundly gifted children have reported that a search for a personal system of moral and ethical belief, and the capacity to consider complex moral issues, may develop in these children much earlier than in children of average intellectual ability (Terman, 1926; Hollingworth, 1931). The *Defining Issues Test (DIT)* (Rest, 1986a) was administered to all subjects of age 10 and above, to assess their levels of moral judgment.

The *Defining Issues Test*, created in 1972, is based on Kohlberg's theories of moral development (Kohlberg, 1958) and was designed to identify the basic conceptual frameworks by which a subject analyses a moral or ethical problem and to assess the conceptual level of the subject's moral reasoning (Rest, 1986a).

The manual reports normative data from over 12,000 subjects from junior high school to adults. No studies are reported using students younger than ninth grade, and the manual reports that the reading level of the test materials is 12–13 years. Although the majority of the subjects of 8 years and above in this study are reading well beyond this age level, it was deemed advisable to restrict the *DIT* to subjects aged 10 years and older.

MEASURES OF PHYSICAL CHARACTERISTICS AND HEALTH

Height and weight

Hollingworth's case studies of 12 children scoring at IQ 180+ found that these children were significantly taller and heavier than were children in the general population (Hollingworth, 1942) and this finding has been replicated in other studies. The children in this study were measured for height and weight and the results compared with Australian norms (Adelaide Children's Hospital, 1982.) The parents' records of subjects' length and weight at birth were compared with the norms for South Australia (South Australian Health Commission, 1986). Results for height and weight were also compared with the results of the Hollingworth (1942) and Terman (1926) studies of gifted children.

Handedness, myopia, allergies

In a study by Benbow and Stanley (1983) of the physiological characteristics of profoundly gifted young mathematicians in the Study of Mathematically Precocious Youth at Johns Hopkins University, it was found that these children were characterized by an unusually high incidence of myopia, left-handedness and allergies. Children in the present study were given the *Edinburgh Handedness Inventory* (Oldfield, 1971) to assess their degree of left-handedness. Discussions with parents and family medical records established the incidence of myopia in the sample. Parents recorded subject children's history of allergies and asthma using the questionnaire on symptomatic atopic disease which was used by

Benbow and Stanley in their allergy study (Johns Hopkins Medical School, 1985) and the results of the two studies were compared.

QUESTIONNAIRES, INTERVIEWS, PARENT RECORDS, LETTERS

Questionnaires

Questionnaires developed for this study were completed by the parents of all 15 subjects to elicit information on the following variables:

Questionnaire 1

Pregnancy and birth details; birth order of subject child and siblings; subject's early speech and motor development; health and sleep patterns (Appendix A).

Questionnaire 2

Ages of parents at birth of subject child; country of origin of parents, grandparents and great grandparents; family income; occupation of parents and grandparents; occupations which characterize the family as a whole; educational levels and estimated level of intelligence of parents and grandparents; honours or recognition received by parents or grandparents; hobbies, interests and salient personal characteristics of parents and grandparents (Appendix B).

Questionnaire 3

Number of hours subject spent daily in voluntary reading over a period of 28 days; titles and authors of materials read; classification of materials read; favourite books of subject; subject's reasons for naming those books as favourites (Appendix C).

Questionnaire 4

Number of hours subject spent daily in computer use and television viewing over a period of 28 days; nature of computer use; nature of television viewing; how family decides which programmes should be watched; subject's interest in music; instruments studied and details of subject's progress; subject's play interests; subject's interest in/participation in sports (Appendix D).

Questionnaires are generally recommended to elicit information on background and demographic questions which can be answered speedily and objectively (Borg and Gall, 1983; Merriam, 1988). However, questionnaires 1 and 2 were also effective in eliciting information which the families needed time to research, for example information on the countries of origin and employment held by grandparents and great-grandparents, and specific details of the subject child's early development. Several families reported that a considerable amount of time and research was undertaken to elicit information such as the occupations, hobbies and interests of the children's grandparents, involving family papers and diaries, consultation with other branches of the family, and letters to relatives in countries from which the families originated. Several parents reported subsequently that they found completing the questionnaires to be a most enjoyable and rewarding experience.

In September 1989, the parents also completed the Synopsis of School History (Appendix K). This facilitated the synthesis of material from taped interviews, letters, school reports and other sources, on the interventive procedures employed by the subject's schools, the attitudes of the parents and children towards these procedures, and the type and extent of academic underachievement observable by the parents. This information has been regularly updated.

The subject children also completed Renzulli's *Interest-a-Lyzer* (Renzulli, 1977) which elicits information on hobbies and interests of gifted and talented children.

A response rate of 100 per cent was obtained for all questionnaires.

Interviews

Merriam (1988) suggested that interviewing is the best investigatory technique when conducting intensive case studies of individuals. At least three interviews of 60–90 minutes in length were held with the parents of each subject child. At least three interviews of 45–90 minutes each (depending on age of child) were held with each of the subject children. Interviews were held generally at approximately six-month intervals. These interviews were used to follow up, clarify and expand on the material elicited through the four questionnaires, the achievement and personality testing, the school reports and all other sources of information. Cannell and Kahn (1953) recommended this use of interviews to validate data obtained from written questionnaires. All interviews were conducted by the author, thus increasing the reliability of the data obtained by this method.

Interviews were also used, however, to elicit the parents' opinions on more sensitive issues such as the child's school history and the match between the school curriculum and the child's abilities, the parents' impressions of the child's relationships with teachers and classmates, and the child's social and emotional development. Similarly, interviews elicited the subject children's views on their progress at school, their feelings about their school experiences, their relationships with teachers and other adults involved in their education, their relationships with other children and their views of themselves and their own abilities.

The need for the researcher to establish, in interviews of this nature, an open and nonjudgmental atmosphere of trust and receptiveness is well documented (Asher, 1976; Borg and Gall, 1983; Yin, 1984; Merriam, 1988). Indeed, Cannell and Kahn (1953) claimed that the effective and facilitative research interview is characterized by three qualities that Rogers (1942) identified as characteristic of the productive counselling atmosphere. These are: a warmth and responsiveness on the part of the interviewer which establishes her/him as genuinely interested in the respondent; a permissiveness in regard to expression of feeling which allows the interviewer to accept the respondent's statements without a moralistic or judgmental attitude; and a freedom from any type of pressure and coercion (in other words the skilful interviewer refrains from intruding his or her own wishes, reactions or biases into the interview situation).

At the same time, I was aware of the risk of what has been termed 'the subjects' deceptive, unaided memories of past events and biases in recall' (Asher, 1976, p. 149). Facilitative, probing questions were used to elicit more detailed and accurate responses.

Semi-structured interviews were employed, a method identified by Borg and Gall (1983) as being the most appropriate for interview studies in education. Semi-structured interviews are guided by a list of questions which are prepared in advance. However, neither the exact wording nor the order of the questions have to be adhered to in the interviews (Merriam, 1988). This allows the interviewer to respond to the interests or priorities of the respondent and to investigate ideas that emerge from the discussion, while still maintaining control over the interview as a whole. Each interview, however, closed with some time spent in unstructured mode so that respondents could introduce topics and concerns which might not have been planned by the interviewer but which they felt were important or relevant.

Guideline questions for the semi-structured interviews with parents and subject children are recorded in Appendices E, F, G (parents) and H, I, J (children). All interviews were audio-taped. Subjects and their parents were assured that the anonymity of the children, their families, their teachers and their schools would be preserved through the use of pseudonyms in any report of the study.

Telephone interviews were used from time to time in order to clarify points of information acquired in the face-to-face interviews and also to maintain contact with those subjects and their families who live at a considerable distance.

The interview is an invaluable tool for eliciting sensitive or detailed information which respondents would be unlikely to disclose in other situations. Patton described the interview as a mechanism for discovering how the people we are interested in have organized the world, and the meanings they attach to events and actions around them. 'The purpose of interviewing, then, is to allow us to enter into the other person's perspective' (Patton, 1980, p. 196).

Parent records/diaries

At a very early stage in this study, I discovered that the parents of a number of subject children had kept diary records of the child's development from an early age. Such record keeping had usually developed as a response to the parent's realization that the child's speech and/or motor development was highly unusual. In some cases, record-keeping had been suggested by a pediatrician or by the Mothers' and Babies' Clinic which the family attended.

I suggested to other parents that they might also consider keeping diary records, from time to time, of events or incidents in their child's future development. Merriam (1988) pointed out that diary records are particularly valuable to the researcher because they are non-reactive: that is, not influenced by the research process. They are a product of the real-life situation in which they developed and are grounded in the context under study. As they are recorded in current time, they can serve as a check against the sometimes deceptive or biased memory of past events.

Diary records are sometimes fragmentary, and this can limit their use by the researcher. However, if the records are written for research purposes, as were many of these accounts, they are more likely to be carefully constructed; the writer is more likely to include information relating to the variables of interest to the researcher as well as information on his own interests and priorities. This procedure counteracts, to some degree, the danger of bias which might otherwise arise from the self-selectivity of material in unsolicited diary records; however, it must still be kept in mind that, because diary records are personal documents, the material is still highly subjective.

Letters

Parents of subject children were encouraged to communicate with me as frequently as they wished, to share information about the developmental progress of the children at school and at home. Several parents found it useful and enjoyable to record incidents and events in letters to me over the months and years of the study. These letters frequently recorded anecdotes which the parents felt were illustrative of a situation or a particular stage in their child's development. Letters, like diaries, are recognized as being extremely fruitful sources of information to the researcher undertaking intensive case study research (Angell and Freedman, 1953).

TEACHER JUDGMENTS EXPRESSED IN SCHOOL REPORTS

Few previous studies of the exceptionally gifted have compared teacher judgment and school reports of these children's school progress with their intellectual ability and academic achievement as measured by intelligence and achievement tests. The few such studies which have been undertaken (Pegnato and Birch, 1959; Baldwin, 1962; Jacobs, 1971) have been focused on children of moderate levels of giftedness and have indicated that teachers grossly underestimate the intellectual and academic capacities of these children.

Australian schools communicate formally with the parents of students not only through parent–teacher interviews but also through written reports on the child's academic progress. These narrative reports, written by the child's class teacher, are generally sent home at least twice per year, and it is customary for parents to keep the reports as an ongoing record of their child's progress through school. The subject children's school reports from different grade levels were examined to analyse the school's perceptions of their levels of ability and their scholastic success and academic standing in the school community. The majority of these school reports also commented on the children's emotional and social development within the school context.

PROCEDURES TO INCREASE RELIABILITY AND VALIDITY

The following procedures were used to increase the internal validity of the research findings.

Triangulation of data

The use of multiple methods and sources of data collection is termed 'triangulation' (Denzin, 1970). Methodological triangulation combines dissimilar methods such as achievement tests, interviews, observations and questionnaires to study the same unit. The level of the children's reading achievement, for example, was established through a standardized test of achievement, the record of spare-time reading compiled over 28 days by the child's parents, the child's own record of favourite books, school reports, interviews with the subject child and his or her parents, and through the direct observation of the investigator.

Multiple observations

Data were gathered over a period of several years, with repeated observations. In some cases, the subject's academic and social development has already been followed over a period of 10–11 years.

Member checks

Drafts of each chapter were reviewed by the parents and others from whom the information was derived to ensure that the account of events reported in this study for each child correctly reflected the participants' perspectives of events and situations. The corrections made through this process enhance the accuracy and thus the construct validity of the case study report (Yin, 1984).

Replication

As discussed earlier in this chapter, the use of replication logic in cross-case studies increases the external validity of multiple-case study research.

The goal of reliability is to minimize the errors and biases in a study. The theoretical objective is to be sure that, if a future investigator followed exactly the procedures described in this research, and conducted the same study with the same children, he or she would arrive at the same findings and conclusions (Yin, 1984). The practical objective is to ensure that future researchers will be able to replicate the study as precisely as possible, using identical procedures to those used in the current study. The instruments and procedures used in the many stages of this study have been described in this chapter. The combination of quantitative and qualitative measures, as has been employed in this project, is a form of triangulation that increases both the validity and reliability of a study (Kidder and Fine, 1987).

PROCEDURES SUMMARY

Subjects were identified on the basis of a score of IQ 160 or above on the *Stanford-Binet Intelligence Scale L-M*. Each subject took the following standardized tests of achievement: the *Neale Analysis of Reading Ability*, the *Westwood Test of Spelling*, and either the *Leicester Number Test*, the *Nottingham Number Test* or the *Cooperative Achievement Test–Arithmetic*. Subjects scoring above the ceiling of these tests took the *Scholastic Aptitude Tests–Mathematics and Verbal*.

Subjects 7 years and older completed the Coopersmith *Self-Esteem Inventory*, and subjects aged 10 years and above took the *Defining Issues Test* of moral development. All subjects were checked for height and weight, and were tested for handedness on the *Edinburgh Handedness Inventory*. Parents of subjects who had a history of allergies or asthma recorded details of the incidence of these conditions on the *Symptomatic Atopic Disease Questionnaire*.

Parents of all subjects completed four questionnaires (Appendices A–D) and were interviewed by the researcher on three occasions (Appendices E–G). Subject children were also interviewed on three occasions (Appendices H–J). Parents kept voluntary written records of aspects of their child's academic and emotional development and these records were made available. Children's school records and school reports from different grade levels were acquired and analysed. Parents completed a summary Synopsis of School History (Appendix K) in 1989 and this has been updated through letters, personal interviews and telephone discussions.

4

EARLY DEVELOPMENT AND PHYSICAL HEALTH

One of the characteristics of the well-developed three-year-old is a tendency to hold conversations with adults as if they were peers.

(White, 1975, p. 173)

A good sense of humor... is a mark of giftedness, but the degree of sophistication of that humor increases with ability. While playing under his mother's bed, one child spontaneously knocked on the bedsprings and said, 'Mommy, are you resting?' She replied, 'Well, I'm trying to.' He retorted, 'Does that mean I'm under arrest?' This would have been amusing from a 9-year-old, but this boy was only 2 years old!

(Silverman, 1989, p. 75)

The word 'precocious' has a specific and idiosyncratic meaning in Australia. In other English speaking countries, the primary usage adheres fairly closely to the dictionary definitions:

precocious: (of a plant) flowering or fruiting early: (of a person) prematurely developed in some faculty

Concise Oxford Dictionary

precocious: forward in development, especially mental development, as a child

Encyclopaedic World Dictionary

'Precocious', therefore, relates to early or advanced development in plants or people. It has no negative connotations, and certainly it says nothing about social behaviour. In Australian educational circles, however, it has taken on a strongly pejorative meaning. A 'precocious' child is one who pushes himself forward in an arrogant or attention seeking manner; who makes an ostentatious display of his talents; who uses his verbal facility to embarrass or demean his teacher and classmates; in short, a conceited or unpleasant child whom people would rather avoid than associate with.

Not surprisingly, given the Australian wariness of anything that savours of intellectual superiority, 'precocity' in Australia has become particularly associated with intellectual giftedness, and skill in language. The delight in word-play displayed by Silverman's 2-year-old would be described, by many Australian teachers, as 'precocious behaviour' – and this would not be meant as a compliment.

It is important to recognize, therefore, that when the words 'precocious' or 'precocity' are encountered in the North American or British literature of gifted education, they refer not to unacceptable behaviour but to unusually early and advanced development. Thus, the 20-year study of outstandingly gifted young mathematicians conducted at Johns Hopkins University and the University of Iowa is called the Study of Mathematically Precocious Youth (SMPY).

In 1989 the University of Melbourne made history by becoming the first Australian university to make an academic appointment specifically in gifted education. I was appointed to the position and spent two very happy years there before accepting my present position as Senior Lecturer in Gifted Education at the University of New South Wales, in Sydney. My title at the University of Melbourne was CHIP Lecturer in Education. CHIP stands for Children of High Intellectual Potential. It is an excellent phrase to describe intellectually gifted children: young people who possess unusual potential, even where adverse environmental or personalogical variables may have combined to prevent that potential flowering into performance.

The search for exceptional ability in pre-school children is, by its very nature, a search for *potential*, as it is not usually possible to see evidence of extremely high performance in the very young. The precocious development of speech, movement and reading are extremely powerful indicators of possible giftedness. Of course, not every child who walks, talks or learns to read before the usual age is even moderately gifted; nonetheless, when these skills develop at extremely early ages, they are generally linked to unusually advanced intellectual development.

The literature on intellectually gifted children, and especially the exceptionally and profoundly gifted, reveals that even in early childhood they display significant and often quite radical differences from the developmental patterns observable in age-peers of average ability. Precocity, however, can be more objectively assessed when the developmental norms for the child's age group are used as a reference point; therefore the early childhood development of the 15 children in this study has been extensively examined and compared both with the results of previous research on the very highly gifted, and with norms for the Australian population of children of their age.

BREAST-FEEDING

The decision whether or not to breast-feed is extremely influenced by cultural prejudices and convictions. What is customary in one decade may have fallen out of favour by the next. Perhaps for this reason, little study has been undertaken on the incidence of breast-feeding among gifted children. Terman (1926), however, in his landmark study of 1,500 gifted children, compared breast-feeding in his gifted group with breast-feeding in an unselected group of 20,000 babies studied by Woodbury at around the same time (1922) and found a considerably higher proportion of breast-feeding in the gifted sample. In particular, mothers of the gifted group breast-fed their babies till much later than did mothers of unselected children.

The incidence and duration of breast-feeding was studied for the children in this study and compared with Australian statistics for the general population. The results showed a striking disparity. A national survey of 84,000 Australian mothers undertaken in 1983 (Palmer, 1985) found that only 10 per cent of infants were still being breast-fed at the age of 12 months. By contrast, 12 of the 15 study children (80 per cent) were still being breast-fed at this age. The mean age at which the study children were weaned totally from the breast was as late as 15 months, and five of the children (33 per cent) were still being breast-fed at the age of 18 months. Indeed, three children were still on the breast at the age of 2 years! Adam was weaned at the age of 24 months, Christopher and Jonathon at 22½ and 25½ months respectively, and Hadley was breast-fed right through till 30 months. Generally the reason given by the parents for this surprisingly late weaning is that they believed that the children should themselves decide when they wished to be weaned; several parents commented on the emotional bonding, contentment and feeling of great peace experienced by both mothers and children during breast-feeding.

BIRTHWEIGHT AND CURRENT WEIGHT AND HEIGHT

The few studies of exceptionally gifted children conducted in the last 20 years have paid only limited attention to the physiological characteristics of the subjects, concentrating rather on the scholastic attainments and histories, and the personalogical characteristics of these children. Hollingworth, however, maintained strongly that highly gifted children were distinctly superior in their physical development, and supported her argument by photographs of gifted children compared to age-peers of average intellectual ability (Hollingworth, 1926) and statistics on the birthweight and weight and height in childhood of her 12 subjects with IQs 180+ (Hollingworth, 1942). Of the 10 subjects for whom such data were available, all were above the mean for height.

Studies of moderately gifted children, however, show conflicting results. The mean birthweight of the 1,500 gifted children in Terman's study (Terman 1926) was two-thirds of a standard deviation above the mean for children in California at that time. Witty, reporting 15 years later on a sample of 50 children with IQs of 140+, recorded that the mean weight of the group in later childhood was 'somewhat greater than the norm' (Witty, 1940, p. 404). Hollingworth (1926) matched 45 intellectually gifted children ranging in IQ from 135–190 with a comparison group of children of IQ 90–110 and found that the gifted children were, on average, 4.2cm (1.7 in) taller than the children of average ability. Parkyn (1948) studying a group of New Zealand children selected on the grounds of high ability found that the median height of the group was 5cm (2 in) above the average for children of similar age. Klausmeier, however, studied 56 high-achieving and low-achieving children in Grades 3 and 5 and found that the means for height and weight of the two groups were approximately the same (Klausmeier, 1958).

On birthweight the children in this study resemble their age cohort very closely indeed. The mean birthweight, irrespective of race, for a sample of 2,894 children born in South Australia between 1981 and 1983, was 3,383 grams with a standard deviation of 581 grams (Chan, Roder and Marcharper, 1984). The mean birthweight for the study sample was 3,363 grams with a standard deviation of 389 grams. Thus, the average birthweight of the study children was a mere 20 grams lighter than that of the general population. This difference is not statistically significant.

During 1987, however, the 15 children were measured for weight and height and the results compared with South Australian norms for children of their age and gender (Adelaide Children's Hospital, 1982). Surprisingly, considering the birthweight statistics quoted above, the gifted group appeared to be rather shorter and lighter than their age-peers. Only 4 of the 15 scored above the 50th percentile in terms of weight; indeed 5 of them scored between the 11th and 25th percentile and 4 scored below the 10th percentile. In terms of height, only 5 of the children scored above the 50th percentile, while 5 scored between the 11th and 25th percentile and 2 scored below the 10th percentile.

This result appeared so contradictory to the findings of Terman (1926) and Hollingworth (1942) that it was decided to undertake a more detailed comparison of the study children with age-peers. The weight and height of the full sample of 28 exceptionally gifted children who had been identified for the study by late 1987 were compared with the weight and height of a control group of children of average intellectual ability matched for gender and age in years and months. A directional t-test for dependent groups was employed in each case.

The results were statistically significant for both weight and height. On average, the study subjects were lighter ($t[27] = 2.926$, $p < 0.01$) and shorter ($t[27] = 4.348$, $p < 0.001$) than their age-peers. Their slighter appearance, when compared with classmates of similar age, may well have contributed towards the reluctance of their teachers and school principals to consider acceleration as an interventive measure for these children. This will be discussed further in later chapters.

EARLY MOVEMENT

Studies of the early movement of gifted and highly gifted children generally report that these children learn to walk, on average, two to three months earlier than their age-peers. A number of studies, however, are marred by a failure to clarify exactly what is meant by 'walking'. The age at which a child walks when led or supported by an adult may be several months earlier than the age at which he is able to walk by himself. The mean age for walking while supported, in the general population, is reported as 11 months, and the mean age of walking unassisted as 15–16 months (Mussen, Conger and Kagan, 1956; Edgar, 1973).

Kincaid (1969) reported that the mean age at which his sample of children of IQ 170+ learned to walk was 11.7 months for girls and 11.8 months for boys. He does not, however, define 'walking'. Hollingworth (1942) noted that for the nine children of IQ 180+ for whom these data were available, the mean age of learning to walk was 13.3 months; however, again 'walking' is not defined. Witty, describing 50 gifted children whose IQs were greater than 140, reported the mean age of learning to walk as 13 months (Witty, 1940). It may be that Kincaid was referring to supported walking and Hollingworth and Witty to walking unaided.

Terman, however, was much more precise in his definition of walking. He employed the earlier definition of Mead (1916) in which walking meant 'to take a step unassisted'. Under this definition, Terman's male subjects began to walk, on average, at 13.10 months, and his female subjects at 12.87 months. This was 'about one month earlier... than Mead's normal children' (Terman, 1925, p. 187). The mean age at which Terman's subjects were able to take several steps unassisted was 14.16 months for males and 14.08 months for females.

Perhaps the most valuable data on the early movement of exceptionally gifted children are contained within the case study literature on individual children. Within these individual case studies the idiosyncratic features of the development of some profoundly gifted children can be much more closely reported and analyzed. Theman and Witty reported on an American negro girl, 'B', with an IQ of 200, who took several steps by herself at the age of 8 months 'under the excitement of running after a dog' (Theman and Witty, 1943, p. 168). Silverman (1989) described a girl of 7 months who stood alone, climbed into chairs unassisted and went up and down stairs by herself. Seven months is the age at which the average child in the general population is beginning to learn to sit without support

(Baldwin, Bouma and Dixon, 1983). The literature on the exceptionally gifted contains examples of quite outstanding physical precocity.

The 15 Australian children conformed to the pattern of unusually early movement among the exceptionally gifted. Mussen, Conger and Kagan (1956) reported that in the general population the mean age for sitting up unsupported is 7–8 months, for crawling 10–12 months, for walking while supported 11 months, for walking unassisted 15–16 months and for running 24 months. Table 4.1 shows that the majority of the study children achieved these developmental markers considerably earlier than their age-peers.

The mean age for sitting up unsupported in this exceptionally gifted sample is 6.2 months, as opposed to 7–8 months in the general population. Jade, Rick, Adrian and Roshni were sitting up by themselves at 4½ months, Adam at 5 months. Indeed, several of the children displayed

Table 4.1 Age in months of achieving developmental markers in early movement

Child	*Sat up unsupported*	*Crawled*	*Walked supported*	*Walked unsupported*	*Ran*
NORM	7–8	10–12	11	15–16	24
Anastasia	7.0	6.0	–	10.0	15.0
Jade	4.5	5.0	9.0	10.0	–
Roshni	4.5	5.25	9.25	9.75	10.5
Adam	5.0	6.5	10.5	12.0	–
Rick	4.5	5.5	8.0	9.25	11.5
Cassandra	8.0	9.0	11.0	12.0	–
Adrian	4.5	10.0	11.5	13.0	–
Ian	6.0	10.0	12.5	13.0	15.0
Richard	6.0	8.0	7.0	9.0	–
Jonathon	7.0	8.5	9.5	12.0	13.0
Christopher	6.5	8.0	9.0	10.5	12.0
Hadley	6.0	6.5	–	12.5	–
Fred	6.0	8.0	–	14.0	15.0
Alice	7.0	7.0	9.0	11.0	14.0
Rufus	9.0	11.5	14.5	18.0	21.0
	$\bar{x} = 6.10$	$\bar{x} = 7.65$	$\bar{x} = 10.06$	$\bar{x} = 11.73$	$\bar{x} = 14.11$
	$\sigma = 1.32$	$\sigma = 1.86$	$\sigma = 1.97$	$\sigma = 2.22$	$\sigma = 2.89$

extraordinary physical precocity in their first months of life. Rick's parents were able to put him into a baby car seat at 16 weeks of age because he had such unusual control over his body and head. At 4½ months he also was mobile in his babywalker. He was walking unassisted at 9 months and running at 11½ months! Jade's parents have photographs of her in a baby-walker at 10 weeks of age. At 4 months of age, her mother discontinued the use of the baby-walker as friends advised her that it might retard Jade's crawling ability. This fear proved groundless; she began to crawl at 5 months and by 10 months was walking unassisted.

Jade's parents attribute her capacity to move around independently at such an early age to her determination to spend as much time as possible interacting with her parents.

> She always wanted to be with us [relates Caroline]. She always wanted to be 'in on' things, checking out what we were doing, copying us, experimenting with things. From an early age she enjoyed playing tricks on us. For example she would mischievously hide things that belonged to us around the house and deny that she'd taken them – and then when we were getting quite cross, after maybe an hour of searching, she'd laugh with delight and lead us to where she'd hidden them. Once, for example, she hid the car keys inside the air conditioner. She was certainly less than 16 months old on that occasion because it was before her sister was born.

Jade's delight in communicating and interacting with her parents was evident from a very early age. Caroline has a photograph of Jade at 3½ weeks old, throwing out her arms with glee and laughing uproariously at her mother, the photographer.

> She loved having her photograph taken, and thought it was a tremendous joke. She seemed different from other babies from the moment she was born, but it was only when she got a little older that we realized how very unusual it was to see a baby of that age laughing and 'playing' with her parents like that.

At 4 weeks of age Jade gave a further demonstration of her already mischievous sense of humour, which amazed and disturbed her parents.

> When she was 4 weeks old we took her to the Drive-In with us one night. She was lying in the back seat of the car in her bassinet, and we thought she was asleep. Mike had a bad cold and he began to cough and surprisingly, from the back seat, came a cough from Jade. This kept on for some time. At first we thought it was coincidence but then we began to realize there was a pattern in it; each of Mike's coughs was followed by a cough from Jade. We began to 'try her out' and sure enough, she mimicked every cough, laughing up at us after each one as if it was a big joke! We were just amazed.

The mean age for crawling among the study children was 7.65 months as opposed to 10–12 months in the general population. By 21 weeks Roshni was crawling on hands and knees in any direction. At 24 weeks she surprised her parents by pulling herself into a standing position while being carried in a portable bassinet. Christopher was able to crawl up and down short flights of stairs by 10 months.

As noted above, the mean age for walking when supported in the general population is 11 months, and the mean age for walking unassisted is 15 months. By contrast, the mean age at which the 15 exceptionally gifted children walked while supported was 10.1 months and the mean age at which they walked unassisted was 11.7 months. It is significant that the early lead of one month which this group displayed in walking when supported increased to a remarkable lead of 3½ months in walking unassisted; in other words, the 'skill gap' in learning to walk, from being supported by an adult to being self-sufficient, was only 1.6 months in the case of these exceptionally able toddlers as opposed to 4 months in the general population. Information on the age at which the children began to run is available for only 9 of the 15 subjects; however, the mean age of running in this group was 14.1 months, a remarkable 10 months earlier than the population as a whole. Not only do these children become physically mobile at remarkably early ages, but the stages of skill development are traversed with exceptional speed.

Several of the children's parents commented upon the unusual sense of balance which their children displayed at an early age. Roshni could stand by herself at 8 months of age and at 9 months could stoop and retrieve a toy without losing her balance. Alice, from 18 months, displayed exceptional balance when climbing and showed no fear of heights. Rick, at 3½ years, could ride a two-wheel bicycle unaided. The parents of these children believe that the precocious development of balance contributed both to their advanced mobility and to their self-confidence in their capacity to move around by themselves.

Only one child in the exceptionally gifted group walked, supported or unassisted, at a later age than the mean for the general population. Rufus walked when supported at 14½ months as against the general population mean of 11 months, and walked unassisted at 18 months as against the general population mean of 15–16 months. Interestingly, Rufus was born 3 weeks prematurely and birth complications led to a neck tumour which necessitated physiotherapy for the first 12 months of his life. It is possible that this had a retardant effect on the development of his gross motor skills; however Rachel, his mother, points out that there is a history of children on her side of the family delaying their unassisted walking until as late as 20 months.

EARLY SPEECH

It is generally recognized that intellectually gifted children tend to display a precocious development of speech.

> The rapid acquisition of vocabulary, quick build-up of relatively complex sentences and precision of speech, interest in words, and desire to experiment with words between, say, one and a half and three years, do seem to be characteristic of later intelligence.
>
> (Vernon *et al.*, 1977, p. 12)

Nevertheless, the interpretation of studies of early speech in exceptionally gifted children is hampered by problems of terminology similar to those encountered in reports of early movement; many of the earlier researchers in gifted education did not define precisely what they meant by 'speech'.

Lenneberg (1967), in *Biological Functions of Language*, stated that the average age at which a child speaks his/her first word is 12 months. By 18 months the average child has a vocabulary of 3–50 individual words, but little attempt is made to link them until around the age of two. Jersild (1960) was one of the first developmental psychologists to make a precise comparison of the speech patterns of bright and average children. He found that at the age of 18 months children of average ability were uttering a mean number of 1.2 words per 'remark' whereas their gifted age-peers were uttering 3.7 words per remark. At 4½ years of age the mean number of words per remark for average children was 4.6 whereas for the gifted it was 9.5. The gifted children were able to link words into meaning earlier and with greater degrees of complexity than were their age-peers.

The classic literature on giftedness, however, tends to employ the terms 'sentences' or 'short sentences' without clearly defining their meaning. Witty (1940) reported that the mean age for speaking in 'short sentences' for his subjects of IQ 140+ was 11.3 months. In his 1964 study of children with an IQ of more than 148, Barbe reported that these children began to speak in sentences between the ages of 12 and 20 months, with a mean of 16 months. Hollingworth (1942) found that her subjects of IQ 180+ began to speak in sentences between the ages of 6 and 19 months, with a median of 14 months, which she described as 'considerably earlier than the norm usually recognized' (Hollingworth, 1942, p. 227).

As with his data on early walking, however, Terman (1926) was somewhat more precise in his terminology. He adopted Mead's 1916 definition of 'talking' as being able to use a word intelligently, associating the idea with the object. Using this definition, Terman defined speech as the capacity to utter at least three unlinked words and found that the mean for this event was 11.74 months for boys and 11.01 months for girls. The mean for talking in 'short sentences', which he did not further define, was 17.82 months for boys and 17.05 months for girls. This, according to Terman, was some 3½ months earlier than the mean for Mead's children of average ability. In short, the literature on giftedness upholds Jersild's contention that the gifted generally learn to speak earlier, and develop complex speech patterns at an earlier age, than do children of average ability. This precocity is particularly noticeable in the exceptionally gifted.

Once again, individual case studies provide some fascinating examples of early speech. Baker (1987) reported on a young Australian girl who began to speak at 7 months of age and who, on her first birthday, greeted her grandparents with, 'Hello, Nanna and Pop, have you come to wish me a happy birthday?' Goldberg (1934) described 'K' of IQ 196, who at 2 years of age could recite the addresses and telephone numbers of 12 members of his family. Hollingworth (1926) reported on 'David' who was talking in sentences at the age of 11 months and who at the age of 8 months exclaimed, 'Little boy!' when his shadow appeared on a wall. The father of Jeremy Heimans, a highly gifted young Australian writer, relates a delicious anecdote of his son at 12 months of age, sitting in his high chair being fed. 'Do you like that, Jeremy?' asked father, and Jeremy replied, 'Actually, not very much.' (Nicklin, 1990).

The parents of the 15 exceptionally gifted children were questioned on the age at which the subject child spoke his/her first meaningful word (other than 'babble') and the age at which the child first spoke in short sentences, i.e. two or more words linked for meaning. They were furthermore asked to record the child's specific vocabulary at different ages in the first two or three years. As mentioned in Chapter 3, several of the parents, realizing that their child was displaying unusual linguistic precocity, had kept diary records of the child's early speech, and these records, often started at the instigation of a pediatrician or nurse from the Mothers' and Babies' Health Clinic, have proven invaluable.

The mean age at which the 15 exceptionally gifted children uttered their first word was 9.7 months of age with a sizeable standard deviation of 4.85 months. The norm is 12 months; thus the mean for this group is 2.3 months earlier than the mean for the general population. However, it should be noted that the distribution of ages is highly unusual because of the size of the range (5–21 months) and the extreme positive skew; for this reason the median, 8.5 months, may well be the more meaningful statistic.

The ages at which these 15 children uttered their first word range from 5 months in the case of Jade and Adam to 18 and 21 months in the case of siblings Jonathon and Christopher Otway. Chris and Jonathon were the only children in the entire sample who uttered their first word at an age later than 13 months! Indeed, when Christopher was 18 months old and showed no inclination to produce meaningful speech his mother, Elizabeth, was warned by the Mothers' and Babies' Health Clinic that this might well be an indication of intellectual retardation. Ironically, Christopher is one of the three children in the full study whose ratio IQ is calculated at 200+! Jonathon's IQ is 170. It is interesting to note that the other two children who score at or above IQ 200, Adrian and Ian, also spoke surprisingly late compared to the other children in the sample; Adrian uttered his first word at 13 months and Ian at 12 months.

Robinson (1987) reports that the mother of a young child whose speech seemed unduly delayed was so anxious for him to utter his first word that when he did, at the age of 20 months, and in fact said, 'Look! Squirrel eating birds' food!' she drove the child straight down to his father's office and asked him to repeat the words for his father – whereupon the child said (with some degree of irritation?) 'I just told Mama squirrel eating birds' food!' None of the Australian parents reports such a sudden or dramatic arrival of speech!

It is difficult to arrive at an accurate assessment of when the exceptionally gifted children began to speak in short sentences, because so many of the parents report that the children moved from single words to complete sentences without passing through the usual transition stages. Adam, for example, spoke his first word at 5 months of age and 2 months later was talking in three- or four-word sentences. His mother, Georgina, recalls the astonishment of supermarket attendants as Adam, aged 7 months, produced a running commentary on the grocery items as she wheeled him past the shelves in the supermarket trolley!

A frequent comment by the parents is that their children's speech was phonetically clear and grammatically accurate from the earliest months. 'Her speech was extraordinarily clear right from her first words at the age of 5 months,' says Caroline, of Jade. 'I can't recall anyone ever asking me to interpret her speech.' Holly Bond notes the same of Hadley:

> His early speech, which began at the age of 6 months, was very clear and people frequently remarked on this. In fact his early speech attempts were remarkably accurate and on the few occasions that Robert or I did correct his pronunciation or his use of a word he seemed to note and apply the correction immediately.

Sally Baker noted the same precision and speed of self-correction in Ian:

> Once he decided he was going to talk he went from single words to complete sentences with incredible speed and with virtually no transition stage. And there were very few pronunciation errors: 'koaka' for 'koala' and 'manadin' for 'mandarin' are the only two I can remember. As for correctness of grammar; most children carry on for some time saying 'he comed' or 'I falled', but Ian only had these stages momentarily and then it was straight on into absolute accuracy. Grammar was just instinctive.

Cassandra and Roshni were raised in bilingual families. Cassandra's first words, at the age of 8½ months, were in English, but by 13½ months she had a vocabulary of over 25 words which she could use interchangeably in both English and Hungarian. Most of Roshni's early speech, which commenced at 6 months, was in Punjabi, the first language of her father; however by 10 months of age she could identify and name several household objects in both Punjabi and English, the first language of her Australian mother, and by 14 months of age she could name most parts of her body in both languages. She could recognize, and name, the major colours in Punjabi and English by 14 months and by 24 months could count up to 30 in both languages.

Early and fluent speech is linked, in the study children, to quite remarkable feats of memory. Sarah Singh recalls Roshni singing herself to sleep at 18 months with nursery rhymes. By 12 months of age Adam delighted in reciting passages from books which he had memorized by hearing them read; 'imitation reading', comments Georgina, wryly. Ian knew all the words of the song 'My Grandfather's Clock' by the age of 23 months. Perhaps the most astonishing feat of memory was that of Marion, one of the children in the total sample, who surprised her parents, at the age of 2½, by reciting verbatim the lengthy Australian poem 'The Man from Ironbark'. Marion adored this poem and had learned it by heart through having it read to her almost daily, at her request.

Several parents commented on the children's ability to understand adult speech from a very early age. At 10 months Roshni would respond with what her mother describes as 'a very definite 'YES" to direct questioning. Jan Ward says of Rick, 'He understood a great deal of speech by 12 months and would listen intently to adult conversation.' By the age of 18 months Rick could explain to his mother that he had a sore throat and could describe the source of the pain precisely, without having to point.

The research literature contains numerous references to the unusually mature and sophisticated vocabulary of exceptionally gifted children (Langenbeck, 1915; Terman and Fenton, 1921; Hollingworth, 1942). This facility for selecting the precise word or phrase from an enriched and colourful vocabulary characterizes almost all the study children. Alice, aged 2½, called to her grandmother to look at her 'reflection' in a pool. Ian announced to a family friend at the age of 2 years 4 months, 'My father is a mathematician and my mother is a physiotherapist.' At 3 years 7 months Roshni told her mother, in great excitement, 'When I'm 18 I'm going to graduate from University like Daddy!' It will be interesting to test Roshni's prediction!

As can thus be seen, not only did the children develop the capacity to move around and explore for themselves several months earlier than their age-peers of average ability, but their very early speech enabled them to express their ideas, seek information through questioning, and interact verbally with their parents and other family members at an age when other children are only beginning to experiment with oral communication. Both early movement and early speech have contributed significantly to these children's capacity to acquire and process information. Reading, a third and significant source of knowledge acquisition, also developed at remarkably early ages in this subject group and will be discussed in depth in Chapter 6.

SLEEP HABITS

The majority of studies of intellectually gifted children seem to suggest that they require less sleep than do their age-peers (Pickard, 1976; Webb, Meckstroth and Tolan, 1983). Interestingly, Terman found the converse; in his 1926 study the gifted group required rather more sleep than the general population of children of their age. The difference was small at 6 years of age but by age 12 it had increased to the point where the gifted slept, on average, 45 minutes more per night than their age-mates of average ability. Freeman, however, in her study of children enrolled and not enrolled in England's National Association for Gifted Children, found that the target group (mean IQ 147) had significantly 'poorer' sleep patterns than either of the control groups (mean IQs 134 and 119) (Freeman, 1979).

Parents in this study were asked to indicate whether the subject children seemed to need less sleep, about the same amount of sleep, or more sleep in comparison with their siblings or with other children with whom the parents were familiar. Ten of the 15 children (66 Stanford-Binet per cent) were reported as needing less sleep. Three children (20 per cent) were reported as needing the same amount of sleep; however, these included Christopher and Jonathan Otway, both of whom are subjects of this study and who were being compared with each other! Only two of the 15 children, Cassandra and Roshni, were said to require more sleep than their age-peers.

Several of the parents indicated that their subject child had slept very little, even as a baby, and commented that the wakefulness seemed to be related to a reluctance to 'switch off' from the stimulus of interaction with his/her surroundings. Anastasia's parents claim that even as an infant she never slept during the day. Undue wakefulness seems to have had little effect on the alertness of the children, but it certainly proved a trial to their parents! From an early age Jan and Tony Ward were concerned about Rick's lack of sleep.

> As a baby his sleeping habits were shocking [says Jan]. By 4½ months of age he wouldn't sleep for a longer period than 1½ hours, day or night. He wanted to be where the 'action' was all the time! Things got so bad that when he was 19 weeks old I took him to a pediatrician asking for help. But it was no use; he simply didn't need the sleep. In fact [Jan adds ruefully] the pediatrician said there was nothing

wrong with the baby, but offered me a sedative to help me cope with him!

PHYSICAL HEALTH AND HANDEDNESS

Generally, gifted children appear to be a physically robust group whose health is considerably superior to that of the general population. Even before the publication of Terman's 1926 report, Davis, conducting a survey of teachers and supervisors in 18 states of the USA, found that the gifted were much less likely to be absent from school for reasons of ill-health than were their classmates of average ability (Davis, 1924).

In Terman's 1926 study 74 per cent of the mothers of the gifted group rated the children's health in the first year as 'excellent' or 'good'. (This statistic was not reported for the control group.) School reports rated the health of the gifted pupils as much superior to that of the control group; only half as many of the gifted group suffered from frequent headaches, and symptoms of 'general weakness' were reported almost 30 per cent less frequently for the gifted as for the controls. Defective hearing was approximately 2½ times as frequent among the control group as among the gifted students. In the incidence of childhood infectious diseases, however, the gifted group did not differ significantly from students of average ability.

Witty (1940) in his study of children of IQ 140+ reported that 68 per cent of his gifted subjects reached or exceeded the median of his control group on various measures of general health. Hollingworth (1942) rated her subjects of IQ 180+ as having excellent health. Hill and Lauff (1957) surveying the health of gifted children in the United States found that they had significantly fewer childhood illnesses than the general population of schoolchildren.

The research of Terman did much to lessen the then prevailing view of the gifted as physically weak, undersized youngsters prone to ill-health. Terman did report, however, that 25 per cent more cases of defective vision were found among the gifted group than among the controls (Terman, 1926), and this tendency in the gifted towards myopia is confirmed in further studies. In a recent survey of 150,000 adolescents aged 17–19, Belkin and Rosner of the University of Tel Aviv found that only 8 per cent of subjects scoring at or less than IQ 80 were myopic, as opposed to 27.3 per cent of those scoring at or above IQ 128 (*Those who get passes*, 1989).

Benbow (1985a), in a study conducted in Baltimore and Iowa, reported that myopia, together with left-handedness and symptomatic atopic disease (i.e. allergies), was highly correlated with extreme intellectual precocity. Benbow studied more than 400 students who had scored 700 on the *Scholastic Aptitude Test–Mathematics* or more than 630 on the

Table 4.2 Health profiles

Child	*Childhood illnesses*	*Vision or hearing problems*	*Accidents or operations*	*Symptomatic atopic disease*
Richard	Mumps Chickenpox	None	None	None
Adrian	None	Myopic in right eye	None	None
Christopher	Chickenpox	None	Broken right arm Blocked tear ducts	Chronic asthma Severe, recurrent allergic rhinitis
Jonathon	Chickenpox	None	None	Recurrent asthma Recurrent allergic rhinitis
Ian	Chickenpox	None	Broken left arm	Recurrent allergic rhinitis
Rick	German measles Chickenpox	None	Tonsillectomy	Mild asthma in early childhood
Adam	None	None	Broken right arm	Mild atopic dermatitis
Rufus	Ear infections	Mild hearing loss	Operations on both ears	Mild atopic dermatitis Severe allergies to certain antibiotics
Jade	German measles Chickenpox	None	None	Mild allergic rhinitis
Roshni	Chickenpox Croup and lactose intolerance in infancy	None	None	Food allergies in infancy
Cassandra	Chickenpox	Mild hearing loss	None	Seasonal atopic dermatitis Mild allergic rhinitis
Anastasia	Tonsilitis	None	None	None
Alice	German measles	None	Accident to nose at age 4 Deviated septum	None

Table 4.2 (continued)

Child	*Childhood illnesses*	*Vision or hearing problems*	*Accidents or operations*	*Symptomatic atopic disease*
Fred	None	None	None	Severe recurrent allergic rhinitis and sinusitis have caused Fred to miss significant periods of school Moderately severe food allergies Mild atopic dermatitis
Hadley	Early jaundice necessitated blood transfusions	None	None	Penicillin allergy

Scholastic Aptitude Test–Verbal before age 13: these students represent the top 1 in 10,000 of their age group on mathematical or verbal reasoning ability. She found that over 50 per cent of these students were myopic, as opposed to 15 per cent of the general population, that the frequency of left-handedness (15 per cent) was twice that found in the general population, and that 53 per cent suffered from symptomatic atopic disease as opposed to the 20–25 per cent that could be predicted from general population statistics. The significant over-representation of Asians in the population studied by Benbow should be recognized when considering the incidence of myopia among her subjects; however, with regard to this factor Benbow states: 'Because left-handedness is less accepted in [Asian] cultures, Asians were tabulated separately. It was not considered necessary to study the Asians separately on the other variables, as no significant differences between Asians and non-Asians were seen' (Benbow, 1985a, p. 3).

Health profiles of the 15 children reported here are displayed in Table 4.2.

None of the 15 children has had a serious or ongoing illness. As stated earlier, Rufus, in infancy, had a neck tumour which necessitated physiotherapy. Hadley, in his first week of life, became jaundiced as a result of incompatibility with his mother's blood and required two blood transfusions; however, no ill effects arose from this and his health through later childhood has been excellent. The group has had a surprisingly small incidence of childhood accidents. Alice, at age 4, decided to experiment in the use of a playground slide by coming down it face first; she collided heavily with her brother's head and the resultant trauma to her nose has left her with minor respiratory difficulties. Adam has had a greenstick fracture of the right arm. Christopher broke his right arm rather more dramatically at 5 years 9 months (and displayed his plaster cast with glee: 'Look, Miraca, my arm and the cast and the edge of my sling make an isosceles triangle!'). Ian's dramatically worded but precisely detailed account of his accident, at age 9 years 6 months, in which he notes, 'probably because of the slope [of the street], I fractured my radius' appears in Chapter 9. Only Rufus has had recurring health difficulties. He had numerous ear infections from age 3 till 10½ and required grommets in his ears twice during this time; this has left him with a slight hearing loss, although his hearing is still assessed as within the normal range.

Of the 15 children, 6 have had no contagious childhood diseases, 6 have had one childhood disease (five cases of chicken-pox, one of German measles) and 3 have had two such diseases (mumps and chicken-pox in the case of Richard, German measles and chicken-pox in the case of Jade and Rick). Consultations with three pediatricians have established that the incidence of contagious disease in this group is probably somewhat below what would be expected in the general population of children their age. This is contrary to what might be expected, given that several of the children have entered school at ages earlier than customary (see Chapter 8) and have thus been exposed to the risk of childhood contagious diseases for a longer period than have their age-peers in the general population.

As mentioned earlier, Benbow (1985a) found an astonishingly high incidence of myopia, left-handedness and symptomatic atopic disease in students displaying exceptional mathematical or verbal reasoning ability. The parents of the 15 children were asked to report any tendency towards myopia, either diagnosed or suspected. Only one child of the 15 displays any signs of myopia at this stage; this is Adrian who is short-sighted in one eye. Indeed, of the full sample of 40 children only two, Alexander and Noel, have ever worn spectacles, and in Noel's case this was for a period of only two years, to correct a temporary astigmatism.

All children in the study were administered the *Edinburgh Handedness Inventory* (Oldfield, 1971), to measure the degree to which they are right-handed, left-handed or ambidextrous. This was the instrument used by Benbow in her 1985 study; the results are therefore directly comparable. Of the sample of 15, only one child, Jonathon, is left-handed (6.7 per cent). Of the sample of 40, only four (10 per cent) are left-handed. This is not significantly different from the incidence of left-handedness (7.2 per cent) noted by Oldfield in the general population (Oldfield, 1971).

The parents also completed, for their children, the *Questionnaire on*

Symptomatic Atopic Disease (Johns Hopkins Medical School, 1985) which was used by Benbow to assess the incidence of this condition in her 1985 study. Symptomatic atopic disease is clinically defined as 'a triad constellation of atopic dermatitis, allergic rhinitis and allergic asthma' (Adkinson, 1988, p. 1).

Fully 11 of the 15 children (73 per cent) were reported to have symptomatic atopic disease. This is an even greater proportion than the 53 per cent incidence among Benbow's extremely precocious reasoners, which Benbow has already identified as significantly higher than the incidence in the general population of the United States. At this time it has not been possible to identify research on the prevalence of symptomatic atopic disease in the Australian child population from which a comparison of population statistics could be made; however it could probably be safely assumed that an incidence of symptomatic atopic disease in this exceptionally gifted Australian group which is 20 per cent higher even than that identified by Benbow in a similar, American, population, indicates an over-representation of these conditions in the study sample. Statistics available on the incidence of asthma, one of the conditions in Adkinson's 'constellation', indicate that 10–12 per cent of Australian children in the age range covered by this study are asthmatic (Mellis, 1987), whereas three of the 15 subjects (20 per cent) suffer from this condition.

Not only the incidence but the severity of symptomatic atopic disease is notable in the subject children. The *Questionnaire on Symptomatic Atopic Disease* requires parents to assess and list the severity of the child's condition (asthma, atopic dermatitis, allergic rhinitis, and food or drug allergies) on a scale of 0 (negative history) to 6 (severe active ongoing problem). Five of the 11 children (45 per cent) with a history of symptomatic atopic disease had one or more condition listed at level 5 or 6.

As can be seen, for every medical condition discussed in this chapter, save for symptomatic atopic disease, the children in this study are equal to or superior to the general population in terms of physical health.

SUMMARY

In contrast to the findings in much of the literature on the intellectually gifted, the children of this study are, on average, significantly shorter and slighter than their age-peers. However, their physical health is excellent; none has had a serious illness and the group has had a surprisingly small incidence of childhood accidents and contagious diseases. Their tendency towards symptomatic atopic disease, however, is far greater than that found in the general population.

The children showed remarkable precocity in the development of speech and movement. They learned to sit up, crawl, walk and run markedly earlier than their age-peers, and several were speaking in three- or four-word sentences before their first birthday. Their early speech was characterized by an unusually mature and sophisticated vocabulary and by quite remarkable feats of linguistic memory.

In these exceptionally and profoundly gifted children the precocious development of speech and movement has contributed significantly to their capacity to acquire and process information and has strengthened crystallized intelligence. It has also meant, however, that the child's 'difference' from age-peers has been identifiable from an unusually early age, not only to his parents but to neighbours and other community members. In egalitarian Australia, intellectual precocity in a young child is not generally admired!

5

FAMILY CHARACTERISTICS AND FAMILY HISTORY

The parents valued academic achievement and were models of intellectual behaviour. They were typically more highly educated than the average parent, and most had professional occupations. They believed that it was important for their children to develop their own interests, but expected them to do well in school. Most of the [children] were aware, even in elementary school, that eventually they would be going to college.

(Gustin, 1985, p. 294)

Even in their leisure time, the parents chose activities that required practice and learning. Favorite hobbies or avocations were rarely passive, non-participatory activities such as watching television. The parents were more often attracted to avocations that involved active participation such as carpentry, gardening, sewing, sports, reading history or literature, playing musical instruments, travel, photography. When they were spectators instead of participants, as in attending concerts or sporting events, they studied and discussed the performances of others to increase their own knowledge, skill or appreciation of the activity.

(Sloane, 1985, p. 440–1)

Definitions and models of giftedness developed in the last 10 years view giftedness as superior potential rather than superior performance, and acknowledge that the actualization or thwarting of a young child's potential may arise from factors quite outside his or her control. As was discussed in Chapter 2, Tannenbaum, in his psychosocial model, defines giftedness in children as 'their potential for becoming critically acclaimed performers or exemplary producers of ideas' (Tannenbaum, 1983, p. 86). Tannenbaum considers the influence of general and specific abilities, nonintellective factors, environmental factors and 'chance' or happenstance, and proposes that the potential for excellence, which he terms giftedness, is produced by an overlap of all five factors. Gagné (1985, 1991a) defines giftedness as superior competence or aptitude, and talent as superior performance, and proposes that a cluster of catalytic factors, including personalogical and environmental variables, interact to facilitate or impede the translation of the individual's giftedness (potential) into talent (performance).

The family and its role in moulding the gifted child's attitudes, values and aspirations may well be the most significant factor in talent development. Both Tannenbaum and Gagné regard the family as one of the most important environmental influences on the child's academic and social development. If the family does not value, encourage and facilitate the growth of the young child's gifts, they will not develop, in later life, as talents. Indeeed, in Bloom's study of 120 young adults who had achieved eminence, at an unusually early age, as pianists, sculptors, swimmers, tennis players, research mathematicians and research neurologists (Bloom, 1985), the role of the school appears to have been less than the home influences, including parenting style, and the encouragement of mentors who took a personal, as well as professional, interest in the fostering of the student's exceptional abilities.

This is not to say that the influence of the school is not important. As will be seen in later chapters, if the school does not seek to identify and foster the abilities of exceptionally gifted children or, worse still, if the school or the education system works actively to prevent the gifted student from progressing at her own level and pace, no amount of support, love and encouragement from home will compensate for the lack of a supportive educational framework. Nonetheless, we must not undervalue the influence of the home climate, the family values, the parental expectations, and the modelling of hard work, commitment and love of learning. All these interact with demographic variables such as family size, the intellectual and educational status of siblings, parents and grandparents, and the cultural and social allegiances of the family, to influence the development of the child's potential.

BIRTH ORDER AND FAMILY SIZE

Previous studies of highly and exceptionally gifted children which examine the issues of birth order and family size suggest that an unusually high proportion of highly gifted children are first-born and come from small families. There has been much debate on the possible reasons for this, and the implications for the academic and social development of the children. Certainly, although we cannot ignore the extremely strong influence of heredity in the manifestation of exceptional intelligence (Plomin, 1989) family demographics such as birth order and family size can maintain a strong influence over the degree to which a child's innate capacities can be fostered. As early as the mid-nineteenth century, Francis Galton, in his classic book *Hereditary Genius: An Enquiry into its Laws and Consequences* (1869) noted that a surprising number of the 'great men' of previous generations had been the eldest children, or eldest sons, of their families. Although Galton maintained that exceptional ability was very largely a function of heredity, he was ready to acknowledge that environmental variables such as family position seemed to contribute to a young man's chances of success. (Galton, writing in 1869, embraced the belief of many of his era that women were intellectually inferior to men; consequently he was much less interested in studying the achievements of 'great women'!) Galton pointed out that first-born children are more likely to be treated as companions rather than subordinates by their parents, that they are given responsibility at an earlier age and are therefore more likely to develop independence of thought, and that in families less well-endowed financially they would be likely to have more living space, better care and better nourishment in their earlier years than would their younger siblings.

Over 100 years later Albert (1980) investigated the family positions of a number of American Presidents and Vice-Presidents, British Prime Ministers and American Nobel Laureates, and noted that more than 75 per cent were first-borns or had what he termed 'special positions' in the family – for example, the eldest son, the oldest surviving son in the family, or the youngest child born after a space of several years. '"Special" in these cases covers two conditions; the position of the child in regard to his psychological role and treatment, and position in regard to the place of the family in society and its prevailing commitment to achievement' (Albert, 1980, p. 93). Ninety per cent of American Presidents had 'special' family positions. Albert theorized that birth order can determine the child's psychological or social role within the family, with the first-born receiving greater encouragement to adopt a leadership role or seek independence, and proposed that where the first-born child already possesses a special aptitude, these family dynamics may combine with the child's gift to encourage the optimization of his or her potential.

As discussed in the previous chapter, the early and superior acquisition of language strengthens crystallized intelligence and permits the child to express sophisticated ideas and questions at a much younger age than is usual. Pfouts (1980) believed that first-borns have more and closer interaction with their parents than do later-born siblings, resulting in superior language acquisition. Pfouts further suggested that first-born children tend to be incidentally 'trained' by their families into a parent-surrogate role, and act as interlocutors between their parents and younger siblings, a facilitative role which fosters leadership qualities and develops still further their command of language. The majority of the children in this study adopt a noticeably warm, protective and nurturant stance towards their younger siblings.

Certainly the literature on exceptionally gifted children notes a predominance of first-borns. Terman noted that 60 per cent of the children in his sample were only children or the eldest in their families, and commented that the number of children in these families was considerably below the mean for California families at that time (Terman, 1926). Hollingworth (1942), in her study of 12 children of IQ 180+, reported that for the 11 children for whom birth order was known, no fewer than 10 were eldest or only children, while the mean number of children in this group of families was 1.6. Sheldon (1954) noted that in his study of 28 New York children scoring at or above IQ 170, the subjects tended to be first-born, while 12 (43 per cent) were only children. The mean number of children in this group of families was 1.75. Kincaid (1969), reporting on 561 children whose IQs were above 150, found that 50 per cent were only or first-born children and that the mean number of children in the families was 2.7.

More recently, Silverman and Kearney (1988), studying 23 Colorado children with IQs above 170, reported that 15 (65 per cent) were oldest or only children, while the mean number of children in the families was slightly over 2.0. VanTassel-Baska (1983), investigating the highly gifted young mathematicians and linguists identified by the 1982 Midwest Talent Search, found that half the top scorers were the eldest children of two-child families, although Benbow and Stanley reported that for a sample of almost 900 11-and 12-year-old participants in the 1976 Talent Search conducted by the Study of Mathematically Precocious Youth (SMPY), the families were found to average slightly more than three children, substantially greater than the then current national mean of 1.7 (Benbow and Stanley, 1980).

Interestingly, a study of 1,618 high school students who were finalists in the American National Merit Scholarship Competition (Altus, 1966) found that for this gifted group, whose mean scores were three standard deviations above the mean for the general population, fully 60 per cent of finalists from families of two, three, four or five children were first-born – and this did not even include only children, who for some reason were omitted from the statistics! However, the researchers reported that birth order seemed linked to aptitude only at the highest levels of ability. For the much larger group of high school students who were eliminated from the competition in the first round of testing, birth order and scores did not appear to be related.

Despite the separations of time and culture, the families in the present study are remarkably similar to the families of exceptionally gifted children reported in the majority of previous studies. Within the group as a whole, 29 of the 40 children (72.5 per cent) are first-born, with 8 of these (20 per cent) being only children. Of the 36 families, 24 consist of two or fewer children, while the mean number of children in the family is 2.14. Of the 15 children introduced in this book, 11 (73 per cent) are first-born, although only two children, Anastasia and Rufus, are only children. Adam is included in the group of first-borns because, although he is strictly speaking a second child, there is a 14-year gap between Adam and his older sister, Anne, who has lived away from home, at boarding school and university, since before his birth. This has given Adam a 'special family position', as described by Albert (1980) in that he has been given many of the responsibilities, and has adopted many of the roles, of the eldest child. The mean number of the children in the 14 families reported here is 2.42. Nine of the 15 families consist of two or fewer children, four families have three children and two have four. Table 5.1 displays the birth order and IQ of the 14 children reported here, together with their siblings. Although the mean number of children is slightly greater than that reported in some previous studies, the families still tend to be small; only two families have more than three children. The tendency for exceptionally gifted children to be first-born is even stronger in this Australian sample than in the majority of previous and current American studies.

AGE OF PARENTS AT BIRTH OF SUBJECT CHILD

The literature on intellectual giftedness suggests strongly that the gifted tend to be children of older parents. In Terman's sample (Terman, 1926),

Table 5.1 Birth order and IQ of subjects and their siblings

Child	*IQ*	*Birth order*	*Siblings and sibling IQs*
Rufus	168+	Only child	
Roshni	162	Eldest of four	Three brothers, IQ 141 and two inf.*
Adrian	175+	Eldest of three	Two brothers, IQ 149 and 175+
Rick	162	Elder of two	Sister, IQ 133
Anastasia	173	Only child	
Christopher	175+	Elder of two	Brother (Jonathon), IQ 170
Jonathon	170	Younger of two	Brother (Christopher), IQ 175+
Fred	163	Elder of two	Sister, IQ 127
Cassandra	167	Younger of two	Brother, IQ 136
Ian	175+	Elder of two	Brother, IQ 140
Adam	163	Elder of two	See notes in text
Richard	160	Eldest of three	Two brothers, IQ 155 and inf.*
Hadley	175+	Youngest of three	Two brothers, IQ 149 and 143
Jade	174	Eldest of four	Sister (IQ 130) and two brothers (IQ 139 and inf.*)
Alice	167	Younger of two	Brother, IQ 140

* inf. = infant: too young to be tested

the mean age of fathers at the birth of the subject child was 33.6 years, with a median of 32.6 years. The mean age of the mothers at the children's birth was 29 years with a median of 28.5 years. In the mid-1980s, Rogers (1986) reported that the mean age of mothers of children of average intellectual ability was 25.4 years. By contrast, in Silverman and Kearney's Colorado sample of children of IQ 170+ (Silverman and Kearney, 1988) the mean age of mothers at the time of the child's birth was 29.6 years, while VanTassel-Baska (1983) reported that in her sample of highly gifted finalists in the 1982 Midwest Talent Search the majority of subjects were born when their fathers were in their early thirties and their mothers in their late twenties. Parents of highly gifted children thus seem to have delayed the birth of their first child by a margin of several years when compared with the general population. Such a delay would be likely to enhance the financial stability of the family; financial security, combined with the maturity of the parents, may well contribute to a more stable, emotionally secure home atmosphere in which talent development would be more readily valued and fostered.

Little research has been undertaken on the family positions or family characteristics of gifted children in Australia. It was decided to compare the ages at which the parents of this study started their families with what was typical for families at that time. The mean age at 1 January 1992 of the first-born children of the 14 families reported here is 13 years 2 months, and the median age 14 years 7 months; accordingly, the Australian Bureau of Statistics was consulted to determine the median age of parents at the first nuptial birth during the years 1976–1980, the period in which the majority of the subject children were born. The median age of Australian mothers at their first nuptial birth during this period is reported at 24 years 8 months (Australian Bureau of Statistics, 1987). Unfortunately, this statistic is not available for fathers.

The parents of the children in this study stand in striking contrast to this statistic for the Australian population as a whole. They compare much more closely with the parents of the intellectually gifted children in the American studies referred to above. The mean age of the mothers at first birth was 27 years 3 months with a median of 27 years 2 months, while the mean age of fathers was 28 years 11 months, with a median of 29 years. As can thus be seen, the tendency to delay the birth of the first child was very strong in this group. The median age of first birth to mothers in this study is 2 years 6 months later than the median age of first birth in the Australian community; indeed, 11 of the 15 mothers delayed having their first child beyond the median age for the maternal population as a whole. Even more significantly, fully 10 of the 15 children reported here (excluding Adam) are first-born; although, as will be discussed later in this chapter, almost all the children in the families of this study are intellectually gifted, in five of the families the exceptionally gifted child was born when the parents were even older. The mean age of fathers at the birth of the subject child is 30 years 10 months with a median of 29 years 8 months, while the mean age for mothers is 29 years 3 months, with a median of 28 years 10 months. As in previous studies, very highly gifted children tend to be born to somewhat older parents.

Nevertheless the range of parental ages at the birth of the subject child is surprisingly wide. Michael and Caroline, parents of Jade, were 21 years 11 months and 19 years 5 months old respectively at her birth, while Edward and Georgina, parents of Adam, were 39 years 2 months and 38 years 5 months of age when he was born. Thus the range of parental ages at the birth of the subject children is approximately 18 years.

INTELLECTIVE AND EDUCATIONAL STATUS OF SIBLINGS AND OTHER FAMILY MEMBERS

There has been very little systematic study of the intellectual level of siblings or other family members of highly or exceptionally gifted children. Because of constraints of time and funding, Terman was unable to test all the siblings of his subject group; indeed fully 500 of the siblings remained untested. It is notable, however, that even with this restriction of sample, he was able to comment (Terman, 1926) that the number of families with two children in the gifted study was more than 1,200 times the number that would be expected by chance! In only a few cases does Hollingworth (1942) report the IQ of siblings of her subjects with an IQ of 180+; however, in all reported instances the siblings were themselves intellectually gifted, with IQs ranging between 138 and 167. Silverman and Kearney (1988) reported on 10 families in Colorado and Maine who have had two or more children scoring in the IQ range 170+. Thus the literature reveals a strong tendency for siblings of highly gifted children to score within or close to the IQ range generally accepted as designating intellectual giftedness. Indeed, in a study of 148 families in which one child had been identified as scoring at or above IQ 120, Silverman and Waters tested the siblings and found that in fully 83 per cent of the sample *all* the children in the family scored at or above this level (Silverman and Waters, 1987).

Any discussion of the siblings of intellectually gifted children must take into consideration the effect of regression towards the mean; a marked regression should be expected for extremely high scores. For the children of IQ 180+ in Hollingworth's 1942 sample, a mean sibling IQ of 140 could be expected from the regression effect; yet, as reported above, the sibling IQs in this sample ranged from 138 to 167. It is fascinating to note that both in Hollingworth's study and in other studies of the highly gifted the IQ scores of the siblings significantly exceed the score which would be predicted from the regression effect. Exceptionally gifted children are likely to have highly gifted siblings.

As discussed in Chapter 3, the *Slosson Intelligence Test (SIT)* was used in this study to assess the intellectual level of all siblings who were of an age to be appropriately assessed by this instrument. The results are shown in Table 5.1. In two cases (Christopher's brother Jonathon, who is himself one of the children reported here, and Edmund, the younger brother of Adrian), the children scored at the ceiling of the test, and to conform to the recording procedure used with the subjects themselves, the IQ scores of these siblings are reported here as 175+. With this constraint, the calculation of mean IQs for the sibling group is not appropriate; the median IQ of the sibling group, however, is 140, with scores ranging from 127 to 175+. In all cases but one, that of Penny Campbell, sister of Fred, the siblings scored at or above IQ 130 on the *SIT*. Interestingly, Penny has since been diagnosed as having a significant loss of vision; the depression of IQ scores (though not of intellectual ability itself) among children who have a visual or auditory loss is well documented (Whitmore and Maker, 1985; Caton, 1985; Hellerstein, 1990).

Within this study the total subject group includes four pairs of siblings. Thus 40 children, but only 36 families, are represented.

As has been discussed earlier, standardized tests are used less widely in Australia than in North America or Britain. Many Australian teachers are reluctant to employ objective measures of ability or achievement to assess a child's intellectual and academic functioning, preferring to make a judgment on the basis of the child's classroom performance. Teachers are notoriously ineffective at recognizing intellectual and academic giftedness among their students (Pegnato and Birch, 1959; Jacobs, 1971; Gear, 1976; Tannenbaum, 1983) and many bored, underachieving, culturally different and socio-economically deprived gifted children remain unidentified because of their teachers' biased perceptions of giftedness (Baldwin, 1985; Borland, 1986; Braggett, 1985b; Commonwealth of Australia, 1988). Given this problem, and in the absence of widespread ability or achievement testing, teachers and parents would do well to note that where one child in a family has been identified as highly gifted, there is a very high probability of his or her siblings possessing high intellectual potential, even if this is not yet reflected in high levels of classroom performance.

While the few existing studies of highly gifted children have reported their intellective status in terms of IQ, similar data are not readily available for their parents. Indeed, in the earlier studies such as those of Terman (1926) and Hollingworth (1942) psychometric testing either had not been developed at the time of the parents' childhood or was in its infancy. For this reason, many previous researchers have had to content themselves with an examination of the educational status of the older family members.

Parents and grandparents of the intellectually gifted, and especially the highly gifted, comprise a group whose educational status is significantly in advance of that of the general population. Twenty-six per cent of Terman's sample came from families where one or both parents held a college degree. Terman had no comparative data for the proportion of adults of corresponding age in the general population who were college graduates, but commented, 'it is doubtful whether it would be more than one-fifteenth or one-twentieth of the proportion found for this group' (Terman, 1926, p. 81).

Hollingworth, researching in the 1930s, found that 33 per cent of the fathers and 42 per cent of the mothers of her subjects of IQ 180+ held a college degree (Hollingworth, 1942). In Sheldon's sample of children whose IQs were above 170, studied in the 1950s, 68 per cent of the fathers and 43 per cent of the mothers were college graduates (Sheldon, 1957). Kincaid (1969) noted that in his highly gifted group 57 per cent of fathers and 32 per cent of mothers had graduated from college, while a remarkable 27 per cent of fathers and 5 per cent of mothers held graduate degrees. Barbe (1964) reported significant differences between the educational status of parents of highly gifted (IQ 148–174) and moderately gifted (IQ 120–135) children. Sixty-eight per cent of the fathers of highly gifted boys and 53 per cent of the fathers of highly gifted girls had college degrees as opposed to 52 per cent of the fathers of moderately gifted boys and 41 per cent of the fathers of moderately gifted girls. More recently, VanTassel-Baska reported that a remarkable 30 per cent of the fathers of the 1982 Midwest Talent Search finalists held doctorates.

Generally, the intellective or educational status of grandparents of gifted students is not addressed in the literature. Terman, however, did investigate the educational status of the grandparents of his sample. Of the 692 grandfathers for whom educational data were available, 140 (20.2 per cent) had a college degree. Even more surprisingly, 28 of the 691 grandmothers for whom educational data are available (4 per cent) were college graduates (Terman, 1926). Goertzel and Goertzel (1962) and Albert (1980) emphasized the importance and value placed on education by the grandparents and parents of men and women who have risen to eminence (VanTassel-Baska, 1983), and the average educational status of both fathers and mothers of the 23 children of IQ 170–194 in Silverman's Colorado study has been shown to be a Bachelor's degree plus one year of graduate study (Silverman and Kearney, 1988).

Because of the Australian wariness of objective testing, few Australian adults would have taken an IQ test, and fewer still would be aware of their score. Given this, it is surprising that IQ scores are available for one parent of no fewer than nine of the 15 children in this study. The scores are self-reported, and are thus subject both to reporter bias and to the vicissitudes of memory over time, as in most cases the tests were taken in childhood. However, the reported IQ scores range from 120 to 160, with a mean of 141.

None of the grandparents was able to report an IQ score. However, the parents were asked, in Questionnaire 2 (see Appendix), to estimate what they believed to be the intellectual level of the subject children's grandparents (their own parents) on a Likert Scale with classifications ranging from very superior to very inferior. Seventy-nine per cent of the grandfathers and 71 per cent of the grandmothers in the sample were rated as of superior or very superior intelligence. The possible bias inherent in such reporting is recognized; however, the results will be discussed later, in the light of the educational attainments of the group and the positions they generally hold in business and community life.

Given the absence of objective data on the intellectual levels both of the children's grandparents and of 22 of the 28 parents reported here (it should be remembered that Christopher and Jonathon, being siblings, share one set of parents!), it may be more appropriate to adopt the procedure used by previous researchers and estimate the intellective characteristics of the group through an examination of their educational status. As with the parents of highly gifted children studied over the last 50 years in North America, the educational level of these Australian parents is very significantly beyond that of people of their generation in the general population.

In Australia, young adults who enter undergraduate study at university generally do so at the ages of 18 or 19. As there is a 20-year age span between the youngest and oldest parents in this study, this group reached the ages of 18–19 in the years between 1960 and 1980. However, 15 (54.6 per cent) of the parents turned 18–19 during the five years from 1965 to 1970; consequently the Australian Bureau of Statistics was consulted for data on the proportion of the Australian population attending university during that period.

Australia as a society is much less oriented towards tertiary study than is America, and Australia has for many years admitted a much smaller proportion of her population to university than has the United States; until very recently only a small minority of Australians entered university. Australian elementary school teachers, for example, are not required to hold a degree and the considerable majority of elementary school teachers hold a three-year diploma of teaching gained from a College or Institute of Advanced Education; indeed a survey of 500 teachers in New South Wales state (government) schools in 1990 found that 22 per cent were two-year trained (Hennessy, 1992). A national survey undertaken in 1982 found that only 43 per cent of Australian school principals held any form of academic degree, and only 12 per cent held Masters or Ph.D. qualifications. The proportions were even smaller within the state education systems: only 24 per cent of principals in government schools held a degree, and only 3 per cent a graduate degree (Chapman, 1984). As can be seen, university qualifications are viewed as somewhat less important in Australia than in North America or Britain.

In 1967, 7.1 per cent of males and 3.3 per cent of females in the 17–22 age group were students at Australian universities, that is, 5.2 per cent of the population of people of this age (Australian Bureau of Statistics, 1984). Over 80 per cent of the student population were in undergraduate courses; even at this date relatively few Australian students go on to pursue post-graduate study. The parents of this study stand in striking contrast to these statistics. Twelve of the 14 fathers (86 per cent) and 7 of the 14 mothers (50 per cent) are university graduates, and 3 of the fathers (21 per cent) have doctorates. A further 2 fathers and 4 mothers have vocational diplomas in teaching, nursing and paramedical fields, which necessitated attendance at a College of Advanced Education or Institute of Technology for a minimum of three years. Thus all 14 fathers and 11 of the 14 mothers (79 per cent) have tertiary (post-secondary) education qualifications.

As in Terman's 1926 study there is a significant difference between the educational status of the subjects' parents and grandparents. Only 5 of the 28 parents (18 per cent) left school before the age of 18, yet of the 51 grandparents (out of a possible 56) for whom educational information is available, 26 (51 per cent) left school before this age and 13 (25 per cent) completed fewer than 10 years of school. Despite this, 7 of the 51 grandparents (13.7 per cent) hold university degrees; this is more than twice the proportion found in the general population of the time. A further 6 grandfathers and 5 grandmothers hold a vocational or trade diploma; thus a surprising 46 per cent of the grandfathers and 24 per cent of the grandmothers have tertiary education qualifications. Given the statistics quoted above on the very small incidence of university attendance among Australians of their generation, this would tend to support the parents' estimation that the grandparents are generally of superior or very superior intelligence.

Given the unusually high educational status of the parents and grandparents of the subject children, it is hardly surprising that the families have placed a high value on the importance of the children receiving an education which will optimize their exceptional intellectual and academic potential. The older family members know from experience that an appropriate educational programme can make all the difference between an extraordinary but untapped potential which is given no opportunity to develop and flourish, and outstanding academic performance leading to deep personal satisfaction.

PARENTS' OCCUPATION, INCOME AND SOCIAL STATUS

The literature on the occupational status of the parents of gifted and highly gifted children reveals them as occupying professional and managerial status to an extent far exceeding their proportion in the general population. Terman noted that no fewer than 29 per cent of the fathers of his gifted subjects were classed as 'professional' under the categorization employed in the United States Census report, whereas only 2.9 per cent of the general population of Los Angeles and San Francisco were classified in this group (Terman, 1926). Fifty per cent of the fathers of Sheldon's 28 subjects of IQ 170+ were classified as 'professional' (Sheldon, 1954).

In Hollingworth's sample of children of IQ 180+, of the 10 fathers for whom occupational data are available, 6 were college professors, accountants or journalists, while of the mothers 2 were teachers, 1 was a scientist and 1 a statistician (Hollingworth, 1942). Among the parents of finalists in the 1982 Midwest Talent Search, VanTassel-Baska found professional careers highly represented, especially among fathers, 20 per cent of whom were business managers and 15 per cent college professors (VanTassel-Baska, 1983). Although 44 per cent of the mothers of this group were full-time home-makers, 18 per cent were teachers and 8 per cent nurses.

Barbe's comparative study (1964) of highly and moderately gifted children provides no data on the occupational status of the subjects' mothers. However, a considerable majority of the fathers were rated by the school authorities as being in the 'higher professional' and 'professional' categories. As in the case of educational status, significant differences appeared in the occupational ratings of fathers of highly gifted and moderately gifted children. Seventy-one per cent of the fathers of highly gifted boys and 61.8 per cent of the fathers of highly gifted girls were rated in the higher professional or professional categories as opposed to only 54.9 per cent of the fathers of moderately gifted boys and 44.2 per cent of the fathers of moderately gifted girls (Barbe, 1964).

As can be seen, the literature suggests that parents of children identified as highly gifted come mainly from the professional groups in society, with a significant representation from business management, education and medicine. Generally the socioeconomic status of the families is described as 'moderate' (Hollingworth, 1942) or 'comfortable' (Terman, 1926), although Sheldon (1954) noted that the mean annual income of the parents of his exceptionally gifted subjects, including the income of those mothers who worked outside the home, was about 3.6 times that for employed urban males. However, as will be discussed shortly, these statistics should be treated with caution.

In common with the parents of highly gifted children reported in previous studies, parents in the present study tend to hold professional and managerial positions which are regarded as high-status occupations within the Australian community. Table 5.2 displays the occupations of parents of the 15 children reported here.

As can be seen from Table 5.2, the occupations and occupational status of the parents of this Australian sample closely mirror that of the parents of highly gifted children in the United States, as revealed by the research literature. Seven of the study parents (25 per cent) are in medical or paramedical professions, 4 (14 per cent) are educators and 7 (25 per cent) hold managerial positions, no fewer than 5 being managers of their own businesses. Nine of the 14 mothers (64 per cent) are occupied full-time with home duties, or work outside the home only on a part-time basis. Twelve of the 14 fathers (86 per cent) hold occupational positions ranked within the top 4 groups (upper professional, graziers, lower professional and managerial) of the 17 occupational groups defined by the Australian National University's *Occupational Status Scale* (Broom *et al.*, 1977).

However, it is in the occupational status of the children's grandfathers, rather than their parents, that a pattern emerges which was noted by both Terman (1926) and Hollingworth (1942) in their own longitudinal studies – the tendency for relatives of highly gifted children to achieve unusual professional success and rise to positions of considerable eminence in their chosen fields. The occupations of the grandparents reveal a significant over-representation, among the males, of senior business and managerial positions. Eleven of the 28 grandfathers (39 per cent) are business managers; in several cases they are managing directors of their own companies. Two of the grandparents, who have moved through the administrative ranks within government organizations, now hold the most senior administrative positions within their own states. One other grandfather is a professor of medicine in a major university. In Australia, unlike the United States, the title 'professor' is rarely awarded to an academic; it is reserved to define and honour the most senior members of a university school or faculty. The current occupational status of the grandparents, who are nearing, or have reached, the end of their working lives, could be seen as giving a more accurate picture of the capacity for success in business of the family members of this group than can the occupational status of the children's parents who may not yet have attained their full potential.

PERSONAL CHARACTERISTICS AND PERSONAL ACHIEVEMENTS OF FAMILY MEMBERS

Much of the research into the achievements, characteristics and values of family members of the gifted have concentrated on the families of persons who have already achieved eminence (MacKinnon, 1965; Albert, 1980; Bloom, 1985). Few studies have sought to analyse these characteristics in

Table 5.2 Occupation of parents

Child	*Father's occupation*	*Mother's occupation*
Adrian	Paediatric specialist and consultant	Formerly high school math/physics teacher. Now home duties
Richard	Computer consultant	Formerly primary school teacher Now manages own business selling data storage products
Hadley	Manager in a Public Service department	Formerly clerk in Public Service department. Now home duties
Chris Jonathon	Personnel manager of industrial corporation	Pharmacist working both in large hospital and in retail outlet (part-time)
Cassandra	Medical practitioner specializing in child neurology	Medical practitioner in general practice
Ian	Mathematician and computer consultant	Physiotherapist (part-time)
Anastasia	Financial planning/ insurance marketing	Formerly secretary/ receptionist. Now home duties
Adam	Manager of own small real estate business	Registered nurse
Roshni	Medical practitioner (general practice) Also runs export/ import business	Formerly registered nurse Now part-time book-keeping, but mainly home duties
Alice	Chairman and managing director of large importing firm	Formerly private secretary to company director. Now mainly home duties, but also co-director of company
Fred	Statistician/researcher	Formerly research officer in Public Service department Now home duties
Rick	High school teacher	Primary school teacher
Rufus	Psychologist employed by Public Service	Management of accounts department in legal office (part-time)
Jade	Self-employed builder	Formerly credit manager Now mainly home duties but also self-employed agent for children's entertainers

the families of highly gifted children who may not yet have achieved their potential. Those studies which we do have available, however, reveal the parents and grandparents of the highly gifted as enthusiastic pursuers of knowledge who worked to instill in their children a love of learning, a valuing of academic success, and a desire to fulfil their scholastic and personal potential. Terman (1926) and Hollingworth (1942) noted that the parents of their subjects valued education, success in business, and hard work, and communicated these values to their children. Getzels and Jackson (1962) found that parents of their high IQ children placed more emphasis on scholastic achievement than did parents of the creatively talented. Sheldon (1954) in his study of children of IQ 170+ noted the particular influence of the grandparents in exhorting the children to achieve the highest levels of academic success of which they were capable. Silverman and Kearney (1988) reported that the parents of students whose IQs were above 170 held high aspirations for their children, spent a great deal of time reading and encouraged in their children the spirit of intellectual inquiry which was very much a feature of their own lives.

In his study of 120 adults who achieved excellence in various cognitive, artistic and athletic fields, Bloom (1985) noted the extent to which the values espoused by their parents emphasized doing one's best, striving for excellence, persisting in the face of difficulty or hardship, and seeking to achieve one's potential. Sloane, analysing the home influences in the talent development of Bloom's subjects, wrote:

> Doing one's best – whatever the task – was very important in these homes. It was not enough to stay busy. Emphasis was placed on doing the best one is capable of. Once goals were attained, there was pride in achievement, the reward for a job well done. Some of the parents were known as 'perfectionists'; nearly all set high standards for the successful completion of a task.
>
> (Sloane, 1985, p. 440)

The families of this study reflect these values very strongly.

Several of the families are distinguished by a string of academic prizes, scholarships and other awards achieved both at school and at university, and this propensity for success and recognition seems to be translated, even in their non-academic life, into a capacity for achieving recognition in whatever field they enter.

The Lins family exemplifies this trend. Keith, Cassandra's father, won several academic prizes both at school and as an undergraduate, and distinguished himself at graduate level by winning a scholarship to facilitate overseas study, while her mother, Livia, won three scholarships at school as well as gaining prizes for language and literature. Both are now successful physicians. Cassandra's paternal grandfather held a senior medical administrative position in a major hospital and was awarded a civil honour for his services to medicine in the Queen's Birthday Honours List; her maternal grandfather built up, from nothing, a number of large and prosperous textile firms. Two of her uncles are well-known authors in Hungary, while a cousin is a concert pianist. These talents are manifested strongly in Cassandra herself; she has a remarkable gift for writing and after only three years of piano tuition she attained Grade 8 standard and performed publicly with her music teacher playing a Mozart piano concerto.

The family of Richard McLeod displays a similar pattern. Alasdair, Richard's father, won several academic prizes at university and was subsequently awarded a major scholarship to study in Britain both for his M.Sc. and for his Ph.D. in computing control systems. Alasdair's sister, Richard's aunt, topped her final year in law school and was, at one time, the youngest junior partner in any legal firm in her state. His maternal grandfather is a former business manager and telephone technician, whose hobby is inventing. To assist one of his daughters, a hospital sister, he invented a light which could be attached to a thermometer for use on night duty. Richard's mother, Ursula, is the only mother to know her IQ; it is 143. She is a former teacher who is currently managing her own successful and swiftly growing data storage products business. Interestingly, this family is descended on the paternal side from Charles Darwin and is, accordingly, linked to the Wedgwood, Cowper and Huxley dynasties through familial links which were noted by Galton in his seminal work *Hereditary Genius* (Galton, 1869).

Ian Baker's family places a high value on academic success. Ian's father and one of his uncles have Bachelor of Science degrees, a second uncle has a Bachelor of Chemical Engineering and his mother was awarded the prize for academic excellence in her final year at high school and has a University Diploma in Physiotherapy and a Graduate Diploma in Advanced Manipulative Therapy. One of Ian's cousins topped his undergraduate year in organic chemistry, while a second cousin scored full marks in his state's physics and chemistry examinations for university entrance. This love of learning and pride in scholarship is also translated into the family's business enterprises. Ian's paternal grandfather, who holds a senior administrative position in telecommunications, won the top prize in his business management course. His maternal grandfather was managing director of a large department store in the state's capital.

The family of Roshni Singh is similarly noted for academic success. Juspreet, Roshni's father, spent his childhood and adolescence in Singapore. He gained entrance to the Singapore National Junior College, where even to apply a student must have gained distinctions in all high school subjects. He now holds Bachelor's degrees in Medical Science, Medicine and Surgery, which he gained while on a national scholarship. Sarah, Roshni's mother, topped her class all the way through high school and gained her Diploma of Nursing with distinctions or credits in every subject. Sarah began study towards a Bachelor of Law degree in 1983, but gave up the course on finding herself pregnant with Roshni. Juspreet's family, in Singapore, places a high value on success both in study and in business. Roshni's paternal grandfather, a highly successful businessman with offices throughout South-East Asia, has received many honours from the Sikh community in Singapore, while one of her uncles has won a national prize for literature and is a well-known poet. Two Singapore cousins are in special classes for gifted children. On the Australian side, her maternal grandfather is a senior administrator in the parliament of his state and has represented Australia in many conferences of British Commonwealth countries, while her maternal grandmother worked as personal secretary to several senior politicians, including the State Premier.

As indicated earlier, a surprising 86 per cent of the fathers and 50 per cent of the mothers are university graduates. However, several families have achieved remarkable success in the business and professional world with little scholastic assistance.

Douglas Marlow, the father of Alice, went no further in his academic career than the second year of a mechanical engineering course, while Bianca, her mother, left school at the age of 14 and took one year at business college. None of Alice's grandparents remained at school after the age of 14. Yet, in terms of performance in the business world, they are unquestionably the most successful of the families. Douglas is Chairman and Managing Director of an importing, distributing and retailing company with 130 employees and an annual turnover in excess of $80,000,000. His father, who founded the family group of companies, is a man of remarkable and varied talents. In every area of business, sport or local politics in which he has become involved, he has risen to positions of senior responsibility; indeed, the affectionate nickname by which he is known to company employees is 'father'. He is a former organizer of one of Australia's largest and most lucrative national sporting events, and, in earlier days, was the builder of Australia's first fully certified homebuilt aircraft. During the war, he was in charge of engineer officer training for the Royal Australian Air Force.

Douglas Marlow has inherited many of his father's gifts, including his dynamic involvement in business and sport. Douglas has won four Australian national championships in his particular field of sport and has held many sports chairmanships. Alice has inherited Douglas's quiet determination and also the capacity for organization which characterizes both her father's and her mother's families. Bianca Marlow's father owned his own building materials business and was extremely successful financially. The Marlow family is distinguished for its contributions both to the business world and to the community at large. One of Alice's great uncles is chairman of the board of a national industrial commission, and one of her great-grandfathers has received many public accolades for his skills in Church business management, drama and music.

In Questionnaire 2, the parents were asked to list those qualities which they felt were highly characteristic of the children's grandparents, both in business and in their personal lives, and these responses were followed up in the second parent interview.

By far the most frequently listed characteristic was a cluster of traits incorporating kindness, helpfulness, compassion and the ability to relate to, and gain the confidence and respect of, others. These qualities were noted in no fewer than 46 per cent of the grandparents. Qualities of zeal, task commitment and perseverance were listed in 30 per cent of cases. As might be expected from the research of Galton (1869) and MacKinnon (1965) these characteristics were noted mainly in those persons who had already achieved high honour or success in the academic or business world. High levels of organizational and administrative skill, the capacity to make keen and accurate judgments, and an unusually facilitative memory were also seen as characterizing this group. A fourth cluster of traits which were listed for 20 per cent of the grandparents were honesty, integrity and loyalty in business and personal life. Negative characteristics were also listed; the tendency to dominate the lives of their families was noted in four of the grandmothers, and five of the grandparents were described as argumentative or opinionated. However, the dominant impression received from this listing of traits is of a group who are loved, admired and valued by their families, their friends and their acquaintances in both their business and their personal lives.

A striking characteristic of both the parents and the grandparents is their propensity to become involved in service clubs and charity organizations. These people give their time and talents freely to help others. They serve on the committees of Rotary, Lions and other service associations, they work for or organize Meals on Wheels, and they undertake voluntary work for their Church or school. Because of the talent for organization and administration which many of them possess, they tend to occupy leadership positions in these clubs or associations and spend much of their free time in voluntary and unpaid service.

The grandparents of Christopher and Jonathon exemplify this trend. Their paternal grandmother is the District Commissioner for their city's Girl Guide troops and as part of her responsibilities she assists with the organization of the large charity concert which the Guides arrange each year. Her husband, a retired toolmaker, builds the scenery for the concert. The boys' maternal grandfather is the Area Co-ordinator for Neighbourhood Watch, and spent 12 years as the Chairman of the local elementary school Council and several years as Vice-President of the Council of the local high school.

Roshni's maternal grandfather, despite the extremely heavy calls on his time in his state parliamentary position, has worked voluntarily for many years in organizations committed to the support and welfare of physically and intellectually handicapped children. He spent seven years as the organizer of his state's annual Charity Quest to assist neurologically impaired children, with the support of his wife who served on several of the committees associated with the Quest. Several of these parents of exceptionally gifted children undertake voluntary work to assist organisations for children who are intellectually impaired, as well as working voluntarily for the Gifted Children's Associations in their own states.

The reality of these parents' concern and support for the handicapped and the economically deprived stands in striking contrast to the stereotypic Australian perception of parents of the gifted as over-ambitious and selfish individuals whose only concern is to promote the interests of their own children.

The interests and hobbies of the parents are many and varied. As in previous studies of the parents of highly gifted children, reading is a primary interest, listed as extremely important by 40 per cent of the parents. Computers, listening to and playing music, electronics and gardening were also strongly represented, and the grandparents also indicated an enjoyment of cooking and craft work. Australia is a highly sports-conscious society, and 64 per cent of the parents and 36 per cent of the grandparents indicated that they had a sporting hobby. Sailing, fishing, cycling, tennis, golf and orienteering are especially popular. This interest is not surprising, as several parents held sporting championships in their youth. One father was a member of the Australian Junior Ski Team while still at school, while another represented his state in rugby at junior level. The outstanding sports achievements of Alice's father, Douglas Marlow, have already been discussed.

It is interesting to note that the sporting interests of the parents and grandparents, like those of the children themselves, as will be reported in Chapter 7, tend to be sports which can be played alone or in small groups, and in which, consequently, the individual has a higher degree of control over the development of his or her own abilities.

The quotation from Sloane which commenced this chapter commented on the tendency among the parents of exceptionally able children to choose interests and hobbies which required practice and learning, and to study the performance of others to perfect their own skill and increase their enjoyment. Many of the parents in this study have acquired a high degree of expertise in their hobbies and leisure interests. Sarah Singh has a remarkable gift for writing. Tony Short, father of Anastasia, has restored the family's 80-year-old house with a skill and flair worthy of a professional decorator. Bonnie Seng is a gourmet cook. Holly Bond, mother of Hadley, creates, and sells, exquisite china painting; the family home is decorated with her work and with the tapestries woven by Hadley's grandmother. The parents bring to their own undertakings the pursuit of excellence, the striving for success, the concern for detail and precision, and the pleasure in talent development that they seek to inculcate in their children.

A number of parents had so many interests that they found it difficult to list them all.

> I have so many interests that it would be easier to tell you what I am *not* interested in! I don't have time for hobbies as I have *accomplished* four children before the age of 26, plus worked in an outside occupation (credit management) until Mark's birth 5 months ago, and I am still running my own business as an agent for kids' entertainers. I am still completely involved! However, some of my interests are biology, astrology, astronomy, geography, psychology, history, museums, etc., etc., etc.
>
> (Caroline Vincent, mother of Jade)

Several parents indicated that their major interest was in the upbringing and education of their children.

> Writing for pleasure is my idea of total luxury – I would like to write a book eventually. I love swimming for fitness and pleasure. However, most importantly, bringing up my children is my greatest pleasure and accomplishment! Giving all I can to them and meeting the challenges they provide gives me great satisfaction. Although I will definitely pursue my own interests and development when the children are older, above all my most basic need has always been to be a mother, and I love it! Gifted education and education generally is very important to me because of its obvious relevance to my children's lives.
>
> Juspreet thrives on his business pursuits as a challenging, stimulating and exciting occupation. He is very involved with the Sikh community and attends functions and regular temple meetings. He plays kirtan (religious music) at the temple and has regular practice sessions at our home with other Punjabi friends. He devotes as much time as possible to being with our children and specifically ensuring their ongoing involvement in Sikh activities and contact with their community to encourage a sense of belonging and an awareness of their religion, culture and identity.
>
> (Sarah Singh, mother of Roshni)

Interestingly, both Caroline and Sarah, each of whom has been extremely successful both academically and in business, view their children as their greatest accomplishments.

COUNTRY OF ORIGIN OF PARENTS

Early studies of the family background of moderately and highly gifted children reported quite fully on the ethnicity and countries of origin of family members. Terman (1926) reported a significant over-representation of Jewish and Scottish families in his sample, and an under-representation of Asians. In discussing the latter finding, however, he reported, 'In regard to the absence of Chinese, it should be noted that the Oriental schools which the Chinese children attended were not canvassed' (Terman, 1926, p. 56). He followed this comment with a discussion of several studies which showed Asian students as comparing equally or favourably with American students on tests of intellectual capacity.

Hollingworth, in her 1942 study of profoundly gifted children in the New York city area, noted that their parents were predominantly of Jewish and British birth. Witty, conducting a genetic study of 50 children whose IQs were above 140, found a strong representation of Jews, English and Scots (Witty, 1940).

Studies of highly gifted children during the last three decades have, however, paid scant attention to the question of ethnicity or country of birth. It is only recently, with cross-cultural research projects such as those of Stanley, Huang and Zu (1986) and Moore and Stanley (1988) that attention has once more been drawn to trends in the ethnic distribution of exceptional giftedness. Stanley, Huang and Zu have established that highly able young Chinese mathematicians tested before their thirteenth birthday, in Shanghai, on a standard Chinese translation of the *Scholastic Aptitude Test–Mathematics (SAT–M)* significantly outscored American children of similar ages tested as part of Johns Hopkins University's annual talent search for mathematically precocious youth. The mean score for Asian boys was 630 (within a possible range of 200–800) against the American mean of 417, while the mean score of Asian girls was 614, compared to the American mean of 383. In Stanley's words, these are 'astoundingly high statistics' (Stanley, Huang and Zu, 1986, p. 12). Moore and Stanley (1988) studied the first 292 members of the Johns Hopkins Study of Mathematically Precocious Youth subjects who scored 700+ on the *SAT–M* before age 13, and found that 68 (22 per cent) of this group were of Asian ancestry – a remarkable 15 times the percentage of Asians in the United States population at that time. Shortly after, Lupkowski and Stanley (1988) extended the Moore and Stanley study to include *all* 523 American youths who had scored 700 before age 13. They found that 27.3 per cent reported their family background as Asian-American – an over-representation by a factor of about 18.

In a plenary address at the annual Congress of the American National Association for Gifted Children in November 1985, Sternberg reported that the number of students of Asian background in American programmes for gifted children exceeded the normative expectation from population figures by a factor of five. Entrance to programmes for gifted children in the US is usually set at a level to accommodate moderately gifted children, rather than the highly or exceptionally gifted; thus an interesting pattern seems to be developing: an over-representation of Asian children by a factor of five in the population of moderately gifted students and by a considerably greater factor – 15 or over among the exceptionally gifted. A student has to be extremely gifted mathematically to score more than 700 on the SAT–M by the age of 13; only 4 per cent of college-bound 17- and 18-year-olds in the United States attain such a score!

Do similar patterns appear in Australia? Such data as we have at this stage suggest that the matter is certainly worth pursuing. In 1989 the Department of Education of Australia's most populous state, New South Wales, released a document reporting the scores of the top 500 students in the 1988 Higher School Certificate (HSC), the state's external examination for university entrance (Susskind, 1989). Fully 19.9 per cent of the family names of children on this list are Asian. As, in 1988, the percentage of Australian residents born in Asian countries was only 4.04 per cent (Australian Bureau of Statistics, 1990), this is an over-representation by a factor of 4.93 – virtually the same over-representation as was reported by Sternberg for the population of Asian-Americans in programmes for the (moderately) gifted. Examination of the lists of top scorers in the New South Wales HSC for the two subsequent years (NSW Board of Studies, 1990; NSW Board of Studies, 1991), reveals that this over-representation has actually increased to a factor of 5.85 in 1989 and a factor of 6.87 in 1990.

In early 1990 the Secondary Education Authority of the State of Western Australia published the names of the 51 students who had gained special Awards and Certificates for outstanding results in the 1989 Certificate of Secondary Education, the Western Australian equivalent of the New South Wales Higher School Certificate (Mossenson and Marsh, 1990). Children with Asian family names comprise 15.32 per cent of this group – an over-representation by a factor of 3.5. However, the proportion of Asian family names in the lists of students who gained the most prestigious of these prizes, the General and Subject Exhibitions and Awards, is even more remarkable. Of the 51 students recognized for truly outstanding scholastic results 16 (31.4 per cent) have Asian family names – 7.2 times more than could be predicted from the population statistics.

In the following year, 1990, a very similar proportion of Asian students appeared in the awards lists for the General and Subject Exhibitions and Awards. Of 49 students receiving these highly coveted prizes, 17 (34.7 per cent) had Asian family names – an over-representation by a factor of 7.29 (Mossenson, 1991).

Is there a still greater over-representation among exceptionally gifted children? The Australian Bureau of Statistics was consulted to determine whether the ethnicity and/or country of origin of the parents in this study mirrored the proportions found in the Australian community as a whole. Unfortunately, the most recent statistics available (Australian Bureau of Statistics, 1990) confine themselves to an analysis of the country of birth of persons now resident in Australia; the question of ethnicity as such is not addressed. Thus, to ensure direct comparability with the statistics for the country as a whole, it is necessary to classify the parents of the subject children in terms of their country of birth, rather than their ethnicity or racial affiliation.

When a comparative analysis is made of the country of birth of the study parents and the country of birth of persons currently resident in Australia, a pattern of over and under-representation appears that is so striking that it has been decided to report on an analysis of the parents of all 40 children who were participants in the study in 1990 (the most recent year for which the relevant Australian Bureau of Statistics data are currently available) rather than examining only the 15 children more intensively reported here. As the study includes four sibling pairs, we are examining data on 72 parents rather than 80.

The Asian-born parents in this study originated from China, Hong Kong, India, Malaysia and Singapore. The statistical data on persons resident in Australia in 1990 who were born in these specific countries indicate that the Australian population at that time included 65,000 persons born in China, 58,200 born in Hong Kong, 60,400 born in India, 77,600 born in Malaysia and 26,900 born in Singapore. Given that the total Australian population in 1990 was estimated by the Bureau of Statistics as 17,086,200, it can be seen that persons from the countries of origin of the Asian-born parents represented only 1.69 per cent of the Australian population.

All other things being equal, one might have expected 1.69 per cent of the parents in this study to have this Asian background. Instead, 19 of the 72 parents (26.4 per cent) were of Asian origin, a difference by a remarkable factor of 15.6! This is very close to the over-representation of Asian-Americans – by a factor of 18 – in Lupkowski and Stanley's sample of extremely gifted young mathematicians. The Australian studies quoted above would seem to mirror the American findings with amazing fidelity; an over-representation of Asian-Australians among the moderately gifted by a factor of at least 5, and among the exceptionally gifted by a factor at least three times greater than this! It can be seen from this that the increase in frequency is not a matter of a few percentage points, but of orders of magnitude seemingly between 5 and 20. Apart from the fact of the difference itself, the sheer size of the difference is startling. Furthermore, the difference increases with the level of potential and/or performance, suggesting sub-population differences in whatever factors 'power' intellectual potential and achievement.

Statistics on the over-representation of Asian-Australians in the study during 1988 were reported at the Eighth World Conference on Gifted and Talented Children (Gross and Start, 1989). At that time the statistics were even more startling, showing an over-representation by a factor of *21.66*! The downward shift in this statistic between 1988 and 1990 arises from two factors. The first is that the proportion of parents of Asian birth decreased slightly with an increase in the total sample of children from 31 to 40. The second factor, however, which had much greater impact on the statistics, was the enormous increase, between 1988 and 1990, in the number of immigrants from the five countries from which the Asian-born parents originate. The proportion of Australian residents born in China, Hong Kong, India, Malaysia and Singapore rose from 1.34 per cent in 1988 to 1.69 per cent in 1990 – a growth of 26 per cent over two years! Indeed, the influence of this factor on the downward shift in the study's Asian over-representation between 1988 and 1990 can be shown by the fact that the drop of 27 per cent, from a factor of 21.6 to a factor of 15.6, matches almost exactly the 26 per cent increase in Asian immigrants over the same two-year span.

As mentioned earlier, in the studies of Witty (1940) and Hollingworth (1942), the researchers noted an over-representation of Scottish and English children. A similar pattern appears in this study. Whereas the percentage of the Australian population in 1990 born in the United Kingdom (Scotland, England, Wales and Northern Ireland) is 7.14 per cent, 21 of the 72 study parents (29 per cent) were born in these countries – four times that which would be predicted from the population statistics.

By contrast, the children of parents born in Australia are under-represented. Fully 78 per cent of the Australian population, but only 40 per cent of the parents of this study (29 of the 72), were born in that country – only 0.51 of what would be predicted from an examination of population statistics.

To return for a moment to the remarkable over-representation of Asian children in this study of exceptionally gifted students in Australia; we have discussed, and will be discussing in much greater depth in later chapters, the problems of social isolation and rejection which confront the exceptionally gifted children because they differ so radically from their age-peers in their intellectual and emotional development, their interests, their play habits, their hobbies and even their speech. Given that Asian immigration to Australia has become an extremely sensitive issue, both politically and socially (Ching-Hwang, 1986; Wood, 1991; McLelland, 1992), and considering the overt hostility towards Asian immigrants displayed by sections of the Australian community (Harris, 1987), one must ponder whether a significant proportion of exceptionally gifted children in Australia may be distrusted, feared or rejected on ethnic as well as intellective grounds.

A CAVEAT – THE INFLUENCE OF TEACHERS' PERCEPTIONS OF GIFTEDNESS

One of the earliest observations of the over-representation of Asians in the higher ranges of intellectual capacity was that of Jensen (1969) in his now famous paper in the *Harvard Educational Review*. Approbrium was heaped on Jensen's head for that paper mainly because of its identification of a lower mean IQ score for Black Americans than for Whites. In the ensuing political hubbub Jensen's second finding went virtually unnoticed: that the mean IQ score of Asian-Americans was fully half a standard deviation *above* the mean score for Caucasians. The significance of this is immense when one is dealing with gifted children, as the further one gets from mean scores, the greater is the disparity revealed by such basic population differences.

To illustrate this point: in a normal population with a mean IQ of 100, and a standard deviation of 15, 228 children in every 10,000 would have an IQ score two standard deviations above the mean, that is, a score of IQ 130 or higher. However, with a mean shift upwards of half a standard deviation, as reported by Jensen for Asian-Americans, no fewer than 668 children in 10,000 would score in the IQ 130+ range. Many American gifted programmes which employ an IQ criterion for entrance set their entry level at IQ 130; in this situation, 6.68 per cent of Asian children would be eligible to enter these programmes on the basis of IQ as opposed to only 2.28 per cent of Caucasian children – an over-representation by a factor of 2.93. Yet Sternberg reports an over-representation by a factor of 5! Why do American gifted programmes contain almost twice the number of Asians than could be statistically expected even from Jensen's projections?

The children of this study have scored at or above IQ 160 on the *Stanford-Binet Intelligence Test L-M*, an instrument with a mean of 100 and a standard deviation of 16. Thus, these children score at least 3.75 standard deviations above the mean. Fewer than 9 children in 100,000 score at or beyond this level. However, if we shift the mean upwards by 0.5 of a standard deviation, to investigate the implications of Jensen's findings, and if we assume the standard deviation for the Asian population to be the same as that for non-Asians, then the criterion score of IQ 160 for entrance to this study becomes only 3.25 standard deviations above the new mean. Beyond this point lie not 9, but 58, children in 100,000. If Jensen's findings regarding a higher Asian mean are correct, and if they hold good for the Asian-Australian population as well as for Asian-Americans, then we could expect to find Asian-Australians over-represented in the study by a factor of 6.5. Yet the over-representation actually found is an astonishing *15.6*!

Why are there so many more Asian children in American programmes for the gifted, and in this Australian study of the exceptionally gifted, than could be predicted even using statistics more favourable to the Asian population?

With regard to the present study, one must always keep in mind that the subjects were not drawn at random from the Australian population, nor for that matter from the populations of South Australia, Victoria, New South Wales, Tasmania and the Australian Capital Territory. These children were referred to the study by psychologists, teachers or parents who recognized their remarkable intellectual abilities. They are, therefore, the exceptionally gifted children who had not fully succeeded in concealing their abilities, or who had, for whatever reason, been accurately identified as exceptional.

Furthermore, as has been discussed in Chapter 3, they represent a minority of Australian children in the age-range and IQ range covered by the study, comprising only one-third of the theoretical population of children of IQ 160+ in the five states from which they are drawn, and less than one-quarter of the theoretical population of such children in Australia as a whole. We have no guarantee that the racial, gender or socio-economic distribution of the study sample mirrors the distribution of these variables in the larger group of exceptionally gifted children who have not yet been identified.

In the absence of widespread ability or achievement testing, intellectually gifted Australian children who are correctly identified as gifted by their schools tend to be those who conform to the highly stereotyped view of giftedness held by the majority of Australian teachers. The gifted child is generally held to be the student who works hard, achieves at or near the top of his class, and displays a keen enjoyment of school and learning. This is one of the reasons why a high proportion of the children who were referred to this study *by their schools* were referred in the first few years of schooling on the basis of their early enthusiasm and outstanding performance in class, before the patterns of boredom, deliberate under-achievement and lack of motivation which now characterize them had time to become established.

Despite the resentment towards Asian immigrants expressed by sections of the Australian population, they are generally perceived as extremely hardworking, committed to self-improvement, eager to make the most of their abilities and talents, and devout in their belief that education is the key to a fuller and richer life-style for their children.

> Education, the getting of wisdom, is incorporate within their religious values and practices, just as learning is an act of worship in the orthodox Jewish system... They are becoming a threat to the low-grade hedonism and delicious mediocrity of [the Australian] lifestyle.
>
> (Harris, 1987, p. 12)

The behaviours that characterize Australia's Asian migrants are very much akin to the behaviours that Australians have been taught to associate with the intellectually gifted. In addition, the Asian-Australians in the present study seem somewhat more resistant to intellectual boredom and peer pressure to conform than do their Caucasian counterparts. All things considered, it is hardly surprising if teachers are more successful in identifying gifted Asian students than they are with gifted Australians, and this, together with the higher proportion of gifted Asian students suggested by Jensen, could go some way towards explaining the over-representation of Asian-Australians in this study.

The stereotyped Australian perceptions of giftedness have almost certainly influenced the socio-economic distribution of the sample. In Australia, giftedness is overwhelmingly seen as a middle-class phenomenon (Goldberg, 1981; Braggett, 1985b; Start, 1987). As discussed in Chapter 2, high intellectual ability is associated, in the minds of many Australians, with economic and social prestige. Principals of schools in working-class neighbourhoods frequently report that they have no gifted children in their schools. Unfortunately, rather than countering this outdated and class-ridden perception, Australian politicians and Teachers' Unions all too often endorse it.

Chapter 2 noted the remarkable assertion of Joan Kirner, at that time a member of the Legislative Council of the state of Victoria but later to become Minister for Education and State Premier, that 'gifted programmes' featured among the means whereby 'a ruling class stays dominant both in education and in the shaping of [Australia's] political economy' (Kirner, 1984, p. 5). Di Foggo, President of the Australian Teachers Federation, who told Charles Boag that her Union was not against gifted children *per se* – 'just' the allocation of resources to them – defended the Federation's opposition to selective schools for able students on the ground that ability grouping would lead to 'a stratification in the community' (Boag, 1990, p. 49). In a speech criticizing what he viewed as an elitist spirit in gifted education, Giles, then Director of Studies in the South Australian Education Department, invoked the negative connotations of social privilege by using the politically loaded metaphor of 'an exclusive gentleman's club'. 'A great deal of time and effort has gone into debate in recent years about how many should belong to 'The Club' and by what criteria its members should be elected' (Giles, 1983, p. 70).

The following year, writing in *Education*, the newspaper of the New South Wales Teachers' Federation, West described the State Education Department's Opportunity Classes, full-time self-contained classes for gifted children in fifth and sixth grade, as 'set up to cater for a small elite... to provide a last refuge for white Anglo-Saxons' (West, 1984, p. 266). Parents of opportunity class students, and students themselves, responded with angry letters refuting West's allegations and describing the multicultural and mixed socio-economic compositions of the Opportunity Classes.

> Half the children in my class come from migrant and various religious backgrounds.
>
> (Pressick, O.C. student, 1984, p. 288)

> You might think that I am the son of a doctor or a lawyer from an Anglo-Saxon family. I am not. I am a Greek son of an average every day carpenter. My parents migrated from Greece, and the reason why *I* am writing this letter is because my parents have not got the language abilities to write it.
>
> (Korsanos, O.C. student, 1984, p. 384)

The Federation, however, saw no reason to alter its perception of giftedness as circumscribed by race and class. In 1990 Poulos, then editor of *Education*, described gifted children seeking entrance to a university programme as 'the sons and daughters of middle-class yuppies trying to steel [sic] more and more privileges under pretentions to greater abilities bestowed on them not by their class position but by God himself' (Poulos, 1990a, p.8).

Not surprisingly, therefore, the majority of Australian teachers work on the assumption that gifted students are middle-class children who are well-dressed and neatly groomed, whose parents hold professional or management positions, who achieve high levels of academic success, who are motivated to study and who willingly accept the values of their teachers and the school. Not surprisingly, the children who were referred to the study by their teachers are, in the main, children who at least in their early years of schooling conformed to this pattern. (Ian Baker was not identified as gifted by his teachers but by the psychologist who was brought in to test him so that the school could refer him to a special school for uncontrollable children. The school attended by 14-year-old Beatrice, of IQ 180, refuses to accept that her intellectual abilities are anything out of the usual; Beatrice, who is being treated for clinical depression, was referred to the study by her psychiatrist.)

Studies of the highly and exceptionally gifted have indicated a much greater variability in IQ range among boys than among girls. McNemar and Terman (1936) postulated that the ratio of boys to girls above IQ 160 would be 2:1. Terman's gifted group contained 19 boys, but only 7 girls, of IQ 180 and above (Terman, 1925). Of Hollingworth's 12 profoundly gifted subjects, only 4 were girls. The children in this study conform to this pattern. Of the 15 children reported here, only 5 are female; in the total sample, of the 8 children who score at or above IQ 175, only 2 are girls.

Silverman (1986) has pointed out, however, that the three highest scoring subjects in Terman's gifted sample were female, and has suggested that the imbalance between males and females recorded in studies of the intellectually gifted may arise from sampling bias; where studies are conducted on referred samples, such as those of Terman and Hollingworth, the researcher may acquire a sample which does not truly represent the gender distribution of the underlying population. This may well be true in the case of the present study. Australian research (Brown, 1983; Gross, 1983) suggests that teacher bias results in a significant numerical dominance of boys in Australian programmes for the gifted; a similar bias may have resulted in a greater number of exceptionally gifted boys than girls being referred for inclusion in this study.

It must be acknowledged that the distribution of gender, racial origin and social class in this Australian study reflects strongly the characteristics of the exceptionally gifted children described in previous research studies. However, a major difficulty with referred populations (and even the children in Terman's landmark study were initially referred for testing by their classroom teachers) is that those children who are identified as gifted tend to be children who conform, at least at the time of their referral, to the community's subjective and often biased perception of what gifted children should be like. It is highly probable that, as with the selection of Terman's gifted sample, Australian children from low-status socio-economic or racial groups would be less often identified as possessing high intellectual potential. There are almost certainly children of truly exceptional intellectual capacity who are living in economically deprived conditions and who, under the subjective procedures by which Australian schools identify, or fail to identify, intellectual giftedness, may never have their abilities recognized or fostered.

SUMMARY

As in previous international studies of exceptionally gifted children, the children in this study tend to be the first-born of small families whose parents have deliberately delayed starting a family until the completion of tertiary study or through a desire for increased financial security. Their parents and grandparents are, in general, more highly educated than the majority of people of their generation, and they tend to be employed in professional occupations or, if in business, in managerial positions. Children whose parents were born in Asia are very significantly over-represented. It must be emphasized, however, that in any population of gifted children referred for study by their teachers, children who conform to teachers' rather stereotyped perceptions of giftedness and talent tend to be nominated in numbers out of proportion to their presence in the population as a whole. It is, therefore, not surprising that the children who were referred to the study *by their teachers* should in general be boys from middle-class and professional families, who come from cultures which value learning and scholastic achievement, and who, at least at the time of their identification, enjoyed school and were experiencing high levels of academic success.

In their spare-time occupations the parents of the children in this study closely resemble the parents of gifted students in previous studies such as that of Sloane (1985) whose quotation begins this chapter. In their hobbies, as in their professions, they participate enthusiastically, are keenly involved, and select avocations which demand, or at least permit, the development of high levels of skill. Even in their leisure occupations they model for their children the pursuit of excellence and the enjoyment of a task well done. Many have won local or national recognition for their contribution to their selected avocation; several have represented their region, their state or even their country in their chosen sport.

A significant proportion of these parents of exceptionally gifted children spend much of their spare time in voluntary and unpaid service in organizations for children who are intellectually or physically handicapped.

6

ACADEMIC ACHIEVEMENT LEVELS

A major component of the learning style of this group is the ability to skip steps in learning and to take giant intuitive leaps. Highly gifted children often surprise adults by arriving at insightful conclusions without being able to describe the steps they took to get there. ('I just figured it out!') The need to show their work in a precise, linear fashion is at cross purposes with their learning style. They may get a visual image of an intricate set of relationships and be unable to translate their thinking process in such a manner that others can follow it.

While their age-mates are comfortable working with concrete material, highly gifted children are more at home with abstractions. They may have difficulty concentrating on isolated fragments of information, analyzing bits of learning by phonics, or memorizing facts by rote. Yet they manipulate abstract symbol systems with ease and become animated when dealing with complex relations involving many variables. They are systems *thinkers.*

(Silverman, 1989, p. 75)

Exceptionally gifted children may demonstrate precocious intellectual, psychomotor and psychosocial development remarkably early in life. As was shown in Chapter 4, most of the children in this study were independently mobile at an age when their age-peers of average ability are still dependent on the help of their parents, and were expressing themselves fluently in complex sentences while age-peers were still mastering the skills of linking words into phrases. In common with other extremely gifted children in previous studies, they acquired the skills of reading, writing, spelling and counting some years earlier than would normally be anticipated; indeed, the majority of these young Australians entered elementary school with the literacy and numeracy skills that one would normally expect from a student in third or fourth grade.

EARLY DEVELOPMENT OF READING

One of the most powerful indicators of extreme giftedness is early reading. Terman found that one of the few variables on which the exceptionally gifted children (IQ 170+) in his gifted group differed from the moderately and highly gifted was the very early age at which they learned to read. Almost 43 per cent of Terman's sub-group of children of IQ 170+ was reading before age 5, compared with 18.4 per cent in the sample as a whole, while 13 per cent of the IQ 170+ group had learned to read before age 4 (Terman and Oden, 1947).

Leta Hollingworth confirmed that it was early reading that most clearly differentiated between moderately and exceptionally gifted children (Hollingworth, 1926). Of Hollingworth's 12 subjects of IQ 180, four were reading at age 2, three at age 3 and three at age 4 (Hollingworth, 1942). The remaining two children were reading before entering school, but precise age levels were not recorded.

VanTassel-Baska (1983) studied 270 students aged 13 and 14 who had achieved scores of 630 on the *Scholastic Aptitude Test–Mathematics* or 580 on the *Scholastic Aptitude Test–Verbal* in the Midwest Talent Search. Although IQ scores were not recorded for this sample, their verbal and mathematical precocity is indicated by the observation that their *SAT* scores place them within the 90th percentile on this test which is standardized on college-bound seniors. VanTassel-Baska found that 80 per cent of this group was reading by age 5, and 55 per cent by age 4.

The case study literature contains numerous examples of extremely precocious readers, such as 'Madeline', who taught herself to read at age 3 without parental assistance. 'Reading seems to be born in her,' Madeline's mother is reported as saying. 'The maturity of her interpretations and expression in reading has always been a source of surprise and comment by others' (Burks, Jensen and Terman, 1930, p. 269). By the time Madeline was 7 years old, her parents' main concern was 'to keep her doing something else than reading' (Burke, Jensen and Terman, 1930, p. 269).

Terman, in a unique retrospective study of the childhood of Francis Galton, relates that Galton was reading by age 2½ (Terman, 1917). In a letter to his sister Adele, written the day before his fifth birthday, Galton wrote: 'My dear Adele, I am 4 years old and can read any English book. I can say all the Latin substantives and adjectives and active verbs, besides 52 lines of Latin poetry.' Terman comments that if Galton could indeed read any English book at such a tender age, he was without doubt as far advanced in his reading as the average English or American 10-year-old of that era. Terman's assertion might, in turn, come as a sharp shock to English or American teachers of 10-year-olds in the 1990s!

A characteristic that almost seems to define the profoundly gifted child is what I have termed 'spontaneous reading' (Gross, 1989a): reading which is untaught and unrehearsed and which seems to appear full-blown in the child without the stages of its development, whatever they be, being perceptible either to onlookers or, in some cases, to the child herself. 'Betty Ford', reported by Terman and Fenton (1921) and the prodigiously gifted child author Marjory Fleming (Malet, 1946) seem to have 'caught' reading in this way, as did Terman's 'Madeline'.

Marjory Fleming, a prodigiously gifted young writer who lived in Scotland at the start of the nineteenth century and died in 1812, one month before her ninth birthday, kept copious journals in which she recorded her thoughts and feelings, as well as a remarkable collection of poems and short stories. At the age of 6, Marjory recorded in her journal the strange experience which had accompanied her acquisition of reading three years earlier. She was brought up in a household where learning and scholarship were valued and where reading was modelled as a pastime which brought great joy and satisfaction. By the age of 3, Marjory deeply envied her older brother's patent delight in being able to read for himself, while she was still dependent on being read to. One day she was staring at the print of a book which she desperately wanted to read when she suddenly found that the letters before her were no longer meaningless squiggles; they 'jumped out at her, saying *The Mouse and other Tales*'. Her first emotion was complete bewilderment and a little anxiety; however, this soon changed to delight as she found that she could, without effort, read the book right through. Marjory had not been taught the mechanics of reading at any time.

As has been discussed earlier, the children in this study developed the capacity to move around and explore their environment several months earlier than their age-peers of average ability, while the remarkably early development of speech enabled them to gain information on many topics through incessant questioning of their parents and other family members at an age when other children are only beginning to experiment with oral communication. Both early movement and early speech contributed significantly to these children's capacity to acquire and process information. A third contributor to the children's enhanced capacity to acquire knowledge has been the astonishingly precocious development of reading.

As mentioned in Chapter 4, some early studies of speech and movement in young children have been flawed by the researcher's failure to define precisely what he or she meant by 'talking' and 'walking'. To avoid falling into the same trap, let me explain what I mean by 'reading'. A young child who is shown the picture of a cat with 'cat' written underneath, and responds by saying the word, is not necessarily reading. She may be responding to the pictorial clue, rather than decoding the word. It is only when the child is able to recognize and pronounce the word 'cat' in another context, with no pictorial clue to assist her, that we can be sure that she is responding to, and analysing, the collection of printed symbols which make up the word 'cat' rather than the picture of an animal with which she is well familiar. Therefore, for the purposes of this study, reading is defined as the ability to decode and comprehend more than five words from a printed source *without* the use of pictures as textual clues. Even using this definition, which is more cautious than many employed in studies of early readers, the early acquisition of reading in the study children is quite dramatic. Of the 15 subjects, 4 were reading before their second birthday, 6 before their third birthday, 2 before their fourth birthday, 2 before their fifth birthday, and 1, Alice Marlow, shortly after her fifth birthday.

The parents uniformly report that their children were fascinated with reading from an early age. Reading is a primary interest of this group of parents, and they read to their children from the earliest months. Not surprisingly, the children responded with a passionate interest in books. In several cases 'book' or 'read' were among the first words the child learned to say; indeed, most of the parents report that the young child demanded to be read to at every opportunity.

> On her first birthday she was given Dr Seuss's *ABC Book* which she loved me to read to her over and over again because of the funny rhymes. I must have read it hundreds of times. I can picture Roshni toddling towards me with her arm stretched out to me holding a book. It was a pastime that we both enjoyed because it meant, for me, a time when I didn't have to rack my brains for something else to keep her occupied and happy, and one where I could sit down and be completely relaxed.
>
> (Sarah Singh, mother of Roshni)

Nine of the 14 families report that their subject child learned to read either with no assistance or with only minimal assistance from the parents. Adrian and Fred taught themselves to read before their third birthdays by watching *Sesame Street*. Adrian's reading came as a complete surprise to his parents; at the age of 1½ they found him playing with another child's alphabet blocks, arranging the letters in alphabetical order. A few months after his second birthday they found him using the portable typewriter which stood in his father's study; he had copied a whole page of a children's book laboriously with one finger!

These 'self-taught' readers received much of their stimulation from street signs, labels in supermarkets or names of shops. Ian, at age 2, was able to differentiate among the labels of his beloved collection of old 45-rpm records and audio cassette tapes, and entertain himself independently by playing his favorite music. The development of Ian's reading has been remarkable. Before his third birthday he had become fascinated with road maps, and by 3½ his mastery of reading was such that he would use the street directory of the city in which he lived to plot a new route from his home to play-school or to a friend's house and then, with the directory closed in his lap, he would navigate his father through the new route as his father drove in accordance with Ian's directions. 'Second on the right will be Cedar Avenue; then take the first left down Wallace Terrace and left again on to Park Street and you'll be there.' At the age of 4½ his knowledge of his neighborhood was so encyclopedic that he was able to direct a stranger, who was lost, to a destination several streets away. Nor was his reading confined to road maps; as related earlier, at pre-school as a 4-year-old Ian read stories to the other children by holding the book in front of him, for the others to see, and reading upside down!

The remaining five families report that they gave moderate amounts of assistance in the development of their child's reading. In three cases (Adam, Rick and Anastasia), the mothers encouraged the child to recognize individual words with the use of flash-cards. The mothers of Rufus and Richard encouraged their children to help them write small books, so that they could use stimulus materials that had specific meaning for the individual child. By age 4½, Rufus was reading from material with quite sophisticated syntax, written by himself with assistance from Rachel. When Rufus's reading was assessed by an educational psychologist at age 5½, he was found to be reading at a 10-year-old level.

However, several parents report that they were strongly advised by friends that they should not assist the development of their children's reading in any way. Livia Lins was told by Mike and Cassandra's pre-school teachers that she must on no account try to teach them to read at home, and she obeyed this injunction, believing that the teachers' professional opinion must be correct.

> For a long time before Rufus entered school he was asking me, 'Can I read? Can I learn to read?' and people were telling me, 'You mustn't teach him! You mustn't teach him!' This was mainly friends who were teachers who saw him at playgroups and thought he was too advanced and were always saying to me 'Oh, you mustn't do this or that' because they assumed I was pushing him. So I deliberately held him back so that I would do the right thing. Eventually I gave in to the pressure from Rufus because he was so desperately anxious to learn to read, and I made him these little reading books, but I didn't let him read nearly as much as he wanted to and I have always regretted that. I wish now that I hadn't held him back. My friends were wrong and I should have trusted my own judgment.
>
> (Rachel Street, mother of Rufus)

Bianca Marlow had not been specifically advised against teaching Henry and Alice to read, but she avoided it on the assumption that to do so would create difficulties for the school at a later date.

> Alice could read a few words before she went to school, but her

> reading didn't really take off until she was formally taught by her teachers. And yet I don't know; she may have been reading earlier than that without letting us know. She's a funny little thing, very secretive. She often hides things she can do.

Alice is indeed a self-contained, private little person, and the development of her reading abilities in the first two years of school was certainly unusually accelerated.

Many exceptionally gifted children display an almost overwhelming desire to learn to read. Marjory Fleming's pleas to be taught were steadfastly refused by her family; the sudden and spontaneous 'arrival' of Marjory's ability to read at the age of 3½ angered her mother considerably (Malet, 1946). Terman reported that the assistance reluctantly given by some of the parents of his gifted group was given 'only in response to urgent solicitations on the part of the child' (Terman, 1926, p. 272). Many of the Australian parents speak of the strategies their children employed at remarkably early ages in their eagerness to teach themselves to read. David Otway reports that even before the age of 2 Christopher had realized that letters could be grouped into words; he would line up letters from his plastic alphabet and besiege his parents with requests to read aloud the 'words' he was forming. Richard and Roshni insisted on having the same passage read to them repeatedly until they had memorized it so precisely that they could 'read' it back to their parents. Richard, before age 2, would become upset if Ursula tried to point to the words as she read, and would push her hand off the book. His preferred strategy was to have his mother stop in the middle of a sentence, and then, himself, point to the word she had stopped at.

> Around the time of her second birthday Roshni had several favorite books that she took pleasure in 'reading' to us. She had memorized the gist of the stories after several adult readings. After this period began she went through a stage where she insisted that any new book she received was read to her several times concurrently [sic] with the aim of memorizing it immediately so that she could 'read' it back to us.
>
> (Sarah Singh, mother of Roshni)

> Before the age of 2, Hadley knew every word of Beatrix Potter's *The Tale of Peter Rabbit*. He'd loved the story and had asked me to read it to him many, many times. How do I explain this – one day Hadley simply took over and 'read' the entire book, word perfect. I was utterly amazed. I assumed he was using picture cues, but the incredible thing was that he was also mimicking my way of reading; he had my enthusiastic expression and emphases down perfectly. I remember at the time experiencing a feeling of eerie magic. He

> repeated this feat many times for the family, totally absorbed in the atmosphere he was creating. I recall, too, at times like that, having the feeling that what we were seeing of Hadley's talents was only the tip of the iceberg.
>
> (Holly Bond, mother of Hadley)

The skills of writing also tended to develop early in this group of children. Just before his third birthday, Rufus copied out a sign saying 'EXIT' for his den. Christopher and Jonathon, from age 3 onwards, had regular reading and writing sessions with their father, at the boys' eager request. At 3 years 10 months Roshni wrote a letter to her grandmother on the family's personal computer: 'Hello Grandma, How are you, love Inshor'. When questioned on the unusual spelling of her name, she explained she was writing it backwards as a joke! When Roshni was 4 years 9 months of age, Sarah converted to the Sikh religion and she and Juspreet decided to be 'remarried' in the temple according to the rites of her new faith. Roshni, who was extremely excited by the coming ceremony, drew a picture of her parents in the temple and wrote beneath it: 'My Mummy and Daddy are geting mared tomoro [sic]'.

By the time they entered school, most of the study children had the reading skills of children several years their senior. Georgina and Edward Murphy estimate that by the time Adam was 3 years old he would already have been able to read the first passage of the Neale Analysis of Reading, the standardized test used to assess the reading achievement of the younger subjects in this study. Christopher was reading children's encyclopedias before his fourth birthday. 'By age 4½ he knew what countries were in what continents and what their capitals were,' reports David. When he entered school at age 5, Christopher had a reading age of 10 years and was reading the daily newspaper with great enjoyment. Elizabeth Otway and Jan Ward are convinced that a major facilitator of the early development of Christopher's and Rick's reading skills was the fact that they slept so little. 'Because it was almost impossible to get Rick to sleep during the day I started him on flash cards for the sake of something to keep him occupied,' says Jan, who is a primary school teacher. 'He was off the flash cards and on to books in no time. By 2½ he was reading the sort of books you'd give to a child in first grade.'

Although early reading is generally recognized as a powerful indicator of intellectual giftedness, some researchers question its validity as a predictor of scholastic success. Braggett (1983) proposes that many children who display unusually accelerated reading development in early childhood may not retain this capacity but may, rather, be 'developmental spurters' whose early advantage is diluted, during the years of elementary schooling, by poor teaching and/or by an alteration of relationships within the home. Braggett claims that 'developmental spurters' are 'possibly the largest single group of gifted children we may identify in the school' (Braggett, 1983, p. 14).

The persistence, over time, of exceptional reading accuracy and comprehension skill in these exceptionally gifted children indicates that they are by no means 'developmental spurters'. In every case, the reading development of these children has followed the pattern reported in the studies of Burks, Jensen and Terman (1930), Hollingworth (1942), Durkin (1966) and VanTassel-Baska (1983) and in the numerous individual case studies of precocious readers (Terman and Fenton, 1921; Hirt, 1922; Witty and Coomer, 1955; Feldman, 1986; Gross, 1986); that is, the precocity in reading which was such a salient feature of the child's early development has persisted, and in many cases increased, through the children's elementary school years. What *has* decreased in several instances, however, has been the opportunity accorded to these children to display their precocity in the classroom situation. As will be discussed in later chapters, the majority of these exceptionally gifted children have been required, from Grade 3 onwards, to read from the same school texts and materials as their chronologically aged peers. Assessments of developmental changes in gifted students should not be made from an examination of their school performance alone; the apparent 'levelling out' of the academic achievements of a gifted child may arise from the expectations and requirements of the class teacher. The gifted child whose leisure time reading is several years in advance of her classroom achievement is not a 'developmental spurter' but rather a child who has been prevented, either by peer pressure or by the imposition of an inappropriate curriculum, from displaying her true reading interests or achievements in the school situation.

During 1988 and 1989 the scholastic achievement of the study children was assessed using standardized tests of mathematics, reading and spelling. The tests themselves are reported and discussed in Chapter 3. Reading achievement was assessed using the *Neale Analysis of Reading* which is designed to assess the reading accuracy (RA) and reading comprehension (RC) of children aged 6–13 years. Children who scored at the ceiling of this test both for reading accuracy and for reading comprehension were subsequently tested using the *Scholastic Aptitude Test–Verbal (SAT–V)* which is standardized on American 17–18 year-olds planning to enter university. The range of the *SAT–V* in scaled scores is 200–800, with a mean which varies around 500 depending on the cohort tested in any year.

Table 6.1 displays the age at which the 15 children learned to read and their reading achievement levels in elementary school compared with their chronological age at the time of testing.

As can be seen from Table 6.1, the reading achievement of the 15 children while at elementary school is at least three or four years in

Table 6.1 Age of beginning reading and reading achievement levels in elementary school

Child	*Age at which child learned to read*	*Chronological age at time of later reading assessment*	*Reading age or test score*	*Test employed*
Adrian	Before age 2	9 yrs 9 mths	380V	SAT–V
		12 yrs 10 mths	590V	SAT–V
		13 yrs 9 mths	660V	SAT–V
		14 yrs 9 mths	740V	SAT–V
Adam	18 mths	5 yrs 3 mths	8 yrs 6 mths	Neale RA
		7 yrs 5 mths	11 yrs 6 mths	Neale RA
		7 yrs 5 mths	11 yrs 8 mths	Neale RC
Anastasia	19 mths	7 yrs 7 mths	12 yrs 1 mths	Neale RA
		7 yrs 7 mths	12 yrs 7 mths	Neale RC
Ian	Before age 2	9 yrs 2 mths	13 yrs 6 mths	Neale RA
		9 yrs 2 mths	12 yrs 5 mths	Neale RC
Hadley	18 mths	7 yrs 7 mths	12 yrs 2 mths	Neale RA
		7 yrs 7 mths	11 yrs 1 mths	Neale RC
Roshni	2 yrs 9 mths	4 yrs 11 mths	8 yrs 2 mths	Neale RA
		4 yrs 11 mths	7 yrs 4 mths	Neale RC
Fred	2 yrs 6 mths	12 yrs 1 mths	500V	SAT–V
Richard	2 yrs 9 mths	11 yrs 11 mths	360V	SAT–V
Rick	2 yrs 7 mths	5 yrs 8 mths	8 yrs 11 mths	Neale RA
		5 yrs 8 mths	9 yrs 1 mths	Neale RC
Christopher	2 yrs 3 mths	11 yrs 4 mths	580V	SAT–V
Rufus	3 yrs 9 mths	13 yrs 11 mths	360V	SAT–V
Jonathon	3 yrs 3 mths	9 yrs 1 mths	12 yrs 10 mths	Neale RC
		9 yrs 1 mths	12 yrs 9 mths	Neale RC
Cassandra	4 yrs 6 mths	11 yrs 1 mths	350V	SAT–V
Jade	4 yrs	7 yrs 2 mths	10 yrs 2 mths	Neale RA
		7 yrs 2 mths	11 yrs 1 mths	Neale RC
Alice	5 yrs	8 yrs 0 mths	11 yrs 11 mths	Neale RA
		8 yrs 0 mths	12 yrs 3 mths	Neale RC

Neale RA = Neale Reading Accuracy
Neale RC = Neale Reading Comprehension
SAT–V = Scholastic Aptitude Test – Verbal

advance of their chronological age. Fred, Christopher and Adrian scored above the mean on the *SAT–V* before the usual age of graduation from elementary school. Roshni, before the age of 5, had the reading capacities of a Grade 3 student. Anastasia and Hadley, at 7½, had reading skills more usually encountered in Grade 7.

EARLY DEVELOPMENT OF NUMERACY

The precocious development of reading, and a passionate love of reading, seems almost universal in exceptionally gifted children. Many extremely gifted students display an associated precocity in the development of numerical skills. The children in Terman's gifted group, for example, were, on average, advanced by several years in their mathematics achievement (Terman, 1926). Sixty-nine per cent of the mathematically gifted students identified in the 1983 and 1984 Midwest Talent Searches were performing basic mathematical operations before school entry (VanTassel-Baska, 1989).

The literature on exceptional giftedness records some truly remarkable case studies of mathematical precocity in pre-school and elementary school students.

Several of Hollingworth's subjects of IQ 180+ displayed exceptional mathematical precocity (Hollingworth, 1942). By the age of 7 'Child A' could square any number up to 100, solve problems in ratio, and calculate series of operations such as: 'Take 2, square it, square that, divide by 4, cube it, add 17, take the square root, add 7, square it, square it, give the result'. Hollingworth adds that such a calculation would take the boy around 5 seconds! Hollingworth's 'Child D', a gifted artist, was so enthralled with numbers that even in dealing with colour he turned to mathematics and awarded a numerical value to each of the 300 shades with which he worked. By the age of 12 'D' had completed university entrance requirements in arithmetic, algebra, geometry and trigonometry.

Roedell describes a 3½-year-old boy who was told that his young cousin was two years younger than he, and responded by saying, 'Oh, when she is 3 I'll be 5, and when she is 4, I'll be 6...' and continuing the calculation up to the age of 12 (Roedell, 1989, p. 19).

William James Sidis, the profoundly gifted young man who lectured to the Harvard Mathematical Club on fourth-dimensional bodies at the age of 11, had, by age 9, already mastered algebra, trigonometry, geometry and differential and integral calculus (Montour, 1977). Norbert Wiener, generally recognized as the father of cybernetics, was doing university maths while still at elementary school, and graduated from Tufts College at fourteen years of age (Wiener, 1953).

Since 1971 the Study of Mathematically Precocious Youth (SMPY), based at Johns Hopkins University and the University of Iowa, has conducted comprehensive longitudinal studies of elementary and secondary school students who display extremely precocious mathematical reasoning. Mathematically gifted students are offered 'a varied combination of accelerative possibilities' (Stanley and Benbow, 1986, p. 375) and allowed to select an optimum combination designed to respond to their individual needs. The numerous SMPY publications record the success of these individualized programmes which often involve quite radical levels of mathematical acceleration, and record the remarkable mathematical development of some of the young prodigies with whom SMPY has worked (Stanley, 1976a; Stanley and Benbow, 1983; Brody, Assouline and Stanley, 1990).

A curious feature of the literature on extreme mathematical precocity is that, whereas parents of linguistically precocious children are able to recall in considerable detail the various stages in the development of the children's reading skills, the parents of mathematically precocious students are less likely to have documented the stages in their children's acquisition of the skills of numeracy. The parents of the Australian children conform to this pattern. The majority of the parents can recount the age at which the child was able to 'recite' lists of numbers in sequence but few are able to assess the age at which he or she first displayed an understanding of arithmetic processes. Accordingly it is not possible to construct a table in which the age at which the child learned to manipulate numbers could be compared with his or her mastery of mathematical skills later in childhood. This is regrettable, as the results of standardized testing of mathematics achievement during the elementary school years, which will be reported later in this chapter, indicate that the majority of the study children display a remarkable precocity in mathematics as well as in reading.

A number of the parents are, however, able to recount significant stages in the development of their children's numerical skills. Hadley, at about 18 months of age, became fascinated with the maths drill programs used by his older brothers on the family computer. Robert Bond recounts Hadley's enjoyment of simple addition programs. Hadley would work out the answer to a question with the help of plastic beads and type it into the computer, laughing with delight when the displayed response showed that his calculation had been correct. From his earliest years, he showed a remarkable capacity for estimation. Holly Bond has recounted, in Chapter 1, Hadley's remarkable feat, at the age of 22 months, in guessing the length of time she and he had been out walking. 'When he came out with a very casual "Oh, about 26½ minutes," I was astonished and excited,' said Holly, 'and I decided to test this ability again over the next few weeks. Sure enough, his estimates were invariably extremely accurate.'

Like Hadley, Adrian could do simple addition and subtraction before the age of 2, and by age 4 was multiplying two-digit numbers by two-digit numbers in his head. Richard, at 3 years 9 months, surprised Ursula by asking, 'Why isn't thirty called twenty-ten?' His capacity, at age 4, to count mentally in binary, octal and hexadecimal has been related earlier. Sally and Brock Baker report that numbers had taken on a fascination for Ian by the time he was 4 years old. 'He seemed to have quite a good understanding of numbers up to 1,000 at this age and was constantly asking us for sums. We went through a stage where his first question on waking every morning, for many months, would be a request for some kind of sum.' Christopher's prodigious talent for numbers showed itself shortly after the age of 3; when he started pre-school at age 4, he was capable of Grade 4 maths work and within three weeks of his starting formal schooling at age 5 his maths ability was assessed as average Grade 5 level. At 5 years of age Rick was handling, with ease, division problems such as 3721 ÷ 6.

The mathematics achievement of the 15 children was assessed using one or more of a number of standardized tests of arithmetic or mathematics achievement which have been fully described in Chapter 3. In each case, off-level testing was employed, in response to the accelerated development of the subjects. The *Leicester Number Test*, standardized on English 7-and 8-year-olds, was used to assess the maths achievement of the 5- and 6-year-olds in this study. The *Nottingham Number Test*, standardized on English 9- and 10-year-olds, was used to assess the 7- and 8-year-olds. The *Cooperative Achievement Test–Arithmetic (CAT)*, standardized on Grade 7, 8 and 9 students in junior high schools in the United States, was used to assess the children in the middle and upper grades of elementary school, while the *Scholastic Aptitude Test–Mathematics (SAT–M)*, standardized on American high school seniors intending to enter university, was used to assess those elementary school students who scored at the ceiling of the *CAT*. Like the *SAT–V*, the range of the *SAT–M* in scaled scores is 200–800, with a mean which varies around 500 depending on the age cohort tested in any year.

Table 6.2 displays the mathematics achievement level of the 15 subjects compared with their chronological age at the time of testing.

As can be seen from Table 6.2, the majority of the children have mathematics achievement levels at least two years in advance of their chronological age. This is particularly impressive in the cases of Roshni and Rick, who at ages 5 and 6 respectively had developed arithmetic skills more usually encountered in children three years their senior. However, the most notable statistic arising from this analysis of the children's mathematics achievement is that fully five of the 15 subjects have scored above the mean on the *Scholastic Aptitude Test–Mathematics*, at or below the age of 12 years 1 month. Given that this test is standardized on American

Table 6.2 Mathematics achievement levels compared with chronological age

Child	*Age at time of testing*	*achievement score*	*Standardized test employed*
Adrian	8 yrs 10 mths	760M	SAT–M
Adam	7 yrs 8 mths	82nd %ile of 9-year-olds 61st %ile of 10-year-olds	Nottingham
Anastasia	8 yrs 1 mth	90th %ile of 10-year-olds	Nottingham
Ian	9 yrs 11 mths	560M	SAT–M
Hadley	7 yrs 7 mths	99th %ile of 10-year-olds	Nottingham
	7 yrs 9 mths	78th %ile of Grade 7s	CAT
Roshni	5 yrs 5 mths	98th %ile of 7-year-olds 84th %ile of 8-year-olds	Leicester
Fred	12 yrs 1 mth	640M	SAT–M
Richard	12 yrs 6 mths	780M	SAT–M
Rick	6 yrs 6 mths	94th %ile of 8-year-olds	Leicester
		68th %ile of 9-year-olds	Nottingham
Christopher	11 yrs 4 mths	710M	SAT–M
Rufus	13 yrs 11 mths	590M	SAT–M
Jonathon	8 yrs 6 mths	77th %ile of Grade 7s	CAT
Cassandra	11 yrs 0 mths	50th %ile of Grade 7s	CAT
Jade	7 yrs 2 mths	85th %ile of 7-year-olds 50th %ile of 8-year-olds	Leicester
Alice	8 yrs 6 mths	94th %ile of 10-year-olds	Nottingham

SAT–M = Scholastic Aptitude Test – Mathematics
CAT = Cooperative Achievement Test – Arithmetic

17- to 18-year-olds intending to enter university, this is a truly remarkable feat. Indeed, three of the subjects, Adrian, Richard and Christopher, have already been accepted as members of the 'Study of Mathematically Precocious Youth (SMPY) 700–800 on *SAT–M* Before Age 13 Group'.

The schools' response to these children's remarkable levels of mathematical precocity will be discussed much more comprehensively in

Chapter 8. Some illustration is appropriate here, however, of the truly prodigious mathematical talent of a number of the subjects.

By the age of 6, having taught himself BASIC from a computer manual, Adrian had written several computer programs on mathematical problems. He achieved his first publication shortly after his eighth birthday, when a mathematics journal printed a program he had written to calculate perfect numbers. At the age of 8 years 10 months he achieved the phenomenal score of 760 on the *SAT–M*. He spent six weeks in June–August 1989 at the Research Science Institute for academically gifted mathematics and science students held at George Washington University in the United States. This residential programme offers mathematically brilliant young scholars the opportunity to undertake individual research under the guidance of internationally renowned research scientists and mathematicians. Adrian was the only Australian invited to participate. He celebrated his fourteenth birthday in the United States in the company of exceptionally gifted young mathematicians from Germany, France, Mexico, India, the United Kingdom and other nations, and graduated from university with his Bachelor of Science degree shortly after his fifteenth birthday.

Christopher achieved the remarkable score of 710 on the *SAT–M* at the age of 11 years 4 months. He was disappointed with this score, as his scores on the two practice tests which he had taken had been 760 and 780, and he felt that test anxiety had reduced his test score to what, for him, was a less than acceptable level. To restore his spirits, I attempted to explain to him the significance of having scored 2.1 standard deviations above the mean on a test standardized on students six to seven years his senior. The conversation between Christopher (CO) and myself (MG) is reported verbatim.

MG: Look, Chris, do you know what the mean of a set of scores is?

CO: Oh yes, it's the average of the scores.

MG: Okay, now do you know what I mean if I talk about a standard deviation?

CO: Not really, but I can make a guess. I think it would be the average of all the differences from the mean.

MG: Chris, how on earth did you come at that? You're not quite there but you're awfully close.

CO: Well, the standard is sort of the *expected* score, isn't it, so it would be a kind of average in a way, and deviations are differences from the standard, so standard deviations would have to be the average of all the differences of the different scores from the mean.

From a child of 11 with no experience of statistics, this is a remarkable response. Chris has not, of course, correctly defined the standard deviation but he has intuitively grasped the concept of variability and the standard deviation's role as a measure of distance from the mean. I related this incident to Professor Julian Stanley of the SMPY Project, who promptly sent Christopher a letter commending him on his 'cleverly close' solution and enclosing a proof that the sum of the deviations of measures about their arithmetic mean is always zero (Stanley, 1988).

Many Australian schools encourage their mathematically able students to participate in Australia-wide mathematics competitions sponsored by two commercial firms, Westpac and IBM. Several of the study children have won prizes in the state and national sections of these competitions. Christopher, at age 10, was placed second in his state's section of the IBM maths competition, in which he was competing at Grade 10 level; he has received credits or distinctions in either the Westpac or IBM contest each year since first participating in 1983 at the age of 7. Normally students are not permitted, by their schools, to enter these competitions before Grade 7. Hadley's school entered him, at age 7, in the Primary Schools Mathematics Competition conducted annually within his state; entry to this contest is normally limited to Grade 6 students.

SPELLING AND WRITTEN LANGUAGE

Several of the children in this study have expressed their concern that throughout their school career teachers have repeatedly contrasted the maturity and richness of their vocabulary and the sophistication of their written language with a seeming immaturity in spelling. Accordingly, the spelling achievement of the children was assessed, during 1988 and 1989, using the *Westwood Spelling Test*. This test, described in Chapter 3, is designed to assess the spelling achievement of children aged 6 to 15½ years. It was thus judged suitable to assess the levels of spelling of all but the most verbally gifted of the study children. The children's levels of achievement on the *Westwood Spelling Test* are recorded in Table 6.3, compared with their chronological ages at the time of testing.

As can be seen from Table 6.3, all 15 of the children have spelling achievement levels which are considerably in advance of their chronological ages; indeed in seven cases (47 per cent) the child's spelling age is four or more years in advance of his/her chronological age. These children are excellent spellers.

Nevertheless, nine of the 15 reported, in personal interviews, that they are frequently criticized, by their teachers, for what the teachers term 'careless' spelling errors. These children admitted good-naturedly that they could, at times, be more careful in proof-reading their written work. However, several expressed a strong belief that their teachers' criticisms of their spelling are unduly harsh, given that the vocabulary they use in

Table 6.3 Achievement levels on *Westwood Spelling Test* compared with chronological age

Child	*Chronological age at time of testing*	*Spelling age on Westwood Spelling Test*
Adrian	Not tested	SAT–V 500+
Adam	7 yrs 5 mths	9 yrs 8 mths
Anastasia	7 yrs 7 mths	11 yrs 11 mths
Ian	9 yrs 2 mths	15 yrs 6 mths
Hadley	7 yrs 7 mths	12 yrs 6 mths
Roshni	4 yrs 11 mths	7 yrs 4 mths
Fred	Not tested	SAT–V 500
Richard	11 yrs 0 mths	15 yrs 3 mths
Rick	6 yrs 4 mths	7 yrs 10 mths
Christopher	11 yrs 6 mths	15 yrs 6 mths
Rufus	11 yrs 8 mths	13 yrs 5 mths
Jonathon	8 yrs 6 mths	13 yrs 5 mths
Cassandra	9 yrs 10 mths	15 yrs 3 mths
Jade	7 yrs 3 mths	9 yrs 5 mths
Alice	6 yrs 10 mths	9 yrs 6 mths

stories, essays and other class assignments is so much more sophisticated than that of their classmates and thus more prone to mis-spellings. Four of the children stated frankly that when they are doing written work for a teacher whom they feel is over-critical of their spelling, they will select simpler words which they are sure of being able to spell correctly, rather than risk chastisement by mis-spelling a more complex word which they know would be more appropriate to the context.

Samples of the written language of three of the children are reproduced below, with spelling and punctuation unaltered.

Foul Play at Midnight

> The sharp glistening cutlass plundered in the dimmed room. The ghastly Doctor of Homocide was laughing gleefully until he heard police sirens near the desolate location in which he committed his last murder. Desperately, the Doctor sped from the factory into a camouflaged escape vehicle. Alas, the tyrant roams again.
>
> (Rufus, aged 11)

(This was Rufus's entry in a contest, run by a major newspaper, which challenged readers to write a mini-saga in 50 words.)

(Untitled)

(The following passage forms part of a 'gothic romance' written by

Cassandra for her personal enjoyment. The hero, Jonus, has proposed marriage to Adeline, who is many years older than he.)

> 'No, child. I couldn't marry you. You know that.'
> Jonus stared into her face, feeling as if he had had a blow across his head with a metal bar.
> 'Child?' he murmered.
> He pulled himself together and said, 'Then I must go away. Forever.'
> Adeline watched as he hung his head and trudged back to his home, his whole body limp and exhausted with all the emotional strength draining out like water. She sighed slowly and went into her house.
>
> ---
>
> Jonus sat in his green kingdom of leaves and grass. He glanced at his body. It was thin and bony from malnutrition and too much exercise. These last few days he had tried to empty his head of all the memories of his home town. He had concentrated on the woodpecker which was pecking at its tree, and the squirel which was collecting nuts for the winter.
>
> (Cassandra, aged 11)

A 'P' Story

> Ploto the platapus invited emey emu to his place. They played pluck the plump plums. Plop plop on the plate the plentiful plums droped. Plainly they needed a plan. They planted a plank on a plastic platfome. Please said a plump plumber fixing a plug – dont let those plums drop on me. 'yes' said Ploto the platapus. Plop plop the plums fell on the plump plumber.
>
> (Adam, aged 6)

The minor spelling errors in these passages of prose should not distract the reader from the atmosphere of humor, melodrama or pathos which the writer is trying to evoke by his/her deliberate choice of language or use of phrasing. The linguistic skill employed by Adam in his platypus story at the age of 6 stands in vivid contrast to the work of a child three years his senior, which was placed adjacent to Adam's story in a school publication.

> The seagull glides above the shore,
> Thinking the whole place was a bore,
> So he started looking for fun
> but a man started shooting at him with a gun,

he hid behind some trees
but he found that the tree was full of bees,
he ducked down behind a bush and counted to one
and shot the man with his gun.

(Boy, aged 9)

The forced juggling with tense and metre to accommodate the needs of the rhyme scheme is characteristic of children of this age, but the result is clumsy and the poem itself holds little coherence or sense. Perhaps its virtue, for the teacher who chose to publish it, lies in the fact that it contains no spelling errors!

COMPARISON OF ACHIEVEMENT LEVELS IN READING, MATHEMATICS AND SPELLING

It is instructive to compare the levels of achievement of the study children in different subject fields. As in some cases the standardized tests of mathematics, reading and spelling were administered at intervals of some months, it is not always possible to make a direct comparison of a child's achievement level in one subject as against his achievement level in other subjects.

What are more directly comparable, however, are the levels of the child's advancement in the three subject fields, that is, the difference between the child's chronological age and the age level relative to his achievement on the various tests. These differences are displayed in Table 6.4. As the *Neale Analysis of Reading*, the *Westwood Test of Spelling*, the *Leicester Number Test* and the *Nottingham Number Test* are normed in age equivalents, it is possible to calculate the child's degree of advancement in years and months by subtracting his chronological age from his achievement age. The *Cooperative Achievement Test–Arithmetic*, however, is normed in grade equivalents, and the *Scholastic Aptitude Test–Mathematics* does not permit of interpretation in either age or grade equivalents. Accordingly, it is not possible to calculate with any degree of precision a child's degree of advancement on the two latter tests and scores on these tests are simply recorded as a percentile of a given grade level cohort (*CAT*) or as a scaled score (*SAT–M*).

A striking characteristic of these exceptionally gifted children is the sheer breadth of their talent. Each of the 15 children reported here displays achievement levels at least one year in advance of his or her chronological ages in all three subject areas. Adrian, Ian, Hadley, Fred and Christopher achieve, in all three areas – reading, mathematics and spelling – at levels four or more years beyond their chronological age. Particularly in the younger children – Hadley, at age 7 and Ian, at age 9

Table 6.4 Children's degrees of advancement in reading, mathematics and spelling

	Advancement beyond chronological age		
Child	*in reading*	*in mathematics*	*in spelling*
Adrian	SAT–V 660 at age 13	SAT–M 760 at age 8	SAT–V 660 at age 13
Adam	RA: 4 yrs 1 mth RC: 4 yrs 3 mths	3 yrs 0 mths	2 yrs 3 mths
Anastasia	RA: 4 yrs 6 mths CA: 5 yrs 0 mths	2 yrs 6 mths	4 yrs 4 mths
Ian	RA: 3 yrs 10 mths RC: 3 yrs 3 mths	SAT–M 560 at age 9	6 yrs 3 mths
Hadley	RA: 4 yrs 7 mths RC: 3 yrs 6 mths	78th %ile of Grade 7 (CAT) at age 7	4 yrs 11 mths
Roshni	RA: 3 yrs 3 mths RC: 2 yrs 5 mths	3 yrs 0 mths	2 yrs 5 mths
Fred	SAT–V 500 at age 12	SAT–M 640 at age 12	SAT–V 500 at age 12
Richard	SAT–V 360 at age 11	SAT–M 780 at age 12	SAT–V 360 at age 11
Rick	RA: 3 yrs 3 mths RC: 3 yrs 5 mths	3 yrs 0 mths	18 mths
Christopher	SAT–V 580 at age 11	SAT–M 710 at age 11	4 yrs 0 mths
Rufus	RA: 16 mths RC: 16 mths	80th %ile of Grade 7 (CAT) at age 11	21 mths
Jonathon	RA: 3 yrs 9 mths RC: 3 yrs 8 mths	77th %ile of Grade 7 (CAT) at age 9	4 yrs 11 mths
Cassandra	SAT–V 350 at age 11	50th %ile of Grade 7 (CAT) at age 11	5 yrs 5 mths
Jade	RA: 3 yrs 0 mths RC: 3 yrs 11 mths	12 mths	2 yrs 2 mths
Alice	RA: 3 yrs 11 mths RC: 4 yrs 4 mths	2 yrs 6 mths	2 yrs 8 mths

RA = Neale Reading Accuracy RC = Neale Reading Comprehension

– such remarkable levels of academic advancement indicate a truly exceptional potential for scholastic success.

This potential, however, is not always recognized by the school, or even by the child herself. Jade was surprised and delighted by her score on the *Leicester Number Test*; she had frequently been told by her teacher, and consequently believed, that she was 'weak' in maths. Christopher, aged 11, was amazed by his score of 580 on the *SAT–V* as his teachers had led him to believe that while his mathematical abilities were phenomenal, his verbal skills were only slightly superior to those of his age-peers. The parents of the children in this study speak feelingly of their frustration in having to convince teacher after teacher, as their child passes through school, that the child's academic talent is not confined to the subject field in which it is most immediately visible.

THE AUSTRALIAN VIEW OF GIFTEDNESS AS FIELD-SPECIFIC

The reluctance of schools and teachers to recognize the breadth of these children's talent owes much to the perception, held by many educators in Australia, that the academic ability of the intellectually gifted child is generally manifested in *one* specific field of talent, rather than in several subject areas.

As noted earlier, the major models of giftedness which have powered this field of education since the early 1960s have emphasized that giftedness is a multi-faceted construct, and that children do not need to be gifted 'across the board' but may have the potential to excel in a single performance area. Almost without exception, however, these definitions also alert the practitioner that many gifted children may excel in several or all of the areas under consideration. The Marland definition, for example, emphasizes that gifted children have the potential to demonstrate high performance in any of its six areas of ability 'singly or in combination' (Marland, 1972, p. 2). Gagné (1985, p. 108) defines giftedness as 'competence which is distinctly above average in one or more domains of ability' and talent as 'performance which is distinctly above average in one or more fields of human performance'. Gagné further points out that giftedness in even a single domain of ability can contribute to excellence in several fields of talent.

There are undoubtedly some gifted students whose exceptionality does rest in a single area of endeavour. However, there are many more who excel in several areas. In general, empirical studies of gifted and talented students which have assessed the children's abilities and achievements through standardized testing as well as through teacher judgment have established that in the considerable majority of cases gifted students equal or exceed the norms for children of their age *in most areas* of academic development (Terman, 1926; Barbe, 1956; Witty, 1958, DeHaan and

Havighurst, 1961). The interlinkage of academic aptitudes is especially noticeable in studies of the highly and exceptionally gifted, such as Terman's sub-group of subjects of IQ 170+ (Burks, Jensen and Terman, 1930), Hollingworth's longitudinal study of children of IQ 180+ (Hollingworth, 1942), and the SMPY investigations of mathematically precocious students (Stanley, 1976b). It is not surprising, therefore, that the children of this study possess multiple talents. Rather, it is of concern that in so many cases their teachers should view their ability as unidimensional.

Many researchers including Robinson (1977), Renzulli (1978), Tannenbaum (1983) and Feldhusen (1986) have argued, wisely, that we should try to identify and cater for able students with specific talents as well as those who possess all-round ability. Underachieving gifted students, for example, may display a high level of expertise in a field of special knowledge and interest, while displaying little ability or interest in other subject areas (Whitmore, 1980). Unfortunately, some Australian teachers misinterpret these caveats as implying that gifted students rarely possess multiple talents; these teachers are consequently reluctant to acknowledge that children such as Adrian, Christopher or Hadley can possess exceptional talents in many subject areas, or that others such as Ian, Anastasia or Richard can display truly remarkable levels of giftedness in a specific subject field and still perform at a level years ahead of their age-peers in all other areas.

The Australian perception of giftedness as field-specific has been strengthened by its inclusion in a number of state policy documents. The New South Wales Government has gone so far as to generate, for its own use, separate definitions of giftedness and talent based on this premise.

> Gifted students are those with the potential to exhibit superior performance across a range of areas of endeavour.
>
> Talented students are those with the potential to exhibit superior performance in one area of endeavour.
>
> (New South Wales Government, 1991, p. 3)

The New South Wales Government strategy for the education of gifted and talented children is, in my view, by far the most far-sighted and potentially productive of any of the Australian state policies in gifted education. It is unfortunate, however, that the policy developers have chosen to construct a definition which is grounded neither in the research on human abilities nor in gifted education, and which can only strengthen the existing misconception, among many teachers, that the majority of highly able students are talented only in one field or subject area.

Grinder (1985) has traced the development, through the eighteenth and nineteenth centuries, of the belief that genius was a symptom of hereditary degeneration (Lombroso, 1891) or neuropathology (James, 1902) and that in consequence intellectually gifted persons were likely to be eccentric, deficient in moral stamina, or lacking in emotional stability. Even Terman, in the early years of his career, worked on the premise that children of extraordinary intellectual potential tended towards emotional instability (Terman, 1905). Hollingworth noted the prevalence of this view in the early 1930s, but astutely recognized it as 'founded on nothing more substantial than the human craving for a just nature that will somehow penalize the lucky and equalize biological wealth' (Hollingworth, 1931, p. 4). However, whereas few American educators in the 1980s would seriously suggest that intellectual giftedness is correlated with emotional instability, this belief is still powerful enough in Australia for a group of educational researchers to list it, in 1981, as one of the factors which militate against the establishment of appropriate educational programmes for intellectually gifted children (Australian Schools Commission, 1981).

Only a few weeks ago I was phoned, in my university office, by a lady seeking advice on her son who was, by her account, seriously underachieving in elementary school. As she described him, the boy indeed seemed extremely intelligent but absolutely uninterested in the curriculum that was being offered to him. Her main concern, however, seemed to be to assure me that, although extremely bright, he was 'normal'. Several times in our fifteen minute conversation she used phrases such as, 'He's not one of these weird kids you read about', 'His behaviour isn't deviant in any way' and 'He's very bright but quite emotionally healthy and I want to keep him that way.' Feeling that it might be useful for both her son and herself to be able to meet other gifted students and their parents, I suggested that she might contact her local association for gifted and talented children, and arrange for him to attend some of their weekend enrichment classes. 'Oh no,' she blurted out. 'I don't want to meet a lot of peculiar people.'

The Australian view of giftedness as field-specific, coupled with the powerful stereotype of the gifted child as one whose emotional development must be stringently monitored, strengthens the existing tendency of many Australian teachers to work from a deficit model in their response to intellectual giftedness. Rather than developing curricula to enrich and enhance the gifted child's identified area of talent, or being alerted, by the discovery of one talent, to the possible existence of others, the Australian teacher is more likely to look for an area of academic weakness which she can work to rectify. Adam Murphy, since entering school at age 5, has been subjected to continual intervention designed to 'neaten' his handwriting, while his advancement in reading and mathematics, four years and three years respectively beyond his chronological age, has never been adequately addressed; this has been despite the Education Department psychologist's assurance to Adam's class teachers that his handwriting is normal for his age and requires no remediation. Where a child has no visible area of academic weakness, as in the case of Rick Ward, the school may decide that, in order to forestall possible emotional difficulties in later years, his academic progress should be deliberately decelerated in order to decrease the gap between his achievements and those of his age-peers.

The schools' response to the academic abilities of the children in this study, including the use of inappropriate and unnecessary remediation procedures, will be discussed at length in Chapter 8.

SUMMARY

Hollingworth (1942) and Terman (1925) proposed that early reading was one of the most powerful indicators of possible intellectual giftedness. Both the children of IQ 170+ studied by Terman and the subjects of IQ 180+ followed by Hollingworth read at very early ages. Of the 15 children in this study 14 were reading before their fifth birthday, and 10 began reading before their third birthday. Adrian, Adam, Anastasia and Ian read before the age of two.

Nine of the 14 families whose children read before school entry report that the child learned to read either with no assistance or with only minimal assistance from the parents. Several of the parents were strongly advised by their friends not to assist their children's reading development in any way, even although the children were actually asking to be shown how to read! These 'self-taught' readers received much of their stimulation from street signs, labels in supermarkets, or names of shops. Adrian and Fred taught themselves to read by watching *Sesame Street*. The remaining five families report that they gave moderate amounts of assistance in the development of their child's reading.

In the homes of these 15 families reading is modelled by the parents as a valued and loved activity. Twelve of them have more than 500 books in the home, and five families have more than 1,000 books. Reading was named by 40 per cent of the parents as one of their most enjoyable leisure-time activities, and these parents undertook deliberately to pass on this enthusiasm by reading to their children from the earliest months. Not surprisingly, the children responded with a passionate interest in books. In several cases 'book' or 'read' was one of the first words the child learned to say, and most of the parents report that the young child demanded to be read to at every opportunity.

The experience of these parents reveals that there is little to be gained from 'withholding' reading from a child who has already demonstrated unusually high intellectual potential, and is asking to be shown how to read. Rewarding the eagerness of such a child by giving him or her moderate amounts of assistance in recognizing and decoding letters is not 'pushing'; it is simply acknowledging that the child is ready, rather earlier than his age-peers, to begin acquiring the skills of reading. Exceptionally gifted children who have demonstrated a precocious development of speech and movement are likely to develop reading skills considerably earlier than their age-peers.

It is important to note that the children have not been 'developmental spurters'. The precocity in reading which became evident at remarkably early ages has stayed with them through their school careers. Even those children who at school are required, by the constraints of an inappropriate curriculum, to read books which are suitable for their age-peers of average ability, are reading at home, with full comprehension and enjoyment, books written for children several years their senior. It is important that the teachers of such children provide them with materials appropriate to their reading levels and reading interests, undeterred by the erroneous supposition that the child's advancement in reading is temporary and will 'plateau' in later years.

Many of the children display quite remarkable degrees of mathematical precocity and five of the 15 scored above the mean on the *SAT* at or before the age of 12. Their exceptional gift for maths was clearly visible even in early childhood.

Several of the children report that their teachers regularly complain about their 'poor' spelling. All 15 of the children, however, have spelling achievement levels considerably in advance of their chronological ages and more than half display the spelling achievement that one would expect from children more than four years their senior. It would seem that their teachers are noticing only the occasional errors in the children's writing and failing to notice that their written vocabulary and syntax are in fact many years in advance of their age.

The sheer breadth of these children's abilities contradicts the Australian perception of giftedness as field-specific. As in many other studies of intellectually gifted students, all 15 children display achievement levels in advance of their peers on all the academic variables studied here. Five of the subjects achieve four or more years beyond their chronological age in maths, reading and spelling. Their teachers, however, persist in viewing them as gifted only in the subject area in which their precocity is most immediately noticeable.

7

READING DEVELOPMENT AND RECREATIONAL INTERESTS

When your mind feels restrained and boxed in on four sides with superficial teachers, boring school days and no challenge whatsoever, I recommend the world's best antidote. This secret remedy is simply reading. Books truly open up whole new worlds. When your own life becomes dull and monotonous, you can easily delve into someone else's through books. I can throw myself, mind and body, into a good book and watch reality slip away. There is so much to be learned – limitations at school shouldn't stop you. Remember, books are a great place to visit, and, you know, sometimes I wouldn't mind living there.

(Gifted high school student writing in *On Being Gifted*, 1978, p. 34)

When Emma was in Grade 7, her mother commented that she had completely floored one of her school friends by wanting to discuss the Czechoslovakian struggle for freedom from the U. S. S. R. Emma has since decided that there are more acceptable topics of conversation, such as clothes and boys.

(Bowmaker, 1991, p. 16)

It is futile and probably wholly unsound psychologically to strive to interest the child above 170 IQ in ring-around-the-rosy or blind man's buff. Many well-meaning persons speak of such efforts as 'socializing the child' but it is probably not in this way that the very gifted can be socialized.

(Hollingworth, 1926, p. 272)

As has already been described, the majority of the children in this study had developed, by the time they entered school, the reading accuracy and reading comprehension skills of children at least three years their senior. By the time they were 5 years of age, they had access, through the books, magazines and newspapers in the home, to information, views and attitudes which many of their age-peers would not encounter until half way through elementary school. The accelerative influence of this early access to an 'information bank' normally reserved for children several years their senior is evident in almost every area of development addressed in this chapter; the children's hobbies, their enthusiasms, their preferred reading materials, their play interests and their friendship choices resemble those of children four or five years older than they. It is appropriate, therefore, that this chapter should commence with an analysis of the reading habits and interests of the subject group.

The love of reading, and its importance to the children, can hardly be over-estimated. Five of the 15 children have stated that reading is the most important thing in their lives. Many of them echoed the sentiments expressed by the American high school student whose comments head this chapter.

One of the questionnaires completed by the children and their parents, Questionnaire 4, (Appendix D), sought information on the children's play interests and spare time activities. As part of this questionnaire, the children were given a list of eight leisure time activities generally enjoyed by elementary school students, and were asked to order the activities from 1 to 8 in terms of their own personal preferences; thus the activity which the child enjoyed most of the eight listed would be ordered '1' while the activity enjoyed least would be ordered '8'. The eight activities which the child was required to order were listed in Question 31 as follows:

Reading
Sports
Puzzles, board games or video games
Playing music or listening to music
Working with computers (but not video games)
Writing, drawing or painting
Radio or TV
Playing, socializing

By far the most highly favoured activity was reading. Responses to this question will be analysed more fully later in this chapter; it is, however, interesting to note that even the activity which was rated in second place, playing with puzzles, board games or video games, came nowhere close to approaching the popularity of reading. VanTassel-Baska, from whose survey of the 1982 Midwest Talent Search Finalists this question was taken, also found that reading was listed as the favourite leisure pastime by the majority of her respondents (VanTassel-Baska, 1983).

The parents in this study actively foster their children's love of books and valuing of reading. In a study of the home environment of extremely gifted mathematical and verbal reasoners, Benbow found that approximately 56 per cent of the families which she surveyed owned more than 500 books, as compared to only 12 per cent of a comparison group of families of moderately gifted children (Benbow, 1985b). An even greater proportion of the Australian families – 80 per cent – have more than 500 books in the home, and 33 per cent have more than 1,000 books.

FREQUENCY AND EXTENT OF READING

As might be expected from these findings, all 40 children in the study are frequent and copious readers. In June 1988, Questionnaire 3: Reading Record (Appendix C) was sent to the parents of the subject group. This questionnaire was modelled on one which was sent by Terman in the early 1920s to the parents of his subject group (Terman, 1926) and sought the following information:

— Parents were requested to record the amount of time the child spent in voluntary reading each day. Reading undertaken at school or for other formal study requirements was not included.
— Parents were requested to record each day, for a period of four weeks, every book, journal or magazine which the subject child read for pleasure.
— Parents were requested to classify each book read by the child according to the Classification Table supplied with the Questionnaire (Appendix C).
— Children were requested to list, to a maximum of 10, books which were their special favourites. These did not have to be books which the children read in the four-week period of record-keeping; however, they had to have been read during the previous two years.
— The children were asked to write, for each of these favourite books, a short paragraph explaining why they had particularly enjoyed it.

This Reading Record differs in two respects from the reading questionnaire developed by Terman. Firstly, Terman required the parents of his subjects to record their children's reading over a period of eight weeks. The present study limited the survey period to four weeks because of a concern that a longer period of supervision might put undue pressure on the children's mothers, the majority of whom work outside the home on a full-time or part-time basis. Secondly, Terman required the parents of his subjects to record the time which the child spent in reading each day, and the type of books read, but he did not require the authors and titles of the books to be recorded. The present study, by contrast, sought daily listings of the specific books, journals and magazines read by the subjects, in the belief that this more detailed survey would permit a more comprehensive analysis of the children's reading interests.

A number of the parents commented that making this survey of their child's reading habits had been an instructive and illuminating experience; before beginning the survey they had not been fully aware of the extent and frequency of their child's reading. Several parents described, in some embarrassment, the difficulties that can arise when a child becomes so immersed in a specially favoured book that he refuses to be separated from it even on shopping expeditions, trips to the dentist or visits to elderly relatives.

> Some of my friends tell me about the difficulties they have in getting their children to read. The problem we have with Alice is to get her to *stop* reading long enough to do anything else – like going to the shops or doing her piano practice! If we go out, no matter for how short a time, a book or a couple of books go in the car with us. It is very difficult to make a proper record of the amount she reads because very often we find her reading at the same time as doing something else.
>
> (Bianca Marlow, mother of Alice)

The parents of 10 of the 15 children reported that their child read so much and at so many different times of the day that the hours recorded on the reading record may not have represented the full extent of his or her voluntary reading; for example, several commented that their child regularly read during the night hours during periods of wakefulness, or in the early morning before rising. The unusual sleep patterns of the subject children were discussed in Chapter 4.

Typical of the parents' comments was that of Joseph, father of Gabrielle, one of the children in the total sample. Gabrielle was, at the time, 6 years 2 months old.

> She usually reads for at least an hour a night in bed, at a rate of about 90–100 pages an hour, as well as intermittent reading during the day (in between other projects – she is nearly always busy). We find it quite difficult to maintain an adequate supply of suitable literature, and she does quite a bit of rereading (which she likes). Not infrequently, one of us will go down to her room at 2 or 3 a.m., to find her reading, having already finished an entire book! We discourage this, as she tends to be rather grumpy the next morning – she needs her sleep!

Data on the frequency and amount of reading among the exceptionally gifted children of this study should therefore be regarded as a conservative estimate of the actual time these children spend in reading for pleasure.

Table 7.1 details the average number of hours per week which the children were reported as spending in voluntary reading over a four-week period between June and August, 1988.

As mentioned earlier, the parents of Terman's gifted group kept a record, over the space of two months, of the amount of time the children spent reading *at home* each week, the number of books which were read, and the type of books which the children selected (Terman, 1926). The results were compared with those of a control group of children of similar

Table 7.1 Average number of hours per week spent in reading for pleasure, compared with means of Terman's 1926 study

Child	Chronological age at time of survey			
	5–6 years	*7–8 years*	*9–10 years*	*11–12 years*
Jade	9.5			
Roshni	5			
Rick	3			
Anastasia	7			
Adam	6.75			
Hadley	4			
Alice		6.5		
Jonathon		7.5		
Cassandra			10	
Ian			2.25	
Adrian				9
Rufus				6.5
Christopher				7.5
Fred				17
Richard				6
Terman's mean: boys	2.9	7.2	9.6	10.44
Terman's mean: girls	2.9	6.16	8.29	9.97

age. The number of hours spent in voluntary reading by the gifted group increased from six hours per week at age 7 to 12 hours per week at age 13. The average 7-year-old in the gifted group read more books in the two-month period than the mean of the control group for any age up to 15, and the average number of books read by the gifted group at age 8–9 was three times that for the control group at the same age. The teachers of the gifted group rated 88 per cent of this group as reading more than the average, as opposed to only 33 per cent of the control group (Terman, 1926).

Teachers participating in a later study undertaken by Witty and Lehman of 50 subjects whose IQs ranged from 140 to 183, reported similar results. The amount of time the gifted subjects spent in reading far surpassed that spent by age-peers of average ability (Witty and Lehman, 1936).

Anderson, Tollefson and Gilbert (1985) examined the frequency and type of reading among 276 gifted students in Grades 1–12. In this study the average number of books per month decreased significantly as the gifted children passed through school, from 19.5 in primary grades to 3.3 in senior high school. These figures are no doubt influenced by the increasing length and complexity of books selected as children mature. However, the study also revealed a shift in attitude towards reading as a pastime; whereas 90 per cent of the elementary and junior high students reported that they read chiefly by personal choice, only 65 per cent of the senior high students gave personal choice as their primary reason for reading.

When the subjects of the present study are categorized in terms of the age-ranges used by Terman for his reading survey of the gifted group (Terman, 1926) the resultant subgroups are so small as to render even non-parametric statistical procedures inappropriate. Nevertheless, it is fascinating to compare the individual scores of the 15 children with the mean scores of the Terman group in each age-range. Each of the six children aged 5–6 years spends more time per week in reading than did the average child of that age in Terman's gifted group, while in the three older age-ranges, Jonathon, Alice, Cassandra and Fred also read more than did the average child of their age in Terman's gifted sample. Comparing the subjects of the two studies across age-ranges, 10 of the 15 children (67 per cent) exceed the mean number of hours spent reading by their gifted age-peers in Terman's study more than 60 years previously. This is an astonishing result. One might surely have expected that the enticements of television, videos and personal computers, which were not available to the children of Terman's study, would have decreased the reading time of many of these present-day children.

Although the data on the subject group as a whole are extremely useful, allowing some degree of comparability with the results of the previous reading surveys discussed in the literature review, the greater value of the reading record lies in the insights it provides to the reading habits of the subjects as individuals. By far the most prolific reader of the group was Fred Campbell, who at age 11 was reading for an average of 17 hours per week, almost twice as much as any other boy in the study. Yet Fred's mother, Eleanor, commented, in a letter accompanying the completed questionnaire, that the time Fred spent in reading had declined significantly in the previous few months since acquiring a personal computer!

By contrast Ian, aged 9, who five years previously had been reading stories to his classmates at pre-school, had reduced his personal reading to two hours per week, because one of his other interests had supplanted his love of reading. Ian's early preoccupation with road maps has developed to the point where it dominates his waking hours. Cartography is his joy and his obsession. By the age of 10, Ian could identify and classify, in terms of the Department of Main Roads descriptors, any major or minor road in his home city of 1 million people. He was almost as skillful in his analyses of the road systems of other states. When he was not absorbed in his collection of Australian street directories, he was drawing maps to demonstrate his theories of how the road systems and traffic flow of various suburbs could be improved. During his spare time, such as it was, he worked on extremely complex maths puzzles (he scored 560 on the *Scholastic Aptitude Test–Mathematics* at the age of 9 years 11 months) and listened to music. It is doubtful whether he could have fitted in the time to read more than he did.

NUMBER OF SOURCES READ FROM PER WEEK

During the initial months of the study, when I was getting to know the children and their families, several of the parents mentioned to me, as a curiosity, that their children tended to read from a number of different sources concurrently, rather than finishing one book or magazine before starting another. This was borne out by the results of the Reading Record questionnaire.

> Something that Alice does all the time is have several books going at once. It is annoying to us, but she seems to handle it with ease and jumps from one book to another with no trouble at all!
>
> (Bianca Marlow, mother of Alice)

Table 7.2 records the number of different sources from which the study children read during the survey period, averaged across the four weeks.

As Terman did not require the parents of his gifted group to record the number of books read each day by these children, it is not possible to compare the variability in the number of reading sources of the children in the Californian and Australian studies. It is interesting to note, however, that when the number of hours spent in reading per week (Table 7.1) is compared with the number of sources read from (Table 7.2) a pattern emerges which was also noted by Anderson, Tollefson and Gilbert

Table 7.2 Average number of sources read from per week

	Chronological age at time of survey			
Child	*5–6 years*	*7–8 years*	*9–10 years*	*11–12 years*
Jade	10			
Hadley	6			
Roshni	18			
Rick	9			
Anastasia	2			
Adam	13			
Jonathon		24		
Alice		6		
Cassandra			9	
Ian			4	
Richard				5
Fred				4
Christopher				22
Rufus				5
Adrian				9

in their 1985 survey of the reading habits of gifted children in Grades 1–12; the children read from a wide number of sources in the early years of schooling, but fewer books are read as they move into the later years of elementary school and progress through their secondary education. In the present study four children in the two younger age groups read from more than 10 sources during the course of the week, compared with only one child from the two older groups. However, a closer analysis of the Reading Records themselves reveal that whereas the 5-year-olds and 6-year-olds generally read shorter books which could be completed, and often are, in the course of an evening, the older children select longer and more complex books which might take several days to read. Indeed in the case of children aged 9 years and older, much of their reading is adolescent or adult fiction which the child of average ability would require some weeks to digest – always supposing, that is, that the average child could master the language and concepts!

The results of the Reading Record display considerable variability even among children in the same age group. In the 11–12 age group Fred, who was deeply absorbed in the lengthy science fantasy chronicles of David Eddings and Stephen Donaldson, read from only four sources per week, finishing one text before progressing to the next; by contrast Christopher, whose tastes were much more eclectic, ranging from Dickens and the Brontës through to the *Asterix* comics and a wide array of newspapers and journals, read from an average of 22 sources per week. Like Alice Marlow, Christopher chooses to keep several books 'in play' at any time; he selects from several different and equally satisfying sources rather as in the course of a wine-tasting the connoisseur of fine wines will savour, with appreciation and restraint, the bouquets of various great vintages. In the 5–6 age group Hadley, who was at that time absorbed in the children's mystery novels written for 9- to 12-year-olds by English author Enid Blyton, read from only six sources per week, whereas Roshni, who was in fact only 4 years 8 months old at the time of the survey, read from an average of 18 sources per week and would happily read, in the course of an evening, four or five books at a 6- or 7-year-old reading level.

READING INTERESTS AND FAVOURITE BOOKS

Terman (1926), in his study of the reading interests of his gifted subjects, found that the gifted group read over a much wider range of material than the control group. Nevertheless, books on mystery and adventure comprised 37 per cent of the gifted group's total reading over the two months of the reading survey, while informational fiction, including the classics, comprised 13 per cent, and fairy tales, folk tales and legends allowed for another 7 per cent. Lists of specially favoured books, kept by each child in the gifted group, contained a high proportion of books which are today considered classics, such as Stevenson's *Treasure Island* and *Kidnapped*, Dickens' *Oliver Twist* and *David Copperfield* and the high adventure novels of Dumas. Ten years later, Witty and Lehman (1936) confirmed the interest of gifted children in mystery and adventure, and noted the rising interest in detective fiction.

Although Terman was interested in comparing his extremely gifted subjects of IQ 170+ with the total gifted group on their early reading development, he made no formal analysis of differences in their reading habits or interests. What is available to us, however, is a series of case study analyses of seven gifted juvenile writers whom Terman discovered in the course of his wider investigations (Burks, Jensen and Terman, 1930). The mean IQ of this group was 165 with a range of 148–188. Although this group displayed wide and mature reading interests, their favourite authors at the age of 10 and 11 were Stevenson, Scott, Dickens, Swift, Tennyson and Bunyan! Terman also describes a 7-year-old with a mental age of 13 whose favourite reading was Gibbons' *Decline and Fall of the Roman Empire* (Burks, Jensen and Terman, 1930).

Terman (1926) noted that the most striking contrast between the gifted group and the control group was in the age at which different books were read. Books that were preferred by the control group children aged 11 or 12 were read with enjoyment by the gifted child of 8 or 9. The precocity in reading development which was so noticeable in the pre-school gifted child persisted through the elementary school years which were the focus of the first phase of Terman's study. Like the children of the present study, the Terman subjects were not 'developmental spurters'.

How have the reading interests of highly gifted children changed over the last 50 years?

In the first years of the 1980s, Flack, comparing the reading interests of 10 highly gifted Indiana adolescents, noted that 'every subject listed science fiction and/or science fantasy as his or her favourite literature form or genre' (Flack, 1983, p. 219). Two years later Kolloff (1985) reported on the reading preferences of 201 gifted students in Grades 3–9. These students displayed an overwhelming preference for science fiction (preferred by 40 per cent of the subjects), fantasy (36 per cent) and mystery (34 per cent). Surprisingly, although only 2 per cent of the sample actually stated that they preferred the classics, 43 per cent listed books which would be considered classics in their lists of favourite books. The highly gifted students studied by VanTassel-Baska (1983) were avid readers with 75 per cent of the students listing reading as their favourite leisure-time activity. Interestingly, the reading interests of VanTassel-Baska's subjects differed very little from those of Kolloff's (1985) moderately gifted sample, with 54 per cent listing science fiction as the preferred genre, 29 per cent listing fantasy and 24 per cent mystery. Only 4 per cent of the students listed the classics as a favourite genre; however, the discrepancy which

Kolloff noted between the percentage reporting the classics as a favoured genre and the considerably larger percentage actually listing specific 'classic' novels as personal favourites could suggest that children in the 1980s may be unclear as to the precise meaning of the term.

As noted earlier, the parents in the present study kept records, over the four weeks of the reading survey, of every book, newspaper, journal or magazine read by their subject children, and classified each reading source using a table provided with the Questionnaire (Appendix C). This has enabled a thorough analysis of the reading choices of individual children at this period of their lives.

Like the gifted groups studied by Terman (1926), Witty and Lehman (1936) and VanTassel-Baska (1983), the subjects of this study read over a wide area. Typical of the group was Jonathon, aged 8 years 9 months at the time of the survey, who was reading folk tales and legends, adult sports magazines, children's and adults' reference books and encyclopedias, adventure, fantasy, humour and children's comics. The children read a considerable amount of nonfiction, although the interest in biography which was reported by Terman did not appear so strongly in this group.

Amongst the 5- and 6-year-olds both boys and girls showed a strong preference for fantasy and adventure stories. The adventure and mystery novels of Enid Blyton were extremely popular and were read during the four weeks by four of the six children in this age range, although Blyton's *Toytown* books such as the *Little Noddy* stories, which were written specifically for children of this age, had already been outgrown. Nature and animal books were popular with both sexes, as were children's reference books. The boys enjoyed myths and legends from other cultures, while the girls preferred the same story themes couched in the form of fairy tales. These findings, apart from the popularity of Blyton, who is not represented to any significant extent in the American studies, are congruent with those of the studies discussed previously.

By contrast, findings for the 9- to 10-year-old and 11- to 12-year-old age groups demonstrate a distinct shift away from the reading interests displayed by gifted age-peers in studies conducted before 1980. The 7- to 8-year-old boys showed a strong preference for adolescent and adult comic books such as the *Asterix* series, in which humour is based in satire or parody; this type of humour was not readily available to children at the time of the Terman (1926) or Witty and Lehman (1936) studies. However, these boys conformed in some degree to the earlier studies by displaying a liking for factual texts on chemistry, geology and technology. The 7- to 8-year-old girls had developed an interest in mystery, particularly detection of the *Agaton Sax*, *Encyclopedia Brown* genre. Both genders enjoyed the whimsical humour of Roald Dahl.

The 9- to 12-year-olds continued to enjoy *Asterix* and other pictorial humour such as the *Garfield* comic books. However, the most significant development in the children's reading interests during this period is what can justifiably be termed a fascination with the more serious modes of adult science fiction and science fantasy by authors such as Arthur C. Clarke and Stephen Donaldson. This absorbing interest in science fantasy is often heralded by an earlier involvement with the 'middle-earth' novels of Tolkein and the *Narnia* series of C. S. Lewis. The high level of interest in science fiction mirrors the findings of VanTassel-Baska and Flack in their 1983 studies of highly gifted mathematical and verbal reasoners.

The children were required to list up to 10 books which they regarded as personal favourites, and write, for each, a short paragraph explaining their choice. These books must have been read, or reread, at some time during the previous two years.

It is when these 'favourites' lists are analysed that it becomes evident that these exceptionally gifted children differ radically from the moderately gifted children of previous studies, both in the books which they nominate as favourite reading and in the age at which they read these books. Adam, at 6 years 10 months, read during the four-week period, and nominated as favourites, Lewis Carroll's *Alice in Wonderland*, Charles Kingsley's children's classic *The Water Babies* and Arthur Ransome's *The Picts and the Martyrs*. Anastasia, also aged 6 years 10 months, read Robert Louis Stevenson's *Child's Garden of Verses*, *Moomin Summer* and *Moomin Madness* by Tove Jansson, and a whole series of *National Geographic* magazines. Fred, aged 11 years 4 months, was devouring the adult science fantasy novels of David Eddings. Christopher, aged 11 years 5 months, voluntarily listed books which he had read, and particularly valued, over the previous six months; the list included *David Copperfield* and *Nicholas Nickleby*, *Jane Eyre*, *Wuthering Heights*, *Tess of the D'Urbervilles* and the collected short stories of American author O. Henry.

Terman, in 1926, noted that the children in his gifted group tended to read books which were preferred by children of average ability some three years older than they. Each of the 15 children of the present study was reading, with full comprehension and enjoyment, literature which is written for, and preferred by, young people five to seven years their senior. This can lead to severe problems of salience and possible social rejection should the exceptionally gifted child try to share his reading interests with age-peers. It would have been extremely difficult for Christopher to find another 11-year-old with whom he could discuss his keen interest in the social problems of Victorian England as portrayed in the novels of Charles Dickens. It would be virtually impossible for a child like Anastasia, who at 7½ discovered with delight Richard Adams' *Watership Down*, to find another 7-year-old with whom she could share her pleasure in the subtleties of language and dry humour of this novel.

THE IMPACT OF 'HIGH FANTASY'

A striking finding of this study is the virtual absence of the classics from the children's list of reading preferences. This stands in vivid contrast not only to the case studies of exceptionally gifted children undertaken in the first half of this century (Dolbear, 1912; Terman and Fenton, 1921; Goldberg, 1934) but also to the 1980s studies of Kolloff (1985) and Van Tassel-Baska (1983). Apart from Adam's selection of Charles Kingsley's *The Water Babies* and Christopher's enjoyment of Dickens and the Brontës, the classics are quite unrepresented. The historical novels of Sir Walter Scott, which featured so strongly in the reading lists of Terman's prodigious young writers (Burks, Jensen and Terman, 1930) and the profoundly gifted children studied by Hollingworth (1942), are ignored by these extremely gifted children, 50–60 years later.

The emotional and moral development of exceptionally gifted children will be discussed at length in Chapter 9; however, it is important to note at this time the general agreement among previous researchers studying the exceptionally and profoundly gifted (McElwee, 1934; Hollingworth, 1942; Zorbaugh, Boardman and Sheldon, 1951) that these children develop, at an early age, a precocious interest in matters of morality and religion. Hollingworth found that religious questioning, the search for a personal system of morality and 'a definite demand for a systematic philosophy of life and death' (Hollingworth, 1942, p. 280) generally begins when a child reaches a mental age of 12 or 13; the majority of the children of this study would have attained a mental age of 12 by the chronological age of 7½.

It is natural that the social isolation which is often reported as characterizing extremely gifted children (Burks, Jensen and Terman, 1930; DeHaan and Havighurst, 1961; Janos, 1983) coupled with their hunger for reading, should lead them to turn to books for answers to the moral questions that besiege them. The novels of Scott, Hugo and Dumas, which appeared so frequently in the reading choices of the profoundly gifted young people of the 1920s and 1930s, pose moral and ethical questions which might be particularly attractive to exceptionally gifted children whose intellectual precocity and accelerated moral development urge them to develop a personal belief system at a much younger age than is customary. If this need is still characteristic of the extremely gifted, and if the highly gifted children of recent studies are not turning to the classics to serve this need, it is interesting to speculate whether another literary genre may have replaced the classics for the children of the 1980s.

Kolloff's 1985 survey and the present study differ from the studies of the first half of this century in the prominence of what Halstead (1988) terms 'high fantasy' both in the children's day-to-day reading and in their lists of favourite books. For children in the younger age groups, 'high fantasy' encompasses C. S. Lewis's *Chronicles of Narnia*, the Madeleine L'Engle series which begins with *A Wrinkle in Time*, and Ursula LeGuin's *Earthsea Trilogy*. For the older children it is characterized by Ray Bradbury's *Martian Chronicles*, the *Dune* series of Frank Herbert and Stephen Donaldson's *The Chronicles of Thomas Covenant, an Unbeliever*.

The frequency with which the term 'chronicles' is used either as a title or a descriptor of these series is no accident; the series trace the moral or ethical growth of the key characters within the framework of the development of a society, and the passage of time is frequently used as a metaphor for personal or societal growth. This tradition springs directly from the great classics of earlier times; the powerful contrast of the ethical growth of Jean Valjean placed against the crumbling French society of *Les Miserables* can be compared with Virgil's technique in portraying the growth of his hero Aeneas towards moral maturity by placing it against the collapse of Trojan society. Exceptionally gifted children are able to recognize and appreciate this structural technique while, at the same time, glorying in the power of the story and identifying with the heroic figure whose triumph over hardship and doubt forms the core of the adventure.

There are many points of resemblance between high fantasy and the classics. Both may be based on an accounting and analysis of the relationships between humans and superior beings, with the humans striving against seemingly impossible odds to live up to the high ideals and honour the moral requirements which the 'gods' place upon them. The relationship between the children and the Christ-figure, Aslan, in *The Lion, the Witch and the Wardrobe* exemplifies this. In both genres a 'quest' predominates, with the protagonists drawn into the adventure often by forces beyond their control; the quest of the three children in L'Engle's *A Wrinkle in Time* parallels in many ways the pursuit of the Holy Grail in the Arthurian legends.

Both genres take their themes from the battle between good and evil; the heroes strive to attain abstract goals of honour, justice or moral perfection; soliloquies characterize both genres, both as a means of carrying the story forward and as an opportunity for the hero to reflect on the moral or ethical dilemmas which confront him. Both set their tales in lands or kingdoms divorced by time and/or space from the era of the reader; for Scott, this was Scotland of the Middle Ages or the war fields of the Crusades, while for Arthur C. Clarke and Ray Bradbury it is the cities and plains of Mars. Both genres employ battles as a metaphor for the fight against evil; significantly, these often take the form of formal passages of arms, governed by the medieval rules of chivalry. This convention may be highly attractive to the perceptive and sensitive child of high intelligence who is aware of, and perturbed by, the suddenness of death in modern warfare. A consistent theme in both the classics and high fantasy is that the evildoer is given time to repent, and true repentance may lead either to forgiveness or to an amelioration of an otherwise severe punishment. This appeals to the strong sense of justice and 'fair play' which is so much a characteristic of exceptionally gifted children (Hollingworth, 1926; Janos and Robinson, 1985).

The fascination which high fantasy holds for the majority of the 9- to 12-year-olds in this study suggests that this genre satisfies an intellectual and emotional need for these children. It may well be that exceptionally gifted children of the present day use high fantasy much as their counterparts of the 1920s and 1930s used the novels of Scott, Stevenson and Dumas, to fuel and satisfy their moral questioning.

FREQUENCY AND TYPE OF TELEVISION VIEWING

Very little research has been undertaken on the television viewing habits of intellectually gifted children. In the mid-1980s, however, three researchers decided, independently, to investigate the issue. In the United States, the Nielsen rating information on television viewing for 1985 indicated that children during that year watched alarmingly large amounts of television. Children aged 2–5 years watched an average of 28½ hours of television each week, while children aged 6–11 watched approximately 26½ hours (Nielsen, 1985).

The research undertaken during that year, and the subsequent year, however, suggests that gifted children watch considerably less television than do children of average ability. Abelman (1986), comparing 364 gifted children and 386 'traditional' [*sic*] children aged between 4 and 13 years found that the gifted children typically consumed two hours less television *each day* than did the control group.

Further differences have been found even among children at different levels of giftedness. Benbow (1985b) compared the home environments and toy preferences of two groups of gifted children – 252 *extremely* gifted mathematical and verbal reasoners (13-year-olds who had scored either 700+ on the *SAT–M* or 630+ on the *SAT–V*), and 205 moderately gifted students of similar ages (children who had scored at the 97th percentile on *in-grade* achievement tests). Benbow found significant differences in the television viewing habits of the two groups. Two-thirds (68 per cent) of the extremely precocious students reported watching less than two hours of television per day, compared with only a quarter (23 per cent) of the moderately gifted. Approximately 29 per cent of the moderately gifted students watched five hours or more of television per day, compared with only 5 per cent of the extremely precocious.

No Australian studies have been identified which examine the television viewing habits of gifted children, and the commercial firm which conducts research on the viewing habits of Australian children for the television media has indicated that it does not collect data on the amount of viewing undertaken by children, but only on the preference ratings of specific programmes (McNair Anderson, 1989). However, in Questionnaire 4: Television and computer use, play interests and spare-time activities, the children's parents were asked to record the time which their subject child spent watching television each day over a period of 14 days, to name each programme watched by the child, and to indicate which family member made the decision to view each programme. Table 7.3 depicts the average number of hours per week spent in watching television.

As noted above, the American Nielsen records for 1985 indicated that children aged 6–11 watched, on average, 26½ hours of television each week (Nielsen, 1985). All 15 of the exceptionally gifted subjects watch much less than this; five of the children watch five or fewer hours of television per week. As mentioned earlier, Benbow established, in her 1985 study of the television viewing habits of extremely precocious mathematical and verbal reasoners, that 68 per cent of these children watched fewer than two hours of television per day (14 hours per week if this is averaged across a seven-day week), as opposed to 23 per cent of a control group of moderately gifted children. Fourteen of the 15 study children have television in their homes; 12 of the 14 (86 per cent) watched television for fewer than 14 hours per week. This group uses television even less than Benbow's extremely gifted young people in the United States.

Table 7.3 Average number of hours spent per week in watching television

	Chronological age at time of survey			
Child	*5–7 years*	*8–9 years*	*10–11 years*	*12–13 years*
Jade	1.5			
Adam	2			
Hadley	13			
Roshni	2.5			
Rick	9			
Anastasia	1.5			
Jonathon		20		
Alice		9.5		
Rufus			9	
Cassandra			5	
Ian			10	
Fred				8
Christopher				21
Adrian				8.5
Richard				0*

* Richard's family does not have television

Table 7.4 gives a breakdown of the types of programme watched by the 15 children during the first week of the television survey.

Of the 129.25 hours collectively spent viewing during the first week of the television survey, 22.25 hours (17 per cent) were spent watching news, current affairs programmes and documentaries such as film of wild life safaris or travel. Family programmes, especially British and Australian series such as *Rumpole of the Bailey*, *Fawlty Towers* and *A Country Practice*

Table 7.4 Hours spent watching different types of programme during first week oftelevision survey

Child	*News/ Current events*	*Family shows or series*	*Quiz/ game shows*	*Sport*	*Children's programmes*	*Other*
Adrian	4.5	1.0			0.5	
Jade					0.25	
Alice	3.5	8.5	1.00			
Rufus	1.25	3.25	0.25			3.75
Roshni	0.25	1.0			2.5	
Rick		1.5	0.5		4.5	1.5
Anastasia		1.0			1.0	
Christopher	5.0	3.0	2.5	1.5	7.5	3.0
Jonathon	3.0	8.5	2.0		7.0	
Cassandra		4.0				
Fred	1.5	4.5				1.5
Ian	0.75	4.25	5.25	0.25	9.0	
Adam	2.0					
Hadley	0.5	6.0	1.5	3.25	0.5	
*Richard**						

* Richard's family does not have television

were extremely popular, occupying 46.5 hours, or 36 per cent of viewing time; however, several parents made a point of reporting that their children were not permitted to watch Australian or American soap operas! The relative lack of interest in sporting programmes (4 per cent) is surprising, given the almost obsessive sports-consciousness of the Australian population; however, as will be discussed later in this chapter, children in this study do not find sport particularly enthralling, either as participants or as spectators.

Programs developed specifically for children are also popular, accounting for 32.75 hours or 25 per cent of viewing time. Six of the 15 parents reported that their children were not permitted to watch cartoons; on the other hand, as will be discussed, Sally Baker at one stage 'prescribed' cartoons for Ian as a form of behavioural therapy. Game shows occupy

10 per cent of viewing time. These are generally adult quiz shows which challenge the viewer's general knowledge or reasoning ability, and parents of the older subjects report that their children enjoy pitting their wits against the adult contestants. The remaining category, 'other', generally consists of films or telemovies, and accounts for 8 per cent of viewing time.

Roderick and Jackson (1986) compared the television viewing habits and family rules of 65 matched pairs of gifted and non-gifted American students aged 9–13 years. Both that study and that of Abelman (1986) found that the parents of the more highly able students tended to monitor their children's television viewing much more closely than did the parents of the control group. Furthermore, these parents were more likely to discuss with their children the possible emotional impact of programmes which featured physical or emotional violence, whereas the parents of the non-gifted children were much less likely to 'become involved in or actively exercise control over their children's consumption, interpretation and use of television information' (Abelman, 1986, p. 27).

Like the parents of gifted students in the studies of Abelman (1986) and Roderick and Jackson (1986), the parents in this study take a keen interest in their children's television viewing, and decisions on what will be viewed by the children are generally made by the parents and children together. The parents' responses to Questionnaire 4, and their comments in my interviews with them, established that these mothers and fathers feel strongly that it is their responsibility to monitor, and when necessary veto, the viewing choices of their children. However, these decisions are not made on authoritarian grounds; rather they reflect a thoughtful and balanced approach by the parents to the question of how best to ensure that their children can benefit from the best that television can provide without being adversely influenced by its negative aspects. 'We monitor Hadley's viewing out of a concern for his welfare,' says Holly Bond, 'and to ensure that he keeps a balanced outlook on what television has to offer. We discourage too much viewing because there are so many other valuable things to do.'

> On the rare occasions when Henry and Alice do ask to watch something that we consider unsuitable we discuss the content with them and explain why we think it is inappropriate, and then suggest alternatives. We do this because we want to protect them for as long as possible from the 'wrong' type of viewing.
>
> (Bianca Marlow, mother of Henry and Alice)

David and Bonnie Seng limit the viewing of Adrian and his brothers to encourage participation in other activities.

> After 7.30 p. m. we encourage them to turn off the TV and do some school work or music practice. We believe in giving our children a

> controlled mixture of freedom and guidance so that they can learn to make the correct decisions for themselves later on in their lives.

Elizabeth and David Otway have definite views on the programmes which they feel are appropriate for Jonathon and Christopher.

> If we don't think a programme is appropriate we won't let them watch it. We think it better that they have controlled viewing rather than uncontrolled viewing. We don't think that as children they are capable of making appropriate value judgments or criticisms. There is a real danger in the blind acceptance of apparent reality.

Six of the 15 sets of parents expressed a specific concern that television programmes contain too much gratuitous violence, and indicated that they monitor their children's viewing to guard against this.

> We work on the assumption that the values they are exposed to on television have an influence on children, and we are concerned about the desensitization to violence and suffering that can even arise from too much exposure to TV news. We try to protect Mike and Sandy [Cassandra] from fearful experiences and at the same time we try to foster a critical approach towards the values and information the children are exposed to on TV so that they will be less likely to take things at face value.
>
> (Keith Lins, father of Mike and Cassandra)

Caroline and Michael Vincent have similar views. 'We are concerned about the fact that so many children are becoming accustomed and hardened to violence. We don't want our children influenced in this way.' Rachel and Daniel Street, parents of Rufus, express their concern regarding the influence of television on children's social behaviour and morals.

The parents of Roshni, Cassandra, Christopher and Jonathon, and Rick are concerned about the possible effect of 'long periods of passively watching indifferent programmes ' (Cassandra's father) on the creative imagination of their children.

> We have noticed a definite and negative effect of some of the cartoons or 'ghost-buster' type programmes. Rick will sometimes reproduce the ideas from these programmes in his writing and we notice that these stories are much less creative and original than the ideas he takes from his own imagination.
>
> (Jan Ward, mother of Rick)

The family of Richard McLeod does not have television. 'It makes children intellectually lazy,' says Richard's mother, Ursula.

Nevertheless, the majority of the parents believe that television, used wisely, can be a positive influence on their children's education and intellectual growth. The parents of 13 of the 15 children have commented specifically on ways in which television documentaries or educational programmes have enhanced their children's general knowledge or widened their horizons in exposing them to other regions of the world or other cultures. Caroline Vincent buys videos of books which Jade has read and enjoyed. The families of Adrian, Roshni and Ian use moderate amounts of television as a relaxant. 'I'll quite often remind Roshni if there is something on TV that I think she'll like,' says Sarah Singh, 'or if I want her to relax, "switch off" or unwind. She would rarely bother to remember for herself.'

Unlike the other mothers, Sally Baker has deliberately encouraged Ian to watch the early morning cartoon shows. As was briefly described in Chapter 1, and will be discussed more fully later, Ian's elementary school experience was a saga of educational mismanagement, and his extreme intellectual frustration and social isolation have given rise to social behaviours which can make him extremely difficult to live with. For his first few years of schooling, mornings were a trial for the whole family as Ian struggled to conquer his loathing for school and his extreme reluctance to get out of bed, while at the same time fighting the psychosomatic disturbances of abdominal pain, migraine or nausea which sometimes accompanied his emotional distress. Sally encouraged Ian to rise at 7.00 a.m. and spend the next 45 minutes bathing himself in the mindlessness of the cartoon shows. 'He uses it as a "wake-up" much as I use a shower,' she explained at the time. 'Without the cartoon session he is often extremely reluctant to get out out of bed and he is not too pleasant to those around him when he does.' Ian, at age 9, achieved a mental age of 18 years on the *Stanford-Binet Intelligence Scale* (a ratio IQ of 200) and a score of 560 on the *Scholastic Aptitude Test–Mathematics*. At school, in his Grade 4 class, he was required to do Grade 4 maths.

Like the gifted subjects of the surveys conducted by VanTassel-Baska (1983), Abelman (1986) and Roderick and Jackson (1986), the children in this study show little real enthusiasm for television. The gifted children studied in the three earlier surveys tended to express only moderate interest in television. Amongst the highly gifted finalists in the 1982 Midwest Talent Search, only 7 per cent indicated a preference for television viewing, as compared to 75 per cent who indicated that their favourite leisure pastime was reading (VanTassel-Baska, 1983). Of the eight general interests which the 15 exceptionally gifted children were required to place in order of preference (Question 31, Questionnaire 4) television viewing was rated as the activity enjoyed least!

COMPUTER USAGE

In Questionnaire 4: Television and computer use, play interests and spare-time activities, parents were asked to report on aspects of their child's computer use at school and at home.

All 15 of the children had access to computers at school. Only six of the 15, however, had a computer in their own classroom; in the majority of cases the school holds the computers in a central area such as a computer room or resource centre to which classes or individual students go on a rostered basis for 'computer sessions'. This necessarily limits the amount of time each student may spend in computer use; on average, the subject children spent 1½ hours per week in computer contact at school.

Computer use in school was largely confined to 'learning games' based on maths, spelling and other school subjects, although eight of the 15 families reported that the teachers also used skill building programs designed to develop the students' mathematical abilities on an individual basis. In only nine classrooms was the computer used as a word processor to facilitate children's writing. In four classrooms the children were permitted to use a print program to make greeting cards and posters. Such programming as the children have learned has generally been acquired at home, through self-teaching from manuals with assistance from those parents who have adequate levels of computer literacy. Ian, who taught himself BASIC programming some years ago, and whose computer management skills are considerably in advance of the rest of his class, was at one stage provided with what his teacher termed 'extension work' in computing; this consisted of testing out available software for the teacher and advising her on which programs were appropriate for use by his classmates! 'There appears to be no lack of equipment and software, but no proper teaching in the subject,' comments Brock Baker. 'He has the ability to go further in programming but without appropriate guidance he is stuck at the level he's at now.'

Fred Campbell, who at the time of this computer use survey was spending an average of 30 hours per week on his personal computer at home, received a maximum of two hours per week of computer instruction at school. Like Ian, Fred received little educational acknowledgment of his talent for computing, but was expected to use his gifts in the service of the school.

> 'He helps the teachers with word processing,' reports Eleanor Campbell, a little wryly, 'and when guests come to the school they use him to demonstrate student use of computers! I am negotiating with the school for him to do Pascal programming by himself in Semester 2 instead of the computer awareness the rest of the class is doing.'
>
> (Eleanor Campbell, mother of Fred)

The parents are generally unimpressed with the quality of computer education in their children's schools. Computer usage is generally seen as lacking in intellectual content, circumscribed by the teachers' lack of computing skill and knowledge, and limited further by constraints of time and finance. David Otway is an exception; he has no complaints about computer use in the school attended by Christopher and Jonathon. 'Computers are constructively and intelligently used as a tool rather than as an end in themselves,' he says. 'For example, in Chris's economics class they use a PC for simulation exercises.'

At home, however, the children have fewer constraints on their computer usage. All 15 families own a personal computer. Eleven of the 15 children have been using computers at home for two years or longer and six of them began using computers before the age of 4. The children spend an average of seven hours per week in computer use at home, more than four times the amount of computer contact available, on average, at school.

Generally the children put their home computers to a much wider range of usage than they are able to do with the computers they work with at school. Seven of the 15 children have taught themselves programming, with varying degrees of assistance from manuals or their parents. Twelve of the 15 use the home computer as a word processor, whereas only nine children make use of this function at school. Although the majority of the children enjoy what Ursula McLeod and Holly Bond dryly term 'arcade games', they also use skill building programs in mathematics, language and spelling; indeed several of the parents reported that their children enjoy this activity at home much more than at school because they are able to progress further through skill levels without being interrupted by classmates demanding their turn on the computer. Fred Campbell uses the graphics capability of his home computer to further his outstanding artistic talents, and its sonic capabilities to compose music.

The parents of nine of the 15 subjects believe that their child has an unusually high aptitude for computing and computer work. Adrian's talent is acknowledged and provided for; he has been studying computing science part-time at university since the age of 10. Rufus, at age 5, undertook computer enrichment classes for gifted children provided by the local university. The abilities of Alice and Fred are acknowledged in school reports. As related above, Ian's teacher recognized his capacities and used him as an adviser on appropriate software for classroom use.

The parents of Roshni, Hadley, Anastasia and Christopher are influenced in their perception by the speed at which their children have mastered computer processes. 'Hadley has been an independent computer user since he was 3 years old,' says Holly Bond, 'and a pretty competent touch typist since 5. He seems to have a much higher aptitude than his age-peers.' 'She picks up everything she is told with remarkable speed and doesn't forget anything,' says Sarah Singh when Roshni turned 6. 'She is always enthusiastic to learn new things and new applications for the computer. What strikes me most, probably, is the "normality", for her, of using a computer. She takes it in her stride and it is as normal as any other activity she is involved with, only probably more fun!'

Edward Murphy reports on Adam's remarkable capacity to synthesize new information.

> 'He was anxious to learn BASIC but this isn't provided for at school. However, we luckily had a tutor program that contained instructions, and also obtained a book from the library. In a matter of days, without help from us, he had developed a rough program that produced an addition sum and told you whether your answer was right or wrong. This, I believe, was a program of a dozen lines. His latest creation, this evening, after an hour on the machine, was a program of a train moving along the screen continuously, which consisted of about 100 lines, albeit with some repetition.
>
> Again it clearly demonstrated to us this ability of almost instantly grasping a technique and leaping ahead with it. He now understands BASIC programming better than I do!' (Adam at this stage had just had his eighth birthday.)

The availability of a personal computer in the home, and the time to use it, may compensate to some degree for the restrictions of time, computer availability and adequate teaching to which the children are subjected at school. The question remains, of course, as to what happens to undisplayed computing potential which may be possessed by classmates whose parents may be unable to provide computing facilities in the home!

INTEREST AND PARTICIPATION IN SPORT

Australia is an extremely sports-conscious society and children are introduced at an early age to a culture which values both participation in team sports and the enthusiastic support of local or national sporting groups. Unlike the majority of Australian children of their age, the children studied here have little enthusiasm for sport, either as participants or as spectators. Only four of the 15 children are members of a school sports club or sports team, and only five are members of a community (for example, church) sports club or team. However, these children who do play sport tend to display extremely high levels of ability. Fred Campbell won his school's swimming championship within his age-group, and was placed third in his age-group within his entire school district. Alice, at 8 years of age, was already an outstanding horsewoman. Roshni, aged 5, swam as well as the majority of the 7-and 8-year-olds in her class, while Rick, at age 6, was already proficient in freestyle, backstroke and breaststroke. Cassandra, at age 10, was invited to train for her state swimming squad, but decided not to accept the offer.

The sports played by the 15 children tend to be those, such as swimming, tennis and horse-riding, which do not require team participation and in which, consequently, the individual has a higher degree of control over the development of his or her own abilities. Hadley Bond is the only truly committed sportsman of the group, playing for his local T-ball team in summer and for a community soccer team in winter, and also enjoying cross-country running. Even so, when Holly Bond speaks of Hadley's enjoyment of ball games, the behaviours she describes are skill building exercises rather than purely physical 'romps' with a ball which are more characteristic of young children. Hadley was 7 years old at the time.

> He spends a great deal of time with a ball in his hands – throwing, spinning, catching, etc. I would say it's his favourite pastime. Sometimes a ball goes to bed with him! He enjoys balloons, too, for much the same reasons.

The Bonds are the only family in the study which watches a significant amount of sport on television; Hadley and his older brothers, Adrian and John, watched nine hours of Australian Rules Football across the 14 days of the television viewing survey. The only other subjects who watched *any* sport during the viewing survey were Christopher (two hours) and Ian (45 minutes). In Question 31 of Questionnaire 4, which required the subjects to list eight leisure-time activities in order of preference, a surprising 40 per cent of the children named sport as the *least* favoured activity and another 13 per cent listed it in seventh place. Surprisingly, children rating sport in this unfavourable light are not necessarily untalented in this area; Roshni and Fred, whose superior abilities in swimming are described above, and Alice, who excels at horse-riding, listed sport as their least favourite activity, while Cassandra, who was invited to train for her state swimming squad, rated it as her seventh of eight preferences. In this group of children a high level of talent in sport does not necessarily indicate a high level of interest or enjoyment.

Much of the schoolyard conversation in Australian elementary schools centres on the children's own sporting performance, the fortunes of the major league football or cricket teams which are eagerly followed by the majority of Australian families, and the more humourous or dramatic incidents in the previous evening's television programmes. These highly gifted children, who have little interest in sports either as participants or as spectators, and who watch much less television than their class-mates, may be at a considerable social disadvantage unless they can acquire enough sporting knowledge to be able to contribute, to some degree, to the conversation. Tannenbaum, in his study of adolescent attitudes towards academic brilliance, found that the hostility shown by teenagers of average ability towards the intellectually gifted was moderated to a degree where the gifted student also possessed a high level of talent or interest in sport (Tannenbaum, 1962). It may be that the children of this study are paying lip-service to the Australian sporting ethos for the sake of peer-group acceptance.

INTEREST AND TALENTS IN MUSIC

The literature on giftedness indicates a strong link between exceptional intellectual potential and musical talent. All 10 of Flack's highly gifted subjects (Flack, 1983) and almost 50 per cent of VanTassel-Baska's Midwest Talent Search finalists (VanTassel-Baska, 1983) had at some time taken instrumental lessons. Twelve of the 15 Australian children (80 per cent) learn a musical instrument; indeed, seven of the 15 learn two instruments and two of the girls, Anastasia and Alice, are members of their state's section of a prestigious national girls' choir. The piano is the most popular instrument and is played by nine of the children, while Richard and Rufus learn trumpet, Cassandra, Richard and Christopher learn flute, Jonathon plays clarinet, Alice and Hadley enjoy the recorder, Jade plays violin and Rufus is an enthusiastic student of the electric organ.

None of these children displays a musical talent of the level of exceptionality which characterizes their academic work. However, fully seven of the 15 children are described, by their instrumental or vocal teachers, as having unusually high levels of musical ability. Hadley learns recorder in a group of children two years older than he who, furthermore, had been learning for two years before he joined the group as a beginner; yet his teacher notes that he masters the work with ease and seems to have an exceptional memory for note sequences. Roshni's piano teacher comments on her remarkable memory to retain instructions, and the speed with which she masters new work. Alice's choir teacher has told the Marlows that she has an exceptional ear for music. Jonathon was invited to join the leading boys' choir of his state; he declined the invitation with regret as the timing of the choir practices coincided with his piano lessons and it was not possible to alter his piano schedule. Cassandra is an outstanding pianist; although at age 10 she had been learning for only three years she had already attained Grade 8 in piano and performed publicly with her music teacher playing a Mozart piano concerto. Richard, at age 10, had one of his flute compositions used as a test piece in a master class for adult musicians at the Conservatorium of Music in his state. 'He was so embarrassed for the professional flautists who were criticized by the tutor for not interpreting the piece as the composer had intended,' says Ursula McLeod, Richard's mother. Like many other exceptionally gifted children, Richard is acutely sensitive to the feelings of others.

HOBBIES, PLAY INTERESTS AND FRIENDSHIP CHOICES

The hobbies and play interests of exceptionally gifted children have a powerful influence on their friendship choices. Whereas the play of young elementary school children of average ability involves predominantly simple sensori-motor activity, the play interests of the gifted centre on games of intellectual skill. In his study of 561 children scoring at or above IQ 150, Kincaid (1969) noted that the favourite activities of these children included discussions, visits to museums, puzzles and listening to foreign language records. Hollingworth's subjects of IQ 180 frequently reported a liking for bridge, chess and other competitive board games (Hollingworth, 1942).

Gifted girls tend to be less interested in doll-play than are their peers of average intelligence. Hollingworth related that when she asked a 7-year-old girl of IQ 170 why she did not care to play with dolls, the girl replied, 'They aren't real. The doll that is supposed to be a baby doll is twice as big as the one that is made like a mother doll' (Hollingworth, 1931, p. 10). This rejection of doll-play can be a considerable hindrance to socialization; for young girls role-play with dolls may play a major part in establishing the parameters of relationships. For the gifted child, however, the search for logic and structure may supersede the desire for social intercourse.

An additional barrier to normal socialization with age-peers may arise from the profoundly gifted child's enjoyment of leisure activities which are completely outside the realms of interest or capability of the average child. Zorbaugh and Boardman (1926) described a boy, 'R', of Stanford-Binet IQ 204, who began to design and make books at the age of 3 and who had applied to the United States patent office for two patents by the time he was 8 years old. Hollingworth's 'Child D' was, at age 7, composing, typing and selling a regular playground newspaper. 'Betty Ford', the prodigiously gifted child author described by Terman and Fenton in 1921, had written an anthology of 200 stories and poems by the time she was 7. At age 6, Australian maths prodigy Terence Tao wrote a computer program to produce Fibonacci numbers (Gross, 1986). At 12, this child's spare-time activities included translating Douglas Adams' *The Hitch-Hiker's Guide to the Galaxy* into Latin (Gross and Start, 1989).

Information on the leisure activities preferred and avoided by the children in the present study was acquired in the interviews both with the children and with their parents. The children, however, were also asked to complete Renzulli's *Interest-a-Lyzer*, a questionnaire designed to elicit information on the hobbies and interests of gifted children (Renzulli, 1977). Although several of the children commented that they found the *Interest-a-Lyzer* somewhat boring and, as Richard, aged 11, said politely, 'a bit stereotyped in its perception of the sorts of things kids are interested in,' their responses to the items certainly illustrated how radically the interests, ideas and perceptions of these exceptionally gifted children differ from those of their age-peers.

This chapter has already discussed the unusually mature and sophisticated reading interests of exceptionally gifted children. Question 2 of the *Interest-a-Lyzer* asks children to pretend that some day they will be the author of a famous book, and invites them to describe the theme and topic of the book. Predictably, because of the fascination which 'high fantasy' holds for this group, six of the 15 children chose to place their imagined contributions to literature within this genre. However, all six went beyond the requirements of the exercise and discussed the plot and title of the book with great enthusiasm. Nine-year-old Jonathon's fantasy would have as its hero an adventurer seeking the lost city of Atlantis. Adrian's science fantasy would rest on 'a medieval perception of the future' and would be entitled *Gems of Knowledge*. Cassandra's novel, entitled *Where the Moon Meets the Sand*, would be set in a fantasy world where 'strange creatures would have stranger adventures'. Christopher's science fiction adventure would centre on 'humans on another planet who rebel against humans who have not left earth'.

Question 10 of the *Interest-a-Lyzer* required the children to imagine that they had been given a job as a feature writer on a newspaper, and asked them to select three 'feature columns' from a suggested list of 25 as being those which they would prefer to write. The feature columns from which the subjects were required to choose included many which might be expected to appeal to elementary school children, for example pet care, book reviews, crossword puzzles, movie reviews and popular music. As young Richard might have predicted, however, the study children paid scant attention to the more conventional offerings. Rather, the columns which attracted the highest response were 'Maths puzzles' with 15 votes out of a possible 90, 'Humour' with 14 votes, and 'Political cartoons' with 11. 'Games and activities for children' drew 8 votes, 'Science facts' and 'Stock market analysis' 6 each, and 'Book reviews' 5. No child selected 'Movie reviews', 'Horoscope', or 'Personal advice'. Rufus commented that if he were a journalist he would choose none of the options proposed by Renzulli, but would prefer to write a column on election reviews and polls!

Question 9 of the *Interest-a-Lyzer* asked the children to pretend that their community was going to have a 'career day', and asked them to select the three occupations which they would like to study for the day. As with their literary interests, the job interests of these children tended to reflect their intellectual maturity rather than their chronological age. Even among the 5- to 6-year-olds the usual childish choices of train-drivers, soldiers, stewardesses or pilots were conspicuous by their absence. Roshni, who had just turned 5, wanted to spend the day with a doctor. Rick, aged 5 years 11 months, wanted to be a computer operator. Hadley, just past his seventh birthday, wavered between a gardener, the Prime Minister and a TV director. Generally the occupations selected were of high status, both socially and financially. Medicine and computer programming were the most frequently selected occupations, but science, politics and economics were each selected by three children. There was little difference between the occupations selected by boys and girls; indeed Jade and Cassandra were interested in finding out about the police force. Jonathan, aged 9 years 1 month, mischievously wrote 'politician – comedian' with arrows linking the two! Richard said he'd like to spend the day with a Public Servant (Civil Servant in Britain) so that he could find out whether they really read books all day. Failing that, he would follow a politician around for the day to find out what they did apart from smiling and shaking hands. Ian, predictably, wrote:

First choice: Highways Department top planner.
Second choice: Highways Department second top planner.
Third choice: Highways Department third top planner.

No child showed any interest in being a teacher! It is tempting to speculate on links between this lack of interest in teaching as a profession and the less than inspiring teaching to which many of these children have been subjected. Interestingly, however, a study of 3,000 14-year-olds in Melbourne's state schools (McGuigan and Start, 1991) found that it was children of modest intellectual capacity, rather than bright or gifted students, who indicated an interest in entering teaching.

The 'leisure-time activities' section of Questionnaire 4 listed 12 toys and games in general use among elementary school children, and asked the children to indicate their personal feelings about each on a five-point Likert scale ranging from 'very strong dislike' (1) to 'very strong liking' (5). The 12 toys/games were listed as follows:

electronic toys,
construction toys,
dolls,
cuddly toys,
cars, trucks,
pretend or fantasy games,
puzzles,
educational toys,
board games,
games involving ball play,
games involving mock fights,
games involving 'chasing'.

When the mean preference scores for the 12 games/toys are ordered from least enjoyed to most enjoyed, the activity enjoyed least, with a mean preference score of 2.6 is 'games involving mock fights' while the activity most enjoyed, with a mean preference score of 4.4, is 'board games'. Interestingly, these are the two activities most immediately identifiable, in children's minds, with competition. Like the exceptionally gifted children studied by Burks, Jensen and Terman (1930), Hollingworth (1942) and Silverman (1989), the Australian subjects enjoy the challenge of pitting their wits against other able children and adults in games of intellectual skill, but dislike and reject physical competitiveness; seven of the 15 subjects indicated a strong or very strong dislike of games involving mock fights, while another four expressed a lack of interest in them. The lack of interest in sport identified in Question 31 is confirmed in Question 30 with two children indicating a strong dislike of ball games and a further five expressing neutrality towards them.

The four games most strongly favoured were, in order of popularity: board games; pretend or fantasy games; puzzles; and electronic toys. Construction toys, cars and trucks, and mock fights attracted little interest. In interviews with the author, several children expressed a deep enjoyment of fantasy or 'pretend' play. For Adrian, this takes the form of what he terms 'book-based games' such as *Dungeons and Dragons* – structured play governed by complex rules and dictated by hierarchies of power and authority. For Cassandra the need is satisfied by dressing up in her room at home and enacting fantasies which she herself creates. 'I like thinking – pretending – imagining,' she says. Cassandra requires no audience for her fantasies; she enjoys her own company and is stimulated by her own imagination. Sarah Singh notes Roshni's deep enjoyment of fantasy play. 'She loves playing with her younger brother Harjeevan,' says Sarah. 'They are happy for hours playing imaginary games, acting out roles, setting up fantasy situations and playing out the idea together.'

Gifted children prefer games of intellectual skill where new ideas and strategies can be developed and trialled (Terman, 1926; Witty and Lehman, 1927; Hollingworth, 1931) while children of average ability feel more secure with games where such rules as exist are clearly defined and closely adhered to. This can cause conflict when the highly gifted child, who may perceive the illogicality or irrelevance of the rules, seeks to overturn them either to improve the game or simply for the intellectual stimulation of the ensuing argument (Gross, 1989b).

Because of these factors, the play of the highly gifted tends to be an uneasy compromise between their own interests and abilities and their desire to be accepted into the social group. Children who are less willing or less able to make such a compromise may prefer to invent solitary intellectual games which often centre on fantasy and imagined adventure. A significant number of intellectually gifted children create imaginary playmates or imaginary countries, in an attempt to satisfy their need for companionship or social interaction at their own level and within their own interests (Terman, 1926; Hollingworth, 1926). The interest in fantasy games among the study children has already been discussed.

The games which extremely gifted children invent for their own personal enjoyment may appear deceptively simple to the uninitiated observer, but may have remarkable degrees of complexity. Hadley, for example, is one of only two children of the 15 who expressed a strong liking for cars and trucks. Hadley, at 7 years of age, had a collection of 120 model cars with which he played on a regular basis. His favourite game was racing as many as 70 of the cars against each other on a dirt track in his garden. However, the structure of the race was complex, and progressed through a process of elimination heats based on the speed and distance each car had travelled. A single race meeting could take up to several hours.

It is interesting to speculate how many other exceptionally gifted children may have invented games of considerable structural complexity which are not recognized as such by casual observers. If Hadley had played this game in the school yard it is probable that passing teachers would have remained quite oblivious to the intricate interweaving of the variables of size, mass and friction which lent such challenge and delight to the exercise. They might well have seen the activity as merely a small boy playing with cars.

The majority of the children of IQ 180+ studied by Hollingworth had conspicuous difficulties with play in early childhood. These children were unpopular with their age-peers 'because they always wanted to organize the play into some complicated pattern with some remote and definite climax as the goal' (Hollingworth, 1931, p. 9). Children of 6 years old are not generally responsive to the promise of delayed gratification and are unlikely to be drawn to sustained, complex games which lead to remote goals. Hadley's 7-year-old age-peers would be unlikely to understand the interests and objectives which underpin his car races. Furthermore, children of average ability characteristically resent the attempts of the gifted child to reorganize their play. It can be exceedingly frustrating for a 5-year-old of average ability, to whom the ritual of a game may not be distinguishable from the game itself, to have a gifted age-mate insist on restructuring the rules and conditions of play. The gifted child may feel he is removing illogicalities from the play, or altering the rules to introduce new and greater challenges; however, for the average child, whose vision is narrower, the very fabric of the game is being destroyed. It is significant that Hadley played his car games by himself; he did not attempt to explain them to his age-peers.

It can be particularly hurtful to the exceptionally gifted child to realize that the activities which he finds absorbing arouse no enthusiasm or interest in his age-peers. 'Seymour', a boy of IQ 192 reported by McElwee (1934), was given a chemistry set at age 7½ and immediately tried to establish a chemistry club among the boys in the neighbourhood; to his chagrin he found not one child to share his interest. Ian Baker, whose enthusiasm for cartography and road systems has been described earlier, has developed a new and allied interest, but he has no one with whom to share the excitement of his discoveries. The following is an extract from a letter to me from Ian's father, Brock, in August 1989, when Ian was 10 years 4 months old.

> When I last wrote to you I didn't mention the latest passion that His Nibs has taken up with his usual total dedication. WATCH OUT, STATE TRANSPORT AUTHORITY, YOU'RE BEING HEAVILY SCRUTINIZED. Yes, he's taken up learning all the bus, train and tram routes. He can now tell you how to get from anywhere to anywhere right across the city via public transport. This includes the route numbers, the roads travelled on and the stop numbers to board and alight. He's also produced a document on the Word Processor called 'All You Need to Know About the S.T.A.', which he has built up from the S.T.A. Route Maps and his street directory. Every route is listed with the roads along which the bus travels. In the case of the trams and trains, he includes the stops. His latest trick is to produce route time-tables for routes of interest. These he builds up from the S.T.A. timetable, the route map and his street directory. He finds it all so fascinating and naturally is a bit miffed when no one else is interested. The relations, however, show interest and consequently end up being snowed under by the vast quantities of documents he heaps upon them.
>
> (Brock Baker, father of Ian)

Enclosed with the letter from his father was a short missive from Ian in which he had detailed, with great precision, two alternative routes by which I could travel from my new home in a Melbourne suburb to my then place of employment at the University of Melbourne, a distance of some seven miles. Both routes were accurate in every detail; indeed the route which Ian advised as his personal recommendation was the route which I had been travelling for several weeks after a period of trial and error! Ian lives in another city several hundred miles from Melbourne; he had designed the two alternative routes entirely with the use of a Melbourne street directory.

Research over the last 60 years has demonstrated convincingly that intellectually gifted children tend to seek out, for companionship, either older children or children of the same age who are at similar stages of intellectual development (Davis, 1924; Burks, Jensen and Terman, 1930; Hollingworth, 1931); thus the exceptionally gifted child is likely to seek out, as friends, children several years older than himself. O'Shea (1960) noted that in several studies conducted over a number of years no variable correlated more highly with friendship choices in children than mental age, and that this stood considerably above any other factor.

The search for like minds and like companionship appears to begin in very early childhood. Hubbard (1929) observed a heterogeneous group of 3-year-olds at nursery school, measuring the children both in terms of the number of times the children chose each other as spontaneous play companions and in terms of the length of time they spent together as a group. When she calculated the correlation between mental age and spontaneous group participation, Hubbard found that children who played together most often showed a correlation of 0.41 with mental age, while for those who played together longest the correlation was a remarkable 0.62.

Difficulties arise, however, when the highly gifted child is unable to find intellectual peers with whom to interact. Terman's study of the play interests of those children in the gifted group who scored above IQ 170 established that they were much more solitary in their play than were children clustering around IQ 140 (Burks, Jensen and Terman, 1930). Hollingworth attributed this isolated play to the difficulties experienced by the highly gifted child in finding playmates who are 'appropriate in size and congenial in mentality' (Hollingworth, 1936, p. 278). She noted that the majority of children testing above IQ 160 played little with other children unless special opportunities were found, such as those provided in a special, full-time class for the intellectually gifted or through a programme of grade advancement.

Where the gifted child's gravitation towards intellectual peers in older age groups is not facilitated by the school, or where it is actively thwarted through the school's insistence that the child remain full-time with chronological peers, there is a strong tendency for exceptionally gifted children to become social isolates, preferring the intellectual stimulation of their own thoughts and play to the tedium imposed by continual interaction with children whose intellectual and social development, ideas, interests and enthusiasms are still at a level which they themselves outgrew several years previously.

Fred Campbell speaks feelingly on the social advantages of acceleration. Throughout Fred's years at elementary school he was a social outcast, mocked and derided by the other children for his remarkable mathematical abilities (he scored 640 on the *SAT–M* at 12 years 1 month), his artistic talents and his interests in psychology and philosophy. Two weeks after his eleventh birthday, Fred was permitted to grade-skip straight into secondary school. 'It's the best thing that has ever happened to me,' affirms Fred. For the first time, he was able to associate freely with children whose ways of thinking and viewing the world were more closely aligned with his own. His classmates, who were one to two years older than he, accepted him as one of them. He was no longer socially rejected and, like other boys of his age, he now had friends to stay for the weekend or to 'sleep over', a normal experience for most children of 11 or 12 but one rarely experienced by the exceptionally gifted child who is isolated from intellectual peers in the regular classroom.

The parents of the study children, and the children themselves, report that the students whom they seek out as preferred play companions are two to four years older than they. Fred, at age 12, had as his closest friend another computer enthusiast aged 16. The neighbourhood friend with whom 10-year-old Ian played most regularly was a highly intelligent boy of 12. Jade, at 6 years of age, took little interest in the play and activities of her classmates and sought out in the schoolyard her friend Joan, who was 9 years old and in Grade 4.

> This used to cause some tremendous social difficulties because there were days when Joan would prefer to play with her own classmates, and on these days Jade would come home sobbing bitterly that Joan didn't like her any more. As a matter of fact I suspect that Joan was being put under a lot of social pressure from her own classmates who didn't like her playing with 'the little kid'. If only Jade could have been grade-skipped to a level nearer Joan's age. When Joan would come round here at weekends there was no difficulty at all; it was only at school, where social pressures intervened, that the difficulties arose.
>
> (Caroline Vincent, mother of Jade)

After a brief period of adjustment to the accelerative procedure, Roshni Singh, aged 5, settled happily into her Grade 2 class of 7- and 8-year-olds.

> She loves it and has really 'arrived' socially [reported Sarah Singh, three months after Roshni's second acceleration]. The other children now treat her as a peer or equal and seek to include her in their activities. This week she was invited to two birthday parties, and both groups of children were small in number so that it seems obvious that her popularity has really increased. Children invite her to their homes and for outings while signs from school about her social activities are very positive, for example, other children asking her to be their best friend or writing stories about her being their friend.

As will be comprehensively discussed in Chapter 9, the exceptionally gifted children who have been accelerated in grade placement by two or more years express a strong belief that they are now more appropriately placed both academically and socially. They are now able to work and play with the children whose companionship and friendship they sought in previous years. When they were in lower grades, and thus occupying a position of social inferiority in the hierarchy of the schoolyard, they were greeted with derision, or at best a grudging acceptance, by the older children with whom they wished to associate; however, once they were accelerated to the same grade level, and could thus be viewed as occupying the same stratum in the social hierarchy as their older friends, they were readily accepted and valued for their academic talents. This suggests that children of average ability may reject younger gifted children on the basis of their inferior grade placement rather than on their comparative youth. If this is so, it provides a powerful contradiction to the argument that young accelerands will be socially rejected by the older children in the classes they seek to enter.

SUMMARY

The children of this study are copious and avid readers. Despite present-day distractions of television, videos and personal computers, several of them read more than did the average child of their age in Terman's study, more than 60 years ago. Furthermore, whereas the children in Terman's sample generally read, for pleasure, books which were preferred by children of average ability some three years older than they, these exceptionally gifted children are reading literature which is written for, and preferred by, young people five to seven years their senior. It is ridiculous for teachers to suggest that such children would gain any benefit or enjoyment from reading, in school, texts which are appropriate in level and content for their age-peers.

Perhaps the most significant finding regarding the reading interests of these children is their fascination, from age 9 onwards, with the more serious modes of adult science fiction and science fantasy. The many points of similarity between 'high fantasy' and the classics have been discussed in this chapter, and it is suggested that the moral and ethical questions which are posed in the high fantasy novels of C. S. Lewis and Madeleine L'Engle and, in the case of the older children, those of Stephen Donaldson, David Eddings and Frank Herbert, might make these books particularly attractive to exceptionally gifted children whose intellectual precocity and accelerated moral development urge them to develop a personal belief system at a much younger age than is customary.

The literature on the television viewing habits of intellectually gifted children suggests that the gifted child watches considerably less television than do his age-peers of average ability (Benbow, 1985b; Abelman, 1986). Of eight leisure-time activities which the 15 children were asked to list in order of preference, television viewing was rated as the activity enjoyed least! Twelve of the 14 subjects who have television in the home watch for fewer than two hours per day. Family programmes, especially British and Australian series such as *Rumpole of the Bailey*, *Fawlty Towers* and *A Country Practice*, were popular, as were news programmes and documentaries, adult quiz programmes and programmes made especially for children.

Several parents reported that their children were not permitted to watch cartoons, or American and Australian soap operas. The children showed a relative lack of interest in sporting programmes. Like the parents of gifted students in the studies by Abelman (1986) and Roderick and Jackson (1986), the parents of these children take a keen interest in their children's television viewing, and decisions on what will be viewed by the children are generally made by the parents and children together.

All 15 of the families own a personal computer, and the children spend an average of seven hours per week in computer use, more than four times the amount of computer contact which, on average, they have at school. Several of the children have taught themselves programming at home, from manuals, with moderate amounts of assistance from those parents who have adequate levels of computer literacy. Neither the children nor their parents are impressed with the quality of computer instruction available in the children's schools.

Although several of the children display high levels of sporting talent, they display little interest in sport either as participants or as spectators.

The 15 children enjoy listening to and making music. Fully 12 of them play a musical instrument and seven play more than one. No fewer than seven of the children are described, by their instrumental or vocal teacher, as having high levels of musical ability.

The leisure-time interests and play preferences of the subjects are radically different from those of their age-peers of average ability. They actively dislike play which involves 'mock fights' or other forms of physical competitiveness and, like the exceptionally gifted children of previous studies, prefer games of intellectual skill where ideas and strategies are matched against each other. Several children express a deep enjoyment of 'pretend' or fantasy play. Because their interests and modes of play are so different from those of their age-peers, the majority of these children prefer to play with children several years older than they. Where this is not permitted by the school, or where the older children are reluctant to accept them, the children often revert to solitary play. The games which they invent for their own entertainment are often quite remarkable in their complexity.

8

SCHOOL HISTORY

The advantages of early recognition, appreciation and, if possible, measurement are apparent in the study of this small group of exceptionally intelligent children. Although all were identified fairly early in their lives, there are very different degrees of adaptation to school and society, ranging from opposition and truancy, through indifference, to rapt and enthusiastic preoccupation...

The cases that have achieved most contented and socially useful adaptation are those in which parents, teachers and principals have made use of special gift identification, have sought educational guidance, have personally fostered and supervised the child's development and the solution of his adjustment problems, or have taken advantage of such experimental classes for exceptional children as the schools have offered at the time.

Among the cases herein reported the clearest ones of easy and useful adjustment occurred when the exceptional child became a member of an experimental group comprised of others of his approximate kind.

(Hollingworth, 1942, p. 234–5)

The exceptionally gifted children described in the preceding chapters differ radically from their age-peers on almost every variable. The remarkably early development of movement and speech gave these children a considerable advantage in acquiring and processing information, and thereby strengthened crystallized intelligence. This advantage was further enhanced by the astonishingly precocious development of reading; 14 of the 15 children entered school with the reading skill and experience of children several years their senior. In the majority of cases the child's astonishing verbal abilities were accompanied by a mastery of the skills of numeracy which clearly qualified him, at age 4 or 5, to undertake the maths curriculum more usually offered to 7- or 8-year-olds. The children's reading interests, their hobbies and enthusiasms, their play preferences and their friendship choices were so incompatible with those of their classmates that from their first few weeks at school the majority of the subjects experienced extreme difficulty in establishing positive social relationships with other children of their chronological age.

As discussed earlier, the normal distribution predicts that children scoring at and above IQ 160 on the *Stanford-Binet L-M* will appear in the population at a ratio of fewer than 1 in 10,000. If the average elementary school teacher were to enjoy a career lasting for 40 years, and if her average class size over that period were to be 40 students, the likelihood of that teacher encountering a child of IQ 160+ during her entire professional career would be less than one chance in seven. Employing the same parameters, the likelihood of this teacher encountering a child of IQ 180+, such as Adrian, Christopher or Ian, would be 1 in 625!

Students such as the children described here are, thus, anomalies within the system. They are unexpected, they do not 'fit' and the majority of schools are not set up in terms of class structure, curriculum, teacher training or teacher expectations to provide for their particular learning needs. They differ significantly from their age-peers, and those differences, intellectual, academic and social, are readily observable. It might be expected, therefore, that the schools in which these children enrol would have acknowledged the infrequency of such an enrolment, and the astonishing academic capacities of the child, by making a differentiated curricular or organizational response.

Unfortunately, the schools' responses to the children's academic and social needs have generally been very far from adequate.

THE SCHOOL'S RESPONSE TO EARLY READING

The precocious development of reading in the 15 children has been described in considerable detail in Chapters 6 and 7. Children in Australia, like British children, enter kindergarten or pre-school (the terminology differs between states) at age 4, and graduate to formal schooling at age 5 – at least one full year earlier than their counterparts in the United States. No fewer than 14 of the 15 children were reading fluently and with excellent comprehension by the time they entered school; indeed 12 of the 15 had been proficient readers since 3 years of age.

Nevertheless, in only four cases of the 15 did the school make *any* accommodation for the fact that the child had entered school already reading. Richard McLeod, who before the age of 3 had demonstrated the reading skills of a 5-year-old, was permitted to enrol in school at the age of 4 years 10 months – two months early – specifically on the grounds of his remarkable reading development. All went well for the first few weeks, until the class teacher commenced pre-reading exercises with the other 5-year-olds, and insisted that Richard participate.

> He was forced to endure all of the pre-reading experience with the whole class, and when I went up to school to remind them gently that he could indeed read at a level some years beyond this, and that

> indeed this was why they had taken him in early, the teacher was extremely hostile. I soon discovered that the school believed that Richard was advanced only because we had taught him ourselves. They accused us of 'pushing' him and warned us that what we were doing was incredibly harmful.
>
> (Ursula Mcleod, mother of Richard)

A disturbing finding of this study has been the tendency of these exceptionally gifted young readers to conceal their abilities in an attempt to simulate the reading capacities of their classmates. No fewer than 10 of the 15 parents reported that their children actually stopped reading, or deliberately decreased the quality and quantity of their reading, after a few weeks in school. Hadley Bond, who had been reading since the age of 18 months, entered school at 5 years 6 months and promptly began to mimic his classmates in selecting picture books, or books with only a few words of text, from the classroom bookshelves. Despite having been given access to a psychologist's assessment conducted some months before, which placed Hadley's full scale IQ on the *WPPSI (Wechsler Preschool and Primary Scale of Intelligence)* at 150, his class teacher took his reading performance at face value, and some months passed before the school recognized and responded to his exceptional reading abilities.

During his first few months at school Ian Baker particularly disliked having to read aloud and would mumble and stumble over words to such a degree that his teacher remained quite unaware that only a few months previously he had been assisting his pre-school teacher by reading to the class. It was not until Sally Baker intervened by explaining to his teacher that he had just finished reading, at home, E. B. White's *Charlotte's Web* that the school responded by permitting him to move beyond the Reception Grade reading programme.

Roshni Singh stopped reading on entry to pre-school, at age 3 years 4 months, and stopped again on entry to formal schooling at 4 years 4 months. Like Richard, Roshni had been permitted early entry to school on the basis of her accelerated reading capacities, yet her teacher showed no concern when her reading appeared to regress dramatically in the first few weeks of school.

> This particular teacher expected nothing of Roshni's exceptional ability, and gave nothing in return. Her biggest concession was to bring a dictionary into class for Roshni's use towards the end of the year. The whole curriculum of this class seemed to be based on what the least able child could be expected to manage. In maths, for example, the children were allowed to count to 20, but not beyond. Roshni could count to 30 in both English and Punjabi before she was two!
>
> (Sarah Singh, mother of Roshni)

The parents of Hadley, Ian, Richard and Roshni felt secure enough in their relationship with the school to discuss these difficulties with the class teacher. In the majority of cases, however, the parents of children who had stopped reading decided not to mention the problem to their child's teacher for fear they would be disbelieved, and their child penalized. These parents watched in concern as their child worked through weeks of 'reading readiness' exercises while, at home, he or she read books normally enjoyed by 7- or 8-year-olds; yet they did not have the confidence to explain to the class teacher that her reading programme was unsuited to the needs of their child. As Australian schools, in general, do not employ standardized achievement testing to assess students' academic abilities, the teachers of these young children continued to rely on their flawed perception of the children's reading aptitudes, and the majority of the children spent their Reception or Kindergarten year reading, in class, at a level three or four years below their true capacity.

EARLY ENTRY TO FORMAL SCHOOLING

Numerous studies (Worcester, 1955; Hobson, 1979; Alexander and Skinner, 1980) have shown that when under-age gifted children are admitted to formal schooling on the basis of intellectual, academic and social readiness, they perform as well as, or rather better than, their older classmates. However, schools considering early entrance generally focus their attention solely on whether the young child will be mature enough to cope with the demands of the school day. A requirement of equal importance, but usually given much less consideration, is that the school which enrols a young child of exceptional ability must provide a curriculum that is academically rigorous, intellectually stimulating and flexible enough to meet the demands of the child.

Surprisingly, considering the fierce Australian opposition to academic acceleration (Goldberg, 1981; Cross, 1984; Gross, 1984; Victorian Teachers' Union, 1986; Boag, 1990; Poulos, 1990), seven of the 15 children in this study were permitted to start formal schooling before the usual age of entry. In two cases, that of Adrian and Hadley, the experiment was less than successful; in each case the failure arose from a lack of flexibility on the part of the school, rather than from immaturity or unreadiness in the young child. As was told in Chapter 1, Hadley missed the cut-off date for school entry by a mere two weeks and, in acknowledgment of this, his State Education Department allowed him 'visitor's rights' in the Reception class of a primary school a few miles from his home. Despite having admitted Hadley to the class on the basis of his phenomenal mathematical and reading abilities, the school was quite unwilling to adapt the curriculum to his needs. Hadley was bored and resentful and the experiment continued for only two weeks.

> There was little point in carrying on. He was learning nothing he hadn't taught himself two years before, he was hating it, and we didn't want him to start his school experience feeling that it was a complete waste of time.
>
> (Holly Bond, mother of Hadley)

A few months later, at the 'legal' age of 5½ years, Hadley enrolled in a different state school which acknowledged his educational needs by allowing him to enter at Grade 1 rather than Reception level, an immediate grade-skip of 12 months.

By the age of 3, Adrian Seng was displaying the reading, writing and mathematical abilities of a 6-year-old, and a prestigious independent (private) primary school agreed to enrol him in Reception at the age of 3 years 6 months. The experiment, however, was not a success. Intellectually Adrian was very far in advance of his 5-year-old classmates; socially, however, he would have needed a great deal of support, encouragement and understanding from his class teacher if he were to cope successfully with a six-hour school day. This understanding and flexibility were, unhappily, not forthcoming; his teacher was unable to cope with Adrian's intellectual and social needs and complained to the principal that he distracted the other children. After several weeks the Sengs and the principal agreed that Adrian should be withdrawn from school. Eighteen months later, he entered a State Education Department school at the usual age of 5, by which time he had completed, in home study, the first six years of the elementary school mathematics curriculum.

It should be noted that at no other time in Adrian's school and university career of extremely radical acceleration (he obtained his Bachelor of Science degree in 1991 at age 15) have the Sengs been told that his presence has been a distraction to other students. Proctor, Feldhusen and Black (1988), in their published guidelines for early admission of intellectually gifted children, emphasize that the receiving teacher of an early entrant must have positive attitudes towards early admission and be willing to assist the young child to adjust to the new situation. The receiving teachers of Hadley and Adrian were unable to respond effectively to the needs of young but brilliant children.

Three of the children, Hadley, Rick and Jade, entered school early on the recommendation of educational psychologists associated with their State Education Departments or Kindergarten Unions, who had conducted psychometric assessments of the children, and were thus aware of their remarkable intellectual and academic potential. Their parents, also, were convinced of the need for early entry; Hadley had been reading since the age of 18 months, Rick since 2½ years of age and Jade since 4; all three children preferred, as playmates, children several years older than they, and all were socially and emotionally mature beyond their years. The principal of Jade's school was eager to enrol her; the principals of the schools which Hadley and Rick wished to enter were extremely dubious but agreed reluctantly on the basis of the psychometric evidence. In the four other cases of early entrance the initial approach to the school was made by the parents of the subject children, who met varying degrees of obstruction from the school administration before the child was somewhat grudgingly admitted. In only one case of the seven did the principal or the receiving teacher display any familiarity with the literature on early entrance of intellectually gifted children; indeed, several of the parents reported that they had to argue persuasively against the principal's strong conviction that early entrance and acceleration were proven causes of psychosocial disturbance in children and would lead to social and emotional distress in later years. It says much for these parents' powers of persuasion that their children were indeed admitted!

Several of the children have been the victims of appalling organisational or bureaucratic mismanagement. Rick Ward was tested on the *Stanford-Binet Intelligence Test*, by a psychologist in private practice, at the age of 2 years 9 months, and was assessed as having a mental age of 4 years 4 months and an IQ of 147. On the basis of this assessment, coupled with the precocious development of his literacy and numeracy skills, he was permitted to enter kindergarten (pre-school) at the age of 3 years 4 months, fully 8 months earlier than the usual age of entry. Rick's reading and mathematics skills were allowed to blossom at kindergarten and it became increasingly obvious to the kindergarten director and teachers that here was a child of truly exceptional intellectual capacity. At the age of 3 years 11 months he was retested on the *Stanford-Binet* and this time achieved a mental age of 6 years 6 months and an IQ of 162. On the basis of this second assessment both the kindergarten director and the assessing psychologist advised the Wards that they should start to look for a school which would accept Rick into formal schooling some time after his fourth birthday.

Children may enter schools run by the South Australian Education Department at any time between their fifth and sixth birthdays; the Department is adamant, however, in its refusal to enrol children before the age of 5 years. Nevertheless, Rick's parents, being themselves teachers employed by the Education Department, were aware that the Department's then current 'Policy regarding fostering gifts and talents among children' (South Australian Education Department, 1983) contained the proviso that opportunities should be made available for pre-school children with gifts and talents [*sic*] to undertake activities within junior primary school classes. This meant that even if Rick could not be formally enrolled in school before the age of 5, he might be able to attend school part-time, and participate in Reception class activities, if a school could be found which would be prepared to accept him.

The search for an Education Department school which would recognize and respond to the Departmental policy on fostering gifts and talents took several months.

> Negotiating with schools was the most incredibly time-consuming business. We took along the psychologist's report, a statement from the kindergarten to the effect that they believed Rick was ready for formal schooling, and a letter from the State Gifted Children's Association confirming that he regularly attended their programmes for gifted pre-schoolers, but the schools either hadn't heard of the Departmental policy on 'gifts and talents' or weren't prepared to comply with it. We only found one Education Department school that was prepared to consider admitting him, and that was further from home than we would have liked. However, we jumped at it when, after a lot of deliberation, they agreed to take him on a part-time basis for three days a week. Actually, the principal and the receiving teacher were quite positive about it when they met Rick and realized how bright he really was.
>
> (Jan Ward, mother of Rick)

Rick entered formal schooling on a part-time basis at the age of 4 years 6 months. After only three days, however, the Wards were informed of a further difficulty. In general, South Australian elementary schools are not subject to geographic zoning restrictions; by coincidence, however, the particular school which had agreed to accord Rick 'visitor's rights' had been placed under a special restriction which required it to limit attendance to children living within certain geographic boundaries. Rick and his parents lived just outside the area which the school was now permitted to service. The principal expressed her regrets but explained that the Education Department had instructed her that the Wards must obtain a letter of exemption from the Department's Area Office before she could allow Rick to visit classes within her school. Jan Ward describes the ensuing events.

> We were quite simply stunned. It was like a slap in the face. We contacted the Area Office immediately but we were given the bureaucratic run-around; no one seemed to know whose responsibility it was to handle Rick's case, or even which office should be dealing with it. Meanwhile, Rick had to return to kindergarten, because the school principal didn't feel she could risk taking him back into school until she had the letter of exemption. So there the poor little beggar was; he'd left kindy a couple of weeks before to go up to 'big school' with the teachers and the other kids feeling happy for him and

congratulating him, and now here he was back among them with his head hanging as if he'd failed or done something wrong. It was a cruel and insensitive way to treat a child.

It took two full months for the Education Department administrators to come to the decision that a special exemption might be made for Rick. Having seen what 'big school' was like, he was unhappy at kindergarten, and he questioned me continually about when he was going to be allowed to go back and be with his new friends. At one point, in desperation, I managed to get through on the phone to one of the senior administrators who was handling the case, and asked him whether the Department might surely be prepared to make allowances for children with special needs. 'What do you mean, special needs?' he said. 'He doesn't have a speech impediment or one limb, does he?' Obviously he didn't consider giftedness a special need.

GRADE-SKIPPING AND SUBJECT ACCELERATION

VanTassel-Baska (1985) identified five essential elements of a successful gifted programme: content acceleration to the level of the child's abilities; thoughtfully planned, relevant enrichment; guidance in selecting courses and directions; special instruction with the opportunity to work closely with other gifted youth; and the opportunity to work with mentors who have high-level expertise in the child's area of giftedness.

Few educators would argue against the provision of enrichment, guidance in selecting appropriate courses, and mentorships. Ability grouping, however, is much less willingly accepted, and in Australia, as well as in Britain and the United States, many teachers and parents are strongly opposed to acceleration.

Few interventive procedures have been so comprehensively and rigorously studied as has academic acceleration. This concern for evaluation has arisen largely from the prevelance of the misconception, among teachers, that the social and emotional development of accelerated children is endangered and that the process is likely to leave 'gaps' in their academic development which will slow them down in subsequent grades (Southern, Jones and Fiscus, 1989). Far from offering support to these beliefs, the research on acceleration contradicts them strongly. A meta-analysis by Kulik and Kulik (1984) of 26 controlled studies of academic acceleration showed that accelerated gifted students significantly outperformed students of similar intellectual ability who had not been accelerated. Furthermore, research finds no evidence to support the notion that social or emotional problems arise through well-run acceleration programmes, and suggests that we should concern ourselves rather with the maladjusting effects that can arise from inadequate intellectual challenge (Daurio, 1979; Gallagher, 1976; Robinson, 1983; VanTassel-Baska, 1986). A survey of 21 mathematically precocious boys who had been radically accelerated found that, in comparison with equally talented youths who had not been accelerated, the accelerands had higher educational aspirations, believed that they had used their educational opportunities more effectively, and felt that their educational programme had had markedly positive effects on their social and emotional development (Pollins, 1983).

At the time of the Terman study (Terman, 1926) acceleration was probably the most common interventive strategy used by schools to foster the talents of intellectually gifted youth. Indeed, this was acknowledged by Terman in his instruction to teachers participating in the initial survey that they should nominate for intelligence testing not only the brightest student in their classes, but also the youngest. 'Take age into account. Of two pupils who seem to be about equally exceptional, but who differ one or more years in age, the younger is probably the more intelligent' (Terman, 1926, p. 21). Of the 12 children of IQ 180+ studied by Hollingworth (1942), 11 were grade-skipped in school and no fewer than seven were radically accelerated; in other words these seven children were promoted by three or more grade-levels.

Acceleration is much less commonly employed in Australia. A major causative factor is the lack of awareness, among teachers, of the academic and social benefits, to gifted children, of this practice. There is a paucity of Australian research and reporting on acceleration. An annotated bibliography of Australian writings on giftedness, creativity and talent, comprising 676 entries dating from the 1930s, features only seven entries on acceleration and, of these, no fewer than five report on a single acceleration programme, that of University High School in Melbourne (Braggett, 1986a). As a result of this lack of awareness, and the failure of teacher training institutions to introduce student teachers to the characteristics and needs of gifted children, many Australian teachers draw their perceptions of special programmes for the gifted at least in part from American television soap operas featuring special classes of precocious adolescents, or 16-year-olds in medical practice! The decision of the Academic Board of the University of New South Wales to establish an Early Entrance Program for exceptionally gifted high school students was greeted by a hysterical outburst in the editorial of *Education*, the journal of the New South Wales Teachers Federation, which unwittingly illustrated the source, and level, of the writer's perceptions of gifted children.

> It appears that the Board has succumbed to the Talented Child Brigade who have been pushing their middle-class wheelbarrow all the way to the University. One wonders whether the members of the

> Board held special video screenings of all these B-rated movies about the whiz kids before arriving at their decision to admit these kids?... After all, poor old Albert Einstein would have missed out, replaced no doubt by the sons and daughters of middle-class yuppies trying to steel [sic] more and more privileges under pretensions to greater abilities bestowed on them, not by their class position but by God himself.
>
> (Poulos, 1990a)

The article is illustrated with a caricature of the inn scene from *The Student Prince*, in which a toddler in a jumpsuit is shown standing on a bar-room table clutching a baby's bottle while, surrounding her, male students in quasi-military uniform quaff beer from steins and carol 'Drink! Drink! Drink!'

A further cartoon in the next issue of the journal, which depicted the gifted child attired in an academic gown, waving a violin and clutching a sheaf of documents headed '$E = MC^2$', was accompanied by the following astonishing commentary. Grammar, punctuation and syntax have been left unchanged.

> EXCEPTIONAL PROVIDED FOR CHILDREN. If you are 'talented' you will earn your stripes in the public arena and not through some back-door. If you are the most 'Gifted' you will certainly top the state in the (Higher School Certificate) no matter what age. But my guess is that you will not top the state, you never do because you are chosen via shonky tests from Organisations that peddle and profit from liberal individualism under the banner of the Talented Children Inc.
>
> (Poulos, 1990b)

Indeed, teacher concern about the possible maladaptive effects of acceleration is frequently encouraged by naive and inaccurate pronouncements from the Teachers' Unions. The policy document of the Victorian Teachers' Union warns educators that where schools employ acceleration 'serious social and emotional adjustments often occur in the short term and frequently in the long term' (Victorian Teachers' Union, 1986, p. 90). This is directly contradicted by 60 years of educational research.

Although acceleration is rarely offered to moderately gifted Australian children, the majority of the exceptionally gifted children studied here, 10 of the 15, have been grade-skipped at some time in their elementary school history. In a few cases, the grade-skip has been proposed by the school after careful consideration of possible alternatives, and has been supplemented with subject acceleration in one or more academic areas, participation in pull-out programmes, or some other attempt to individualize the curriculum in response to the child's particular needs. Jonathon, for example, was permitted to grade-skip from Grade 4 to Grade 6, and in Grade 6 started German with the Grade 8 students. In Grades 2, 3 and 4 he participated in a pull-out programme for children talented in maths and science. Fred Campbell was permitted to graduate from elementary school two weeks after his eleventh birthday (a grade-skip of 12 months), and in Grade 8 took Grade 11 chemistry and Grade 11/12 maths. Fred was permitted to 'collapse' Grade 9 and 10 studies into a single year, and entered Grade 11, in January 1991, a few days after turning 14, two years earlier than is customary.

Hadley, after his abortive attempt at early entry, was permitted to skip Reception class and enter Grade 1 at the age of 5½. At first the school assumed that the grade-skip, coupled with in-class enrichment, would satisfy Hadley's needs, including his insatiable hunger for problem-solving in mathematics; however, when it became obvious that a different approach was required, he was permitted to go to the Grade 2 classroom for maths and Grade 3 for computer education. At the end of his Grade 1 year the school permitted him to make a second grade-skip straight into Grade 3. A further grade-skip at the end of Grade 4 allowed him to enter Grade 6 at the age of 8 years 8 months, three years younger than the majority of his new classmates.

In the majority of cases, however, the accelerative programme offered to the children has been a token grade-skip of one year. Feldhusen (1983) advises an eclectic approach to programming for the gifted in which acceleration, enrichment and extended learning opportunities are employed within an integrative framework, adaptable to the cognitive and affective needs of the individual. By contrast, the single year grade-skip has generally been used, with the study children, as a last-ditch attempt to alleviate boredom or social isolation when several other strategies have been tried and have proved ineffective. It is thus a reactive, rather than a proactive measure, and is more likely to have been undertaken where the parents of the subject child have familiarized themselves with the literature on acceleration and have been prepared to assert themselves with the school administration.

> It has been an uphill battle all the way, and we are sure that the school agreed to accelerate Adam partly because they couldn't think what else to do with him and partly because they hoped it would keep us quiet.
>
> (Edward Murphy, father of Adam)

> The idea of acceleration came from us totally and we decided it was a necessity when Roshni was being 'switched off' in Reception and was under-achieving ridiculously. She made no progress in maths for the whole year in class, while at home she was sailing through

> work in number, space and measurement that we knew was part of the Grade 2 and 3 maths curriculum, and loving every minute of it. She was a different child at home when she was being allowed to develop at her own pace and level. We read all the literature we could find on acceleration before deciding it was the only option and before approaching the school.
>
> (Sarah Singh, mother of Roshni)

The success of radical acceleration as an interventive procedure for exceptionally and profoundly gifted children is well-documented (Hollingworth, 1942; Benbow, Perkins and Stanley, 1983; Robinson, 1983; Gross, 1986). By contrast, in all six cases where acceleration has been confined to a 'token' grade-skip of one year (Richard, Adam, Rick, Jade, Anastasia and Alice) the children report that the boredom, loneliness or social isolation which they experienced before the grade-skip has been alleviated only momentarily or not at all. It is doubtful whether taking a 7-year-old who is reading *Watership Down* and grade-skipping her to work with 8-year-olds will provide more than a temporary alleviation of her distress.

Radical acceleration: Adrian and Christopher

A small minority of the subject group has been radically accelerated in response to their truly phenomenal intellectual and academic abilities. This small group includes Adrian Seng and Christopher Otway. Both boys have been assessed on the *Stanford-Binet L-M* as having mental ages at least twice their chronological ages (a ratio IQ of at least 200) and both are members of the Study of Mathematically Precocious Youth's cohort of students who have scored at or above 700 on the *SAT–M* before their thirteenth birthdays. The acceleration programmes of these two children are thoughtfully planned and carefully monitored responses to the boys' intellectual, academic and social needs.

Adrian's abortive attempt at early entrance to elementary school has been described earlier in this chapter. Even at this early stage, when he was 3½ years of age, he was displaying the mathematical capabilities of a 6-year-old, and by the time he made his second attempt at early entrance, shortly after his fifth birthday, he had mastered virtually all the maths curriculum of his state elementary school system. His parents, David and Bonnie Seng, had familiarized themselves with the literature on acceleration and on the education and psychology of the gifted, and had realized that an age-linked progression through school would be intellectually and socially disastrous for their son. Fortunately, the principal of a nearby elementary school shared their belief, and Adrian entered into a programme of flexible progression designed by his parents and the school in partnership, and monitored by both. This programme consisted of a combination of grade-skipping and subject acceleration, designed to enable Adrian to experience the work of each grade-level, but compacted in such a way that he was able to move through two grade levels in any one year. By the time Adrian was 6½, he was attending Grades 3, 4, 6 and 7 for different subjects, and had friends, with whom he played in the schoolyard, from each grade level he worked at.

Adrian's mathematical achievements soon outpaced the abilities of the elementary school staff and at the age of 7½ he was permitted to attend the local high school (which enrolled students from Grades 8–12) for part of each day, working in maths at Grade 11 level with children seven years older than he. The rest of the day was spent in Grade 5 and 6 in his elementary school. Adrian is a modest and unassuming boy with an unusually open and friendly nature, and he became extremely popular with both his elementary school and high school friends, while his teachers found him a delight to work with. By the time he was 8 years of age, he was taking maths, physics, English and social studies at high school, moving flexibly between classes at Grade 8, 11 and 12 level, while continuing to attend elementary school part-time.

At age 8+, having informally sat and passed university entrance mathematics, Adrian began first-year university maths, initially in independent study and later under the guidance of faculty members from his local university. His parents and the principal of the elementary school had, by this time, reluctantly decided that this school had little more to offer him, and just before his ninth birthday he made a smooth transition from elementary school and began to spend one-quarter of his time at university and the remaining three-quarters at high school, working in several science subjects in Grades 10, 11 and 12 while taking humanities and general studies with Grade 8. By the time he was 12 his studies at university included fourth-year algebra, second year physics and second-year computer science. At the age of 14 he graduated from high school to devote himself to full-time university study.

Adrian has an absorbing thirst for knowledge. As he gained each university entrance qualification he used the time thus saved at high school to take on another subject. As the pace with which he masters new work is immeasurably faster even than that of his classmates at university, he has been able to maintain a radically accelerated programme which is equally remarkable for the breadth of its content. By age 14, he had passed university entrance examinations in mathematics, physics, chemistry, biology and English, and completed university courses in areas such as mathematical physics, quantum mechanics, discrete mathematics, linear and abstract algebra, Lebesgue integration, electromagnetic theory, optics, and several areas of computing science. At high school he was taking classical studies, modern European history and Latin at Grade 12, and German at Grade 10. During the last three years he has won several international prizes in mathematics. He completed the requirements for the Bachelor of Science degree shortly after his fifteenth birthday, and while still 15, entered B.Sc. Honours (post-graduate) study in pure mathematics. Adrian will commence Ph.D. study at age 17.

From his earliest years Christopher Otway displayed prodigious talents in mathematics and language. He taught himself to read at 2 years of age, and before his fourth birthday he was reading children's encyclopedias and had acquired a level of general knowledge that would be unmatched by the majority of Grade 5 or 6 students. His maths abilities developed almost as precociously. Shortly after his third birthday he spontaneously began to devise and complete simple addition and subtraction sums, and by the time he entered kindergarten (pre-school) at the usual age of 4 he was capable of working, in mathematics, at Grade 4 level.

Christopher was tested by a Kindergarten Union psychologist at 4½ years of age and was assessed as having a mental age of 7 years. (A subsequent assessment at age 11 established a mental age of 22 years and thus a ratio IQ of 200). However, his parents did not wish for, or seek, early entrance for the lad. By the time Christopher enrolled in the local state elementary school a few weeks after his fifth birthday, he had the maths achievement level of a Grade 5 student.

Like the parents of Adrian Seng, Elizabeth and David Otway had studied the literature on intellectual giftedness and were aware of the educational and psychosocial benefits of acceleration. Accordingly, they suggested to the principal of Christopher's school that he might be a suitable candidate for grade-skipping or subject acceleration. The principal and teachers had recognized Christopher's remarkable abilities within a few days of his enrolment, and readily accepted that he required a curriculum considerably differentiated in pace and content from that usually offered to Grade 1 students. Consequently, Christopher was withdrawn from his Grade 1 class for a few hours each day to join the Grade 2 children for English and the Grade 5s for maths. It soon became evident, however, that even this intervention did not address the full extent of Christopher's advancement and the following year, as a Grade 2 student, he went to the Grade 7 class each day for maths.

For the first two years of Christopher's elementary schooling, radical subject acceleration within his own school building proved an effective and sufficient response to his remarkable gifts in mathematics. As in the case of Adrian Seng, however, major difficulties arose when Chris's skill and knowledge in maths developed beyond the point where they could be adequately addressed by the staff of the elementary school. Only a few weeks into Grade 3, it became obvious that even the Grade 7 maths extension work which he was being offered in private tutorials with the principal was no longer sufficient to meet his needs.

After much thought, and in consultation with the principal of Christopher's elementary school, the Otways transferred him, half way through his Grade 3 year, to a large school in the neighbourhood which enrolled students across all grades from Reception to Grade 12. In response to his accelerated abilities in maths and language, the receiving school decided to enrol him in Grade 4 rather than Grade 3 – an immediate grade-skip of 12 months. To complement the grade-skip, the school was only too willing to continue his subject acceleration in mathematics and, as an additional response to his evident musical aptitude, permitted him to start lessons in flute, a curricular offering usually reserved for students in Grade 8 and above. The following year Christopher entered Grade 5, but was enrolled in Grade 9 for maths and started Indonesian lessons with the Grade 8 students.

Christopher's programme of subject acceleration has been extremely successful; at 12 years of age he was based in Grade 9 with students two and three years older than he, but took physics, chemistry, economics and English with the Grade 11 classes. The following year, rather than accelerate to Grade 12 for individual subjects, he chose to 'repeat' Grade 11 in different curriculum areas, this time taking humanities and foreign language subjects. As was related in Chapter 1, in October 1991, aged 14 years 11 months, Chris sat university entrance examinations in maths, chemistry, physics and economics, with an average mark of 98 per cent. In 1992 he will complete his final year of high school, sitting university entrance exams in legal studies, accounting, English, biology and Australian Studies. When he graduates from high school, at age 15, he will have undertaken a remarkable range of subjects from which he can choose those which he will study at university.

Christopher could, if he wished, have sat for university entrance mathematics at the end of 1989 and would undoubtedly have achieved extremely high grades, as his scaled score on the *SAT–M* at the age of 11 years 4 months was already 710; however, both Chris and his parents felt that for social reasons it was best that he postpone university enrolment for a few years. He will enter university a few weeks after his sixteenth birthday.

As mentioned earlier, Chris was assessed on the *Stanford-Binet* a few days after his eleventh birthday. The psychologist's report indicates the phenomenal level of his ability.

> On the *Stanford-Binet Intelligence Scale*, at the age of 11 years 0 months, Christopher obtained a mental age of 22 years. This meant that he had in fact passed virtually all the items on the test, right up to Superior Adult Three. Even here, however, it was obvious that Chris had not really reached his ceiling on some of the items. This gives him an intelligence quotient of at least 200... To extend the

testing established on the *Stanford-Binet*, I also used the *WAIS–R (Wechsler Adult Intelligence Scale)*, which is the adult intelligence scale most widely used. Here Chris performed at the absolute maximum for abstract reasoning and arithmetic, placing him in the 'very superior' range even compared with adults. At this level we started to pick up some relative weaknesses, in that his spatial skills are in the 'superior' rather than the 'very superior' range compared with an adult. However, obviously given that he is only 11 years of age, this too is an exceptional score. My belief is that Chris is a boy of very rare talent. Certainly I think the testing today was limited by the ceilings on the tests, rather than by Christopher's ability.

(Psychologist's report on Christopher Otway, aged 11)

The relative merits of acceleration and enrichment have been much debated. Many researchers (Goldberg, Passow, Camm and Neill, 1966; Sisk, 1979; Feldhusen, 1983) conclude that the most effective interventive technique is a combination of these, and other, strategies. Christopher has been fortunate in that his school has married his programme of radical acceleration to an enrichment programme in English, creative thinking and problem-solving, contained within pull-out classes. Additionally, during 1989, he participated in a cluster group programme for academically able Grade 8 and 9 students, organized by a local teachers' college. Further enrichment and extension in mathematics has been provided by permitting him to enter state and national maths competitions at much younger ages than is generally permitted. At the age of 10 was he placed second in his state's section of the national IBM mathematics competition, in which he was competing at Grade 10 level!

Terman and Oden (1947), in their follow-up research on the young adults of Terman's gifted group, argued forcefully that for students who display exceptional levels of intellectual giftedness the more conservative accelerative procedures, such as a grade-skip of a single year, are unlikely to be sufficient to meet their intellectual or social needs; for such students Terman and Oden, like Hollingworth (1942), advised several grade-skips spaced appropriately throughout the student's school career. The individualised educational programmes offered to Adrian and Christopher, which combine grade-skipping with a graduated programme of subject acceleration, answer the requirements of Terman and Oden, and respond effectively to the intellectual, academic and social needs of these profoundly gifted young men.

It is significant that both these cases of radical acceleration have occurred where an influential member of the school staff has had some previous knowledge of the research literature in gifted education. The principal of Adrian's primary school had a keen interest in gifted education for some years before Adrian's enrolment, and had been receiving the newsletters of his state's Association for Gifted and Talented Children, which reported on developments in the field both in Australia and overseas. The principal of the school to which Christopher transferred had spent several months on a study tour of the United States, observing programmes for gifted and talented youth in several states, and had been particularly influenced by the work of Stanley and his colleagues in the Study of Mathematically Precocious Youth (SMPY) at Johns Hopkins University. In addition, the two-grade acceleration of Roshni, who at 6 years of age was working happily in a Grade 3 class with children aged 8 and 9, was facilitated by a member of the teaching staff of her school who, in the words of Sarah Singh, 'was familiar enough with the characteristics of highly gifted children to the extent that she knew that my arguments and numerous quotes from the recent literature were legitimate'.

OTHER INTERVENTIVE PROCEDURES

Stanley (1979), in an analysis of contemporary North American practice in educating the gifted and talented, identified four types of enrichment commonly used by schools in attempts to respond to the needs of gifted children: busywork; irrelevant academic enrichment; cultural enrichment; and relevant academic enrichment. Busywork consists of loading the gifted child with a greater quantity of the work given to his classmates, in an attempt to keep him occupied. Irrelevant academic enrichment is the provision of enrichment work which is not related to the child's specific talents, such as offering classes in contract bridge to a child whose talents lie in mathematics or the sciences. Cultural enrichment consists of a lateral extension into a field which the child might not otherwise encounter, such as learning a foreign language or playing a musical instrument. Relevant academic enrichment, which Stanley proposes as the most appropriate form of enrichment intervention, requires the provision of a programme specifically designed for the individual and responsive to his talents, such as encouraging a mathematically gifted 9-year-old to investigate and report on the number systems of ancient civilizations.

Braggett reported on the curriculum content of Australian enrichment programmes purportedly established for gifted students.

> I have witnessed so many enrichment sessions over the past two years that I could now be forgiven for believing that enrichment refers to one of three different approaches: (a) library research on dinosaurs, space travel or the solar system, often supported by carefully presented diagrams and pictures, (b) computer awareness programmes that often include LOGO or BASIC language, or (c) process writing as advocated by Donald Graves. Another group of

> teachers believes that an excursion must be involved to meet Renzulli's Level 1 prescription, with a high percentage choosing a stream or river as the enrichment target or, alternatively, the local museum if it is raining. I hasten to add that all these activities may be educationally legitimate provided there is a valid rationale for them.
>
> (Braggett, 1985a, pp. 16–17)

Such activities may indeed be educationally valid as enrichment for the gifted where they address the specific talents and interests of the children for whom they are prescribed. Where this is not so, they can best be described as irrelevant academic enrichment (Stanley, 1979), activities which may keep the gifted child occupied for a period of time and offer a temporary alleviation of boredom, but which neither acknowledge nor foster his or her specific aptitudes or interests.

With a few fortunate exceptions, the in-class and pull-out enrichment programmes offered to the children of this study have been of the type described by Braggett. In the last three or four years, many Australian pull-out programmes for the gifted have purported to offer 'creative thinking' or 'problem-solving skills'. Questioned on the content of the 'creative thinking' sessions offered in their 'enrichment' programmes, the study children generally report that these consist of poetry writing, designing greeting cards, and brain-storming alternative uses for a brick. 'Problem-solving skills' include work with tangrams, puzzles devised by Edward de Bono, presented randomly and out of context, and brain-storming alternative uses for a brick! The children are, on the whole, less than enthusiastic about the content of the pull-out programmes offered by their schools, while they view the 'enrichment sheets' or 'problem-solving booklets' which some of their teachers hand out on a whole-class basis, as unchallenging, repetitive and a waste of time.

Both Braggett in 1984, and the Senate Investigatory Committee more recently, found that much of what passed as curriculum for the gifted in Australia comprised in-class enrichment or pull-out programmes (Braggett, 1986b: Commonwealth of Australia, 1988). The Richardson Study (Cox and Daniel, 1986) which examined provisions for the gifted in the United States, was strongly critical of pull-out programmes as a less than effective interventive procedure which offered a temporary and partial response to an ongoing dilemma. VanTassel-Baska, alluding to the fact that the typical time-frame allotted to enrichment through pull-out is no more than 150 minutes per week, described the procedure as an 8 per cent solution to a total problem (VanTassel-Baska, 1989). The Richardson Study claimed, in addition, that pull-out programmes encouraged the regular classroom teacher to feel herself absolved of responsibility towards her gifted students, the furtherance of whose talents thus became the responsibility of the resource room or specialist teacher.

The pull-out programme offered by the school attended by Rufus has several serious structural flaws. In a letter to the parents of students invited to participate, the pull-out provision is described as a 'revolving door' programme. However, contrary to the recommendations of Renzulli and his colleagues who designed the Revolving Door identification and enrichment model (Renzulli and Smith, 1980; Renzulli, Reis and Smith, 1981), students are given no opportunity to participate in decisions on their placement in, or withdrawal from, the programme; they enter and leave at semester breaks at the discretion of the teachers in charge. It is stated in the parent letter (with underlining for emphasis!) that students participating in the gifted programme are expected to complete all the normal classwork and homework set by their subject and home-room teachers; it might have been hoped that selection into the gifted programme, which takes place in class time, might imply an acknowledgment that the student had already mastered much of the basic content of the subject in which he was receiving enrichment! Students are selected for the programme on the Renzullian criteria of a high level of general ability, task commitment, and creativity (Renzulli, 1978); creativity, however, is defined in the parent letter as 'swiftness in completion of a task'!

These difficulties, in common with many other flaws which beset Australian programmes for gifted students, arise from a lack of awareness, among many well-meaning and committed teachers, of current research in the education and psychology of gifted children. For example, as stated earlier, because the research journals in gifted education are less freely available in Australia than in the United States, the negative critiques of Renzulli's 'three-ring' conception of giftedness, Enrichment Triad instructional model and 'Revolving Door' identification scheme, which have been published in the last few years (Jellen, 1983; Kontos, Carter, Ormrod and Cooney, 1983; Gagné, 1985; Jellen, 1985; Borland, 1989; Jarrell and Borland, 1990), have been slow to make their impact on Australian educators, and schools which base their enrichment and identification strategies on these models are frequently unaware that Renzulli's theories are being called seriously into question.

Table 8.1 displays the interventive measures which schools have employed to foster the intellectual and academic talents of the subject children.

At first glance the tally of interventive procedures employed with these intellectually and academically gifted children appears impressive. It should be borne in mind, however, that these children are young people of truly exceptional intellectual potential. At 5 years old, the usual age of entry into formal schooling, even the *least* intellectually advanced member of this group would have been functioning at the intellectual level of an

Table 8.1 Interventive procedures employed by schools to foster the talents of the children in this study

Child	*Early entry*	*Grade-skipping*	*Subject acceleration*	*Pull-out programme*	*Other*
Adrian	Yes	Yes	Yes		Yes
Jade	Yes				
Alice		Yes		Yes	
Rufus				Yes	
Roshni	Yes	Yes	Yes		
Rick	Yes		Yes	Yes	
Anastasia	Yes	Yes		Yes	
Christopher		Yes	Yes	Yes	Yes
Jonathon		Yes	Yes	Yes	
Cassandra				Yes	
Fred		Yes	Yes	Yes	Yes
Ian		Yes	Yes	Yes	Yes
Adam		Yes	Yes	Yes	
Richard	Yes	Yes	Yes	Yes	Yes
Hadley	Yes	Yes	Yes		Yes
Total	7	11	10	11	6

8-year-old, while Adrian, Christopher and Ian were functioning, intellectually, at the level of the average child of 10. In every case the parents of the subjects report that this intellectual precocity was accompanied by a passionate love of learning, a desire to explore and investigate new knowledge, hobbies and interests more usually associated with children several years their senior, and a preference for the companionship of older children. Academically, socially and emotionally they were more than ready for formal schooling. Yet only seven of the 15 children were permitted early entrance to formal schooling, and in three of these cases, those of Adrian, Hadley and Rick, the school's mismanagement of the situation was such that the attempt had to be postponed or abandoned.

Surprisingly, 10 of the children have been permitted to skip a grade. However, as was discussed in Chapter 6, the academic attainment levels of these children, as established by standardized tests of achievement in reading, mathematics and spelling, are many years in advance of their chronological ages. Fourteen of the 15 children have reading achievement levels more than three years in advance of their chronological age, while eight of the 15 are advanced by more than four years. In mathematics, 12 of the 15 children are advanced by more than three years, while seven are advanced by more than four years; indeed, no fewer than five of the subjects have scored above the mean on the *Scholastic Aptitude Test–Mathematics*, standardized on 17–18-year-olds, before the usual age of graduation from elementary school! Of the 13 subjects tested on the

Westwood Spelling Test, seven had spelling ages four years in advance of their chronological ages, and four were advanced by five or more years. There is little point in offering students such as these a token grade-skip of one year unless the school is prepared to complement this with subject acceleration at least in those areas where it is most urgently required. Nevertheless, in only seven of the 10 accelerative cases has the grade-skip been combined with subject acceleration, and in only one case of the seven, that of Adrian, has this subject acceleration addressed the full extent of the child's academic advancement.

The most common means of intervention employed by the schools serving these extremely gifted children was the pull-out enrichment programme, experienced by 11 of the 15 children. A disturbing finding, which will be discussed later in this chapter, is that in the majority of cases the pull-out provision was offered for only one or two years, and that in several cases the programme itself was disbanded by the school, not because of the educational weaknesses of this model but for political or ideological reasons. As discussed earlier in this chapter, the curricula of the pull-out programmes were generally viewed, by the children, as unstimulating and irrelevant to their particular fields of talent.

Current Australian awareness of, and attitudes towards, ability grouping of gifted children are vividly illustrated by the finding that the bibliography of Australian writings on giftedness, creativity and talent, edited by Braggett in 1986, contains only four entries under the headings 'ability grouping', 'grouping' or 'streaming' and of these four entries, three were written in the 1930s and one in 1964! Furthermore, no distinction is made between the three methodologies: the index reads 'Ability grouping (see Streaming)'. Under the heading 'special classes/schools' appear only 27 entries, 13 (48 per cent) of which describe the full-time self-contained 'Opportunity C' classes for intellectually gifted elementary school students in the state of New South Wales (Braggett, 1986b).

While most Australian states permit a certain degree of ability grouping and a minority of states, such as New South Wales and Northern Territory, have created a limited number of full-time self-contained classes for the gifted, the Ministry of Education of the state of Victoria has issued a strong caveat against grouping on ability within its schools.

> The task of ensuring effective access requires that schools... ensure that test-scores and general measures of ability are not used to stream students into particular classes, and that classes are organized to cater for students with a range of previous learning.
>
> (Education Department of Victoria, 1984, p. 13)

The Australian wariness of ability grouping stands in striking contrast to the attitudes prevailing in other Western societies. Influenced by a considerable body of empirical research on the positive effects of ability grouping on both the academic and social development of gifted students, virtually every internationally recognized authority on the education and psychology of the gifted has recommended that intellectually gifted children should be grouped together for a significant proportion of their class time (Hollingworth, 1942; Barbe, 1957; Kulik and Kulik, 1982; Tannenbaum, 1983; Webb, Meckstroth and Tolan, 1983; Feldhusen, 1985; VanTassel-Baska, 1985).

The extremely positive effects on academic achievement when gifted students are grouped for instruction has been re-emphasized by the recent meta-analytic research of Karen Rogers (1991). The American National Research Center on the Gifted and Talented has published the following six recommendations for practices involving ability grouping.

- Students who are academically or intellectually gifted and talented should spend the majority of their school day with others of similar abilities and interests.
- The Cluster Grouping of a small number of students, either intellectually gifted or gifted in a similar academic domain, within an otherwise heterogeneously grouped classroom can be considered when schools cannot support a full-time gifted programme (either demographically, economically or philosophically).
- In the absence of full-time gifted programme enrolment, gifted and talented students might be offered specific group instruction across grade levels, according to their individual knowledge acquisition in school subjects, either in conjunction with cluster grouping or in its stead.
- Students who are gifted and talented should be given experiences involving a variety of appropriate acceleration-based options, which may be offered to gifted students as a group or on an individual basis.
- Students who are gifted and talented should be given experiences which involve various forms of enrichment that extend the regular school curriculum, leading to the more complete development of concepts, principles and generalizations.
- Mixed-ability Cooperative Learning should be used sparingly for students who are gifted and talented, perhaps only for social skills development programmes.

(Rogers, 1991, pp. xii–xiii)

It is of concern that these recommendations, excellent as they are, should have closed with the suggestion that Cooperative Learning, which is acknowledged as unsuited to the academic needs of gifted students (Robinson, 1990), should be used in social skills programmes. Here again we have a fine group of researchers who seem unaware of the extent to which the psychosocial development of gifted students differs from that of their age-peers of average ability. Coleman (1985) found that 'avoiding answering questions about moral or ethical concerns' (p. 182) was one of the most common behaviours adopted by gifted students to camouflage their intellectual abilities.

These researchers who have made a special study of the intellectual and emotional needs of exceptionally and profoundly gifted students have emphasized that, if these children are to avoid severe psychosocial disturbance arising from salience and social isolation, some form of on-going ability grouping is imperative (Carroll, 1940; Hollingworth, 1942; DeHaan and Havighurst, 1961; Kline and Meckstroth, 1985; Janos and Robinson, 1985; Silverman, 1989).

After many years of studying and serving the exceptionally and profoundly gifted, Hollingworth became convinced that these children should be permitted access, on a full-time basis, to other students at similar stages of intellectual, social and emotional development. She became a staunch and persuasive advocate of the establishment of full-time self-contained classes for children of exceptional intellectual potential (Hollingworth, 1926, 1936, 1942; Hollingworth and Cobb, 1923, 1928). Hollingworth reported on 'Child C', a boy of IQ 190, who was consistently rejected by other children until he was transferred to a special class for gifted children where the median IQ was 164. In this class he was able, for the first time, to make social contacts with other children who shared his abilities and interests, and within a short time he was one of the most popular and respected class members (Hollingworth, 1942).

Despite the overwhelming evidence on the advisability of homogeneous grouping of highly gifted students, not one of the exceptionally gifted children in this study has experienced any form of full-time grouping with intellectual peers.

EXAMPLES OF INAPPROPRIATE EDUCATIONAL PROGRAMMING

The school histories of several of the 15 children are text-book examples of educational mismanagement.

Ian Baker

Ian Baker entered the Reception class at his local state elementary school two months after his fifth birthday. Ian's phenomenal abilities in number and language, and his remarkable gift for cartography, have been described in this and previous chapters. During his first few months in school no allowance was made for his mathematical abilities, and only after his parents had gently informed the teacher that he had just finished reading

E. B. White's *Charlotte's Web* was he permitted to forego the reading readiness exercises undertaken by the rest of the class.

Ian was bored, deeply unhappy and restless at school, but his parents were not informed of any serious behavioural problems. However, as was described in Chapter 1, after Ian had been at school for some eight months, the school administration asked for a meeting with Brock and Sally Baker. In this meeting the parents were rather brusquely informed that Ian was uncontrollable in class, that he was displaying bouts of frightening physical violence towards other children, and that the school wished to have him psychometrically assessed with a view to transferring him to a school for behaviourally disturbed children. This special school was attached to the psychiatric department of a large children's hospital. 'We were totally devastated,' says Brock Baker. 'We felt as though we had managed in 5½ years to bring up a violent criminal who was about to be expelled from school before he had completed one year.'

In some ways, however, the news of Ian's aggressiveness at school confirmed a concern which Brock and Sally already had about aspects of his behaviour at home.

> We had always felt that Ian was reasonably bright, and we had noticed that whenever he became bored he stormed around the place like a caged lion looking for a fight. When he was in that mood he became physically aggressive and verbally nasty towards anyone in reach, especially smaller children. When he was mentally stimulated, then his behaviour improved considerably. Accordingly, we were only too happy to have him assessed. We felt sure that if he was indeed identified as bright and in need of further stimulation, then the school would respond to this. In addition, any help the psychologist could give us to improve our handling of Ian at home would be most welcome!

Ian was assessed on the *Stanford-Binet Intelligence Test* at the age of 5 years 11 months and was found to have a mental age of 9 years 10 months and an IQ somewhere in excess of 169. (Subsequent testing at the age of 9 years established a mental age of 18 years and a ratio IQ of 200.) To complement the *Stanford-Binet* testing, the educational psychologist administered a test of reading achievement and found that Ian's reading accuracy and comprehension were at the 12-year-old level – an advancement of more than six years. The psychologist confirmed Brock and Sally Baker's belief that Ian's emotional swings were directly related to the amount of intellectual stimulation he was receiving, and emphasized the importance, for the emotional health of such an exceptionally gifted child, of providing him with academic work at sufficiently challenging levels, and with the companionship of children of like abilities and interests. He referred Ian to the State Association for Gifted and Talented Children, and recommended to the school that it establish some form of enrichment and extension programme to respond to Ian's intellectual and social needs.

At first, the school, and Ian's class teacher, responded to the challenge with enthusiasm.

> Ian's teacher, who had never had such a student in her class before, took it upon herself to stimulate Ian and did not force him to do the same work as the others if he did not want to. She scoured resource centres looking for suitable curriculum material and put in a great deal of extra work to ensure that the problem of boredom did not recur. Ian stayed with this teacher right through Grade 1 and Grade 2 and she gave him a variety of really stimulating maths tasks – some of them right up at Grade 8 level. In addition, the principal was very encouraging towards the gifted children in the school. He set up special pull-out sessions, taught both by himself and other staff members, which Ian and several others in the school attended. These two years could not have been better for Ian, and as a result the whole family benefited.
>
> (Brock Baker, father of Ian)

Unfortunately, this situation was relatively short-lived. Shortly after the start of the year in which Ian entered Grade 3, the elementary school principal retired, and the school was led until the end of the year by a temporary 'acting' principal. The pull-out programme for gifted and talented students, which had been happening less and less regularly during the last few months of the old principal's stay, was finally disbanded. During the first semester, Ian's teacher permitted him to work on an individualized maths programme using a Grade 7 mathematics text; however, he received no guidance or assistance, and no other children to work with, and during the second semester, with little encouragement to continue, Ian gradually reverted to the Grade 3 maths curriculum of his classmates.

> Ian has a very frustrating attitude of never telling us what is happening at school except to say that it is boring, so it was well into the year before we realized what was happening. All the negative behaviours had returned and our home life was gradually turning sour again, but we had assumed that the school, having found what worked for Ian, would be keeping up the good work. When we finally got it out of him that there no longer was a pull-out programme and that he was back to doing Grade 3 maths, we were appalled.
>
> (Brock Baker)

The new principal was a politically alert young woman who was aware of the hostility of the Australian teacher industrial unions towards special programming for the gifted, and the disapproval of gifted programmes openly voiced by a number of influential senior administrators in the state Education Department. She was also made aware, by her new staff, that they had 'had enough of gifted children and special programmes for the gifted', which they felt had been foisted upon them by the old principal. The Bakers sought an interview to ask her if something could be done to alleviate Ian's boredom and frustration. She was not unsympathetic, but was adamant that Ian should not receive any special programme or provision that was not offered to the other children in the school. She stated frankly to Brock and Sally that it would be 'political suicide' for her to establish gifted programmes within her school.

Ian completed Grade 3 in a quiet fury of anger, intellectual frustration and bitterness. The verbal and physical aggressiveness returned in full spate; however, as he was now two years older than he had been in Grade 1, he was able to maintain a tighter control on his emotions while at school, and his teachers remained quite unaware of the emotional toll levied on the child. At home, however, he released all his frustration and resentment and he became, in Brock's words, 'almost impossible to live with'.

This situation lasted for the remainder of Grade 3 and through the whole of Grade 4. The Bakers made regular visits to the school to plead with the teachers and the principal to provide some form of intellectual stimulation for Ian, but they were met with vague promises of enrichment which never, in fact, materialized.

During his Grade 4 year, Brock and Sally decided to have Ian reassessed by an independent psychologist with a special interest in intellectually gifted children. Accordingly, at the age of 9 years 3 months Ian was assessed firstly on the *Wechsler Intelligence Scale for Children (WISC–R)* and subsequently on the *Stanford-Binet L-M*, the scale on which he had first been tested at age 5. Ian ceilinged out on the *WISC–R*, scoring scaled scores of 19 (the maximum possible) on all subscales of both the verbal and performance subtests. On the *Stanford-Binet* Ian, in the words of the psychologist's report, 'sailed through all the items through to the highest level of all, Superior Adult Three. Here he did start to fail on some tests, but nevertheless his IQ came off the top of this scale also.' Ian scored a mental age of 18 years 6 months, exactly twice his chronological age, and thus a ratio IQ of 200. In addition, the psychologist administered standardized achievement tests of maths, reading and spelling. Ian's reading and spelling were at adult level, and on the *British Ability Scales* maths test, he scored more than five years above his chronological age.

The psychologist was appalled to hear that a child of such exceptional talent was being forced to plod through a lockstep curriculum with other Grade 4 students. Her written report, reproduced in part in Chapter 1, expressed her extreme concern that Ian was required to undertake the regular curriculum with age-peers, and recommended, quite unequivocally, that for his educational and psychological welfare, he urgently needed acceleration, especially in the area of maths. The report was ignored.

Half way through Ian's Grade 4 year, it became clear to the Bakers that there was little hope of his school, under the new principal, ever re-establishing its programmes for, or its interest in, highly able students. Brock Baker wrote to me describing his frustration.

> During the last year and a half we feel that Ian has only been marking time and has not been advancing at a rate comparable with his ability. We consider this to be far from satisfactory. So much so that we are considering moving Ian to another school, but are being quite frustrated by the almost total lack of interest shown by the schools so far contacted. In most cases the principals are aware of the problems that can stem from having gifted children in the school, but do not have special programmes for such children and are not prepared to set them up... The only time a gifted child gets fair treatment, let alone special treatment, is when there is an individual teacher prepared to do extra-curricular work to seek out and provide the stimulating material for these students. The education system in this state is in no way geared towards helping gifted children. In fact it actually works against them.

After months of searching, the Bakers found an independent (private) school which promised to provide some form of special programming for Ian. They would not permit him to grade-skip, nor were they prepared to agree to subject acceleration until they had observed, for themselves, the level at which he was capable of working; accordingly Ian enrolled in Grade 5, with his chronological age-peers, in February 1989. The following month, for the purposes of this study, he took the *Scholastic Aptitude Test–Mathematics* and achieved a scaled score of 560, a remarkable performance for a child of 9 years 11 months. This achievement is even more impressive when one considers that since Grade 2 he had received no formal instruction in maths beyond that appropriate to his chronological age!

Despite its assurance that Ian's academic needs would be addressed, his new school was at first slow to make appropriate provision and, in Sally's words, 'we had to do our fair share of reminding them of the promises they made before he was enrolled, which were the basis for our decision to enrol him!' A request to the principal that he be permitted to take maths with the Grade 7 class was met with the response that there would be little point in this as his achievement level was already many years ahead of Grade 7! However, during the first semester of Grade 5 he was permitted to participate in pull-out programmes for mathematically gifted children in Grades 5–7, and when his Grade 5 teacher admitted, with commendable courage and honesty, that she simply did not have the skills or knowledge to extend his phenomenal maths capacities within the regular classroom, the school sought, and found, a mentor for him. This was a maths teacher from the senior school, who has authored several maths texts and is regarded as extremely able in his field. This teacher worked with Ian in a mentorial relationship for the rest of the year, taking him through the Grade 8 and 9 maths curriculum, and filling in the gaps in his knowledge. The target was to bring Ian up to the Grade 10 standard in maths so that the following year, 1990, he could work with the Grade 10 students in a programme of subject acceleration.

This indeed occurred. In 1990 Ian, aged 10, was based with the Grade 6 students but undertook maths with the top stream of Grade 10. The school swiftly recognized the academic and emotional benefits that arose from his maths acceleration, and proposed to the Bakers that Ian should skip Grade 7 and go straight into Grade 8 at the start of 1991. To complement the grade-skip, the school, with the Bakers, designed a programme of subject acceleration in Ian's areas of particular strength. This found him, at the age of 11 years 10 months, based in Grade 8 but taking maths and computing with Grade 11, science with Grade 10 and social studies with Grade 9.

In 1989 the school entered Ian, along with other mathematically gifted students, in two Australia-wide maths competitions. Normally students are not eligible to enter these competitions before Grade 7; however, in recognition of Ian's phenomenal abilities, he was permitted to enter while still in Grade 5. In both competitions he out-performed all other entrants from his school. Ian was jubilant but slightly dazed.

> His achievements in these competitions finally meant that he received some public recognition for his scholastic abilities. The certificates and trophies were presented at school Assemblies, and, in addition, his achievements were referred to during the Junior School Principal's annual report presented on Speech Day. This was the first time in Ian's life that anyone had publicly acknowledged and praised his abilities. For Ian, and his parents and grandparents, Speech Day was a very high High.
>
> (Brock Baker)

The Bakers have been relieved to note that certain unpleasant physical symptoms which plagued Ian for some time dissipated with the disappearance of the intellectual frustration. 'As the anger and aggressiveness lessened,' says Sally, 'so did the blinding headaches, and the nausea and the stomach pains. He is a different child.'

Ian Baker's mathematical ability is certainly on a par with that of

Christopher Otway and may well equal that of Adrian Seng. Unlike Adrian and Chris, however, his astonishing potential has largely been ignored by the education system; indeed, for a substantial proportion of his elementary schooling, his progress in maths has been deliberately suppressed. It is unfortunate that he had to suffer through four years of appalling educational mismanagement before his astonishing intellectual abilities were at last acknowledged.

Rick Ward

The bureaucratic mismanagement which attended Rick Ward's early entrance to elementary school has been outlined earlier in this chapter. When Rick was finally permitted to maintain his 'visitor's rights' in the Reception class, the principal and receiving teacher acknowledged that, even though he was fully a year younger than many of his classmates, his numeracy skills were far beyond that of the other students, and at Jan and Tony Ward's request he was permitted to accelerate to Grade 1 for maths, and undertake additional maths enrichment in the Reception class at other times. This provision was continued and extended when he entered Grade 1; indeed, he was permitted to take maths with the Grade 3 students, a subject acceleration of two years.

At first this arrangement worked happily; however, during the second half of the Grade 1 year the structural arrangements for Rick's subject acceleration began to break down. More often than not the Grade 1 teacher would forget to remind Rick that it was time for him to go to the Grade 3 classroom for maths, or the Grade 3 teacher would forget to send for him. No 5-year-old, no matter how intellectually precocious, should have to take responsibility for the management of his school day. Rick missed more and more of his maths acceleration classes and, in the words of Jan Ward, 'neither of the teachers seemed to show any concern about this'. Indeed, when Jan expressed her own concern to the Grade 3 teacher her response was, 'Well, it doesn't really matter, does it? I mean, it's not as if he's behind.'

As in the case of Ian Baker, problems re-emerged with the arrival of a new school principal. This new administrator adopted a firm stance against any form of academic acceleration, and at the start of Rick's Grade 2 year Jan Ward was informed that his accelerated maths programme would cease forthwith and that, furthermore, although Rick had been attending the Grade 3 class for maths the previous year, this year he would do Grade 2 maths with his Grade 2 classmates. Jan protested that this would require him to repeat the work which he had successfully completed two years previously; the principal considered this point and finally conceded that he might be permitted to do maths 'extension sheets', but only when he had completed his regular class work. Jan Ward explains the principal's rationale for this decision.

> She spent quite a long time talking to me about the importance of ensuring that a child is 'happy' in school, and explaining that from her point of view 'happiness', rather than academic acceleration, was the first priority for Rick. She seemed to feel that these were mutually exclusive. She admitted that Rick was 'exceptional in some areas' but questioned whether his abilities would be of any use to him if he did not learn to 'use them creatively'. She followed this up by announcing that he would be better off if he consolidated his maths ability by using concrete materials instead of doing the work in his head!

Under the new structures imposed to ensure Rick's 'happiness', he was bewildered and unhappy. The Grade 2 maths bored him; he had mastered it with ease two years earlier. When he asked his Grade 2 teacher whether he could take the 'extension sheets' home to show Jan, she refused with the comment, 'I don't want your mother helping you at home.'

Next, the school began to encourage Rick to moderate his reading achievement so that it would be more in line with his classmates.

> His teacher allows the children to bring books from home to read in class, but for the last few weeks when he has arrived at school with the novel he has been reading, she has told him that she would rather he bring along shorter books with more pictures, which would be more 'enjoyable' for him. I'm sure she thinks that I am interfering with Rick's choice of book, but I'm not. He is now frightened of taking his own choice of book to school in case he gets into trouble.
> (Jan Ward)

The situation was complicated by the principal's insistence that all children, regardless of their level of mastery, should use concrete materials in mathematics. Rick's teachers tried hard to discourage him from working out maths problems in his head instead of using the materials provided to assist him.

> His maths lessons for the past month have consisted of finding different ways of making up different amounts of money, and then counting out the change for one dollar. The teacher insists that the children should count up the change concretely using the plastic coins. Rick does it the other way round; he does the subtraction sum in his head and then picks up the plastic coins which make up the total. I have tried to explain to the teacher that to Rick all maths becomes a sum to be worked out mentally, even if it is a worded problem-solving task, but she still becomes so openly concerned

> when he does this, and speaks to him sternly in front of the other kids, that on occasions he comes home in tears. The change in him since last year is really disturbing. He has gone from being a happy, confident, stimulated little boy to a child who is bewildered and uncertain of what is expected of him.
>
> The lady is not a bad teacher. The kids love her and parents of children who are having learning difficulties have the utmost respect for her. It's just that her philosophy of education and her teaching methodologies don't match Rick's academic or emotional needs.
>
> (Jan Ward)

Rick mastered long multiplication and long division before his sixth birthday. If this situation had continued, with Rick being forced to conform to the maths curriculum of the grade level in which he was enrolled, three years would have passed before he was formally introduced to either.

In 1992, however, Rick's Grade 5 year, Jan and Tony withdrew him from the government primary school and sent him, after much heart-searching, to a private school which has a reputation for academic rigour and excellent programmes for able students.

> It is very expensive, and we hope we can keep it up, but with both of us working we think we can. We do feel resentful that we should have to go outside the state system to get an appropriate education for Rick, but we felt we just had to do something. Last year was totally wasted. He had no pride in his work and he was just coasting along. His maths wasn't being challenged. He *still* hadn't been introduced to long division, which he knew in Grade 1!
>
> He's only been at the new school for a few weeks, but already you can see the difference. Last year he couldn't have cared less. Now he's just beginning to take an interest in work again. He's taking pride in the way he looks when he goes off to school. His whole attitude is different.
>
> (Jan Ward)

Adam Murphy

Bloom (1985), in his study of 120 adults who had achieved success in cognitive, artistic and athletic fields, reported that many of his subjects had changed schools several times in childhood before finding an educational environment which facilitated the development of their particular talents. No fewer than 10 of the 15 children in the present study have changed schools at least once during their elementary schooling to escape an educationally repressive environment. Richard McLeod, aged 12, is currently attending his fourth school in seven years. His parents withdrew him from a small but exclusive private school to which he had won a scholarship entitling him to full remission of fees, when it became apparent that the school had no intention of fostering the outstanding talent for mathematics which had won him the scholarship. 'The fee remission helped us financially,' says Ursula McLeod, 'but it was like a free meal in a lousy restaurant.'

Perhaps the most poignant example of the search for an appropriate education is that of the Murphy family. Edward and Georgina Murphy are the oldest parents in the study; Adam was born when Edward was 39 and Georgina 38 years of age. Both parents have a deep and abiding love of the countryside and shortly after Adam's birth they were able to realize a dream which they had cherished for many years; they sold the complex of small businesses which they had worked for 12 years to establish, and moved to an isolated but very beautiful region of their state to live in semi-retirement.

When Adam entered kindergarten at 4 years of age the Murphys thought it best that they let the teacher know that he was a competent and enthusiastic reader and had been so since the age of 3.

> She smiled at us as if what we had said was a social pleasantry rather than a piece of information that might help her with his education, and we soon found that this was, indeed, the attitude taken by the kindergarten staff. Matters were complicated by the fact that Adam had already passed though the stage of having to read aloud, and now preferred to read silently, so when the teachers did notice him poring over a book, they assumed he was simply looking at the pictures.
>
> (Georgina Murphy)

The situation improved markedly when Adam entered school shortly after his fifth birthday. As is common in small country schools in Australia, the entry class comprised pupils in Reception, Grade 1 and Grade 2. After the first few weeks, Adam's teacher sought an interview with the Murphys and told them that he was easily the brightest child she had encountered in her teaching career. At the suggestion of this teacher, Adam was tested by an Education Department psychologist, who subsequently informed the teacher, and Adam's parents, that on the *Wechsler Intelligence Scale for Children–Revised (WISC-R)* he had achieved a full-scale IQ of 155. (Subsequent testing on the *Stanford-Binet* established an IQ of 162.) His teacher responded to this information by allowing Adam to work with the Grade 1 students and, in the following year, treating him as if he were in Grade 2. By this means Adam was able to complete the work of the first three grades of elementary school in his first 18 months of formal schooling. Adam thrived on the intellectual stimulation, the academic challenge and the warmth and encouragement of this teacher who delighted in the visible flowering of his talents.

At the end of the year in which Adam completed the Grade 2 curriculum, the principal and school staff met with the Murphys to discuss the provision that should be made for him during the following 12 months. The principal explained that the school would have two classes containing Grade 3 pupils – a composite (split) Grade 2/3 class and a composite Grade 3/4. Edward and Georgina felt strongly that, since Adam was already working in mathematics at Grade 4 level, he should enter the Grade 3/4 class where his abilities in both maths and language could be extended. The principal demurred; he explained that both he and his teaching staff had serious concerns about the psychosocial risks attendant on acceleration, and that they would much prefer Adam to enter the Grade 2/3 group, where there would be less of an age gap between him and his class-mates. The principal promised, however, that for maths and some aspects of English Adam would study with the Grade 3/4 class, at Grade 4 level, and that if this proved effective both academically and socially he could transfer to the Grade 3/4 class on a full-time basis later in the year.

As discussed earlier, it is of paramount importance in any case of acceleration that the receiving teacher should be sympathetic towards the accelerative process, and be prepared to assist the child to adapt to the new situation. The Grade 2/3 class which Adam entered was taught by two teachers, each on a part-time basis, and each made it clear to Adam and to his parents that they believed that he was too young for the class and should have remained in Grade 2. With such negative attitudes on the part of his home-room teachers, Adam's promised subject acceleration to Grade 4 was out of the question. Indeed, the Grade 2/3 teachers seemed to take pleasure in picking up any slip in spelling, maths or reading, or any minor infraction of class rules, and presenting it to the Murphys as evidence that Adam was socially immature and of moderate academic ability. The psychologist's assessment of Adam as having a reading age of 12 was rejected as irrelevant, and Adam was presented with readers and other texts at Grade 2 level. The contrast between the enthusiastic acceptance and encouragement he had experienced only a few weeks previously, and the continual criticism and disapproval to which he was now subjected, had an intensely depressive effect on Adam both emotionally and intellectually. 'Quite simply,' says Edward Murphy, 'he stopped learning.'

As in the case of Ian Baker, Adam's boredom, depression and intellectual frustration manifested itself in negative behaviours at school and at home. His teachers reported him as arrogant, disruptive and unmannerly. At home, he was aggressive and short-tempered towards his younger sister. However, as the year progressed he lost even the will to rebel. He began to conform to the requirements of his teachers and the academic standards of his classmates. His teachers were delighted with the 'improvement' in his behaviour, and expressed their approval to Edward and Georgina.

Half way through the school year, Edward Murphy expressed his fears in a letter to me.

> What I find hard to tell them, because I can't define it, is that he has lost, or rather is no longer able to display, the 'spark' that he always had. This was the sharpness; the quick, often humorous comment; the sudden bubbling over of enthusiasm when he starts following through a series of ideas. It is rather like a stone with many sharp edges; they have knocked these edges off and as a result he is rolling more smoothly in class and they are happy about that. I feel that they have caused him to bury an important part of himself. It is still there; it bursts out at home now and again, but he has learned to keep it hidden. I hope you know what I mean, because I have tried to explain it to the teachers and I fail every time. They believe they have had great success, but I know they are depressing some vital spark.

Two months after this letter was written the Murphys sold their home in the country and moved back to the city. They had become convinced that if Adam were to receive an education commensurate with his needs they would have to live in an area where they would have a wider choice of schools. After discussions with several state and independent schools, Adam enrolled in Grade 3 at a large private school which provided pull-out programmes for gifted students. The Murphys were in hope that the school would accelerate Adam to Grade 4, at least for maths, but the principal was cautious and wanted behavioural evidence that Adam's ability was truly exceptional. Unfortunately, neither the curriculum of the regular classroom nor the horizontal 'enrichment' provided in the pull-out programme contained any element of accelerated instruction; consequently Adam had no opportunity to display the full extent of his advancement in maths and language. Indeed, he lost the urge to do so. The school took this as confirmation that Adam had 'levelled out' and that his current grade placement was adequate to his educational and social needs.

Ironically, the one area in which Adam *was* permitted to accelerate was in his membership of the school's competitive chess team. He is an extremely talented player and the school regularly matched him against much older students from other schools. There was no suggestion that he would suffer social or emotional distress through training regularly with team-mates who are several years his senior; yet, the school continued to refuse him any form of academic acceleration on the grounds that it might result in emotional damage in later years! Perhaps in chess the 'risk' of acceleration was offset by the prestige that accrues to the school through Adam's success in competitions!

Shortly before Adam's eighth birthday, he, his parents and his younger sister, Mary, took a skiing holiday in the Australian Alps. Adam, who had never skied before, took to the sport like a duck to water. Like many of the study children he has an unusually developed sense of balance (see Chapter 4) and the ski instructor told Georgina and Edward that the speed of his learning was quite remarkable. Edward Murphy wryly compared Adam's learning on the ski slopes to his learning in the classroom.

> With Adam's skiing he went from being an absolute beginner to mastering the Intermediate runs in only five days. He was allowed almost a free rein and advanced up through the classes according to his ability. His morale, enthusiasm, commitment and social behaviour were bubbling along on a high. We have rarely been more proud of him. I have never seen him tackle anything with such DETERMINATION. Interestingly, on his first day, which consisted mainly of falling over and trying to stagger up hill, he was very silent, not talking to anyone, just gritting his teeth with an 'I am damn well going to master this' attitude. An occasional burst of annoyance but always short lived and then back into it. And always, he wanted to achieve more. Contrast this with his performance at school!

On the ski-slopes, Adam was permitted to move through the levels of learning according to his ability and achievement. The level and pace of instruction were dictated by the level and pace of his mastery of the required skills, rather than by his chronological age. He had to strive for success, and he was allowed to make mistakes and learn from them. He was praised for his achievements but no one tried to hold him back when he himself wished to strive for the 'more' that he knew was in him. Above all, no one told him to hold back or ski more slowly in case he sped ahead of the others in his ski class.

Adam is now in Grade 6. He is excelling academically but finds it extremely difficult to make friends and, indeed, his social behaviour has deteriorated significantly. The principal has advised the Murphys to enrol him in a counselling programme for 'children without friends' run by a private psychologist. The programme aim is 'to improve children's peer relationships and social behaviour by teaching them new social skills and social attitudes in a small group'. Adam's social skills and attitudes are completely acceptable at chess or on the ski-slopes, where he has access to older children and a stimulating environment. His teachers seem unwilling to consider that in appropriate grade placement could be a factor in his social isolation at school.

No fewer than seven of the 15 children have participated in pull-out enrichment programmes which have been disbanded by the school for other than educational reasons. In the cases of Ian and Rick, described above, the programmes were discontinued by an incoming principal whose ideological beliefs did not support the provision of special programmes for the gifted. A pull-out programme in one of the schools attended by Richard McLeod was abandoned because of political pressure from the parents of children not enrolled in the programme.

> In an attempt to save the programme, the school began to include more and more of the children, but as the ability range of the kids in the programme broadened, the curriculum had to be watered down to such an extent that it made a mockery of the whole issue. Eventually the programme was disbanded. The political pressure on the principal and staff was just too great.
>
> (Ursula McLeod)

The school attended by Roshni Singh informed her mother Sarah, at one stage, that it intended to introduce a pull-out programme for Roshni and other gifted children within the school.

> However, they are so worried about the charge of elitism and the political consequences that they have backed down on the idea, and what they have introduced instead is a programme of individualized research in which all the children are included. The individualization consists of being able to select your own topic for research. We've been told that this will extend the gifted children because they will select topics at their own level.
>
> (Sarah Singh)

Sarah and Juspreet have since moved Roshni to a different school which is maintaining her grade acceleration (at age 8 she is in a composite Grade 5/6 class) while also permitting her subject acceleration (she does her maths with the Grade 6 students) and allowing her enrichment in computing and ability grouping in English.

Numerous researchers in the education of the gifted (Tannenbaum, 1983; Fetterman, 1988; Feldhusen and Baska, 1989) have discussed the necessity of finding a balance between inclusive identification procedures – those which will admit to a programme all children who could benefit academically from being included – and the indiscriminate admission, for political or social reasons, of children who are unlikely to cope with the extended or accelerated curriculum and who will necessarily act as a brake on the progress of the very students for whom the gifted programme is intended. Australian educators need to take heed of these caveats.

Earlier in this chapter we outlined the five elements which VanTassel-Baska (1985) identified as being necessary for the success of a gifted programme: content acceleration to the level of the child's abilities; thoughtfully planned, relevant enrichment; guidance in selecting courses and directions; special instruction with the opportunity to work closely with other gifted youth; and the opportunity to work with mentors who have high-level expertise in the child's area of giftedness. Of the 15 children, only one, Adrian Seng, has enjoyed an educational programme which contains all five elements.

UNDERACHIEVEMENT

Many studies over the last 20 years have reported alarming incidences of underachievement among the intellectually gifted (Pringle, 1970; Painter, 1976; Whitmore, 1980, Supplee, 1990). Several causes of underachievement have been identified, among them being teacher indifference, curriculum requirements which grossly underestimate the gifted child's potential or existing standards of achievement, lack of motivation, an educational climate that decries or fails to provide healthy competition, and lack of encouragement from home (Seeley, 1989). Indeed, Tannenbaum has succinctly and accurately defined underachievement as 'a single syndrome representing diverse etiologies' (Tannenbaum, 1983, p. 223–224). For the purposes of this study underachievement is defined as performance in class at a level significantly below that which is predicted by the child's performance on standardized tests of achievement in the subject area under consideration, or general academic achievement at a level significantly below that which is predicted by the student's intelligence quotient.

The causes of underachievement in the children of this study will be analysed and discussed in Chapter 9. However, it is important to note, in this discussion of the children's school programmes, that in interviews with the author, 14 of the 15 children have stated frankly that, in class, they are working significantly below their true ability level. Only Adrian believes that his educational programme allows him to achieve his full potential. In general, the parents of the children concur with these views.

Underachievement in many gifted children remains unnoticed because their school achievement is acceptable, or even well above average, by general standards. In 1989 both Fred Campbell and Hadley Bond commented that they were fully aware that their current schools were making a genuine effort to meet their educational and social needs. Both children had been permitted to grade-skip by two years and both had been provided with a carefully planned programme of subject acceleration. Nevertheless, neither boy was being enabled to work in mathematics at the level of his tested achievement. Fred, at age 12, took Grade 11 maths, a subject acceleration of four years, yet his scaled score on the *SAT–M* one month after his twelfth birthday was a remarkable 640.

He was undoubtedly capable of university level mathematics, and if underachievement is measured by the disparity between potential and performance, Fred was probably underachieving by a margin of at least three years. Hadley, at 7 years 10 months, achieved the 78th percentile score for American Grade 7 students on the *Cooperative Achievement Test–Arithmetic*, yet in class he was taking Grade 4 maths. Hadley was working with children two years older than he, but in terms of his tested maths achievement he was underachieving by a margin of at least two years.

The academic underachievement of the children who have not been accelerated is a matter of most serious concern. Ian Baker, at the age of 9 years 11 months, scored 560 on the *SAT–M*. His class teacher, in insisting that Ian complete the Grade 4 maths curriculum with his age-peers, was requiring him to underachieve by a margin of some seven years.

Twelve of the 15 children report that at various times during their school career they have deliberately concealed their abilities for peer acceptance. Cassandra's teachers are aware of this and have discussed it with Keith and Livia Lins; however, they are doing little to dissuade her from the practice.

> She deliberately holds herself back to fit in with the others. Many times she does not want to learn new concepts at home – for example, although she is interested in algebra she does not want me to teach it to her – as she knows she will be bored stiff at school when the rest of the class is taught them. She already finds it difficult to listen when the same concepts are repeated over and over in class.
>
> (Livia Lins, mother of Cassandra)

> In a way, Fred doesn't mind his underachievement. He is a non-competitive person and has no desire to be top of his Grade. At least he is not intellectually frustrated as he was in elementary school, and he is so happy to have friends, as he does now, that he doesn't see underachievement as a major problem.
>
> (Eleanor Campbell, mother of Fred)

> We feel Richard underachieves because, after years of having his abilities suppressed at school, he has come to feel that achievement isn't really important. Peer acceptance is also probably an issue. Certainly he has never been happier or more at ease with himself than now. He has friends and he's content just to drift along.
>
> (Ursula McLeod, mother of Richard)

Ursula is aware, however, that when faced with a challenge which excites him, Richard can throw off his lethargy and respond with a surge of energy which recalls his former love of learning.

When Richard is challenged it seems he can do just about anything. For example, earlier this year we wanted him to sit for the state scholarship exam and we were trying to think of something that would inspire him to do his best. A few years ago the joy of achievement would have been sufficient incentive, but that doesn't work for Richard any more. So we offered to buy him a new personal computer, which he had been asking for, if he topped the state in the scholarship competition. We also pointed out that although his maths is certainly exceptional, his English could do with some work; you will remember, Miraca, that when you recently retested him on the SAT his verbal score was exactly the same as it had been 12 months before.

Well, he rose to the challenge. He spontaneously suggested that we buy him some sort of vocabulary book, and took it upon himself to study Webster's Wordpower, a book of prefixes, suffixes, root words and extended vocabulary. He spent a total of about three hours, self-motivated and really concentrating, finishing all sections of the book except the large vocabulary section. When he came back from the exam, he said it had helped a lot and that he'd been able to finish the speed reading and reading comprehension sections. He topped the state and got his personal computer!'

OPPOSITION OR HOSTILITY FROM TEACHERS

A disturbing finding of this study is the overt or veiled hostility which the majority of the parents have experienced from teachers or school administrators. Ursula McLeod encountered this within a very few weeks of Richard's admission to school, when she tactfully suggested to his teacher that he be permitted to 'skip' the reading readiness programme as he had been reading since before the age of 2. The teacher countered by accusing Ursula of teaching Richard to read, and warning her that gifted children were often damaged by parental pressures to learn. 'You leave him to me,' she said firmly. 'It's my duty to pluck the tall poppies.'

Sarah and Juspreet Singh faced active opposition from Roshni's pre-school teachers over the child's remarkable reading capacities. Roshni had been permitted to enter pre-school at the age of 3 years 4 months and was consequently the youngest child in her class of 3-, 4- and 5-year-olds. Sarah was concerned that Roshni was being given large cut-out letters as an introduction to the alphabet when she had, in fact, learned the alphabet off by heart shortly after her second birthday. Indeed, she could already read as well as the average second-grade student. After much negotiation Sarah managed to persuade the pre-school teachers to allow her to take small books home from the classroom library. 'They were pretty unstimulating, frankly,' says Sarah, in retrospect, 'but they were better than sandpaper letters.' Matters came to a head, however, when the pre-school teachers found that in four weeks Roshni and Sarah, at home, had worked through their entire reading programme for the year. They confronted Sarah in indignation. The principal intervened on behalf of the teachers. 'If you do all the work with her at home,' she explained, 'what will the teachers have left to do with her here?' Neither the teachers nor the principal would accept that a 3-year-old who could complete the year's reading programme in one month might require a differentiated educational provision.

No fewer than six of the 15 parents report that they have experienced various degrees of obstructiveness from teachers or school administrators who have countered requests for assistance by claiming that they themselves were parents of gifted children who succeeded academically without intervention. 'There was no child brighter than the principal's son,' says Ursula McLeod, wryly. 'He had just won a half-scholarship to a prestigious private school. Heaven forbid another child's success should detract from his.' Rachel Street decided to seek the support of the principal when Rufus's Reception class teacher admitted in genuine distress that she had not been able to teach Rufus anything he did not already know, and that she feared he had been bored all year.

> She was a lovely and caring lady, and I simply wanted to discuss possible ways in which the school could ensure that he would be more stimulated the following year. But the Principal pooh-poohed my concern. 'I have a bright son who is 21 now and he grew up all right; you are just worrying too much.'
>
> (Rachel Street, mother of Rufus)

Equally disturbing is the frequency with which teachers claim that they have taught many pupils who are as bright, or brighter, than the subject children. Caroline Vincent is deeply concerned that almost since her entry to school at 4 years of age, the majority of Jade's teachers have ignored the psychologist's assessment which places her IQ at 174, her reading interests which are those of a child several years her senior, and her extreme difficulties in forming social relationships with age-peers, and have insisted that she is no more able than the other 'bright' children within her class. Holly Bond notes that it is the teachers who have appeared most threatened and uncomfortable with Hadley's phenomenal maths ability who have been most anxious to assure her (and themselves) that there are many children in the class who are brighter than he.

> Even after formal testing had established that at age 6 Adam had the reading ability of a 12-year-old, his teachers insisted that they had lots of good readers in the class. In a meeting with his class teachers, when we were proposing a grade-skip and they were giving us all

the academic and social reasons they could rake up for why it wouldn't work, one of the teachers said, quite suddenly, 'Of course, I believe we have a number of children in the school as intelligent as Adam, if only we had bothered to have them tested.' They had seen the psychologist's report, we had already discussed the low incidence of children with IQs of 160+, they knew the level of rarity they were dealing with – 1 in 10,000 – but they were still able to come up with a comment like that!

(Edward Murphy, father of Adam)

It's really disturbing, when you realize what this sort of thing implies – that either these teachers have NO idea of the implications of such exceptionally high IQs, or that they are so determined to reduce the magnitude of the differences between the highly gifted kids and the others in the class that they will quite deliberately cut down the tall poppies to do so.

(Caroline Vincent, mother of Jade)

Several of the parents report a lack of support or practical assistance from those employees of the state Education Departments whose special responsibility it is to advise on the needs of highly able children.

We have tried to clarify our thoughts as to the best direction to take, but this has been hindered by a lack of direction in these matters by the Education Department staff we have contacted. In a recent letter to my brother I remarked that after all this time I have at last discovered what the Department's official policy on the gifted is. Their official policy appears to be not to have an official policy; and their unofficial policy is to prevent inquirers from finding out what the official policy is.

(Edward Murphy)

Many of the parents express extreme frustration with teachers' lack of knowledge and awareness of the needs of intellectually gifted children, and their unfamiliarity with the research literature in this field.

What we find beyond comprehension, is that in other professions individuals seek to improve their knowledge; Georgina will come home and look up the latest on some matter that has arisen at the hospital; doctors will refer patients to specialists and abide by their findings; but these teachers tell us on the one hand that they know nothing about the education of gifted kids, and then proceed to tell us the way it should be done! They blame the lack of inservice training, but the material is there to be read, the specialists are there to be asked; why don't they have the professionalism to find out?

(Edward Murphy)

One of the major difficulties is that the considerable majority of teachers in Australia have had not so much as a single lecture on gifted and talented children in their pre-service training (Start, 1985). Thus, the considerable majority of teachers teaching gifted children in cluster groups, pull-out classes or even self-contained classes for gifted students have had no opportunity for training in gifted education.

Of even greater concern is that, where Australian education departments have appointed teachers to be consultants in gifted education, these appointments have frequently been made without sufficient consideration of the applicants' previous experience in developing special curricula and/or special programmes for gifted students, their knowledge of current research and practice in Australia and overseas, their familiarity with the literature in the field, or indeed whether they have undertaken *any* academic coursework on the education or psychology of the gifted! Some of the gifted education consultants have done an excellent job; others have been able to offer little support to the teachers and parents who have sought assistance from them. A keen interest in gifted children and attendance at two or three conferences, although laudable, do not of themselves qualify a teacher to inservice her colleagues and advise on the education of the gifted students in the surrounding schools. Consultants in the education of intellectually handicapped, blind or hearing impaired students are not appointed with such cavalier disregard for training, experience or aptitude. It is little wonder that the teachers and parents of the study children have had such limited assistance from the consultants and 'support teachers' appointed to advise on the education of the gifted.

The degree to which teachers in Australia are unaware of the training in gifted education available to (or required by) teachers in other parts of the world may perhaps be illustrated by the report of a high school teacher, published in the newsletter of her state's Association for Gifted Children, on the 8th World Conference on Gifted and Talented Children, which was held in Sydney, Australia, in July 1989.

> My second impression from the conference is difficult to express verbally. It concerns the look of horror reflected in the faces of overseas delegates as they learned that selective schools in New South Wales did not have their staff selected too... Apparently, overseas, where schools or classes involve students with special abilities, the teachers have special training.
>
> (Wilson, 1989, p. 5)

SUMMARY

Although Adrian, Christopher, Hadley (at last!) and Fred are currently served by educational programmes which address most of their intellectual and social needs, the majority of the children are not so fortunate. Seven of the 15 children were admitted to school before the usual age of entry; however, in the majority of these cases the receiving teacher ignored the children's identified achievement levels in maths and reading and required them to participate in the reading readiness and number familiarity programmes of the Reception class. Six children have been permitted to make a 'token' grade-skip of one year, but the school has generally assumed that the grade-skip will, by itself, be sufficient to address their academic needs. Not one of the 15 children has been in a self-contained class of gifted students, the intervention recommended by Hollingworth (1942) as being the most appropriate response to the academic and social needs of the exceptionally and profoundly gifted. The schools attended by Ian (formerly), Cassandra and Rufus have attempted to address their intellectual and social needs through pull-out programmes while insisting that the children remain full-time with age-peers; prescribing pull-out for a child of IQ 200, without associated acceleration, is as realistic a response as applying a band-aid to a shark-bite.

The parents of 12 of the 15 subjects believe that their children are working significantly below their true ability level in at least one or two subject areas, while the parents of nine of the children state that in *no* academic subject area is their child being permitted to work, in class, at the level which he or she has attained on standardized achievement tests. The parents of these children have either given up their attempts to persuade the school to recognize their children's exceptional talents, or continue to negotiate with their child's teacher in the hope, if not the conviction, that their perseverance may eventually have some effect. These parents share a sense of loss and bewilderment which was expressed most feelingly by Caroline Vincent, mother of Jade, when Jade was 7 years old. Jade has now moved to a new school, where she is somewhat happier and is slowly and tentatively learning to make friends with her new classmates.

> I feel very negative about Jade's school experience. We have seen her go from an extroverted, confident and happy 3-year-old whose abilities took our breath away, to a negative, often bitterly unhappy 7-year-old. She has lost her zest for learning and achievement. She is totally different from the child I would have predicted she would be. It seems incredible to me that the school should expect her to be excited about the curriculum they offer her, which is years and years below her level, and what makes it worse is that because she won't respond to the basic work, nothing in the way of acceleration or enrichment is being done for her. It's a vicious circle. I am so afraid that she will never feel fulfilled, and yet I feel powerless to do

anything because I feel like I am fumbling around in the dark and I don't know where the switch is.

9
PSYCHOSOCIAL DEVELOPMENT

I have come to the conclusion that the degree of my difference from most people exceeds the average of most people's difference from one another; or, to put it more briefly, that my reactions to many things don't conform to popular patterns.

(Joad, 1947)

My life is spent in a perpetual alternation between two rhythms, the rhythm of attracting people for fear I may be lonely and the rhythm of getting rid of them because I know that I am bored.

(Joad, 1948)

One of the most popular radio programmes in Britain in the 1940s and 1950s was *The Brains Trust*, in which a panel of intellectuals and entertainers, chosen for their skill with words and ideas, would debate questions raised by an audience or sent in by listeners. Over the years, many became household names, including the scholar and philosopher Professor C. E. M. Joad, whose thoughtful response to almost any question, 'It all depends on what you mean by...' was greeted by the audience with the delighted and affectionate laughter with which they would greet the catchphrase of a favourite comedian. Many of his listeners would have had little understanding of the urge which prompted the preamble – Joad's need to define the question, to delineate the grey areas, and to clarify precisely those aspects to which he felt he could respond; in the minds of radio audiences, 'It all depends on what you mean by...' became Joad's lietmotif: something you could depend on for a chuckle of recognition before you settled down to try to understand his answer.

As can be seen by the quotation above, Joad recognized his difference from the mass of his fellowmen, and the degree of his difference. It was typical of the great scholar that his analysis of the degree of difference has almost a statistical flavour! Linked to this knowledge was the ever-present longing for congenial companionship, and the rueful awareness, bought with experience, that he was unlikely to find it.

The 15 exceptionally gifted children described in the preceding chapters differ significantly from their age-peers in their intellectual, academic, social and emotional development. The precocious development of literacy and numeracy skills resulted in these children entering school with levels of reading and mathematics achievement which would not normally be acquired until they had progressed through several elementary school grade levels. Even although the majority of the children spontaneously moderated their reading performance, or even stopped reading altogether, in an attempt to disguise the differences between themselves and their classmates, the magnitude of the difference was such that it was almost immediately recognized by the other children, if not always by the class teacher!

The difficulties in socialization which arose out of the academic discrepancies were intensified by the sophistication of the reading interests, hobbies and play preferences of the exceptionally gifted children. As a result, the majority experienced extreme difficulty, from their earliest days at school, in establishing positive social relationships with their classmates. Although, as is related in previous chapters, 10 of the schools responded by permitting the children a modest degree of academic acceleration, in the majority of cases even this response was not enough to provide them with a peer group of children at similar stages of intellectual or emotional development. Twelve of the 15 have admitted to underachieving deliberately in an attempt to win peer group acceptance.

Many psychologists and educators studying the gifted and talented have emphasized the importance, to the realization of intellectual potential, of a positive self-concept and a high level of self-esteem (Hollingworth, 1926; Carroll, 1940; DeHaan and Havighurst, 1961; Tannenbaum, 1983; Foster, 1983; Feldhusen and Hoover, 1986). Self-concept, as defined by Feldhusen (1986), is 'a set of perceptions, interpretations and evaluations of self and one's own talents, abilities and liabilities' (Feldhusen, 1986, p. 120). Self-esteem, an affective aspect of self-concept, is a personal judgment of worth or value expressed in the attitudes a person holds towards himself and his actions, and is largely derived from the positive or negative feedback the individual receives from significant others, such as teachers, parents and classmates, about the value or effectiveness of his actions (Foster, 1983).

Coopersmith (1981) warned that people whose perceptions of their performance do not match their personal aspirations may evaluate themselves over-harshly, even when their attainments are markedly superior to those of their colleagues. 'These persons are likely to report feelings of guilt, shame, or depression, and to conclude that their actual achievements are of little importance' (Coopersmith, 1981, p. 4). Not surprisingly, researchers have found that the self-esteem of gifted children is significantly associated with personal satisfaction and efficient social and academic functioning (Purkey, 1970; Dean, 1977; Feldhusen and Hoover, 1986).

There is general agreement among researchers that academic underachievement in intellectually gifted children is strongly linked to lowered self-esteem and self-concept (Raph, Goldberg and Passow, 1966; Whitmore, 1980; Tannenbaum, 1983; Davis and Connell, 1985). Pringle (1970) found that the majority of the intellectually gifted children referred to her on the grounds of emotional maladjustment had teachers who had seriously underestimated their intellectual ability and had transferred these negative perceptions to the children. Carroll (1940), Hollingworth (1942), DeHaan and Havighurst (1961) and other researchers studying exceptionally and profoundly gifted children have noted that from the early years of elementary school these children have generally acquired a perception of themselves as 'different' and that this perception is generally linked, in the child's mind, with an extremely negative self-image.

Studies of the self-concept and self-esteem of intellectually gifted children produce conflicting results. Several studies (Colangelo and Pfleger, 1978; Tidwell, 1980; Karnes and Wherry, 1981) have suggested that children identified as intellectually gifted have higher levels of self-esteem and self-concept than children not so identified. Other studies (Glenn, 1978; Bracken, 1980) have found no such superiority. A number of studies comparing gifted children enrolled in special programmes with equally able students not so enrolled have identified diminished self-esteem within the gifted group (Rodgers, 1979; Fults, 1980), while others (Coleman and Fults, 1982; Kolloff and Feldhusen, 1984; Feldhusen, Saylor, Nielson and Kolloff, 1990) have observed an enhanced self-esteem among the gifted in special programmes. Kulik and Kulik (1982) in a meta-analysis of the research to that date on ability grouping in secondary schools found that the self-concept of gifted students was more favourable in grouped classes.

Many studies on the self-concept and self-esteem of gifted children are difficult to interpret because of the failure of the authors to report subscale scores. The *Coopersmith Self-Esteem Inventory (SEI)*, for example, contains four subscales, each measuring a different aspect of self-esteem: these are home–family; school–academic; social self–peers; and general self-esteem (Coopersmith, 1981). The literature on the intellectually gifted suggests that while the majority of highly gifted children enjoy unusually positive and supportive family relationships (Getzels and Jackson, 1961; Tannenbaum, 1983; Bloom, 1985), their social relationships with age-peers are fraught with difficulty (Austin and Draper, 1981; Janos, 1983; Roedell, 1984). It would be instructive had some of the studies noted above compared the subjects' scores on the home-parents and social self-peers subscales of the *SEI*. Such a comparison might assist in clarifying the seeming disparities in the results of apparently similar studies. Yet the majority of researchers restrict themselves to reporting the full-scale summary scores, with no discussion of perceived variations among different aspects of self-esteem.

The self-concept scale most frequently employed in Australia is the Piers-Harris *Children's Self-Concept Scale* (Piers and Harris, 1969). However, some doubts have been cast as to the suitability of this scale for use with intellectually gifted students. Janos and Robinson (1985) suggested that the norms of the Piers-Harris scale may significantly underestimate the scores of children not identified as gifted. Tidwell (1980) tested 1600 gifted tenth-grade students on both the Piers-Harris *Self-Concept Scale* and the Coopersmith *Self-Esteem Inventory* (Coopersmith, 1981). Whereas the self-concept scores of these gifted children exceeded norms on the Piers-Harris scale, their mean self-esteem score was within the normal range on the Coopersmith *SEI*. It was decided, therefore, to err on the side of caution by measuring the self-esteem of the children in this study on the Coopersmith *SEI*.

The Coopersmith *Self-Esteem Inventory (SEI)* (Coopersmith, 1981) was designed to measure evaluative attitudes towards the self in social, academic, family and personal areas of experience. The School Form of the *SEI*, used in this study, yields a total score for overall self-esteem as well as separate scores for the four subscales which allow for variance in perception of self-esteem in different areas of experience.

The self-esteem of 12 of the 15 children was measured using the Coopersmith *SEI*. At the time of testing, Roshni Singh, who was still only 5 years of age, and Rick Ward, aged 6, were too young to be assessed effectively with this instrument. An attempt was made to assess Adam Murphy in May 1989, when he was 7 years 8 months old, but this attempt was unsuccessful. Adam's bitter unhappiness and ongoing intellectual frustration have been related in Chapter 8. Since Grade 3 his teachers have tended to repress, rather than foster, his academic capabilities, and he has experienced extreme difficulty in establishing positive peer relationships. Adam has always been reluctant to discuss his social difficulties or his resentment of his unrewarding school programme except in the very warm and supportive relationship he enjoys with his parents, and this reluctance to express a negative opinion was reflected in his performance on the *SEI*. The *SEI* incorporates an eight-item lie scale, which functions as an index of defensiveness or 'test-wise-ness'. A high score on the lie scale is generally viewed as an indication that the child is selecting what he believes to be the more socially acceptable response, rather than being honest in his self-appraisal. A high lie score sheds doubt on the validity of the subject's responses to the *SEI* as a whole. Adam visibly viewed completion of the *SEI* as a distasteful task, and hurried through the test, almost appearing to score the items at random. However, Adam scored on six of the eight lie scale items; this included responding 'That's like me' to statements such as, 'I never worry about anything', 'I always do the right thing', and 'I never get scolded'. Adam's reluctance to discuss negative experiences and emotions, and his desire to appear in the most positive light on the *SEI*, are not characteristic of the subject group as a whole. His attitudes may have resulted from the determined efforts of his Grade 3 teachers, as described in Chapter 8, to make Adam adopt an unrealistically positive view of his school programme, and conform to the behaviours, attitudes, and social values of his age-peers.

The *Self-Esteem Inventory* provides subscale norms for students at three grade levels – United States Grades 3, 6 and 9. Because a number of the children have been permitted to skip one or more grades, scores achieved by them have been compared with the mean scores of children of approximately their chronological age, rather than the mean scores for the grade level in which they were enrolled at the time of testing. For example, the scores achieved by Fred Campbell, who was 12 years 1 month of age but enrolled in Grade 8 at the time of taking the *SEI*, have been compared with the mean scores for American Grade 6 students, rather than Grade 9.

In the following pages, the children's raw scores on the various subscales, as well as their global scores, are expressed as z-scores. The z-score indicates how many standard deviations a raw score is above or below its mean. The scores of 68 per cent of the population could be expected to fall within the normal range of between +1.00 and –1.00. Fewer than 16 per cent of children could be expected to score below –1.00 and 2.28 per cent should score below –2.00. The same proportions would be expected for scores above +1.00 and +2.00. A z-score below –1.50 indicates a disturbingly low level of self-esteem, as fewer than 7 per cent of children could be expected to achieve so low a score. It is important to note that the raw scores of the subject children are not being compared with the mean scores for the study group itself, but with the mean scores of the standardization sample.

Table 9.1 displays the subscale and global scores of the children on the Coopersmith *Self-Esteem Inventory*. It has been most illuminating to compare the children's self-esteem scores on each of the four subscales.

Total self-esteem

Janos, Fung and Robinson (1985), reviewing the literature on the self-concept and self-esteem of intellectually gifted children, report that the majority of studies reveal these children as showing satisfactory, if not necessarily superior, levels of self-esteem when compared with children not identified as gifted. If global self-esteem scores are considered in isolation, without reference to the associated subscale scores, the children

Table 9.1 Scores on the Coopersmith *Self-Esteem Inventory*

Child	*Home–family*		*School–academic*		*Social self–peers*		*General self-esteem*		*Total self-esteem*	
	x	z	x	z	x	z	x	z	x	z
Anastasia	12	+0.56	12	+0.47	2	−2.59	38	+1.0	64	+0.22
Ian	14	+1.05	12	+0.47	4	−1.97	40	+1.26	70	+0.63
Rufus	14	+0.69	14	+1.26	6	−1.14	36	+0.25	70	+0.34
Christopher	14	+0.69	12	+0.68	6	−1.14	28	−0.57	60	−0.30
Jonathon	16	+1.54	12	+0.47	12	+0.53	42	+1.53	82	+1.45
Richard	16	+1.17	10	+0.09	6	−1.14	42	+0.88	74	+0.61
Fred	16	+1.17	12	+0.68	16	+1.71	50	+1.70	94	+1.91
Adrian	16	+1.17	10	+0.09	12	+0.57	44	+1.08	82	+1.13
Cassandra	16	+1.17	14	+1.26	12	+0.57	36	+0.25	78	+0.87
Alice	14	+1.04	14	+1.06	6	−1.34	30	−0.05	64	+0.22
Hadley	8	−0.41	12	+0.47	14	+1.16	40	+1.26	74	+0.90
Jade	8	−0.41	8	−0.70	6	−1.34	20	−1.37	42	−1.29

x = Raw score
z = Difference between raw score and mean of standardization sample, expressed as a z score

in this study could be viewed as conforming to this fortunate pattern. If scores within the area comprising one standard deviation above and below the mean, that is, z-scores between −1.00 and +1.00, are considered as falling within the 'normal' range, then fully eight of the 12 children show average levels of self-esteem, a further three children show superior levels of self-esteem and only one child, Jade, with a z-score of −1.29, can be considered as having a self-esteem score significantly below the mean for her age-peers.

Even at this early stage of the analysis, however, it is noteworthy that of the three subjects scoring more than +1z on total self-esteem, two, Adrian and Fred, are students whose schools have permitted multiple grade-skipping combined with subject acceleration, while the third, Jonathon, has been permitted a single year grade-skip combined with subject acceleration in several subject areas. Jade, on the other hand, with an IQ of 174, had been permitted neither acceleration nor enrichment by her school and for several years had severe problems of intellectual frustration and social isolation. The difficulties confronting Jade will be discussed later in this chapter.

Home–Family

Studies of the family background and family characteristics of highly gifted children have emphasized the unusually warm, close and mutually supportive relationships enjoyed by these young people and their parents (Hollingworth, 1942; Sheldon, 1976; Bloom, 1985). I have had a matchless opportunity to observe, over a number of years, the interactions between these children, their parents and their siblings. As with the families of the highly successful scholars, sportsmen and musicians studied by Bloom (1985), the homes of the study families are child-centred; the parents are very much aware of the children's hobbies and interests, and family life tends to be arranged around their music lessons, chess club involvement, and other activities. However, the children are by no means over-indulged; in most of the families the children have specific household responsibilities, and a prompt and willing performance of these duties is seen as an important contribution to the smooth running of the family home. The children are viewed very much as individuals; although in the majority of families the exceptionally gifted child is unarguably more talented than his/her siblings, the abilities of each child in the family are valued and fostered. There seems to be very little sibling rivalry; the visitor to the home becomes quickly aware that these are families which recognize the unusual gifts of one member and joyfully foster these gifts, while working to optimize the abilities of all. As with the families of the gifted mathematicians and scientists studied by Goertzel and Goertzel (1962), the family climate is authoritative, rather than authoritarian; although the parents require high standards of behaviour, these rules are predicated on a belief that all family members, adults as well as children, should act with courtesy and consideration towards all persons with whom they interact. It may well be this training which has allowed the majority of the children to respond with tolerance and grace to the neglect and discourtesy shown them by the teachers and administrators responsible for their education!

The maximum possible raw score on the home–family subscale of the *Self-Esteem Inventory* is 16 points. Perhaps not surprisingly, given the family atmosphere described above, fully five of the 12 children recorded this maximum score, three more recorded a score of 14, and one scored 12. Seven of the 12 subjects scored more than +1.00z, and the remaining five scored within the normal range.

It is often assumed that the parents of the academically gifted 'push' their children to succeed in school. In interviews with the author, the parents of fully 13 of the 15 children have reported that at some time during the child's elementary schooling they have been accused by teachers or school administrators of 'pushing' the subject child, of over-emphasizing academic work at the expense of the child's social development, or of being overly ambitious for the child's scholastic success. Two of the eight items on the home–family subscale specifically address this issue. Item 11 requires the test-taker to respond 'Like me' or 'Unlike me' to the statement, 'My parents expect too much of me'. Item

22, which requires a similar form of response, states, 'I usually feel as if my parents are pushing me'. Fully 11 of the 12 children responded 'Unlike me' to Item 11 and Jade, the one child who did agree with the statement, qualified this by commenting that she felt her parents expected too much of her in doing jobs around the house! Eleven of the 12 children responded 'Unlike me' to Item 22 which specifically addresses the question of parental 'pushing'. Indeed, during the testing sessions this item prompted several of the children to comment spontaneously to me that, far from feeling 'pushed', they felt that their parents were the only people who offered them praise, reward or encouragement!

For 10 of 12 subjects a high score on the home–family subscale contributed significantly to their positive scores on the index of total self-esteem.

School–academic

It might be expected that these children, whose academic performance, as measured by standardized tests of achievement, is so significantly superior to that of age-peers, would score highly on the index of self-esteem related to school and academic work. Yet, whereas none of the children scored below the normal range on this subscale, only three recorded z-scores of more than +1.00. In contrast to their performance on the home-family subscale, none of the children recorded the maximum score of 16 points.

It should be borne in mind, however, that the academic self-perception of many of these children has been significantly influenced by the views of their classroom teachers who have generally failed to recognize and respond to the children's remarkable gifts. As has been related in Chapter 6, Christopher was delighted but surprised when he achieved a score of 580 on the *Scholastic Aptitude Test–Verbal* at the age of 11 years 4 months; he had always been told by his teachers that, while his mathematical ability was exceptional, his verbal abilities were only average for his age. Jade was surprised and relieved on hearing that she had scored at least one year above her chronological age on the *Leicester Number Test*; she had been frequently told by her teacher, and consequently believed, that she was 'weak' in maths.

The school reports which the children are given to take home to their parents, although generally positive, give no indication that the teachers are aware of the remarkable academic potential of the subjects. The report form used by the school attended by Jade, who at age 7 scored more than two years in advance of her chronological age on the *Westwood Spelling* Test, required the student's class teacher to classify his or her performance in each subject area as below, at, or above grade level. Jade's teacher classified her performance in spelling as 'at grade level'. Anastasia's Grade 3 report stated: 'She is to be commended on achieving the Grade 2 and

3 objectives in mathematics. She now needs to consolidate in this area, and build up her speed and efficiency'; Anastasia, at the age of 8 years 1 month, scored at the 90th percentile for 10-year-olds on the *Nottingham Number Test*! Adam's Grade 3 report indicated that he could 'record addition and subtraction up to 20'; in fact, Adam was already performing at this level in his first year of school! The teachers of Adam, Anastasia and Jade, and indeed of the majority of the 15 children, did not recognize these students' academic precocity because the undemanding work they were presented with offered them no opportunity to display their ability. 'Nor will they discover this if they don't offer these children work that really will reveal their true capacities,' says Edward Murphy, in frustration. 'If you ask a 5-year-old and a 12-year-old to add 2 and 2, and they both answer '4', does that mean they have the same ability in maths?'

Interestingly, the three children who achieved z-scores of more than +1.00 are Rufus and Cassandra, who have received no form of academic acceleration, and Alice who has been permitted a token grade-skip of one year. These three children are working, in class, at levels which do little to challenge their intellectual or academic abilities. They complete the work with ease and their performance is well beyond that of their classmates. Their academic superiority has never been challenged and they have no classmates whose intellectual ability approaches their own, with whom they may compare themselves. By contrast, Adrian, Christopher and Fred, who have been permitted a combination of grade-skipping and subject acceleration, and who have been academically and intellectually challenged, display more modest, but still positive, levels of academic self-esteem. These three children compare their academic performance at school or university with that of their colleagues who are several years their senior. They still out-perform their classmates, but they have to work to achieve their success. The school–academic self-esteem scores of Adrian, Chris and Fred contradict the belief that children who are accelerated will become conceited about their academic ability.

Social self-peers

Hollingworth (1926) defined the IQ range 125–155 as 'socially optimal intelligence'. As was briefly discussed in Chapter 1, she found that children scoring within this range were emotionally well-balanced and controlled, of good character and able to win the confidence and friendship of their classmates. She claimed, however, that above the level of IQ 160 the difference between the gifted child and his or her age-peers is so great that it leads to special problems of development which are correlated with social isolation, and noted that these difficulties seem particularly acute at ages 4 through 9 (Hollingworth, 1942). Gallagher (1958), comparing the friendship patterns of children scoring above and below IQ

165+, noted that the exceptionally gifted children tended to have greater problems of social acceptance than did children scoring between 150 and 164. Burks, Jensen and Terman, comparing the psychosocial development of children of IQ 170+ with that of the gifted group as a whole, concluded that the exceptionally gifted child 'has one of the most difficult problems of social adjustment that any human being is ever called upon to meet' (Burks, Jensen and Terman, 1930, p. 265).

As has been discussed in Chapter 7, the majority of the study children have experienced extreme difficulty in establishing positive social relationships with age-peers. The extremely negative perceptions which these children hold both of their own social skills and of their probable image in the eyes of other children are reflected in disturbingly low levels of social self-esteem.

Of the 12 children reported here, no fewer than seven have z-scores of below –1.00 on the social self-peers subscale. Indeed, Anastasia made the disturbingly low score of –2.59, and Ian Baker, whose school experience has been discussed in Chapter 8, and who was tested at a time when he was being held lock-step with age-peers, scored –1.97. Fewer than five children in 1,000 could be expected to score lower than Anastasia, and fewer than three in 100 lower than Ian. Once again, the only children achieving z-scores of greater than +1.00 are radical accelerands – Fred, who entered Grade 9 one week after his twelfth birthday, and Hadley, who had completed Grade 4 at 8 years 5 months. Indeed, of the five children achieving a positive z-score, four have been grade-skipped by at least one year.

Five of the eight items on the social self-peers subscale address the issue of social acceptability. The majority of these exceptionally gifted children are poignantly aware of the extent to which they are rejected and disliked by their age-peers. Only four of the 12 children responded 'Like me' to the statement 'I'm popular with kids my own age'. Only four agreed with the statement 'Kids usually follow my ideas'. Fully seven of the 12 identified with the statement 'Most people are better liked than I am' and, disturbingly, five children, almost half this group, responded 'Like me' to the statement 'Kids pick on me very often'. Hollingworth (1931) noted the tendency for school bullies, particularly those of below average intelligence, to reserve their particular venom for younger children of exceptional intellectual ability. Only four of the children identified with 'I am a lot of fun to be with'; ironically, these were Adrian, Christopher, Fred and Hadley who have experienced double grade-skips!

In both Australia and the United States many teachers and parents argue against acceleration from a conviction that moving a child away from chronological age-peers will lead to social and emotional disturbance. As has been discussed in Chapter 8, teachers and administrators in several of the schools attended by the study children have refused to accelerate these students, or award them more than a token grade-skip of 12 months, for fear that this will lead to the children being rejected by their age peers. By contrast, it is the children who have been accelerated by more than one year who show the healthiest social self-concept. The schools attended by these young people have tried to create for them a peer group of children whose levels of intellectual, academic and emotional development approximate their own. As a result, these accelerands are able to work and socialize with other children who share, or can at least empathize with, their interests, their delight in intellectual inquiry, and their ways of viewing the world. These children are confident in their relationships with classmates. They are no longer rejected for being different. They know they are liked, and their opinions valued. They have been able to assume positions of social leadership. They feel they are 'fun to be with'. They are enjoying the social pleasures of childhood while, at the same time, experiencing the intellectual satisfaction of challenging academic work.

General self-esteem

Whereas the home-family and social self-peers subscales of the *SEI* measure the child's view of his relationships with others, the general self-esteem subscale assesses the individual's own view of how he or she copes with life. The child is asked to respond 'Like me' or 'Unlike me' to statements such as: 'I can make up my mind without too much trouble', 'There are a lot of things about myself I'd change if I could', 'I can usually take care of myself', 'I often wish I were someone else' and 'If I have something to say, I usually say it.'

On the whole, the children exhibited positive levels of general self-esteem. Six of the 12 recorded z-scores at or in excess of +1.00, and only Jade, with a z-score of –1.37, showed a disturbingly negative self-perception. Again, radical accelerands Fred, Adrian and Hadley were among the students recording scores significantly above the mean. Surprisingly, considering his very low score (–1.97) on the social self-peers subscale, Ian Baker has been able to retain a very positive general self-image (z = +1.26).

Nevertheless, it is interesting to note that, despite the positive levels of general self-esteem displayed by the group as a whole, and despite the healthy self-concept displayed by the radical accelerands on home-family, social self-peers and general self subscales, three children of the 12 identified with the statement 'It's pretty tough to be me'. These are Adrian, Christopher and Ian, the children whose ratio IQ scores are at or in excess of IQ 200.

Exceptionally gifted children are aware that they are different, but for the profoundly gifted, those students scoring above IQ 180, that awareness is acute. The sense of salience is expressed most feelingly by an anonymous 16-year-old writing in the American Association for Gifted Children's publication *On being gifted*.

> Now, let's be blunt. We are not 'normal' and we know it; it can be fun sometimes but not funny always. We tend to be much more sensitive than other people. Multiple meanings, innuendos and self-consciousness plague us. Intensive self-analysis, self-criticism, and the inability to recognize that we have limits make us despondent. In fact, most times our self-searching leaves us more discombobbled [confused] than we were at the outset.
>
> (American Association for Gifted Children, 1978, p. 9)

In a study of self-concept, self-esteem and peer relationships among intellectually gifted children, Janos, Fung and Robinson (1985) found that self-esteem scores of children who saw themselves as being 'different' from age-mates were significantly lower than those of children who had no such perception of difference. These authors proposed that it is possible that the mere awareness of their intellectual superiority and atypical interest patterns might be sufficient to diminish self-esteem in the intellectually gifted. The continual awareness of 'difference' and salience experienced by profoundly gifted children, even when they are fortunate enough to enjoy supportive family and peer relationships, and a school programme which at least partly addresses their intellectual and academic needs, must indeed make it 'tough to be them'.

To summarize, if only the global scores are examined, the children of this study score, in general, within the normal range on total self-esteem. However, the most telling insights come from an examination of the subscale scores. Whereas these children's scores on home-family self-esteem are unusually high, and their scores on general and school-academic self-esteem are generally above the mean, their scores on social self-peers are disturbingly low. Children displaying the highest levels of self-esteem on the social self-peers and general subscales are those who have been radically accelerated.

THE INFLUENCE OF SELF-CONCEPT ON THE MOTIVATION TO EXCEL

Bloom, in his study of 120 adults who achieved excellence in cognitive, artistic and athletic fields, identified three characteristics as critical to success: (a) an unusual willingness to undertake a remarkably high workload in order to achieve at a high level; (b) a determination to reach the highest standards of which one is capable; and (c) the ability to learn new techniques, ideas or processes in the talent field more rapidly than the average (Bloom, 1985). It is notable that the first two characteristics are motivational.

Bloom claimed that the motivation to achieve was not inbuilt in his subjects; it manifested itself after several years of instruction, and was strongly influenced by early socialization and training. Feldman (1986) in his studies of young prodigies in natural science, musical composition, prose writing and chess, highlighted the remarkably high levels of motivation displayed by the children; indeed he claimed that the quality which defined them most forcefully was the passion with which excellence was pursued.

Foster (1983) proposed that a necessary condition for the development of the drive to excel is a secure self-concept. He further suggested that the development of intimacy, a relationship of mutual support, concern and valuing, is a necessary correlate of the development of a strong sense of self-esteem.

One of the measures of the supportiveness and intimacy of a relationship is the extent to which the significant others in an individual's life provide him with accurate, honest and detailed feedback about his standard of performance. This accurate and unbiased feedback, however, is often withheld from the intellectually gifted child. The average child often downplays the superiority of the gifted by providing false feedback about the true extent of his gifts and talents. If this false feedback is accepted and internalized by the gifted child, he may, as Coopersmith (1986) suggested, develop a self-concept based on underrating himself, his abilities and his value to society. Particularly in a society such as Australia, where the highly egalitarian social ethos is based, in large part, on 'cutting down the tall poppies' (Ward, 1958; Goldberg, 1981; Start, 1986; Feather, 1989), there is a very real danger that the gifted student will receive deliberately misleading information about his abilities and potential not only from classmates but also from teachers. Where feedback from both teachers and age-peers is invalidated because of envy or lack of understanding, or where the teacher prefers to conceal from the gifted child the true extent of his advancement, the gifted receive a negative and unrealistic view of themselves and their potential, and this false image may result in poor self-esteem and lowered self-concept.

Foster (1983) proposed that a secure and healthy self-concept is a necessary condition for the development of the drive to excel. Feldhusen and Hoover (1986) proposed that the inter-linkage of intelligence, self-concept and self-esteem may engender the strong motivational force essential for high-level production. 'This conceptualization therefore implies a relationship, in gifted individuals, between self-concept, self-esteem and a realization of intellectual ability or potential' (Feldhusen and Hoover, 1986, p. 141). A corollary of this theory would propose that where a child who is known to be intellectually gifted is not demonstrating high-level performance, we might suspect that her exceptional cognitive abilities are not supported by healthy levels of self-concept or self-esteem.

CHILDREN WHOSE POTENTIAL IS LARGELY UNREALIZED

With the possible exception of Adrian, none of the 15 children has achieved his or her intellectual or academic potential. However, the children whose schools have failed most dismally to address their academic needs are Richard, Adam, Rufus, Roshni, Rick, Jade, Anastasia and, until very recently, Ian.

The boredom and unhappiness suffered by Richard McLeod for much of his school career has been discussed in Chapters 7 and 8. Until he entered high school, Richard never knew the emotional security of a warm and friendly relationship with a classroom teacher who valued his abilities and tried to foster them. Rather, his teachers would load him with 'busywork', especially in mathematics, to keep him occupied and quiet while they concentrated on teaching the other children. As a consequence, Richard believed that he was of little value either as a student or, because of the social ostracism he received from his age-peers, as a class-mate. Richard's emotional distress grew so severe that in 1987, when he was 10 years old, his parents pulled him out of school for three months and taught him at home. Currently, in the final grades of high school, Richard is somewhat more stimulated academically (although still performing many years below his true capacity; he scored 780 on the *SAT–M* at 12 years 6 months), and both he and his mother say, with relief, that his social relationships with classmates have never been better; yet Richard still recorded a significantly depressed z-score, –1.14, on the social self-peers subscale of the Coopersmith *SEI*. As was discussed in Chapter 8, Ursula McLeod is concerned that Richard has lost his drive to excel; whereas he formerly worked for the glow of success and achievement, early in 1989 he had to be 'bribed' to try his hardest in a scholarship exam with the promise of a new computer if he topped the state.

The changes in Anastasia's attitude to school, and the swift decline in her popularity with peers have caused severe concern to Alison and Tony Short. Anastasia is a born leader and organizer. In this she resembles the majority of the study children. One of the items on Renzulli's *Interest-a-Lyzer* asks the children what job they would prefer to do in a class play; it is no coincidence that they overwhelmingly selected actor, director or business manager, the roles which involve visibility and decision making! No child chose the 'behind scenes' tasks of building scenery, or designing or making costumes. In her personal life, however, Anastasia would like to take all these roles, and on a skiing holiday in 1989 she was able to do precisely that. She was the only child staying at the ski resort during the week of her holiday, and as a delightful, engaging 8-year-old with sparkling eyes, a ready wit and an infectious giggle she was so endearing that the adults, holiday makers and resort staff alike, took her to their hearts. Anastasia decided that she would write and produce a play to entertain the guests, and this she did. She devised the play, produced it, directed it, wrote out the programme, made tickets, distributed them, told people where to sit and played the leading part on stage. The play involved audience participation; caught by the charm and enthusiasm of the little girl, they willingly joined in the fun and acted out the parts she designed for them as the play progressed. For Anastasia it was an evening of pure magic.

However, while this level of enthusiasm, vibrancy and breathtaking all-round talent may be readily accepted on a holiday spree, Anastasia's classmates find it difficult to live with on a daily basis. It may be her very versatility which irks them; her reading interests are completely beyond their comprehension, she is a superb actor and a skilled musician, she thinks at a level and speed that silences them, and it has not yet occurred to her that she might be more popular if she were to moderate her performance.

> Versatility is one of the few human traits which are universally intolerable. You may be good at Greek and good at painting and be popular. You may be good at Greek and good at sport, and be wildly popular. But try all three, and you're a mountebank. Nothing arouses suspicion quicker than genuine, all-round proficiency.
>
> (Dunnett, 1961, p. 383)

Whatever the cause, Anastasia is only too well aware that the other children dislike and resent her. She recorded the disturbingly low z-score of −2.59 on the social self-peers subscale of the *SEI*.

Hollingworth believed that, even when an exceptionally gifted child possessed outstanding leadership potential, the chances of him or her being permitted to realize that potential were slight. She pointed out that the child or adult selected as the leader of a group is likely to be more intelligent than, but not too much more intelligent than, the average of the group led, and stated that a child whose IQ is more than 30 points above the average of the group of which he is a member is unlikely to become a popular leader (Hollingworth, 1926). For this reason she proposed that children of 'socially optimal intelligence' were more likely to become the leaders of the peer group, while children of IQ 170+ were too intelligent to be understood by the majority of their age-peers. Forty years later, Gibb (1969) suggested that leaders must not exceed their followers by too wide a margin of intelligence, as very great discrepancies hinder the unity of purpose of the group, and because the highly intelligent have interests and values remote from those of the general membership. Anastasia's talent for organization and leadership may never be fulfilled.

The loneliness, unhappiness and frustration of Ian and Adam have been recounted in previous chapters. These problems are intensified for these boys, and for Jade, by a trait which Hollingworth (1942) noted as being particularly characteristic of exceptionally gifted children; they find it extremely difficult to 'suffer fools gladly'. The explosions of blind fury to which Ian was prone in his early years arose from his frustration at being unable to communicate to his classmates ideas which to him were obvious, but which to them were quite incomprehensible. Brock and Sally Baker noticed that it was particularly younger children who aroused Ian's anger. Edward and Georgina Murphy notice that when Adam is particularly frustrated he becomes more than usually aggressive towards his younger sister. Jonathon, Cassandra, Hadley and Alice do not seem to suffer from this particular frustration; perhaps this is because they have older siblings who are also intellectually gifted, with whom they can discuss their ideas. Hadley's three grade-skips have given him further access to older children to whom he can relate intellectually. Holly Bond reported after his second grade-skip that he had entered 'a social wonderland'.

> He is well accepted and has made lots of good friends... Robert and I had an interview yesterday with the Principal and his class teacher. It was so different to previous years. They say he is a well-rounded, well-balanced little boy who is modest and as mature as any other Grade 4 child. He shows initiative, happily joins in everything, and is becoming an increasingly popular individual. He is popular despite being clearly top of the class.

Hollingworth warned, however, that exceptionally gifted children have to learn to accept that the majority of persons they will encounter in life are very different from themselves in thought and action. 'The highly intelligent child must learn to suffer fools gladly – not sneeringly, not angrily, not despairingly, not weepingly – but *gladly* if personal development is to proceed successfully in the world as it is' (Hollingworth, 1942, p. 299).

There is no doubt that, no matter how appropriate are the interventions made for these children in school, they will live, as adults, in a world where the vast majority of people they will encounter will find it difficult to relate to their remarkable intellectual capacities, their atypical interests and their radically different ways of responding to moral and ethical questions. This does not mean, however, that the school should absolve itself from the requirement to make the extremely gifted child's passage through childhood as trouble-free as possible; a child who receives affection and approval from other children is learning and practising the skills which will assist her to form sound social relationships in adulthood. A child who is ostracized by her peers has little opportunity to practise these skills.

Chapter 8 closed with a poignant quotation from Caroline Vincent, mother of 7-year-old Jade. Caroline and Michael watched in despair and with a feeling of powerlessness as Jade changed from a vibrant, confident and happy 3-year-old with a delight in acquiring new knowledge, to a sad little girl who developed totally negative attitudes towards school and her classmates, and was often bitterly unhappy. Her school offered Jade, with an IQ of 174, neither acceleration nor enrichment. Indeed, although she was permitted to enter school 12 months before the usual age, and her reading developed at a remarkable pace with the encouragement of the principal and the Reception Grade teacher, at the end of that year the teacher suggested that Jade repeat the Reception Grade. This suggestion was not made on intellective grounds – the teacher recognized that Jade had progressed far beyond the rest of the class both intellectually and in her academic achievement – but because she was rather small and the teacher felt that if she repeated the year she would be with other children who were closer to her in physical size.

Jade had found the work of the Reception class boring in the extreme. The children had been learning the alphabet, one letter at a time, while Jade had mastered the alphabet at age 3.

> I couldn't bear to think of her sitting through all that again. I had noticed an actual slowing down of her intellectual curiosity and love of learning right from halfway through the Reception grade. I was worried, already, that this would intensify if they made her repeat the year. So I stood my ground and demanded that she be promoted to Grade 1 in the normal way, and fortunately they agreed.
>
> (Caroline Vincent)

Academically and socially, Jade had serious problems in Grade 1.

> She wouldn't settle, she was disruptive, she was hitting children, stealing their pencils, and things like that. I found out about this when the class teacher called me up for an interview, and out it all came. The awful thing was: when she saw how upset I was, she said, to comfort me, 'Well, at least it's not as bad as it was last year when she was hitting the other children with a stick.' Apparently this had been going on all through the Reception year but no one had told me; I suspect the Reception class teacher didn't want to admit it because she didn't want to recognize it as a sign of boredom or frustration. I was mortified. I had had no idea. I know just how the parents of the child called 'Ian Baker' felt when they were called up to school and told that he was being violent towards the other

> children. I can empathize with so much of their experience, because Jade has been through so many of the same things.
>
> (Caroline Vincent)

Many of Jade's problems stem from her extreme lack of self-confidence, and fear of failure. In contrast to her delight in new experiences in early childhood, she became more and more reluctant to undertake new tasks in case she would perform at a level below that which she herself considered satisfactory. Like many exceptionally gifted children, she sets herself extremely high standards, and then agonizes over whether she can attain them.

> With Jade, the thing is that with every stage you have to build up her confidence; she always assumes that she can't do something and is unwilling to try; but once she realizes that she *can* do it, then there's no stopping her. Once she has grasped the concept her understanding is just incredibly swift and deep, and she's off and away.
>
> (Caroline Vincent)

A major problem, however, is that whereas Caroline and Michael were prepared to take the necessary time to reassure Jade to the point where she will risk failure by trying the new work, some of her earlier teachers did not see the necessity for this. They were aware that part of her reluctance to work lies in a lack of confidence, but they did not take the time to encourage and support her to the point where she would make the attempt. As a result, Jade's work in the classroom has been far inferior to her levels of demonstrated achievement on standardized tests administered by an educational psychologist and by me in the course of this study, and some of her teachers have been extremely reluctant to believe that she is, indeed, as gifted as the tests would indicate. For most of her school career Jade has had no friends in her own class and she has been lonely, socially isolated and deeply depressed. Three years ago she started lying, stealing and physically attacking her younger sister and brothers. Her parents arranged for her to see a therapist in an attempt to reduce her anger and hostility.

> The therapist irritated Jade intensely by talking to her as if she was a small child, and then blamed her depression and emotional difficulties on the fact that she had started school early! She kept saying, 'She's an 8-year old, just treat her like an 8-year-old.'
>
> (Caroline Vincent)

Jade's z-score on the social self-peers subscale of the Coopersmith *SEI* was −1.34.

In 1991 Caroline and Michael moved Jade, and her sister and brothers, to a small private school which has a special interest in gifted and talented children. Jade is somewhat happier in school and is beginning to develop the self-confidence she needs to make friends with some of her new classmates. However, she is still unwilling to display the full range, or extent, of her abilities to her teachers or age-peers.

Earlier in this chapter a corollary was proposed to the Feldhusen-Hoover conception of giftedness as a conjunction of intelligence, self-concept and self-esteem interacting to engender the strong motivational force essential for high-level production (Feldhusen and Hoover, 1986). This corollary proposed that, where a child who is known to be intellectually gifted is not demonstrating high-level performance, we might have cause to suspect that her exceptional cognitive abilities are not supported by healthy levels of self-concept or self-esteem. As discussed in the preceding pages, Ian, Adam, Jade, Anastasia and Richard, who are working, in the classroom, at levels significantly below their tested levels of achievement, have z-scores of below −1.00 on the social self-peers subscale of the *SEI*, and all are reported, by their parents, to have lost the motivational drive that characterized them in early childhood. This finding strengthens and enhances the Feldhusen Hoover conception of intellectual giftedness. An inappropriate and undemanding curriculum, and the requirement to work at the level of age-peers, have not only imposed underachievement on these children, but have also engendered the conditions of low self-esteem and poor motivation which serve to ensure that underachievement continues.

MORAL DEVELOPMENT

Researchers studying the highly and exceptionally gifted have noted that these children are frequently found to have unusually accelerated levels of moral development. Terman (1926) reported that on tests of 'trustworthiness' and 'moral stability' the average child of 9 years of age in his gifted sample scored at levels more usually attained by children aged 14. Hollingworth noted, in her subjects of IQ 180+, a passionate concern for ethical and moral issues, and a deep and unusually mature interest in questions of origin, destiny, and man's relationship with God (Hollingworth, 1942). She recounted the experience of a highly gifted girl of 8 who asked her parents, 'What is it called when you can't make up your mind whether there is a God or not?' and who, on being told that this was termed agnosticism, expressed a wish to join the 'Agnostic Church'. Hollingworth compared this child's dissatisfaction with the established Church with that of Goethe who at the age of 9 devised a religion of his own in which God could be worshipped without the help of priests (Hollingworth, 1942). She illustrated the preoccupation with moral questions of good and evil which characterizes exceptionally gifted children by describing a 6-year-old boy of IQ 187 who wept bitterly after reading 'how the North taxed the South after the Civil War' (Hollingworth, 1942, p. 281).

Carroll, in his study of children of IQ 170, discussed the capacity of these young people to understand the gradations in moral and social values.

> Nothing to them is ever wholly white, or wholly black, wholly right or wholly wrong... The really great humanists are not found among bigots of limited intelligence, but among those who have sufficient intellectual capacity to realize that all values are relative.
>
> (Carroll, 1940, p. 123)

The research and writing of Kohlberg, which links moral and cognitive development, has had a considerable influence on psychologists and educators studying the psychosocial development of the intellectually gifted. Kohlberg's model, which was strongly influenced by the cognitive stage theory of Piaget, proposes that a child's acquisition of moral judgment passes through six stages of development which are themselves contained within three clearly defined levels of moral growth (Kohlberg, 1963).

The first level, of *pre-conventional* thinking (Stages 1 and 2), is characterized by a self-centred perspective of morality; at this level the child follows rules to avoid punishment, rather than from any abstract concern for order or fairness. Similarly, helping others is seen as 'good' because it will probably result in reward or reciprocal assistance.

The second, or *conventional*, level (Stages 3 and 4) is characterized by a societal perspective; a child or adult functioning at this level will be influenced in his decisions by the moral values of the family, group, community or culture of which he is a member.

A person functioning at the highest, or *post-conventional* level of moral development (Stages 5 and 6) will base his judgment upon his autonomous views of the universal ethical principles on which be believes a good society *should* be based. Such a person will eschew conventional principles of morality; his decisions and actions will be based on what Webb, Meckstroth and Tolan (1983) have described as 'moral principles beyond conformity'.

> People in these upper levels are the leaders, creators and inventors who make major contributions to society, and who help reformulate knowledge and philosophy, often changing major traditions in the process... Those who have reached the highest levels of moral development may go beyond the law as well, sometimes sacrificing themselves, and often changing the world's perception of the law,

> and finally the law itself. Gifted children may set themselves on such a course early in life.
>
> (Webb, Meckstroth and Tolan, 1983, p. 179)

Several studies (Arbuthnot, 1973; Grant, Weiner and Ruchton, 1976; Maccoby, 1980) have found significant correlations between scores on individual or group tests of intelligence and high scores on measures of moral development. While the majority of adults do not progress beyond the second, or conventional, level of moral judgment, Boehm (1962) and Kohlberg (1964) found that intellectually gifted children were able to make complex moral judgments much earlier than their age-peers, while some highly gifted elementary school children functioned at the 'principled', post-conventional level normally attained by fewer than 10 per cent of adults. Thorndike (1940), studying the moral judgment of 50 highly gifted children aged 9–12, found that the levels of moral development exhibited by these children correlated much more closely with their mental ages than with their chronological ages. Janos and Robinson (1985) report on an earlier, unpublished study in which, using the *Defining Issues Test* (Rest, 1979) as a measure of moral judgment, they compared a group of 24 radically accelerated university students aged 11–18, and two groups of gifted high school students who had not been accelerated, with a group of typical university students. All three groups of intellectually gifted students exhibited significantly higher levels of moral judgment than did the typical undergraduates.

The *Defining Issues Test (DIT)*, is based on Kohlberg's principles of moral development, and was designed to identify the basic conceptual frameworks by which an individual analyzes a moral or ethical problem, and to assess the conceptual level of his or her moral reasoning (Rest, 1986a).

In the *Defining Issues Test* a subject is presented with six moral dilemmas in the form of short stories; each story is accompanied by a list of 12 'issues' or questions that an individual might consider in making a decision about what ought to be done in the situation. The subject must evaluate each issue in terms of its importance in helping him come to a conclusion about what he would do if placed in the situation portrayed in the story. The subject must then select the four issues which would have the greatest influence on his decision. The issues are written in such a way as to represent 'the different considerations that are diagnostic of different schemes of fairness (i.e. moral judgment stages)' (Rest, 1986a, p. 196); the issues, indeed, comprise a set of alternatives that require the individual to choose between different concepts of justice.

The *DIT* lends itself to different forms of scoring; according to the manual (Rest, 1986a) the score most often used by researchers is the P index, P standing for 'principled morality', the level of moral judgment equating with Kohlberg's post-conventional Stages 5 and 6. The P index is interpreted as the relative importance that subjects attribute to issues reflecting the highest levels of moral reasoning. It is calculated by summing the number of times that Stage 5 and 6 issues are chosen as the first, second, third or fourth most important consideration, weighting these ranks by 4, 3, 2 and 1 respectively. The score, expressed as a percentage, can range from 0 to 95.

The *DIT* is not generally used with elementary school children, as successful administration requires the subject to have a reading age of at least 12 years (Rest, 1980b). However, given the research reported above on the accelerated development of moral judgment in highly gifted elementary school children, it was decided to use the *DIT* to assess the moral development of Adrian, Christopher, Rufus, Richard, Cassandra, Fred, Jonathon and Ian, whose chronological ages at the time of assessment were 10 years and above. The mental ages of the children at the time of administration were at least 16 years and all had the reading accuracy and reading comprehension skills of young people several years their senior.

Table 9.2 compares the P scores of moral judgment recorded by the Study children on the *Defining Issues Test* with the mean scores for American junior high school, high school and college students.

Although all eight children were, at the time of administration, below the mean age of American junior high school students, all record principled morality scores on the *Defining Issues Test* which are above the mean for this population, and five of the children record z-scores of at least

Table 9.2 Ages of subjects and P scores on *Defining Issues Test*, compared with norms for American students

			Z-scores compared with American students		
Child	*Age*	*P score*	*Junior high*	*High school*	*College*
Christopher	12 yrs 2 mths	24	+ 0.78		
Rufus	11 yrs 8 mths	26	+ 1.10		
Fred	12 yrs 1 mth	48	+ 4.59	+ 1.64	+0.32
Adrian	13 yrs 4 mths	20	+ 0.14		
Ian	10 yrs 0 mths	30	+ 1.73	+ 0.11	
Richard	11 yrs 10 mths	34	+ 2.37	+ 0.45	
Cassandra	11 yrs 1 mth	24	+ 0.67		
Jonathon	12 yrs 3 mths	50	+ 4.90	+ 1.80	+ 0.48

Note The Z-scores were derived from comparison with norms for American students. Means and Standard Deviations for the above groups were:
Junior high, $\bar{x}$ = 19.1, SD = 6.3, for males,
$\bar{x}$ = 19.8, SD = 6.3, for females;
High school, $\bar{x}$ = 28.7, SD = 11.8;
College, $\bar{x}$ = 44.1, SD = 12.2.

+1.00. Indeed, the P scores of Fred, Ian, Jonathon and Richard are so elevated that they are also above the mean for American high school students, and both Fred, aged only 12 years 1 month, and Jonathon, aged 12 years 3 months, actually scored above the mean for college students!

It is interesting to note that of the five children who recorded z-scores of more than +1.00 on the *DIT* norms for junior high students, three children, Rufus, Ian and Richard, had significantly depressed scores on the social self-peers subscale of the Coopersmith *Self-Esteem Inventory*. Ian, at age 10, scored above the mean for high school students on the DIT but recorded a disturbingly low social self-peers z-score of –1.97. Neither Ian nor Rufus had at this time been permitted any form of acceleration, and Richard's token grade-skip of one year still leaves him with classmates who are far below him in terms of intellectual, social and emotional development. On the other hand, Fred, who has scored above the mean for college students on the *DIT*, recorded a z-score of +1.71 on the social self-peers subscale of the SEI; Fred has been radically accelerated, and is able to work and socialize with children who share his abilities and interests. Jonathon, whose social self-peers z-score was +.53 has been grade-skipped and enjoys a further one year subject acceleration in maths and a two year subject acceleration in German.

It may be that, where exceptionally gifted children have not been accelerated to be with children at similar levels of intellectual and social development, significantly elevated levels of moral development may intensify their awareness of thinking and feeling in ways that set them apart from their age-peers. The loneliness and bewilderment of Ian Baker is more readily understood when one considers that at age 10 he was capable of moral reasoning at levels which characterize Kohlberg's post-conventional stages, while his classmates may well have been functioning within Stages 1 and 2, where rules are followed not from an appreciation of their value, but simply to avoid punishment. Ian's views on ethical and moral issues such as justice, fairness, personal responsibility, and responsibility toward others, are so far removed from those of his age-peers that it is quite unrealistic to expect him to understand their perspective, or to expect them to understand his. He is already functioning at a level which few of his classmates will ever attain.

Until Fred Campbell was permitted to accelerate from elementary school to high school one month after his eleventh birthday, his school experience was one of bitter unhappiness. He was tormented by his age-peers for being different. They mocked his interest in psychology and philosophy. They were unable to understand his passion for mathematics. Not even his sporting talent saved him, because at heart Fred was not particularly interested in sport and was not willing to participate in the Monday morning post-mortem of the weekend's games. Fred's actions, reactions and opinions, when he tried to express them, were utterly alien to their system of values. They taunted, derided and attacked him mercilessly, and made his life a misery. At the age of 12 years 1 month, Fred was displaying the level of moral judgment attained by the average college student; it is probable that 12 months earlier, at the end of his elementary school involvement, he would have been functioning above the mean for high school students. As with Ian, Fred's level of moral judgment was so vastly superior to that of his classmates that it is unrealistic to expect that normal social relationships could ever have been established while he remained with age-peers. By contrast, when Fred's general and subject acceleration permitted him to work and socialize with children four and five years older than he, the discrepancies between the intellectual and moral development of Fred and his classmates were not so obvious, and he was not only accepted by his classmates, but actively valued as a colleague and friend.

Many of the children have shown, from early childhood, a strong tendency to question rules and to rebel against practices which they consider unjust or unfair. The reluctance of Adam and Ian, in their first few years of school, to accept rules and restrictions which they considered irrelevant or invalid, has been discussed in previous chapters. Ian is plagued by a continual compulsion to challenge school or family rulings with which he does not agree, but he has not yet developed the social skill to do this with subtlety.

> We know he's very gifted and we're continually amazed by what he can understand and how quickly he can understand it, but... sometimes we still find it hard to believe that he can really be as bright as that, especially since we see the things he does which are really stupid, like parent baiting rather than parent manipulating which his younger brother can do much better!
>
> (Brock Baker)

The ongoing difficulties which Jade and Adam have experienced at school arise partly from their frustration with what they view as stupid and unfair restrictions. The continual questioning and challenging of traditions which their age-peers take for granted sets these children even further apart from their classmates and often leads to social rejection.

Several of the research studies on the highly gifted (Burks, Jensen and Terman, 1930; Hollingworth, 1942; Zorbaugh, Boardman and Sheldon, 1951) have noted that exceptionally gifted children display high standards of truth and morality, and can be overly judgmental towards other children or adults who do not appear to be measuring up to these standards. They have a very low tolerance of hypocrisy, and, because of their keen powers of observation and analysis, they can pick up, very speedily, discrepancies between what an adult says and what he does. They pick up, much earlier than children of average ability, the sobering truth that their teachers and parents, like all other adults, have character flaws, and this realization, arriving before the child has developed a level of social maturity which could assist him or her to deal with it, can be extremely disturbing.

At age 7, Alice Marlow had a class teacher who made no secret of her dislike and resentment of the child. Alice relates that one morning, as the children were milling around the classroom door waiting to go out, the teacher trod accidentally on Alice's toes, and, when she discovered that it was Alice's foot under her own, intensified the pressure, grinding her heel into the child's instep. Alice quietly but firmly states that she believes the teacher's action was deliberate. A year later, she still recalled the incident with something approaching horror. That the violence was directed at herself did not disturb her as much as the realization that a teacher who was supposedly dedicated to caring for her charges would so far forget her moral responsibilities as to try to harm a child.

The unusually high value placed by exceptionally gifted children on truth and morality may affect their scores on the lie scales of various personality tests. The lie scale built into the Coopersmith *Self-Esteem Inventory* contains items which state, 'I always tell the truth', and, 'I like everyone I know'. Interestingly, four children, Christopher, Ian, Hadley and Anastasia, responded 'Like me' to the first item. Elizabeth Otway endorsed Christopher's perception.

> It's true. He *does* always tell the truth, and frankly, it is no great asset. He seems to have a real need to be completely truthful, and it is not always appreciated by the people he's with. On the very few occasions when he *has* told a white lie, a 'social' lie, it has bothered him so much that later in the conversation he has admitted that he lied, and has explained how he really feels about the issue. To be honest, people find this much more disturbing than the original impulse to lie, which everyone has.

It is interesting to speculate whether the social difficulties experienced by Ian and Anastasia may be due to their uncompromising honesty; both can be tactless in the forthright expression of their views. It may be that the parents and teachers of exceptionally and profoundly gifted children should explain the convention of the 'social lie', and assist them to temper honesty with social judgment.

The second lie scale item mentioned above, 'I like everyone I know', received affirmative responses from Christopher and Hadley. Interestingly, this is a perception that I myself have developed of Chris through my conversations with him over a number of years. He knows that his intellectual capabilities, and in particular his talents in mathematics, are prodigious, but this has never caused him to view the children or adults with whom he interacts in a lesser light. Indeed, he seems to focus on the positive, rather than the negative, aspects of people. This does not stem from any social naivety; he recognizes and rejects arrogance, intellectual laziness, and hypocrisy, and is particularly disturbed when he notes these qualities in teachers; however, he genuinely seems to find something to like and admire in everyone he meets. Hadley took the *SEI* after his second grade-skip; in his 'social wonderland', as Holly described it, relationships were coloured by the roseate hue of his new happiness.

These results suggest that those lie scale items on the *SEI* which address questions of ethics or personal morality may function differently for exceptionally and profoundly gifted children than for children of average intellectual capacity.

PASSION FOR DETAIL AND PRECISION

Several researchers have noted, in the highly gifted, a passion for detail and precision (Hollingworth, 1942; Webb, Meckstroth and Tolan, 1983; Kline and Meckstroth, 1985). 'Nearly everything matters, and it matters that it matters' (Kline and Meckstroth, 1985, p. 25). Because the exceptionally gifted tend to view events holistically, and because their extremely sensitive perception makes them keenly alive to aspects of events that the average person would not even be aware of, they sometimes experience difficulty in editing their narration of an event to select only those aspects which will be relevant or interesting to the listener. The following letter, quoted in full, was written to me by Ian Baker during one of my periods of residence in the United States. Ian was 9 years 4 months old. The 'whatchamacallit' to which Ian refers was Renzulli's *Interest-a-Lyzer* which he was to have completed, in common with the other children, and sent with the letter, but which, like Richard, he found rather boring and consequently delayed in completing. In the end, his mother resorted to a spot of emotional blackmail; Ian was not permitted to write to Miraca, which he enjoyed, until he had completed the *Interest-a-Lyzer*! Place names and the name of the hospital have been changed to protect Ian's identity; however, his spelling and punctuation are left unchanged.

> This letter was meant to be sent with the whatchamacallit. However, I shall not stop sending letters in the future. Mum wouldn't let me prepare this thing before the whatchamacallit was posted.
>
> My father's oldest son (me!) has broken his left arm. It happened at Seaville on Sunday the eighteenth of September. I fell over in the gutter of Ocean Terrace (look it up!) and, probably because of the slope, I fractured my Radius. Mum wouldnt believe me, until we reached the bakery and I was very pale. Mum had another look and my arm was bent at an angle of about 30 degrees. I ate a bit of the

pie, and one of the people from the bakery drove us to the district hospital. Bill stayed with some of his friends.

I had some x-rays and Mum's estimation (30 degrees) was correct. A temporary plaster was put on and my grandparents (who were in Newtown and drove to Seaville on very short notice), drove Mum and me to the Children's Hospital (Casualties Section). I had to wait for about ten minutes before they started to attend to me. They took Mum and me to a room and I went to have some more x-rays while Mum told my grandparents what was happening and that they could go home. They came back to our place and fed the Cats (these were the neighbour's who were on Holidays) and I went to sleep while Mum discussed something with a doctor. I woke up. Mum discussed matters with a nurse while I was asleep again. Both asked me a few questions about whether I knew what was happening. I answered both correctly. After the nurse had come, she gave me some tablets and I went off to another place. The tablets sent me to sleep. I woke up and I was wheeled to Operating Theatre One. I had a rubbery needle put in for injections. It did not hurt that way (as much!). The operation was done in about ten minutes. I spent stacks of time in the Recovery room, then I recovered and threw up in the bed. They were not quick enough with the vomit bowl! Everything had to be changed. I went back to my ward (8C) and went to sleep.

On the next day, around 9.16., the orthopaedic surgeon came around. I was allowed to go home now. We waited till Dad came, and then I went home. My piano playing/practice is ruined: I can only use five notes now, so I don't bother, and my typing speed has dropped to twenty-eight words per minute (28 w.p.m.) on average (four paragraphs) and 32 w.p.m. on rate (one paragraph). My old speed was around 33 w.p.m. and my maximum speed was 36 w.p.m. on average and 40 w.p.m. on rate.
Best regards,

Ian.

To a psychologist or educator, especially one who is interested in the traits and characteristics of gifted children, and can see how the passion for detail, the humour, and the verbal fluency which characterize these children are reflected in Ian's letter, this account is a delight. To another 9-year-old, however, it would be intensely boring, unsatisfying or even irritating. The 9-year-old of average ability would want to focus on whether there was blood, whether an ambulance came, what happened on the operating table, and whether it hurt. Ian shows little concern for the dramatic aspects of the event; his concern is to detail precisely for his reader the locus of the event, the cause of the accident, the family arrangements (I know, through this study, the family members mentioned), details of his stay in hospital, and the effect of the incident on his unusually advanced typing skills, of which he is rightly proud. There is little in Ian's account to interest or impress a child of his own age. The insistence on precision, which also characterizes Ian's passion for road maps and transport route maps, is yet another 'difference' which sets the exceptionally gifted apart from age-peers. The complexities of route time-tabling and the intricacies of the road systems doted on by Ian in his transport studies leave his age-peers cold; as related in chapter 7, he can find no one outside his own family with whom he can discuss the topics which absorb him.

SUMMARY

When the children's scores on the sub-scales of the Coopersmith *Self-Esteem Inventory* are compared, it can be seen that, while the total self-esteem scores of most of the children fall within the normal range, the majority record scores on the social self-peers subscale which are significantly below the mean for age-peers of average ability. Research suggests that an awareness of the differences between themselves and the majority of their age peers can have a depressing and demotivating effect on the intellectually gifted. As has been discussed in this and previous chapters, the exceptionally gifted children in this study differ from their age-mates on almost every variable examined. The children are aware that they are disliked and rejected by their classmates and this intensifies existing problems of self-concept. A further difference lies in their accelerated levels of moral development; on questions of moral or ethical significance, these children's reactions are radically different from those of their age-peers and resemble those of junior high, high school or college students.

There are readily identifiable differences between the levels of self-esteem of students who have been radically accelerated and those who have been retained with their age-peers or with children only 12 months their senior. General self-concept and social self-concept are very much stronger in radical accelerands. Children whose educational programme requires them to work at academic levels which do not provide adequate intellectual challenge show disturbingly depressed levels of self-esteem and motivation.

It is now generally understood and accepted that a child's level of social and moral development is more highly correlated with his mental age than with his chronological age (Hallahan and Kauffman, 1982; Tannenbaum, 1983; Janos and Robinson, 1985). Intellectually gifted children differ from their age-peers in their social and emotional development as much as in their intellectual and academic characteristics. The difficulties confronting the exceptionally gifted students in this study have been exacerbated by the reluctance of their schools to allow them access to other children who share their levels of intellectual, moral and psychosocial development. In the absence of a peer group of children who share their abilities, interests and values, they have to try to forge some links to the group of age-peers with whom they have been placed. This places the gifted child in a forced-choice dilemma. If he is to satisfy his drive for excellence and achievement, he must risk sacrificing the attainment of intimacy with his age-peers. If the pursuit of intimacy is his primary need, he must moderate his standards of achievement, conceal, to some extent at least, his intellectual interests, and conform to a value system that may be seriously at variance with his own level of moral development, to retain the approval of the group in which he has been placed. In the child or adolescent of average ability the drives towards intimacy and achievement are compatible, indeed complementary. The gifted, however, must be one of the few remaining groups in our society who are compelled, by the constraints of the educative and social system within which they operate, to choose which of two basic psychosocial needs should be fulfilled.

A number of the children have shown, at various times during their school career, moderate to severe levels of depression. For some, this has been alleviated by a more appropriate grade-placement. For others, the loneliness, the social isolation and the bitter unhappiness continue. The plight of these children recalls another quotation from the gifted adolescents interviewed for the American Association for Gifted Children's book *On Being Gifted*.

> Too early in my life, I felt that I didn't want to be human anymore. I didn't want to die, yet continuing on in the state I was in wasn't hittin' on nothin'.
>
> (American Association for Gifted Children, 1978, p. 18)

10

THE EXCEPTIONALLY GIFTED: RECOGNITION AND RESPONSE

Where the gifted child drifts in the school unrecognized, held to the lockstep which is determined by the capacities of the average, he has little to do. He receives daily practice in habits of idleness and daydreaming. His abilities are never genuinely challenged, and the situation is contrived to build in him expectations of an effortless existence. Children up to about 140 IQ tolerate the ordinary school routine quite well, being usually a little young for grade through an extra promotion or two, and achieving excellent marks without serious effort. But above this status, children become increasingly bored with school work, if kept in or nearly in the lockstep. Children at or above 180 IQ, for instance, are likely to regard school with indifference, or with positive distaste, for they find nothing to do there.

(Hollingworth, 1931, p. 5)

When Leta Hollingworth wrote this, in 1931, it was customary for even moderately gifted students to have been grade advanced. She acknowledges this in her comment that they were likely to be a little young for the grade they were in through having had 'an extra promotion or two', and she attributes these children's tolerance of the lockstep curriculum to this early intervention. Moderately gifted children in the 1990s, however, are much more likely to be retained in the regular classroom with age-peers; we can no longer assume that they 'tolerate the ordinary school routine quite well'.

The situation for exceptionally and profoundly gifted children is much as it was in the 1930s. School offers them very little. In elementary school they learn little that they have not already taught themselves several years earlier. The majority are likely to be found in the regular classroom with perhaps the token offering of a pull-out programme for two hours each week, or a single grade-skip. As Hollingworth observed (1942), in the regular elementary school classroom moderately gifted children waste half their time; extraordinarily gifted children waste practically all their time.

This book has traced the intellectual, academic, social and emotional development of 15 remarkable young people from their early childhood to the present day. Only one child, Adrian, has completed his secondary education; the others are still undertaking their elementary or secondary schooling, experiencing, in the majority of cases, educational programmes which are totally inadequate to their needs.

As can be seen from the preceding chapters, the children in this study differ quite radically, in many ways, not only from children of average ability but even from their moderately gifted age-peers. In terms of intellectual capacity alone Richard, Roshni and Adam, with IQs between 160 and 162, differ from moderately gifted children of IQ 130 to the same degree that the latter differ from children of average ability, while Ian, Chris and Adrian with IQs of 200+, are as far from the moderately gifted child as he or she is from an intellectually disabled child of IQ 60. The curriculum and programming structures which might be offered to moderately gifted students are not sufficient, by themselves, for the needs of the extremely gifted. Equally, of course, interventions such as radical acceleration, which are designed specifically for the extremely gifted, would be inappropriate, both academically and socially, for moderately gifted students.

MODELS OF GIFTEDNESS

The model or definition of giftedness adopted by a school or education system will naturally determine the identification procedures which will be used and the type of child who will be identified.

Very few of the children in this study would be recognized as gifted under any model which incorporated motivation or task commitment as an integral component of giftedness. Ian was identified only when his rebellious and violent behaviour caused his school to have him tested with a view to placement in a special school for behaviourally disturbed children. Richard shows little motivation at school and had to be coaxed with the promise of a new computer before he would study for the scholarship which would assist his parents with school fees. The parents of Adam, Jade, Ian and Rick have shared, in these chapters, their concern at their children's demotivation and their fears that the children's intellectual curiousity and love of learning might have been so depressed by years of underachievement that it might never return. Fred speaks of his loathing for school, his depression and his loneliness, which lasted for six years until he was permitted early entry to secondary schooling. Hadley Bond rejected school after two weeks.

These children can hardly be described as task committed, yet they are among the most gifted children ever studied. Their experiences illustrate and reinforce the inappropriateness of the Renzulli 'three-ring' model of giftedness (Renzulli, 1978) for the identification of underachieving or demotivated gifted students – which necessarily, as the research discussed in this book has shown, includes the considerable majority of highly, exceptionally and profoundly gifted children. Yet, as was discussed in Chapter 2, the Renzulli model has had considerable influence on policy development in gifted education in Australia. Rufus's school, like many others, selects students for its 'gifted and talented' programme on the Renzullian criteria. As Rufus, a quiet-natured child, has been somewhat more successful in concealing his boredom than some of the other study children, he was deemed 'task committed' and gained entry to the pull-out programme. Most of the children in this study would not have been admitted.

The concerns of several researchers regarding the limitations of the 'three-ring' model were summarized in 1989 by Borland.

> It is inadequate for practical purposes. It appears to be based on a questionable reading of the research marshalled in its support, and this results in a definition that attempts to carry too much weight on its slender shoulders. Moreover, the consequences of using this definition are such that only those children who are *already succeeding* in the regular classroom are likely to receive special services. What is needed is a definition that rests on a firmer foundation of scholarship and logic, and is better considered in terms of the effects of utilizing it. Happily, definitions of giftedness exist that meet these criteria.
>
> (Borland, 1989, p. 15)

Two of the definitions which Borland next discusses as meeting the requirements of scholarship, logic and practicability are those of Abraham Tannenbaum and Françoys Gagné, which have been discussed at length in Chapter 2. Both models focus on 'the links between promise and fulfilment' (Tannenbaum, 1983, p. 95). Both recognize the influence of personalogical and environmental variables on the translation of potential into performance.

Gagné's model presents giftedness as 'exceptional competence in one or more domains of ability' and defines talent as 'exceptional performance in one or more fields of human activity' (Gagné, 1985, p. 111). In terms of their levels of tested intelligence, all 40 of the children in this study are outstandingly gifted in the intellectual domain; yet many do not demonstrate exceptional academic performance within the classroom setting. Psychosocial constraints such as lack of motivation, severely depressed social self-esteem, the pressure to underachieve for peer acceptance, or social isolation and loneliness, have combined with environmental barriers such as an unsupportive school climate, inappropriate identification procedures, and the Australian wariness of intellectual precocity, to hinder the translation of aptitude into achievement. Within the Gagné model these children are gifted but not yet talented.

The facilitative or obstructive influence of chance, which is such a powerful element in Tannenbaum's psychosocial model, appears as a striking factor in the school careers of several of the children. If the principal of Chris Otway's school had not won a Fullbright Fellowship to study educational provisions for the gifted in the United States, and had he not visited Julian Stanley and Camilla Benbow of the Study of Mathematically Precocious Youth and seen at first hand the advantages of acceleration, it is extremely doubtful whether Christopher would have been permitted the radical acceleration which has allowed him to develop his phenomenal abilities. If the psychologist brought in to test 5-year-old Ian Baker had not already been aware of the measurement issues involved in testing young gifted children, he might have used the more generally employed *WPPSI (Wechsler Preschool and Primary Scale of Intelligence)* to assess Ian instead of the *Stanford-Binet*, and the full extent of Ian's abilities, and consequently the full extent of his boredom and intellectual frustration, might never have been revealed.

Equally, chance can determine the teacher a child is placed with, or the direction in which a school's philosophies will proceed. If the interview panels which appointed the new principals to the schools attended by Rick and Ian had happened to select administrators who were less ideologically opposed to special provisions for the gifted, these children might not have had their special programmes terminated, and their early years of schooling might have been very different.

APPROPRIATE IDENTIFICATION PROCEDURES

One of Australia's national sporting heroes was, and is, the great cricketer, Sir Donald Bradman. Bradman's achievements as a batsman are legendary. Yet, according to one of his biographers, (Derriman, 1989), during his high school cricket career, even when he was making 300 not out, no one realised how prodigiously talented he was. He was incomparably better than anyone he had ever played with or against, but in the country town where he lived there was no yardstick by which talent of his calibre could be measured. It was not until he was observed by Bill O'Reilly, an older cricketer who had spent some time in Sydney, that the phenomenal extent of his talent was recognised; O'Reilly had a more valid means of comparison.

In much the same way a teacher may come to realize that an exceptionally gifted student is the brightest student she has ever taught, and yet may still have no conception of the true extent of the child's talent. If our ablest young people are to be accurately identified and assisted, our teachers must be trained in recognizing and estimating *levels* of giftedness.

The *National Report on Identification*, produced for the United States Government in 1982 by Susanne Richert and her colleagues, noted that extremely gifted students were a group particularly at risk for non- or misidentification.

We discussed, in Chapter 1, the tendency for schools to develop identification protocols and establish programmes designed for the moderately gifted, in the expectation that all levels of giftedness will be thus identified and catered for. A major difficulty is that many of the 'trait lists' published both in texts on gifted education and as commercial materials, and used as identification aids by teachers, focus on the behavioural traits and characteristics of moderately gifted students. A further problem is that these lists, with few exceptions, concentrate on the positive characteristics of the moderately gifted achiever and ignore the negative behaviours often displayed by highly gifted students whose schools have failed to make appropriate provision for them.

Research suggests that, particularly in the early years of schooling, parents are considerably more effective in identifying gifted children than are teachers (Baldwin, 1962; Jacobs, 1971; Ciha, Harris, Hoffman and Potter, 1974). Extremely gifted children tend to display such precocious development of speech, movement and reading that their parents generally realize, long before their child reaches school age, that he or she is unusually advanced. As Chapter 4 relates, 10 of the 15 study children were walking independently before their first birthday, fully three months earlier than is usual, and the mean age at which the children uttered their first words was 9.7 months, as against a population mean of 11–12 months. Five of the children were reading before their second birthday and 10 were reading before they turned 3. However, parents of such extremely precocious youngsters are often reluctant to admit to teachers that their child displayed such unusually early development for fear that they will be disbelieved and classed as 'pushy mums'. The considerable majority of the parents in this study did not tell their child's kindergarten teacher that the child was already an avid and fluent reader, and a further proportion report that when they did try to discuss their children's accelerated development with teachers, they were disbelieved.

The parents of extremely gifted children can be a valuable resource in the successful identification and assessment of their child's abilities. Given that deliberate underachievement can begin as early as the first few weeks of school, teachers or principals enrolling children into formal schooling should question parents on the developmental history of their child, with particular reference as to whether the child may have already learned to read. This procedure would give the parent of the early reader 'permission' to acknowledge that her child is, indeed, different and in need of early recognition and intervention. Furthermore, as discussed in Chapter 5, the presence of one exceptionally gifted child in a family should alert both the teacher and the parents to the strong possibility that siblings are also intellectually gifted.

Teacher, parent, peer and self-nomination, when used appropriately and with care, can contribute significantly to the effectiveness of a schools's identification procedures. Of even greater value, however, in the identification of intellectually and academically gifted students, are standardized tests of ability and achievement. These objective screening measures, used in conjunction with subjective procedures such as nomination, anecdotal records, trait lists and other indices, can mesh together to create a comprehensive and effective identification and assessment process (Richert, Alvino and McDonnel, 1982; Tannenbaum, 1983; Feldhusen and Baska, 1989).

This combination of objective and subjective procedures will enable schools to make a more accurate assessment of the true attainment levels of exceptionally gifted children who may be underachieving in the regular classroom through lack of challenge, inappropriate grade placement, or a desire to conceal their abilities for peer acceptance. Exceptionally gifted children tend to have the potential for high level performance in several academic subjects, and teachers should be alerted, by the discovery of one talent, to the probable existence of others.

As discussed in Chapter 3, however, a major problem in the use of standardized tests with extremely gifted students is the phenomenon of 'ceiling effect'. This occurs when the test is too easy for the group taking it, the group as a whole scores near the top of the scale with very little variance, and it becomes impossible to discriminate between the individual scores. In a paper outlining measurement difficulties in evaluating programmes for the gifted, Archambault (1984) warned that ceiling effects are likely to be operating if the mean score for any given group is more than three-quarters of the maximum possible score. This will almost certainly occur if highly gifted students are tested on any instrument designed to assess the intellectual or academic capacity of normal children of their chronological age.

A further problem arises when a child scores near the ceiling of a test of achievement and we wish to retest later in the year to measure possible gain. Not only is the test's capacity to measure gain restricted by the low ceiling but, what is worse, due to an artifact of measurement error called 'regression towards the mean', the second score might actually be lower than the first, falsely implying a decrease in ability or achievement.

Educators or psychologists wishing to assess the capacities of the extremely gifted should take care to select an instrument with an unusually high ceiling or, where such an instrument does not exist, use off-level testing – that is, tests standardized on an age-group some years older than the student whom they wish to test. As Chapter 3 relates, off-level testing was used for virtually every academic variable examined in this study.

Ceiling effect comes into play not only in achievement testing but in IQ testing also. As was discussed earlier, group tests of intelligence, which generally have ceilings in the 130s or 140s, are impractical for the assessment even of highly gifted children. Furthermore, the majority of individual IQ tests, such as the *Wechsler Intelligence Scale for Children–Revised (WISC–R)* also have ceilings which are too low to assess the intellectual capacity of many highly gifted students and are quite impractical for the assessment of the exceptionally or profoundly gifted. Several of the children in this study who scored in the high 140s on the *WISC–R* subsequently scored at 160+ on the *Stanford-Binet*. Daniel, one of the most profoundly gifted of the 40 children, achieved a IQ of 154 on the *WISC–R* but when tested on the *Stanford-Binet L-M* at the age of 9 years 5 months achieved a mental age of 18 years 8 months and thus a ratio IQ of 198. Unfortunately, many school counsellors or guidance officers insist on using the *WPPSI* or *WISC–R* to assess an extremely gifted child even when the child has already scored in excess of IQ 160 on the *Slosson* and is therefore almost certainly beyond the *WPPSI* or *WISC–R* ceiling.

The criticisms of the new *Stanford-Binet Revision IV*, and discussions of its inappropriateness for use with highly gifted students, have been set out in Chapter 3. *The Stanford-Binet Intelligence Scale L-M* should be used, rather than the newer test, when the tester has any reason to suspect that the child being tested may be of very high intellectual potential. As Silverman and Kearney have advised (1989), in cases where a child obtains three subtest scores at or near the ceiling of any current instrument, he or she should be retested on the *Stanford-Binet L-M*, and ratio scores should be computed for any child who scores beyond the test norms. In this study, scores above IQ 157 on the *Slosson Intelligence Test* have served as an excellent predictor of scores above IQ 160 on the *Stanford-Binet L-M*.

SAMPLING ISSUES

There are inherent limitations in any study of a population which is characterized by its scarcity. Individuals scoring at and above IQ 160 on the *Stanford-Binet L-M* appear in the population at a ratio of fewer than 1 in 10,000. Australia is a nation of only 17 million people; thus elementary school children scoring at IQ 160 and above comprise a theoretical population of fewer than 180. In a community such as Australia, where a number of the most influential education systems and teacher industrial unions maintain an active opposition to standardized ability and achievement testing, it is no easy task to identify a subject group selected on the basis of scores on measures of intellectual capacity. Indeed, the very fact that, in the absence of widespread testing, this study has identified one-fifth of the theoretical population of exceptionally gifted children in Australia in the age range covered by the study, suggests that the assertions of researchers such as Burt (1968), Robinson (1981) and Feldman (1984) that there are a greater number of children at extremely high levels of intelligence than is predicted by the normal curve, may be well founded.

Because of the scarcity of children scoring at or above IQ 160, it has not been possible, in this study, to employ random selection from a large subject pool. The 40 children in this study have been referred by psychologists, teachers or parents who were either aware of the children's remarkable intellectual abilities or who suspected that the children might, indeed, be exceptionally gifted. The subjects of this study, therefore, represent a minority within a minority: extremely gifted Australian children whose abilities have been recognized. Exceptionally gifted children who have been successful in concealing their abilities, or who deviate significantly in their behaviour or origin from Australian teachers' expectations of gifted children, may be under-represented in this study.

The over-representation of children of Asian-born parents and of parents born in the United Kingdom has been reported in Chapter 5 and the implications of this have been comprehensively discussed. The under-representation of children from working-class and socially deprived families is a matter for concern. Research has repeatedly shown that Australians assume that gifted children come from wealthy or financially confortable homes, that they arise from the dominant culture, that their parents are well-educated and that they attend private, rather than government, schools. Principals of schools in economically disadvantaged neighbourhoods frequently report that they have no gifted children in their schools (Goldberg, 1981; Braggett, 1985; Commonwealth of Australia, 1988). The insistence by many of the teachers' unions that gifted students come only from middle-class families of the dominant culture has done little to improve the situation. There are certainly children from economically disadvantaged families who would readily qualify for entry to this study; however, given the attitudes described above, it is hardly surprising if their teachers fail to recognize them.

Coupled with these biased and inaccurate perceptions is a pervasive belief among Australian teachers that standardized tests of ability and achievement are invariably biased against students from disadvantaged backgrounds. Teachers are generally unaware of the widespread use, overseas, of non-verbal tests of general ability specifically to identify intellectually gifted students from cultural and racial minorities. If we are to find the underachieving gifted among our minority and disadvantaged groups it is time we stopped looking for 'gifted behaviours' and started looking for gifted children.

The search for subjects in this study has been limited by geographical constraints. American readers of this text may not be aware that although Australia occupies a land mass equivalent to that occupied by the United

States without Alaska, the population is less than 7 per cent of the US population, and is concentrated in cities and towns along the narrow fertile strip of coastline. Distances between settlements are immense. Time and travel costs have so far restricted the study to the five eastern states: South Australia, Victoria, New South Wales, Australian Capital Territory and Tasmania. Even so, the land mass involved is equivalent, in American terms, to everything east of a line drawn from Minneapolis to Houston, Texas. The study will, however, be extended to the three remaining Australian states, Queensland, Western Australia and Northern Territory.

TEACHER EDUCATION

Many of the difficulties and hardships which have confronted the 40 children throughout their school careers have arisen from a lack of awareness, among teachers and school administrators, of the characteristics and needs of intellectually gifted children, and of the strategies which schools can employ to optimize their intellectual and academic potential. Well-designed programmes, such as those of Adrian, Chris and Roshni, have tended to arise where the principal, or a teacher in the school, has undertaken some training or inservice in gifted education. There is an urgent need, in Australia, for both pre-service and inservice teacher education in this area.

The *New South Wales Government Strategy for the Education of Gifted and Talented Students*, published in April 1991, makes two important recommendations to principals within its schools.

> All schools should facilitate the participation of all staff members in at least one introductory inservice course addressing the education of gifted and talented students in 1992–93.
> After 1995 all schools, where feasible, should seek to employ at least one teacher who has training in the education of gifted and talented students.
>
> (NSW Government, 1991, p. 11)

The strategy makes the important distinction between inservice and training. Every teacher requires inservicing in gifted education but a teacher who has undertaken an inservice workshop, or even attended several conferences, is not *trained* in the education of gifted and talented children. Training implies a specialist course of study undertaken at a university or other tertiary institution, leading to the award of a degree, post-graduate diploma or certification. Such a course should be led by a faculty member who himself or herself has academic qualifications in gifted education and who has experience in teaching gifted students both in the regular classroom and in special programmes.

The Professional Training Institute of the American National Association for Gifted Children has identified the following components as desirable content in a certification or degree programme in gifted education.

(1) a minimum of four subjects including the following topics:
- nature and needs of gifted and talented children
- identification and assessment
- counselling the gifted
- curriculum development for the gifted
- strategies and materials for teaching the gifted
- creative studies
- programme development and evaluation
- parent education and advocacy training
- gifted students from special populations
- cognitive and affective processing

(2) at least one graduate level course in research procedures

(3) at least one subject focussing on a specialist curriculum area

(4) a practicum involving the instruction of gifted students, supervised by university personnel.

(Feldhusen, 1985b, p. 89)

Over 140 universities in the United States offer Master of Education and Ph.D. degree programmes on the gifted and talented. Research has shown that teachers with specialist post-graduate training in gifted education are significantly more effective in their teaching of gifted students than are teachers who have not undertaken specialist training (Hansen, 1988). Ideally, teachers working with gifted students in special programmes should be trained, rather than merely inserviced, in gifted education. Certainly consultants or support teachers who have special responsibility for advising and assisting teachers to develop programmes for the gifted, should have at least a certification in gifted education, and, wherever possible, a Master's degree with specialization in this field.

APPROPRIATE PROGRAMMING FOR EXCEPTIONALLY GIFTED CHILDREN

Joyce VanTassel-Baska (1989) identified five elements which are essential to the success of a programme for gifted students: content acceleration to the level of the child's abilities; thoughtfully planned, relevant enrichment; guidance in selecting courses and directions; instruction with the opportunity to work closely with other gifted youth; and the opportunity to work with mentors who have high-level expertise in the child's area of giftedness. Of the 40 subjects of this study only Adrian has enjoyed an educational programme which has contained all five elements. However, Adrian's provision with mentors eventuated more because of the interest his prodigious maths ability excited in the mathematics community, than through any deliberate intervention, in this regard, on the part of his school. His mentors have been academics working in the maths faculties of local colleges and universities.

Enrichment by itself, whether offered in the regular classroom or in pull-out programmes, is quite inadequate as an educational response to exceptional intellectual giftedness. However, where enrichment is offered as one component in an educational programme, educators should be aware of the research on inappropriate and appropriate enrichment strategies (Feldhusen and Kolloff, 1978; Stanley, 1979) and should ensure that the enrichment provided responds to and extends the child's academic and intellectual talents.

Ability grouping of academically gifted students is actively discouraged in several Australian states. Yet, as we have discussed in Chapter 8, the research evidence for the effectiveness of ability grouping is extremely powerful. It is absolutely essential for exceptionally and profoundly gifted children if they are to have any chance of finding intellectual and social companionship. Even with radical acceleration, the mental ages of extremely gifted children are still considerably higher than the average student in the classes they have entered, and where ability grouping has been employed in the new class their teachers have generally placed them in the top group in their areas of strength to ensure that they are, indeed, provided with academic challenge and intellectual peers.

Teachers and school administrators should be aware of the empirical research on the positive effects of acceleration; the erroneous supposition that acceleration will cause social and emotional damage has acted as a powerful barrier to appropriate grade placement for several of the children in this study. Acceleration is a valid and appropriate response to the educational and social needs of children whose reasoning capacities and academic achievement are several years beyond those of their age-peers. It is, however, essential that individualized educational programmes be on-going. It is unforgivable that the acceleration programme established for a child should be discontinued or reversed because of the ideological objections of an incoming school principal.

This study has demonstrated, most forcefully, that accelerating exceptionally and profoundly gifted children by a single year is no more effective than retaining them in the regular classroom with age-peers. As Terman and Oden (1947) advised, and has been shown in this study, the extremely gifted respond better to a series of grade-skips spaced appropriately through the child's school career. This exposes the gifted child to a curriculum which more closely approximates his level of intellectual capacity and significantly increases the chances of him forming warm and productive social relationships with other students. In several cases in this study younger children who had been rejected, in the schoolyard, by older students with whom they wished to play, were happily accepted by these students once they had been accelerated into the same class. This suggests that students of average ability may reject younger gifted children on the basis of their inferior grade placement rather than their comparative youth. Once the younger child is viewed as occupying the same stratum in the social hierarchy of the playground, they can be more readily accepted and valued for their academic and other talents.

When they are appropriately placed, extremely gifted children become strongly motivated to achieve. As Feldhusen and Hoover have pointed out (1986), student motivation should be a programme goal, not a condition for programme placement.

It is noticeable that the majority of children who have been radically accelerated have extraordinary levels of mathematics achievement. Children whose most visible talents lie in the area of language are less likely to have their exceptionality acknowledged. Hollingworth pointed out that 'society attends to that which is socially annoying. The school attends to those who give it trouble' (Hollingworth, 1931, p. 3). Teachers too often assume that exceptional ability in language can be fostered though an open-ended curriculum within which the child is permitted to work 'independently' without teacher direction or guidance. The mathematically gifted child, however, gives the school more 'trouble'; it is acknowledged that these children cannot be left so easily to their own devices, and the school is more likely to establish structures within which their progress can be guided and monitored.

It is important to note that the most effective educational programmes offered to the children in this study are those which have been designed through close cooperation among the school, the parents and the child. Several of the parents report that before discussing their child's educational programme with the school, they familiarized themselves with the literature on the academic and social needs of the gifted, and particularly the research literature on acceleration. Several parents subscribe to journals of gifted education and report that they find these extremely valuable both in their discussions with schools, and in their upbringing of the subject children and their siblings. These parents have familiarized themselves with their children's educational and social needs in much the same way as Australian parents of intellectually and physically disabled children have been taught, by the helping agencies, to familiarize themselves with the particular needs and rights of their children.

The exceptionally gifted children in this study are avid readers, and read, with full comprehension and enjoyment, books written for children five to seven years their senior. The training of school librarians should include some component on the reading development and reading interests of the gifted, and in particular the highly gifted who may prefer reading materials which are radically different from those preferred by their classmates. As early as 9 years of age several of the children in this study had developed a deep and lasting interest in the more serious modes of adolescent and adult science fiction and science fantasy, yet books of this genre and level were not generally available in their elementary school libraries.

The principal of one of Sydney's newer selective high schools told me only a few days ago that his new Year 7 intake had almost literally stripped the shelves of his school library in the first two days of the school year. 'They were taking home five or six books at a time,' he said, in good humoured amazement, 'and bringing them back for changing in a couple of days. They must have been starved, in primary school, for reading at their level.' School administrators should ensure that the libraries of elementary schools contain books and other materials of a level and type to provide for the accelerated reading development and interests of highly gifted children; this is particularly necessary for children whose parents may not encourage their love of reading or who may not be able to afford to buy books for their children.

Suggestions that the majority of gifted children are 'developmental spurters' whose accelerated reading development plateaus in later childhood, are not borne out either by this study or by previous studies of the highly gifted. In every case in this study the precocity in reading which was such a striking feature of the children's early development has persisted, and in many cases increased, through the children's elementary school years.

What has decreased for many of these children, however, has been the opportunity to display this precocity in the classroom situation. In the majority of cases the children in this study have been required, from Grade 3 onwards, to read from the same school texts and materials as their classmates of average ability. For this reason their continuing exceptionality is not displayed in the classroom; however, it may still be clearly visible at home, or in weekend programmes for gifted students organized by advocacy groups, where the child's unusual reading interests are accepted without comment or criticism. In several cases the child has appeared, to his or her classroom teacher, to have developed a new, and apparently unrelated, talent.

Jackson (1992) has offered an important insight into the continuity but transmutability of high intellectual aptitude. She proposes that, since the challenge of learning to read exceptionally well may lose its excitement as the young child progresses through the first years of elementary school, he may seek other avenues for the expression of his precocious ability.

Exceptionality in reading is, after all, a precocious talent for decoding and encoding a complex and sophisticated symbol system. Some precocious readers may translate this facility into an enhanced capacity for mathematics, computing, creative writing or music. If a school or teacher insists on the young gifted child reading only those books which can be mastered by age-peers, the child may deliberately choose to transfer her skills to another subject field in the hope that this new expression of talent will be more readily accepted.

Ian Baker's early passion for reading seemed, to his teachers, to disappear in the first few years of school. However, his passion for street directories, fueled by his quite phenomenal skills in map reading and map construction, developed to the point where it dominated his waking hours. No one could tell him to moderate his mapping skills so that he did not get ahead of the class. No one else in the class liked mapping.

Perhaps children who are able to translate their exceptionality in one field of performance into an equally exceptional performance in a second field are those who have developed, to an unusual degree, what Sternberg, in his 'componential' theory of intellectual giftedness, would term 'transfer components' – those skills required for generalizing information from one context to another (Sternberg, 1981). Too often we are led to assume that giftedness is transitory. Braggett has suggested that developmental spurters are 'possibly the largest single group of gifted children we may identify in the school' (Braggett, 1983, p. 14). Renzulli has repeatedly advised that rather than seeking to identify giftedness itself we should be looking for 'gifted behaviour' which may surface 'in certain students (not all students), at certain times (not all times) and in certain circumstances' (Renzulli, 1986, p. 63). However, exceptional intellectual potential is not a 'here today gone tomorrow' phenomenon. It is not transient but rather transferable, and rather than responding to it only when it conveniently presents itself to our notice, we should seek to understand its continuity through its diverse manifestations and transitions as the child matures.

PSYCHOSOCIAL DEVELOPMENT

Exceptionally gifted children fall outside the range of what Hollingworth (1926) defined as 'socially optimal intelligence'. Children of IQ 160 are too infrequent to find congenial companionship unless the school actively assists by creating for them a peer group of students who are closer to them both in mental age and in their accelerated levels of emotional development.

The majority of the children in this study have deliberately underachieved for peer acceptance. Several cannot recall a time in their lives when this has not been an automatic survival mechanism, accepted as a painful but necessary part of living. Some have deliberately moderated their performance in the hope that this will make them more acceptable to their class teachers. Several children have related incidents where a teacher has given inaccurate or erroneous information to the class, and the subject child has remained silent both during and after the lesson, for fear of embarrassing the teacher or diminishing his or her reputation in the eyes of the other students.

In all cases, children who have been radically accelerated, or who have been permitted a single year grade-skip combined with subject acceleration in their area of particular exceptionality, state that they are now much more appropriately placed both academically and socially. Teachers appear to be less threatened by exceptionally gifted students who have been radically accelerated, as their academic achievements can now be viewed against the performance of children several years their senior and, paradoxically, appear less out of the ordinary. In addition, as these children now require less curriculum differentiation, and are thus easier to teach, teachers find their presence less of an irritant.

Except in a few cases, such as that of Ian Baker during his most severe period of emotional distress, the teachers of the children in this study hold most positive views of the children's emotional stability. The school reports speak in glowing terms of the children's cooperation, reliability, fairness, and concern for the rights of others. Like the exceptionally and profoundly gifted children described by Burks, Jensen and Terman (1930), Hollingworth (1942), and Barbe (1964), these Australian children tend to internalize their problems, and the school generally remains unaware of the extent of the child's loneliness, unhappiness and intellectual frustration. The parents in general believe that their children cope remarkably well with the social and intellectual difficulties that confront them, and indeed these children must be possessed of remarkable qualities of emotional strength to cope so successfully with years of educational neglect and lack of understanding.

The children in general display a healthy academic self-concept. Their scores on the school-academic subscale of the Coopersmith *Self-Esteem Inventory* (Coopersmith, 1981) are generally above the mean, although those children who have been radically accelerated, and have had the opportunity to compare their achievement levels with other children at similar stages of intellectual development, display more modest, if still positive scores. However, of the 12 children old enough to be tested on this instrument, seven displayed significantly lowered levels of social self-concept. An important finding of this study is that of the five children recording a positive z-score on the social self-peers subscale, four have been grade-skipped by at least one year.

From their earliest years at school, these exceptionally gifted children have experienced considerable difficulty in establishing positive social relationships with their age-peers. Their exceptional intellectual abilities, their levels of academic achievement, their tendency to think in abstract principles instead of concrete examples, their remarkably accelerated reading interests, and their atypical play preferences, have set them apart from their classmates. Because children tend to select companions and form friendships on the basis of mental age rather than chronological age (Hubbard, 1929; Hollingworth, 1926, 1942; O'Shea, 1960), the exceptionally gifted children in this study have generally sought out, as friends, children several years older than they. Where this gravitation towards intellectual peers in older age groups has been thwarted by the school's insistence that they remain with age-peers, or where their social overtures have been rejected by the older children, the study children have become social isolates, preferring the intellectual stimulation of their own thoughts and play to the tedium imposed by continual interaction with other children whose intellectual and social development, ideas, interests and enthusiasms, are still at a level which they themselves outgrew several years previously. That this isolation results from the absence of congenial companionship rather than from any tendency to misanthropy on behalf of the exceptionally gifted child is demonstrated by the fact that in all cases where socially isolated children have been accelerated to be with intellectual peers, the isolation has disappeared and the children have been able to form warm and supportive relationships with their older classmates.

For the exceptionally gifted children of this study academic acceleration has proved a sound and successful interventive measure. In no case has social or emotional damage arisen from even the most radical accelerative measures; indeed, for children who were previously isolated and rejected it has facilitated the process of socialization. By contrast, it is where schools have decelerated or ignored the children's academic progress to concentrate solely on social needs, that moderate to severe levels of psychosocial damage has become evident. Keeping exceptionally and profoundly gifted children with age-peers is not the way to socialize these children.

THE CHILDREN: WHERE TO FROM HERE?

Let us end as we began, with the children.

Adrian Seng completed his Bachelor of Science degree at age 15 and is now, at 16 years of age, doing post-graduate study in mathematics. Soon he will have to consider where he will do his Ph.D. There is no doubt that universities worldwide will be competing for the privilege of nurturing this astonishingly gifted young scholar.

Fred Campbell will graduate from high school a few weeks before his sixteenth birthday. He will enter university three months later and plans to do a B.Sc. with specialization in maths and physics.

Chris Otway has just made history in his state by gaining a 98 per cent average in his university entrance exams while three years younger than the other candidates. As related earlier, he plans to stay on at school for a further year, taking university entrance study in five more subjects while further developing his skills in piano and flute and enjoying his explorations of the stock market. He will enter university two months after his sixteenth birthday to do a B.Sc. degree in the faculty of maths and computer science in the major university of his state. 'I'll probably do a bit of economics on the side,' he adds, 'and then when I've got the B.Sc. I'll probably do a Bachelor of Economics.'

These three boys have come, or are coming, to the end of their school career. All are fortunate in that they have been permitted (if, in Fred's case, only latterly) to progress through school at their own pace within an educational programme designed specifically to respond to their intellectual and social needs.

The other 12 children whose stories are told here still have several years to go before they graduate from high school – although Richard and Rufus are the same age as Fred and Chris and would certainly have thrived on a similarly accelerated programme. Several of the children are still in elementary school. A minority are receiving thoughtfully designed educational provisions which acknowledge the fact that their educational needs, like their intellectual potential, are highly unusual and in desperate need of recognition. The majority are not.

This study embraces 25 more children whose stories have not yet been told. Their abilities, and their needs, are quite exceptional. As with the 15 children of this book, a minority are receiving appropriate educational provision. Gabrielle has just turned 7. She has an IQ of 168 and her reading, maths and spelling abilities are quite remarkable. At 5 years 8 months she was reading *The Voyage of the Dawn Treader* by C. S. Lewis. By the time she was 6 she was based in Grade 2 but was subject accelerated, several times each week, to Grade 4 for maths and to Grade 5 for English.

> 'She is generally happy at school', says her father, Joseph, 'and her teacher says she is popular with the other children. Interestingly, she is quite definite about whom she likes and doesn't like, and why. She continues to articulate remarkably well her insights into her own feelings and other people's behaviour. Her use of spoken English still seems to me her greatest ability.'

Sally Huang, currently aged 11, has an IQ of 165. She is an extremely enthusiastic and hardworking girl with a phenomenal gift for mathematics. Her school, in a country city, has allowed her radical acceleration through a series of carefully planned and monitored progressions and she is currently in Eleventh Grade, excelling in all academic subjects, as she has done over the last few years. Sally has had a few gentle confrontations, over the years, with teachers who have been reluctant to let her progress at her own pace, but she is a determined young lady who expresses her feelings politely but with a quiet conviction, and in general the teachers have responded positively to her requests. It was Sally who herself requested that she skip from Grade 5 to Grade 7, as she was finding the curriculum and social interactions of the younger class rather unrewarding.

After her acceleration to Grade 9, her mother, Hedy, wrote

> Sally seems to have settled in very well. The school staff are indeed very amazed at how well she has settled in and how well she conducts herself. In fact, she is currently ahead in most of her subjects, and top of her grade most of the time. The teachers in her school seem to be receptive and willing to give her a go. Sally was very happy up until the time when she became ahead of her classmates and was forbidden to go ahead with her extension work. However, her teachers relented after she explained and expressed her frustration and once again she is a happy girl, progressing at her own fast pace.

These, however, are the success stories. What of Stuart and David, two brothers of IQ 170 and 166 respectively, whose school has done nothing in response to their intellectual needs beyond 'enrichment' in the regular classroom? What of Beatrice, of IQ 180, who lives in a small country town and whose remarkable abilities were discovered only when the psychiatrist who was treating her for severe depression decided to have the girl psychometrically assessed? Beatrice's school has refused to accept that she is of anything other than average intellectual capacity. Accordingly the curriculum she is offered is many years below her academic capacity and she is lonely and socially isolated. Beatrice loves learning but loathes school.

What of Daniel, aged 9, with a mental age of 18 and an IQ of 198, who has just made a score of 650 on the SAT–M? The school which he attended for three years believed, and told his parents quite firmly, that he was a child of average ability with a little more strength in mathematics. His mother and father became increasingly concerned at the swift decline in Daniel's interest in school and learning, and his transformation from a bright-eyed, eager child who was fascinated by new knowledge to a bewildered and deeply unhappy little boy who was convinced that his teacher was threatened by him and deliberately laid traps in class to catch him out. 'She doesn't wait for me to give precise answers to questions,' he said, 'and it makes me look silly'. The hostility of a teacher, even if it is imagined, can be terrifying for a small child.

Finally, at the end of Grade 2, Daniel's tolerance came to an end and he told his parents quite firmly that he was not going back to school. His parents are now home-schooling him, under the supervision of the state education authority. He has completed the eleventh grade maths curriculum and is studying high school chemistry and physics.

How can politicians, educators and the teachers' unions realistically justify their unwillingness or unreadiness to provide for children who differ so radically from their age-peers as the children in this study – and whose remarkable gifts, if permitted to flourish, could be of such inestimable benefit, in later years, to the community in which they live?

Brian Start outlines the arguments by which we rationalize our inaction.

> The arguments of equality would impress on the teacher that these children are from the middle class, that they are already advantaged, that to cater for them diverts funds from the needy, that they create a sense of failure among those who do not achieve so well, that they increase class divisiveness, reinforce the ruling class, and the whole gamut of rhetoric from those whose commitment to ideology is greater than to facts, or to children.
>
> There are pedagogical statements such as 'They learn anyway', 'It distorts their childhood', 'It disturbs their peer group relations', 'It turns them into snobs', 'It makes them hypercompetitive', 'Makes them despise the ordinary bloke'. You know them all. You also know that these are statements to justify a position, and that each of them bears little relation to the empirical facts available from research studies overseas.
>
> (Start, 1987, p. 8)

As this chapter was being written, I received a letter from Martin and Deborah Brown, the parents of two highly gifted little boys. The letter speaks for itself.

> My wife and I are employed in connection with the integration of hearing impaired (H.I.) children into mainsteam schooling. As such we service a number of different schools and see children from birth to the end of high school. As such we know the Education Department provisions, and the importance of acceptance within a school environment of 'different' children. We also know how important it is to be tactful and not to be pushy about 'rights' as the effects on the children of tactless and pushy people are terrible.
>
> We found it enlightening that the schools we visit are always sympathetic to the needs and provisions of individual education plans for the hearing impaired child, yet suddenly become antagonistic at the idea of providing an appropriate education for a 'hypothetical' child of similar ability to ours.
>
> We have had comments from principals and teachers ranging

from 'Go to America' to 'It's not fair to the other kids', to 'Yes, they need special help but the staff are against it.'

Any suggestion of grade-skipping is spurned with 'They need socialization with their peers', 'If they can't kick a football properly how can you expect them to fit in with the other kids?', 'The other kids in the class wouldn't like it.'

Yet Michael doesn't play with 5-year-olds. He is comfortable playing with 7- to 8-year-olds. They are his more appropriate social peers.

Being different is a great cross to bear in our society, so it is important that they do not feel that there is something wrong with themselves, or have to be ashamed of their talents.

We are interested only in the principle that they be allowed to develop themselves to be what they are.

BIBLIOGRAPHY

Abelman, R. (1986). 'Television and the exceptional child'. *G/C/T*, 45, 26–28.

Adelaide Children's Hospital (1982). *Standards for height, weight and head circumference from two to eighteen years*. Adelaide, South Australia: Adelaide Children's Hospital.

Adkinson, N. F. (1988). Personal communication.

Albert, R. S. (1980). 'Family positions and the attainment of eminence: A study of special family positions and special family experiences'. *Gifted Child Quarterly*, 24(2), 87–95.

Alexander, P. J. and Skinner, M. E. (1980). 'The effects of early entrance on subsequent social and academic development'. *Journal for the Education of the Gifted*, 3, 147–150.

Altus, W. D. (1966). 'Birth order and its sequelae'. *Science*, 151, 44–49.

American Association for Gifted Children (1978). *On being gifted*. New York: Walker.

Anderson, M. A., Tollefson, N. A. and Gilbert, E. C. (1985). 'Giftedness and reading: A cross-sectional view of differences in reading attitude and behavior'. *Gifted Child Quarterly*, 29, 186–189.

Angell, R. C. and Freedman, R. (1953). 'The use of documents, records, census materials and indices'. In L. Festinger & D. Katz (eds), *Research methods in the behavioral sciences* (300–329). New York: Holt, Rinehart and Winston.

Arbuthnot, J. (1973). 'Relationship between maturity of moral judgment and measures of cognitive abilities'. *Psychological Reports*, 33, 945–946.

Archambault, F. X. (1984). 'Measurement and evaluation concerns in evaluating programs for the gifted'. *Journal for the Education of the Gifted*, 7, 12–25.

Asher, J. W. (1976). *Educational research and evaluation methods*. Boston: Little Brown.

Austin, A. B. and Draper, D. C. (1981). 'Peer relationships of the academically gifted: A review'. *Gifted Child Quarterly*, 25(3), 129–134.

Australian Broadcasting Commission (1988). *The Seven-Thirty Report*. Television news, A.B.C., Melbourne, May.

Australian Bureau of Statistics (1984). *Social indicators No. 4*. Canberra: Commonwealth of Australia.

—— (1987). *Average weekly earnings, states and Australia, 1987*. Canberra: Commonwealth of Australia.

—— (1988a). *Births Australia, 1987*. Canberra: Commonwealth of Australia.

—— (1988b). *Estimated resident population by country of birth, age and sex: Australia June 1986 and preliminary June, 1988*. Canberra: Commonwealth of Australia.

—— (1988c). *National schools statistics collection, Australia 1988: Preliminary*. Canberra: Commonwealth of Australia.

—— (1990). *Estimated resident population by country of birth, age and sex: Australia June 1989 and preliminary June 1990.* Canberra: Commonwealth of Australia.

Baker, J. (1986). 'Uni High's fast lane gets four more years'. *The Age*, Melbourne, Australia, 17 July.

—— (1987). *Gifted children. Warragul and Drouin Press*, Victoria, Australia, 5, 1 December.

Baldwin, A. Y. (1985). 'Programs for the gifted and talented: Issues concerning minority populations'. In F. D. Horowitz and M. O'Brien (eds) *The gifted and talented: Developmental perspectives* (223–249). Washington, DC: American Psychological Association.

Baldwin, J. W. (1962). 'The relationship between teacher-judged giftedness, a group intelligence test and an individual intelligence test with possible gifted kindergarten pupils'. *Gifted Child Quarterly*, 2, 153–156.

Baldwin, D., Bouma, G. and Dixon, B. (1983). *All about Australian children.* Melbourne: Oxford University Press.

Barbe, W. B. (1957). 'What happens to graduates of special classes for the gifted?'. *Ohio State University Educational Research Bulletin*, 36, 13–16.

—— (1964). *One in a thousand: A comparative study of highly and moderately gifted elementary school children.* Columbus, Ohio: F. J. Heer.

Beazley, K. (1984). *Opening ceremony address.* Proceedings of the First Australian National Conference on the Education of Gifted and Talented Children, Melbourne, August, 1983. Melbourne: Commonwealth Schools Commission.

Benbow, C. P. (1985a). *Physiological correlates of extreme intellectual precocity.* Paper presented at 32nd Congress of the National Association for Gifted Children, Denver, Colorado.

—— (1985b). *Home environments and toy preferences of extremely precocious students.* Paper presented at 32nd Congress of the National Association for Gifted Children, Denver, Colorado.

—— and Stanley, J. C. (1980). 'Intellectually talented students: Family profiles'. *Gifted Child Quarterly*, 24(3), 119–122.

—— and Stanley, J. C. (1983). 'An eight-year evaluation of SMPY: What was learned?'. In C. P. Benbow and J. C. Stanley (eds), *Academic precocity: Aspects of its development* (205–214). Baltimore: Johns Hopkins University Press.

—— Perkins, S. and Stanley, J. C. (1983). 'Mathematics taught at a fast pace: A longitudinal evaluation of SMPY's first class'. In C. P. Benbow and J. C. Stanley (eds), *Academic precocity: Aspects of its development* (51–78). Baltimore: Johns Hopkins University Press.

Bergman, J. (1979). 'The tragic story of two highly gifted, genius-level boys'. *Creative Child and Adult Quarterly*, 4, 222–233.

Bloom, B. S. (1985). *Developing talent in young people.* New York: Ballantine.

Boag, C. (1990). 'Our gifted children: bright, bored and ignored'. *The Bulletin*, 15 May, 48–54.

Boehm, L. (1962). 'The development of conscience: A comparison of American children at different mental and socioeconomic levels'. *Child Development*, 33, 575–590.

Borg, W. R. and Gall, M. D. (1983). *Educational research: An introduction. (fourth edition).* New York: Longman.

Borland, J. H. (1986). 'IQ tests: Throwing out the bathwater, saving the baby'. *Roeper Review*, 8(3), 163–167.

—— (1989). *Planning and implementing programs for the gifted.* New York: Teachers College Press.

Bowmaker, P. (1991). *Why Emma? A case study.* Unpublished manuscript.

Bracken, B. A. (1980). 'Comparison of self-attitudes of gifted children and children in a non-gifted normative group'. *Psychological Reports*, 47, 715–718.
Braggett, E. J. (1983). 'Curriculum for gifted and talented children: Needs'. In Commonwealth Schools Commission *Curriculum for gifted and talented children* (9–30). Canberra: Commonwealth Schools Commission.
—— (1984). *An overview of Australian provision for gifted/talented students*. Paper presented to the Third National Conference of the New Zealand Association for Gifted and Talented Children, Christchurch.
—— (1985a). *Education of gifted and talented children: Australian provision*. Canberra: Commonwealth Schools Commission.
—— (ed.). (1985b). *Education of gifted and talented children from populations with special needs*. Canberra: Commonwealth Schools Commission.
—— (1986a). *Talented, gifted, creative Australian writings: An annotated bibliography*. Canberra: Commonwealth Schools Commission.
—— (1986b). 'The education of gifted and talented children in Australia: A national overview'. In K. Imison, L. Endean and D. Smith (eds), *Gifted and talented children: A national concern* (13–27). Toowoomba, Australia: Darling Downs Institute Press.
Brody, L. E., Assouline, S. G. and Stanley, J. C. (1990). 'Five years of early entrants: Predicting successful achievement in college'. *Gifted Child Quarterly*, 34(4), 138–142.
Broom, L., Duncan-Jones, P., Lancaster-Jones, F. and McDonnell, P. (1977). *Investigating social mobility*. Canberra: Australian National University.
Brown, S. K. (1983). 'The sex factor in the selection of intellectually talented youth'. *Education Research and Perspectives*, 10(1), 85–104.
Bruer, M. (1989). 'Sport to get $230 million boost'. *The Age*, 22 August, p. 1.
Burks, B. S., Jensen, D. W. and Terman, L. M. (1930). *Genetic studies of genius* (Vol. 3), *The promise of youth*. Stanford, California: Stanford University Press.
Burt, C. (1968). 'Is intelligence normally distributed?'. *British Journal of Statistical Psychology*, 16, 175–190.
Cahill, N. J. (1989). 'The Senate Select Committee Report on the Education of Gifted and Talented Children: What now?'. *Unicorn*, 15(3), 168–170.
Cannell, C. F. and Kahn, R. L. (1953). 'The collection of data by interviewing'. In L. Festinger and D. Katz (eds), *Research methods in the behavioral sciences* (327–380). New York: Holt, Rinehart and Winston.
Carroll, H. A. (1940). *Genius in the making*. New York: McGraw-Hill.
Caton, H. R. (1985). 'Visual impairments'. In W. H. Berdine and A. E. Blackhurst (eds), *An introduction to special education* (2nd ed. 235–282). Boston: Little, Brown.
Cavalier, R. (1986). 'Preamble: Report to the Senate Standing Committee on the Education of Gifted and Talented Children'. *Hansard*, May 26, 1266–1310.
Chan, A., Roder, D. and Marcharper, T. (1984). *Obstetric profiles of immigrant women from non-English speaking countries in South Australia, 1981–1983*. Adelaide, Australia: Epidemiology Board, South Australian Health Commission.
Chapman, J. D. (1984). *A descriptive profile of Australian school principals*. Canberra: Australian Commonwealth Schools Commission.
Ching-Hwang, Y. (1986). *Chinese Australian: Past, present and future*. Key-note address at National Conference of the Chinese Community in Australia, Sydney, November.
Ciha, T. E., Harris, R., Hoffman, C. and Potter, M. (1974). 'Parents as identifiers of giftedness: Ignored but accurate'. *Gifted Child Quarterly*, 18, 202–209.
Clark, B. (1983). *Growing up gifted* (2nd ed.). Columbus: Merrill.
Colanero, R. (1985). 'Gifts and talents among children from non-English speaking

backgrounds'. In E. J. Braggett (ed.), *Education of gifted and talented children from populations with special needs* (46–49). Canberra: Commonwealth Schools Commission.

Colangelo, N. and Pfleger, L. R. (1978). 'Academic self-concept of gifted high school students'. *Roeper Review*, 1, 10–11.

Coleman, J. M. and Fults, E. A. (1982). 'Self-concept and the gifted classroom: The role of social comparisons'. *Gifted Child Quarterly*, 26, 116–120.

Coleman, L. (1985). *Schooling the gifted*. Menlo Park: Addison-Wesley.

College Board (1986). *10 SATs*. New York: College Entrance Examination Board.

Commonwealth of Australia (1988). *The report of the Senate Select Committee on The Education of Gifted and Talented Children*. Canberra, Australia: Australian Government Publishing Service.

—— (1989). *Going for gold: The first report on an inquiry into sports funding and administration*. Canberra: Australian Government Publishing Service.

Commonwealth Schools Commission (1981). *National Seminar on the Education of Gifted and Talented Children, Melbourne, 8–10 November, 1981: Proceedings*. Canberra: Commonwealth Schools Commission.

Congressional Record (1987). *Record of the United States Congress*, 133, 25, 19 February.

Conway, R. (1971). *The great Australian stupor: An interpretation of the Australian way of life*. Melbourne: Sun Books.

Coopersmith, S. (1967). *The antecedents of self-esteem*. San Francisco: W. H. Freeman.

—— (1981). *Self-Esteem Inventories: manual*. Palo Alto, CA: Consulting Psychologists Press.

Cox, C. M. (1926). *Genetic studies of genius* (Vol. 2) *The early mental traits of 300 geniuses*. Stanford, CA.: Stanford University Press.

Cox, J. and Daniel, N. (1986). 'The Richardson Study: Dissemination and implementation'. In J. F. Feldhusen, M. U. M. Gross and J. Reinhold (eds), *Leadership accessing monographs: Education of gifted and talented youth* (1–29). Indianapolis: Indiana Department of Education.

Creed, K. (ed.) (1986). *Programs for gifted and talented children: Exemplary practices, school-based and system-based*. Melbourne: Commonwealth Schools Commission.

Cross, R. (1984). 'A strategy for enrichment of gifted disadvantaged students in secondary schools'. In K. B. Start (ed.), *First national conference on the education of gifted and talented children, 1983* (143–149). Canberra: Commonwealth Schools Commission.

Daley, P. (1992) 'What has 44 legs and an IQ of 3000?'. *Melbourne Age: Agenda*, 16 February, 2–3.

Daurio, S. P. (1979). 'Educational enrichment versus acceleration: A review of the literature'. In W. C. George, S. J. Cohn and J. C. Stanley (eds), *Educating the gifted: Acceleration and enrichment* (13–63). Baltimore: Johns Hopkins University Press.

Davis, H. (1924). 'Personal and social characteristics of gifted children'. In G. M. Whipple, (ed.), *Report of the Society's Committee on the Education of Gifted Children* (123–144). The Twenty-Third Yearbook of the National Society for the Study of Education. Bloomington, Illinois: Public School Publishing Company.

Davis, H. B. and Connell, J. P. (1985). 'The effect of aptitude and achievement status on the self-system'. *Gifted Child Quarterly*, 29(3), 131–136.

Dean, R. S. (1977). 'Effects of self-concept of learning with gifted children'. *Journal of Educational Research*, 70, 315–318.

DeHaan, R. F. and Havighurst, R. J. (1961). *Educating gifted children*. Chicago: University of Chicago Press.

Denzin, N. K. (1970). *The research act: A theoretical introduction to sociological methods*. Chicago: Aldine Press.

Derriman, P. (1989). 'Bradman: The final portrait'. *Good Weekend: The Age Magazine*, 7 October, 65–73.

Dolbear, K. E. (1912). 'Precocious children'. *Journal of Genetic Psychology*, 19, 461–491.

Dorr, D., Rummer, C. B., and Green, R. F. (1976). 'Correlations between Coopersmith's Self-Esteem Inventory and the California Test of Personality for children in grades four and six'. *Psychological Reports*, 39, 221–222.

Dunnett, D. (1961). *The game of kings*. London: Cassell.

Durkin, D. (1966). *Children who read early*. New York: Teachers College Press, Columbia University.

Eales, C. (1985). 'Talented children from low socio-economic groups'. In E. J. Braggett (ed.), *Education of gifted and talented children from populations with special needs*, (24–29). Canberra: Australian Commonwealth Schools Commission.

Edgar, P. (1973). *Under 5 in Australia*. Melbourne: Heinemann.

Education Department of Victoria (1984). *Curriculum development and planning in Victoria: Ministerial paper No. 6*. Melbourne: Education Department of Victoria.

Educational Testing Service (1964). *Cooperative Mathematics Tests: Arithmetic*. Monterey, California: C/T/B: McGraw Hill.

Eisner, E. (1981). 'On the differences between scientific and artistic approaches to qualitative research'. *Educational Researcher*, 10(4), 5–9.

Feather, N. T. (1989). 'Attitudes toward the high achiever: The fall of the tall poppy'. *Australian Journal of Psychology*, 41(3), 1–30.

Feldhusen, J. F. (1983). 'Eclecticism: A comprehensive approach to education of the gifted'. In C. P. Benbow and J. C. Stanley (eds), *Academic precocity: Aspects of its development* (192–204). Baltimore: Johns Hopkins University Press.

—— (ed.). (1985a). *Toward excellence in gifted education*. Denver: Love.

—— (1985b). 'The teacher of gifted students'. *Gifted Education International*, 3(2), 87–93.

—— (1986). 'A conception of giftedness'. In R. J. Sternberg and J. E. Davidson (eds), *Conceptions of giftedness* (112–127). Cambridge: Cambridge University Press.

—— and Baska, L. K. (1989). 'Identification and assessment of the gifted'. In J. F. Feldhusen, J. VanTassel-Baska and K. Seeley (eds) *Excellence in educating the gifted* (85–101). Denver: Love.

—— and Hoover, S. M. (1986). 'A conception of giftedness: Intelligence, self-concept and motivation'. *Roeper Review*, 8(3), 140–143.

—— and Kolloff, M. B. (1978). 'A three-stage model for gifted education'. *G/C/T*, 4, 3–5, 53–57.

—— Saylor, M. F., Nielson, M. E. and Kolloff, M. B. (1990). 'Self-concepts of gifted children in enrichment programs'. *Journal for the Education of the Gifted*, 13(4), 380–384.

Feldman, D. H. (1979). 'The mysterious case of extreme giftedness'. In A. H. Passow (ed.), *The gifted and the talented: Their education and development*. The Seventy-eighth Yearbook of the National Society for the Study of Education. Chicago: University of Chicago Press.

—— (1984). 'A follow-up of subjects scoring above 180 IQ in Terman's "Genetic Studies of Genius"'. *Exceptional Children*, 50, 518–523.

—— (1986). *Nature's gambit*. New York: Basic.

Fetterman, D. M. (1988). *Excellence and equality: A qualitatively different perspective on gifted and talented education*. Albany, New York: State University of New York Press.

Flack, J. (1983). *Profiles of giftedness: An investigation of the development, interests and attitudes of 10 highly gifted Indiana adolescents*. Unpublished doctoral dissertation: Purdue University.

Foster, W. (1983). 'Self-concept, intimacy and the attainment of excellence'. *Journal for the Education of the Gifted*, 6(1), 20–27.

—— (1986). 'The application of single subject research methods to the study of exceptional ability and extraordinary achievement'. *Gifted Child Quarterly*, 30(1), 33–37.

Fraser, W. (1989). 'Behind Joanna Murray-Smith'. *Good Weekend: The Australian Magazine*, 7 October, p. 102.

Freeman, J. (1979). *Gifted children*. Lancaster, England: MTP Press.

Frey, D. (1978). 'Science and the single case in counselling research'. *The Personnel and Guidance Journal*, 56, 263–268.

Fults, B. (1980). 'The effects of an instructional program on the creative thinking skills, self-concept, and leadership of intellectually and academically gifted elementary students'. *Dissertation Abstracts International*, 41, 29331-A.

Fussell, F. (1983). *Class: A guide through the American status system*. New York: Summit Books.

Gagné, F. (1985). 'Giftedness and talent: Reexamining a reexamination of the definitions'. *Gifted Child Quarterly*, 29(3), 103–112.

—— (1991a). 'Towards a differentiated model of giftedness and talent'. In N. Colangelo and G. A. Davis (eds) *Handbook of gifted education* (65–80). Boston: Allyn and Bacon.

—— (1991b). *There is a difference between giftedness and talent*. Paper presented at the 38th Annual Conference of the National Association for Gifted Children, Kansas City, Missouri, November 8–10.

Gallagher, J. J. (1958). 'Peer acceptance of highly gifted children in elementary school'. *Elementary School Journal*, 58, 465–470.

—— (1976). *Teaching the gifted child* (2nd ed.). Boston: Allyn and Bacon.

—— and Crowder, T. (1957). 'The adjustment of gifted children in the regular classroom'. *Exceptional Children*, 23, 306–312, 317–319.

Galton, F. (1869) *Hereditary genius: An enquiry into its laws and consequences*. London: Macmillan and Co.

Gardner, J. (1961). *Excellence: Can we be equal and excellent too?* New York: Harper and Row.

Gear, G. H. (1976). 'Accuracy of teacher judgment in identifying intellectually gifted children: A review of the literature'. *The Gifted Child Quarterly*, 20(4), 478–489.

Getzels, J. and Jackson, P. (1961). 'Family environment and cognitive style: A study of the sources of highly intelligent and of highly creative adolescents'. *American Sociological Review*, 26(3), 251–360.

—— (1962). *Creativity and intelligence*. New York: John Wiley and Sons.

Gifted Children's Taskforce (1987). *Gippsland Press*, 29 December.

Giles, J. R. (1983). 'Policies and programs for education to foster the gifts and talents of students in South Australia'. In *Education of gifted and talented children in Catholic schools*. Melbourne, Australia: Catholic Education Office of Victoria.

Gillham, W. E. C. and Hesse, K. A. (1970). *The Leicester Number Test*. Nottingham, England: University of Nottingham Press.

—— (1974). *The Nottingham Number Test*. Nottingham, England: University of Nottingham Press.

Glenn, P. G. (1978). 'The relationship of self-concept and IQ to gifted students' expressed need for structure'. *Dissertation Abstracts International, 41*, 2931-A.

Goertzel, V. and Goertzel, M. G. (1962). *Cradles of eminence*. Boston: Little, Brown & Co.

Goldberg, M. L. (1981). *Issues in the education of gifted and talented children in Australia and the United States*. Canberra: Commonwealth Schools Commission.

—— Passow, A. H., Camm, D. S. and Neill, R. D. (1966). *A comparison of mathematics programs for able junior high school students* (Vol. 1). Washington, DC: US Office of Education, Bureau of Research.

Goldberg, S. (1934). 'A clinical study of K., IQ 196'. *Journal of Applied Psychology*, 18, 550–560.

Grant, J. E., Weiner, A. and Ruchton, J. P. (1976). 'Moral judgment and generosity in children'. *Psychological Reports*, 39, 451–454.

Grinder, R. E. (1985). 'The gifted in our midst: By their divine deeds, neuroses and mental test scores we have known them'. In F. D. Horowitz and M. O'Brien (eds), *The gifted and talented: Developmental perspectives* (5–35). Washington, DC: American Psychological Association.

Gross, M. U. M. (1983). 'Gifted girls – are we giving them away?'. *Pivot*, 10(4), 46–47.

—— (1984). 'Accelerating the gifted child'. *South Australian Association for Gifted and Talented Children Newsletter*, 36, 1–8.

—— (1986). 'Radical acceleration in Australia: Terence Tao'. *G/C/T*, 45, 2–11.

—— (1988). 'The acceleration program of Terence Tao: an update'. *Mensa Research Journal*, 25, 46.

—— (1989a). 'Two remarkably gifted child authors'. *The Gifted Child Today*, 12(3), 17–23.

—— (1989b). 'The pursuit of excellence or the search for intimacy? The forced-choice dilemma of gifted youth'. *Roeper Review*, 11(4), 189–194.

—— (1992). 'The use of radical acceleration in cases of extreme intellectual precocity'. *Gifted Child Quarterly*, 36(2), 90–98.

—— (in press). 'The early development of three profoundly gifted young boys of IQ 200+'. In A. J. Tannenbaum and P. N. Klein (eds), *To be young and gifted* New York: Ablex.

—— and Start, K. B. (1989). *'Not waving but drowning'; The exceptionally gifted child in Australia*. Paper presented at Eighth World Conference on Gifted and Talented Children, Sydney, Australia.

Grost, A. (1970). *Genius in residence*. Englewood Cliffs, NJ: Prentice-Hall.

Gustin, W. C. (1985). 'The development of exceptional research mathematicians'. In B. S. Bloom (ed.), *Developing talent in young people*, (270–331). New York: Ballantine.

Hagen, E. (1980). *Identification of the gifted*. New York: Teachers College Press.

Hallahan, D. P. and Kauffman, J. (1982). *Exceptional children*. Englewood Cliffs, NJ: Prentice Hall.

Halstead, J. W. (1988). *Guiding gifted readers from preschool through high school*. Columbus, Ohio: Ohio Psychology Publishing Company.

Hansard (1986a). *Official Hansard Report: Senate Standing Committee on Education and the Arts: Reference: Gifted and talented children*. Sydney, 26 May. Canberra: Commonwealth of Australia.

—— (1986b). *Official Hansard Report: Senate Standing Committee on Education and the Arts: Reference: Gifted and talented children*. Adelaide, Wednesday, 5 November. Canberra: Commonwealth of Australia.

Hansen, J. B. (1988). *The relationships of skills and classroom climate of trained and untrained teachers of gifted students*. Unpublished doctoral dissertation, Purdue University.

Harris, M. (1987). 'The case for our cultural mix'. *The Weekend Australian*, 21–22 November, 12.

Heller, K. A. (1989). *The Munich longitudinal study of giftedness*. Paper presented at Eighth World Conference on Gifted and Talented Children, Sydney, Australia, July.

Hellerstein, L. F. (1990). 'The gift of vision'. *Understanding Our Gifted*, 2(6), 1, 8–10.

Hennessy, K. (1992). *Decision making in primary schools*. Unpublished paper presented at Research Seminar, School of Education Studies, University of New South Wales, 11 March.

Hill, G. E. and Lauff, R. E. (1957). *Identifying and educating our gifted children*. Athens, Ohio: University of Ohio College of Education Press.

Himelstein, P. (1972). 'Review of Slosson Intelligence Test'. In O. K. Buros (ed.), *Seventh mental measurement yearbook*, 1. Highland Park, NJ: Gryphon Press.

Hirt, Z. I. (1922). 'A gifted child'. *The Training School Bulletin*, June, 49–54.

Hobson, J. R. (1979). 'High school performance of under-age pupils initially admitted to kindergarten on the basis of physical and psychological examination'. In W. C. George, S. J. Cohn and J. C. Stanley (eds), *Educating the gifted: Acceleration and enrichment* (162–171). Baltimore: Johns Hopkins University Press.

Hobson, K. (1991). 'The gifted kids' stigma: Moves to address "the Aussie attitude"'. *Canberra Times*, 17 April, 8.

Hollingworth, L. S. (1926). *Gifted children: Their nature and nurture*. New York: Macmillan.

—— (1931). 'The child of very superior intelligence as a special problem in social adjustment'. *Mental Hygiene*, 15(1), 3–16.

—— (1936a). 'The development of personality in highly intelligent children'. *National Elementary Principal*, 15, 272–281.

—— (1936b). 'The founding of Public School 500, Speyer School'. *Teachers College Record*, 38, 119–128.

—— (1942). *Children above IQ 180*. New York: World Books.

—— and Cobb, M. V. (1928). 'Children clustering at 165 IQ and children clustering at 146 IQ compared for three years in achievement'. In G. M. Whipple (ed.), *Nature and nurture: Their influence upon achievement*. The Twenty-seventh Yearbook of the National Society for the Study of Education, Part 2 (3–33). Bloomington, Illinois: Public School Publishing Company.

—— Cobb, M. V. *et al.* (1923). 'The special opportunity class for gifted children, Public School 165, Manhattan'. *Ungraded*, 8, 121–128.

—— Garrison, C. G. and Burke, A. (1917). 'The psychology of a prodigious child'. *Journal of Applied Psychology*, 1(2), 101–110.

—— (1922). 'Subsequent history of E–.; Five years after the initial report'. *Journal of Applied Psychology*, 6(6), 205–210.

Hubbard, R. (1929). A method of studying spontaneous group formation in Thomas, Dorothy and their associates. *Some new techniques for studying social behavior*. Child Development Monograph Number 1. New York: Bureau of Publications, Teachers College, Columbia University.

Hughes, H. H. and Converse, H. D. (1962). Characteristics of the gifted: A case for a sequel to Terman's study. *Exceptional Children*, 29, 179–183.

Jackson, N. (1992). 'Precocious reading of English: Origins, structures and predictive significance'. In A. J. Tannenbaum and P. N. Klein (eds) *To be young and gifted*. New York: Ablex.

Jacobs, J. C. (1971). 'Effectiveness of teacher and parent identification of gifted children as a function of school level'. *Psychology in the Schools*, 8, 140–142.

James, W. (1902). *The varieties of religious experience: A study in human nature*. New York: Longmans, Green.

Janos, P. M. (1983). *The psychological vulnerabilities of children of very superior intellectual ability*. Unpublished doctoral dissertation, Ohio State University.

—— Fung, H. C. and Robinson, N. M. (1985). 'Self-concept, self-esteem and peer relations among gifted children who feel "different"'. *Gifted Child Quarterly*, 29(2), 78–82.

—— and Robinson, N. M. (1985). 'Psychosocial development in intellectually gifted children'. In F. D. Horowitz and M. O'Brian (eds), *The gifted and talented: Developmental perspectives* (149–195). Washington, DC: American Psychological Association.

Jarrell, R. H. and Borland, J. H. (1990). 'The research base for Renzulli's Three Ring Conception of Giftedness'. *Journal for the Education of the Gifted*, 13(4), 288–308.

Jellen, H. G. (1983). *Renzulli-itis; A national disease in gifted education*. Paper presented at the Illinois State Conference on the Gifted, Peoria, Illinois, November 14.

—— (1985). 'Renzulli's enrichment scheme for the gifted: Educational accommodation of the gifted in the American context'. *Gifted Education International*, 3, 12–17.

Jensen, A. R. (1969). 'How much can we boost IQ and scholastic achievement?'. *Harvard Educational Review*, 39(1), 1–123.

Jersild, A. T. (1960). *Child psychology*. Hemel-Hempstead: Prentice-Hall.

Joad, C. E. M. (1947). *A year more or less*, BBC Radio, London, 3 May.

—— (1948). 'Sayings of the week'. *The Observer*, London, 12 December.

Johns Hopkins Medical School (1985). *Questionnaire on symptomatic atopic disease*. Baltimore: Johns Hopkins University.

Karnes, F. A. and Wherry, G. N. (1981). 'Self-concepts of gifted students as measured by the Piers-Harris Children's Self-Concept Scale'. *Psychological Reports*, 49, 903–906.

Kidder, L. H. and Fine, M. (1987). 'Qualitative and quantitative methods: When stories converge'. In M. M. Mark and R. L. Shotland (eds), *Multiple methods in program evaluation* (105–139). New Directions for Program Evaluation No. 35. San Francisco: Jossey Bass.

Kincaid, D. (1969). 'A study of highly gifted elementary pupils'. *Gifted Child Quarterly*, 13(4), 264–267.

Kirner, J. (1984). 'Tackling education: One viewpoint'. *Labor Star*, 5 May.

Kitano, M. K. and De Leon, J. (1988). 'Use of the Stanford Binet Fourth Edition in identifying young gifted children'. *Roeper Review*, 10(3), 156–159.

Klausmeier, H. J. (1958). 'Physical, behavioral and other characteristics of high- and lower-achieving children in favored environments'. *Journal of Educational Research*, 51, 573–581.

Kline, B. E. and Meckstroth, E. A. (1985). 'Understanding and encouraging the exceptionally gifted'. *Roeper Review*, 8(1), 24–30.

Kohlberg, L. (1958). *The development of modes of moral thinking and choice in the years ten to sixteen*. Unpublished doctoral dissertation: University of Chicago.

—— (1963). 'The development of children's orientations toward a moral order: 1. Sequence in the development of moral thought'. *Vita Humana*, 6, 11–33.

—— (1964). 'The development of moral character and moral ideology'. In M.

Hoffman and L. Hoffman (eds), *Review of child development research*. New York: Russell Sage Foundation.

Kolloff, M. B. (1985). *Reading preferences of gifted students*. Unpublished manuscript.

—— and Feldhusen, J. F. (1984). 'The effects of enrichment on self-concept and creative thinking'. *Gifted Child Quarterly*, 28(2), 53–58.

Kontos, S. Carter, K. R., Ormrod, J. E. and Cooney, J. B. (1983). 'Reversing the revolving door: A strict interpretation of Renzulli's definition of giftedness'. *Roeper Review*, 6(1), 35–39.

Korsanos, J. (1984). 'The fuss'. *Education*, 65(19), 384.

Kulik, C. C. (1985). *Effects of inter-class ability grouping on achievement and self-esteem*. Paper presented at the annual convention of the American Psychological Association, Los Angeles.

—— and Kulik, J. A. (1982). 'Effects of ability grouping on secondary school students: A meta-analysis of evaluation findings'. *American Educational Research Journal*, 19, 415–428.

—— and Kulik, J. A. (1984a). *Effects of ability grouping on elementary school pupils: a meta-analysis*. Paper presented at the annual meeting of the American Psychological Association, Ontario, Canada.

Kulik, J. A. and Kulik C. C. (1984b). 'Effects of accelerated instruction on students'. *Review of Educational Research*, 54, 409–425.

—— (1991). 'Ability grouping and gifted students'. In N. Colangelo and G. A. Davis (eds), *Handbook of gifted education*, (178–196). Boston: Allyn and Bacon.

Kusko, J. (1990). 'So your child isn't an Einstein'. *GH*, January, 63–67.

Langenbeck, M. (1915). 'A study of a five-year-old child'. *Pedagogical Seminary*, 22, 65–88.

Leder, G. C. (1987). 'Teacher student interaction: A case study'. *Educational Studies in Mathematics*, 18, 255–271.

—— (1988). 'Do teachers favor high achievers?'. *Gifted Child Quarterly*, 32(3), 315–320.

Lenneberg, E. H. (1967). *Biological functions of language*. New York: Wiley.

Lombroso, C. (1891). *The man of genius*. London: Walter Scott.

Lupkowski, A. E. and Stanley, J. C. (1988). *Comparing Asians and Non-Asians who reason extremely well mathematically*. Unpublished paper presented at the Cornell Symposium on Asian Americans: Cornell University, 5–6 May.

Maccoby, E. E. (1980). *Social development*. New York: Harcourt.

McElwee, E. (1934). 'Seymour, a boy with 192 IQ'. *Journal of Juvenile Research*, 18, 28–35.

McGuigan, K. and Start, K. B. (1991). *High ability dropouts from Victorian secondary colleges*. Paper presented at Ninth World Conference on Gifted and Talented Children, The Hague, 29 July–2 August.

MacKinnon, D. (1965). 'Personality and the realization of creative potential'. *American Psychologist*, 20, 273–281.

McLelland, J. (1992). 'Mother's milk and yum cha'. *Sydney Morning Herald*, 29 January, 10.

McNair Anderson (1989). Personal communication from A. Haydon, Client Service Manager: Media.

McNemar, Q. and Terman, L. M. (1936). 'Sex differences in variational tendency'. *Genetic Psychology Monographs*, 18, 1–66.

Malet, O. (1946). *Marjory Fleming*. London: Faber and Faber.

Mares, L. (1986). *Mixed ability classes and the gifted: What does a teacher need to know?*. Unpublished paper presented at the Third National Conference on Gifted and Talented Children, Hobart, Tasmania, September.

Marland, S. P. (1972). *Education of the gifted and talented, Volume 1: A report to the Congress of the United States by the U. S. Commissioner of Education*. Washington, DC: US Government Printing Office.

Martinson, R. A. (1974). *The identification of the gifted and talented*. Ventura, California: Office of the Ventura County Superintendent of Schools.

Mead, C. D. (1916). *The relation of general intelligence to certain mental and physical traits*. New York: Teachers College Press.

Mellis, C. (1987). *Asthma in the very young*. Sydney: The Asthma Foundation of New South Wales.

Merriam, S. B. (1988). *Case study research in education: A qualitative approach*. San Francisco: Jossey Bass.

Miles, M. B. and Huberman, A. M. (1984). *Qualitative data analysis: A sourcebook of new methods*. Newbury Park: Sage.

Montour, K. (1976) 'Success versus tragedy: Wiener and Sidis'. *Intellectually Talented Youth Bulletin*, 1(19), 3–4.

—— (1977). 'William James Sidis: the broken twig'. *American Psychologist*, 32, 265–279.

Moon, S. M. (1991). 'Case study research in gifted education'. In N. K. Buchanan and J. F. Feldhusen (eds) *Conducting research and evaluation in gifted education*, (157–178). New York: Teachers College Press.

Moore, S. D. and Stanley, J. C. (1988). 'Family background of young Asian Americans who reason extremely well mathematically'. *Journal of the Illinois Council for the Gifted*, 7, 11–14.

Mossenson, D. (1991). Personal letter from Dr David Mossenson, former Director-General of Education of Western Australia, 7 January.

—— and Marsh. C. (1990). 'The state's top students: 1989 Secondary Education Awards'. *The West Australian*, 9 January, 26–27.

Mussen, P. H., Conger, J. J. and Kagan, J. (1956). *Child development and personality*. (3rd edition). New York: Harper and Row.

Neale, M. D. (1966). *Neale Analysis of Reading Ability*. Macmillan: London.

New South Wales Board of Studies (1990). *Top scores in the High School Certificate Examination*. Sydney: New South Wales Board of Studies.

—— (1991). *Top scores in the High School Certificate Examination*. Sydney: New South Wales Board of Studies.

New South Wales Government (1991). *NSW Government Strategy for the education of gifted and talented students*. Sydney: New South Wales Government.

Nicklin, L. (1990). 'The boy who knows so much'. *The Bulletin*, 16 October, 34–35.

Nielsen, A. C. (1985). *Report on television, 1985*. Chicago: A. C. Nielsen Co.

Oldfield, R. C. (1971). 'The assessment and analysis of handedness: the Edinburgh Inventory'. *Neuropsychologia*, 9, 97–113.

O'Shea, H. (1960). 'Friendship and the intellectually gifted child'. *Exceptional Children*. 26(6), 327–335.

Painter, F. (1976). *Gifted children: A research study*. Knebworth, England: Pullen Publications.

Palmer, N. (1985). 'Breastfeeding – the Australian situation'. *National Medical Association of Australia Newsletter, 21(2)*, 3–10.

Parkyn, G. W. (1948). *Children of high intelligence*. Oxford: Oxford University Press.

Patton, M. Q. (1980). *Qualitative evaluation methods*. Newbury Park, CA: Sage.

Pegnato, C. W. and Birch, J. W. (1959). 'Locating gifted children in junior high schools: A comparison of methods'. *Exceptional Children, 23*, 300–304.

Pfouts, J. (1980). 'Birth-order, age-spacing, IQ differences, and family relations'. *Journal of Marriage and the Family, August*, 517–528.

Pickard, P. M. (1976). *If you think your child is gifted*. London: George Allen and Unwin.

Piers, E. (1984). *Piers-Harris Children's Self-Concept Scale: Revised Manual*. Los Angeles: Western Psychological Services.

Plomin, R. (1989). 'Environment and genes: Determinants of behavior'. *American Psychologist*, 44(2), 105–111.

Pollins, L. D. (1983). 'The effects of acceleration on the social and emotional development of gifted students'. In C. P. Benbow and J. C. Stanley (eds), *Academic precocity: Aspects of its development* (160–178). Baltimore: Johns Hopkins University Press.

Poulos, J. (1990a) 'Academic board goes to the movies'. *Education*, 8 October, 71(14), 8.

—— (1990b). 'Editorial comment'. *Education*, 24 October, 71(15).

Powell, P. M. and Haden, T. (1984). 'The intellectual and psychosocial nature of extreme giftedness'. *Roeper Review*, 6(3), 131–133.

Pressick, K. (1984). 'Enjoying school'. *Education*, 65(15), 288.

Pringle, M. L. K. (1970). *Able misfits*. London: Longman.

Proctor, T. B., Feldhusen, J. F. and Black, K. N. (1988). 'Guidelines for early admission to elementary school'. *Psychology in the Schools*, 25(1), 41–43.

Purkey, W. W. (1970). *Self-concept and school achievement*. Englewood Cliffs, NJ: Prentice Hall.

Raph, J., Goldberg, M. L. and Passow, A. H. (1966). *Bright underachievers*. New York: Columbia University Press.

Renzulli, J. S. (1977). *The Interest-a-Lyzer*. Mansfield Center, CT: Creative Learning Press.

—— (1978). 'What makes giftedness? Reexamining a definition'. *Phi Delta Kappan*, 60, 180–184, 261.

—— (1986). 'The three-ring conception of giftedness: A developmental model for creative productivity'. In R. J. Sternberg and J. E. Davidson (eds). *Conceptions of giftedness*. Cambridge, MA: Cambridge University Press.

—— Reis, S. M. and Smith, L. M. (1981) *The Revolving Door Identification Model*. Mansfield Center, Connecticut: Creative Learning Press.

—— and Smith, L. H. (1980). 'The revolving door model: An alternative approach to identifying and programming for gifted and talented students'. *G/C/T*, 15, 4–11.

Rest, J. R. (1979). *Development in judging moral issues*. Minneapolis: University of Minnesota Press.

—— (1980a). 'Development in moral judgment research'. *Developmental Psychology*, 16, 251–256.

—— (1980b). 'The Defining Issues Test: A survey of research results'. In L. Kuhmerker, M. Mentkowski and V. L. Erikson (eds), *Evaluating moral development* (113–120). Schenectady, New York: Character Research Press.

—— (1983). 'Morality'. In J. Flavell and E. Markman and P. Mussen (eds), *Manual of child psychology: Volume 3: Cognitive development* (556–692). New York: Wiley.

—— (1986a). *Defining Issues Test; Manual*. Minneapolis: Center for Ethical Development, University of Minnesota.

—— (1986b). *Moral development: Advances in research and theory*. New York: Praeger.

Reynolds, M., Birch, J. and Tusseth, A. (1962). 'A review of research on early admissions'. In M. Reynolds (ed.), *Early school admission for mentally advanced children* (165–177). Washington, DC: Council for Exceptional Children.

Richert, E. S., Alvino, J. J. and McDonnell, R. C. (1982). *National report on identification: Assessment and recommendations for comprehensive identification of gifted and talented youth*. Washington, DC: Educational Information Resource Center, US Department of Education.

Robinson, A. (1990). 'Point-counterpoint: Cooperation or exploitation? The argument against cooperative learning for talented students'. *Journal for the Education of the Gifted*, 14, 9–27.

Robinson, H. B. (1977). *Current myths concerning gifted children: Gifted and Talented Brief 1–11*. Ventura, California: National/State Leadership Training Institute.

—— (1981). 'The uncommonly bright child'. In M. Lewis and L. A. Rosenblum (eds), *The uncommon child* (57–81). New York: Plenum Press.

—— (1983). 'A case for radical acceleration: Programs of Johns Hopkins University and the University of Washington'. In C. P. Benbow and J. C. Stanley (eds), *Academic precocity: Aspects of its development* (139–159). Baltimore: Johns Hopkins University Press.

Robinson, N. (1987). 'The early development of precocity'. *Gifted Child Quarterly*, 31(4), 161–164.

—— (1992). 'The use of standardized tests with young gifted children'. In P. Klein and A. J. Tannenbaum (eds), *To be young and gifted*. New York: Ablex.

Roderick, J. A. and Jackson, P. (1986). 'T.V. viewing habits, family rules, reading grades, heroes and heroines of gifted and non-gifted middle school students'. *Roeper Review*, 9(2), 114–119.

Roe, A. (1951a). 'A psychological study of eminent physical scientists'. *Genetic Psychology Monographs*, 43, 121–235.

—— (1951b). 'A psychological study of eminent biologists'. *Psychological Monographs*, 63 (14, Serial No. 331).

—— (1953). 'A psychological study of eminent psychologists and anthropologists'. *Psychological Monographs*, 67 (2, Serial No. 352).

Roedell, W. C. (1984). 'Vulnerabilities of highly gifted children'. *Roeper Review*, 6(3), 127–130.

—— (1989). 'Early development of gifted children'. In J. VanTassel-Baska and P. Olszewski-Kubilius (eds) *Patterns of influence on gifted learners* (13–28). New York: Teachers College Press.

Rodgers, B. (1979). *Effects of an enrichment program screening process on the self-concept and other-concept of gifted elementary children*. Unpublished doctoral dissertation, University of Cincinnati.

Rogers, C. R. (1942). *Counseling and psychotherapy*. New York: Houghton Mifflin.

Rogers, K. B. (1991). *The relationship of grouping practices to the education of the gifted and talented learner*. Connecticut: National Research Center on the Gifted and Talented.

Rogers, M. T. (1986). *A comparative study of developmental traits of gifted and average youngsters*. Unpublished doctoral dissertation, University of Denver.

Seeley, K. (1989). 'Underachieving and handicapped gifted'. In J. F. Feldhusen, J. VanTassel-Baska and K. Seeley (eds) *Excellence in educating the gifted* (29–37). Denver:Love.

Selig, K. (1959). *Personality structure as revealed by the Rorshach technique of a group of children who test at or above 170 IQ on the 1937 revision of the Stanford-Binet Scale (Volumes I–V)*. Unpublished doctoral dissertation, New York University.

Sheldon, P. M. (1954). 'The families of highly gifted children'. *Marriage and Family Living, February*, 59–60, 67.

—— (1959). 'Isolation as a characteristic of highly gifted children'. *The Journal of Educational Sociology, January*, 215–221.

Sheridan, G. (1989). 'Wasteland emerges in education reform'. *The Weekend Australian* 29 July, 26.

Silverman, L. K. (1986). 'Whatever happened to the gifted girl?'. In J. Maker (ed.), *Critical issues in gifted education* (43–89). Rockville, MD: Aspen Publications.
—— (1989). 'The highly gifted'. In J. F. Feldhusen, J. VanTassell-Baska, and K. R. Seeley (eds), *Excellence in educating the gifted* (71–83). Denver:Love.
—— (1992) Don't throw away the old Binet. *Understanding Our Gifted*, 4(4), 1, 8–10.
—— Gross, M. U. M. and Kearney, K. (1991). *A cross-cultural comparison of children above IQ 170*. Paper presented at the Ninth World Conference on Gifted and Talented Children, The Hague, 2 August.
—— and Kearney, K. (1989). 'Parents of the extraordinarily gifted'. *Advanced Development*, 1, 1–10.
—— and Waters, J. (1987). *Exploding the myth of the non-gifted sibling*. Paper presented at the Thirty-Fourth Annual Convention of the National Association for Gifted Children, New Orleans, November.
Sisk, D. A. (1979). 'Acceleration versus enrichment: A position paper'. In W. C. George, S. J. Cohn and J. C. Stanley (eds), *Educating the gifted: Acceleration and enrichment* (236–238). Baltimore: Johns Hopkins University Press.
Sloane, K. D. (1985). 'Home influences on talent development'. In B. S. Bloom (ed.), *Developing talent in young people*, (439–476). New York: Ballantine.
Slosson, R. L. (1985). *Slosson Intelligence Test*. New York: Slosson Educational Publications, Inc.
South Australian Education Department (1983). 'Policy regarding fostering gifts and talents among children'. *Education Gazette*, 11(23), 567–571.
South Australian Health Commission (1986). *Pregnancy outcome in South Australia, 1985*. Adelaide, Australia: Epidemiology Board, South Australian Health Commission.
South Australian Institute of Teachers (1985). *Proposed curriculum policy*. Adelaide, South Australia.
Southern, W. T. and Jones, E. D. (1991). *The academic acceleration of gifted children*. New York: Teachers College Press.
—— and Fiscus, E. D. (1989). 'Practitioner objections to the academic acceleration of gifted children'. *Gifted Child Quarterly*, 3(1), 29–35.
Stanley, J. C. (1976a). 'The case for extreme educational acceleration of intellectually brilliant youths'. *Gifted Child Quarterly*, 20(1), 66–75, 41.
—— (1976b). 'Use of tests to discover talent'. In D. P. Keating (ed.), *Intellectual talent: Research and development* (3–22). Baltimore: Johns Hopkins University Press.
—— (1977–1978). 'The predictive value of the SAT for brilliant seventh- and eighth-graders'. *The College Board Review*, 106, 31–37.
—— (1979). 'Identifying and nurturing the intellectually gifted'. In W. C. George, S. J. Cohn and J. C. Stanley (eds), *Educating the gifted: Acceleration and enrichment* (172–180). Baltimore: Johns Hopkins University Press.
—— (1988). Personal communication to 'Christopher Otway', 8 June.
—— and Benbow, C. P. (1983). 'Extremely young college graduates: Evidence of their success'. *College and University*, 58(4), 361–371.
—— and Benbow, C. P. (1986). 'Youths who reason exceptionally well mathematically'. In R. J. Sternberg and J. E. Davidson (eds) *Conceptions of giftedness* (361–387). Cambridge: Cambridge University Press.
—— Huang, J. and Zu, X. (1986). '*SAT-M* scores of highly selected students in Shanghai tested when less than 13 years old'. *The College Board Review*, 140, 10–13, 28–29.
—— Keating, D. P. and Fox, L. H. (eds) (1974). *Mathematical talent: Discovery, description and development*. Baltimore: Johns Hopkins University Press.

Start, K. B. (1985). *A digest of the Australian National Survey of the Education of Teachers on the Needs of Gifted and Talented Children: A report on a report*. Paper presented at the Sixth World Conference on Gifted and Talented Children, Hamburg.
—— (1986a). 'A deprived group thought too clever by half'. *Sydney Morning Herald*, 28 June.
—— (1986b). 'Submission to the Senate Standing Committee on the Education of Gifted and Talented Children'. *Hansard*, 20 May, 822–882.
—— (1987). *Is high intelligence a valid reason for depriving the deprived?* Paper presented at the Seventh World Conference on Gifted and Talented Children, Salt Lake City, Utah.
—— (1991). 'Highlights from Australia'. *Gifted Education International*, 7(30), 158–160.
—— John, R. and Strange, L. (1975). *Provisions for children of high intellectual potential (CHIP Study)*. Paper presented to the Conference of the Australian Association for Research in Education, Adelaide, November.
Stephens, A. (1986). 'Gifted kids are "deprived"'. *The Sun Living Supplement*, 18 February, 2.
Supplee, P. L. (1990). *Reaching the gifted underachiever: Program design and strategy*. New York: Teachers College Press.
Susskind, A. (1986) 'The schools that make children "pompous"'. *Sydney Morning Herald*, 15 March, 4.
—— (1989). 'HSC: The best of the bunch'. *The Sydney Morning Herald*, 10 January, 13.
Tannenbaum, A. J. (1962). *Adolescent attitudes towards academic brilliance*. New York: Bureau of Publications, Teachers College, Columbia University.
—— (1983). *Gifted children: Psychological and educational perspectives*. New York: Macmillan.
—— (1986). 'Reflection and refraction of light on the gifted'. *Roeper Review*, 8(4), 212–218.
—— (1988). *Myths and misconceptions in the education of the gifted*. Paper presented at Conference of the South Australian Association for Gifted and Talented Children, Adelaide, South Australia, 24 April.
Terman, L. M. (1905). 'A study in precocity and prematuration'. *American Journal of Psychology*, 16, 145–183.
—— (1917). 'The intelligence quotient of Francis Galton in childhood'. *American Journal of Psychology*, 28, 209–215.
—— (1925). *Genetic studies of genius: Vol. 1. Mental and physical traits of a thousand gifted children*. Stanford, CA: Stanford University Press.
—— and Fenton, J. C. (1921). 'Preliminary report on a gifted juvenile author'. *Journal of Applied Psychology*, 5, 163–178.
—— and Merrill, M. A. (1973). *Stanford-Binet Intelligence Scale: 1972 norms edition*. Boston: Houghton Mifflin.
—— and Oden, M. H. (1947). *Genetic studies of genius* (Vol. 4), *The gifted child grows up*. Stanford, CA: Stanford University Press.
—— and Oden, M. H. (1959). *Genetic studies of genius* (Vol. 5), *The gifted group at mid-life*. Stanford, CA: Stanford University Press.
Theman, V. and Witty, P. (1943). 'Case studies and genetic records of two gifted negroes'. *Journal of Psychology*, 15, 165–181.
Thorndike, R. (1940). 'Performance of gifted children on tests of developmental age'. *Journal of Psychology*, 9, 337–343.
—— Hagen, E. P., and Sattler, J. M. (1986). *The Stanford Binet Intelligence Scale: Fourth edition. Technical manual*. New York: The Riverside Publishing Co.

'Those who get passes are the ones with glasses' (1989). *Eyecare Australia*, May, 8.

Tidwell, R. A. (1980). 'Psycho-educational profile of 1,593 gifted high school students'. *Gifted Child Quarterly*, 24(2), 63–68.

Totaro, P. (1990). 'Gifted kids may be victimised by peers, warns psychologist'. *Sydney Morning Herald*, 26 June.

Tumin, M. (1983). 'The process of integration'. In G. Klopf and A. Lestor (eds), *Integrating the urban school*. New York: Teachers College Press.

VanTassel-Baska, J. (1983). 'Profiles of precocity: The 1982 Midwest Talent Search finalists'. *Gifted Child Quarterly*, 27(3), 139–144.

—— (1985). 'Appropriate curriculum for the gifted'. In J. F. Feldhusen (ed.). *Toward excellence in gifted education* (45–67). Denver: Love.

—— (1986). 'Acceleration'. In C. J. Maker (ed.) *Critical issues in gifted education*. Rockville, MD: Aspen Press.

—— (1989). 'Profiles of precocity: A three-year study of talented adolescents'. In J. VanTassel-Baska and P. Olszewski-Kubilius (eds.) *Patterns of influence on gifted learners* (29–39). New York: Teachers College Press.

Vaughn, V., Feldhusen, J. F. and Asher, J. W. (1991). 'Meta-analyses and review of research on pullout programs in gifted education'. *Gifted Child Quarterly*, 35(2), 92–98.

Vernon, P. E., Adamson, G. and Vernon, D. F. (1977). *The psychology and education of gifted children*. London: Methuen.

Victorian Teachers' Union (1986). *Policy Statement on Education*. Melbourne: Victorian Teachers' Union.

Ward, R. (1958). *The Australian Legend*. Melbourne: Oxford University Press.

Webb, J. T., Meckstroth, E. A. and Tolan, S. S. (1983). *Guiding the gifted child*. Columbus, Ohio: Ohio Psychology Publishing Company.

West, D. (1984). 'Opportunity for what?' *Education*, 65(14), 266.

West, K. (1987). 'Pride of place for intellectuals'. *The Australian*, 14 October, 15.

Westwood, P. S. (1979). *Helping children with spelling difficulties*. Adelaide, Australia: Education Department of South Australia.

White, B. (1975). *The first three years of life*. Englewood Cliffs, N. J. : Prentice Hall.

White, W. L. (1984). *The perceived effects of an early enrichment experience: A forty-year follow-up study of the Speyer School experiment for gifted students*. Unpublished doctoral dissertation, University of Connecticut.

Whitmore, J. R. (1980). *Giftedness, conflict and underachievement*. Boston: Allyn and Bacon.

—— and Maker, C. J. (1985). *Intellectual giftedness in disabled persons*. Rockville, Maryland: Aspen.

Wiener, N. (1953). *Ex-prodigy: My childhood and youth*. New York: Simon and Shuster.

Wilson, D. (1989). 'After the conference'. *Newsletter of the New South Wales Association for Gifted and Talented Children*, 57, 5.

Wilson, S. (1979). 'Explorations of the usefulness of case study evaluations'. *Evaluation Quarterly*, 3, 446–459.

Witty, P. (1940). 'A genetic study of fifty gifted children'. In G. M. Whipple (ed.) *Intelligence: Its nature and nurture* (401–409). 39th Yearbook of the National Society for the Study of Education.

—— and Coomer, A. (1955). 'A case study of gifted twin boys'. *Exceptional Children*, 22, 104–108.

—— and Lehman, H. C. (1936). 'A study of the reading and reading interests of gifted children'. *Pedagogical Seminary and Journal of Genetic Psychology*, 49, 215–226.

Wood, A (1991). 'Slowing the immigration flow from a torrent to a trickle'. *The Australian*, 17 December.

Woodbury, R. M. (1922). 'The relation between breast and infant feeding and infant mortality'. *American Journal of Hygiene*, 2, 668–687.

Worcester, D. A. (1955). *The education of children of above average mentality*. Lincoln: University of Nebraska Press.

Yin, R. K. (1984). *Case study research: Design and methods*. Beverly Hill, CA: Sage.

Zorbaugh, H. W. and Boardman, R. K. (1936). 'Salvaging our gifted children'. *Journal of Educational Sociology*, 10, 100–108.

—— Boardman, R. K., and Sheldon, P. (1951). 'Some observations of highly gifted children'. In P. Witty (ed.), *The gifted child* (86–105). Boston: D. C. Heath & Co.

APPENDIX A

Questionnaire 1: Early development and physical health

NAME OF CHILD: ______________________________

DATE ON WHICH THIS QUESTIONNAIRE HAS BEEN COMPLETED: ______________

Unless specifically indicated, all the following questions refer to the subject child, i.e. the child who has been referred to the study.

1 Full name of child. ____

2 Date of birth. ______ day ______ month ______ year.

3 Birth order position (e.g. only child, eldest child of three, second child of four, etc.).

____

4 Names and dates of birth of siblings (brothers or sisters).

Name	Sex	Date of birth
__________________________	______	______________
__________________________	______	______________

5 Was child a full-term baby? ______ (If not, please say how many months child was carried.)

6 Were there any unusual conditions of birth. (Prolonged or difficult delivery, use of instruments, etc?)

7 Did mother take any prescribed medication during pregnancy?

8 Was conception medically facilitated in any way? (Medication to increase fertility; in vitro fertilization, etc.)

9 Please describe mother's health during pregnancy.

10 Child's weight at birth. ______________________

11 How did child's birth weight compare with that of other siblings?

12 Child's length at birth. ______________________

13 How did child's length at birth compare with that of other siblings?

14 Child's weight TODAY. (Date on which you are filling out this questionnaire.) ______________________

15 Child's height TODAY. (Date on which you are filling out this questionnaire.) ______________________

16 If child was breast-fed, from what age to what age?

____

If child was bottle-fed, from what age to what age?

____

17 Please give the month and/or year when the child began to:

utter words ______________________

speak in short sentences ______________________

Please give any specific examples you can recall of child's early speech, with (if possible) the child's age at the time.

18 At what age did the child's first teeth appear? ____________

At what age did permanent teeth start to come in? ____________

19 At what age did child start to:

sit up unassisted ______________________

crawl ______________________

walk assisted (holding an adult's hand) ______________________

walk alone (several steps) ______________________

run ______________________

Please give any specific examples you can recall of child's early mobility with (if possible) the child's age at the time.

20 In comparison with other children in the family or other children with whom you are familiar, does the child seem to need:

(a) less sleep?
(b) about the same amount of sleep?
(c) more sleep?

Please tick whichever applies.

21 Did the child have any serious health problems or handicaps in infancy?

22 Does he/she have any serious health problems or handicaps NOW?

23 Has the child had any of the following childhood illnesses: (Please tick any which apply.)

Measles	_____	Age?	_____	Severity?	_____
Mumps	_____	Age?	_____	Severity?	_____
Whooping cough	_____	Age?	_____	Severity?	_____
German measles	_____	Age?	_____	Severity	_____
Chicken-pox	_____	Age?	_____	Severity?	_____
Other	_____	Age?	_____	Severity?	_____

24 Has the child had any accidents or operations? Yes _____
No _____

If yes, please describe including the child's age at the time.

25 Does child have any vision problems? Yes _____ No _____

If yes, please describe the nature of these.

Is the problem corrected by spectacles or other intervention?

26 Does the child have any hearing problems? Yes _____
No _____

If yes, please describe the nature of these.

Is the problem corrected by a hearing aid or other intervention?

27 Does the child suffer from any allergies? Yes _____
No _____

If yes, please describe what form the allergy takes and (if possible) the cause or source of the allergy.

28 Does the child suffer to any degree from asthma?

Yes _____ No _____

If yes, please describe as fully as you can the symptoms, the degree of severity, any medication prescribed and the age at which the child first developed asthmatic symptoms.

29 Is the child: Predominantly right-handed _____

Predominantly left-handed _____

Ambidextrous (writes fluently with either hand) _____

30 (If girl) Has menstruation begun? _____ At what age? _____

(If boy) Has voice changed? _____ At what age? _____

APPENDIX B
Questionnaire 2: Family history

NAME OF CHILD: ______________________________

DATE ON WHICH THIS QUESTIONNAIRE HAS BEEN COMPLETED: ____________

In this questionnaire, all persons specified (e.g. mother, maternal grandfather, sister, etc.) are referred to in terms of their relationship to the SUBJECT CHILD.

1 Date of birth of father ____ day ____ month ____ year

2 Date of birth of mother ____ day ____ month ____ year

3 Age of father at birth of FIRST child ____ years ____ months

4 Age of mother at birth of FIRST child ____ years ____ months

5 Age of father at birth of SUBJECT CHILD ____ years ____ months (if different from 3 above)

6 Age of mother at birth of SUBJECT CHILD ____ years ____ months (if different from 4 above)

Please use this space to make any comments you wish which clarify or enlarge on the information in Questions 1 – 6.

7 Country of birth of father ______________________________

Year of arrival in Australia (if applicable) ____________________

8 Country of birth of mother ______________________________

Year of arrival in Australia (if applicable) ____________________

9 Country of birth of paternal grandfather ____________________

Year of arrival in Australia (if applicable and if known) __________

10 Country of birth of paternal grandmother ____________________

Year of arrival in Australia (if applicable and if known) __________

11 Country of birth of maternal grandfather ____________________

Year of arrival in Australia (if applicable and if known) __________

12 Country of birth of maternal grandmother ____________________

Year of arrival in Australia (if applicable and if known) __________

13 Please record the country of birth and year of arrival in Australia of any of the subject child's great-grandparents for whom you have this information.

14 Father's highest level of education. (Please check)

- Intermediate certificate ____
- Matriculation ____
- Vocational or trade diploma. (Please name) ________________
- Teacher's diploma ____
- First degree from tertiary institution (e.g. University, C. A. E., Institute of Technology, etc). (Please name) ________________
- Master's degree. (Please name) ____________________
- Doctoral degree. (Please name) ____________________

15 Mother's highest level of education. (Please check)

- Intermediate certificate ____
- Matriculation ____
- Vocational or trade diploma. (Please name) ________________
- Teacher's diploma ____
- First degree from tertiary institution (e.g. University, C. A. E., Institute of Technology, etc). (Please name) ________________
- Master's degree. (Please name) ____________________
- Doctoral degree. (Please name) ____________________

16 Using the criteria outlined in questions 14 and 15, please record the highest educational level attained by the following relatives (where this is known).

Paternal grandfather: ______________________

Paternal grandmother: ______________________

Maternal grandfather: ______________________

Maternal grandmother: ______________________

Please use this space to make any comments you wish which clarify or enlarge on the information in questions 14 – 16.

17 (a) What is father's occupation?

(b) Please write brief description of what this job entails.

____

(c) Father's annual salary before tax. Please check range.

Less than $10,000	___	$10,000 – $14,999	___
$15,000 – $19,999	___	$20,000 – $24,999	___
$25,000 – $29,999	___	$30,000 – $34,999	___
$35,000 – $39,999	___	$40,000 – $44,999	___
$45,000 – $49,999	___	$50,000 – $54,999	___
$55,000 – $59,999	___	$60,000 – $64,999	___
$65,000 – $69,999	___	At or over $70,000	___

(d) If father's IQ is known, please record it in this space ___

If the name of the Intelligence Test on which this score was achieved is known, please record it here.

____

(e) Has father received any positions of honour or recognition in academic, business, social or sporting life? (e.g. academic prize, business award, presidency of club or lodge, etc.)

____

(f) What are father's special interests, hobbies or accomplishments?

____

18 (a) What is mother's occupation? (If mother is involved full-time in home duties, record her occupation when she was working outside the home.)

(b) Please write brief description of what this job entails/entailed

____

(c) If mother is currently earning, please check range of her annual salary before tax.

Below $10,000	____	$10,000 – $14,999	____
$15,000 – $19,999	____	$20,000 – $24,999	____
$25,000 – $29,999	____	$30,000 – $34,999	____
$35,000 – $39,999	____	$40,000 – $44,999	____
$45,000 – $49,999	____	$50,000 – $54,999	____
$55,000 – $59,999	____	$60,000 – $64,999	____
$65,000 – $69,999	____	At or over $70,000	____

(d) If mother's IQ is known, please record it in this space.

____

If the name of the Intelligence Test on which this score was achieved is known, please record it here.

____

(e) Has mother received any positions of honour or recognition in academic, business, social or sporting life? (e.g. academic prize, business award, presidency of club or lodge).

____

(f) What are mother's special interests, hobbies or accomplishments?

____

In the following questions, you will be asked to estimate the level of a family member's intelligence, in comparison with the average person. It is important that you compare the family member with the strictly average person, not with the average member of your own family.

19 Please answer the following questions for child's PATERNAL GRANDFATHER.

(a) Age if living. _____ If dead, age at death. _____

(b) His occupation or occupations.

____

(c) Compared to the strictly average person, is/was his intelligence very superior, superior, average, inferior, very inferior? (Circle)

(d) Positions of honour or recognition received by him.

____

(e) His special interests, hobbies or accomplishments.

____

(f) His outstanding characteristics.

______

20 Please answer the following questions for child's PATERNAL GRANDMOTHER.

(a) Age if living. ______ If dead, age at death. ______
(b) Her occupation or occupations.

______

(c) Compared to the strictly average person, is/was her intelligence
very superior, superior, average, inferior, very inferior? (Circle)
(d) Positions of honour or recognition received by her.

______

(e) Her special interests, hobbies or accomplishments.

______

(f) Her outstanding characteristics.

______

21 Please answer the following questions for child's MATERNAL GRANDFATHER.

(a) Age, if living. ______ If dead, age at death. ______
(b) His occupation or occupations.

______

(c) Compared to the strictly average person, is/was his intelligence
very superior, superior, average, inferior, very inferior? (Circle).
(d) Positions of honour or recognition received by him.

______

(e) His special interests, hobbies or accomplishments.

______

(f) His outstanding characteristics.

______

22 Please answer the following questions for child's MATERNAL GRANDMOTHER.

(a) Age, if living. ______ If dead, age at death. ______
(b) Her occupation or occupations.

______

(c) Compared to the strictly average person, is/was her intelligence
very superior, superior, average, inferior, very inferior? (Circle).

(d) Positions of honour or recognition received by her.

____

(e) Her special hobbies, interests or accomplishments.

____

(f) Her outstanding characteristics.

____

23 Have any other family members (aunts, uncles, cousins, great-aunts, great-uncles, etc., of subject child) displayed exceptional ability in any field?

Please use space available on this and following page.

24 What occupations have been most common on father's side of the family?

25 What occupations have been most common on mother's side of the family?

267 What is father's current weight? _____ Current height? _____

27 What is mother's current weight? _____ Current height? ___

APPENDIX C

Questionnaire 3: Reading Record

WEEK 1 2 3 4 (Please circle). Child's name: ____________________

Child's age: _____ yrs _____ mths

— Please record time in hours and minutes.
— Do not record books or materials child has to read for homework or other school responsibilities. Count only materials read voluntarily. Do not include books that you read to your child.
— Record names of newspapers, magazines, journals, etc., but please record both title and author of books.

	Time spent in reading today	*Books, magazines, etc. read today*	*Classification*
Sunday			
Monday			
Tuesday			
Wednesday			
Thursday			
Friday			
Saturday			

CLASSIFICATION TABLE

Fairy stories, folk tales, legends	A
Classical mythology (Roman, Greek, Norse)	B
Science fiction	C

Fantasy	D
Mystery (including detective fiction)	E
Adventure	F
Historical fiction	G
Romance (love stories)	H
Classics (Bront, Stevenson, Dickens, etc)	I
Nature and animal stories	J
Stories of school life	K
Horror	L
Poetry or drama	M
Historical fact	N
Travel	O
Biography	P
Children's encyclopaedia or reference books	Q
Adult encyclopaedia or reference books	R
Science fact	S
Computer/electronics	T
Maths/statistics	U
Sports	V
Humour	W
Comics	X
Any other (please indicate your own classification).	Y

CHILD'S READING PREFERENCES

Child's name: ______________________________

Age: _____ years _____ months

Write the names of up to 10 books which you have enjoyed very much during the last two years. If you remember the author's name, write that also. For each book, write a short paragraph explaining why you particularly enjoyed it.

You will probably need more space than this, so please feel free to add further sheets of your own paper to this one.

APPENDIX D

Questionnaire 4: Television and computer use, play interests and spare-time activities

NAME OF CHILD: ______________________

DATE ON WHICH THIS QUESTIONNAIRE HAS BEEN COMPLETED: ______

— This questionnaire is designed to elicit information on your subject child's out-of-school activities and interests. The television viewing record which is appended to the questionnaire is an important part of this. It asks you to record your child's television viewing over a period of 14 days. Can I ask you, therefore, to start filling in the viewing record on the Sunday after you receive this questionnaire and return it to me, with the completed questionnaire, as early as possible.

— Also appended to the questionnaire is a sheet on which your subject child is requested to record the five television programmes which s/he most enjoys, together with a brief statement about his/her reasons for nominating these programmes. This can be completed either before or during the 14-day viewing record period. In the case of children under 8 years the child may dictate his/her choice of programme and ideas to the parent; however I would prefer it if children 8 years and over did this themselves.

— The programmes which the child records as favourites DO NOT have to be programmes watched during the 14 day viewing period.

1 As a general rule, at what time does your subject child go to bed:

on weeknights? ______ on weekends? ______

2 Do you have any family rules about television viewing? If so, what are they?

____

3 Generally, who decides which television programmes should be watched? (Parents; children; joint decision: sometimes one, sometimes the other?)

4 To what extent and in what ways do you attempt to influence your children's TV viewing?

5 What are your reasons as a parent for doing this?

6 Are there any special benefits you feel your subject child derives from TV viewing?

7 Do you feel TV viewing has any negative effects on your subject child?

8 Does your subject child have his/her 'own' (or shared with siblings) TV or is all his/her viewing done on the 'family' set?

9 If your subject child does have his/her 'own' set, how much control do you exercise over what, and how much, s/he watches?

10 Does your subject child have access to a computer:

(a) at school? ______ (b) at home? ______

If you answered 'Yes' to (a), please complete questions 11 – 14.

11 Is the computer situated in the child's own classroom or in a computer room or other special area?

12 Approximately how many hours per week does your child spend actually using the computer?

13 Please tick the activities which your child undertakes on the computer and describe them briefly.

- 'learning games' (maths, spelling, etc.).

- more serious exercises in maths, spelling, etc.
- word processing (e.g. writing stories).
- printing greeting cards, posters, etc.
- computer programming.
- other.

(If 'other' please describe as clearly as you can, if possible including the name your child gives to the exercise or activity.)

14 What is your own opinion of the school's current use of computers in your child's education?

If you answered 'Yes' to question 10(b), please complete questions 15-20.

15 What make and model of computer do you have at home?

16 How long have you had it?

17 For how many hours per week (approximately) does your subject child use the computer?

18 Please describe as fully as possible the ways in which your child uses the computer. (It may help to use question 13 as a guide.) Please record any commercial packages which your child particularly values or uses a great deal. If your child is involved in programming, please give details of this. If there is not enough space here, please continue on the back of the sheet.

19 Do you consider that your subject child has an unusually high aptitude for computing/computer work? What are your reasons for believing this?

20 Are there any current restrictions on your child's further development in computing? If so, what are they?

21 Does your child belong to any youth organization or Church organization e.g. Junior Red Cross, Scouts or Girl Guides, Scripture Union, etc?

22 Does your child attend any out-of-school clubs focusing on specific hobbies, e.g. science, chess, etc? (Not clubs specifically for gifted children.) Please describe.

23 Does your child attend any out-of-school clubs or programs specifically for gifted and talented children? Please describe.

24 Is your child a member of any competitive or non-competitive sports teams or clubs, e.g. football, orienteering, tennis? Please describe.

- at school
- out of school

25 Does your child have a high degree of ability in any particular sport? Please describe and outline any awards s/he may have won.

26 Does your child play competitive chess or other board games as a member of a regular club or team?

27 Does your child take lessons at school or privately in dance, music, drama, gymnastics, foreign language or other cultural activity?

Activity:

Are the lessons undertaken at school or privately?

How long per week does the child spend in

(a) lessons

(b) practice

For how long has the child been taking lessons?

Please record any examinations passed or standards attained.

Have you at any time been told that the child has unusual aptitude in this activity? When and by whom? Is there any independent evidence (prizes won, public performances, etc.) of unusual aptitude or talent.

28 Approximately how many books does your child possess? (Some may be shared with siblings.) Please round up or down to nearest 25.

29 Approximately how many books do you (parents) own? Please round up or down to nearest 50.

30 This question will list some toys and games which children enjoy to various degrees. Please tick the column opposite each activity to indicate the degree of your child's enjoyment of this activity. (By all means seek your child's help on this.)

Column 1 = very strong dislike

Column 2 = strong dislike

Column 3 = neutral

Column 4 = strong liking

Column 5 = very strong liking

	1	2	3	4	5
electronic toys					
construction toys					
dolls					
cuddly toys					
cars, trucks					
pretend or fantasy games					
puzzles					
educational toys					
board games					
games involving ball-play					
games involving mock fights					
games involving 'chasing'					
other?					

Please ask the subject child to complete questions 31–34

31 Here are a number of activities which some children enjoy doing in their spare time. Please place them in order in which you enjoy them by writing '1' beside the activity you enjoy most, '2' beside your next favourite and so on, down to '8'. You would put '8' beside the one you like least. You can't just say you enjoy them all equally; you must try to put them in order of enjoyment.

Reading ______

Sports ______

Puzzles, board games or video games ______

Playing music or listening to music ______

Working with computers (but not video games) ______

Writing, drawing or painting ______

Radio or TV ______

Playing, socializing ______

32 Now that you have done number 31, you can write in here any activity which you particularly enjoy but which was not included in the list.

33 What games do you enjoy playing in your leisure time at school? (For example, break and lunchtime)? You don't have to restrict yourself to games mentioned in questions 31 or 32.

34 What games do you enjoy playing at home after school and at weekends? Again, you don't have to restrict yourself to games mentioned in questions 31 or 32.

APPENDIX D

TELEVISION VIEWING RECORD

Please record all programmes watched by subject child for two consecutive weeks.

WEEK ______ : Week beginning Sunday ______________ (date).

Child ______________________________

	Name of programme	*Length of viewing*	*Which family member selected this programme?*
Sunday			
Monday			
Tuesday			
Wednesday			
Thursday			
Friday			
Saturday			

APPENDIX E

Parent interview 1

1 Was ______________________ reading before entry to school?

2 What type and levels of books or other materials was s/he reading?

3 When s/he started school, did you tell the teachers that s/he was reading? Why or why not?

4 (How) did the teachers/school discover that s/he could read?

5 Did ______________________ experience any difficulties at school due to his/her early reading?

6 At what age did ______________________ start school?

7 What size and type of school? Government or private?

8 Has the school made any special provisions to cater to his/her talents?

9 Has s/he ever been accelerated?

10 Have any teachers been particularly helpful or responsive to ______________________?

11 Have any teachers been particularly unhelpful or unresponsive?

12 Do you think that ______________________ has ever experienced difficulty because his/her teachers are generally less intelligent than s/he?

13 Do you think s/he is aware of this? What makes you feel this?

14 What wishes or plans do you have for ______________________'s future education?

15 If all the following educational alternatives were available to your child, which would you choose and why?

- A withdrawal (pull-out) program for gifted children.
- A full-time, self-contained gifted class within a normal school.
- A special school for gifted children.
- Child to be able to progress through grade levels and schools (junior primary through to high school) at his/her own rate.
- Child to stay in regular, heterogeneous classroom but progress at his/her own rate.

16 Many parents of gifted children are wary of expressing a wish for special provisions for their child, for fear of seeming elitist. If I had asked you question 15 in a meeting with other parents of gifted children, would you answer the same, or differently?

17 If I asked you question 15 in a meeting of other parents of elementary school children of widely differing levels of ability, would you answer the same, or differently?

APPENDIX F
Parent interview 2

1 Your responses to questionnaire 2 show that members of your family have experienced success and recognition both in business and in their spare-time interests. What personal qualities in these individuals do you feel might have contributed to their success?

2 Do you see any of these qualities in ________________ (subject child)?

3 As ________________'s parents, have you tried to encourage these qualities?

4 What do you see as ________________'s strengths – academic and personal?

5 What do you see as his/her relative weaknesses?

6 How has s/he been progressing academically at school since the last time we talked?

7 Has the school made any (further) attempts to match the curriculum to his/her abilities?

8 How do you think s/he feels about school at the present moment?

9 Some studies of exceptionally gifted children have found that they can have difficulties making friends at school. Other studies suggest that they can be quite popular.

What about ________________?

10 (If parent suggests that subject child has problems of social isolation) Do you feel this might be because s/he prefers to be by himself/herself or do you think s/he would really like to be with other children?

11 (Following from 10) Was this characteristic of ________________ when s/he was younger or is it a more recent development?

12 Some studies suggest that highly gifted children prefer the companionship of older children. Others suggest that they prefer to be with children of their own age or younger.

What about ________________?

13 What type of child does s/he prefer as a companion?

14 Some gifted children when they are very young have an imaginary friend – a pretend child or animal, or even an imaginary country. Did ________________ ever have anything like that?

15 Does ________________ have or has s/he ever had a mentor – an adult outside the school and the immediate family who has had a significant influence on the development of his/her talent?

16 (If 'Yes' to 15.) How has the mentor helped in this regard?

17 (If 'Yes' to 15.) How do you think ________________'s relationship with the mentor differs from or resembles his/her relationship with his/her teachers at school?

APPENDIX G
Parent interview 3

1 How has ________________ been progressing academically at school since we last talked?

2 Has the school made any (further) attempts to match the curriculum to his/her abilities?

3 How much has the school involved you in planning his/her school program?

4 How do you think s/he feels about school at the present time?

5 How are his/her current relationships with classmates?

6 How are his/her current relationships with teachers at school?

7 Has ________________ ever experienced any hostility from other children or teachers, or from other community members, that you feel arose from a resentment of his/her exceptional abilities?

8 (If 'Yes' to 7). Do you think this has had any effect on his/her academic performance, or his/her feelings about his/her abilities?

9 Some parents of gifted children report that they themselves have

experienced varying degrees of resentment from community members, or even members of their families, because of their child's unusual abilities. Have you experienced anything like this?

10 (For parents of Asian or Eurasian origin). Have you or your children experienced any hostility towards you on racial grounds?

11 (If 'Yes' to 10). Is it possible that the resentment ________________ experiences is related to his/her being Asian, rather than towards his/her abilities?

12 Your answers to Questionnaire 4 suggest that ________________ prefers to play games which involve quite a lot of intellectual challenge. Was s/he like this as a young child or is this a more recent development?

13 Some studies of exceptionally gifted children suggest that they have difficulties in dealing with other children's slower thinking in play situations. One researcher phrased it as difficulty in 'suffering fools gladly'. Other exceptionally gifted children seem to have much less difficulty with this. How does ________________ handle it?

14 Some studies suggest that exceptionally gifted children like to ask quite 'deep' questions about religion, the origin of man, where the human race is going... that kind of thing. Other exceptionally gifted children don't seem to have these interests.

What about ________________?

APPENDIX H
Child interview 1

1 Let's pretend that your teacher says you can choose one particular school subject or activity and do as much of it as you like for the whole of the next week. It has to be something you already do in school. What subject or activity would you choose?

2 What do you particularly enjoy about that?

3 Now the opposite. Let's pretend that the teacher says you can choose one subject or activity to leave out completely for the whole of the next week. What subject or activity would you choose?

4 Why would you particularly choose to leave that out?

5 What part of the school day do you like best? Why?

6 What part of the school day do you like least? Why?

7 A lot of children say they find school a bit boring from time to time. Do you find school boring a lot of the time, sometimes or only rarely?

8 What particular aspects do you find boring?

9 What do you think is your strongest subject, academically?

10 Do you think you could handle harder work in that subject if it was offered to you?

11 Have you ever asked your teacher to give you more challenging work?

12 Is there any school subject that you have difficulty with and feel you would like more help with?

13 In your Interest-a-Lyzer you said you'd like to invite ________, ________________ and ________________ to be your classroom teacher for a day. Why did you choose these particular people?

14 In what ways do you think ________________ (any name from 13) would differ from your present teacher?

15 If you could change anything you wanted about your present class or school, or the work you do at school, what changes would you make?

Additional questions for children who have experienced acceleration or other interventive procedures.

16 Your school has accelerated you/ placed you in a withdrawal program/ given you enrichment work. Has this made a difference to your feelings about school?

17 Has it made a difference to the level you are able to work at?

18 What are the benefits and disadvantages of your special program?

APPENDIX I
Child interview 2

1 Is there anything that happened at school in the last few weeks that you found particularly enjoyable or interesting?

2 (If 'Yes') In what ways did that event differ from the things that usually happen at school?

3 What is the most interesting thing that has happened to you outside school in the last few weeks?

4 Are there any similarities between that event and ______? (Answer to 1)

5 In the classroom do you usually work very quickly or at a moderate speed, or do you take your time?

6 Do you tend to finish your work before the other children in your class, finish around the same time, or finish a little after them?

7 (If 'finish before'). How do you spend your time when you're waiting for the other kids to catch up?

8 (If 'a little after') How do you think the teacher feels about your speed of work?

9 (If 'a little after') Is there any particular reason why you prefer taking your time over the work?

10 Some very bright kids are a little shy of letting people see that they're bright, and try to 'play it down' in class. Others quite enjoy being recognized as bright. How do you feel?

11 (If 'play it down') What are some of the things you do to 'play down' your abilities?

12 (If 'play it down') Do you think the teacher knows you're 'playing down' your abilities?

13 (If 'play it down') Do any other kids in your class realise it?

14 Do you ever get teased or bullied because of being bright?

15 How do you get on with the other kids in the class?

16 (If answer indicates few or no friends, or a significant degree of social rejection.) Some kids prefer to be on their own; they really prefer their own company to being with other kids. Other kids don't mind *too* much about being alone but would quite like to join in with the others now and again. How do you feel?

17 Do you like to be with kids your own age, or do you prefer to be with kids a bit older or a bit younger than you?

APPENDIX J
Child interview 3

1 Is there anything that happened at school in the past few weeks that you found particularly enjoyable or interesting?

2 (If 'yes') In what ways did that event differ from the things that usually happen at school?

3 What is the most interesting thing that has happened to you outside school in the last few weeks?

4 Are there any similarities between that event and ______? (Answer to 1)

5 What sort of games do you play in your free time at school? At home?

6 What sort of games do you *prefer* to play?

7 Sometimes kids have an imaginary friend or even an imaginary country that they make up stories about – another 'pretend' child, perhaps, or a 'pretend' pet. Sometimes the imaginary friend can seem almost real! Have you ever done that?

8 Imagine that you have a friend at school who shares all your particular interests and ideas. The teacher lets you work with

him/her in class on work of your own choice. What would you be likely to do?

9 You also play with this 'ideal friend' in the playground at break and lunch. What games would you play, or how would you spend your time?

10 Your mother lets you have your ideal friend over for the weekend. What sort of thing would you do?

11 Back to school for this question! Some people say that teachers who teach bright kids should be very bright themselves. Other people say it doesn't matter as long as the teacher is willing to let the bright kid work at his/her own pace. What do you feel about this?

12 Do any of your teachers stand out in your mind as having been particularly helpful or responsive to you?

13 (If 'yes' to 12.) Do you think (that teacher) was also very bright?

14 Have you ever felt you were being held back, or have you ever felt a bit irritated, by a teacher's lack of knowledge in a subject?

15 Have you ever secretly felt that a teacher might not be as bright as you yourself?

16 What qualities do you feel a teacher should have to be a particularly effective teacher for bright kids?

APPENDIX K
Synopsis of School History

CHILD: ______________________

Date of completing this synopsis: ____________

Your answers to these questions are almost certainly already on tape, so you do not need to give extensive written responses. However, if you want to enlarge on something and there is not enough space here, please feel free to write on the back of the sheet or add extra sheets of paper.

1 At what age did the subject child enter school? Give month and year of entry. If this was earlier than the usual age, please explain briefly how the early entry came about. Was it preceded by early entry into pre-school? Who suggested early entry to school? If it was your idea, did you have difficulty in persuading the school to agree?

2 Apart from early entry, has your subject child experienced any form of acceleration? Was this grade-skipping or subject acceleration? (Subject acceleration is where the child stays with his own grade level for most of the time but moves to a higher grade for part of the day or week to work at higher levels in a specific subject area.) Describe the form of acceleration your child has undertaken. State the grade levels involved in his/her acceleration and the year/s (e.g. 1987) in which this occurred.

3 Did the idea of acceleration come from you or from the school? Please enlarge.

4 Has your child ever been involved in a school withdrawal program for gifted children? If so:

- **at what grade level?**
- **for how many hours per week/ how many weeks per year?**

- As far as you can, describe the curriculum of the withdrawal program.
- As far as you can, decribe the procedures by which students were selected for the withdrawal program.

5 Has the school arranged for any other form of special program for your child? Please describe the program.

6 If your child entered school already reading, what accommodation did the school make to cater for this?

7 To what extent have you, as a parent, been involved in helping plan the school's program for your child? How much difficulty have you had in persuading the school to let you become involved?

8 Do you feel that your child is working in school at a level that truly reflects his/her abilities? Please enlarge on this.

9 If you feel your child is underachieving, do you feel that this is because the school curriculum/program does not challenge him/her, or do you feel s/he may be underachieving deliberately for peer acceptance?

10 How old will your child be at the end of this month, and what grade is s/he in?

11 Please use this space to make any further comments you wish on your child's experience at school over the last few years. If you wish, you can write a resume of his/her experience or your views on his/her experience.

INDEX

The children studied in the research project, the subject of this book, are referred to by pseudonyms and entered under Christian names in the index.